The Archaeology of
the Transjordan
in the Bronze and
Iron Ages

Rudolph Henry Dornemann

Milwaukee Public Museum

The Milwaukee Public Museum, Milwaukee, Wisconsin — A.A.M. accredited
An educational and cultural resource of Milwaukee County

Library of Congress Catalog Number 83-61718
ISBN 0-89326-053-3

Typography via telecommunications by Parnau Graphics, New Berlin, Wisconsin
Printing by Robert M. Young Company, Milwaukee, Wisconsin

To Meredith

TABLE OF CONTENTS

LIST OF TABLES

LIST OF ILLUSTRATIONS

ABBREVIATIONS

AA   Amman Tomb A, L. Harding,
            "Two Iron Age Tombs, 'Amman,"
            *Quarterly of the Department of
            Antiquities of Palestine,* XI
            (1945).

AAA   *Liverpool Annals of Archaeology
            and Anthropology,* Liverpool.

AAS   *Les Annales archéologiques de
            Syrie* or *Annales archéologiques
            Arabes Syriennes* (after 1965).

AASOR   *Annual of the American Schools
            of Oriental Research.*

AB   Amman Tomb B, L. Harding,

"Two Iron Age Tombs, 'Amman," *Quarterly of the Department of Antiquities of Palestine,* XI (1945).

AC   Amman Tomb C, L. Harding, "Two Iron Age Tombs in 'Amman," *Annual of the Department of Antiquities of Jordan,* I (1951).

AD   Amman Tomb D, L. Harding, "Two Iron Age Tombs in Amman," *Annual of the Department of Antiquities of Jordan,* I (1951).

ADAJ   *Annual of the Department of Antiquities of Jordan.*

AE   Amman Tomb E, R. W. Dajani, "An Iron Age Tomb from Amman," *Annual of the Department of Antiquities of Jordan,* XI (1966).

AF   Amman Tomb F (Unpublished).

AFO   *Archiv für Orientforschung.*

AG   Amman Tomb G (Jebel el Qusur, unpublished).

AJA   *American Journal of Archaeology.*

AN   Amman Tomb N, L. Harding, "The Tomb of Adoni Nur in Amman," *Palestine Exploration Fund Annual,* VI (1953).

AM   Amman Museum.

AMB   Amman Middle Bronze Tomb, L. Harding, "A Middle Bronze Tomb at Amman," *Palestine Exploration Fund Annual,* XI (1953).

Amuq, I   R. and L. Braidwood, *Excavations in the Plain of Antioch,* Vol. I (1960).

AP   W. F. Albright, *The Archaeology of Palestine* (1960).

APEF   *Annual of the Palestine Exploration Fund.*

APHL   R. Amiran, *The Ancient Pottery of the Holy Land* (1970).

AS, I-V   E. Grant, *et al., 'Ain Shems Excavations (Palestine),* Vols. I-V (1931-39).

ASOR   American Schools of Oriental Research.

Assur   A. Haller, *Gräber und Grüfte von Assur* (1954).

BA   *The Biblical Archaeologist.*

Babylon   O. Reuther, *Die Innenstadt von Babylon (Merkes)* (1926).

Balu'a   W. Ward and M. Martin, "The Balu'a Stele: A New Transcription with Paleographic and Historic Notes," *Annual of the Department of Antiquities of Jordan,* VIII-IX (1964).

BASOR   *Bulletin of the American Schools of Oriental Research.*

Beth Shemesh   E. Grant, *Beth Shemesh* (1929).

Bethel   J. Kelso, *The Excavations of Bethel (1934-1960)* (1968).

Beziehungen   W. Helck, *Die Beziehungen Ägyptens zu Vorderasien im 3. und 2. Jahrtausend v. Chr.* (1962).

BMB   *Bulletin du Musée de Beyrouth.*

BSP   G. M. Fitzgerald, *Beth-Shan,* Vol. II: *The Four Canaanite Temples of Beth-Shan,* Part II: *The Pottery* (1930).

Byblos, II   M. Dunand, *Fouilles de Byblos Tome II (1933-1938)* (1958).

BZ, II   O. Sellers, *et al., The 1957 Excavations at Beth-Zur* (1968).

CAH   *Cambridge Ancient History.*

CP   P. Cintas, *Ceramique punique* (1950).

CPP   J. G. Duncan, *Corpus of Dated Palestinian Pottery* (1930).

DA   H. J. Franken, *Excavations at*

Deir 'Allā, Vol. I (1969).

Dhiban, I — W. Reed and F. Winnett, *Dhiban Excavation Reports* (1964).

Dhiban, II — A. D. Tushingham, *The Excavations at Dibon (Dhibân) in Moab, 1952-53* (1972)

E.B. — Early Bronze.

Ebla — P. Matthiae, *Ebla, un impero ritrovato* (1977).

EEP, I — N. Glueck, *Explorations in Eastern Palestine*, I (1933).

EEP, II — N. Glueck, *Explorations in Eastern Palestine*, II (1934).

EEP, III — N. Glueck, *Explorations in Eastern Palestine*, III (1939).

EEP, IV — N. Glueck, *Explorations in Eastern Palestine*, IV (1951).

Fara (S) — F. Petrie, *Beth-Pelet I (Tell Fara)* (1930).

Gaza, I-IV — F. Petrie, *et al.*, *Ancient Gaza*, I-IV (1931-34).

Gerar — F. Petrie, *Gerar* (1928).

Gibeah — L. A. Sinclair, *An Archaeological Study of Gibeah (Tell el-Fûl)* (1960).

Hama, II — E. Fugmann, *Hama, fouilles et recherches de la Fondation Carlsberg 1931-1938)*, Vol. II, Part I (1958).

Hama Cem. — P. J. Riis, *Les Cimetièrees à Crémation: Hama, fouilles et recherches de la Fondation Carlsberg 1931-1938* (1948).

Hawam — R. W. Hamilton, "Excavations at Tell Abu Hawam," *Quarterly of the Department of Antiquities of Palestine, IV* (1935).

Hazor, I-IV — Y. Yadin, *et al.*, *Hazor*, I, II, and III-IV Plates (1958-61).

IA — Irbed Tomb A, R. W. Dajani, "Iron Age Tombs from Irbed," *Annual of the Department of Antiquities of Jordan*, VIII-IX (1964).

IABS — F. James, *The Iron Age at Beth Shan* (1966).

IB — Irbed Tomb B, R. W. Dajani, "Iron Age Tombs from Irbed," *Annual of the Department of Antiquities of Jordan*, VIII-IX (1964).

IC — Irbed Tomb C, R. W. Dajani, "Iron Age Tombs from Irbed," *Annual of the Department of Antiquities of Jordan*, VIII-IX (1964).

ID — Irbed Tomb D, R. W. Dajani, "Iron Age Tombs from Irbed" *Annual of the Department of Antiquities of Jordan*, VIII-IX (1964).

IEJ — *Israel Exploration Journal*.

ILN — *Illustrated London News*.

IM — Irbed Museum.

JEA — *Journal of Egyptian Archaeology*.

Jericho, I-II — K. M. Kenyon, *Excavations at Jericho*, Vol. I (1960) and Vol. II (1965).

JESHO — *Journal of Economic and Social History of the Orient*.

JN — Jebel Nuzha Tomb, R. W. Dajani, "Jabal Nuzha Tomb at Amman," *Annual of the Department of Antiquities of Jordan, XI* (1966).

JNES — *Journal of Near Eastern Studies*.

JPOS — *Journal of the Palestine Oriental Society*.

KM — Kerak Museum.

LA — *Liber Annuus*.

Lachish, III — O. Tufnell, *Lachish III: The Iron Age* (1953).

L.B. — Late Bronze.

M — Meqabelein Tomb, L. Harding, "An Iron Age Tomb at Meqabelein," *Quarterly of the Department of Antiquities of Palestine,* XIV (1950).

MA	Madeba Tomb A, L. Harding, "An Early Iron Age Tomb at Medeba," *Palestine Exploration Fund Annual, VI* (1953).
MB	Madeba Tomb B, M. Piccirillo, "Una tomba del Ferro Ia Madeba," *Liber Annuus, XXV* (1975).
MAD	Madeba Museum
M.B.	Middle Bronze.
MEG, I	R. Lamon and G. Shipton, *Megiddo I Seasons of 1925-34* (1939).
MEG, II	G. Loud, *Megiddo II Seasons of 1935-39* (1948).
MEG T	P. L. O. Guy and R. Engberg, *Megiddo Tombs* (1938).
Nasbe	J. C. Wampler, *Tell en-Nasbeh,* Vol. II: *The Pottery* (1947).
Nebo	S. J. Saller and B. Bagatti, *The Town of Nebo (Khirbet el Mekhayyat)* (1949).
Other Side	N. Glueck, *The Other Side of the Jordan* (1940).
Palestinian Figurines	J. B. Pritchard, *Palestinian Figurines in Relation to Certain Goddesses Known through Literature* (1943).
Pella, I	R. H. Smith, *Pella of the Decapolis I* (1973).
PEFA	*Palestine Exploration Fund Annual.*
PEFQS	*Palestine Exploration Fund Quarterly Statement.*
PEQ	*Palestine Exploration Quarterly.*
QDAP	*Quarterly of the Department of Antiquities of Palestine.*
RB	*Revue Biblique.*
River Jordan	N. Glueck, *The River Jordan* (1946).
SA	Sahab Tomb A (Unpublished).
SAOC	*Studies in Ancient Oriental Civilization.*
SB	Sahab Tomb B, L. Harding, "An Iron Age Tomb at Sahab," *Quarterly of the Department of Antiquities of Palestine,* XIII (1948).
SC	Sahab Tomb C, R. W. Dajani, "A Late Bronze-Iron Age Tomb" Excavated at Sahab, 1968, *Annual of the Department of Antiquities of Jordan,* XV (1970).
SS, III	J. W. Crowfoot, *et al., Samaria-Sebaste,* Vol. III: *The Objects* (1957).
Tarsus, II	H. Goldman, *Excavations at Gözlü Kule, Tarsus,* Vol. II: *Bronze Age,* (1956).
Tarsus, III	H. Goldman, *Excavations at Gözlü Kule, Tarsus,* Vol. III: *Iron Age* (1963).
TBM, I	W. F. Albright, *The Excavations of Tell Beit Mirsim,* Vol. I (1932).
TBM, IA	W. F. Albright, *The Excavation of Tell Beit Mirsim, Vol. IA: Bronze Age Pottery of the Fourth Campaign* (1933).
TBM, II	W. F. Albright, *The Excavation of Tell Beit Mirsim,* Vol. II: *The Bronze Age* (1938).
TBM, III	W. F. Albright, *The Excavation of Tell Beit Mirsim,* Vol. III: *The Iron Age* (1943).
Timna	B. Rothenberg, *Timna: Valley of the Biblical Copper Mines* (1972).
UB	C.-M. Bennett, "Fouilles d'Umm el-Biyara," *Revue Biblique,* LXXIII (1966).
VT	*Vetus Testamentum.*
ZDPV	*Zeitschrift des Deutschen Palästina-Vereins.*

PREFACE

The last five years have seen a great increase in archaeological activity in the Transjordan and publications are beginning to appear on projects conducted in the past decade. This manuscript was completed in 1970 and has been revised and up-dated to include relevant references through 1978. Trips by the author to Amman in 1974, 1975, 1977 and 1978, and a review of recent publications indicates that what has been said here is still valid and in need of serious consideration by those who are concerned with the archaeology of Syria and Palestine. We have not up-dated our work beyond 1978 for now, since to do so would require still longer delays in its publication.

The topic of this monograph was suggested as a dissertation topic to Professor Helene J. Kantor of the Department of Near Eastern Languages and Civilizations at the University of Chicago in the spring of 1968. The proposal received her approval and enthusiastic encouragement. The historical, cultural and archaeological problems involved in the scholarly treatment of this topic became vivid to me during my residence in Amman, Jordan in 1965-1967. My position there as Archaeological Advisor to the Department of Antiquities on a United States Aid to International Development tourism project necessitated considerable travel. In this way, I became well acquainted with most of the geographical areas of the country. At that time I also became acquainted with much of the artifactual material (published and unpublished) which had come to light in the past two decades.

With Professor Kantor's encouragement I wrote to Professor G. Ernest Wright, who was at that time President of the American Schools of Oriental Research, to explore the possibility of support from that organization to return to Amman and gather materials for this monograph. I had hoped that the Thayer Fellowship which I had delayed for several years and finally given up could be applied in some way to this undertaking. Although this proved to be impossible, the American Schools of Oriental Research was looking for someone to set up a research center in Amman. My interests and those of the Schools overlapped, resulting in my appointment as the Schools' Annual Professor at the Amman Research Center for the academic year 1968-69. A modest amount of money was included in the budget for excavation on the Citadel of Amman. It was my hope that such excavation could provide important information for this monograph if a stratified sequence of artifacts could be obtained upon which the largely unstratified artifacts from the Transjordan could be ordered.

The successful completion of this monograph could never have been accomplished without the support and encouragement of the officers and officials with whom I worked, or represented, in the years 1968 and 1969. Consequently, I must acknowledge my debt to the following persons and institutions: Professors G. Ernest Wright, Edward F. Campbell, and John Marks, Mr. Thomas Newman and the Trustees of the American Schools of Oriental Research for the appointment which allowed me and my family to reside in Amman for a year and for the suport of my field activities; the Oriental Institute of the University of Chicago and its past directors, Professors Robert M. Adams and George R. Hughes, for their encouragement and aid, and for granting me a leave of absence from work on the publication of the Amuq Phase K-O pottery. Also, I am indebted to Dr. Hughes for his aid, understanding, and patience during the year in which my dissertation was written in Chicago. I am grateful to the then Acting President, Abd al-Karim Khalifa; Secretary General, Hassan al-Nabulsi; Dean Mohammed es-Samra, Drs. Abdul-Karim Gharaibeh, Fawzi el-Fakhrani, Ahmed Fakhri, Aida Aif, Messrs. (now also Drs.) Khair Yassine and Assem Barghouti, and officials of the University of Jordan for their support and/or participation in the Amman Citadel excavations in 1968 and 1969 (which is further acknowledged below) and for the use of the University's facilities. I thank the former Minister of Tourism and Antiquities of the Hashemite Kingdom of Jordan, Salah Abou Zeid, for the issuance of the permit for excavations on Jebel Qala'. I would like to thank Mr. Jacob Oweis, a former director of the Department of Antiquities of the Hashemite Kingdom of Jordan, for his encouragement, active support, and the joint participation of his department in the Amman Citadel excavations, as well as for his permission to publish Amman tomb F and permission to photograph museum objects and include such photographs in this monograph. Messrs. Safwan et-Tell, Yousef Alami, and Sami Abadi of the Department assisted in matters of excavation and the handling of finds. Messrs. Ahmed Odeh and Rafiq Dajani of the same Department graciously permitted me to examine unpublished finds from their excavations and include some remarks here. The curators of the Amman, Jerash, Irbed, Madeba, and Kerak Museums assisted in the examination and photography of museum objects and extended their hospitality. The then director of the Tourism Authority of the Hashemite Kingdom of Jordan, Mr. Ghaleb Barakat, granted permission to include two maps (figures 2 and 3) in this monograph.

A considerable debt must also be acknowledged to those who advised, guided, and assisted in the preparation of this monograph in its form as a Ph.D. dissertation. The members of my dissertation committee: Professor Helene J. Kantor, Chairperson; and Professors Maurits van Loon and Stanley Gevirtz gave freely of their advice and knowledge. Advice on specific problems must also be acknowledged from other Oriental Institute and Department of Near Eastern Languages and Civilizations members; specifically, Professors Robert J. Braidwood, Klaus Baer, Carl De Vries, Hans Güterbock, and Mr. Carl Haines. A debt to Professor Paul W. Lapp, deceased, must be acknowledged for discussing with me specific problems dealing with the pottery and stratigraphy of certain Transjordanian sites.

Fellow students Elizabeth Carter, David Nasgowitz, and Harold Wolff offered a number of suggestions which were incorporated in our discussion. The technical assistance of Janice Nasgowitz in editing and typing the final dissertation copy must also be acknowledged. The drawings were done by Attah Alaiwat and my father William Dornemann. The former was also responsible for the field drawings upon which our architectural plans are based. Family and in-laws provided many hours of labor in proofreading and typing in the preparation of drafts of the monograph as well as providing the funds for typing and editing. The completion of this monograph would have been impossible without the encouragement and help of my wife, Meredith. She spent many hours typing and proofreading as well as relieving me of many burdens so that more of my time could be spent in writing and study.

Finally, I would like to express my thanks to fellow staff members at the Milwaukee Public Museum, particularly to its director, Kenneth Starr, for his encouragement in the completion of the manuscript, its editor Mary Garity for her efforts in seeing to the production of the manuscript, to Carter Lupton for his assistance in editing and proofreading, and to Karen Heerhold and Roberta Blanks for the typing of the manuscript.

Milwaukee   May 1981

CHAPTER I

INTRODUCTION

Objectives and Emphases of Monograph

It is at present scarcely possible to provide more than an historical framework for most chronological periods in the Transjordan. Though this monograph will depend upon historical facts and accounts as its framework, it will, of necessity, deal primarily with the archaeological material available from this area. Detailed study of the artifactual assemblages has provided the basic sequence of cultures and the fundamental delineation of these cultures.

Limitations are placed on the discussion of each period by the kind and amount of the archaeological evidence, as well as its availability. The Bronze Age is poorly represented, and for the most part its history is little more than an abstraction from the scanty archaeological evidence. Since much of the evidence for Bronze Age habitation is still unpublished, the discussion and analysis of details will be limited. The material which has been found in the last few decades is, however, far too important to ignore, so it will be surveyed briefly. This survey will provide a background for our discussion of the Iron Age.

In comparison with the Bronze Age, the evidence for the Iron Age is much more abundant. The Transjordan can now be seen as a cultural entity in relation to its neighbors, although neither all centuries of its history nor all its geographical areas are uniformly documented. Most of the discussion will center on pottery because it is the most plentiful and useful body of material. A considerable amount of additional information can be gained from an analysis of figurines, small objects, sculpture, etc. A broader base is thus attained for an understanding of the area's Iron Age assemblages than is possible for the Bronze Age.

The pottery discussion will deal first with vessels found in the Amman district, since this area offers the greatest amount of material, and then with the vessels found in the other areas of the Transjordan. Most of the vessels were found in tombs, so it is imperative to direct the analysis toward the development of a typological sequence. The typological sequence will be supported by stratified material wherever possible and will be made as inclusive as possible by adding forms available only in sherd collections.[1] An analysis of vessel decorations provides information which is supplementary to the analysis of forms. It is fortunate that the published Iron Age phases at Deir 'Allā and the sherd evidence from our 1969 Amman Citadel sounding are now available to provide links between the two distinct sequential units into which the Amman district material falls.

Considerable attention has been given to foreign parallels of Transjordanian artifacts. In the past much of the discussion has been presented from a Palestinian point of view. This is still valid in many ways since there is evidence that considerable contact existed between Palestine and the Transjordan in most periods.

Comparison of the artifacts of both areas helps to highlight the characteristic features of each. The discussion of parallels with neighboring areas other than Palestine also illustrates those features of the assemblage which are distinctly local to the Transjordan (specifically, without good Palestinian or other parallels) as well as features which have a wider significance. A re-examination of the archaeology and culture of this area on the basis of the evidence which has been found in the past two decades, in contrast to the surface material upon which previous statements were based, is clearly desirable at this point in time.[2]

In the past two decades a small collection of inscriptional material has come to light in the Transjordan in addition to the important artifactual material. The inscriptional material, though significant in the linguistic and paleographic information it provides, is quite limited in its historical value. The written evidence which had

---

[1]Our pottery illustrations are numbered in order on the photographs, figures 46 through 50 and 61 through 83. The profile drawings are similarly numbered in order on figures 50 through 60. Many sherds are illustrated both in photograph and drawing; in such cases, they are referred to in the text only by their sherd numbers (numbers assigned solely for the purposes of this monograph) and these numbers are underlined on the figures. Where only a photograph or drawing are illustrated, the figure number has also been included in the reference.

The sherd numbers and illustration numbers on the remaining plates are always positioned in the lower left corner of the illustration. Locus numbers have been placed in the lower right corner in the case of the 1969 sounding sherds. The first sherd from a locus is designated in this manner and subsequent sherds are to be considered from the same locus until a new locus number is designated. Where reference is made to museum collections or publication numbers or levels, this information is also placed in the lower right corner. Where type numbers are indicated, these numbers are positioned in the upper left corner of an illustration.

No consistent scale is used for plates 20-31 but a 1:5 scale is used for sherd illustrations.

[2]We have, in Chapter III (pp. 25-26), given the reasons for our use of a modified version of W.F. Albright's chronological scheme. We have also used this scheme for the Bronze Age because it is presently more acceptable to us than any other and it makes uniformity possible throughout this monograph.

previously been available had been incorporated into the major works by Martin Noth[1] and William F. Albright,[2] as well as in studies by students of Albright.[3] The archaeological evidence, on the other hand, demands some major shifts in current thinking about the Transjordan.

Summary of Archaeological Research in the Transjordan

A succession of famous explorers surveyed the Transjordan, or parts of it, with increasing exactitude from Ulrich J. Seetzen in the first decade of the nineteenth century to Nelson Glueck in the 1930's and 40's. The earlier explorers concentrated their efforts on the recording of such imposing architectural remains as those of the Decapolis cities, Araq el Emir, Petra, and the desert castles. Substantial and obvious remains of earlier periods, like the standing pillars of Ader or Lejjun or the vast dolmen fields, also received their attention and comment. Nelson Glueck contributed greater precision in determining the full range of habitation throughout the history of the entire area. The idea of collecting surface pottery from the sites throughout the area was new. When basic pottery sequences were worked out by excavators in Palestine, diagnostic criteria became available by which the general chronology of settlement could be established on specific sites as well as over larger areas. Unfortunately, little follow-up excavation was done on any of these sites until quite recently, and in the past two decades many new surveys have been conducted over specific areas of the Transjordan.[4] The British and American Schools in Jerusalem did undertake a few soundings on tells of the earlier periods in addition to several seasons of excavation at Tell el Kheleifeh (1938-40). However, the largest archaeological undertakings in the area at Beidah, Jerash, Khirbet et Tannur, Teleilat Ghassul, Mount Nebo, and Amman dealt mainly with periods falling on either side of the time range of this monograph.

Glueck's survey, and the similar reconnaissance on a smaller and less comprehensive scale by the British, French, German, and American Schools in Jerusalem, led to greater precision in the identification of sites through the comparison of their ceramic evidence for periods of habitation with geographical position, size of settlement, present name, and all historical citations. The accuracy of site identification was increased tremendously in this way, but it is not possible to judge at present what the percentages of error are for all but the most obvious sites. The best examples of the difficulties of identification that beset Palestinian archaeologists are the search for ancient Gath and, in the Transjordan, the proposed identification of Tell Deir 'Allā with Succoth. Arguments for the latter were presented by Glueck,[5] but since then the excavations on the site have led to a different conclusion, namely the identification of this site with ancient Gilgal.[6]

Though Glueck's work[7] went far beyond that of his predecessors in the Transjordan, uncertainty still exists in the interpretation of surface survey

[1]Martin Noth, *The History of Israel* (2nd ed.; New York: Harper and Brothers, 1960) and "Beiträge zur Geschichte des Ost-Jordanlandes," *Beiträge zur biblischen Landes und Altertumskunde,* Vol. III (1949).

[2]William Foxwell Albright, *Archaeology and the Religion of Israel* (5th ed.; New York: Anchor Books, 1969); *From the Stone Age to Christianity* (2nd ed.; New York: Anchor Books, 1957); and *The Jordan Valley in the Bronze Age* ("AASOR," Vol. VI; New Haven: ASOR, 1926).

[3]Nelson Glueck, *The Other Side of the Jordan* (New Haven: ASOR, 1940); *The River Jordan* (Philadelphia: The Westminster Press, 1945); "The Civilization of the Edomites," *BA,* X (1947), 77-84; A. H. van Zyl, *The Moabites* ("Pretoria Oriental Series," Vol. III; Leiden: E. J. Brill, 1960); George M. Landes, "The Material Civilization of the Ammonites," *BA,* XXIV (1961), 65-86; and "A History of the Ammonites" (unpublished Ph.D. dissertation, Department of Near Eastern Studies, Johns Hopkins University, 1956).

[4]The major survey projects which are noted extensively in publication or which were published before 1978 are: James Mellaart, "Preliminary Report on the Archaeological Survey on the Yarmuk and Jordan Valley for the Point Four Irrigation Scheme," *ADAJ,* VI-VII (1962), 126-57; Henri de Contenson, "The 1953 Survey in the Yarmuk and Jordan Valleys," *ADAJ,* VIII-IX (1964), 30-46; materials from a 1965-1966 Shu'eib-Heshban survey are included in Kay Prag, "The Intermediate Early Bronze-Middle Bronze Age: An Interpretation of the Evidence from Transjordan, Syria and Lebanon," *Levant,* VI (1974), 69-116; Siegfried Mittmann, "Beiträge zur Siedlungs- und Territorialgeschichte des nördlichen Ostjordanlandes ("Abhandlungen des Deutschen Palästinavereins," Weisbaden: Otto Harrassowitz, 1970); Walter E. Rast and R. Thomas Schaub, "Survey of the Southeastern Plain of the Dead Sea, 1973," *ADAJ,* XIX (1974), 5-53; Moawiyah Ibrahim, James A. Sauer, and Khair N. Yassine, "The East Jordan Valley Survey, 1975," *BASOR,* CCXXII (1976), 41-66; Robert Iback, Jr., "Archaeological Survey of the Hesbân Region," *AUSS,* XIV (1976), 119-26 and "Expanded Archaeological Survey of the Hesbân Region," *AUSS,* XVI (1978), 201-14; Terry M. Kerestes, John M. Lundquist, Brian G. Wood and Khair N. Yassine, "An Archaeological Survey of the Three Reservoir Areas in Northern Jordan, 1978," *ADAJ,* XXII (1977-78), 108-35; and David W. McCreery, "Preliminary Report of the A.P.C. Township Archaeological Survey," *ADAJ,* XXII (1977-78), 150-62. The very recent surveys in ancient Moab and Edom, and in the Beqa' northwest of Amman, did not appear in published form before 1979.

[5]Nelson Glueck, "Three Israelite Towns in the Jordan Valley: Zarethan, Succoth, Zaphon," *BASOR,* XCIII (1943), 2-23.

[6]Henk J. Franken, *Excavations at Tell Deir 'Allā,* I ("Documenta et monumenta orientis antiqui," Vol. XVI; Leiden: E. J. Brill, 1969), pp. 4-8.

[7]Nelson Glueck, *Explorations in Eastern Palestine,* I ("AASOR," Vol. XIV; New Haven: ASOR, 1933); *Explorations in Eastern Palestine,* II ("AASOR," Vol. XV; New Haven: ASOR, 1934); *Explorations in Eastern Palestine,* III ("AASOR," Vols. XVIII-XIX; New Haven: ASOR, 1939); and *Explorations in Eastern Palestine,* IV (2 parts; "AASOR," Vols. XXV-XXVIII; New Haven: ASOR, 1951).

material. Admittedly, the general periods of occupation can be outlined, but extreme caution should be observed until the results of the survey have been corroborated by the excavation of a considerable number of well-chosen sites. As will be shown below, recent finds have considerably undermined some of the general conclusions drawn at the end of Glueck's survey. Actually, they supplement the work of the survey and most often affect the interpretation of the evidence rather than calling into question the evidence itself. In assessing the material which Glueck has published, the problems are few, though some are rather critical. The major difficulty comes when theories are built around what was not found. The positive evidence is, in general, still reliable with minor adjustments, but the negative evidence has in many ways proved to be misleading.[1]

Evidence from Surface Surveys as Opposed to Evidence from Stratified Excavation and the Necessity of Discussing Transjordanian Assemblages in Relation to Palestine

The conclusions of Glueck's survey have not yet been adequately checked because insufficient excavation has been conducted to provide the required stratified pottery sequences. It is still necessary to rely heavily upon Palestinian material to organize materials from the Transjordan. It remains to be shown how closely materials from opposite sides of the Jordan correspond. There is now enough clear evidence which can be paralleled between the two sides of the Jordan to show that artifacts characteristic of each period are present. There is not enough evidence, however, to document the complete assemblage of every period. As more material becomes available, particularly stratified material, difficulties have increased rather than decreased because the peculiarities and variations become clearer. The problem, then, is to assess whether the differences are due to regional variations or to incomplete knowledge of the Palestinian assemblages. In some periods, where our documentation is fair, we can begin to show regional variations, though their meanings cannot yet be fully assessed. This is the case specifically in the Middle Bronze II B-C and Iron Age II periods. In other time ranges, like the end of the Early Bronze and the beginning of the Middle Bronze, the transitional period from Late Bronze to Early Iron or the Neo-Babylonian and Persian periods, the interpretation of the archaeological evidence is unclear and much debated so that many possibilities exist for correspondence between Palestine and the Transjordan. For example, in Palestine, in the first of these problem periods, it has not been shown conclusively which of two alternatives is

correct: (1) whether a clear break exists between the end of the Early Bronze Age tradition and the beginning of the Middle Bronze Age tradition or (2) whether a significant overlap exists between the two. How, then does this affect the picture of what went on in the Transjordan?

The conclusion of Nelson Glueck that:

During most of the following M.B. II period and much of the L.B. period, both in the Jordan Valley and in the Transjordan, there seems to have set in a sharp decline of permanent settlement, accompanied by a lessening and centralization of sedentary population at a comparatively few fixed and strongly fortified points. In North Gilead and in the Jordan Valley, this decline seems to have taken place mainly between the middle of the 18*th* and the 15*th* centuries B.C., while in the rest of the Transjordan south of the Wadi Zerqā it seems to have extended between the 20*th* and the 13*th* centuries B.C.[2]

has been widely repeated and if true would indicate a major difference in the settlement patterns of Palestine and the Transjordan during the second millennium B.C. As additional information becomes available this conclusion will require constant reevaluation. Equally serious consideration must, however, be given to an alternative possibility that MB I, IIA, B, C and L.B. settlements will be found to exist in the Transjordan in roughly the same frequency that they have been found to exist in Palestine. Currently, there is only scattered and scanty evidence for the existence of these periods in the Transjordan and only more work will show to what extent these gaps can be filled.

We must remember that in Palestine, generally, the amount of excavated E.B. material greatly exceeds the amount of MB IIA material. Therefore, Glueck's statement of a considerable decline in the density of occupation in the Transjordan from E.B. to MB II could be said to be the case in Palestine also. The MB IIA period is not well represented in Palestine at the present time,

---

[1]An illustration of the difficulties which can be expected to arise when the negative evidence of surface surveys is compared with evidence from an actual excavation was pointed out by Paul W. Lapp in a report on Araq el Emir. "The excavation in the village underlines the dangers of building archaeological arguments from silence. A careful surface exploration did not reveal traces of Iron I occupation, to say nothing of Early Hellenistic, Middle Bronze I-IIA, Early Bronze, and Chalcolithic. These last four horizons were not even encountered in two squares which reached bedrock in the spring, and no evidence for Iron I fortifications appeared until fall. While a sobering experience for one attempting to set down archaeological conclusions, it also provides a perspective of expectation for what might appear 'from silence' in future work at 'Araq el Emir." Paul W. Lapp, "The 1961 Excavations at 'Araq El-Emir," *ADAJ*, VI-VII (1962), 80-89.

[2]Glueck, EEP, IV, Part I, 423.

and one is thus led to wonder what surprises may be in store for us with increased investigation of the Transjordan.

One final remark must be made on the relative sophistication of the cultures in the Transjordan in comparison to those in Palestine. All too often, the Transjordan is seen merely as the distant borderland, the land in constant threat of nomad incursions and devastation, or as just a land of nomads. Consequently, it is often thought of as a wild, poor, and more primitive cultural area. We hope the following discussion will show that a change of thinking is needed here. In the past, such views were encouraged by a lack of information and there was nothing to refute such possibilities. It is becoming quite clear that, with increased research, the Transjordan can be clearly distinguished from Palestine. But when we examine the distinguishing features presently available, they do not indicate poverty in contrast to Palestine. In fact, there are signs of relative prosperity and a greater similarity with the more cosmopolitan centers of the seacoast.

The Question of Settled as Opposed to Non-Settled Populations in the Transjordan

Most of the references to the Transjordan in scholarly discussions mention the presence of nomadic or, less specifically, non-urban populations. This is most frequently the case in discussions of the Bronze Age but less so in the Iron Age. Since nomadism has played a large part in the recent history of the Transjordan, this has been built into the history of every period where our information fails, almost as an easy explanation to cover our lack of knowledge. There are many questions, however, for which we need answers before we can really understand the problems of interaction between urban and non-urban populations. Is it really valid in most cases to try to distinguish between materials that originated in urban rather than non-urban settings? If so, to what extent and in what way? How significant or great are the differences between settled and nomadic populations in times of highly developed urban societies in an area? Do such population groups share a common culture, heritage, descent, standard of living, etc., or are these features substantially different? Are the two groups mutually dependent or not? Is the situation different when there is only a small urban element in an area? Most archaeological handbooks contain facile answers to many of these questions, based on parallels with horse or camel nomads from medieval to modern times. It is true that when Burckhardt[1] was traveling in the area the balance between urban and non-urban was heavily on the side of the latter. One

must remember, however, that he did meet with a considerable number of established villages and some large towns which were not of nomadic tradition, as for example Ramtha, Irbed, Ajloun, Sûf, Salt, Kerak, Shobak, Tafile, Ma'an, Aqaba, and many others, as well as way stations on the pilgrimage route to Mecca. A great variety of relationships is possible between urban and bedouin groups within a given geographical setting. The relative strengths of the parties and their traditions would tend to create a unique relationship in each area.

In contrasting settled populations with nomads, it must be remembered that it was not unusual for the townspeople to move to the fields in harvest time to perform the necessary manual labor, and to move out to their flocks in the spring to help with the milking of the sheep and goats. At such times it would be normal for these townspeople to live in tents or caves. There are college-educated men from the Transjordan who can remember living just such a life when they were young. On the other hand, the bedouin are not ignorant of basic farming knowledge, and often the difference in standard of living, traditions, and mode of life is basically the preference of a tent to a mud-brick house.

The majority of the nomads in the Transjordan are limited by the needs and pace of their sheep and goats and are clearly distinguishable from the camel nomads who traditionally range far deeper into the desert and are correspondingly fewer in number. Who has ever undertaken a study to find out what percentage of the flocks which are pastured in the Transjordan in any particular period belong to townfolk as opposed to nomads? The sheep, of course, cannot exist in the actual desert and are confined to the fertile lands or the marginal regions. The marginal regions cannot really be expected to harbor and support the masses of nomads which, archaeologists too often find, inundate a settled area and bring a civilization to a close. The usual parallel for such an incursion, and what is supposedly the latest of these incursions, is the Arab invasion. But how much of the strength and character of the new civilization, as well as of the population, actually came out of the desert and how much of what previously existed was left intact and gradually modified? We might ask, did the Moslem conquest bring a new wave of immigrants to reoccupy all the sites of the Transjordan and all the other places bearing typical early Islamic pottery? Certainly not!

Can the Transjordan really be considered as a border between Palestine and the desert? Where is the boundary of the desert? Surely, the fertile

[1]John Lewis Burckhardt, Travels in Syria and the Holy Land (London: John Murray, 1822).

uplands of Edom, Moab and Ammon were as inviting and as capable of sustaining a population as most areas in Palestine. Are more bedouin to be found in the desert fringes or in the rough terrain between the Jordan Valley and the higher plateaus? Why should the hill country east of the Jordan be more inviting to nomads than that west of the Jordan? What is the precise picture in Palestine itself between nomad and villager, between the inhabitants of the hill country and those of the plains — even today? It was very interesting in the spring of 1969 to see how far into the desert the green fields of wheat and barley stretched—almost to the line of the Early Islamic desert castles! Seemingly, the limit to agriculture in the area, in a year of good rainfall, is the amount of labor available to till the soil and harvest the produce.

To build theories on modern analogies, it is easy to take the present circumstances as a point of departure rather than those which existed thirty years ago and earlier. For years now, there has been a drive to settle the bedouin and to register and educate them. The pendulum has swung in favor of the mudbrick house as opposed to the tent. The major barriers to movement now lie at the Jordan and force a closer connection with areas north, south and east. The outlets to the sea are now Beirut and Aqaba rather than Gaza or Haifa. The "King's Highway" is still important, but it is really overshadowed by the "Desert Highway" (roughly from Mafraq south to Zerqa, Amman, Qatrana, Ma'an and Aqaba). Unless impassable trade barriers have been erected, there tends to be a great similarity in the products found in most stores throughout Syria, Lebanon, Jordan and the Arabian Peninsula. How often in past history did a similar situation occur? Little work has been done to test this possibility, for example, for Crusader times when it might have been expected to occur. There may be some valid parallels in the Roman period when there was political turmoil in Palestine. The "King's Highway" and the "Desert Highway" flourished at this time and part of the reason may have been security in the transport of goods. Going back further in time, the same may have been possible from about the ninth to the fifth centuries B.C.

In emphasizing the importance of the trade routes one should not forget that, though they can stimulate and probably raise the cultural level of an area, a solid local economic base must exist. Nelson Glueck's remarks concerning the Nabataeans,[1] usually considered the epitome of a trading nation, make this point very well and act as a caution to us in viewing other periods.

> The day has passed when the entire development and the great wealth of the Nabatean kingdom can be ascribed exclusively to the caravan trade

from Arabia northward which was largely in their hands. They did engage in caravan trade to a great extent, to be sure, but they also engaged in industry, and both intensively and extensively in agriculture as we have seen. Petra cannot merely be understood as a "caravan city" as it has frequently been called; it was also the center of a great agricultural area whose products were marketed in Petra.

The last few paragraphs should be enough to illustrate that it is high time that some reevaluation of theories dealing with the desert and the sown be undertaken, preferably by nonarchaeologists. It may be well to set aside theories of invasion and conquest by peoples supposedly recognizable behind certain ceramic traditions and/or alluded to in vague references among the historical material, presently at hand, until the archaeological material is on a firm footing in both Palestine and Transjordan, and until the answers to some of the above questions have been spelled out clearly.[2]

The Geographical Units in the Transjordan

Some observations on the geography of the area are in order at the close of these general remarks. The area under consideration here coincides with the east bank portion of the modern Hashemite Kingdom of Jordan. Though the Jordan River originates north of the Sea of Galilee, we will not mention the area east of this line and north of the Yarmuk River, since until recently almost nothing in the way of archaeological evidence[3] has been available to go with the scanty historical references to this area for the Bronze and Iron Ages. To the east and south of the fertile areas of the Transjordan, so little is known, until one gets into Arabia proper, that we cannot deal with this area either. It is not necessary to elaborate greatly on the historical geography of this area since a thorough job has been done recently by Yohanan Aharoni[4] and others, and many of

---

[1]Glueck, Other Side, p. 158.

[2]The appearance of new components in a ceramic assemblage and the destruction of specific settlements has frequently been attributed to incursions of nomadic or seminomadic groups like the Amorites. The validity of such hypotheses has been questioned recently by a number of scholars. An excellent review of the evidence and reconsideration of the problem with strong negative conclusions is presented in Thomas L. Thompson, *The Historicity of the Patriarchal Narratives* (Berlin: Walter de Gruyter, 1974).

[3]Only the material published in a brief report on excavations at Tell Ashtara is presently available. Ali Abou Assaf, "Tell Aschtara in Süd Syrien. Erst Kampagne, 1966," *AAS*, XVIII (1968), 103-22.

[4]Yohanan Aharoni, *The Land of the Bible*, trans. A. F. Rainey (Philadelphia: The Westminster Press, 1967), pp. 31-37, 57.

Glueck's remarks remain valid. It should be pointed out, however, that much of what was said by earlier writers like George Adam Smith must be handled very critically or discarded. The best example of this is Smith's description of the Jordan Valley which leads to the following conclusions:

> Why, then, have towns always been so few in the valley? and why has it so much deserved the name of wilderness? The reasons are three. From early spring to late autumn the heat is intolerable, and parches all vegetation not constantly watered. At Pella and opposite Jericho we found the temperature in July at 104°; it has been known to rise in August to 118°. The Arabs of the Ghôr, the Ghawârineh, are a sickly and degenerate race. It is not to be wondered at, that the Israelites who possessed the hills on either side should prefer to build their cities there, descending to the valley only for the purposes of sowing and reaping their harvests. This is what many Samarian villages now do, as well as the bedouin of Moab and the peasants of Gilead.
>
> Again, in ancient times the valley was infested with wild beasts. . . . A still more serious hindrance to settlement of population in the Jordan Valley was the frequency with which it was overrun by Arabs.[1]

The implication of such a description is that no settlement amounting to much is to be expected in the Jordan Valley and that the valley would have provided an effective barrier between east and west. This has proved to be far from true and, in fact, quite the opposite was probably the case.

The country can quite simply be divided into three parallel north-south zones: the Jordan Valley — Wadi Arabah rift; the high plateaus of Edom, Moab, Amman, and Irbed; and the rough hill country which forms the transition between them. All three areas are cut deeply by rifts which drain eventually to the west in the valley. These rifts finger out into the hill country and the plateau with a gradual increase in altitude until they merge with the level of the eastern district.

Taking the north-south and east-west divisions into consideration, we have subdivided our area into ten distinct units, as illustrated in Figure 1: (1) the Irbed district, (2) the northern Jordan Valley, (3) the southern Jordan Valley, (4) the northern hill country of Gilead, (5) the southern hill country of Gilead, (6) the Amman district, (7) the area south of 5 and 6 down to the Wadi Mujib, (8) the area between the Wadis Mujib and Hesa, (9) the area south of the Wadi Hesa to the edge of the desert, and (10) the Arabah. These units seem to hold together on grounds of historical geography (see pages 27-29, 182 and 183) and seem to be natural geographical units. Presently their borders cannot be shown to play more than a minor role in distinguishing archaeological assemblages, though in the future this may change.

Some of the peculiarities that are evident in specific areas should be pointed out. The Jordan Valley is still a rather poorly investigated area, but it is quite rich, as it can support agriculture the year round with the aid of some form of irrigation. Jericho, Beth Shan, and Khirbet Kerak illustrate the important role of this area throughout history and it is difficult not to assume that in most periods both sides of the Jordan Valley formed a cultural unit. Each bank was undoubtedly influenced more by the hill country directly above it rather than that across from it, but to a large extent it should be expected to be a melting pot. This can be well illustrated for most of the periods dealt with here. Throughout the Early Bronze Age the tomb materials from Bab edh Dhra' and Jericho are closely parallel. In the E.B. III period Tell Shuna (north) illustrates a Khirbet Kerak ware site equal in importance to Beth Shan and Khirbet Kerak itself. At the end of the Early Bronze Age, the material from Tell Ikhtenu (south), a site which almost balances Jericho in location at an equal distance and position east of the Jordan, parallels the material from Tell es Sultan, Jericho very closely. Middle Bronze II tomb material from Jericho shows features which are uncommon in Palestine but usual in Amman. Finally, at the end of L.B. and the beginning of the Iron Age, the pottery from Tell Deir 'Allā is very close to that of Beth Shan, not very far away across the valley, but it also has features which are distinctly Transjordanian. Certainly contacts along local roads, as well as along international routes are in evidence. Together they provided active intercommunication throughout the valley so that the material culture became quite uniform throughout. On the east bank of the Jordan, then, we can expect a definite Transjordanian character in the local assemblage but, unlike the higher areas to the east, there is greater evidence for Palestinian influence. This influence would seem to be determined primarily by features adopted in the whole of the Jordan Valley.

The natural terrain of the hill country makes easy passage difficult and forests, still existing in some areas today, must have provided additional impediment to travel in antiquity. Few sites actually fall in this area, except along the water courses.

The fertile plains of the upper plateau are broken up into large natural units which would be expected normally to have contained cultural units also. Certainly, the western stretches of

[1]George Adam Smith, *The Historical Geography of the Holy Land* (7th ed.; New York: A. C. Armstrong and Son, 1901), pp. 489-90.

canyons formed by the rivers Hesa, Mujib, Walla, Zerka, and Yarmuk form great natural barriers, but to the east these canyons gradually become less steep and merge into rolling country. If the edge of the cultivated land does not extend far into the desert at a particular time, the natural barriers serve well, but if they extend quite far, the natural borders gradually disappear.

There has been sufficient discussion of the geographical peculiarities of these areas in the past, but three points should be stressed. First, the "Desert Highway" must have played a role equally as important as that of the "King's Highway." It avoided difficult terrain, was not far from settled areas (yet did not pass through them with the resultant difficulties of tolls, etc.), and could be traveled with greater speed. This was undoubtedly the route which the Nabataeans and Ammonites used intensively and was also probably the route along which the Israelites moved in their exodus from Egypt to reach the borders of Moab from the Arabah.

The second point is that the richest and densest settled area was that in the north, the Irbed district. Though the Yarmuk borders this area on the north, it really forms an effective barrier only to the northwest; while direct north and northeast afford easy communication across the rift and form the gateway to Syria. Unfortunately, this area and the Hauran are, as mentioned above, virtual blanks both archaeologically and, to a large extent, historically. This area can easily be expected to have had a fairly uniform culture, one which was more cosmopolitan than that in areas further south, unless of course the trade routes extended this cultural sphere to the area of greatest contact with it.

The third point deals with the southern end of the area and its effect upon the rest. The various competing overland or overseas trade routes leading from Arabia came out around the head of the Gulf of Aqaba. In either case, the questions is: where did the articles of trade go from here? Did they go directly across to the Mediterranean coast, to Egypt, into Palestine, or up the Transjordan to Syria? The demand from all of these areas for the products of Arabia is clear, and the products they used as means of exchange must have accompanied the caravans on their outbound journey. This traffic would have affected the Transjordan either in profit derived in providing goods and services to the caravans and traders, in the amount of duty exacted from caravan transit, or in profit derived by its traders if they became involved in the handling of the traffic. Quite possibly the greatest influence exerted on the Aqaba region came from the fulfillment of another outside demand, namely for copper. The copper mining area in the Arabah was undoubtedly in constant use. Solomon's undertakings in the area were later followed by those of the Edomites, and he probably took over an industry which had been exploited by Egypt and local peoples for millennia. The recent find of a Temple of Hathor at Timna underscores this, as well as the find of a hoard of copper objects of the Chalcolithic period near Engedi. Basil Hennessy speculates concerning the effect of a Palestinian copper industry on Egypt at this early date.[1] The existence of such an industry, which is suggested by the Engedi finds, would provide an explanation for the Palestinian contacts with Egypt at this time. In any case, the inhabitants of this area seem to have had enough contact with Egypt for such contact to have colored their culture to some extent. It will be important to know, eventually, how much of a catalyst to civilization in the Transjordan this copper industry was at the beginning of the Iron Age, when the working of iron as well as copper may have played an important role in the Transjordan.[2]

---

[1]Basil Hennessy, *The Foreign Relations of Palestine during the Early Bronze Age* (London: Bernard Quaritch Ltd., 1967), p. 86.

[2]This would be true of other areas in the Transjordan as well. Ancient iron mines are said to have been found near Ajlun, and other areas look equally promising, though no geological study is presently availble upon which to base any serious argument along these lines. The Ajlun district is just to the east of sites like Deir 'Allā, Beth Shan, and Tell es Sa'idiyeh, where metal working seems to have been an important occupation. The recent survey and excavations in the Ajlun area have not provided evidence for mining activity in the Iron Age. Robert A. Coughenour, "Preliminary Report on the Exploration and Excavation of Mugharat el Wardeh and Abu Thawab", *ADAJ*, XXI (1976), 71-78.

The historical evidence for the Bronze Age in the Transjordan is extremely limited and, for the most part, consists of little more than an exposition of the cultural sequences of the area. Consequently, the historical evidence will not be discussed until the end of this chapter, where it can be seen in the context of the archaeological material. There, it will also serve as background to the Iron Age discussion and make clearer the changes and transition from the Bronze to the Iron Age.

Any discussion of the Bronze Age must be seen in the light of the conclusions drawn by Nelson Glueck as the result of his survey of the Transjordan and reappraisals of that view based on evidence which has come to light since then.

Glueck's conclusions in respect to the radical decline in settlements which he posits for the Middle and Late Bronze Ages, have been quoted above (p. 11). These conclusions represent some of Glueck's latest statements on the subject and are less conservative than his earlier statements.[1] In contrast to a severe decline in occupation which Glueck proposes, W. A. Ward and M. F. Martin would see a continuation of sedentary populations in the Transjordan through the period of the Egyptian Empire in Palestine.[2] Glueck suggests that part of the reason for the decline was a result of destruction caused by the Hyksos.[3] It is precisely this period which has now been given a definite character through scattered finds in the Transjordan.

Glueck has also posited gaps in the Early Bronze settlement of the Transjordan, but his conclusions are qualified with suspicions that they will be filled in the future.[4] With the sherd evidence which Glueck illustrated, the sherds illustrated here, and a knowledge of the tomb and excavated settlement material which has come to light in the past two decades, it is now possible to define the artifactual assemblages of the Transjordan. The extent to which these assemblages were common throughout the area, however, is still not clear.

Early Bronze Age

Table 1 illustrates the nature of the evidence (Tomb, settlement, or surface material) which is available presently in the ten geographical units we distinguished above and which are illustrated on Figure 1.

Since there currently are a number of chronological schemes for Bronze Age Palestine and since these schemes are constantly being adjusted,[5] it is difficult to maintain one's arguments for a particular scheme for any length of time. In this monograph we have basically opted for a Bronze Age scheme used by W. F. Albright, G. E.

TABLE 1. BRONZE AGE SETTLEMENT IN THE TRANSJORDAN

Area	EB I	EB II	EB III	EB IV	MB I	MB IIA	MB IIB	MB IIC	LB I	LB II
1	o				o	o			-	-
Arqub el Dhahr	x		x	x						
El Husn				x	x					
Irbed								x	x	x
Fo'arah						x	x			
Mughair						x	x			
2	-	-	-	-	-	-	-	-	-	-
Shuna (north)	x	x	x	?						
Ghor Canal Tombs	x	x	x	x						
Deir 'Allā								?	o	o
T. es Sa'idiyeh	?	-	-	?					?	o
Pella				-	-	-	x	-	x	x
3	-				-				-	-
T. Ikhtenu	-	?	?	o	o	-	-	-	?	?
4 & 5					-	-				-
6	-	-	-	-	-	-	-	-	-	-
Amman	-	-	-	-	x	-	x	x	x	-
Yaguz	x	?	?							
Safut							-	-	-	-
Sahab	xo					x	xo	o		o
7				-	-					-
Mt. Nebo		?	x				x	x	?	?
Jellul	-	-	-		?	-	-	-		
Madeba										-
Kh. Iskander	?	?	o	o	o					
Aro'er				o	o					o
8	-	-	-	-	-					
Ader				o	o					
Bab edh Dhra'	x	xo	xo	x	x					
9					-	-				-
Petra					(scarab)					
10					-	-				-
(Timna)										o

Tombs	x	Sherds	-
Settlement	o	Probable Sherds	?

---

[1] Glueck, *EEP*, I, 81-82; *EEP*, II, 138; *EEP*, III, 268; and *Other side*, pp. 114-15.

[2] William A. Ward and M. F. Martin, "The Balu'a Stele: A New Transcription with Palaeographic and Historic Notes," *ADAJ*, VIII-IX (1964), 19-20.

[3] Glueck, *Other Side*, p. 124.

[4] Glueck, *EEP*, III, 268.

[5] See particularly William G. Dever, "The EB IV-MB I Horizon in Transjordan and Southern Palestine," *BASOR*, CCX (1973), fig. 1 for a table which summarizes various schemes for the end of E.B. and the beginning of M.B. as of 1973.

Wright and Nelson Glueck in the 1930s. We have discussed our preference for an Iron Age scheme below on pages 25-26. One of the major areas of dispute is the end of the Early Bronze Age and the beginning of the Middle Bronze Age. We are using the MB I designation purely for the initial phase of the Middle Bronze Age and using EB IV to designate the end of the Early Bronze Age but without subdivisions for the time being.

Bab edh Dhra' Tombs

The major portion of the earliest excavated Bronze Age material from the Transjordan currently comes from Bab edh Dhra'.[1] An intial phase of EB IA[2] has no published parallels on either side of the Jordan. The stratigraphic position of the entire EB IA phase in relation to EB IB is established by superimposed burials.[3] The method of burial is uniform with one exception, tomb A71W.

> The usual pattern is a circular shaft appearing below 50 cm. to one meter of the surface wash. Blocking slabs at the base of the shaft cover the entrances from one to five chambers. There is a 50 cm. step down to the floor of the dome shaped chamber. In the center of the typical chamber was a heap of bones lying on a mat, with the long bones of several adults and perhaps a child neatly laid on the pile. To one side was a line of skulls or skull fragments. Surrounding these and lining the walls were from ten to seventy-five pots usually nested and stacked. One or two stone cups were common but never more.[4]

Briefly, the vessels can be described as follows:

> They are all skillfully handmade vessels of the same ware and have a burnished red slip. . . . The handled cups, simple bowls, and two-handled jars dominate the typology. Uncommon forms include kernoi, ladles, and chalices. . . . The incised decoration and tiny handles and protuberances are also common.[5]

An early stage of this ceramic seems to be indicated in tombs A76W and A45 where both burnishing on the plain vessel surface or burnishing over a red wash commonly occur and where the workmanship is cruder than is normal in other tombs. Tomb A71W is placed at the end of the period, and there the burial practice was one of successive articulated burials with the earlier burials pushed back as each new interment was made. This is the burial practice common at Jericho in Kenyon's Proto-Urban tombs.[6] Crude examples of red band-painted vessels, occurring at Jericho, are also present in A71W.[7] One shaft tomb seemed to have a contemporary deposit of both EB I parallel band-painted pottery

[1]The recent excavations at Jawa, near Azrak in the northeast of Jordan, have uncovered a spectacular settlement which began at the end of the Chalcolithic period and extended into the Early Bronze Age. Very little pottery is published so far in the preliminary reports, so it is difficult to be certain of the exact date within this time range for the construction of the defense system with its gates and tower or the construction of the elaborate, impressive water collecting system. See Svend Helms, "Excavations at Jawa (A Preliminary Report)," *ADAJ*, XVIII (1973), 41-44; "Jawa Excavations 1974: A Preliminary Report," *Levant*, IX (1977), 22-35.

The excavations at Sahab have now also revealed an extensive Chalcolithic settlement which continued into the beginning of the Early Bronze Age. Fuller publication is needed before we can compare this material with the assemblages from Jawa, Teleilat Ghassul, Bab edh Dhra', and other sites. Domestic occupation was found both in caves and above the ground surface: Moawiyah M. Ibrahim, "Archaeological Excavations at Sahab, 1972," *ADAJ*, XVII (1972), 23-36; "Second Season of Excavations at Sahab, 1973," *ADAJ*, XIX (1974), 55-61 and 187-98; and "Third Season of Excavations at Sahab, 1975," *ADAJ*, XX (1975), 69-82 and 169-78.

[2]Paul W. Lapp, "Bab edh-Dhra' Tomb A76 and Early Bronze I in Palestine," *BASOR*, CLXXXIX (1968), 34-38.

[3]Though Lapp used the terminology common in the United States, as opposed to the proto-urban designation, he dismissed G. E. Wright's criterion for defining EB IA as too limited in scope to form a separate assemblage. Wright's basic component of this assemblage is a sequence of grey-burnished forms, mostly bowl and cup shapes. The sequence and its dating have been questioned by Roland de Vaux ("Palestine During the Neolithic and Chalcolithic Periods," *CAH*, Vol. I, Chapters ixb, v-viii [Cambridge: Cambridge University Press, 1966], pp. 35-39) and Lapp added to this questioning by underlining Wright's suggestion of an overlap between red and grey-burnished techniques and demonstrating that the latter was probably done in imitation of basalt vessels. The specifics of the shape of the Bab edh Dhra' grey-burnished vessels are contrary to the sequence proposed by Wright with supposedly late deep-bowl forms occurring here in clearly early contexts. See also P. W. Lapp, "Palestine in the Early Bronze Age," in *Near Eastern Archaeology in the Twentieth Century*, edited by James A. Sanders, (Garden City: Doubleday and Company, Inc., 1970), pp. 101-24.

[4]Paul W. Lapp, "The Cemetery at Bab edh-Dhra', Jordan," *Archaeology*, XIX (1966), 109.

[5]Lapp. *BASOR*, CLXXXIX, 21-24.

[6]Lapp, *Archaeology*, XIX, 109.

[7]*Ibid.* It is very interesting that where this type of pottery was found at Jericho in tomb A 94, vessels typical of Bab edh Dhra' EB IA were also found. This tomb is considered by Lapp to be the only one of Wright's EB IA tombs which did not contain either EB IB or C material as well.

and a typical EB II lattice-painted juglet. There were several other EB II shaft tombs, but most of the material contemporary with the walled city, EB II and III, comes from mass disarticulated burials in what Lapp called "charnel houses" of one or two stories. This method of burial is currently unique, but the ceramic material and other finds duplicate very closely those of the Jericho tombs. The charnel houses in many cases are built over shaft tombs.[1] Only preliminary publication is available at the present time.[2]

Albright and Lapp mention a type of burial which is thought to be characteristic of the final, EB IV, phase at Bab edh Dhra'. These are single interments with a pile of stones or "cairn" over the burial. Lapp did not publish such a tomb and most of our evidence for "cairn" burials from this site comes from a collection of pottery published by Albright. This pottery was associated with what was thought to be a "cairn" burial which had been robbed.[3]

Tombs from Other Sites

The tomb material from Arqub el Dhahr is the largest body of E.B. material aside from Bab edh Dhra'.[4] Most of the vessels date from the end of the Late Chalcolithic to EB I. It is interesting that here in the northern Transjordan we have the red-lined painted pottery typical of Ai and the Ophel tombs, including some extremely elaborate examples. Grey-burnished ware (Esdraelon ware) is also present, however. It is difficult to determine the precise date of the latest pottery from this tomb. Though it seems to be a chronologically homogeneous unit, the presence of Khirbet Kerak ware makes its attribution a problem. An EB III date is indicated by the Khirbet Kerak ware but if this were not present, a late EB III to EB IV date would seem most appropriate.

The whole of the Early Bronze period is again represented at Tell esh Shuna (north)[5] and of particular interest is an abundance of Khirbet Kerak ware, though this is not found everywhere on the tell. The material from the earliest soundings on the site by de Contenson shows clearly that it must be considered with Khirbet Kerak and Beth Shan as a major Khirbet Kerak ware site. Early Bronze II material similar to that from Tell esh Shuna has been found in a cave near Tell el Husn.

Evidence of Architecture and Soundings on Tells

The town at Bab edh Dhra'[6] is badly eroded but two superimposed defense networks were found.[7] The earliest one was of mud brick and over it was a later wall of massive stone-rubble construction which is said to be twelve meters thick on the west side. The town itself came to an end about 2300 B.C. or slightly later. A vast area around the town was covered with layer upon layer of very poor domestic dwellings, apparently after the main settlement had ended inside the walls of the city.[8]

In the latest phase of the town, a few potsherds of a type typical of the latest type of burial in the cemetery were found. This belongs to what Lapp called the Intermediate Bronze Period but is now considered EB IV by Schaub and others. The burials pockmark the earlier structures and consist of single articulated burials covered with a cairn of stones.

Heavy stone defenses were also found at Khirbet Iskander, but the period of their use is not

[1]Lapp, *Archaeology*, XIX, 109.

[2]A considerable number of tombs in the Bab edh Dhra' cemetery had been excavated prior to Paul Lapp's work and are published by Sylvester Saller, "Bab edh-Dhra'," *LA*, XV (1964-65), 137-219.

[3]W. F. Albright, J. L. Kelso and J. Palin Thorley, "Early-Bronze Pottery from Bâb edh-Dhrâ' in Moab," *BASOR*, XCV (1944), 3-13 and Lapp, *Archaeology*, XIX, 106. Recently R. Thomas Schaub has published an EB IV tomb from Bab edh Dhra'. He provides little additional evidence for the "cairn" burials aside from the mention of a single piece of pottery found with tomb A1 which was of this type. Tomb A54 is a stone lined shaft tomb which had been used successively for multiple burials, the latest of which were still in articulation. A second similar EB IV tomb, A52, is also mentioned. The long EB shaft tomb tradition clearly continues into E.B. IV but the chronological relationship between these tombs and the "cairn" burials is still uncertain. R. Thomas Schaub, "An Early Bronze IV Tomb from Bab edh-Dhra'," *BASOR*, CCX (1973), 2-19.

[4]Peter J. Parr, "A Cave at Arqub El Dhahr," *ADAJ*, III (1956), 61-73.

[5]Henri de Contenson, "Three Soundings in the Jordan Valley," ADAJ, IV-V (1960), 12-31 and figs. 1-18.

[6]The tell was originally considered by W. F. Albright to be an enclosure more for settlement during religious pilgrimages than for normal habitation. William F. Albright, "The Archaeological Results of an Expedition to Moab and the Dead Sea," *BASOR*, XIV (1924), 2-12.

[7]Paul W. Lapp, "Bab edh-Dhra'," Newsletter no. 8 of the ASOR (1965), p. 3.

[8]The EB IV occupation outside the walls after the EB III occupation ended, is mentioned again recently by Schaub, *BASOR*, CCX (1973), 2. Excavation is continuing at Bab edh Dhra' on the defenses and on areas inside and outside these walls. More details should be available soon as well as information on the two-acre EB III town site at Numeira, 7 kilometers south of Bab edh Dhra'.

indicated in the preliminary report.[1] House walls and limited architectural evidence has been found at a number of sites which are discussed below as continuing through the EB IV and MB I periods.

Remains of a row of large standing stones were found a short distance to the east of the walled settlement at Bab edh Dhra' by W. F. Albright. Remains of similar rows of stones have also been found at Ader, Khirbet Iskander and Khirbet Lejjun.[2] In each case, the row of stones seems to be associated with E.B. settlement, but unfortunately no other evidence is now available to help us understand how they were originally used.

At Khirbet Iskander, Parr supposes that an earlier sequence of Early Bronze occupation exists below the EB IV-MB I layers he excavated. Early Bronze material has been found at Amman but none has been published. Recent excavations have not exposed any E.B. occupation levels, but unstratified pottery from various places on the citadel shows that such occupation once existed on the site. Figure 46:3-8 shows E.B. I-II grain-wash; figure 46:20, E.B. handle; figure 46:18-19, EB flat bases; number 2, E.B. II-III plate rim; and figure 46:1 indicates Late Chalcolithic-EB I material (similar to Arqub el Dhahr nos. 19, 23, 39).

Early Bronze IV — Middle Bronze I Settlements

A number of sites have yielded material of the end of the Early Bronze period and of the Middle Bronze I period. This material was also extremely common in Glueck's surface survey in the south. It has usually been stressed that in the Transjordan this material is associated with architecture, which is only rarely the case in Palestine. This has led to the assumption that permanent settlement persisted longer in the Transjordan and that MB I settlements may have continued parallel with the MB IIA of Palestine. Unfortunately, the evidence that exists is not yet available for study, so it is again only possible to make some observations.

Four tells have yielded information for this time range, though in most cases from rather restricted soundings. The most complete, but quite limited, publication is of the material from Ader.[3] The closest parallels to much of this material are still from Tell Beit Mirsim. Ader C corresponds roughly to Tell Beit Mirsim J, B to I, and A to H. The B and C, ceramic material from Ader is characterized by thick and often widely-spaced burnish. Combing is frequent; at times burnishing and combing seem to be combined into what looks like incised comb burnishing. Ledge handles are usually of the envelope type, but some pushed-up ledge handles still occur. Plastic bands with thumb indentations are very common, and the rilled-rim bowls and hole-mouth rims are usual. The use of burnishing, surface combing, ledge handles, and red slip indicates a continuation of the E.B. tradition. The variety of shapes which are decorated with the thumb-indented bands is much greater than that at Tell Beit Mirsim and such decoration is also frequent at Ader. Only two sherds of incised straight and wavy line decorations have been published (in these examples it is done with a single incised line rather than the combing, parallel incised line technique, called band-faced-combing by Glueck); both are from Phase A.[4]

It is hard to tell how this material compares with Khirbet Iskander since the published evidence is too limited, though Parr promises interesting conclusions as a result of a careful pottery analysis. Some band face-combing decoration is present, as well as an unusual (Iron I looking) painted sherd. A significant comment by the excavator is that along with the typical MB I pottery there exists clearly contemporary material carrying on Early Bronze traditions At Tell Ikhtenu (south), the Early Bronze Age pottery tradition also continued side by side with pottery similar to Kenyon's EB-MB pottery from the tell

---

[1]Peter J. Parr, "Excavations at Khirbet Iskander," *ADAJ*, IV-V (1960), 128-33.

[2]Khirbet Lejjun has not yet been excavated but clearly has at least an EB II-III occupation. The location of the site shows a deep penetration into the desert which is not apparent again until the Iron Age. Occupation in such an isolated location raises a considerable number of questions concerning the population density in the Early Bronze Age and the kind of agriculture which was practiced to provide subsistence for the population of the area. Glueck's theories of E.B. settlement, in which he supposes that most of the farming areas of many settlements were included within the enclosure of the heavy town fortifications (Glueck, *Other Side*, p. 123), are questionable and again based at best on negative evidence. I see no reason to suppose that sites in the Transjordan will not conform to the normal pattern of settlement as is evidenced in a similar barren steppe area at Tell Arad. There a large E.B. town has been revealed by excavation and its means of sustenance in a dry area are equally problematic. The researches on the elaborate water utilization system at Jawa should be a great help in understanding the ecological adaptations which are necessary for such settlements.

[3]Ray L. Cleveland, *The Excavation of the Conway High Place (Petra) and Soundings at Khirbet Ader* (2 parts; "AASOR," Vols. XXXIV-XXXV; New Haven: ASOR, 1960), Part II, pp. 79-97.

[4]This decoration is actually quite rare, if the relative number of sherds of this type illustrated by Glueck from his entire survey is an indication. Most of these sherds were actually found in the Jordan Valley.

at Jericho.[1] This pottery was associated with several phases of "a fairly well-built, large village of rectangular houses arranged in moderately orderly blocks divided by narrow unpaved streets."[2]

Little in the way of architecture was preserved at Aroʻer. In the earliest phase, VI B, no architecture was associated with the layers excavated in a small sounding. The phase VI A exposure was slightly larger and remains of domestic architecture were encountered. The features indicated above for Ader are characteristic at Aroʻer as well, with Ader B generally equated with Aroʻer VIB and A to VIA respectively. Pottery is present in sufficient volume for Olávarri to demonstrate a development in bowl forms, as well as in cups, cooking pots and other forms. The red-burnished tradition continues throughout but a shift in color and thickness of slip is noticeable. The bright reds of VIB become lighter and often tend to a yellowish shade in VIA. The slip becomes thinner in VIA.[3]

Early Bronze IV — Middle Bronze I Tomb Material

Only a few scattered tombs belonging to the end of E.B. and MB I have been excavated in the Transjordan. The tomb found at el Husn is extremely interesting because it also is characterized by the continuation of the Early Bronze Age pottery tradition together with MB I pottery.[4] Some of the otherwise unique vessels from tombs 877A2 and 1098A at Megiddo are present here also. In general, some shapes are clearly E.B. though a majority are MB I. A red wash or a burnished red surface occurs frequently. The unusual combination of incised and painted decoration has its closest parallels on vessels from the Megiddo tombs cited above.

The Amman tomb, from Jebel et Taj, does not show such a strong E.B. character and is similar to the MB I (EB — MB tomb material from Jericho and Dhahr Mirzbaneh.[5] This tomb would seem then, to be later than the El Husn tomb. We have mentioned the EB IV tombs found at Bab edh Dhraʻ which are the latest tombs in that cemetery (p. 11 above).

Amman Citadel Early Bronze IV — Middle Bronze I Sherds

Some additional evidence for EB IV — MB I occupation in Amman can be illustrated from our sherd material. Figure 46:22-25 shows several examples of envelope-ledge handles,[6] figure 46:9-10 pictures burnished jar sherds showing the junction of the neck and shoulder,[7] and number 17 shows finger pushed up band decoration on a rim.[8]

Middle Bronze I Material and Syrian Parallels

Unlike the above-mentioned EB IV — MB I material, the very latest evidence of this time range is represented only by sherds. Unfortunately, not enough has been published from the tell soundings to document this stage stratigraphically. The sherds of this type are characterized by what Glueck calls band face-combing decoration[9] but this decoration is called comb-incising in the Amuq.[10] The number of such sherds found in the Jordan Valley and in the Transjordan once seemed to indicate a greater

[1]J. Basil Hennessy, "British Archaeology Abroad," *Antiquity*, XL (1967), 130.

[2]Kay Prag, "The Intermediate Early Bronze-Middle Bronze Age: An Interpretation of the Evidence from Transjordan, Syria and Lebanon," *Levant*, VI (1974), 97. It will be very important, some day, to learn how this rather shallow occupation on the south mound of Tell Ikhtenu relates stratigraphically to the higher mound to the north, which probably contains a complete Early Bronze sequence. Prag indicates that basically the two phases at Ikhtenu (south) parallel other sites in the following manner: the earliest phase, Phase I = ʻAroʻer 6B = Ader B = Iskander 3 and Phase II = ʻAroʻer 6A = Ader A. Many parallel forms are illustrated or discussed in a limited fashion in the preliminary reports of these sites and some regional variation is also evident. Band face-combing appears in very limited quantity in the latest phases mentioned. At Ikhtenu, unlike the other sites, the red-burnished tradition of the Early Bronze Age does not occur in Phase II.

[3]Emilio Olávarri, "Fouilles a ʻAroʻer sur l'Arnon," *RB*, LXXVI (1969), 230-259.

[4]G. Lankester Harding, "An Early Bronze Age Cave at El Husn," *PEFA*, VI (1953), 1-13.

[5]Paul W. Lapp, *The Dhahr Mirzbaneh Tombs* ("ASOR Publications of the Jerusalem School, Archaeology," Vol. IV; New Haven: ASOR, 1966). Additional Middle Bronze Age I tomb materials from Amman are mentioned as having been found near the Sports City and several pieces are illustrated in Yusuf Alami, Peter Dassel, Fawzi Zayadine and Siham Balqar, *The Ancient History of Amman* (Amman: Department of Antiquities, 1975), pp. 19 and figures 1 and 2.

[6]Glueck, *EEP*, III, pls. 13:1; 14:1, 11; 18:2, 3; EEP, IV, pl. 17:2, 5, 7.

[7]Glueck, *EEP*, IV, pl. 109:1, 2.

[8]Glueck, *EEP*, III pl. 13:8, 10.

[9]Glueck, *EEP*, II, 124.

[10]Robert J. Braidwood and Linda S. Braidwood, *Excavations in the Plain of Antioch*, I ("OIP," LXI; Chicago: University of Chicago Press, 1960), p. 464, fig. 363.

popularity here than in Palestine. The recent tomb excavations at Jericho[1] and Gibeon,[2] and the work at the tells of Bethel[3] and Hazor,[4] however, indicate that it should be considered equally popular in Palestine. Pottery decorated with comb-incising seems to occur simultaneously in Syria and Palestine and can be found at the same time in Egypt and Iran. In Palestine and Egypt it seems to be short-lived, but in Syria it is the most common type of decoration in the first half of the second millennium. The best parallels to the early Palestinian material actually come from Ras Shamra (the beginning of Ras Shamra II:1)[5] and Qadesh.[6]

The band face-combing decoration is often lumped together with certain varieties of painted and incised wares of the Amuq[7] and elsewhere. Contemporary decoration with parallel painted lines bordering a painted wavy line occurs at Megiddo[8] and elsewhere. The relation of these wares and decoration techniques is not yet clear, but they seem to be emerging as chronologically distinct and had best be kept separate for the present. Thus, wares with incised wavy lines over painted bands seem to be stratigraphically earlier than the comb-incised wares in the Amuq, Hama, and recently, Tell Mardikh. In the Amuq, pottery decorated with incised wavy lines over painted bands is published in I, J and the second mixed range,[9] at Hama in levels J5-1,[10] and at Tell Mardikh in level IIB2.[11] In the Amuq, the comb-incised decoration is published in the second mixed range, with only rare, possibly intrusive, sherds in I and J,[12] but it most common in Phases K and L; at Hama it is found in levels H5-1;[13] and at Tell Mardikh it is found in levels IIIA and IIIB.[14] At Hazor and other sites in Palestine it clearly continues through MB II.[15] Some painted decoration consisting of wavy lines between parallel lines is found in the Amuq in Phase J and the second mixed range.[16] A cup sherd, decorated with incised wavy lines over painted bands, was found in area A (Str. XVIII) at Hazor,[17] together with late E.B. material. Similar sherds were also found by Glueck on sites in the Jordan Valley.[18]

Though a good portion of the Palestinian and Syrian ceramic from the end of the Early Bronze to the end of the Middle Bronze II does not correspond, the above does show that parallels to the Syrian wares of MB II can be found in Palestine and Transjordan. They must, however, be carefully identified and separated from the MB I material. The Palestinian occurrences should indicate what is most probably true in the Transjordan also; that is, that we should expect some such Syrian MB II wares to be found with local MB II material. Despite the addition of new components in the EB IV assemblage which subsequently form the basis of the MB I assemblage,

[1]Kathleen M. Kenyon, *Excavations at Jericho* (2 vols.; Jerusalem: British School of Archaeology, 1960 and 1965), pp. 180-261; II, pp. 33-202.

[2]James B. Pritchard, *The Bronze Age Cemetery at Gibeon* (Philadelphia: University of Pennsylvania Museum, 1963), figs. 19:7; 30:20; 33:38-41; 34:5; 35:2, 3; 56:3-5; and 57:1.

[3]James L. Kelso, *The Excavations of Bethel (1934-1960)* ("AASOR," XXXIX; Cambridge: ASOR, 1968), pls. 31:16, 18, 20-24; 111:A.

[4]Yigael Yadin, *et al., Hazor III-IV* (Jerusalem: Magnes Press, 1961), pls. CCLIX:22-24; CCLXVI:18.

[5]Claude F. -A. Schaeffer, *Ugaritica*, II ("Institute français d'archéologie de Beyrouth Bibliothèque archéologique et historique," Tome XLVII; Paris: Librairie Orientaliste Paul Geuthner, 1949), p. 241, fig. 101:35.

[6]Maurice Pézard, *Qadesh* ("Haut-commissariat de la République française en Syrie et au Liban, Service des antiquities et des beaux-arts, Bibliothèque archéologique et historique, "Tome XV; Paris: Librairie Orientaliste Paul Geuthner, 1931), pl. XXXV, fig. 2.

[7]Braidwood and Braidwood, *Amuq*, I, pp. 443, fig. 342:4, 5, 6, 7, 9; p. 444, fig. 343:16, 17; p. 445, fig. 344:13-16; p. 464, fig. 364:5, 6; and 365:2-10.

[8]P. L. O. Guy and Robert M. Engberg, *Megiddo Tombs* ("OIP," XXXIII; Chicago: University of Chicago Press, 1938), pls. 11:29-33; 12:1; 15:1, 2, 6-9; 20:13; 33:3, 5; 33:10.

[9]Braidwood and Braidwood, *Amuq*, I, p. 443, fig. 342:4, 5, 6, 7, 9; p. 444, fig. 343:16, 17; p. 445, fig. 344:13-16; p. 464, fig. 364:5, 6; and 365:2-10.

[10]E. Fugman, *Hama, fouilles et recherches de la Fondation Carlsberg 1931-1938* ("Nationalmuseets skrifter," IV: København: National museet, 1958), Vol. II, Part 1, pp. 64, fig. 74; 69, fig. 85: 74, fig. 93; 77, fig. 98; 80, fig. 103; 82, fig. 106.

[11]A. Davice, M. F. Squarciapine, P. Fonzaroli, M. Liverani, P. Matthiae, G. M. Scandone, *Missione archeologica italiana in Siria, Rapport preliminare della campagna 1966 (Tell Mardikh)* ("Università degli studi di Roma," Serie archeologica, XIII; Roma: Istitut di studi del Vincino Oriente, 1967), pl. LX:2-5 and now Paolo Matthiae, *Ebla, un impero ritrovato* (Torino: Giulio Einaudi, 1977), fig. 21.

[12]Braidwood and Braidwood, *Amuq*, I, p. 442, fig. 341:8-10; p. 465, fig. 366:3.

[13]Fugman, *Hama*, II, 89, fig. 109; 90, fig. 110; 95, fig. 117; 98, fig. 120; 101, fig. 124; 104, fig. 127; 108, fig. 132; and 111, fig. 139.

[14]Davice, *et al., Missione archeologica italiana in Siria*, pls. LII and LIII, and Matthiae, *Ebla*, figs. 37, 38, 40 and 41.

[15]Yadin, *et al., Hazor*, III-IV, pls. CCLIX:22-24; CCLXVI:18.

[16]Braidwood and Braidwood, *Amuq*, I, p. 443, fig. 342:2, 3.

[17]Yadin, *et al., Hazor*, III-IV, pl. CLVI:1, 3.

[18]Glueck, *EEP*, IV, pl. 35:14.

many characteristics of the earlier, established Early Bronze tradition continue throughout the period. This underscores the reason for the quandary, expressed in the introduction, over the pros and cons of an overlap between the end of the Early Bronze and Middle Bronze I. The Syrian material is actually very sparse for the size of the area involved, and we have clear evidence for distinct geographical variation within it.

Middle Bronze II A

Presently the evidence of the Middle Bronze II A period is confined to material from two tombs found at Fo'arah and Mughair, both a short distance north of Irbed, and from surface sherds.[1] The pottery and objects from these tombs have good parallels at sites where contemporary material was found. Most typical are the carinated bowls and deep round-sided bowls, but here they had a brown rather than a red slip. In the Fo'arah, tomb there are several interesting shapes which currently have their parallels only at Megiddo in Level XIV.[2] These are two large piriform-shaped storage jars and a small jar, all with unique beveled rims. MB II B material was also found in this tomb. Most of the MB II material identified by Glueck came from sites along the Wadi Zerqa and in the Jordan Valley. Sherds designated as MB II A were found in certain areas of the town settlement at Araq el Emir.[3] Only a few more sherds from Amman can be added here, to include that city at the head of the Wadi Zerqa.

The Amman sherd material which can clearly be labeled as MB II A is paralleled at Tell Beit Mirsim and is similar to a portion of the material which Glueck called MB II A. There are a number of jar and bowl rims (nos. 45, 46, 48) and a number of flattened loop handles (nos. 26, 29 and fig. 47:27, 29-31) with an uneven grey-brown wash, which in places allows the cream slip beneath to show through.[4] Some body (fig. 47:32-36) and bowl rim sherds are of a similar ware and surface treatment. The streaky decoration resembles Early Bronze grain-wash, but a comparable date seems out of the question here.

Other base and body sherds show a similar effect, but the colors are reversed with the grey-brown showing through the unevenly applied cream wash. There are a number of sherds which seem now to date to MB II B, but which may eventually be found to occur in MB II A also. These are a series of bowl rims with cream wash and two jar rims which are of a steel-grey ware. These are similar to many of the Amman MB II sherds but have a pinkish-red slip (no. 47 and fig. 48:51-55, 57). Several body sherds of storage jars of similar ware and surface treatment were found, and

some of these showed a range in color from this pinkish-red to cream (fig. 48:56, 58, 63). Several sherds of the same ware were covered only with a cream slip; some were of vessels with thinner walls. Three of these sherds bore incised decoration with good parallels at Tell Beit Mirsim in Stratum D.[5] A MB II B-C date for the group of sherds under discussion seems most likely at present, but unfortunately there is a fairly close parallel for only one of the storage jar rim profiles, and this is from Stratum XIII at Megiddo.[6]

Middle Bronze II B-C

Before continuing on to discuss the remainder of the MB II sherd material from Amman, it would be helpful to discuss the whole vessels which are available from the Transjordan and then to describe the sherds by analogy wherever possible. At least four tomb groups of MB II B-C date have so far been found in Amman, but unfortunately only one has been published.[7] The scarabs and cylinder seals from two other tombs have been published,[8] and much of the material is on display in the Amman National Museum and the University of Jordan Archaeological Museum. Fortunately, the unpublished material

[1]A "caravanserai" has recently been excavated at Jawa, see the articles mentioned in footnote 2, page 27 above. Spectacular architecture, preserved to a second story and with many corbelled roofs still standing, has been presented in these preliminary reports. If the few sherds which are illustrated are indicative, contact with Syria is unmistakable. Clear MB II A forms are present while others seem to reflect the end of the Syrian Early Bronze Age tradition.

MB II A sherds have been published from the recent excavations at Pella: Robert Houston Smith, *Pella of the Decapolis*, I (Wooster: College of Wooster, 1973), pp. 197-98, and are mentioned as having been found in the earliest level of a tomb in Area A at Sahab: Ibrahim, *ADAJ*, XVII, 27.

[2]Gordon Loud, *Megiddo, II, Seasons of 1935-39* ("OIP," LXII; Chicago: University of Chicago Press, 1948), pls. 12:20-22; 13:1, 2.

[3]Lapp, *ADAJ*, X, 88-89.

[4]William Foxwell Albright, *The Excavations of Tell Beit Mirsim in Palestine, Volume I, The Pottery of the First Three Campaigns* ("AASOR," XII; New Haven: ASOR, 1932), p. 6:1-3.

[5]Albright, *TBM*, I, pl. 11:1-6, 8.

[6]Loud, *MEG*, II, Plates, pl. 18:1-3.

[7]G. Lankester Harding, G. R. Driver, B. S. J. Isserlin, and O. Tufnell, "Four Tomb Groups from Jordan," *PEFA*, VI (1953), 14-26.

[8]William A. Ward, "Scarabs, Seals and Cylinders from Two Tombs at Amman," *ADAJ*, XI (1966), 5-18.

can be easily described by paralleling it to Jericho tomb material and material from the published Amman tomb. Until full publication of all the tombs becomes available, it would be best to avoid greater detail and not attempt fine distinctions along the line of Miss Kenyon's recent five-fold division of her MB II.[1] The vessels in the published tomb consisted of small, open, deep, inturned, shallow, carinate, tripod, three-loop-footed, and spouted bowls; a small chalice, chalice-like vases, one-handled vases, and a tall vase; round-bottomed and elongated dipper juglets; oil juglets (cylindrical juglets), piriform, and other juglets with button bases; and finally dipper flasks, small flasks, lamps, a cooking pot, and water jars. A few round, flat, or disc bases occur but ring bases or low trumpet-foot bases are most common. Most of the vessels are of a light colored ware. The exceptions are one bowl, some juglets, and the large storage vessels. The use of a cream slip is common, though occasionally a white or a buff slip is used. Painted decoration is in some shade of red and, in most cases, is on a light slip. The most common decoration is merely parallel lines. In two cases there are wavy lines placed between parallel lines and the tall vase has much more elaborate decoration. One sherd is decorated with the band face-combing common in MB II in Syria. Only one of the piriform juglets is decorated with incised decoration and no good examples of characteristic MB II B chalices occur. The latter facts, coupled with the elaborate decoration of the tall vase, led Isserlin to remark that the date of this tomb covers only the later portion of MB II, and that it possibly extends into the beginning of the Late Bronze age.[2] The extension into L.B. I must have been slight, however, since no Cypriote or Mycenaean imports were found.

The remaining Amman tombs help cover the MB II B-C period completely. Good chalices (most typical in Megiddo Stratum XII[3] and X[4]) occur, as do more piriform juglets (again, incised decoration on these juglets is rare). Several different red-line decorated bowl forms occur and there are now a good number of the chalice-like vases with the same red-line decoration. These are strongly reminiscent of Khabur ware vessels in decoration and shape, but not in base forms. The vessels from the Khabur area have very small bases, almost reduced to button bases.[5] The Syrian vessels which are related to Khabur ware forms are very similar to these vessels from Amman.[6] Much more material is necessary before any connection between these areas can be shown, though chronologically they seem to fall within the same time range. The repertoire of red-on-cream or -white decoration is growing and the most interesting are: two bowls with painted decoration inside, one with a red cross (similar to a bowl from Beth Shemesh Tomb 12),[7] the other with two parallel lines with a wavy line just below the rim; three jars with loop handles on the shoulder, one similar to number 89 of the published tomb but with more elaborate decoration, one similar to number 90 but of a more rounded profile, and a larger jar similar to number 91 but with a much narrower neck and decorated with red painted bands; and a tripod-loop footed vase with fine red-orange decoration similar to that on vessel number 4C61 from layer C of tomb 4 at Jericho,[8] though the Amman example is much better executed. Similar fine decoration is found on a white-slipped bowl (though with bichrome painting in red and

[1]Kenyon, *Jericho*, I, pp. 262-518; II, pp. 203-478. A majority of the vessels mentioned on pages 42-44 have now been published and labeled as Middle Bronze tomb B from Amman, as opposed to tomb A, which is the tomb published by Harding. Michelle Piccirillo, "Una tomba del Bronzo Medio at Amman?" *LA*, XXVIII (1978), 73-86. On the whole there are more fine vessels present in this tomb and the percentage of decorated vessels is higher than in tomb A. Five of these vessels have very fine, and in several cases very intricate, decoration. The major differences in the occurrence of specific vessel shapes are the inclusion of only one flat-based, cylindrical juglet (where 14 were present in tomb A), several elongated dipper juglets and three chalices with sharply carinated sides (where none are present in tomb A). The bowl with the cross painted on its interior is included in this tomb as well as seven alabaster jars. All of the scarabs from this tomb dated between the thirteenth and sixteenth Egyptian dynasties according to Ward. The publication of this tomb provides an additional grouping of vessels but adds little more to our discussion of the date of this material.

A jug of Middle Bronze Age II date was found in a pocket in bedrock in the recent excavation on Jebel Qala': Crystal-M. Bennett, "Excavations at the Citadel (El Qal'ah) Amman, Jordan," *Levant*, X (1978), p. 8. The jug most closely resembles Syrian vessels of this period except for the low pedestal base. The jug is decorated (apparently in red/brown paint) with three bands of straight and wavy lines on the neck and shoulder. A snake, molded in clay and covered with punctate decoration, was applied to the handle.

[2]Harding, *et al.*, *PEFA*, VI, 34-36.

[3]Loud, *MEG*, II, Plates, pl. 29:1-5.

[4]*Ibid.*, pl. 44:23-27.

[5]Barthel Hrouda, *Die bemalte Keramik des zweiten Jahrtausends in Nordmesopotamien und Nordsyrien* ("Istanbuler Forschungen," XIX; Berlin: Verlag Gebr. Mann, 1957), pl. 7:6, 8.

[6]*Ibid.*, pl. 13:3, 4.

[7]Grant, *Beth Shemesh*, pp. 148-49 and no. 136.

[8]John Garstang, "Jericho: City and Necropolis," *AAA*, XX (1933), pl. XVI, no. 10.

brown) from Megiddo, Stratum IX.[1] A number of similar white-slipped bowls, without decoration, were found at Megiddo in Stratum IX[2] and in tombs 251, 855, 1100B, D, 1145B, etc.[3] Such bowls are very common in Amman where the surface decoration also is very much at home, as it is to a lesser extent at Jericho.

The Amman tomb material can now be paralleled very closely to the whole range of Kenyon's MB II material at Jericho, and this fact is clearly underlined by the evidence of the scarabs from these tombs.[4] At Jericho the scarabs range from the XIIIth through the XVIIth dynasties, and exactly the same range is true of the scarabs from Amman.[5] This evidence gives good bracketing dates to the material under discussion and indicates that the material spans the entire period. The metal objects from the Amman tombs add little to our discussion and merely represent what is to be expected in this period.

Two tombs have recently been excavated on the citadel in Irbed with a date range of MB II through L.B. Cylindrical and piriform juglets are clear MB II indicators here. An unusual flaring chalice, without pedestal foot but merely on a ring base, is also unquestionably Middle Bronze. Three vessels, two bowls and a one-handled jar, have the red band decoration on white slip, but their profiles have no exact parallels in the Amman tombs. Another bowl with similar decoration, however, has an exact parallel. The tomb from Fo'arah, mentioned above, extends in time down into the MB II period. Three bowls with tripod-loop legs were found here. Two of these have a burnished brown slip like that on the MB II A vessels but the third, which is almost identical to one of the others in shape (one of these vessels has a very short neck), is covered with a white wash and has red paint decoration similar to vessel number g.1 of Jericho tomb 5.[6]

The remaining two larger groups of MB II B-C material come from a tomb at Wadi Abu en Naml near Mount Nebo and from the foundation deposit of the "temple" found near the Amman Airport.[7] The Wadi Abu en Naml pottery was very badly corroded, but the date is clear and together with the scarabs indicates that the whole of MB II B-C is covered in the deposit. The material from the temple at the Airport in Amman is apparently very rich. Some of the vessels are on display in the Amman Museum, but none there belong to this period. The pertinent pieces here are the published scarabs from this deposit. These range in date, according to William A. Ward, from the seventeenth to the thirteenth century B.C.[8] No architecture of the Middle Bronze period has yet been found on the site. An examination of scarabs in the Amman and Jerash Museums yielded the interesting information that scarabs ranging in

date between the XIIIth and XVIIth dynasties were found at the following places: Pella, Jerash, Heshbon, Al Wir, Kufr Sum, and Petra.

Finally, the Amman sherd material, which can be illustrated as an addition to this body of evidence, can be added here. There is a typical cooking pot rim (no. 86) and a typical double-strap handle of a piriform or cylindrical jug (no. 105). There are a number of body sherds (figs. 48:59-62, 64, 66, 67, 69-73; 49:75-77) usually of hard grey ware with cream or white slips, most of which are decorated with red paint; a carinated bowl sherd with white slip but no paint (no. 79); several bowl rims (fig. 48:70, 71); a jar rim (no. 74); several ring bases (nos. 82, 84 and fig. 49:83); and a flat base (no. 80). Two similar sherds bear much more elaborate decoration. One is a fragment of a bowl base which has, on its interior, a design in orange paint on a white slip (fig. 48:72). The design seems to contain fish and a stylized water pattern. The second sherd (fig. 48:65) is of buff ware, but it has no slip and is decorated with brown paint in a series of parallel lines with zig-zags between them. There is a sherd of a decorated carinate bowl (fig. 48:73) which is similar to two of the bowls from one of the Irbed tombs, mentioned above, and an example from Megiddo Stratum XII.[9] Finally, there is a one-handled jar (no. 78) similar to number 89 of the published Amman tomb. Its decoration is different, consisting of three parallel bands at the junction of neck and shoulder, a band at the carination of the vessel with something more complicated than a checker-

---

[1]Loud, *MEG*, II, Plates, pl. 54, no. 18.

[2]*Ibid.*, pl. 53:16.

[3]Guy and Engberg, *MEG T*, pls. 26:12; 43:22; 47:8; 48:11, 12; 50:9, 10; 52:3; etc.

[4]Diane Kirkbride, "Scarabs", in Appendix E of Kenyon, *Jericho*, II, pp. 580-661.

[5]Ward, *ADAJ*, XI, 5-18.

[6]Garstang, *AAA*, XX, pl. XXXI, left.

[7]Vessels said to come from Zerqa are in the collections of the Pontifical Biblical Institute in Jerusalem: Piccirillo, *LA*, XXVIII, 83 and Amiran, *APHL*, photos 155 and 156. Sherds dated to MB II B-C (and a few later sherds of LB I, LB II and Iron I) were found in Area II, Plot A in the East Cemetery at Pella: Smith, *Pella*, I, pp. 168-70, 174-75 and 198-99. Two tombs were found in the same area and are given date ranges of 1600-1550 for Tomb I and 1700-1650 for Tomb 4: *Ibid.*, pp. 170-74, 198-210 and pls. 35-40, 46-57, 61-62, 81-82 and 88-89.

[8]William A. Ward, "Cylinders and Scarabs from a Late Bronze Temple at 'Amman," *ADAJ*, VIII-IX (1964), 47-55.

[9]Loud, *MEG*, II, Plates, pl. 28, no. 20, but without the band of dots.

board design (similar to the design on the tall vase no. 46 from the Amman tomb) beneath, and two vertical bands of the typical parallel and wavy-line decoration which divide the area between rim and carination. The paint in this case is maroon.

As was said above, fine subdivisions of this material would be premature at present, but several observations should be made. (1) The tombs without L.B. material contained no Cypriote imported wares. (2) There seems to be an evolution in the use of a light slip with the brown-maroon-red-orange painted decoration which we have lumped together above merely as red paint. In the paint, only brown color seems to have chronological value. It seems to be early and is usually on a buff or unslipped surface. There seems to be no chronological importance to the use of orange or red or maroon paint after the beginning of the period, but there seems to be a development in the light slip. A cream to yellow-cream color appears to be less frequent at the end of the period where a white slip becomes more common. The cream and white slips, which seem to be earlier, are not evenly applied and usually let the surface color beneath show through. This effect may have been produced by burnishing, since the slip is very fast and does not come off easily. The white paint on the sherds that apparently come from the end of the period seems to be thinner and more evenly applied. It washes off fairly easily in some cases, apparently where there has not been burnishing, or yields a very bright white color where it has been very evenly burnished.[1]

The material listed above documenting the MB II period in the Transjordan, must now be related to that which Glueck had available to him. He mentioned that sites like Jellul, el Misna', and el Medeiyineh probably had a continuous occupation from E.B. through the Iron Age, but considered this exceptional. Glueck does not consider that the occupation of the Transjordan was uniform, but posits a sharp decline in settlement between the twentieth and thirteenth centuries B.C. in Edom, Moab, and parts of Ammon,[2] between the eighteenth and thirteenth centuries B.C. along the Wadi Zerqa,[3] and between the eighteenth and fifteenth centuries in the Jordan Valley and Northern Gilead.[4] A portion of the material called MB II A must be retained as such (similar to that illustrated above), with the exception of a good portion of the painted pottery. Where this pottery is illustrated for sites in the Jordan Valley, it is classed merely as MB II which avoids difficulty. The sherds, numbers 7, 11, and 13, plate 13; 15, plate 14; 4-7, plate 15; and 13, plate 17 illustrated by Glueck, EEP, III (illustrated as coming from the Wadi Zerqa but unfortunately not by site), however, fall together with the MB II B-C material described above. As a consequence, the material from Amman can on this basis be said to have similarities throughout the surrounding area. Also note, then, that Glueck's own sherd evidence, with dating adjustments on the basis of the Amman and Jericho tombs, indicates that at least the Amman district was heavily settled during MB II A-C. The Wadi Abu en Naml tomb, Irbed tomb, and the scattered sherds and scarabs from elsewhere indicate that at least a moderate amount of settlement existed in the Transjordan during the Middle Bronze Age.

When the first Amman tomb material was found, it was not considered enough to change the existing opinions on settlement in the Transjordan, and one tomb was not considered to be unusual if found in basically nomadic territory. This statement has been reiterated recently by George Landes with a part of the above mentioned material available. He still retains with Albright, the view of nomadic populations and no established cities in the area.[5] The material presented above is sufficient in quantity and scope to make a serious challenge to such a theory and to cause doubts that such a wealth and variety of vessels could have been left in the tombs of nomads. he standard of living indicated by the tombs could possibly be attained by nomads, but the manufacture and transport of materials deposited in the tombs would pose a considerable problem for nomadic people. The burial inventory and custom, apparently, did not differ greatly from that of settled cities like Jericho.

Middle Bronze Glacis at Amman and Safut

Other evidence is available to support the urban character of at least part of the Transjor-

---

[1] The earlier uneven application of the slip is very close in effect to surface appearance of some types of alabaster vessels of a stone which is usually considered Egyptian. The clear white alabaster vessels of local stone, common in the Late Bronze, seem similar to the later variety of white washed vessels. In the latter, there is some overlap in vessel shape but, in the former, there are only rare parallels. If there is an imitation of stone here, it is only for texture and surface treatment and not, possibly until the end of the period, in the imitation of vessels. It is interesting to note that the working of alabaster vessels seems to have centered in several places in the Jordan Valley, near Beth Shan and just east of the Dead Sea, see Immanuel Ben-Dor, "Palestinian Alabaster Vases," QDAP, XI (1941), 93-112.

[2] Glueck, EEP, III, 268.

[3] Glueck, EEP, IV, Text, p. 423.

[4] Ibid.

[5] George M. Landes, "The Material Civilization of the Ammonites," BA, XXIV (1961), 67.

danian occupation. In 1953, a "sloping plastered 'glacis' revetment, resting on natural rock and crowned by a wall," was revealed by a cut through the south end of Tell Safut by the new Jerash-Na'ur highway.[1] Landes adopted a "wait and see attitude" until this material has been clearly published and considered it of little enough importance to warrant change of interpretation.[2] Glueck's surface survey did not reveal MB II material on this site, but some MB II sherds, mostly of the hard grey ware with orange-pink slip discussed above, were found in a visit to the site with a small group in the spring of 1969. Unfortunately, the glacis has not received additional publication and on our one visit to the site its existence could not be confirmed since the cut has been weathered so as to make any features indistinguishable. In the light of a recent find from Amman, the presence of a glacis here must be considered as highly likely. In Amman in the fall of 1968, the Department of Antiquities was clearing north of the "Roman-Hellenistic" wall of the citadel to give a better, unobstructed view of that wall for touristic purposes.[3] In the process of this work, a number of stone wall foundations were found which ran out beneath and beyond the "Roman-Hellenistic" wall. In the spring of 1969, some soundings were made by the author west of this area to gain more information about this defense system. Much more work needs to be done to increase the knowledge of this area but the outline of the occupation in this area is fairly certain. In some places above bedrock in area III, Early Bronze sherds were found but no construction has been found to go with them. Above the brown layer which contained these sherds was a thick layer of sterile *huwwar* composition which had once formed a glacis (fig. 8:1-4). It came up against two intersecting stone foundations of what must have been the walls at its summit (fig. 8:3, 4 and fig. 5). These two walls, E and F on figure 5, intersect at an angle which indicates that it is either the junction of a lower city wall with a citadel wall or, more likely, that we have a fort, similar to the one exposed by Sellin at Ta'annek,[4] extending out beyond the line of the city wall. A third possibility, that of the junction of the city wall with a gateway, also exists. Unfortunately, the stones inside the wall are currently quite jumbled (fig. 9:1, 2) and are in a shallow deposit above bedrock. A second line of larger stone foundation blocks runs over wall E but on a slightly different line. This wall foundation, here called wall D, had no connection with the glacis and was separated from it by a layer of earth (figs. 8:3 and 9:2). The glacis material was cut almost horizontally and was covered by two Iron Age layers which probably correspond to the basic divisions in our sounding to the west (fig. 8:2-4).

The remains of a house wall of the Iron Age can be seen in the section above the glacis and outside the line of the earlier walls. The date of wall G (fig. 8:1, 2) is uncertain. It may be part of a defense system to which wall H also belongs or it may be a fairly recent wall. The important point here is that this wall is situated in such a way that it may reasonably be considered an extension of the Iron Age wall to the east. Also, Iron Age occupation extended beyond the earlier walls and this indicates either that wall F (with which there is no associated pottery at present) is earlier than the Iron Age or that the line of the wall was moved early in the Iron Age.

The sherd material from this area is sparse but enough was found in secure context to aid in the dating of the glacis phase. The glacis construction itself forms a good Middle Bronze Age dating criterion. Middle Bronze sherds were found around and between walls D and E. A distinctive MB II flask was reconstructed from sherds and several of the typical M.B. red painted on white slip sherds discussed above, were found between the walls close to bedrock. Very few sherds were found in the jumble of stones inside walls D and F, but several of these were red painted on a white slip. The remainder of the sherds were probably M.B., although some may have beeen L.B.; no Iron Age material was found here. More excavation is needed here but the basic history of occupation is clear.

The theory of nomadic control of the Transjordan in MB II with the exclusion of urban settlement can now be dismissed, and urban settlement, at least in the areas where the above MB II material has been found, must be expected. The role of the nomadic population in the area is an unknown factor in almost any period, and how it interacted with the M.B. urban population is a matter on which judgment should be suspended until conclusive evidence is available. Since this evidence is obviously not now available, most of the speculation and comment about it should be set aside.

---

[1]Farah S. Ma'ayeh, "Recent Archaeological Discoveries in Jordan", *ADAJ*, IV-V (1960), 114.

[2]Landes, *BA*, XXIV, 67.

[3]The excavator, Mr. Ahmed Odeh, and former Director of the Department of Antiquities of Jordan, Mr. Jacob Oweis, have consented to the inclusion of this material in this monograph; the photographs are my own. Unfortunately, they were taken after a week of rains that came just after the suspension of excavation.

[4]Ernst Sellin, *Tell Ta'annek* ("Denkschriften der Kaiserlichen Akademie der Wissenshaften in Wien, Philosophisch-historische Klasse", Band 50; Wien: Carl Gerold's Sohn, 1904), p. 43, plan III.

Late Bronze Age

The evidence for the Late Bronze Age, with the exception of some stratified sherds from Aroʿer and Deir ʿAllā, and a number of unstratified sherds from other sites, comes from tomb deposits found in Amman, Irbed, Pella, and Tell es Saʿidiyeh, and the "temple" at the Amman Airport. A relief fragment called the Shihan stele, found by F. de Soulcy between Dhiban and Shihan in 1851, may possibly be dated to this period though a number of scholars have suggested an earlier date, in the Early Bronze Age.[1] Our discussion is limited because very little of this material is published. It is evident from the Irbed tombs and the tell material from Deir ʿAllā, that L.B. clearly continues on with the M.B. tradition. Late Bronze material is scattered throughout the Transjordan and seems to be as well established as the M.B. assemblage.[2] A surprising amount of imported Mycenaean and Cypriote pottery is present, and the local wares (though seemingly having some peculiarities in contrast to Palestine), on the whole, can be paralleled in Palestine.

Presently only one tomb, Irbed D,[3] has been published, as has some of the pottery from the storerooms surrounding the L.B. temple at Deir ʿAllā.[4] This provides information concerning the end of the Late Bronze Age, but no published material is available to document its beginning (though considerable material exists). The clearest carry-over from M.B. into LB I seems to be the late M.B. variety of white slipped ware. We have seen how the creamy-white ware with reddish paint must be considered MB II B and C, but the length of its continued use in LB I is problematic. It is difficult at this point to determine in which half of the sixteenth century B.C. vessels with such decoration should be placed, and thus whether they should actually be considered MB II C or LB I. An excellent example of this difficulty is provided by the sherds which Glueck collected at Tell Deir ʿAllā.[5] He dated most of these sherds MB II, though a few were given a wider range of MB II to LB I. Franken, as a result of his excavations, rejected completely the MB dating and considered LB I rather than MB II as the date of the initial settlement of that site.[6] Franken must be considering this ware as purely Late Bronze, or as dating to the end of the sixteenth century, while Glueck's dating was at least a half-century earlier. None of the sherds upon which Franken bases his argument have yet been published, but the sherds collected by Glueck can easily be placed at the end of the sixteenth century.

Figure 50 illustrated two LB I examples of this ware;[7] number 117 has a soft, somewhat fugitive, white slip and red-painted decoration while number 122 has a very hard grey ware with a

[1]The relief was dated to the Late Bronze Age in its publication by René Dussaud in 1912 but W. F. Albright and recently, in a review of the evidence Olga Tufnell, "The Shihan Warrior," *Iraq*, XV (1953), 161-66, suggest an earlier date, in the Early Bronze Age. The stele will undoubtedly remain an enigma until comparative Bronze Age materials are available from the Transjordan. The kilt and hair style clearly show dependence on Egyptian conventions dating back as early as the fourth dynasty but the curl at the back (though difficult to interpret) and the stance of the man holding the spear still have their closest parallels in Hittite art. It is dangerous to try to push the roots of a local Egyptianizing art style into the Late Bronze Age, when strong Egyptian and northern influences affected the Transjordan, until more evidence is available. Tufnell's argument for the date of the spear is inconclusive (see similar shaped spear heads of the proper size illustrated in Du Mesnil Du Buisson, *Baghouz* [Leiden: E. J. Brill, 1948[, Pl. LXI) and we would see the spear, and probably this relief as well, best paralleled by the "Baʿal stele" from Ugarit, Claude F. A. Schaeffer, "Les fouilles de Minet el-Beidah et de Ras-Shamra, quatrieme campagne (printemps 1932)," *Syria*, XIV (1933), 122-24, pl. XVI.

[2]A small amount of additional material has been published recently. Late Bronze II sherds were found at Pella in Area II A, particularly in the "tube installation" between Tombs 1 and 4: Smith, *Pella*, I, pp. 174-75 and 211-12. A number of imported Mycenaean vessels (two-handled piriform jar and several stirrup jars), a number of LB II imitations of Mycenaean vessels (stirrup jars, pyxides and flasks), a number of typical LB II bowls, jars and jugs similar to those found in the Irbed tombs and a number of forms which are found in both LB II and Iron I (dipper juglets, flasks, bowls and lamps) were found at Sahab in Tomb C, which was first used in LB II and continued in use into Iron II: Rafiq W. Dajani, "A Late Bronze-Iron Age Tomb Excavated at Sahab, 1968," *ADAJ*, XV (1970), pp. 29-34. A Mycenaean krater sherd was found in the Department of Antiquities excavations at the tell at Sahab in 1975: Ibrahim, ADAJ, XX, p. 178, fig. 3. This sherd was found in Area E where substantial walls of an important LB II building were encountered, *ibid.*, pp. 78-80. Finally, a Late Bronze Age tomb has been excavated in the Beqaʿ Valley, northwest of Amman. Mention is made of the work by Robyn Brown, Patrick McGovern and others in James A. Sauer, "ACOR, Amman: Director's Report 1976-77," *American Schools of Oriental Research Newsletter*, No. 4, 1977, p. 9.

[3]Rafiq W. Dajani, "Iron Age Tombs from Irbed," *ADAJ*, VIII-IX (1964)," 99-101 and pls. XXXVIII-XL.

[4]Henk J. Franken, "Excavations at Deir ʿAllā, Season 1964," *VT*, XIV (1964), pls. III, VI, and VII.

[5]Glueck, *EEP*, IV, Plates, pls. 40-42.

[6]Franken, *DA*, p. 19.

[7]These sherds were at the Jerash Museum and came from tombs at Pella.

bright white burnished slip and bright red-painted bands. This sherd is of the imitation "Cyrpiote"-like bowls similar to those found in the Amman M.B. tomb (nos. 14 and 17). Numbers 80, 82, 84 and figure 49:83 are base sherds of similar bowls found on the Amman Citadel. The date range of such bowls is, then, MB II C to LB I.

Aside from the Jericho tombs, vessels decorated with red paint on a creamy-white slip are not very common. A number of good examples, recently found at Shechem,[1] are clearly similar to the vessels and sherds under discussion here. However, since they are not very numerous, it seems as if they were an imported ware and the Jordan Valley and the Transjordan may prove to be the major producers of vessels decorated in this manner. At Shechem, the date of these sherds is MB II C.

Imported Wares

The significant new feature in LB I is the large number of foreign vessels. Only a few were found in the Irbed tombs (bilbils and a painted Mycenaean bowl sherd), but Pella, Deir 'Allā, and the Amman airport "temple" yielded a large quantity of such vessels.[2] Few forms common in Palestine seem to be missing here. Fifteenth through thirteenth-century pottery forms are well illustrated in the building's foundation fill and three phases of use. The Cypriote pottery imports consist of Base Ring I, Red Lustrous Wheel-made and White Slip II wares. The Mycenaean vessels with a range from Mycenaean II A through III B are even more numerous and consist of the following: medium and small sized storage jars, pictorial kraters, alabastra, stirrup jars, flasks, cups and bowls (the latter two forms are curiously present only as a small percentage of the total).[3] Imported Egyptian, Cretan and Palestinian stone vessels were found in the excavation[4] as were gold, bronze and ivory objects.[5]

The amount of foreign pottery present in the Transjordan during this period is greater than at any other time prior to the Hellenistic period. It is interesting that these vessels were found not only in the Jordan Valley but also farther east. As a result, we see a far greater penetration of commerce from the Mediterranean toward the desert areas. The decipherment of Linear B script and the reading of tablets bearing such writing helps in identifying some of the commodities which were handled in these containers, such as oil, honey, wine, etc.[6] Whether such products were in demand in the Transjordan, whether they were merely transferred through trade, or whether some of the products used to fill them originated in this area cannot be determined at present. It seems, however, that the international trade connections were as strong and profitable here as in Palestine.

Local Pottery

The repertoire of local shapes is much the same as in Palestine, but a local preference seems to be indicated in the popularity of certain forms. A number of vessels seem to be imitations of foreign forms. The most frequent among these are the one-handled pitchers with cylindrical necks, obvious imitations of the large Cypriote bilbils. In

---

[1]Lawrence E. Toombs and G. Ernest Wright, "The Fourth Campaign at Balâtah (Shechem)," *BASOR*, CLXIX (1963), 60, fig. 26.

[2]The designation "temple" for the building at the Amman airport is not universally accepted. Volkmar Fritz, "Erwägung zu dem spätbronzewzeitlichen Quadratbau bei Amman," *ZDPV*, LXXXI (1971), 140-52 argues against such a designation and reviews the pertinent literature. His architectural discussion of the building and comparisons with known temple plans leads to the conclusion that the heavy construction was suited more as a tower than as a temple. We are impressed with the architectural arguments and are also inclined to this interpretation. The small rooms (seemingly better suited for use as subsidiary chambers), and the difficulty they present for movement in the structure, seem best suited for a taller, solid structure designed for safe storage. How the tower structure functioned in relation to the remains of burned human bones in layers outside the structure, as mentioned in the preliminary report by J. Basil Hennessy, "Excavation of a Bronze Age Temple at Amman," *PEQ*, XCVIII (1966), 155-62 and again well documented in the most recent work by Larry G. Herr, "The Amman Airport Excavations, 1976" *ADAJ*, XXI (1976), 109-11 remains to be seen when a detailed analysis of the bone is published. Whether or not the tower served a funerary purpose (for the storage of funerary gifts?) and stands as our earliest example of the funerary tower so well known around Amman, Jerash and Palmyra roughly 1500 years later, may never be answered on the basis of evidence from this site alone.

[3]The lists of vessel forms and dates have been revised in accordance with a detailed publication of the Aegean pottery by Vronwy Hankey, "A Late Bronze Age Temple at Amman: I. The Aegean Pottery," *Levant*, VI (1974), 131-59. Unfortunately the local pottery is not yet published so the date of the earliest pottery is still unclear though the range for the Mycenaean wares begins in the Late Bronze age and not earlier.

[4]Vronwy Hankey, "A Late Bronze Age Temple at Amman: II. Vases and Objects Made of Stone," *Levant*, VI (1974), 160-78.

[5]Hennessy, *PEQ*, XCVIII, pls. XXXIV-VI.

[6]M. Ventris and J. Chadwick, *Documents in Mycenaean Greek* (Cambridge: Cambridge University Press, 1956), pp. 323-32.

some cases, the body is rounded like the Cypriote vessel, but usually there is a slight carination in the body. These pitchers are often covered with a red or brown wash and are hand-burnished. Occasionally, they bear painted decoration in wide horizontal bands which are broken up in various ways in a fashion which is common on Palestinian jars at this time. Irbed tomb D, numbers 10, 11, and 13,[1] provides examples of such shapes though without decoration. Small bilbils, pyxides, and stirrup jars are only rarely imitated locally. There are a number of jars of the common local forms, but they have the up-tilted, pierced lug handles.

The most common vessel is the two-handled jar[2] like numbers 14 and 15 from Irbed tomb D. In most cases, the bottom of the handle comes down against the body carination and the neck is elongated. There are a number of variants of this jar type, but the difference is only a matter of proportions. The decoration is the same as that which is normal in Palestine. The other local shapes are large one-handled jars, trefoil-mouthed jugs, storage jars with typical MB II-LB handle placement, kraters, chalices, flasks, elongated dipper juglets, typical L.B. lamps, and typical L.B. carinated bowls (by typical here, we mean typical of Palestine). Only the flasks need additional comment. There are many flasks of a size ca. 20 cm. long which are also common in Iron I. Many of the flasks from Pella, however, are very large, ca. 50 cm. This size is quite unusual in Palestine. The decoration of these flasks is similar to that which is common in Palestine.

Figure 50:115-23 illustrate the contrasting color range on vessels with painted decoration. The sherds, again, are from the Jerash Museum and most probably come from Pella. Figure 50:118 and 123 illustrate a continuation of dark on light decoration but in this case the ware and slip are tan and the paint is brown. The decoration is as well executed as it was earlier. Sherds shown on figure 50:115, 116, 119-21 illustrate black and white painted decoration on a red background. The designs, division of the surface, etc., are all in keeping with the typical L.B. tradition in Palestine and again are very well executed.

Finally, mention must be made of several unique forms from the storerooms surrounding the L.B. temple at Deir 'Allā[3]. The style of decoration differs sharply from that described above. It closely resembles that which will be shown below to belong primarily to the twelfth century B.C. Some of the lamps show a slight ledge at the sides (frequent in Iron I), the goblets are of the shape common to these same strata at Megiddo in Strata VII-VI[4], the chalices are of a form common to these same strata at Megiddo, and the sinous-sided bowl, most common in Iron I, already ap-

pears. The detailed publication of a final report is needed before the earliest appearance of these features can be determined.

Late Bronze Sherds from the Amman Citadel

A small collection of Late Bronze Sherds from unstratified contexts on the Amman Citadel clearly illustrates the occupation of the site in this period. Number 105 illustrates the double-strap handle of a jug and figure 50:102-104 illustrate a number of other jug handles, all with oval cross sections. Number 92 is a sherd from the lip of a dipper juglet. Typical bases are illustrated as numbers 94, 95 (ring base) and figure 50:98 (the stump base of a typical storage jar). A storage jar handle is illustrated as number 99.

The remaining sherds illustrate L.B. painted decoration. Most of these are bichrome (figs. 49:76, 77; 50:107, 110-12, 114) with grey to black and red to orange paint on a light (tan to brown) background. One sherd is very heavily burnished (fig. 50:114) and one has a creamy-tan slip (fig. 50:109), reminiscent of the earlier light slipped wares. One sherd (fig. 50:101) is very exciting in that (though it is very small) it illustrates a piece of a typical New Kingdom Egyptian blue-slipped ware vessel.[5] Such vessels are extremely rare in Palestine. Figure 49:76 is a fragment of "Ajjul Ware."[6] It is important to note that this ware, which is one of the earliest indicators of the increased international connections at the beginning of the Late Bronze Age, is also to be found in Amman.

General Remarks and Comments on the History of the Bronze Age

The historical references which illustrate activities in Bronze Age Transjordan are extremely limited until we reach the Late Bronze, but even

[1]R. Dajani, *ADAJ*, VIII-IX, pls. XXXVIII and XXXIX.

[2]*Ibid*, pls. XXXVIII-XL.

[3]Henk J. Franken, "The Excavations at Deir 'Alla, Season 1964," *VT*, XIV (1964), pls. VIb and VIIb.

[4]Loud, *MEG*, II, Plates, pls. 72:14, 15; 79:11; and 87:1-3.

[5]As for instance at Gurob; Guy Brunton and Reginald Englebach, *Gurob* (London: British School of Archaeology in Egypt, 1927), pl. XXXVII:42L; William L. A. Loat, *Gurob* (London: Bernard Quaritch, 1905), pl. I:13 and 15; Flinders Petrie, *Kahun, Gurob and Hawara* (London: K. Paul, Trench, Trübner and Company, 1890), pl. XXI:41-43, 46.

[6]Flinders Petrie, *Ancient Gaza*, IV (London: British School of Archaeology in Egypt, 1934), pls. XLII, XLIII, XLIV, XLV.

there the evidence is limited. The earliest references are confined to the Biblical accounts of the invasion of the Transjordan and the Jordan Valley by foreign kings at the time of the patriarch Abraham,[1] some possible place names in the Execration Texts,[2] and perhaps some places mentioned in the story of Sinuhe.[3] These references provide meager evidence upon which to gain an insight into the history of the area at that time. The major difficulty in considering the Early and Middle Bronze periods is the problem raised in the introduction, namely the relationships which existed between urban and non-urban populations. Unfortunately, the artifactual evidence surveyed here contributes little to this discussion other than to indicate that the area cannot be considered as open exclusively to nomads or non-urban populations for any great length of time. Bab edh Dhra' and Tell Ikhtenu lead us to expect that further excavations, within and against the outside of the city walls, will yield information either to prove a symbiosis between urban and non-urban populations from EB II-MB I or to indicate a clear break in occupation, if it existed. Such excavation would help considerably in defining the character of the Bronze Age settlement in the Transjordan.

The most striking feature of the Early Bronze Age is the use of charnel houses in the cemetery at Bab edh Dhra'. This practice cannot yet be paralleled elsewhere and it is impossible, on the basis of the evidence now available,[4] to do more than speculate on its cultural significance.

In the light of the above discussion, the references to the Transjordan in the Late Bronze Age can be seen in two ways. If we follow Glueck's views, as reviewed above, we have to see a sudden resurgence of urban settlement in the thirteenth century B.C. as a transitional phase prior to the establishment of the Iron I assemblage. If, on the other hand, Ward and Martin's proposal is followed, a vague, transitional thirteenth-century assemblage need not concern us, but rather a full-fledged L.B. assemblage. It has been shown above that a distinct M.B. assemblage exists in the Transjordan, as does a distinct L.B. assemblage. The historical references must then be seen in this context.

The primary evidence provided by the literary sources is a collection of place names. If the identifications are correct, most of the L.B. places were already mentioned in the Execration Texts. The first mention of Egyptian military action in the area comes from the time of Ramses II[5]. At Timna in the Wadi Arabah, the copper mines were exploited by Seti I and his successors (at least as late as the reign of Ramses V). This suggests heavy Egyptian involvement in the Jordan Valley. Ramses II's and Ramses III's campaigns against *S'r* (Edom)[6] are another indication that Egypt may have exerted considerable cultural influence in the Transjordan, as Ward and Martin's interpretation of the Balu'a stele suggests.[7]

The El Amarna letters dealing with the Jordan Valley also mention the sites of Pella and Hamath (Tell el Hammam on the Yarmuk River) and indicate further exactly how these cities took part in the internecine affairs of Palestine. The Biblical record of the movement of the Israelite tribes through the Transjordan[8] and the obstacles they met on the way in the form of distinct political entities, provides additional important information. The political institutions mentioned in this account should be seen as well established entities bearing the distinct character of a strong L.B. tradition, rather than recently established or vaguely defined entities. The follow-

---

[1]Genesis 14.

[2]Wolfgang Helck, *Die Beziehungen Äygyptens zu Vorderasien im 3. und 2. Jahrtausend v. Chr.* ("Äygyptologische Abhandlungen," Band 5; Wiesbaden: Otto Harrassowitz, 1962), pp. 49-67.

[3]"The Story of Si-nuhe," trans. John A. Wilson; *Ancient Near Eastern Texts*, ed. James B. Pritchard (2nd ed.; Princeton: Princeton University Press, 1955), pp. 18-22.

[4]Lapp, *Archaeology*, XIX, 106-8.

[5]Wilson in Pritchard, *ANET*, pp. 253-258. If the homeland of some of the Shosou mentioned in the texts from the time of Thutmoses II and onward are to be localized in the Transjordan, then we would have evidence for Egyptian involvement in the area at least this early, Raphael Giveon, *Les bédouins Shosou des documents Égyptiens* (Leiden: E. J. Brill, 1971), pp. 9-10, 219-20. Under Amenhotep III (*ibid.*, pp. 26-28) and Ramses II (*ibid.*, pp. 71-77) specific toponyms within the Shosou territory are mentioned. For a detailed review and additional supplementary material see William A. Ward, "The Shosu 'Bedouin'," *JESHO*, XV (1972), 35-60.

[6]Ward and Martin, *ADAJ*, VIII-IX, 20-1.

[7]The recent find of a commemorative scarab of Amenhotep III near Petra provides additional concrete evidence to document the existence of Egyptian influence in the Transjordan prior to the XIXth Dynasty, William A. Ward, "A Possible New Link between Egypt and Jordan during the Reign of Amenhotep III," *ADAJ*, XVIII (1973), 45-46 and pls. XXVIII-XXX. The extent of the Egyptian influence can only be a matter of speculation at this point but "Since the reign of Amenhotep III was generally peaceful until his later years, it is evident that his commemorative scarabs may have been sent to important towns by way of a 'public announcement' of unique events during his reign" (*ibid.*, p. 46).

[8]Numbers 20:14-24:25.

ing states were encountered: Edom, Moab (south of the Arnon), the Amorite Kingdom of Sihon, and Bashan. It is interesting that Bashan (primarily north of the Yarmuk) is so closely connected with the northern part of the Transjordan. This is not surprising, however, since many names of cities of this area are found in the Amarna letters[1] and some of these appear as early as the Execration Texts.[2] A long established political unit in this area thus seems quite clearly to have existed.[3]

It is difficult to say at this point how the Israelite incursion affected the Transjordan, since it comes somewhat earlier than the time when a radical change in the local assemblage occurs. A detailed discussion below will present what can be illustrated as an early twelfth-century assemblage and the following Iron I assemblage. New features definitely occur at the very end of L.B. and, as we noted below, there is a sudden end to the importation of foreign pottery vessels. In the Jordan Valley, at least, this occurred while there was continued Egyptian domination, but not later than Ramses VI, the latest attested Egyptian ruler in Palestine before Shishak. How the Israelite conquest is to be seen in relation to these factors cannot be stated with certainty at this point,[4] but it may at least have been responsible for breaking some trade connections and causing unsettled conditions which gave rise to the parochial character that was to characterize the occupation in this area for many centuries.

[1]Helck, *Beziehungen*, p. 191.

[2]*Ibid.*, pp. 49-67.

[3]Stelae erected by Seti I and Ramses II at Tell el Shihâb and Sheikh Sa'id respectively, in this area indicate a similar situation in regard to Egyptian dominance as that which existed farther south. See Bertha Porter and Rosalind L.B. Moss, *Topographical Bibliography of Ancient Egyptian Hieroglyphic Texts, Reliefs, and Paintings*, Vol. VII: *Nubia, The Deserts, and Outside Egypt* (Oxford: Griffith Institute, Ashmolean Museum, 1962), 383.

[4]Several recent discussions have dealt with the Egyptian records and Biblical texts dealing with Egyptian and Israelite relations with the Transjordan. Several articles have been mentioned above but to these the following should be added: Kenneth A. Kitchen, "Some New Light on the Asiatic Wars of Ramesses II," *Journal of Egyptian Archaeology*, L (1964), 47-70; John van Seters, "The Conquest of Sihon's Kingdom: A Literary Examination," *Journal of Biblical Literature*, XCI (1972), 182-97; Magnus Ottosson, *Gilead: Tradition and History* ("Coniectanae Biblica: Old Testament Series," No. 3; Lund: C.W.K. Gleerup, 1969).

A number of reconstructions of the history of the Transjordan in the thirteenth century B.C. are possible. If the Israelite conquests in the area are to be dated to this century, then it would seem that they may well have to be seen in the broader context of a power struggle between Egyptians and Hittites. Kitchen proposes early thirteenth century B.C. dates for the Ramses II conquests of Moab and Edom, as well as Bashan (Kitchen, *JEA*, L [1964], 69-70). We might then consider the conquests of Sihon and Og to be inroads into the Egyptian sphere by factions allied to the Hittites, while Edom and the remainder of Moab continue to be secure in the Egyptian sphere. So secure in fact, that the Israelite forces do not confront them. The Israelite victories would then serve to negate inroads of northern influence and at worst provide a non-aligned buffer area. Ramses III later reasserts the Egyptian presence in the Transjordan apparently only in Edom and Moab.

CHAPTER III

IRON AGE: INTRODUCTION AND
HISTORICAL SKETCH

The amount and variety of material available for the Iron Age greatly exceeds that from the Bronze Age. Most of our discussion will again center on the pottery vessels. The remaining finds will be brought into the discussion on the basis of the chronological sequence determined by the pottery. Complete vessels from tomb groups, and occasionally from stratified excavation, will be studied first and then the sherd evidence will be used to supplement or better illustrate the types represented by the complete vessels.

Since the information concerning the stratigraphic context of complete vessels is very limited, we are forced to arrange this material typologically. Three major problems must be faced in creating such a typology and fitting it into one of the chronological frameworks which have been proposed. First, no stratified burials were observed in any tomb, so that it is difficult to assess the length of time a tomb was in use. As a result, where unusual vessels occur it is difficult to date them by relying on associated objects in the same tomb. Second, the Iron Age tomb groups presently known from the Transjordan can clearly be separated into two groups but there is a gap in time between them. One group, which will be called Sequence I, falls into the first two centuries of the Iron Age; the other, Sequence II, belongs primarily to Iron II and extends somewhat into Iron III. The few tombs which fall between Sequences I and II have been assigned to the phase with which there is the greatest overlap. Though the relative chronological position of the tomb groups is clear, it is difficult to give a definite terminal date to each. A chronological range may be assigned to most of the vessels in a tomb group but, since no firm evidence exists for the exact dates specific types actually came into or went out of use, we can safely outline only clusters of types. Third, the chronological distribution of these tomb groups does not fit satisfactorily into any of the accepted divisions that have been proposed for the Iron Age.

It would be ideal if we could do away with period designations and divisions altogether and replace them with century or half century dates. Unfortunately, if this were done on the basis of our present knowledge of the Transjordan it would indicate a greater precision than actually exists. In some cases, we are able to date tombs or vessels with some confidence to a narrow time range, but it is far safer, for the present, to give a date as late Iron I than to try to fix it precisely in the second, third, or fourth quarter of the tenth century B.C.

Three major rival chronological frameworks are summarized in Table 2. We have decided, for the present, to follow basically the chronological framework of W.F. Albright, since the majority of the Palestinian parallels we will be citing are published in accordance with this scheme and the sequences of occupation on most other Palestinian sites have been arranged according to it.[1] Where we happen to differ with this framework, we will be able to explain our deviations easier than with any other.

TABLE 2. PERIOD DIVISIONS OF THE IRON AGE

	Loud and Shipton[2]	Aharoni and Amiran[3]	Albright[4]	
300				300
400	Late Iron	Persian	Iron III	400
500				500
		Neo-Babylonian		
600				600
700		Israelite III		700
800	Middle Iron		Iron II	800
900		Israelite II		900
1000	Early Iron II		Iron I	1000
1100	Early Iron I	Israelite I		1100
1200				1200

All three schemes acknowledge a break around 600 B.C. (or 587 B.C.). Albright differs from the others in making his early dividing point at 900 B.C. rather than 1000 B.C. Loud and Shipton create a further division in their Early Iron. Though we will argue below that a distinction should be made between twelfth century artifacts and those which precede and follow them, we do not feel that this is sufficient reason to warrant adopting this scheme. The Loud-Shipton Middle Iron period of 400 years seems much too long and is in need of division. It is very tempting to accept the arguments which Aharoni and Amiran put forward for their subdivision around 840 B.C.

---

[1]Albright, AP, p. 112.

[2]G. Ernest Wright, "The Archaeology of Palestine," *The Bible and the Ancient Near East,* ed. G. E. Wright (Garden City: Doubleday and Company, Inc., 1961), pp. 94-101.

[3]Shipton, *SAOC,* XVII, 4 and Loud, *MEG,* II, Text, p. 5.

[4]Yohanan Aharoni and Ruth Amiran, "A New Scheme for the Subdivision of the Iron Age in Palestine," *IEJ,* VIII (1958), 172.

[5]Albright, *AP,* p. 112.

Unfortunately, as will be shown below, the artifactual evidence from the Transjordan is so meager in the late ninth and early eighth centuries B.C., that it is now impossible to document any change at that time. Also, the validity of adopting an "Israelite" chronological framework between 1200-587 B.C. in the Transjordan is doubtful.

The choice of either 1000 B.C. or 900 B.C. as a main division in the Iron Age is a major problem. We have already stated a preference for Albright's divisions but we must indicate two reservations. First, one must acknowledge that there are strong arguments against the choice of the 900 B.C. date for the change from Iron I to Iron II. A major consideration for the date of this change is an attempt to see a reflection of the historical and political factors in the archaeological materials. It is, however, difficult to see such reflections, except in the most obvious instances. If political changes brought with them sweeping social and economic changes (and these often were reflected in trade and other foreign contacts, with either a depressing or stimulating effect); then, and only then, would a reflection of this be expected to appear in our artifactual material. A great effect on the artifactual record of Palestine would not be expected by the dividing of the Israelite monarchy; but rather it would be expected that such an effect would be much more evident at other times, namely, the establishment on a firm basis of the United Monarchy and the period of resurgent prosperity under the Omrid dynasty. The Aharoni-Amiran divisions coincide with the latter situation in the change from Israelite II to III. Divisions at both 840 and 900 B.C. cannot be substantiated but it is possible to argue for a change at 1000 B.C. rather than at 900 B.C.

The second reservation is that ceramically the greatest change which occurs in the Iron Age is the introduction and primary use, in its latest part, of red wash and burnish decoration. If Albright's divisions are used, the red wash and burnish decoration occurs both at the end of Iron I and throughout most of Iron II. The use of the 1000 B.C. date comes closer to utilizing the innovation in decoration as an indicator of change by confining its use primarily to the period after 1000 B.C.

In such a case, it is tempting to revert to the Loud-Shipton divisions and accept the Aharoni-Amiran division at 840 B.C. It is best to avoid this for the time being, however, since the 1000 B.C. date must be used as a round number, though it comes closest to the date of the introduction of red wash and burnished decoration. Also, the introduction of this surface treatment and its place of original use have not yet been pinpointed. Greater clarification of this matter is, then, needed before a definitive statement is possible.

It is for these reasons that Albright's framework is being used as our basic point of reference for the present. Hopefully, in the not too distant future evidence will be sufficient to permit the use of general numerical dates and to avoid the difficulties of rival chronological divisions. Consequently, the attempt will be made below to rely as much as possible on the Transjordanian evidence itself for divisions.

In addition to the discussion of the chronological framework that will be followed below, the historical framework must also be indicated. Problems of literary interpretation will not be dealt with at length, nor will the attempt be made to extract from ancient written documents all the available information about the Transjordan in the Iron Age. As noted in the general introduction, this has been done by a number of scholars and a repetition of it, even with slight re-emphasis, would not yield enough new information to warrant its inclusion here. The provision of a framework within which our archaeological discussion can be viewed and upon which we can base certain discussions below is all that is intended. In some instances, the archaeological evidence suggests or requires a modification in the understanding of events referred to in literary sources or provides an additional perspective in viewing these literary references.

Source material is derived from four different areas: Egypt, Palestine, Mesopotamia, and the Transjordan itself. The Egyptian references are the least plentiful and concern only the beginning of Iron I and the Persian period. The Biblical text provides the greatest amount of information and, despite the fact that it presents an often biased (Palestinian) view of events, it presents the best coverage of events that exists. The Mesopotamian, namely the Neo-Assyrian, Neo-Babylonian, and Persian sources, are few in number and begin only in the ninth century B.C. A number of inscriptions of varying length on stone and bronze, ostraca, and inscribed seals constitute the epigraphical evidence from the Transjordan. The discussion will begin where it was ended above in the discussion of the Late Bronze Age. There is very little evidence, either from the Transjordan or elsewhere, that indicates continuing Egyptian contact with the Transjordan beyond about 1140 B.C. It would be difficult not to see the situation, sketched above for the Jordan rift, perpetuated until the termination of the Egyptian XXth dynasty's power in Palestine. References to Pella or Hamath are not attested in the twelfth century B.C., and all we can say is that at Timna Ramses V (1145-1141 B.C.) is the latest attested Pharaoh and Ramses VI (1141-1134 B.C.) the last at Beth Shan. The vase from Deir 'Allā[1] with the inscription of Queen Taousert is the only firm twelfth century inscriptional evidence from the Transjordan. Only the two Ramesside scrabs from the Madeba Iron I tomb A, a similar seal from Sahab tomb C, and possibly the Balu'a stele (see pp. 153-154 below) may provide additional evidence.

The Israelite incursion into the Transjordan[2] took place well within the Late Bronze Age. The accounts of the exploits of the Israelite Judges as well as those of Saul and David would be included in the archaeological period of Iron I. The contacts and conquests of various Israelite and Judean kings, as well as the kings of Damascus, that are cited in the Biblical records all fall within Iron II. The interplay between the various areas of the Transjordan and those nations which exercised control over any part of it for some length of time have been abstracted, in tabular form in Table 3. For this purpose, the Transjordan has been subdivided into the geographical areas which we designated above on page 19 (illustrated in fig. 1), namely: (1) the Irbed district, (2) Northern Jordan Valley (between the Yarmuk and the Zerqa Rivers), (3) Southern Jordan Valley (between the Zerqa River and the Dead Sea), (4) Northern Gilead, (5) Southern Gilead, (6) Ammon, (7) Northern Moab (the Moabite-Gadite contested area north of the Wadi Mujib), (8) South Moab (Moab proper, between the Wadi Mujib and the Wadi Hesa), (9) Edom, and (10) the Arabah. We have included the names of the rulers of the individual kingdoms, where they are known, and the numbers 11-16 are placed opposite a particular date to indicate the kingdom which controlled a specific area at that time: (11) Israel; (12) Judah; (13) Aram-Damascus; (14) Assyria; (15) Babylonia; (16) Persia; and (17) Egypt. The chronological chart (Table 3) has been adapted from H. G. May's Oxford Bible Atlas[3] and includes the dates assigned by W. F. Albright[4] and E. R. Thiele (in parentheses). On the chart, areas under local control have no other numbers within the range of time that such control existed. When area numbers are indicated in parentheses, they indicate possible control, except in the case of (14), which indicates tribute-paying, subjugated areas of the Assyrian Empire. Those areas which were not incorporated into the provincial organization but were allowed to maintain their local dynasties (in some cases even to perpetuate their control over neighboring districts) are also shown without additional numbers, as areas under local control.

It is difficult to assess the fortunes of the inhabitance of the eastern side of the Jordan Valley, and northern and southern Gilead in the twelfth and eleventh centuries B.C., and later during the divided Israelite monarchy. In the chart, an attempt has been made to indicate the nations which dominate an area, where specific historical references indicate this. There is a problem, however, in understanding the nature and length of such domination. In the twelfth and eleventh centuries, major political pressures were at work. (1) There was an attempt on the part of the people within various districts to maintain their independence with aid from west of the Jordan River. (2) There was an attempt on the part of neighboring Transjordanian states, like Moab and Ammon, to claim some or all of these areas as their rightful possessions.[5]

The most effective control of the Transjordan by a Palestine power occurred under David, but this gradually deteriorated under his successor, Solomon. Domination was effectively duplicated by Jeroboam II, but proved to be ephemeral. The Mesha Stone inscription alone, of all the fragmentary inscriptions found in the Transjordan, is of sufficient size to illuminate a chapter in local history, tradition, and motivation from the point of view of a local ruler. It is far more difficult to understand the nature and effect of the Aramean domination of certain areas. It is important to

---

[1]Franken, *DA*, p. 19.

[2]See pp. 60-62 above.

[3]Herbert G. May, *Oxford Bible Atlas* (London: Oxford University Press, 1962), pp. 16-17.

[4]We have given our reasons above for following W. F. Albright's chronological divisions in our discussion and for the sake of uniformity include his dating of individual rulers here also. The year dates of Mesopotamian rulers have been brought up to date on the basis of suggestions made by Professor John A. Brinkman, see John A. Brinkman, "Mesopotamian Chronology of the Historical Period," an appendix to A. Leo Oppenheim, *Ancient Mesopotamia* (Chicago: University of Chicago Press, 1964), pp. 341 and 347.

[5]This occurs first in the case of the Moabite state under its king, Eglon (Judges 11:1-12:7), where there was an attempt to dominate the areas here designated as 2-5 and 7. Later, at the time of Jephthah (Judges 3:15-30), the Ammonite state tried to dominate the same areas. These are only two illustrations, among many, of attempted expansion by particular states with the purpose of dominating areas which were not normally under their control in the Iron Age. In the case of the Israelite domination of specific areas, their claim would be based on the conquest at the time of Moses. In the case of Moab, Ammon, or Bashan, the claim would go back to rulers of the Bronze Age who once dominatd extended kingdoms. The territories dominated by the Israelites would be considered lands that were lost temporarily but considered rightfully theirs. If the political record of inter-city or inter-district struggle dates back substantially beyond the accounts related in the Biblical record, then we can expect additional rationalizations to have existed for substantiation of claims of conquest and domination.

TABLE 3.   RULERS AND POLITICAL DOMINATION OF TRANSJORDANIAN AREAS

1	2	3	4	5	6	7	8	9	10	Dates	Israel (11)	Judah (12)	Foreign-based Empires
										1200			*Egyptian XXth Dynasty* (17)
				6					17	1190			1184-1182 Setnakhte
										1180			1182-1151 Ramses III
										1170			
		(8)	Jeph-	(6)		(6)				1160			1151-1145 Ramses IV
			thah							1150			1145-1141 Ramses V
										1140			1141-1134 Ramses VI
										1130			
										1120			
										1110			
										1100			
			Ehud	(6)		(8)	Eglon			1090			
										1080			
										1070			
										1060			
										1050			
										1040			
										1030			
		(8)								1020	Saul 1020-		
						(6?)				1010			
					Nahash	(8?)				1000	David 1000-		
		6	6		Hanun					990			
11-12	11-12	11-12	11-12	11-12	11-12	11-12	11-12	11-12		980			
										970			
										960			
								Hadad		950			*Egyptian XXIIth Dynasty* (17)
										940	Solomon -922		
										930			941?-920? Shishak
13	13	13	13	13		8		(11)	9	920	Rehoboam 922(931)	922(931) Jeroboam I	
										910	Abijam 915(913)	901(910) Nadab	
										900	Asa 913(911)	900(909) Baasha	
										890			*Neo-Assyrian Empire* (14)
										880		877(886) Elah	883-859 Ashurnasirpal II
	12	11			(Ruhubi)	12				870	Jehoshaphat 873(870)	876(885) Zimri	
	12	12	12	11-12			Mesha	11		860		(885) Tibni	
13	13	13	13		Ba'sha	8			11	850	Jehoram 849(848)	876(880) Omri	
12	11-12	12	11-12			(12)				840	Ahaziah 842(841)	869(874) Ahab	
										830	Athaliah 842(841)	850(853) Ahaziah	858-824 Shalmaneser III
13	13	13	13			13				820	Jehoash 837(835)	849(852) Jehoram	
										810	Amaziah 800(796)	842(841) Jehu	
										800		815(814) Jehoahaz	823-811 Shamshi-Adad V
12	12	11-12	12	11-12		8				790		801(798) Jehoash	810-783 Adad-nirari III
										780	Uzziah 783(767)	786(782) Jereboam II	
						12	(12)	11	11	770			782-773 Shalmaneser IV
		(9)								760			772-755 Ashurdan III
					(11)	8		(14)	9	750		746(753) Zechariah / 745(752) Shallum	754-745 Ashurnirari V
										740	Jotham 742(740)	745(752) Menahem / 738(742) Pekahiah / 737(740) Pekah	744-727 Tiglath-pileser III
										730	Ahaz 735(732)	732(732)- Hoshea	
14	14	14	14	14	Sanîpu (14) (Zakir)	(14)	Salamanu (14)	Kaush-malaku (14)	(14)	720	Hezekiah 715(716)	721(723/22)	
	(8)	(6)		(6)						710			
					Bod-El		Kammusunadbi			700			726-722 Shalmaneser V / 721-705 Sargon II
								Aiarammu		690	Manasseh 687(687)		704-681 Sennacherib
										680			680-669 Esarhaddon
					Ammi-nadab I / Hissal-El		Musuri Kemoshalta	Qaushgabri		670			668-627 Ashurbanipal
										660			
										650			
					Ammi-nadab II					640	Amon 642(642)		*Neo-Babylonian Empire* (15)
					(Hanan-El)					630	Josiah 640(640)		626-624? Ashuretililani
										620			-612 Sinsharishkun
										610	Jehoahaz 609(609)		611-609 Ashuruballit II
15	15	15	15	15		15	15	15	15	600	Jehoiakim 609(609)		625-605 Nabopolassar
					Ba'lys					590	Jehoiachin 598(598)		604-562 Nebuchadrezzar II
										580	Zedekiah 597(597)-		*Persian Empire* (16)
										570	587(586)		561-560 Amel-Marduk
										560			559-556 Neriglissar
										550			556 Labashi-Marduk
										540			555-539 Nabunaid
16	16	16	16	16	16	16	16	16	16	530			(559) 538-530 Cyrus II
										520			529-522 Cambyses II
										510			521-486 Darius I
										500			
										490			485-465 Xerxes I
										480			
										470			
										460			464-424 Artaxerxes I
										450			
										440			
										430			424 Xerxes II
										420			
										410			
										400			423-405 Darius II
										390			404-359 Artaxerxes II
										380			
										370			
										360			
										350			358-338 Artaxerxes III
										340			337-336 Arses
										330			335-331 Darius III

28

note its presence in the chart, in view of our discussion below of the influence from the north on art styles in the Transjordan. One of the most important factors which is taken up extensively below is the nature and date of the Assyrian influence in this area. Once again the chart indicates the pertinent facts, and a development can be traced to a point at which these areas are ultimately incorporated into a provincial administration.

Only a few further points need to be stressed here. First, there is an indication that definite units existed, within the contested areas, which accommodated themselves to the power struggles. Mazar indicates that the "Land of Tobiah," connected with the Tobiad family in Hellenistic and Persian periods, is probably to be identified with the "Land of Tabel (*māt Ta-ab-i-la-aia*)"[1] mentioned in a cuneiform document found at Nimrud.[2] It is tempting to connect this further with the land of Tob where Jephthah took refuge many centuries earlier.[3] In the Nimrud document, the land of Tabel borders on "*māt Gi-di-ra-aia*," which is plausibly connected with the later "Gadora (Γαδωεα), which is the capital of Perea (Jewish Transjordan) in the days of Josephus.[4]" Both of these areas border the Ammonite state and at times may have been under its control, as is indicated by the mention of Tobiah as the "Ammonite servant" by Nehemiah.[5]

Mazar's discussion also indicates that Judean and Israelite families held large tracts of land in the Transjordan and were able to maintain these, as well as their influence at the Judean or Israelite courts.[6] As land owners in the Transjordan, they apparently were treated as private citizens and could sustain their holdings even when these areas were not politically controlled by Israel or Judah. On several occasions, the Israelite king was forced to take refuge in the Transjordan. After the death of King Saul, his son Ishbosheth established his capital at Mahanaim.[7] Later, King David fled to Mahanaim when he was forced to leave his capital in Jerusalem when his son Absalom led a revolt against him.[8] In the early part of the reign of Jeroboam I the Israelite capital was again shifted to the Transjordan, this time to Penuel.[9]

Finally, it must be mentioned that the Tobiad family plays a prominent role in the Aramaic correspondence, dating to the Persian period, which has been found at Elephantine in Egypt.[10] This, together with ostraca from Tell el Kheleifeh of the same period,[11] provides historical documentation concerning events in the Transjordan and indicates that a decline in population or culture in the Persian period cannot be safely assumed without further substantiation.

---

[1]Benjamin Mazar, "The Tobiads," *IEJ*, VII (1957), 137-45 and 229-38.

[2]H. W. F. Saggs, "The Nimrud Letters 1952, Part II," *Iraq*, XVII (1955), 131-32, No. XIV.

[3]Judges 11:3.

[4]Mazar, *IEJ*, VII, 238. In this connection it should be mentioned that Wolfgang Helck in his *Die Beziehungen Äygyptens zu Vorderasien im 3. und 2 Jahrtausend v. Chr.* (Äygyptologische Abhandlungen," Band 5; Wiesbaden: Otto Harrassowitz, 1962), pp. 201-203, cites the mention of a *qa-d(u)-[r]* in a list of place names of the time of Seti I. Helck stresses that this site is to be located in the Transjordan and identifies it with Gadara (the Decapolis city identified with modern Umm Queis),

but we must also point out the possibility of the identification with a site farther south.

[5]Nehemiah 6:14.

[6]Mazar, *IEJ*, VII, 232-35.

[7]II Samuel 2:8-12.

[8]II Samuel 17:24.

[9]I Kings 12:25.

[10]A. Cowley, *Aramaic Papyri of the Fifth Century B.C.* (Oxford: Oxford University Press, 1923).

[11]Nelson Glueck, "Ostraca from Elath," *BASOR*, LXXX (1940), 3-10; LXXXII (1941), 3-11. W. F. Albright, "Ostracon No. 6043 from Ezion-geber," *BASOR*, LXXXII (1941), 11-15.

CHAPTER IV

IRON AGE SEQUENCE I (EARLY MATERIAL)

Provenience of Pottery

The pottery corpus on figures 20 to 31 illustrates the complete forms which have been published to date with the addition of photographs of similar pieces from the Madeba, Amman, and Irbed Archaeological Museums. These vessels come from tomb groups excavated at Madeba, Amman (Jebel Nuzha), and Irbed, and from the Iron Age phases A-L of Deir 'Allā. Additional tombs with pertinent material have been found near Mt. Nebo, at Sahab, Amman (Jebel Qusur), Pella and along the line of the East Ghor canal. Some of this material will be mentioned, though without illustrations. Additional related vessel types and decoration styles will be illustrated by drawings of profile types and photographs of sherds from Amman. Our dicussion will also include sherd materials collected by the author on sites other than Amman, as well as from survey reports published by others.

Pottery Shapes

Though certain shapes clearly indicate the position of a specific tomb group within our sequence, some uncertainties remain since the work is done primarily on a stylistic or typologic basis. The published pottery sequence from Deir 'Allā does not span the entire sequence under discussion, but it is of the greatest help here in firmly fixing most questionable pieces and in substantiating the typological sequence. The stratified sherds from the 1969 Amman Citadel sounding overlap the latest types from the tomb groups and must begin very soon after the end of the published Deir 'Allā sequence. The unpublished phase M Deir 'Allā material should be parallel to it.

Beginning of Sequence I: The Jebel Nuzha Tomb

The earliest tomb of the Iron Age sequence is the Jebel Nuzha tomb from Amman. Many of the shapes found here are similar to those from other tombs in this sequence, but there are a good number of shapes which are unique. Within the last five years, more published pottery has become available for comparison so that now the stratigraphic position of this tomb is considerably clearer. Previously, it would have been very tempting to date the earliest material in this tomb to the thirteenth century B.C. on the basis

of many features which are close to the Late Bronze tradition.[1] The total absence of the imported Cypriote and Mycenaean wares that are normally found in Late Bronze Age contexts argues against such dating.[2] It could be argued that such imported L.B. objects were not carried as far east as Amman, but the evidence illustrated above from the airport "temple" in Amman clearly illustrates that such vessels were as common here as in the Jordan Valley. Also, L.B. Mycenaean sherds were found in the predominantly Iron Age tomb excavated at Jebel Qusur, in Amman,[3] and whole vessels were found in the tomb excavated in 1968 at Sahab, about eight miles southeast of Amman.[4] The picture here seems to be like that of Megiddo Stratum VI, where band-painted decoration is the most common decoration, and forms very close to the L.B. tradition occur but no LB II imported wares are present. The publication of more pottery of Level VI from Beth Shan, together with some of the pottery from Deir 'Allā, helps clarify and substantiate a situation which is much the same as that of Strata VII and VI at Megiddo (and less clearly seen at other sites). Beth Shan Level VI is now thought to coincide closely with Dynasty XX in Egypt.

The last major building of the Late Bronze temple at Deir 'Allā contains a faience vase bearing the cartouche of Ramses II and the name of his Queen, Taousert. The next level belongs to a short-lived attempt at rebuilding the site. In this level, the excavator notes a change in pottery; but, unfortunately, very little of it is published. This was mentioned above in connection with the tomb deposits at Pella and Irbed. Imported pottery, apparently, was still present and this level is still attributed to the Late Bronze by Franken.

---

[1]This was done in the publication of the tomb group. Rafiq W. Dajani, "Jebel Nuzha Tomb at Amman," *ADAJ*, XI (1966), 48-52.

[2]Two examples of squat vases with two pointed-lug handles were found, and similar vases and a stirrup vase were found in Madeba tomb A to be discussed below. Both types of vases are normally found in Iron I contexts in Palestine and represent types produced in that period and not survivals from the Late Bronze Age.

[3]Only the coffins found in this tomb have been published so far; see p. 146, footnote 1.

[4]See page 20, footnote 2 above for reference to R. Dajani's publication of Sahab Tomb C.

This level, however, and the first four Iron Age levels (A-D) are probably to be considered contemporary with Beth Shan VI. It will be important to compare the pottery of the last phase of the Late Bronze from Deir ʿAllā, when it is available, with the Beth Shan pottery to see if a distinction should also have been made at the latter site. Also, one would like to know whether it compares solely to Level VI material at Megiddo or whether it should be attributed to the very end of Stratum VII. It is important to note the possibility of Late Bronze pottery occurring later than 1200 B.C. without an admixture of Iron Age wares. The presence of Granary Type Late Mycenaean IIIC pottery at Irbed and the slanting loop handles of the Pella tombs are best explained by this also. A positive statement on this matter must be deferred, pending Franken's full publication of his material.

It is interesting that painted decoration similar to, but yet distinct from the Late Bronze tradition is found in Beth Shan VI, the latest L.B. material at Deir ʿAllā, and Deir ʿAllā Iron Age levels A-D. The Jebel Nuzha tomb contains almost all of the painted pottery that is published from this early part of the Iron Age. Painted decoration, and its implications, will be discussed more fully below.

Important Features of the Jebel Nuzha Tomb

The pottery of the Jebel Nuzha tomb is much more sophisticated and better made than is usual for pottery of the twelfth or eleventh centuries from either the Transjordan or Palestine. A comparison between the vessels from the Jebel Nuzha tomb and Deir ʿAllā illustrates this contrast. The careful analysis of the Deir ʿAllā pottery indicates the basic reasons for the decline which can usually be noted. There was a change in the consistency and preparation of the clay used for potting; there was a temporary loss of the mastery of the fast wheel (the mastery of the fast wheel had been on the decline throughout the Late Bronze Age from a height in MB II); coiling or form-molding techniques were now commonly used to construct the vessels; and less precision was exercised in the drying and firing procedures. Though this constitutes a degeneration of methods, the ones which were used were satisfactory enough to produce dependable and usable pottery. A turnette was employed for some of the vessels, but a faster wheel was not used again until the end of Sequence I, and then only rarely.[1]

Shapes Relating to or Continuing the L.B. Tradition

The jar, figure 27:27, is a shape which was seen in great variety in the Transjordanian L.B. repertoire above and is an isolated example here. A second two-handled jar is typologically later with a lower carination and a shifting of the handles away from the carination to the base of a short narrow neck. There are six other jars, figure 26:30-35, with shapes similar to that of the jar in figure 27:27 but they have only one handle, in most cases beginning low on the shoulder and terminating at the rim. Though jars, figure 26:33-35, resemble L.B. shapes, no such jars have yet been published from L.B. contexts. Unpublished Tell es Saʿidiyeh parallels have been cited[2] for one of these jars and it is considered L.B. Until the context from which this jar comes can be examined, there is no way of knowing whether it is from a fourteenth, thirteenth or twelfth century deposit. The decoration on two of these jars, figure 26:33 and 35, is also unlike L.B. decoration, except for some of the latest L.B. at Deir ʿAllā[3]. Excellent parallels for this vessel shape, both with and without handles, are found in Period I of the cremation cemetery at Hama (ca. 1200-1075 B.C.).[4] This date coincides with our dating here and other features present in this Jebel Nuzha tomb are also found in Period I at Hama, namely, several bowl profiles and base types.

The small seemingly Mycenaean or Mycenaean style vases were mentioned above, but these and similar vessels of this time range should be subjected to very minute analysis to determine, if possible, whether they were truly imports from a great distance or local products. The lack of other imported vessels and the assimilation of other features from such vessels to locally produced vessels at this time suggest that they are not truly imports. At Megiddo, such vases continued in use through Stratum V.

The two-handled flasks, of which fifteen examples were found (not all have been illustrated here), are very difficult to distinguish from L.B. examples. Some are plain (or possibly their decoration is worn off), some have the usual concentric circle decoration on the sides (fig. 30:30-32), and others show more elaborate decoration (fig. 30:17-22). The highly decorated examples, in all but one case, have rather complicated linear geometric patterns which will be discussed below. Similar decoration occurs in the Sahab tomb where cup-spouted flasks (similar to Megiddo

[1]Franken, *DA*, pp. 67-80.

[2]Dajani, *JN*, p. 51.

[3]Franken, *VT*, XIV, pls. VI b and VII b.

[4]P. J. Riis, *Les Cimetières á Crémation, Hama fouilles et recherches de la Fondation Carlsberg 1931-1938* ("Nationalmuseets skrifter," Vol. I; København: Nordick Forlag, 1948), figs. 23, 25, 26, and 63.

Str. VI; Loud, *MEG*, II, Plates, pls. 74:16; 80:7, and 86:11) are also found.[1] The corpus illustrates the variety that exists in the positioning of handles on these flasks. All of the examples are two-handled. No one-handled flasks have yet been found contemporary with Sequence I.

There is a variety of elongated or pointed dipper juglets and jugs from this tomb. There is also a series of jugs and juglets of similar shape but with small ring or disk bases. Such an attachment of bases is unique. The pointed dipper juglet is a common feature of the Middle and Late Bronze Age assemblages but only one, figure 25:10, has the shaved sides and very pointed base which seem to be most typical of the end of L.B. Figure 25:9 and 11 seem to be of the type found both in Megiddo Strata VII and VI. The duplication of the latter type of juglet form in a larger jug (fig. 25:18-21 occurs only in Stratum VI at Megiddo and a few examples have been found here, (9 out of 160 vessels) is unusual. A similar jug is on exhibit in the Irbed Museum (fig. 25:22). Several of the jugs and juglets do not have the simple pinched spout, but are handleless and more elaborate with a carination beneath the rim (fig. 25:5-7). Some of these approach the form which becomes common later in the Iron Age; compare forms on figure 40:2 and 3. The lamps consist of two types, one with a simple up-curving side, without a folded-over ledge (fig. 31:1-6), and the other with slightly folded-over sides (fig. 31:10-13). Both types occur at the end of the Late Bronze Age but the former is the normal type for that period and the latter the one which becomes most common later in the Iron Age. The corpus shows the persistence of both types throughout Sequence I.

The use of a ring base is very common (fig. 21:4, 5, 8, 9, etc.), but in the later tombs of this sequence it is far less common. The high ring bases (fig. 21:10-12, 14) are frequent here, but extremely rare in the other tombs.

There is a series of deep bowls with round sides that form an almost hemispherical shape (figs. 21:4, 5, 8-15; 22:11-13). The size of these bowls varies from small to quite large and almost all are ring based; some have very high ring bases. The rims are very simple, and the little variation that occurs can be seen in the corpus. Concentric circle decoration appears on several of these bowls, most of which are said to be light red in color. The best parallels that have yet been published were cited above from Hama, but more will be said below regarding their date in the discussion of decorations.

The vessel which seems to be a cooking pot, figure 24:24, is not very clear either in drawing or photograph. If it is a cooking pot, it is as unique in this context as the simple out-turned rim is nor-mal for much earlier MB II or LB I contexts, though not in such a shallow, open form.

The high-footed bowl, or chalice, figure 24:8, has parallels at Deir 'Allā in Phase B (fig. 24:9) and at Megiddo in Strata VII and VI. The common features are trumpet feet, relatively straight sides, and flat-ended rims. The Jebel Nuzha bowl, however, has a longer base with a long solid column below the bowl which is not found on the others. The high-footed bowls of the end of the Late Bronze at Deir 'Allā[2] seem to offer the best parallels, but the absence of drawings to accompany the published photographs lends a degree of uncertainty.

The final shape to be discussed here is a miniature two-handled jar. Three examples of such jars are illustrated in figure 30:5-7. Similar jars exist throughout the Iron Age in Palestine with modifications of the basic shape.[3] Unpublished examples from Pella and Tell es Sa'idiyeh apparently come from LB II contexts. If more exact information on these tombs bears this out, there will be another shape which continues from L.B. into the Iron Age.

Remaining Jebel Nuzha Forms

The remaining forms are: (1) a number of bowls of simple profile, (2) two deep two-handled carinated bowls, and (3) two small jugs. These groups will be discussed separately since they have close parallels in the Madeba tombs, which is to be discussed next. The overlap in forms between the Madeba and Jebel Nuzha tombs is illustrated by these forms as well as the appearance in the Madeba tombs of four of the nine basic forms discussed above. Only one additional form was found in the Madeba tomb A which is a common Late Bronze Age form but which did not occur in the Jebel Nuzha tomb.

Restatement of Chronological Position of Tomb

The greater number of surviving L.B. forms in comparison with the Madeba tombs indicates an earlier date for this tomb. The continuation of painted decoration, which is very rare at Madeba, further emphasizes this. Better techniques of manufacture are also indicated in these vessels. It seems best to characterize this tomb material as within the Iron Age (shortly after 1200 B.C.),

---

[1]The designs have been included in Table 5, pp. 174-85 and four cup-spouted flasks are illustrated in R. Dajani, *ADAJ*, XV, pl. XII.

[2]Franken, *VT*, XIV, pls. VI b and VII a, b.

[3]Loud, *MEG*, I, pl. 9:23 and 24.

but very much transitional between the Late Bronze and Iron Age traditions. It is similar to Beth Shan VI in clearly showing the overlap, while distinct from Megiddo VI in its duration. At Megiddo, a fifty-year gap is postulated between Strata VI and V because of abrupt changes in form and decoration which appear in V without transition.[1] A range of 100 years from 1200 to 1100 B.C. seems to be the closest approximation of the date of the Jebel Nuzha tomb that can be given now.

The Madeba Tomb A

This tomb can be considered characteristic of the early centuries of the Iron Age. The gap in time which separates it from the end of the L.B. is clear when it is compared with the Jebel Nuzha tomb. The L.B. features which occur here seem to have been integrated into, and become an integral part of, this Iron Age assemblage. The "Mycenaean" shapes, the squat vases (fig. 30:12-15), and stirrup jar (fig. 30:8) illustrate this most clearly. The inspiration for the shape is clear, but the ware is thicker and similar to that of most of the other vessels in this tomb. Most of these vessels seem to be undecorated (or the decoration has been worn off) and the stirrup jar has a red slip which is not found on the imported vessels. The flasks provide the majority of the painted vessels (fig. 30:17, 24-29, 31, 32, and 33). The spiral or concentric circle design is the most common, but two flasks are more elaborate (fig. 30:17 and 34) though not nearly as elaborate as the Jebel Nuzha examples.[2] The decreased use of painted decoration is evident and goes along with the almost total lack of decoration on other vessels.[3] There is a greater variety in the placement of handles on these flasks than on those from Jebel Nazha. The dominant type, as was the case at Jebel Nuzha, is illustrated by figure 30:24-29. The placement and orientation of the handles on figure 30:34 were not found at Jebel Nuzha but are common in L.B. Figures 30:31 and 32 have sloping strap handles which occur at Megiddo in Stratum VI. Such handles are considered to be of a type which continues to be used until much later in the Iron Age. The narrow necks on figure 30:17, 31, 32, and 34 are unusual elsewhere. One of these flasks, one which happens to be published in photograph as well as line drawing, illustrates finer ware and painted decoration.

Only a portion of a dipper juglet was found. It has the simple elongated form seen above, figure 25:9 and 11, on a Jebel Nuzha juglet.

A large number of deep bowls were found in this tomb. All but one of these had two loop handles which extended from the carination to the rim. The rims, with one exception, are simple.

They curve in uniformly and then back slightly, so that the rim diameter is less than that of the carination. Some of the shapes, figure 23:21, 23, and 26, resemble L.B. kraters but, as is the case with the other bowls, they are undecorated and examples with more than two handles do not occur. The carinations on these bowls are at about mid-height and are rounded. A high carination seems to be a specific Iron Age feature and this nearness of the carination to the rim forces the handles to extend beyond the vessel's greatest diameter. The two similar bowls from Jebel Nuzha (fig. 23:15 and 20) had a fairly sharp carination. The profile of these bowls conformed to that of the typical L.B. carinated bowl. The features we have mentioned so far are firmly connected to both the L.B. and Iron Ages.

The other deep bowls are illustrated in the Sequence I illustrations, pls. 20-31. Three of them show a variety of ledge handles (fig. 23:5, 8 and 10 = [11]). One bowl (fig. 23:12) has a handle on one side and a spout on the other which is similar, except for the rim profile, to a slightly later vessel from Tell Beit Mirsim B₃.[4]

Most smaller bowls have simple rounded profiles or a slight variation thereof. Other bowls have a carination, more or less pronounced, with a flaring or out-turned rim above. The sharply carinated forms, like figure 22:14, 19, and 28, resemble L.B. forms while those with a slight carination and short rim, figure 22:2, 3, 25, 26, and 30, are what Albright calls "wavy-rim bowls" at Tell Beit Mirsim[5] and are characteristic of his

[1]Shipton, *SAOC*, XVII, p. 5.

[2]Thirty flasks are published among the Sahab Tomb C vessels: R. Dajani, *ADAJ*, XV, pls. X-XII and the decoration patterns which are clear on these flasks have been included on Table 5, pp. 174-85.

[3]Harding does note, however, that traces of red lines were found on some of the vessels but this is not illustrated in the drawings. It is impossible to say if this refers to the painted flasks or to other vessels. Such red-line decoration would be in keeping with what was found at Jebel Nuzha and at Megiddo in Stratum VI. Technical changes in the clay seem incompatible with earlier methods of surface finish and painting, with resulting difficulties in application and adhesion of the decoration. This seems gradually to have led to the abandonment of earlier methods of applying the decoration, see Franken, *DA*, p. 173. The normal undecorated L.B.-Early Iron ware of Timna and its vicinity is very similar to the materials discussed here from Madeba, Beno Rothenberg, *Timna: Valley of the Biblical Copper Mines* (London: Thames and Hudson, 1972), figs. 30 and 45, particularly the deep bowls, jars, pinched-lip jug and pixide forms.

[4]Albright, *TBM*, I, pl. 50:9.

[5]*Ibid.*, pp. 63 and 64.

Iron I. Most rims are not elaborate but are simply rounded or pointed at the top. Figure 20:18, 26, and 28 show a flattened horizontal top which is much more common later. The "wavy-rim" profile is also evident in medium-sized to large bowls where it is sometimes modified to a very rounded shoulder and a very short, almost vertical, rim (figs. 23:2[=3], 5[=6], 8[=9], 10[=11], 22 and 26. It is evident from the chart that the remaining bowls from the Jebel Nuzha tomb, which we did not discuss above, have the same features as these Madeba bowls. The only difference is that several of these bowls are also decorated on the interior with painted concentric circles.

The ring base is even rarer in bowls than in other shapes, and the majority have simple flat or rounded bases. Though obscure in the drawings, disk bases are also fairly common at Madeba but it is difficult, except in obvious cases, to distinguish them from flat bases. The disk bases become very common at the end of our present sequence, in the Irbed tombs and the Amman sherd material. At Jebel Nuzha the disk base clearly occurs only on the unique elongated jugs figure 26:37 and 38 (and less clearly on the similar juglets, figure 25:13 and 14), underscoring the presence of a significant shift between the beginning and the end of Sequence I. The ring base is also uncommon in this group, with only one occurring at Jebel Nuzha and three at Madeba tomb A.

Only a few jars occur in Madeba tomb A. They all have short necks and rounded profiles. The placement of handles and lack of carination in these vessels stand in clear contrast to the few examples from the Jebel Nuzha tomb and earlier L.B. vessels. The carination on the smaller jar, figure 26:30, is paralleled in the bowl, figure 24:23. Similar low carinations are typical of the two jugs, figure 26:1 and 31, at Jebel Nuzha. Such forms seem to be characteristic of this stage in our sequence. The spouted jug, figure 27:18, seems to be an early example of a common Iron Age form but, unlike most of the later examples, the spout is placed opposite the handle rather than at the side of the jug. Cylindrical spouted jars are relatively rare in Palestine but more common in Syria, as exemplified at Hama and in the Amuq.[1] The last form to be discussed from this tomb is the storage jar. No such large vessels were found at Jebel Nuzha and more will be said on the basis Iron Age, particularly in Stratum V at Megiddo. An example from phase L, at Deir 'Allā, figure 29:9, is contemporary. The parallels suggest that this jar is among the latest forms present in Madeba tomb A.

Irbed Tombs A, B, and C

The three tomb groups from Irbed are clearly set off from the tombs discussed above by the frequent use of burnishing and a red slip, and by many new shapes. Thus, it would, consequently, be tempting to place these tombs in Sequence II, except that few of the shapes overlap with anything found there and much of this material falls within the range of the Deir 'Allā phases J - L. Each tomb group contains only a small number of vessels and the great overlap of forms indicates a similar time range for all. Hand and wheel burnishing are said to occur, as does one example of circular burnishing and several examples of vertical burnishing (on jugs). Some vessels have rounded bases but flat cut bases are the most frequent. Only one is said to have a disk base and two have ring bases. The great majority of the shapes are very simple. Continuity with the earlier tombs is indicated by this preponderance of flat bases and by the simple profiles. No decoration, aside from red wash, is found on these vessels and light red seems to be more popular than darker shades.

Distinctive Forms

Several round-bottomed bowls occur (several show the "wavy-profile" rim), two are carinated, and only one example is sharply inturned. The simple forms have fairly close parallels above. Figure 20:12 from tomb A and figure 20:7, 25, and 30 from tomb B are bowls with inturned sides, but they have almost vertical rims which are new. The profile of the deep bowl, figure 23:4, is close to 23:2 from the Madeba tomb and the rim is similar to figure 23:5 (=6) and 10(=11) at Madeba. The two carinated bowls, figure 22:35 and 36 from tomb B, could at first glance be mistaken for L.B. vessels. However, the proportional length from the carination to the rim is straighter, more vertical, and longer than is normal in L.B. Similar carinated bowls have been found in the Amuq and elsewhere in Syria. In the Amuq, they have been found at Chatal Hüyük in levels 4 and 5. Their date range on that site can be placed, at present, approximately between 1000 and 750 B.C.

The elongated dipper juglets (fig. 25:17, 18) are like those discussed above. There are two round-bottomed juglets (figure 25:23, 24) which, though paralleled in the corpus (figure 25:25-33, 35), have longer handles and necks. The same lamp types occur here as those found in the Madeba and Jebel Nuzha tombs, with the peculiarity that

---

[1]Riis, *Hama Cem.*, p. 53, fig. 40; p. 63, figs. 71, 72; and p. 66, fig. 83. Many examples were found in the Amuq. To cite only a few of them, we can mention Area I at Chatal Hüyük where this form occurs in levels 4-8 (which cover part of Iron I and II).

in most cases the spouts are elongated.

The most characteristic new form for these tombs is a one-handled juglet with a long neck and a handle attachment at mid-neck, figure 26:5, 13-16.[1] All such jugs are of black-burnished ware. One of the juglets has a small pointed base and the others have button bases.

These tombs are unique in exemplifying the importance of this shape, since it is also found on larger jugs which are rare elsewhere. The surface colors of these jugs (fig. 27:4, 5, and 20) are cream, buff, red, and light red. Juglets of this shape from the Amman and Madeba Museums are illustrated in photograph in the corpus. They also illustrate a range in color.

Three other juglets (fig. 26:18-20), two decanters (fig. 27:13 and 17), and a strainer jug (fig. 27:21) exemplify the attachment of the upper part of the handle to the center of the neck. In each case, there is a ridge around the neck at the height of the handle attachment. One of these is a black-on-red Cypriote juglet, a very common imported vessel in Palestine. In Cyprus such juglets are given a date range of 850 to 700 B.C., but Syrian vessels of this type are said to appear already around 1050 B.C.[2] Four decanters are illustrated from the Madeba and Irbed Museums. Such decanters continue in use into Sequence II, where a few one-handled Cypriote juglets also occur, and illustrate the closest similarities that exist between vessel types of Sequence I and II.

The three storage jars (fig. 28:9-11) are uniform in profile with slightly blunted pointed bottoms, short slightly out-curving necks with small rolled rims and two large handles attached at the sides. The handle attachment is lower and its bottom joins the body at a sharper angle than the L.B. types. Two of these jars (fig. 28:9 and 11) have a small third handle which rises from the top of the shoulder to the side of the neck. This extremely unusual feature seems to be another illustration of the use of the typical handle which has been seen on the jugs.

Tomb B contained two kraters which were almost identical in form though different in size. This shape is similar to figure 23:28 of the Madeba tomb, where there seems to be the beginning of a thickened collar.[3] The kraters from Madeba tomb A, however, are two-handled while the Irbed kraters have four handles. The incised lines on the rims of the Irbed kraters are unique but suggestive of smaller jar rims illustrated in the Amman sherds and also present at Deir 'Allā. This will be dealt with in greater detail in the discussion of jar rims, type LXX, from the 1969 Amman Citadel sounding. The Deir 'Allā and Amman rims are not vertical but at an angle and bear molded ribs rather than incised lines. Four-handled kraters from the Madeba Museum are

also shown in the corpus. These vessels are quite different, as they are much taller with necks proportionately more narrow.

The final form in need of discussion is the strainer, figure 22:51. It is a one-handled tripod cup with holes pierced through the body below the neck. A variety of such vessels is illustrated in photographs from the Amman, Irbed, and Madeba Museums (fig. 22:45-50) and the small legs of such vessels were found in the 1969 Amman sounding. Strainer cups are discussed below as part of Sequence II, but most of the examples included there have a specific shape (closest to the example shown in this sequence from the Irbed Museum), which is defined below. Most of our examples here are distinct from these later cup strainers in either having a tall elongated shape or a narrow neck formed by a constriction not very far below the rim. Some cups show both features.

Several other forms found in these tombs are included in the corpus. They do not warrant individual attention since either their relationship to similar forms is obvious or they are unique but without any particular significance.

Some overlap in form with Madeba tomb A has been pointed out, but the greatest similarity was a basic simplicity. In most cases where shapes were similar, the red wash and burnishing indicated something entirely new in the Irbed tombs. Consequently, a short space of about 50 to 100 years should be placed between Madeba tomb A and the Irbed tombs. There is no firm date for the end of this sequence and the beginning of the next. Though there is some overlap, the Amman sounding indicates that again there is probably a separation of from 50 to 100 years between these tombs and the beginning of Sequence II. The red-burnished tradition continues in Sequence II to

---

[1]The seemingly latest forms published from Timna have parallels with some Irbed forms. The decorated jugs from Timna correspond most closely to the form of fig. 26:16 from Irbed tomb A. Rothenberg, *Timna*, figs. 46:12, 47:1, 1A, 2, 3 and pl. XXIV. The bowl form, fig. 20:43, from Irbed tomb A is the only Sequence I form which is reminiscent of the decorated tankard published, *Ibid.*, fig. 47:5, and the wide bowls with straight side joining the base at nearly a right angle, *Ibid.*, fig. 31. The latter are very characteristic forms of the "Negev-type, hand-made" pottery.

[2]Einar Gjerstad, *The Swedish Cyprus Expedition* (4 vol.; Stockholm: Swedish Cyprus Expedition, 1948), II, Part 2, p. 435. W. F. Albright, "Correspondence with Professor Einar Gjerstad on the Chronology of 'Cypriote' Pottery from Early Iron Levels in Palestine," *BASOR*, CXXX (1953), 22-26.

[3]G. L. Harding, "An Early Iron Age Tomb at Madeba," *PEFA*, VI (1953), pl. III:57 illustrates this best in a photograph.

its fullest expression. The transition between Sequence I and II is weakly represented at present primarily by this Irbed material. The forms and variety of shapes in Sequence II are clearly different from what exist here. Such small tomb groups must be considered as spanning a rather short period of time, though no evidence exists on the number of interments in each. Without any strong arguments, aside from their general positioning, an estimate of a range of between 1050 and 900 B.C. could be made for these tombs, but this seems a bit long. More will be said about relative datings below.[1]

Additional forms from museum collections are illustrated in our corpus. A majority of these vessels came from Madeba and were found in tomb clearances necessitated by accidental finds during house building operations. Many of these Madeba vessels came from one tomb, which we have designated Madeba tomb B in our text and corpus.[2]

The single L.B. vessel present in the Madeba Museum is a Cypriote bilbil, figure 30:4 (Madeba tomb B). Only four vessels belong exclusively to Sequence II and three of these seem to be early in that sequence. One bowl, figure 32:34, from the published tomb seems to be a very late intrusion belonging near the end of Sequence II, bowl type X (fig. 43). The discussion below will illustrate that the majority of the unpublished vessels have a range later than that of the published ones and continue in use, at least through the early range of Sequence II. Most of the vessels have features which have been stressed as characteristic for Sequence I. The earliest forms are in a minority, and most of the material seems to fall in the range of the Irbed tombs or between the two sequences. Some of the closest parallels have been brought into our discussion above, and with this material we can class a small red-burnished bowl, a Cypriote black-on-red one-handled juglet, long-necked juglets with handle attachment at the middle of the neck, and one-handled jugs.

There is a great variety of one-handled jugs. Some have long cylindrical necks and a shape similar to jugs, figure 27:4 and 5, from Irbed except that the handle goes to the top of the rim (fig. 26:39-42, 45 from Madeba tomb B). Interestingly, the profile of these jugs is identical to decorated Philistine jugs from Tell Farah (south)[3] and from Beth Shemesh.[4] Several larger vessels, figures 26:47 (Madeba tomb B) and 27:1 (Madeba tomb B), 3, are actually one-handled jars and are similar to those of Madeba tomb A, figures 26:48 and 27:2, and Irbed tomb A, figure 26:46, but with slightly longer necks. One series of one-handled jugs exhibits globular bodies, round bottoms, and short necks (fig. 26:21-24 and 26 from Madeba tomb B and fig. 26:25, 27-29). There are no good

published parallels but the ware, lack of decoration, rim shapes, handle attachment, and proportions fit well within this sequence and are foreign to L.B. or the later sequence. Two of these examples are from the Irbed Museum.

Several forms can be placed here on the basis of their presence in phases A-L at Deir 'Alla. Some of these continue in use in the next period and emphasize the extension of the time range of these vessels into the early part of Sequence II. The two forms which do not occur later are: (1) the goblets with flaring rims and high narrow stems. The Madeba examples, figure 24:15 and 16 (from Madeba tomb B), are paralleled by a goblet from Deir 'Alla phase J, figure 24:14.[5] The Amman Museum goblet, figure 24:17, differs only in lacking the carinate ridge near the base. (2) The tripod loop stand bowls from Madeba, figure 24:19 and 20 (from Madeba tomb B), also have a Deir 'Alla parallel, figure 24:21. A complete example was found in phase B and a sherd with one of the stand loops comes from D. The complete bowl from Deir 'Alla is the simplest in form with a plain rim and a flat base (but it also has painted decoration), in contrast to the Madeba bowls with ring bases and upturned rims. One rim is like that seen on other bowls and is most closely paralleled in the Madeba tomb A (fig. 23:5 [= 6]). The other bowl stands at the very end of our sequence and has dark brown paint and burnishing. Later examples of similar bowls from Mt. Nebo are discussed on pp. 59-60.

One-handled cups have been reconstructed in Deir 'Alla phases K (fig. 22:42) and L (fig. 22:43,

[1]Another small tomb group from the Irbed district has been published recently. It was found farther east at Mafraq. We have not disrupted our plates to include illustrations of these 21 vessels. All of the vessels have good parallels in the Irbed tombs and fit well at the end of that time range. There are five simple bowls, five jugs, one decanter, three juglets, a two-handled jar, a krater and five lamps. Only two vessels are decorated with a red wash and there is no indication of burnishing on the vessels. Michele Piccirillo, "Una tomba del Ferro I a Mafraq (Giordania)," *LA*, XXVI (1976), 27-30.

[2]This tomb has recently been published: Michele Piccirillo, "Una tomba del Ferro I a Madeba," *LA*, XXV (1975), 199-224.

[3]J. G. Duncan, *Corpus of Palestinian Pottery* (London: British School of Archaeology in Egypt, 1930), type 64R2.

[4]Elihu Grant and G. Ernest Wright, *Ain Shems Excavations (Palestine)* (5 vol.; Haverford: Privately Published, 1931-1939), II, pl. XLII:9.

[5]Half of the few Iron Age forms found in the 1967 excavations at Pella is represented by two goblets with a ridge near the base, like the phase J Deir 'Alla example: Smith, *Pella*, I, pp. 212-13 and pl. 42:136 and 144.

44) and three examples are illustrated from Madeba tomb B (fig. 22:39-41). Similar cups are found in the middle range tombs of Sequence II, though sherd materials from Dhiban, Umm el Biyara, and Tell el Kheleifeh indicate a continuation of this shape until the first half of the seventh century B.C. Unfortunately, the variation in proportions of all such cups makes it difficult to distinguish an evolution in form. The surface treatment generally is of some help, but both plain and red-burnished examples are present throughout, though examples of the latter, on present evidence, are unusual near the end of Sequence II. The rims, in almost all cases, are close to vertical and tend to have a slight out-curve. This contrasts with a frequent rounding toward the inside at the top which is evident later. The handles on these cups do not protrude from the side of the vessel as far as the later examples. All the examples illustrated here have a definite flat base on which to stand, while later this feature is normal only in the Amman district.

Three unpublished handleless juglets (fig. 25:5-7) are found at Madeba in Sequence I. The ware and shape of two of these indicate that they belong here, but the type has a range and overlap identical with the cups which have just been discussed. Also unique in this sequence is a cooking pot from Madeba (fig. 24:23) which has parallels at Tell Beit Mirsim in Level A.[1]

A series of two-handled jars currently has no parallel. The shape on some is identical with that of the two-handled L.B. jars discussed above, but the ware is typical of this sequence. They are undecorated. A strong indicator of their date is the appearance of a ridge under the rim, a feature which appears frequently in the later forms of this sequence. Several jars (fig. 27:23-25) are of the light-red-burnished ware so frequent in the Irbed tombs, and the shape and handle placement differ from that of the L.B. Instead, the form resembles that of the decanters, and the handles join the upper shoulder to the neck below the rim. Two other jars of this group (fig. 28:1 and 2, Madeba tomb B) are more rounded and one of them has black-line decoration. The proportions, rim profile, and handle placement are close to that of type 9 of Sequence II, as are the painted lines but, except for these, the features have not yet changed significantly from those of the other Sequence I jars. They must, however, be considered as very late in this sequence.

Several unique but rather amorphous forms illustrated in the Madeba Museum have been omitted from the chart. The remaining group of vessels is very interesting, as three of them illustrate a form which provides evidence for expanding foreign connections at this time (fig. 27:6, 7, and 8 from Madeba tomb B). Unfortunately,

there are few Transjordanian parallels at present (several similar vessels were found at Mt. Nebo in tomb 84 but they have different rims) so there is no compelling reason to place these jugs in Sequence II. The appearance of such jugs at Abu Hawam in level IV[2] and Hazor in XB[3] supports an early date for these jugs.[4] The other four jugs (fig. 27:9-12) show a modification of this form in the direction of the decanters discussed above.

Additional Material Contemporary with the First Sequence

Hopefully, two very large and important tomb groups will be published soon to amplify and better illustrate what already exists. These tombs will be less useful for chronological purposes, however, since they contain hundreds of objects and were in use for a long period of time. The earlier of the two tombs is from Sahab, here called Sahab C. It has some good L.B. vessels but the majority are contemporary with our Sequence I. A smaller number of vessels indicates a later use of the tomb within the time range of our Sequence II.[5]

The second tomb is from Jebel Qusur, Amman. It contained sherds of L.B. vessels, but few of the

---

[1]If we had any parallels for such a cooking pot from the Sequence II tombs, we would include it there. Since none were found there, we have left it with the other Madeba Museum vessels of Sequence I. Albright, *TBM*, I, pl. 35:6, 8-11; pl. 55:6, 8, 10-12.

[2]R. W. Hamilton, "Excavations at Tell Abu Hawam," *QDAP*, VI (1935), 28, no. 152.

[3]Yadin, *et al.*, *Hazor*, III-IV, pl. CCCLV:13.

[4]Similar jugs are illustrated from Khirbet Silm and Joya in southern Lebanon, Susannah V. Chapman, "A Catalogue of Iron Age Pottery from the Cemeteries of Khirbet Silm, Joya, Qrayé and Qasmieh of South Lebanon," *Berytus*, XXI (1972), figs. 5:57; 6:33, 178; 7:25 and pp. 153-55. Chapman dates these jugs to the Middle Iron Age.

[5]See R. Dajani, *ADAJ*, XV. Excavation of tombs and settlement remains have been conducted at Sahab by the Department of Antiquities of Jordan since 1971 under the direction of Dr. Moawiyeh Ibrahim; Moawiyah M. Ibrahim, "Archaeological excavations in Jordan, 1971," *ADAJ*, XVI (1971), 113-16 and the preliminary reports from the first three seasons cited on page 10, footnote 1.
In 1946, a tomb containing an anthropoid coffin lid was found at Sahab, Sahab A. Unfortunately, the tomb was cleared by villagers and most of its vessels broken and a few sold. W. F. Albright tried to establish its date but could find little remaining near the tomb site as evidence. The few sherds that he did find, he considered tenth century B.C., but nothing is published to support this dating.

vessels belonging to our Sequence I were found. The most characteristic of the latter is the one-handled juglet type with tall neck and handle joined at mid-neck. Until a full publication is available, it is best to consider the main use of this tomb as beginning at a date late in our Sequence I and continuing in use through the greater part of Sequence II.[1]

Deir 'Allā Sequence

Parallels to Deir 'Allā forms have been mentioned above, but the nature of the Deir 'Allā material now available must be described, and its contribution in substantiation of our typological sequence of vessels must be discussed. The Late Bronze material is partially published in photographs of whole vessels. In these preliminary reports, there is a minimum of discussion of pottery vessels.[2] The very latest material from the L.B. levels is said to be indistinguishable at present from the first Iron Age phase (A). The early Iron Age material has been treated in a recently published final report.[3] Only a few references and illustrations have been given so far about the pottery of the later Iron Age phases.

Some of the L.B. material has been mentioned, particularly in conjunction with the Jebel Nuzha tomb. At present, nothing more can be said concerning this material. On the other hand, the recently published volume is of critical importance. In this volume, the Iron Age material is divided into phases on the basis of significant architectural groupings within the many layers excavated. The Iron Age phases A through M are contemporary with our Sequence I, and phase A is the earliest of these phases.

Summary of Phases

The remains of the L.B. temples mentioned above were riddled with pits from the immediately overlying strata. As a result, the pottery from phase A was mixed with that of the underlying strata. The first four phases are considered "semi-nomadic" settlement of the site for only certain parts of the year. There was no long gap between this occupation and the final L.B. destruction. Further excavation elsewhere on the site may, however, provide a different account of events, since heavy walls were found on the edge of the excavated area. To explore this possibility, excavation on a larger scale was begun on the top of the mound and it is planned to carry this on down for large exposures through the entire history of the site. Unfortunately, the suspension of excavations due to unsettled conditions in the

Jordan Valley has postponed the accomplishment of this objective.[4]

The architectural remains in phases A-D were scanty. There were courtyards, pits, occasional holes for wooden posts, ovens, and furnaces. The evidence led Franken to characterize the settlement as follows:

> All these characteristics give us the picture of a semi-nomadic folk who were itinerant metal workers and came to live in the Jordan valley during the winter months where they could grow a crop, and graze their animals in favorable climatic conditions at a time of year when they were bearing their young. Here they worked their furnaces until it became too hot, whereupon they moved back up into the hills to sell their produce and collect the raw materials for further smelting the following year.[5]

Phases D and E are considered transitional where the "semi-nomadic" settlers were, apparently peacefully, displaced by another group which established a fortified town. This settlement lasted through Phase L. In the area excavated, there were substantial buildings with

---

[1] The presence in this tomb of anthropoid coffins, belonging apparently with the earliest main Iron Age burial, would put them contemporary, ie., tenth century B.C., with a similar coffin lid by which Albright dated the tomb ab Sahab (A; for more about anthropoid coffins see below).

[2] Henk J. Franken, "Excavations at Deir 'Allā in Jordan," *VT*, X (1960), 386-93; "The Excavations at Deir 'Allā in Jordan: Second Season," *VT*, XI (1961), 361-72; "The Excavations at Deir 'Allā in Jordan: Third Season," *VT*, XII (1962), 378-82; "Excavations at Deir 'Allā, Season 1964," *VT*, XIV (1964), 417-22.

[3] Franken, *DA*.

[4] Unfortunately, few sites have been excavated with large enough exposures to give us any information concerning the settlement of distinct groups on a site at the same time. The character of the "semi-nomadic" group is clear and Franken's arguments are sound. The sacred nature of the site may well have been the reason for its existence. A shrine was found in the highest levels and we have mentioned the thirteenth-twelfth century temple above. When the area of the site is compared with the area needed for a shrine, and related structures and dwellings, very little room remains on the site for anything else. The question would be whether a shrine with the settlement of "semi-nomadic" people was supported solely by this and possibly other similar groups or whether such groups merely attached themselves to a shrine which was locally maintained and merely aided in that support. In this case, the nature of the remains in and around the shrine would be extremely interesting from the point of view of what evidence it provides for the type of people maintaining and supporting the shrine.

[5] Franken, *DA*, p. 21.

heavy walls standing along streets and in the latest phases portions of defensive walls (in phase K a tower was also found).

Phase M was not published in Franken, *DA*. Erosion and later graves left only scanty and somewhat questionable evidence for this phase which required amplification through the extension of the excavations. It is stated that phase M seems to belong to a short-lived phase after a gap in occupation, and there was a longer gap after this phase before phase N began. Most of the material from phase M came from a cistern. The few passages describing this material indicate that it should be similar to our material from the 1969 Amman Citadel sounding which is presented below.

Method of Publication of Pottery

A word must be said about the treatment of the pottery in this volume, since it affects the way in which it can be used for comparison, and because it represents a new approach. The authors criticize the traditional methods of publishing pottery from sites in Palestine and Syria for a lack of precision. The detailed discussion and analysis are done by Kalsbeek, who presents the material from the point of view of a potter. It is clear from his discussion that much of the pottery description currently given by archaeologists is irrelevant, not precise enough, or inaccurate. Unless a considerable amount of pottery can be submitted to microscopic and other analysis, its description is not a statement of fact, but a matter of educated guess.

> Once he realizes that the terms 'well fired,' 'well levigated' and 'self slip' are all bestowed by the cataloguer after an examination of the vessel unaided by more than his or her sharp eyes, intelligence and experience, he will doubt very much the usefulness of these epithets, as they are all, more or less, undetectable with the naked eye.[1]

An example of what is meant here is the appearance of what looks like a self-slip on bowls and other vessels which in reality is not a slip at all. Self-slips are difficult enough to distinguish from normal slips or wet-smoothing, but yet another problem is introduced here.

> The 'self-slip,' the greenish-grey colour, is a result of the fusing of sulphuric elements in the fuel used for firing with salts in the clay that rise to the surface of the vessel during the drying out process. It is not a slip added by the potter.[2]

The obvious examples can usually be distinguished, but they do not constitute a very high percentage of any body of sherd material. The

necessity of turning to precise methods of analysis for determining the origin of such peculiarities is obvious.

To the potter, for example, the composition and plasticity of a clay mixture determine how he can handle it and how it will react to firing. Most of the pottery of this series of phases at Deir 'Allā was apparently of a nonplastic type of lean clay. This clay was not usually cleaned well before use. Dung was frequently used for temper, especially in cooking pots. Sands which were not carefully cleaned and sifted beforehand were used. Such inclusions, however, gave interior cohesion to the clay, kept it from drying out too quickly (before and during firing) and kept it from shrinking excessively or cracking during firing.

The method of handling such clay was restricted. It would not hold together if put on a fast wheel so methods like coiling, slab building, or the use of a mold had to be employed. A slow wheel could be used for ease in handling the clay and getting at all sides of the vessel, but it could not be speeded up to pull or shape the clay. The great advantage for those who wanted useable but not necessarily delicate or sophisticated vessels was that they were easily fired, without a requirement for high temperatures, and that there would be a very low percentage of loss during the process of manufacture. Such a description adds a dimension to the pottery we have been discussing and helps to understand what is happening at this time.

Careful examination of the break lines of sherds and other features provides information on the method by which the vessel was built up. The profile drawings of pots do not always provide evidence of the particular techniques employed in the process of production. Mr. Kalsbeek's discussion puts a new perspective on the value of such profiles, if they give the proper information. Under a microscope, a thin section of a rim will show how it has been formed. The basic division which Kalsbeek makes in the types of cooking pot rims illustrates this best. The bodies of cooking pots 1 and 2 are made in the same way:

> The base is made from a lump of lean clay, beaten flat in a saucer-shaped form or mould. The inside of the base is smoothed with a cloth or leather before it is tapped out of the form, and the outside is then worked over with a tool after it has dried further.[3]

The shoulder and rim of type 1 are then formed.

---

[1]Franken, *DA*, pp. 67-68.

[2]*Ibid.*, p. 134.

[3]Franken, *DA*, p. 21.

The shoulder is made by attaching a coil of clay and in a turning movement, adjusting it to the same thickness as the base. The upper part of the flattened coil is turned down on the inside and pressed against the top of the shoulder. The rim is formed by making a second outward fold of the upper part of the coil. This is the cause of the concavity on the inside of the rim; the fold comes down over the bulging part of the outside wall. The top of the rim usually forms a very sharp angle.[1]

In the case of type 2:

More use of the wheel is made for finishing the vessel. After the pot was built, but before the rim was finished, the vessel was turned until the coils forming the shoulder and rim were of the required thickness, and thus the carination tends to disappear. In this way too the shoulder may lose its concave shape.

The rim is simpler than type 1 and directly related to the L.B. type 2, . . . the end of the coil is folded inwards only. The top of the rim is slightly adjusted by pressing down, with the result that sometimes the clay gets pushed either more to the inside or to the outside.[2]

The variations within each type are the result of additional treatment given the rim, or of the shaping of the rim with a stress on a particular feature as it is formed. In the case where a rim is going out of use, though still in use while another type is beginning to displace it, there may be some assimilation of types by the appropriation of a particular feature of one type by the other. A careful statistical compilation of types and variants was undertaken and the results are very interesting. The existence of each variant is shown proportionately in each phase and the shifts in the popularity of each become clear. During phases A to D only cooking pot type 1 was in use and, though its use tapers off, it continues until phase L. Type 2 (variant 2g) begins in phase E and type 3 in phase G. However, in the next phase, H, only stray examples of type 1 continue to appear. One of the variants of type 2 is a revival of the L.B. cooking pot rim. It is curious that it disappeared completely during phases A to D and then reappeared and became more frequent in the later phases K and L. A variant of type 1 occurs only after type 2 appears and is the imitation of the type 2 shape in the manufacture technique of 1.

It is extremely unfortunate that the distinctions made here cannot be followed up by comparisons with other sites. Mr. Kalsbeek admits that some of the type 1 and 2 rims can only be differentiated by thin section analysis under a microscope. The disappearance and eventual reappearance of type 2 cooking pots mean that this type must have continued in use elsewhere

in the meantime. Only when such detailed information is available from other sites will it be possible to know the origins of specific influences. The possibilities of tracing such traits in pot manufacture from one site to another and of seeing the influence of one area upon another are exciting. The money and time required for such analysis to be done for a fairly large scale excavation will put a considerable strain on archaeological budgets, but it may well become a necessity if the ceramic materials of a site are to be fully and meaningfully utilized.[3]

What has been illustrated here as the treatment of one type of vessel, and some of its rim types, has been done for all pottery shapes and all parts of the vessels, bases, handles, etc. The surface treatment and decoration of the vessels have been handled in a similar manner, but these are not very extensive since the decoration on vessels of the period under consideration is very limited.

The fact that the basic types of rims, bases, etc., can only occasionally be ascertained with certainty in other archaeological publications casts serious doubt on the significance of the variations illustrated in these publications. If a discussion is based primarily on major changes and innovations, then it can be considered to be on a firm basis. We have tried to keep these limitations in mind in the discussions presented in this monograph, since most of the evidence we can present here does not meet the standards indicated above.

Difficulties in the Use of Deir 'Allā Publication

The method of publication of the Deir 'Allā pottery creates some difficulties in the use of this material for comparative purposes, as the authors themselves admit.

This different approach to the study of the E.I.A. pottery makes comparison with published pottery from other sites rather more difficult since, as a rule, only shapes can be compared and not the construction behind them. . . . Much more ceramic study will have to be done before a fruitful comparative dating of sites from this period can really be made with any certainty.

---

[1]*Ibid.*

[2]*Ibid.*, p. 124.

[3]More has been done in other areas in the world in the scientific analysis of pottery, but for ancient Near Eastern archaeology this is the first systematic attempt at such a treatment. This volume can only be considered as a start in employing scientific analysis of pottery, as the authors realize, and as more is attempted and investigators experiment with different possibilities, greater precision and meaning should be forthcoming.

All these considerations lead to the conclusion that the material published in this chapter should be primarily taken as an entity in itself. Its usefulness for the purpose of dating material from other sites depends on how thoroughly the potters' work from the sites to be compared is known.[1]

The period and time range of the material under discussion are fixed securely on both external and internal evidence, namely, on general comparative basis with other sites, on well dated objects, and on carbon-14 dates. The nuances of the ceramics of this period are well documented at Deir 'Allā. The problem comes in trying to extend these nuances on comparative grounds to other sites. Such an attempt is discouraging and no greater precision is possible now than there has been in the past. This will continue to be the case until more information is available from other sites.

It has been pointed out above that the information available from Deir 'Allā is extensive where there has been a concentration of effort, but when such detailed information becomes available from elsewhere more will be required from Deir 'Allā also. Three areas in particular need additional attention: description of surface treatment, description of wares, and color descriptions. The lack of a comprehensive treatment here is largely intentional by the authors. Each of these items has been discussed and sample descriptions given. It would have been helpful if the descriptions had been continued for all sherds as unscientific procedures until the time comes when they can be replaced by scientific data and thus, for the time being, still allow comparisons in the traditional manner. The reasons for the omissions are valid. For example, no attempt has yet been made to determine the relation of firing techniques to color variation or the significance which the inclusion of certain substances has on the clay mixtures for purposes of hardness, controlled drying or other reasons. Some of the possible answers have been mentioned, but it is obvious that much more analysis of this material is required and considerable advance in experimental techniques and aims is needed. In treating some problems only in sample cases and making it impossible to handle the material in a traditional manner, the authors would seem to underscore their points and their criticisms of the "traditional manner." Material for comparative purposes can be gained by working carefully from level to level within certain types and comparing them with the information gathered in the statistical charts, but in most cases this is an arduous task which does not repay the effort.

Because of the greater precision which may be possible it is tempting to rely heavily on the Deir 'Allā material, but another limitation soon becomes clear. This material has a very confined time range of about 150 years and it is impossible to document the length of time many specific features were in use, particularly where they continue later than phase L. Discussion of specific features of the transition from L.B. to Iron Age and publication of a selection of the latest L.B. pottery makes only a general and partial understanding of this transition possible. New things seem to be happening in phase M (which comes just after the latest phase published here), but no safe assumption can be made as to its nature. There seem to be some basic shifts, like the beginning of wheel burnishing, which set phase M off and put it with the Amman and other materials. In effect, saying that it comes more and more into the orbit of eastern, specifically Ammonite, culture seems logical and the description given seems to bear this out. Unfortunately, no profiles or statistics are given for phase M, so these will have to be awaited in the next publication.

In phases K and L there is an increase in what are called imported wares, which also seem to be coming from the east, but it is not indicated whether the M material is close to these or whether the "eastern" material continues as a minor imported component in phase M also. The mere identification of such wares does not help much since the particular stage in their development is unknown, namely whether the beginning or termination of a stage is represented, or whether a development of fifty, one hundred or more years preceded this stage elsewhere.

This brings us to a final point, that Deir 'Allā may represent a very confined regional assemblage. This may be a characteristic of the site or a peculiarity of the age. In any case, it again emphasizes the limits which exist for the use of the Deir 'Allā material for comparative purposes.

Some Comparisons with the Deir 'Allā Material

There is a gradual improvement in the quality of the pottery from phases A through L. The painted decoration is confined primarily to phases A to D but, aside from this, a lack of surface treatment is common here and most pronounced in phases E to F. Burnishing on earlier vessels is rare and sporadic until phase G, when it gradually begins to increase. Only when burnishing starts to become common, does overall burnishing also become common on bowls, but after this there is a tendency to give up exterior burnishing.[2] The deterioration of pottery techniques at the beginning of the period has been remarked

[1]Franken, *DA*, p. 176.

[2]Franken, *DA*, pp. 182-84.

upon above, and this is complementary to the evidence from other sites, particularly Madeba. Despite this similarity, a closer look at the various shapes indicates that the tomb material is much simpler and the Deir 'Allā repertoire is more varied and elaborate. Though the bowl and jar rims which exist in the tombs can be found at Deir 'Allā, they do not seem to be the normal or most frequent ones. The comparison of tomb with tell material may be partially responsible for this, however.

A greater difference seems to exist when the base types are compared, but this is partially deceptive because the illustrated profiles do not give any information on frequency of forms. It is difficult to extract an accurate figure from the statistical tables, since this specific compilation is not made, and it is difficult to determine what overlap may exist if statistics from different tables are combined. It seems that only in phases C and D (A can be considered contaminated by L.B. and B is fairly close) are the numbers of ring bases about equal to other bases, while in all other phases they are more numerous. In phases E to K the ratio is around 3:1, except for E which is less. Disk bases are extremely rare throughout, and where they do occur, they are usually called imported, miscellaneous, or the reasons for assigning a specific type number are not clear. It is interesting that the tenth to ninth century material from Amman shows frequent use of the disk base as an established part of the pottery repertoire and may indicate a direction from which importation was being made to Deir 'Allā.

The ring bases are not usually very high and the cross-sections of the rings are often triangular or rounded. A good number of pedestal bases also occur throughout. It should be noted that no good parallels to the high disk bases of the Jebel Nuzha tomb were found at Deir 'Allā in the early phases. This is an additional support to the arguments above and would put this tomb contemporary mainly with the latest L.B. of Deir 'Allā, which appears to have lasted two or three decades into the twelfth century.

In reviewing the shapes from Deir 'Allā which are contemporary with the beginning of our sequence, enough has been said about the bowls. Flask sherds occur in phases A and E. In A, the decoration on the sides is in concentric circles, and in E it is a spiral. Pyxis base sherds were found in phase B and a crude bag-shaped pyxis was found in E. Sherds of similar degenerate pyxides were found at Beth Shan in level VI,[1] which for this and other reasons, must continue late enough to be contemporary with this phase, though probably not much longer. The tripod-loop stand bowl of phase B was mentioned above, and sherds of another one come from phase D.

Elongated and somewhat pointed juglets are found throughout these phases, as seems to be true for the sequence above. Sharply pointed bases seem to occur only as late as C and a later blunted-base type occurs in G to K. Both types of lamps continue throughout, and they have bases formed by paring off the clay with a knife. One of the few examples of "Philistine" pottery was found in phase A. A jug, with a strainer spout and a shape typical for Philistine pottery, bears the best example of such decoration found at Deir 'Allā (and possibly the one example, see below).

There is a very good sequence of goblets at Deir 'Allā which illustrates much more variety than the two basic types mentioned above. The goblet from phase B with relatively straight lines is similar to the late L.B. goblets, but it substantiates the existence of this shape in Iron Age levels, as was argued above for the Jebel Nuzha example. The later goblet shape among the Madeba B vessels has its position confirmed by a complete example from phase J. Sherds of such goblets, however, occur earlier and indicate that this shape has a fairly long duration. The earliest sherd comes from phase E and supports the otherwise questionable occurrence of such a goblet in level VI at Beth Shan, which must be considered as coming from the end of this level. The phase L goblet shows a tendency toward more elaboration of profile.

There are only a few one-handled jars. The one from B (fig. 26:44) shows a continuation of the L.B. tradition in the position in which the handle is attached, the thick neck and the body carination. In phase G (fig. 26:43), the carination is replaced by a rounded side, the neck is narrower and the handle seems to join at mid-neck. There are no precise parallels for this, but it is definitely moving away from the L.B. type and toward the Iron Age shape which is familiar in our Sequence I.

The cooking pot sequence has been mentioned above. It is impossible to be certain of parallels with other sites because it is not known how these pots were formed elsewhere. Rim type 1 does seem to be a type which is common at other sites in the twelfth century B.C.

Type 1 is found all over Palestine in the E.I.A. It already occurs in the 14th cent. B.C. It may well be that these 14th cent. pots will have to be regarded as imported from Trans-Jordan or from the southern deserts, and that they are "fossil" types from nomadic incursions. It is not derived from the L.B. cooking pot.[2]

---

[1]Frances W. James, *The Iron Age at Beth Shan* (Philadelphia: University of Pennsylvania Museum, 1966), fig. 50:3.

[2]Franken, *DA*, p. 122.

It is curious that handles are extremely rare on this type of cooking pot and, though more common on type 2, they are still infrequent. No handles on cooking pots are illustrated for phases A to E. The type 3 cooking pot is also considered, most probably, to be Transjordanian and handles are more frequent on this type. Unfortunately, only a few such cooking pots have been found.

Handles in general are very rare in phases A to D on forms other than large jars and juglets. In phases E to L, they are much more common though still not present in very great numbers. The handle attachment for jugs and jars conforms well with what has been seen above. The jug and jar handles which extend from the shoulder to the top of the rim occur in B and then from E to J. The same forms, with the handle joining at the middle of the neck, occur in G and J and in several cases (in K and J) it joins at a neck ridge. The later neck ridge at the middle of the neck is extremely rare. The authors note that such a neck ridge is normal for the tenth century while for the twelfth to the eleventh centuries the ridge, where it occurs, is just beneath the rim and this is its normal position throughout phases A to L at Deir 'Allā.[1]

The handle attachment at mid-neck was most characteristic above on juglets and these occur in J and K. The one-handled cups are also found in the last phases, K and L. Both forms are not considered among the regular types at Deir 'Allā and the cups are considered as imports. Several new bowl shapes occur as innovations, probably as the result of outside influence, at Deir 'Allā. Some of these seem to be early examples of types which exist in the Amman sounding sherds, and then continue to develop and become modified during the course of our Sequence II. The large bowls, types 17 and 18, have mold-formed bodies. The rim shape 17 increases in frequency from phases E on but gives way to type 18 (which begins in J) in phases K and L.[2] The wide rim profile of 18 is found in layers eleven and eight (Periods I and II respectively) of the Amman sounding, but is relatively rare. Types XLV and XLVI of Sequence II seem to be the later development of these forms though the vessel walls have become thinner. Other rim shapes appearing in phases K and L also occur in the Amman sounding and will be discussed below.

Kraters are represented only in sherds, and there are no good parallels to the deep bowl or krater shapes with handles from Irbed or Madeba. In almost all cases, the section of the rim is preserved above the carination. A curved section is unusual, but normally a straight inward incline is found. The rim usually has an elaborate profile.

A great number and variety of storage jars were found at Deir 'Allā (figs. 28:12, 16, 17; 29:1, 2, 4, 5, 8, 9; 30:1 and 2). In phase A, two whole storage jars illustrate a continuation of the L.B. form, having a long pointed shape but with shorter and less flaring rims. One jar is shorter but still pointed. From phase B on, the shape changes so that it approximates more closely that which was seen above from the Irbed Museum. This shape does occur earlier at the very end of the Late Bronze at Deir 'Allā in storerooms around the sanctuary, but it seems to be rather unusual in that context. The shapes from E to L seem to show the closest parallels. The very elongated jars of phases J and L have no parallels so far in the Transjordan.

Deir 'Allā Chronological Position

The chronological table, page 63, shows the relative position of Deir 'Allā phases in relation to other sites. The above discussion clearly indicates that, despite the difficulties mentioned, the Deir 'Allā phases substantiate the typological sequencd which we constructed above. The C-14 date for the end of the L.B. cella, 1180-1160 B.C., fits well with the 1205-1194 B.C. date for Queen Taousert, whose name was found on a vase in the burnt debris of the cella. If a decade or two are allowed for the attempted L.B. resettlement, a date of roughly 1165 B.C. seems a good approximation, though it is longer than the excavators allow. This requires a slightly later date for phases A to L also. Phases A to D must be kept within the twelfth century and we should follow the excavators' lead in staying close to the estimate of a century for phases E to L. Thirty-five to forty years for phases A to D should be sufficient if not too long. The estimate of phases E to L has been stretched only slightly, allowing around 120 years so that phase L would end about 1000 B.C., which is also what the excavators suggest. In this way, the similarity of types and other parallels that have been noted seem to mesh with the greatest satisfaction.

Balu'a, Aro'er, and Some Dhiban Sherds

Iron Age material contemporary with Sequence I has been found in soundings at the above-mentioned sites. The report on Balu'a states that the pottery indicated an Iron II settlement and two questionable sherds were the only indication that occupation may have gone back as early as

---

[1]Franken, *DA*, pp. 182-83.

[2]*Ibid.*, pp. 157-60.

the end of the Late Bronze Age.[1] In the published pottery, no L.B. and few early Iron I sherds are illustrated. Many of the forms, types LX, LXVI, LXXIV, and LXXVI, are contemporary with forms popular in the 1969 Amman Citadel sounding (see below) and the complete storage jar with a "collar-type rim" (type LX) may date somewhat earlier. At Aro'er only a very brief report has been published and a very limited number of sherd profiles from differing dates in the Iron and Late Bronze Ages have been illustrated. The information is too scanty, and without photographs it is difficult to identify these with certainty. Olávarri mentions that red-burnished slip is not found here as it is in Palestine, but says that little of the fortress pottery of the ninth century B.C. and later is preserved in the area of his sounding. He mentioned instead the use of a white slip without burnishing. It has been seen above that this is common in LB I and can be found also in LB II. The shapes on which this slip is found have not been illustrated and, since the description of the loci is not given, certainty cannot be obtained in the matter. It would be interesting if the use of a white slip continued from M.B. into the Iron Age. It is possible that these sherds belong to earlier wares, since the sounding was in a disturbed area of the defense system, but the few sherds of a similar type that were found in the 1969 Amman Citadel sounding indicate that something unique is present here and more information is needed.

A ring base seems to be most common in what Olávarri considers his eleventh-ninth century B.C. pottery and this would fit more with the Deir 'Allā picture than that at Madeba. The bowl rims have general, but not exact, parallels at Deir 'Allā. The closest parallels seem to be in the earliest phases, particularly in B and C, but Olávarri draws some parallels to the "mensif" bowls, which is what Deir 'Allā types 17 and 18 were called in the preliminary reports. These bowls, as has been seen, are from the end of the sequence so more information must be available in order to know exactly where this material belongs. The large jars 1-5 of figure 2[2] do, however, seem to belong to the end of the Deir 'Allā sequence where new types are coming in, and Olávarri seems secure on the basis of Palestinian parallels. Some of this material must be classed as Iron I even if it cannot be closely paralleled in our Sequence I.

The majority of the Dhiban Iron I forms have no well stratified Transjordanian parallels. Little seems to fall early in our Sequence I but most of the sherd profiles, and particularly the complete vessels, have similarities to forms at Irbed and Madeba which we have placed at the end of this sequence. The majority of the published Dhiban materials fall in the early and middle ranges of Sequence II.[3]

The Western Arabah: Wadi Timna and Surrounding Area

Though the Western Arabah does not fall within the scope of our topic, the recent finds at the site of ancient Timna (the Mene'iyeh of Glueck's survey) are closely related and will be essential, when all the information is available, to our understanding of the end of the L.B. and Iron I in the Jordan rift and the Transjordan. The problem has centered around the dating of the copper mining sites in the area. There has been a considerable change in the dating of the pottery but now, finally, it seems to be secure. In the surveys of Glueck, a specific "Edomite" pottery was defined in conjunction with Albright.[4] This pottery was classed as Iron I. It will be shown below that some of this pottery has now been attributed to late in Iron II.[5] In the recent survey work that was done between 1959 and 1966 by Beno Rothenberg, it was argued that the mining sites were in use primarly in the tenth and ninth centuries B.C.[6]

Excavation at Timna has finally provided enough information for a definitive dating and the evidence from this excavation requires that the earlier material be re-examined. Three distinct pottery types are said to occur: (1) the normal Iron I undecorated pottery (apparently much like that present in the Madeba tomb), (2) a heavy ware with incised decoration that is found in the Negev and the Arabah (and was also well illustrated at Tell el Kheleifeh), and (3) the "Edomite" painted pottery. On this evidence, the copper smelting industry in this area is said to date in the twelfth and eleventh centuries B.C.[7]

[1]John W. Crowfoot, "Soundings at Balu'ah," PEFQS, LXVI (1934), pp. 56-63.

[2]Emilio Olávarri, "Sondages à 'Arô'er sur l'Arnon," RB, LXXII (1965), figure 2.

[3]Though few forms were identified as Iron I in William L. Reed and Fred V. Winnett, The Excavations at Dhibon (Dhībân) in Moab ("AASOR," XXXVI-XXXVII; New Haven: ASOR, 1964), a reanalysis of the stratigraphy and the pottery have resulted in some reattribution of dates: A. Douglas Tushingham, The Excavations at Dibon (Dhībân) in Moab ("AASOR," XL; Cambridge: ASOR, 1972), 21. Only a few of the sherds like Reed and Winnett, Dhiban, I, pl. 73:4, 11, 14; 74:4, 5, and 76:13 seems to belong early in Iron I while more of the Iron I sherds seem to fall at the end of our Sequence I.

[4]Glueck, EEP, II, 123-37.

[5]Nelson Glueck, "Some Edomite Pottery from Tell el-Kheleifeh," Parts I and II, BASOR, CLXXXVIII (1967), 8-38.

[6]Beno Rothenberg, "Ancient Copper Industries in the Western Arabah," PEQ, XCIV (1962), 6-71.

[7]Beno Rothenberg, "Timna," in "Chronique archéologique," RB, LXXIV (1967), 80-85.

Glueck's redating of some of his pottery is not challenged, but "Elle semble un développement plus tardif de la même potterie «de tribu».[1]

Two brief reports in the *Illustrated London News* provide the best description presently available for the exciting finds made at Timna in the summer of 1969.[2] The new datings were amply substantiated by the excavation of a temple of Hathor which contained inscribed material and stone pillars. The original construction of the temple is dated by cartouches of Seti I (1309-1291 B.C.) and Seti II (1214-1208 B.C.) and its last phase dates from the reigns of Ramses III (1182-1151) to Ramses V (1145-1141).[3]

> Les mines du début du Fer n'ont fonctionné qu'au cours des XII-XIᵉ siècles av. J.-C. et nulle part on n'a pu découvrir de témoinages d'exploitation au cours des Xᵉ-IXᵉ siècles ou après. Ceci nous oblige à reconsidérer l'interprétation historique admise qui voyait dans les industries du cuivre de la 'Arabah les Mines du Roi Salomon et à regarder les Edomites, peut-être conjointement avec les Kénites-Madianites, comme les anciens mineurs et fondeurs de cuivre de la 'Arabah.[4]

The latest season indicates that the power of the XXth Egyptian dynasty must have been far stronger in Palestine than has previously been considered the case. The Beth Shan stelae indicate the same, though scholars were reluctant to place too much emphasis on them.

The Egyptian rulers seem to have been the catalysts in the working of the Arabah mines, though how much longer after Ramses V (the last attested ruler at the Timna Temple) the mines continued to be worked is not indicated. The full publication of the excavated material must be awaited to be able to say how much of a role the local population played in determining their own fate there in the thirteenth through eleventh centuries B.C. It will be interesting to see, when the pottery is published, whether there is an assemblage that corresponds to that illustrated by Megiddo VIIA-VI, Beth Shan VI, and Deir 'Allā's latest L.B. and phases A-D.[5]

---

[1]*Ibid.*, p. 84.

[2]Beno Rothenberg, "King Solomon's Mines No More," *ILN* (Nov. 15, 1969), 32-33; Beno Rothenberg, "The Egyptian Temple of Timna," *ILN* (Nov. 29, 1969), 28-29.

[3]Far greater detail is now available in Rothenberg, *Timna*. Additional XIXth dynasty rulers: Ramses II, Merneptah and Taousert and XXth dynasty ruler: Ramses IV are now also listed, *Ibid.*, pp. 163-66.

[4]Rothenberg, *RB*, LXXIV, 85.

[5]A small selection of pottery is illustrated in Rothenberg, *Timna*, figs. 30-32, 35, 45-47, and pls. 41-45, 48-52, 101, XXII-XXIV. Only enough is presented to indicate the three basic types of wares now described as: "primitive, hand-made Negev ware," "Midianite ware," and "normal", wheel-made Late Bronze Age-Early Iron Age ware." Footnote references have been made above to some of the vessels represented, and below, to some of the patterns used on the "Midianite ware."

The most common Timna form is that of the flat-bottomed, decorated bowls. These have not been discussed above for lack of significant parallels in the Sequence I materials. Since the style of decoration has such close parallels to the sub-Mycenaean bowls of the Amuq and Tarsus, one looks for similar parallels in vessel form. Some parallels do exist but for the most part the specifics do not correspond exactly. The Timna flat bases are rare and in the north the tendency is toward pointed, out-tilted, s-profile rims rather than blunt or flat-ended rims on out-tilted vessel sides. The circumflex handle, common in the north, does not occur at Timna where, for the most part, handles are missing. In all the discussion of the "Midianite pottery" from Timna one has to consider the broad area over which this ware must have been common, as illustrated in the archaeological survey of Peter J. Parr, G. Lankester Harding and John E. Dayton, "Preliminary Survey in N.W. Arabia, 1968," *Bulletin of the Institute of Archaeology*, X (1972), 23-61 and pls. 1-31 and the characteristic sherds published in John E. Dayton, "Midianite and Edomite Pottery," *Proceedings of the Fifth Seminar for Arabian Studies* (London: Seminar for Arabian Studies, 1972), pp. 25-38.

"Midianite" sherds have also been identified at Lachish, Tell Jurdur, Tell el Farah, Tell Masos, Yotvata and at Jezirat Faraun, showing an extension from the Arabah and the Red Sea to the Mediterranean coast. The references are compiled in: Yohanon Aharoni, Volkmar Fritz and Aharon Kempinski, "Vorbericht über die Ausgrabungen auf der Hirbet el-Mšāš (Tel Māśôś), 2. Kampagne 1974," *ZDPV*, XCI (1975), 16 and 17; and Jon Kalsbeek and Gloria London, "A Late Second Millennium B.C. Potting Puzzle," *BASOR*, CCXXXII (1978), 47-56.

CHAPTER V

IRON AGE SECOND SEQUENCE
(LATE MATERIAL)

Provenience of Pottery

The pottery corpus on figures 32-42 illustrates the shapes of complete vessels which have been published to date with the addition of photographs of similar objects from the Kerak, Madeba, Amman, and Irbed Archaeological Museums. The pottery included here comes primarily from a total of twelve tomb groups from Amman and the surrounding area. Of the eight tombs found in Amman, four were found on Jebel Joffeh, two on Jebel Qala' (the citadel hill), one on Jebel Quṣur, and one on Jebel Amman. The map, figure 3, shows the location of these hills, Jebel Joffeh is south of the citadel hill with part of the downtown area of present Amman in the wadi between the two. The ancient town was situated in this wadi at least as far back as the Hellenistic Period. Iron Age sherds were found beneath the Hellenistic levels in this area during clearance in front of the Roman Theater.[1] Unfortunately, the deep soundings were restricted and no early architecture was found so it is impossible to know if this area was settled in the Iron Age. This, however, is a possibility. The Joffeh tombs are here called Amman A, B, E, and F.[2] Tomb F was found when a portion of the foundations on the east side of the Roman Theater was cleared to bedrock. Unfortunately, the Roman Theater's foundation trench ran across the western part of the tomb and a medieval Islamic wall, about two meters east of it, ran over the eastern portion. The tomb, as a result, was badly disturbed and most of the finds were concentrated around its somewhat less disturbed blocked entrance on the north.[3]

Tomb D was found on the north slope of Jebel Qala' and the tomb of Adoni Nur, here abbreviated AN, halfway down its southern slope, just opposite the Roman Theater. The Jebel Amman tomb (C) was found southwest of the citadel and the Jebel Quṣur tomb (here Amman G) northeast of the citadel. The remaining four tombs of the Amman district contained objects which were indistinguishable from what was found in Amman itself and can be considered within the mainstream of Ammonite culture. One tomb was found at Meqabelein, about eight kilometers south of Amman.[4] It is situated just on the outskirts of Amman where the jebels and wadies of the capital gradually merge into the surrounding plateau. One of the main roads leading to Madeba and southward would have passed in this direction as it does today (about one kilometer east of the site). A number of significant tombs have been found at Sahab. Tomb B is the one Sahab tomb that has been published,[5] Tomb A had been cleared by villagers with little more than the anthropoid coffin lid from it being preserved, and C, the one which was excavated in the summer of 1968.[6] Sahab is farther from Amman, about eleven kilometers to the southeast, on the edge of the cultivated area, and on one of the major tracks into Amman from the barren steppe and the desert to the east (much as it is today).[4]

Outside of the Amman district the amount of information at our disposal is considerably less. A considerable amount of excavation has been done in the last two decades but, since so little is published (or the material is incompletely published) this material can only be used to illustrate that, on the whole, finds in Amman should not only be classed as Ammonite but for the time being also considered as Transjordanian. In some cases, this material adds some detail to what is available from Amman, but this is rare. There

---

[1] Adnan Hadidi, "The Pottery from the Roman Forum at Amman," *ADAJ*, XV (1970), 12.

[2] Capital letters are used here for the Amman and other tombs in keeping with the way tombs A-D and the Irbed tombs have been published. Tombs A and B: G. Lankester Harding, "Two Iron Age Tombs, 'Amman," *QDAP*, XI (1945), 67-74; Tombs C and D: G. Lankester Harding, "Two Iron Age Tombs in Amman," *ADAJ*, I (1951), 37-40; Tomb E, Rafik W. Dajani, "An Iron Age Tomb from Amman," *ADAJ*, XI (1966), 41-47; Tombs F and G: Unpublished; Tomb N: G. Lankester Harding, "The Tomb of Adoni Nur in Amman," *PEFA*, VI (1953), 48-75.

[3] We include this tomb on the chart and in our discussion below since the former Director of the Department of Antiquties of Jordan, Mr. Jacob Oweis, had kindly given us permission to publish this tomb group.

[4] G. Lankester Harding, "An Iron Age Tomb at Meqabelein," *QDAP*, XIV (1950), 44-48.

[5] G. Lankester Harding, "An Iron Age Tomb at Sahab," *QDAP*, XIII (1948), 92-103.

[6] Now see R. Dajani, *ADAJ*, XV.

[7] Basic information concerning excavations at four additional Iron Age sites in the Amman district are now available in Roger S. Boraas, "A Preliminary Sounding at Rujm El-Malfuf 1969," *ADAJ*, XVI (1971), 31-46; Henry O. Thompson, "The Excavations at Tell Siran (1972)," *ADAJ*, XVIII (1973), 5-14; "The Ammonite Remains at Khirbet al-Hajjar," *BASOR*, CCXXVII (1977), 27-34 and "Rujm Al-Malful South," *ADAJ*, XVIII (1973), 47-50.

are currently preliminary reports on excavations at Umm el Biyara (1965-1966),[1] Tell el Kheleifeh (1938-1940),[2] Pella (1958, 1963, 1967),[3] Tell es Sa'idiyeh (1964-1967),[4] Deir 'Allā (1960-1967), Tell er Rumeith (1962 and 1967),[5] Aro'er (1964), Balu'a (1933), Heshbon (1968),[6] Taiwilan,[7] and Buseirah.[8] All of these sites have yielded Iron Age materials and, together with the earlier Dhiban excavations (1950-1953),[9] and two tomb groups from Mt. Nebo,[10] provide us with information from all areas of the Transjordan. The above sites will be mentioned in our discussion only where pertinent information is available. The most information currently available is from Umm el Biyara, Tell el Kheleifeh, Dhiban and Buseirah. Final reports are available only for Dhiban.

Excavation was undertaken on the Iron Age site of Taiwilan near Wadi Musa in the summers of 1968 and 1969. The information from this site is very promising but only a brief note has been published concerning the first season. The portion of the site excavated so far has yielded material from the eighth to sixth centuries and thus overlaps what has been published for Umm el Biyara and Tell el Kheleifeh. Also, it illustrates the period of most of the painted pottery found by Glueck on this site. A considerable amount of painted pottery was found and we must anxiously await its publication.[11] The excavators hope that excavations on terraces higher up the slope from where they were working will yield occupation earlier in the Iron Age.

Though little Iron Age material contemporary with this second sequence was found in stratified excavation on the citadel in Amman, a considerable number of sherds was collected. These, on the whole, illustrate in detail features of the complete vessels included in the corpus. This sherd material, from the 1968 excavations, from surface collection, and from sherding behind a bulldozer that in 1969 was widening a portion of the road that runs over the citadel, is presented below in a chart of profile types, profile drawings and photographs.

Since little has been published so far from the excavations mentioned above, it is hoped that our chart and sherd material will serve as useful tools in organizing the Transjordanian material and provide an aid for the publication of the material from these sites.

Amman District Tombs

The tombs in this sequence from the Amman district are closely related and overlapping so that they form a good base upon which to work out a typological sequence. There are some firm indicators within this sequence which aid in giving a relative date, but not enough parallel material is available to fix the dates absolutely. The published pottery from Dhiban, Tell el Kheleifeh, and Umm el Biyara supports this sequence. The latter two sites aid considerably in refining the dating at the end of the sequence. Only rarely are Palestinian parallels valuable to us here since so much of the pottery is unique to the Transjordan. The recent publications of Bethel, Tell el Ful, and Beth Zur have broadened our knowledge of seventh and sixth century Palestine and, as a result, provide the bulk of the parallels to our material. The span of time represented by the materials in each tomb group varies. Some tombs were used for a short period of time while others were used continuously for centuries.

Little attention has been given to the technical aspects of this pottery, so the discussion must be confined primarily to differences in shape and, to a lesser extent, decoration. Decoration is more helpful here in the Transjordan than it is for contemporary material in Palestine. Not only does

[1]Crystal -M. Bennett, "Fouilles d'Umm el-Biyara," *RB*, LXXIII (1966), 372-403 and "A Brief Note on Excavations at Taiwilan, Jordan, 1968-1970," *Levant*, III (1971), v-vii.

[2]For the most recent treatment and a full bibliography see: Nelson Glueck, "Ezion-geber," *BA*, XXVIII (1965), 70-87.

[3]Robert H. Smith, "Pella (Tabaqat Fahl)," *RB*, LXXV (1968), 105-12; References to earlier work are given here; also, Smith, *Pella*, I.

[4]A number of preliminary articles have been written. We cite only two here, both from the "Chronique archéologique" section of *RB*. John E. Huesman, "Tell es-Sa'idiyeh," *RB*, LXXV (1968), 236-38. James B. Pritchard, "Tell es-Sa'idiyeh," *RB*, LXXIII (1966), 574-76.

[5]Paul W. Lapp, "Tell er-Rumeith," *RB*, LXXV (1968), 98-105.

[6]Roger S. Boraas and Lawrence T. Geraty, "The Fifth Campaign at Tell Hesbân," *AUSS*, XVI (1978), 1-200 and the listing of previous publications on page 1, in footnote 3 of that report. Reference to the Iron II remains are found primarily in Boraas and Geraty, *AUSS*, XIV, 8-9, 56-60, 77-78; and *AUSS*, XVI, 46-48, 67-69, 110 and 187.

[7]Crystal -M. Bennett, "Taiwilan," *RB*, LXXVI (1969), 386-90.

[8]See references listed on p. 59, footnote 2.

[9]Reed and Winnett, *Dhiban*, I, and A. Douglas Tushingham, "Excavations at Dhibon in Moab, 1952-53," *BASOR*, CXXXIII (1954), 6-26 and *Dhiban*, II.

[10]Sylvester Saller, "Iron Age Tombs at Nebo, Jordan," *LA*, XVI (1965-1966), 165-298.

[11]See p. 86, footnote 12 for a brief mention of the painted pottery which was found in the recent excavation at Buseirah.

the Transjordanian repertoire seem in many respects more sophisticated, it is also distinguished by a richer use of painted decoration. A fast wheel was used in the production of many vessels in Sequence II but the earliest tomb, Amman A, shows that its use was not yet established at the beginning of the sequence. Late in the sequence, however, mastery of the fast wheel is illustrated by some very fine and rather difficult forms.

It appears that toward the end of Sequence II the Transjordanian pottery diverges further from the Palestinian than earlier. In the seventh and sixth centuries, the pottery in Palestine is considered a degeneration of the Iron II forms and decoration. In the Transjordan, there seems to be some new life and regeneration rather than the reverse.

A phenomenon occurs in Amman for which we currently have no evidence in Palestine. This is the appearance in black and very light cream wares of shapes well known in red-burnished ware. Whether this is peculiar only to Amman and its immediate vicinity or is general for the Transjordan cannot currently be shown. Black and light cream burnished vessels have also been found in Syria, especially the Amuq, and indicate a wider presence of such wares, particularly since the shapes on which they occur are common in the local setting and not imported. Black-burnished juglets are commonn in Palestine and were seen in Sequence I. They are, however, relatively rare in the Transjordan during Sequence II. It is interesting that some of the black-burnished vessels resemble basalt bowl shapes and several such bowl fragments, illustrated below, have been found at Amman. The red-burnished and black-burnished parallels are given below. The imitation of Iron II pottery bowl shapes in stone is not unusual as such examples are frequent in Syria and Palestine. It seems reasonable, then, that the color of the basalt vessels could easily have been imitated, especially in the Transjordan where there are several large basalt areas. One lies south of the Wadi Mujib (in the region of Balu'a and Aro'er) and the other on the northern border along the Yarmuk River. An even larger area stretches north of the Yarmuk for most of the distance between Derah and Damascus. Considerable freedom and experimentation is indicated by the intentional production of the black and cream variants of the red-burnished vessels.

The tomb material in this sequence falls roughly into three parts. The earliest consists of Amman tomb D and the two tombs of long duration which also contained Sequence I material, namely the Jebel Quṣur tomb (Amman G) and Sahab C, both of which are unpublished. The remaining tombs fall into two groups: i.e., four late tombs within the last half of the seventh and the sixth centuries, and tombs spanning the time between the other groups. The latter fall primarily within the range of the end of the eighth century and into the beginning of the seventh, but two of these tombs seem to have had a fairly long continuous use.

Earliest Material

Relatively few vessels were found in Amman tomb D, but what was found is very important. Only three Cypriote one-handled black-on-red type (III) juglets have been found in Amman. One is from tomb D and the other two are from tomb G (Jebel Quṣur). Other juglets replace this type in the later tombs. The normal date assigned to these juglets, 850-700 B.C., is an argument for pushing most of the material from the later Amman tombs at least toward the end of this time range. The two-handled jars with short necks, rounded bodies, flat bases, and relatively thick ware (fig. 36:18 and 19) are out of character for this sequence and closer to Sequence I. They resemble most closely the cooking pots from TBM in level A[1] and from Ain Shems in level IIb-c[2] where the ribbed rim is also found. Such one-handled jars are also found in Amman G. Similar ribbed rims were also found in the 1969 Amman Citadel sounding (see the discussion below).

The neck ridge and handle placement are unusual on the jug, figure 36:18, and on the strainer juglet, figure 37:13. Similar jugs, however, also exist in Tell Beit Mirsim level A. It is unusual to see such a neck ridge where the handle joins at the top of the rim rather than at the ridge (as reconstructed here). The ratio of neck to body is greater than usual in figure 38:18. This juglet shares the feature of a slightly pointed base with figure 38:20 and 21 but otherwise have sharply contrasting features. The latter are heavier, illustrate a cruder method of construction and have unusually wide necks which are quite short in proportion to the rough bag shaped bodies. Such vessels are rare (figure 38:19 alone being somewhat close) and seem to represent a phase before the main developments take place in Sequence II. The chronological positioning of this tomb is supported by good parallels at Tell Beit Mirsim in level A and by the fact that earlier materials from the end of Tell Beit Mirsim level B parallel materials from the preceding Sequence I.

Amman tomb G and Sahab tomb C must be published in detail before a definite placement is possible. Some of the vessels have been noted

---

[1]Albright, *TBM*, I, pls. 35:6, 8, 9-11 and 55:6, 8, 10-12.

[2]Grant and Wright, *AS*, IV, pl. LXIV:28-31.

above. The Sahab tomb is the earlier of the two, and bowl shapes in it, including a black-burnished example, indicate an overlap with the published Sahab B tomb.[1] A jar in Amman G with a rim similar to figure 37:13 of Amman D indicates an overlap between these tombs, while the presence in Amman G of a large number of jugs of types 1-8 (which last until the end of our sequence) indicates a continued use for this tomb.

There are a great number and variety of bowl shapes in Sequence II and very few of them show any resemblance to those of Sequence I. Two vessels from Sahab B, figure 33:2 and 8, indicate that the earliest use of this tomb dates to the end of Sequence I. Figure 33:2 is a profile which we will see among the Amman sounding sherds.

Remaining Material

The four latest tombs in our sequence are characterized by vessels which show strong late Assyrian and Neo-Babylonian influences. Many of the forms we will discuss here have only general resemblances in Palestine. Either there seem to be peculiarities here which are not found in Palestine or the contemporary evidence for sixth and seventh-century material in Palestine is not yet illustrated sufficiently. The remaining tombs which cannot be attributed to either end of Sequence II fall between them. On the whole, the pottery of the middle and late ranges of our Sequence II shows an expertise and complete mastery of potting techniques.

Amman tombs B and C alone are confined primarily to the middle range, while E and Sahab B contain both middle and late forms. Amman A is the earliest of the four latest tombs and contains more middle forms than the other three.

There are only a few forms which are confined solely to the middle range. There are, however, a number of forms which change considerably in profile during their periods of use so that earlier and later versions of a basic type become obvious. To separate the discussion of the early and late varieties of each form is difficult, so our discussion will be organized by forms rather than by periods. An attempt will be made to try to outline the development of the most important and obvious types if substantiation for such a development can be found in the Amman district or elsewhere in the Transjordan. In other cases, where insufficient examples exist to demonstrate a sequence, we will only be able to show the presence or absence of a type.

Bowl Forms

Type I and II bowls or platters are very simple forms that are basically straight-sided vessels with flat or slight disk bases and simple rims (fig. 32:1-6 and 7-15). Three examples from Amman tomb C (fig. 32:3, 4 and 7) are paralleled by a bowl in the Madeba Museum and represent the earliest versions of these types. The bowls are taller than the later examples and their bases are close to disk forms. Such bowls were not encountered earlier in the Sequence I materials but the general proportions and bases may be a typologial progression from the forms illustrated on figure 20:20-30. The bowls, predominantly of type I, which are most common at the end of Sequence II are lower, have rounded or pointed rims, and have a slight flare to the sides (fig. 32:8-14). The only painted decoration on types I and II bowls is illustrated by one example, AC:5 (fig. 32:1). The simple cross is done in white-painted lines bordered by black lines.

Types IV and V are a series of incurved bowls where, in all cases, the sides of the bowl are long and the incurve occurs close to the rim. The later forms show a sharper incurve and, in most examples, are very low, almost platelike. In several cases, flat bases occur but these are very small. Usually, the bases are slightly rounded. Type IV is found only in Amman tombs A and N, and Meqabelein and thus comes right at the end of the sequence (fig. 32:17-21). These bowls form one of the types of vessels which may be forerunners of still later types (see sherd discussion below). Their thinness is unusual and the shape resembles the finer, thin Nabataean bowls. Harding makes the point that the presence of such Iron Age bowls in the Transjordan is one of many examples which show that we need not look elsewhere for the place of origin of specific artifactual and cultural features which become characteristic of the Nabataean civilization.[2] Bowl type V resembles type IV in fineness, but on present evidence begins earlier. In addition to the tombs in which type IV was found, it is also present in Sahab B and Amman A (fig. 32:22-27). Its profile differs from type IV in that it has a double curve while type IV is simply turned up. Type V is more round-bottomed than flat, has a much higher side and has a smaller diameter than type IV bowls.

Types XXIV, XXV, and XXX are bowls in which the outer portion of the vessel sides turned up to near vertical stance. Types XXIV and XXV (figs. 32:44-52; 33:1-3) represent bowls with a single inward bend. The rim is thickened and, in most cases, the top is flat and horizontal. Such bowls occurred in the 1969 Amman Citadel sounding, but continued through the late ranges of Sequence II. The type XXV rims, which come

---

[1]Now see R. Dajani, *ADAJ*, XV.

[2]Harding, *AN*, p. 57.

from tombs of the middle and late ranges of Sequence II, show a development which was not characteristic of such bowls earlier, namely, a roughly S-shaped profile. The incurve in the type XXX bowl is formed by two inward bends, the rim is thickened and beveled on the outside, and according to Harding,[1] provides the vessel with "anti-splash" qualities (fig. 33:5-7).

Types XLVI and X: Type XLVI is usually somewhat deeper than the bowls we have discussed so far and type X represents the deepest group. (There are a few individual examples of other deep bowl types below.) Bowl type XLVI has what we will call here a "step-rim." It occurs only in Amman N and the Meqabelein tomb (fig. 33:14-17, 19-23). A great variety of such rims is illustrated below among the sherds and they form the best examples for a type in which red, black, and cream-burnished surfaces are present. Though this type has a confined range here, it should be classed as a variety of the type of rim found in our sounding (where it was relatively rare) and still earlier in a number of the Deir 'Allā type 17 and 18 bowl rims which we mentioned above. Type X bowls again are found only in Amman N and the Meqabelein tomb (fig. 32:30-36). These bowls normally have almost straight sides, disk bases, and a line, rib, or bend just below the rim. Figure 32:35 from AN and a sherd from the same tomb are decorated with a unique border of impressed dots along the rib.

Miscellaneous bowls: Two bowl types, XLVII and XV, represented in the Sahab tomb B are important in that they show the place within our sequence of several other bowl types represented by many sherds from Amman. Again these types are in the time range when red-burnished surfaces are duplicated in black and light cream. We see it here as SB:14 (= fig. 33:24) in buff, SB:15 (= fig. 33:25) in black (both of type XLVII), and SB:6 (= fig. 32:42, type XV) with a pink exterior and black interior. The latter combination of colors is very frequent as we shall see below in burnished examples of the cylindrical jars, types LXXVII and LXXX. A bowl with a rim similar to such cylindrical jar rims from this same tomb, SB:3 (= fig. 41:6), also has the same features of pink exterior and black-burnished interior. Two other deep bowl rims which appear in the Amman sherd material are evident here, SB:20 and 21 (= fig. 41:7 and 8), and exhibit the special feature of black burnishing. An earlier deep bowl, number 39 from Amman tomb C (= fig. 41:10), has a rim similar to SB:20 (for the range of variation in such rims, see the sherd material below) but its colors are brown outside and grey inside.

Several other miscellaneous types of bowls exist that are attributable to the middle range of this sequence. Amman B number 48 (= fig. 33:11)

and Amman A number 5 (= fig. 33:12) illustrate small closed bowls (type XL) with narrow mouths and vertical or near vertical necks. Similar bowls were found at Samaria[2] and Tarsus.[3] Amman tomb C number 9 (= fig. 33:13) is of similar profile except that the opening is widened out and the rim tilted down from a vertical position. Tell el Farah (south) tomb 229 provides an excellent parallel for this bowl.[4] The deep bowls, AB:47 (= fig. 32:28) and AC:10 (= fig. 32:29), are interesting in that the former has a good parallel at Tell Jemmeh where it was found with other vessels that bore strong Assyrian influence.[5] AC:10 is thicker than most of the other bowls and is black burnished. This form appears to be imitating a stone bowl form.

Several isolated vessel types obviously belong to the end of our Sequence II. Two of these, AA:7 and 8 (= fig. 33:29 and 30), are very simple bowls but, interestingly enough, the form is unusual. In this case, we may have imitation of metal vessels since similar vessels in metal are more frequently found. An example of such a vessel in bronze was found in the Meqabelein tomb, number 61, and parallels to this have been cited from Tell Farah, south and north.[6]

Only two additional late bowls need be mentioned here, AA:18 (= fig. 33:9) and AN:88 (= fig. 33:10). Both seem to be good Assyrian period shapes. Amman A, number 18, is similar to the type XXXVII rim to be discussed below. Amman N, number 88, is similar to Assyrian palace type ware with impressed dimples on the side of the bowl. This type of pottery is best illustrated from he recent British excavations at Nimrud,[7] and the shape is best illustrated at Assur from a Neo-Assyrian grave.[8] The brown slip on the Amman

---

[1]*Ibid.*, p. 60.

[2]J. W. Crowfoot, G. M. Crowfoot, and Kathleen M. Kenyon, *Samaria - Sebaste III: The Objects from Samaria* (London: Palestine Exploration Fund, 1957), p. 145, fig. 14, no. 1.

[3]Hetty Goldman, *Excavations at Gözlü Kule, Tarsus*, Vol. III, *Iron Age* (Princeton: Princeton University Press, 1963), pl. 75a:1245.

[4]Duncan, *CPP*, type 23J 12.

[5]Flinders Petrie, *Gerar* (London: British School of Archaeology in Egypt, 1928), pl. XLVII:13.

[6]E. Henschel-Simon, "Note on the Pottery of the Amman Tomb," *QDAP*, XI (1945), 75.

[7]Joan Oates, "Late Assyrian Pottery from Fort Shalmaneser," *Iraq*, XXI (1959), pl. XXXVII:60, 61, 62, and 79.

[8]Arndt Haller, *Gräber und Grüfte aus Assur* (Wissenschaftliche Veröffentlichung der Deutschen Orient-Gesellschaft," 65; Berlin: Verlag Gebr. Mann, 1954), pl. 5s.

bowl is, however, unusual for such ware in Assyria. It is found, however, on some vessels of a similar type of ware at Ta'yinat in the Amuq and at Engedi in Palestine.[1]

Bowl Bases

We have dealt above mainly with rims and profiles and now a few words must be said concerning the bases. It is surprising that in a period when the pottery was quite sophisticated, a ring base was seldom used. We will see a considerable number of pointed based vessels below, but again a ring base is rare. Instead, a flat base and, in a majority of cases, a disk base was used. The prevalence of disk bases will be seen below in the sherd material from the 1969 Amman sounding and seems to be a characteristic for vessels of the Amman district.

Goblets

Only four goblets have been found among the vessels of Sequence II. Two, figure 33:33 and 36, are unique early examples and little more can be said about them. The other two, figure 33:34, 35, fall into the middle range but differ little from the goblets discussed above from the end of Sequence I. The major difference is that the ridge near the base has moved up to form a thickening of the shaft, just below the base of the bowl (fig. 33:34, 35).

Lamps

The lamps in use during this sequence all have a fairly wide rim with horizontal lip, which is a type that was present almost throughout Sequence I. The majority of the bases are still rounded (fig. 42:1-9, 14-17) as before but at the end of the period, most notably in Amman N (fig. 42:18, 19, but also occurring in a few examples at Sahab B, fig. 42:20-26, one in Amman E, fig. 42:33, and two in Amman F, fig. 84:3 and 4), a low flat base occurs. The smaller lamps on a high flat base, as are frequently found in the later half of Iron II in Palestine, are extremely rare so far in the Transjordan (fig. 42:25-33 being the closest Amman district forms).

One very characteristic lamp occurs in the middle range. This type is usually smaller than the other lamps and has been pinched at the middle to give the rim a figure-eight outline when viewed from the top (fig. 42:34-38). Whether this form is Ammonite or Transjordanian cannot be argued on present evidence since it is not yet represented outside of the Amman district.

Cups

We have seen some cups of type 1 at the end of the first sequence (fig. 22:39-44) and these continue on through the middle range of Sequence II. The proportions illustrated by these cups are unique to the Transjordan, figure 33:38-41. Cup type 1 is an unusual form which seems to be a miniature of a type of jug found in Sequence I, figure 26:21-28. At the end of the middle range and through the late range of this sequence, tripod-base cups come into use, cup types 3-5 and 7. Such cups have rarely been found outside of the Amman district (fig. 33:49) and form another distinctive feature of the Transjordanian assemblage. Both the Sahab B tomb and the Amman tomb E provide a great variety of such cups. The Sahab tomb has two cups, numbers 22 and 23 (fig. 33:42, 43), with relatively simple, almost vertical rims. Cups with such rims and rounded sides are currently unique and seem to be the earliest forms of this type of vessel. The other cups from the Sahab tomb represent what could be considered the "classic" profile type 5. Typical features of this form are: a slight carination at the bottom of the cup at the height of the leg attachment and an inturned rim with a rib at the side just below the top. The rim profile is the same as on deep bowls SB:20 (=fig. 41:8) and AC:39 (=fig. 41:10) seen above. Those from Amman E show this "classic" profile but in two cases the cups stand on trumpet bases rather than the three small feet, figure 34:11 and 12.

Tomb Amman A illustrates a broad range of cup forms. Alongside cup types 1, 2 and 5 were found an unusual type with a double rib near the rim, type 4 (Amman A:11 = fig. 33:46) and an example of the latest cup type, type 7 (Amman A:13 fig. 34:18). In type 7, the rim turns straight up, rather than horizontally inward, above the ridge at the top of the vessel side. The handle attachment has shifted from the top of the vessel at the rim to the rib beneath the rim. Both the lower carination and the upper rib are sometimes modified or omitted. Only type 7 cups are present in Amman N (fig. 34:13-17) and the Meqabelein tomb (fig. 34:19). This progression of cup types is a clear sequence which helps define the middle and late ranges of Sequence II. This vessel type is important in itself because it is currently found only in the Transjordan.

Trefoil-Spouted Jugs

A great variety of jugs has been found in the Amman district tombs. The two unpublished

---

[1]Benjamin Mazar, Trude Dothan, and Immanuel Dunayevsky, "Engedi," *Atiqot*, V (1966), pl. XV:1 and 2.

tombs, Amman G and Sahab C, provide a considerable number of additional examples, but these coincide quite well with the jug types illustrated. Almost without exception, the jugs have disk bases and only a few have "step-disk" bases. The proportions vary throughout. Handles were made as single or double straps and there is a consistency in the location of their points of attachment. The only development which can be noted is a change in rims. In all cases, they are pinched to form a pouring spout and in the later examples there seems to be more of a tendency to fold over the pinched-in portions. A majority of the earlier jugs have a bend near the top where the rim usually turns straight up or in, or is rolled over to this point (figs. 34:20-26, 30; 35:1-15 from Amman B, C, and E, Sahab B, and Irbed Museum). The later jugs (Amman A, C, E, and N, and the Meqabelein tomb) do not have the bend near the top of the rim and end in a simple outward flare. Two jugs from Amman E (nos. 19 and 5 = fig. 36:3 and 4) have unusual shapes and resemble the contemporary pinched lamps with a top view figure-eight profile. The decoration on these jugs consists of a slip ranging in color from pink to red and burnishing is usual. Painted or incised-line decoration occurs infrequently and is used primarily on vessels from the latest tombs (five examples from AN, one from M, one from AE, and one from AC). There has been some speculation regarding the place of manufacture of jugs of this type.[1] The consistency of their ware and surface treatment with that of other Amman district vessels, as well as the large number of such vessels found here, indicate that they are locally produced.

Other Jugs

The only jugs of this sequence without trefoil rims were found in Sahab B. The handle placement resembles that of the other jugs, as do the proportions of numbers 51 and 52 (= fig. 36:21 and 22). Sahab B, number 59 (= fig. 36:20) is unique. Numbers 54 and 55 (= fig. 36:23 and 24) are closest in shape to the decanters and side-spouted jugs to be discussed next. The similarity is present both in the shape and in the band-painted decoration.

The jugs which we have placed in types 14-18 are commonly referred to as decanters. In Palestine, the decanter has a long history with little change occurring in its shape. The same seems to be true in the Transjordan except of the very end of Sequence I (figs. 36:25-29; 37:1-10). We saw a number of decanters at the end of Sequence I above and, on the whole, they resemble the majority of the decanters we have here.

The handle placement is uniform, from shoulder or shoulder carination to the middle of the neck; there are usually two carinations on the body with the greatest width coming at the bottom; and only two examples have band-painted decoration. Once again peculiarities are evident from the latest tombs. Amman tomb A and the Meqabelein tomb have short wide jugs which do not occur earlier (fig. 37:5 and 6). Three jugs from Amman N (fig. 37:8-10) are unique. Their angles are formed more sharply than usual and the proportions have changed. The only examples of such distinctive sharp angles in the body of a jug or decanter come from Sidon in the Persian Period (an example is illustrated in the American University of Beirut Museum, case no. 27) and from a sixth-century tomb at Ain Shems.[2] The neck ridge has dropped to near the bottom of the neck and the neck narrows at the top. In all three examples the upper carination is the widest part of the vessel, rather than the lower, and the width is again proportionately greater than the height in contrast to the earlier decanters. In the earlier decanters the body was convex between the two carinations, but in Amman N (especially fig. 37:8) and one example from Amman A (fig. 36:29) the sides are concave.

One decanter from Amman A, number 39 (= fig. 37:11) and sherds of a second, 39a, indicate the late range of the tomb. This vessel is classed as a *lagynos*, a type of Hellenistic vessel common in the second century B.C. Number 39 is considered an import and 39a a local production. Whether this vessel actually dates as late as the second century or should date closer to the other vessels from this tomb cannot be determined at present.

Side-Spouted Jugs

We have seen a number of strainer jugs and one example of a cylindrical-spouted jug at the end of the first sequence above. They are more frequent in the early to middle ranges of Sequence II. Round-bottomed (fig. 37:19-24), disk-based (fig. 37:14-18) and flat based (fig. 37:13) examples were found. The disk-based examples have a profile similar to that of the contemporary decanters and almost all have line and band decoration. Only one such jug was found in a late tomb, Amman N, number 123 (= fig. 37:25). This has a front rather than side spout and an elongated handle. Its profile is unlike any of the above and

---

[1]Chapman, *Berytus*, XXI, 166-67 cites some excellent parallels among the red slip jugs which she indicates are common along the Mediterranean coast from al Mina to Achziv.

[2]Grant and Wright, *AS*, IV, pl. XLVIII:15.

resembles that of an Assyrian goblet. No parallels have been found to the attachment of handle and spout on such a form in Assyria, however. The shape is in keeping with the pointed jars below, but the rim is straight and plain and the neck is wider and only slightly flared. Though it is unique, this jug is in keeping with the other forms from Amman N.

Juglets, Small Jars, and Bottles: Types 2, 3, 5, 7, and 10

The corpus illustrates a variety of such small vessels in Sequence II. We mention only a few important features here. Pinched spouts are more numerous than jugs with rounded necks and rims. The few examples with marked pointed bases come from the beginning of the sequence. Only a few black-burnished juglets are found: Amman B:66, C:24, and Sahab B:45 (= figs. 38:11, 15, and 26: 84:2). Once again a particular type of juglet is found exclusively in the latest tombs: Amman N:116, A:24, and Meqabelein numbers 50 and 51 (fig. 38:7-10). These jugs are elongated and have a loop handle which rises markedly above the rim. None bears painted decoration.

Juglets, Small Jars, and Bottles: Types 11, 12, 14-16

Several distinctive features are found in all of these small vessel types. The general proportions are identical, all have cylindrical necks and round mouths, all have neck ridges (and where handles exist their tops join at this ridge), and only rare examples lack painted horizontal-band decoration. The colors of the slips vary from cream to tan and they are usually burnished. The paint color varies from brown to black. These vessels are confined to the middle range and are not found together with the Cypriote black-on-red juglets (type 10). The ware, decoration, and shape of such juglets are Cypriote-looking (fig. 38:33-50), but no such vessels have yet been found in Cyprus. The shape of the handles and their attachment are similar to those found frequently on Cypriote Type V (rarely on IV) vessels and later, and are common in the Hellenistic and sixth to fourth century B.C. Greek vessels. Similar juglets occur in Palestine and there is no evidence for attributing such juglets to a Phoenician rather than Palestinian or Transjordanian assemblage.

The most numerous vessel in this range of types is the small two-handled jar, type 15. All examples are flat or disk based. Two of the earliest examples, Amman C:36 and 37 (= fig. 38:40

and 41), have the double-carination body profile seen on decanters above. The remainder, also the majority, have globular bodies. The necks are usually elongated and in only two oversized examples, Amman E:125 and 135 (= fig. 38:33 and 34) is the height of the neck not roughly equal to the height of the body. The handle attachment is uniform throughout and its vertical outside portion is nearly straight from the bend to attachment. The placement of the painted-line decoration is illustrated in the corpus.

Types 11, 12, and 13, small bottles and one-handled juglets respectively, are far less numerous than the similar two-handled vessels. Amman E:126 and 26 (= fig. 38:30 and 31) resemble Amman E:135 (= fig. 38:34) but have rounded bottoms. The neck ridge and handle placement indicate that they belong with the types under discussion here. Only one juglet with the profile normal for type 15 is one-handled, Amman C:35 (= fig. 38:32), and, interestingly, it is early. Two small bottles were found in the middle range, type 11, figure 38:28 and 29. The profile is also identical with that of the normal two-handled, type 15, variety. Similar small bottles appeared at the end of Sequence I.

None of the vessels under discussion in this section were found in the late range of tombs. To cite Palestinian parallels from one site as an illustration, we can mention Tell Beit Mirsim where small jars like our type 15 appeared in phase A. The decoration, however, was different in one example[1] and two examples had no painted decoration.

Pointed-based Bottles: Types 17 and 18

Bottles of this type partially overlap the range of the vessel types just discussed. They occur side by side in middle range tombs, but the pointed bottles continue to be found in the late range of tombs. The wares, color, and painted decoration of most are identical. The corpus illustrates the proportions, rim types, and method of decoration. Similar bottles are very rare in Palestine. They have been found at Tell Gorin (Engedi), Tell en Naṣbeh, Tell el Ful, Megiddo, Tell Farah (north), Samaria, and Lachish.[2] Either one or two exam-

---

[1]Albright, *TBM*, I, pl. 39:13, 15, 16, and 17.

[2]Mazar, *Atiqot*, V, 71, fig. 19:14 and 15; J. C. Wampler, *Tell en-Naṣbeh*, Vol. II, *Pottery* (Berkeley: Pacific School of Religion, 1947), pl. 75:1732; R. A. S. Macalister, "Some Interesting Pottery Remains," *PEFQS*, XLVII (1915), pl. II:1; Robert S. Lamon and Geoffrey M. Shipton, *Megiddo I, Seasons of 1925-35, Strata I-V* ("OIP," XLII; Chicago: University of Chicago Press, 1939), pl. 9:1, 4, 6, and 7.

ples are present in each case. The time range for such bottles at these Palestinian sites is seventh to fifth centuries B.C. with the earlier part of this range given most frequently as a date. In Syria, such small bottles have been found at Tarsus[1] and in the Amuq. The examples from Chatal Hüyük and Ta'yinat are numerous. In Syria, these bottles are found to be contemporary with multi-colored glazed bottles of similar shape (most closely resembling Amman E:72 [= fig. 39:5] for this period). A study by E. J. Peltenburg[2] has outlined the range of this glazed material as primarily seventh century and in some cases lasting down to ca. 550 B.C. At Chatal Hüyük, the levels in which this ware occurs cannot be confined satisfactorily to the seventh century B.C. They undoubtedly occur in seventh-century contexts but also appear in levels with sixth-century imported Greek pottery. Some of the latest pottery bottles are decorated more elaborately than the rest. In some cases a change occurs in the wares and paint colors used. These changes indicate a longer period of use, but are unparalleled elsewhere at present.

The number of examples of such bottles in the Amman district is far greater than that found elsewhere. An argument for a long use, extending into the sixth century, is supported by the appearance of a new type, 18, in the latest Amman tombs. This type of bottle appears at Meqabelein and one was found in Amman N. The type 18 bottles are different from type 17 only in their exaggerated length. A jar, intermediate in shape between this type and the jars type 2 below, was found at Babylon in a Persian context. It illustrates the same exaggeration in length of an otherwise normal type.[3]

Imitation Alabastra: Type 19

This type is found only in the latest tombs, Amman A and N, and Meqabelein. Most of the examples show an exaggerated length, as is the case with type 18, and only a few smaller examples occur. The dates given vary from the sixth to the seventh century. This type of vessel is not common but according to von Bissing the alabaster vessels, of which these are imitations, first appear in Egypt, apparently the land where this form was first manufactured, at the end of the eighth century B.C.[4] He dates faience vessels of this type to "Spätzeit" in his catalogue of Egyptian faience vessels,[5] but later modifies this on elaborately decorated examples from Cerveteri in Italy, which he says must date between 700 and 600 B.C.[6] This form is not found in the Assyrian period in Mesopotamia, but it is found at Babylon and is attributed to the Neo-Babylonian

period.[7] This same shape occurs in glass and alabaster in the Meqabelein tomb indicating its popularity and adaptability.

Handleless, Pointed-based Jars: Type 1

Within the same late range are found a number of handleless pointed jars which are similar in shape but proportionately larger than the pointed bottles, type 17. This form has been considered primarily Transjordanian and the majority of the examples are found in the Transjordan (fig. 40:1-6). One example was found at Arad in the final fortress phase, stratum VI, and is considered to be typically Transjordanian by the excavator, Aharoni. Aharoni gives a date of 609 B.C. for the end of this stratum.[8] The same type of jar was found at Tell en Naṣbe,[9] though the proportions do not correspond as exactly to the Amman district vessels as the Arad jar. It is important to note that at this site similar vessels first appear in the sixth century and continue to occur with modification through the Hellenistic period. Red and white painted bands are said to occur on some, a feature which also occurred on some of the AN jars. Other vessels of this general group resemble the type 2 jars discussed below and represent the version of this general type which continues later.

Outside of Palestine and Transjordan this jar shape is very close to that of numerous Assyrian and Neo-Babylonian vessels, primarily within the range of the Tell en Naṣbe types; but again,

---

[1]Goldman, *Tarsus*, III, pl. 84:1079, 1081-83.

[2]E. J. Peltenburg, "Al Mina Glazed Pottery and its Relations," *Levant*, I (1969), 73-88.

[3]Oscar Reuther, *Die Innenstadt von Babylon (Merkes)* ("Wissenschaftliche Veröffentlichung der Deutschen Orient-Gesellschaft," 47; Leipzig: J. C. Heinricks, 1926), p. 35, fig. 44b; p. 65, fig. 109e. An example of an elongated juglet was also found at Tarsus; Goldman, *Tarsus*, III, pl. 84:1086.

[4]W. von Bissing, *Steingefässe* (Vienne: Adolf Holzhausen, 1907), pp. 54, 55, 145, pl. III: 18326, 18325, 18684, 18628.

[5]W. von Bissing, *Fayencegefässe* (Vienne: Adolf Holzhausen, 1902).

[6]W. von Bissing, *Zeit und Herkunft der in Cerveteri gefundenen Gefässe aus ägyptischer Fayense und glasiertem Ton* (München: Bayerischen Akademie der Wissenschaften, 1941), p. 84.

[7]Alabaster vessels of this shape are illustrated in Reuther, *Babylon*, p. 27, fig. 31; pl. 76:148 a and b.

[8]Yohanan Aharoni and Ruth Amiran, "Excavations at Tell Arad," *IEJ*, XIV (1964), 136 and pl. 33:B.

[9]Wampler, *Naṣbe*, pl. 27:444, 446, 447, and 452.

though they are of the general type, there are few examples which duplicate the proportions of these jars exactly. The closest parallels can be found at Nineveh,[1] Nippur,[2] and Assur[3] from the end of the Neo-Assyrian period, from Babylon[4] at an earlier date, and from Warka[5] in Neo-Assyrian and Neo-Babylonian levels. The Nippur and Warka examples are especially good in that they have a ridge between shoulder and neck, a striking feature of Meqabelein numbers 45-47 (= fig. 40:2-4). The rims of the Nippur vessels are simpler than the Amman district types and a metal vessel of the same shape has been found at this site.[6] At Warka, the ridge between neck and shoulder is considered an indicator of date, and the ridge is said to occur in the Neo-Babylonian period but not earlier.[7] This detail presents another good argument for our dating of tombs AN and M, and supports the placement of M in the Neo-Babylonian period.

Handleless, Pointed-based Jars: Types 2 and 3

These jars belong to the same general type of vessel discussed in the preceding paragraphs and overlap the range of jars found in Mesopotamia. The curved lines in the body and neck profile of type 1 are replaced by straighter lines and shorter necks. In Amman N numbers 91 and 92 (= fig. 40:10 and 11), there is a lack of emphasis on the neck which in number 92 is virtually absent (type 3). The other three vessels (type 2) are similar in profile and the Meqabelein examples show somewhat squat knob bases with ribbing (fig. 40:7 and 8). The ribbing affords an excellent parallel to Tell en Naṣbe number 446 and the knob to number 452.[8] This general type of vessel is said to have a few late pre-exilic examples, but their primary occurrence is in the sixth century. The knob base, like on number 452 however, is considered somewhat later and carries through into the late periods. The type 2 Amman district jars should, then, be considered the latest of the two types.

Pointed Based, Two-Handled Jars: Type 6

Only three jars of this type have been found. The one from Amman N (fig. 40:17) is virtually the same as the type 1 jars, with the addition of handles on two sides. The handles on this jar and the Irbed Museum example have the "duck head" profile which appears on vessels of the seventh and sixth centuries B.C. in Assyria and Greece. Such handles are commonly found on the glass version of the alabastra which were also copied in pottery (our type 19 above). We will discuss the example found in the Meqabelein tomb below.

Such jars have been found at Babylon[9] and Assur.[10] The most precise date for such vessels is provided by examples from Fort Shalmaneser at Nimrud. Here the date range would run from the end of the eighth through the seventh century B.C.[11]

Jar Type 7

Another handled jar with wide neck from Amman N, number 118 (= fig. 40:17), is contemporary with the vessels discussed in the preceding paragraphs. There are currently no good Palestinian parallels, but a similar jar was found at Nimrud in association with tablets which could be dated around 640-630 B.C.[12]

Two-Handled, Globular Vases: Jar Type 8

The shape, ware, and decoration of these vessels is very similar to that of the small jars, type 14. The necks are proportionately wider and shorter but the handle attachment and most other details correspond. One good Palestinian parallel exists at Tell Farah (north)[13] and the closest parallels actually come from Motya, Carthage, and other western Phoenician colony

---

[1]R. Campbell Thompson, "The British Museum Excavations at Nineveh," *AAA*, XX (1933), pl. LXXIV:17.

[2]Donald E. McCown and Richard C. Haines, *Nippur*, I ("OIP," LXXVIII; Chicago: University of Chicago Press, 1967), pl. 102:15, type 62.

[3]Haller, *Assur*, pl. 3:1, n, y, and ah; pl. 5:x and aa.

[4]Reuther, *Babylon*, pls. 65:94; 73:117.

[5]Eva Strommenger, *Gefässe aus Uruk von der neubabylonischen Zeit bis zu den Sasaniden* ("Ausgrabungen der Deutschen Forschungsgemeinschaft in Uruk-Warka," 7; Berlin: Verlag Gebr. Mann, 1967), p. 22 and pl. 12:3, 4, and 7.

[6]McCown and Haines, *Nippur*, I, pl. 108:16.

[7]Strommenger, *Gefässe aus Uruk*, p. 22.

[8]Wampler, *Naṣbe*, pl. 27.

[9]Reuther, *Babylon*, pl. 73:128a (Middle Babylonian) fig. 9:0 on p. 14 (Kassite).

[10]Haller, *Assur*, pl. 3:k.

[11]Oates, *Iraq*, XXI, pl. XXXIX:101.

[12]Harding, *AN*, p. 72.

[13]Roland deVaux, "Les Fouilles de Tell el-Far'ah, près Naplouse," *RB*, LVIII (1951), fig. 12:19.

sites.[1] Their date in the western Mediterranean ranges between the seventh and sixth centuries B.C., while de Vaux dates his example to the very end of the eighth century B.C. This is compatible with the occurrence of such vessels in both the middle and late ranges of our tombs and their similarity in shape to the juglets, type 14, of the middle range. Despite the fact that these jugs and the related small jars are Cypriote-looking, no good Cypriote parallels of manufacture and the appearance of similar vessels in the Phoenician colonies would support such a theory. The number of examples of this type of vase and the whole series of vessels of similar proportions, ware, and style from the Amman district make it hard to argue that they are not equally or even more at home in the Transjordan than in Phoenicia. Also, though our knowledge of Phoenician pottery of this period is quite scanty, no similar vessels have been found in Phoenicia and the small jars, type 14, are no more frequent there than in Palestine. Instead, there is a type of small jar with a profile peculiar to the Phoenician area that is used in its place.[2]

Cooking Pots

Four cooking pots were found in this sequence and they belong primarily to the middle range. The general profile is similar, but Amman B:49 (=fig. 41:1) and E:59 (=fig. 41:3) have proportionately larger handles. All of these vessels are of the type dated "after the end of the VII century" by Albright.[3]

Cylindrical Jars and Some Deep Bowls

Only a single example of the cylindrical jar was found in the tombs of this sequence, but a large number of sherds of this jar type has been found at Amman (sherd types LXXVI-LXXIX). This Amman N example helps in determining the date range of such rims, but we cannot go too far on the basis of just one example. The bowl profiles (fig. 41:6-8, 10) serve the same purpose of providing dating links for our Amman Citadel sherd material. We have already mentioned the peculiarities of the ware colors of these vessels and will discuss this further below.

Storage Jars

Two of these jars, M:43 and AN:113 (fig. 4:11 and 13), are identical in profile. Both the necks and the bases of these vessels are out of proportion to the size of the bodies and such small ring

bases could never have been used to support such jars. The handle placements and neck ridges are similar to those on decanters and the size of the handles and necks are more in keeping with such vessels. Specifically, they are almost identical to the decanters of type 18 from Amman N.[4]

Storage jars of this type approach the proportions of the elongated Persian and early Hellenistic jars but parallels are extremely rare. The closest examples come from Tell Gemmeh (ancient Gerar) and date to the XXVI Dynasty of Egypt and the Persian period.[5] Only the ring bases are missing on these jars. The same type is illustrated at Tell el Farah (south) but is dated, possibly incorrectly, to the XXII Dynasty of Egypt.[6]

A shorter version of this type was found at Meqabelein, number 61 (=fig. 41:12). Its neck is wider but it has the same ring base. It is decorated with five zones, each consisting of three parallel impressed lines. Impressed lines also occur on the tall jar M:43 but here they do not seem intentional, but rather created in the manufacture of the vessel. This jar was probably constructed by coiling and the lines formed by the joins between the coils were not later removed by smoothing the surface. It is easy to see in this the beginning of ribbing which eventually became more elaborate and a characteristic feature on jars and cooking pots for more than 700 years

---

[1] Pierre Cintas, *Ceramique punique* ("Publications de L'Institut des Hautes Études de Tunis," III; Paris: Librairie C. Klincksieck, 1950), pl. XXVIII:329, 330, 334, and 338. In only one of the Punic examples is there a ring base. In the other cases, the base is formed by pressing in the center to form a concave base. Several of the Amman examples also do not have ring bases, but one has a disk (AE 123) and one has a flat base (AE 124). The bases typical of the Punic pots are virtually non-existent in our area.

[2] Roger Saidah, "Fouilles de Khaldé," *BMB*, XIX (1966), 58:2 and Cintas, *CP*, LXXIV:65 *et suivantes* [*sic*].

[3] Albright, *TBM*, I, 81, pl. 55:2, 4, 5, 7, 9, and pl. 56:1-3, 10, and 11.

[4] A good parallel found at Tell en Naṣbe (Wampler, *Naṣbe*, pl. 37:665) represents a unique type attributed to the sixth century B.C. on the basis of comparable features on other decanters. Nothing is preserved of the Tell en Naṣbe decanter below the shoulder carination, so we do not know how closely it might resemble the unusual Amman N decanters, type 18, or, possibly, whether it is not a decanter at all but a jar similar to those under discussion here.

[5] Petrie, *Gerar*, pl. LVIII:63h and k.

[6] Flinders Petrie, *Beth-Pelet I (Tell Fara)* (London: British School of Archaeology in Egypt, 1930), pl. XXIX:63k.

from the Hellenistic period on. In the case of the small jar M:61, where the lines are intentional, we cannot consider this unusual. Incised line decoration is well illustrated by our sherd material below.

The fact that we are probably dealing with a period in which the origins of ribbing as a decorative feature emerge is strongly emphasized by jar AN:115 (=fig. 41:9). The preserved portion of the jar illustrates a handleless variety of, apparently, the elongated jar. The low neck ridge is present but below this the surface is ribbed, not in zones, but continuously over the entire surface. On present evidence, it would be best to place these vessels as late as possible in our sequence rather than to place the introduction of ribbing too early and distant from the period of its greatest popularity.

The jar from Amman F (fig. 84:1) is of this type also, but of intermediate size. It is of the black-burnished ware which we have noted as occurring since the middle range of Sequence II. Its use on a type of jar which we must place at the very end of our sequence indicates a surface finish which continues to the very end of Sequence II. In this case, the burnishing is a continuous spiral but with a space between the burnish line.[1]

Whole Vessels from Other Sites

Enough material is available from four other sites to warrant a separate discussion. Unfortunately, it constitutes a small portion of the excavated finds which hopefully will be available soon.

Linguistic material bearing royal names helps in dating the finds in associated levels at Tell el Kheleifeh and at Umm el Biyara. The name Qôs-anal has been read by Glueck on an inscription from level IV at Tell el Kheleifeh,[2] and Qôs-gabar on a seal from Umm el Biyara.[3] The men were contemporaries and the latter is mentioned in the same inscription of Ashurbanipal, dated to 667 B.C., as an Ammi-nadab, king of Ammon. Mrs. Bennett considers Umm el Biyara to be a one period site with a very confined time range of about fifty years in the first half of the seventh century B.C.

An inscribed seal from Amman tomb AN bears the name of one of the kings of Ammon and this Ammi-nadab has been identified with the king of Ammon mentioned in the Ashurbanipal inscription of 667 B.C. Our examination of the pottery, however, favors a later date, in the last half of the seventh century B.C. The slight variation between the dates can easily be reconciled with the contention that his burial took place close to the middle of the century. The finding of an inscribed

bottle in the excavations at Tell Siran has provided a new listing of several Ammonite kings and includes two Ammi-nadabs, two generations apart.[4] If either of these rulers is the one mentioned in the Ashurbanipal inscription, then the suggestion of Thompson and Zayadine to equate him with the first Ammi-nadab is most logical, since there is more room in the known sequence of rulers at this point.[5] The second Ammi-nadab would then date in the last half of the seventh century B.C., the date we would prefer to assign to the ruler mentioned on the seal of Adoni-nur. On the basis of the evidence currently available, we consider this hypothesis to be the most acceptable.

In this context, the Umm el Biyara settlement can be dated to the first half of the seventh century B.C. without difficulty, as Bennett suggests and as our middle range parallels indicate. It can be associated with the date of the Ashurbanipal inscription and Ammi-nadab I. The tomb of Adoni-nur can then be placed in the last half of the seventh century B.C., as our late range parallels indicate, and can be associated with the date for Ammi-nadab II of around 635 B.C.

Level IV at Tell el Kheleifeh may have a longer range and is the only level at this site from which any amount of pottery has been published. The time range of this level may extend as far back into the eighth century as it extends forward into the sixth. Few of the published forms actually overlap with those of our late range, but some are similar and others are definitely contemporary with this range though different.

Of the sites mentioned, the most material is available from Dhiban. The majority of the published forms fall in the early to middle range of our Sequence II. There is no evidence for occupation contemporary with our late range at present.

---

[1]The appearance of such spiral burnishing and ribbing on the same type of jars brings up a point which needs to be emphasized. There is actually little difference in the technique used to produce these effects. The difference is primarily a matter of timing. Burnishing is produced when a tool is applied to a vessel when it is leather hard. If a wetter surface is treated, the tool sinks in rather than rides on the surface. Similar ribbing occurred on vessels in Early to Middle Bronze Syria as a degeneration of burnishing techniques.

[2]Glueck, *BASOR*, CLXXXVIII, Part I, pp. 8 and 9. Earlier references to the reading of the seal are given here.

[3]Bennett, *UB*, pp. 398-401.

[4]See p. 173, footnote 2 for bibliography on the Tell Siran inscription.

[5]See page 28 for the incorporation of the rulers into our chronological chart, Table 3.

Almost all of the published material from Mt. Nebo comes from two large tomb groups.[1] This material is confined to Iron II (though earlier Iron Age tombs have also been excavated in this area) but does not extend as late as the middle range of Sequence II. These tombs, consequently, help fill the gap between our 1969 Amman Citadel sounding material and the majority of our Sequence II material which falls in the middle and late ranges.[2]

Vessels with Parallels to Early and Middle Range Forms Found in the Amman District

Several pottery types, from the four sites under discussion, have a fairly long range and do not provide precise dating criteria. These types, found at the end of our Sequence I, must have continued in use through the early part of our Sequence II into the middle range.

One of the most characteristic forms is that of cup type 1.[3] The other Amman district cup types, however, are not found at these sites. The Mt. Nebo tombs illustrate the largest number of early examples of type 1 cups. The profiles vary somewhat and all examples are of a fairly heavy ware. Both flat and rounded bases are present and the shapes here overlap with those of the far more numerous perforated cups. On the other three sites, flat bases are rare on such cups, but rounded bases are normal. Only one example has a rim which is nearly vertical and in all cases the handles project a considerable distance from the sides.

A second important form is the bottle, type 11. Quite a few examples of these were found at Dhiban and Mt. Nebo but not at the other sites.[4] The Dhiban examples all come from tombs, which may explain their absence elsewhere. All the juglets of this type have a neck ridge and most are decorated with parallel painted lines. The type 15, small jars, and the type 17, pointed base bottles, are presently illustrated only from the Dhiban tombs.[5]

A number of dipper juglets from Dhiban and Mt. Nebo fall into the same time range. Their shapes are not particularly instructive, but at least they do not bear any of the characteristics of the end of the second sequence. A number of flasks were found in the Mt. Nebo tombs. The short, narrow, slightly-flaring neck and the placement of the handles on these flasks were unusual features in Sequence I and had their only parallel there in number 82 (= fig. 30:34) from Madeba tomb A. Several flasks had no handles at all and one, rounded on only one side, had a double rib around the side to hold a suspension cord that passed through the handles.[6]

Most of the lamps from these sites fall into our types 4 and 6 with horizontal topped ledge rims and either rounded or flattened bottoms. Only at Dhiban and Mt. Nebo are there exceptions to this with the presence of a number of other types. The sizes and proportions of the latter vary considerably and it is impossible to say what features may be due to chronological differences. Some of the lamps do not have the horizontal ledge in the portion behind the pinched spout which resembles

---

[1]Saller, *LA*, XVI, 165-298.

[2]In addition to Umm el Biyara, the British School of Archaeology has continued its excavations at sites in the south of Jordan under the direction of Mrs. Crystal-M. Bennett. For a preliminary report of the work at Taiwilan see: Crystal -M. Bennett, *Levant*, III, v-vii and for preliminary reports on the first four seasons of excavations at Buseirah see: Crystal -M. Bennett, "Excavations at Buseirah, Southern Jordan, 1971: A Preliminary Report," *Levant*, V (1973), 1-11; "Excavations at Buseirah, Southern Jordan, 1972: Preliminary Report," *Levant*, VI (1974), 1-24; "Excavations at Buseirah, Southern Jordan, 1973: Third Preliminary Report," *Levant*, VII (1975), 1-19; and "Excavations at Buseirah, Southern Jordan, 1974: Fourth Preliminary Report," *Levant*, IX (1977), 1-10; Bennett dates the occupation at Taiwilan to the seventh century B.C. and the occupations at Buseirah to the end of the eighth, the seventh and possibly into the sixth centuries B.C.

As is the case with the other sites in this section, Taiwilan and Buseirah clearly overlap primarily with our middle range materials. Though the Taiwilan pottery has not been published it is apparently very close to that which was found at Buseirah, particularly with large amounts of similar painted pottery. Complete vessels are published in the second and third preliminary reports from Buseirah. These vessels are similar to vessels from the other sites discussed in this section, particularly: bowls similar to our types I, II, III, IX, X, XXIII-XXV, XXVIII, XXXIII, XL, XLI, XLIII, cups, cooking pots, censers, lamps, a pointed bottle (our type 17), a juglet (our type 15), jugs and decanters. Particularly in the bowl types, there are more variations of forms which are not well documented in the Amman district.

[3]No complete examples have yet been published from Dhiban but a sherd of such a cup is illustrated in Tushingham, *Dhiban*, II, fig. 1:13.

[4]Reed and Winnett, *Dhiban*, I, pl. 77:3, 7, and 8 from tomb 3 and Tushingham, *BASOR*, CXXXIII, 24, fig. 10 from tomb 6.

[5]Reed and Winnett, *Dhiban*, I, pl. 77:1, 2, and 5 (type 15) and 9 (type 17); Tushingham, *BASOR*, CXXXIII, 24, fig. 10 also illustrates both types.

[6]Saller, *LA*, XVI, 222, fig. 20:14, 14a; 276, fig. 34:28-35. Shapes similar to the flask with one flat side and side ribs can be found at Megiddo (Str. IV-I): Lamon and Shipton, *MEG*, I, pl. 36:1, 2; Samaria: Crowfoot, and Kenyon, *SS*, III, 173-74, fig. 24:1-6, and elsewhere in Palestine.

the types 1 and 2 present only in our first sequence, but this may not indicate a chronological difference here. Many Dhiban examples show a blunted end on a very flat-based form which is unique. The most interesting examples are those with high disk or even ring bases, resembling somewhat the frequent Palestinian forms which, as stated above, have few parallels in the Amman district. Most of the lamps of this type are currently found at Dhiban and seem to fall in an eighth to ninth-century B.C. time range.

Several unusual lamps should also be mentioned here. Three lamps with unusual profile and raised on a high stand were found at Mt. Nebo and Tell el Kheleifeh.[1] Two other lamps on stands were found at Tell el Kheleifeh, but they were of the seven-spouted variety.[2] Several lamps of a very unusual and interesting type have been published recently (1969) from Tell el Kheleifeh. These are double compartmented lamps in which lamps of normal profile (but in most cases with disk bases that are uncommon in the Transjordan) are attached over the top of a second bowl. There is an opening in the rim through which the lower compartment can be filled, but there is no opening which actually connects both compartments.[3]

There are a number of bowls which resemble types existing at the end of the first sequence, found in the 1969 Amman sounding and found in the middle range tombs of Sequence II. These bowls have up-turned, vertical rims in most examples. The bases vary from disk to ring base.[4] Only rarely are these bowls said to be burnished, however, and south of the Amman district a white slip seems more common than a red slip or surface color. This surface coloration is presently best documented in the Mt. Nebo tombs.

A number of other vessels were found which are primarily contemporary with the middle range. We mentioned above the small two-handled jars of type 15 (fig. 38:35-50) which have good parallels at Dhiban and Mt. Nebo. A small jar of similar shape comes from Tell el Kheleifeh, but its decoration is very unusual (see discussion below).[5] A number of different small jars and juglets were found at the other sites. One is a rounded juglet similar to AE:94 (type 9, fig. 38:24) from Tell el Kheleifeh[6] and two examples of the same shape, but without handles, come from that site and Umm el Biyara.[7] At the latter site, there are a number of other elongated juglets which have no good parallels elsewhere. Only the short rounded neck is similar to that on the juglets just mentioned.

A few decanters were found; all come from Umm el Biyara. Two are not illustrated but are said to be similar to Sahab B:57.[8] We have no exact parallels for the proportions of the decanter

which is illustrated. It has an elongated, somewhat narrow cylindrical body of equal diameter from top to bottom, in keeping with the proportions of the juglets. Several juglets from Dhiban[9] and Mt. Nebo[10] are narrowed, diminutive decanters but cannot be classed as such. Similar juglets are found at Carthage, but with a rounded bulge in place of the bottom carination. Here they have, however, been given a seventh to sixth-century B.C. date range.[11]

A popular vessel at Dhiban,[12] Mt. Nebo,[13] and Tell el Kheleifeh[14] is a strainer cup with tripod base. We have illustrated at the end of our Sequence I, a number of strainer vessels which had flat bases and mouths narrower than their greatest diameter. The strainer cups may be a modified continuation of this form. The absence of such vessels at Umm el Biyara and from the middle and late ranges of Sequence II in the Amman District indicates that they are in use earlier than the seventh century B.C. Some of these cups resemble in profile those from Umm el Biyara and Tell el Kheleifeh which were discussed above (we have already mentioned the overlap of type 1 cups and such perforated cups at Mt. Nebo) and others have a double-waisted profile. We will see below that at Tell el Kheleifeh there is a similar variation on a well established bowl type which

[1]Saller, *LA*, XVI, 266, fig. 29:1, 2; Nelson Glueck, "Some Ezion-geber: Elath Iron II Pottery," *Eretz Israel*, IX (1969), 56, fig. 2-14.

[2]Glueck, *Eretz Israel*, IX, 55 and 58, 56, fig. 2:12, 13.

[3]*Ibid.*, p. 57, fig. 3:17-24, and p. 59. The photograph of a similar lamp (pl. XII:4-5) from the museum of the Monastery of the Flagellation, Jerusalem, illustrates that the lower compartment in this instance is actually a flask and may indicate that this compartment was intended to hold additional fuel. A similar lamp is now published in Eliezer D. Oren, *The Northern Cemetery of Beth Shan* (Leiden: E. J. Brill, 1973), fig. 42b:17 fig. 72:15.

[4]Bennett, *UB*, p. 387, fig. 2:6; p. 389, fig. 3:2, 4.

[5]Glueck, *BASOR*, CLXXXVIII, Part II, 35, fig. 4:5.

[6]*Ibid.*, Part I, pl. 19, fig. 5:4.

[7]Bennett, *UB*, p. 364.

[8]*Ibid.*, p. 393.

[9]Reed and Winnett, *Dhiban*, I, pl. 77:10, 11.

[10]Saller, *LA*, XVI, 273, fig. 33:8.

[11]Cintas, *CP*, fig. VI:74.

[12]Tushingham, *BASOR*, CXXXIII, 24, fig. 10.

[13]Saller, *LA*, XVI, 269, fig. 32:1-10; 292, fig. 37:1-5; 207, fig. 16:1-22.

[14]Glueck, *BASOR*, CLXXXVIII, Part II, 26, fig. 1:2, 3 and 7; 32, fig. 3:5-10.

probably represents a local variation in these vessel types. Within the time range under discussion, the perforations are in almost all cases confined to one or two rows (with the number of examples of each being about equal).[1] Professor James B. Pritchard argues that the perforated cups and related cup forms were used as censers.[2]

A large number of deep bowls or kraters were found both at Dhiban and Mt. Nebo and are without published Transjordanian parallel elsewhere. There are several examples of tripod-loop bases[3] and other vessels have flat bases. The rims and profiles of the Dhiban vessels are quite simple and the decoration consists of painted bands.[4] Several similar vessels were found in the Mt. Nebo tombs but in most cases, painted decorations and rim profiles are more elaborate.[5] Most of the Mt. Nebo vessels are quite high in contrast to the earlier krater shape, as best exemplified in the Irbed tombs (fig. 24:2-4).[6] Instead, they resemble the Madeba tomb B vessels (fig. 24:5-7) and the lone example from Tell el Kheleifeh.[7] The use of four handles on such vessels is normal.

Most of the discussion of bowl types has been included below in the discussion of sherd materials, but several complete forms should be mentioned here. Type II bowls are not numerous, and again come chiefly from Dhiban[8] and Mt. Nebo.[9] These examples date earlier than the seventh century. The vessels that approach this shape at Umm el Biyara are said to be lids.[10]

Horizontal ledge rim bowls are found at Dhiban[11] and Umm el Biyara[12] and are suggested as parallels to our type XLIX bowl from Meqabelein (fig. 33:27 and 28). They are generally the same, but lack the rounded bases and are more squared at the tops and angles. Bowls of similar profile also occur at Mt. Nebo, but here such bowls (along with bowls of profile types XXV and XLIII) stand on very high ring or trumpet bases.[13]

The type XXXVIII Assyrian period bowl, represented presently in Amman only by a sherd, occurs frequently at Tell el Kheleifeh in Level IV.[14] The latter occurrence suggests that this is another example of a late eighth-century B.C. type which continues at the beginning of the seventh century B.C. but does not seem to continue later than this. This bowl form is best illustrated in Palestine at Tell Gemmeh and Farah (north), though found elsewhere also.[15] The parallels mentioned by Glueck for this type of bowl are not as precise as we would like and must be used with caution.[16] His parallels are with bowls that we have designated as type XLVII (Sahab B: 14 and 15 = fig. 33:24 and 25), type V (Sahab B:16-19 = fig. 32:22-25) and type IV.[17] Our discussions of bowls and sherds of these types indicate that they are all distinct and unrelated types.

Another complete bowl shape type LXIII, which is found frequently as a sherd, has its sole complete example at Tell el Kheleifeh.[18] A few examples of this rim type were found in the upper levels of the 1969 Amman sounding, but not in any of the Amman district tombs. This suggests that its period of use falls into the ninth and eighth centuries B.C. The Tell el Kheleifeh example would seem to fall at the end of this time

---

[1]Additional strainer cups are now also published from Dhiban, Tushingham, *Dhiban*, II, figs. 16:15-18; 23:7 and 11. Only one resembles those illustrated on our fig. 22:45-51, only two have two rows of holes while the rest have three, and one has a moderately high ring base rather than the short tripod legs.

[2]James B. Pritchard, "On Use of the Tripod Cup," *Ugaritica VI*, edited by Claude F. A. Schaeffer ("Institut Français d'archéologie de Beyrouth, Bibliothéque archéologique et historique," Vol. LXXXI; Paris: Librairie Orientaliste Paul Geuthner, 1969), pp. 427-34.

[3]Saller, *LA*, XVI, 243, fig. 25:16-19; 285, fig. 35:8-10.

[4]Reed and Winnett, *Dhiban*, I, pl. 77:14 and 15; Tushingham, *BASOR*, CXXXIII, 24, fig. 10. A similar vessel is in storage in the Amman Museum and is said to be from Jerash.
Now also Tushingham, *Dhiban*, II, fig. 22:13 and 24:26 with parallel band decoration but also fig. 17:7 with the addition of a band with metope pattern 113 and fig. 22:11 with the addition of a band with metope pattern 101 repeated.

[5]Rim profiles resembling our type XXVI, LXIII, LXVIII, LXXIV, and LXXV rims can be found on these vessels.

[6]Saller, *LA*, XVI, 245, fig. 26; 247, fig. 27:1-3; 285, fig. 35:1-5, 11 (6, 7, 12 and 14 are handleless examples).

[7]Amiran, *APHL*, p. 301, photo 326.

[8]Tushingham, *BASOR*, CXXXIII, 24, fig. 10.

[9]Saller, *LA*, XVI, 221, fig. 19:18-27; 276, fig. 34:1-8.

[10]Bennett, *UB*, p. 387, fig. 2:4 and 5; p. 389, fig. 3:3.

[11]Reed and Winnett, *Dhiban*, I, pl. 73:7.

[12]Bennett, *UB*, p. 387, fig. 2:16.

[13]Saller, *LA*, XVI, 215, fig. 18:14, 16-19; 222, fig. 20:1, 3; 273, fig. 33:3, 4.

[14]Glueck, *BASOR*, CLXXXVIII, Part II, 26, fig. 1:5 and 6; 35, fig. 4:1-3, 6-8.

[15]Petrie, *Gerar*, pl. L1, 26w, and x; and Roland de Vaux, "La troisième campagne de fouilles à Tell el-Far'ah, près Naplouse," *RB*, LVIII (1951), pl. XV:1 where they are found in level 1.

[16]Glueck, *BASOR*, CLXXXVIII, Part II, 26 and 35.

[17]The two sherds shown from Glueck, *BASOR*, CLXXXVIII, Part I, pl. 16, fig. 4:7a and b, seem to come from shallow bowls of this type but the bowl profiles are not drawn.

[18]Glueck, *BASOR*, CLXXXVIII, Part I, 19, fig. 5:2.

span, as the ware is very thin and the delicate ring base illustrates a late feature. Fine ware and a similar base are found on a spouted bowl with ribbed rim and single handle. Its shape has a very close parallel at Tell Beit Mirsim,[1] but it has a much earlier (eleventh century) date there.

A large number of bowls were found in the Mt. Nebo tombs and at Dhiban.[2] Among these were a number of simple bowls with rounded sides and bases.[3] Others had profiles similar to that on the cups, type 1, but with straighter rims.[4] Low, sharp-angled examples of the latter in a finer ware were also present and resemble shapes found at Samaria in Periods VI and VII.[5] Deeper carinated shapes with a profile resembling type XXXIII may be late examples and slight modifications of the bowl type found at Irbed, IB:12 and 13 (= fig. 22:35 and 36).[6] Three bowls resemble the type VIII profile illustrated on figure 32:28 but are of earlier, thicker ware and are ribbed over the whole side. Similar ribbed bowls are best illustrated at Tell Gemmeh.[7]

Peculiar types of bowls and censers are presently unique to Tell el Kheleifeh. These vessels are characterized by a band of "dentiled ornamentation" at the carination and usually are made of rather thick ware. Flat based bowls, pots, and trays of very heavy ware are also unique at Tell el Kheleifeh, as far as Transjordanian parallels are currently concerned. We must consider these vessels as local products, possibly of a cultural sub-area in the south which stretches at least from the Arabah[8] on the west and into Arabia[9] in the east.

Few cooking pots have been found and they are similar to those of type 4 found in the Amman district.[10] Only two examples of strainer jugs have been found.[11] This illustrates a sharp contrast to the popularity of this vessel in Iron I. The storage jars at Tell el Kheleifeh provide the primary illustrations currently available for this class of vessel, except for the late Amman district examples discussed above. These are totally different from the earlier vessels[12] and are more in keeping with a tradition continuing on from our better documented Sequence I examples.

A number of sherds at Tell el Kheleifeh illustrate elaborately profiled and elaborately decorated vessels which may be dated later than the other vessels we have discussed here. These sherds come from vessels which are decorated with rows of bosses or other projections.[13] Few good parallels are presently available for such decoration but one bowl and several jars from Mt. Nebo illustrate the presence of similar decoration elsewhere.[14]

---

[1]Albright, *TBM*, I, pl. 50:9.

[2]The additional pottery forms illustrated in Tushingham, *Dhiban*, II, now also provide parallels to the Mt. Nebo tomb material.

[3]Saller, *LA*, XVI, 215, fig. 18:1-9; 222, fig. 20:2; 267, fig. 31:10, 11.

[4]*Ibid.*, pp. 215, fig. 18:12; 267, fig. 31:12, 14.

[5]Crowfoot, Crowfoot, and Kenyon, *SS*, III, 122, fig. 10:8 (Period VI) and 126, fig. 11:17 and 23. The Mt. Nebo examples are illustrated in Saller, *LA*, XVI, 215, fig. 18:10; 267, fig. 31:13.

[6]Saller, *LA*, XVI, 267, fig. 31:16, 18.

[7]Petrie, *Gerar*, pl. XLIX:13d, and Wampler, *Naṣbe*, pl. 54:1203 and 1204.

[8]Glueck, *BASOR*, CLXXXVIII, Part I, 14, fig. 3.

[9]G. Lankester Harding, *Archaeology in the Aden Protectorates* (London: Her Majesty's Stationery Office, 1964), pls. V, VII, VIII, and X.

[10]At Umm el Biyara, they are paralleled to similar pots at Tell Beit Mirsim (Albright, *TBM*, III, pl. 19:1-4).

[11]Saller, *LA*, XVI, 235, fig. 23:24, 25.

[12]Glueck, *Eretz Israel*, IX, 52, fig. 1:2-7.

[13]Portions of four storage jars, but without preserved rims, are illustrated in Tushingham, *Dhiban*, II, fig. 19:1-4.

[14]Saller, *LA*, XVI, 242, fig. 25:10, 12, 13, 15; 273, fig. 33:7.

TABLE 4. CHRONOLOGICAL TABLE OF ARCHAEOLOGICAL
SITES OF THE IRON AGE

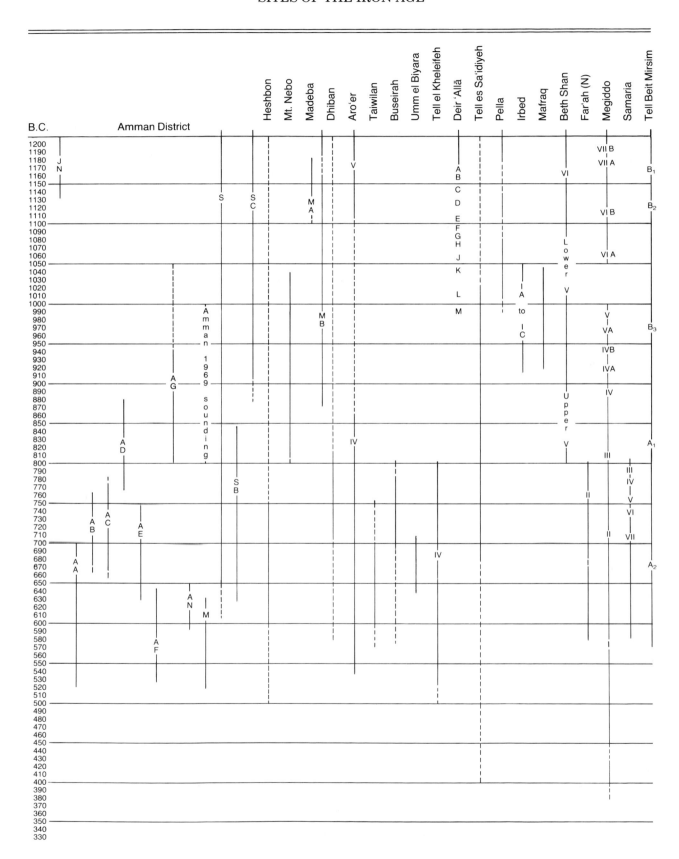

CHAPTER VI

PAINTED POTTERY OF THE IRON AGE

Aside from the Philistine pottery of Iron I, painted pottery plays a minor role in Palestinian ceramics during the Iron Age. The surface surveys in the Transjordan, however, yielded a high percentage of painted pottery and led to the designations of specific Edomite and Moabite painted wares by Albright, Glueck, and others. A very high degree of similarity to these Moabite and Edomite wares is illustrated by examples in figures 66 to 71 from Amman. This, in conjunction with the painted vessels from the Amman district tomb groups, illustrates that most of these painted wares were not confined to either Edom or Moab but were present throughout the Transjordan. In searching for parallels, it became evident that much of this painted pottery was represented by examples in Palestine. In some cases, it occurred frequently and in others it was rare. There seems to be greater contact with the seacoast and, though very poorly represented at present, with Syria. The date of much of this pottery has been a question, but in most cases it can now be dated with relative certainty. The occurrence of specific patterns at the beginning and end of the Iron Age indicates that we are dealing with a fairly constant tradition, despite certain modifications.

Unfortunately, only a small portion of this pottery was found in excavations. Significant contributions should be made by the publication of the remainder of the Tell el Kheleifeh pottery as well as that from the recent excavations at Umm el Biyara, Taiwilan and Buseirah.[1] Much of the so-called Edomite pottery was originally considered Iron I, but recently there have been arguments to redate much of it in the range of eight through sixth centuries B.C. When one re-examines the sherds, it becomes clear that some are early and others late.[2]

Simple Band-Painted Decoration

The most common decoration throughout the period is the application of parallel bands or lines of paint. This primarily is found on the body of the vessel (usually on the inside of bowls and on the outside of closed vessels), but occasionally occurs on rims also (nos. 433, 437 and 438). At the beginning of the period it appears in concentric circles inside bowls, particularly in the Jebel Nuzha tomb. It is also evident on flasks (where a variant spiral motif is often found) and on the outsides of chalices (DA phase L), jars, small jugs, and pyxides. The effect is always dark on light with a range of paint colors from red to black, and tan or buff to red for the ware. At Deir 'Allā in the earliest Iron Age phases, two colors are occasionally used in alternate bands. There is some division of the vessels' surfaces into decorated and undecorated zones, but it is not usually well planned. Either the entire surface is filled with fairly evenly spaced bands or many bands are grouped tightly together and an isolated band left elsewhere on the pot (e.g., Deir 'Allā phase A, fig. 47:3, and 5-8; phase B, fig. 51:62-64, 52:1; phase C, fig. 54:119; Jebel Nuzha tomb nos. 1, 2, 3, 7, 51, 53). The grouping of lines is already apparent early (JN nos. 4, 5, and 6) and remains prevalent throughout the time in which red-washed and red-burnished wares are in common use (starting with around Deir 'Allā phase G, fig. 65:60; phase L, fig. 75:88).

The use of parallel-line decoration increased considerably at Megiddo at the end of Stratum VII and in Stratum VI, and at contemporary Beth Shan in level VI. We remarked above on the similarities in these levels with the Jebel Nuzha tomb, where parallel-line painted decoration was most frequent. Deir 'Allā and the Madeba tombs illustrate how this painted decoration then declines.[3] The painted decoration on the inside of bowls becomes extremely rare. A glance at our table of decorative designs (Table 5) shows that many of the designs which apparently worked well on a round area were applied to the inside of bowls as well as to the sides of jugs. The few painted bowl sherds from the Amman 1969 sounding and Tell Beit Mirsim, level B$_3$, illustrate some of the latest bowl sherds decorated in this manner. (Only the plain cross, design 252, is found in Sequence II bowls.) Design 255, found at Tell Beit Mirsim,[4] is a variant of design 258 with circles in the center instead of a square. A bowl with groups of concentric circles was found in the same level. This decoration was found in the 1969 Amman Citadel sounding, no. 67:369.

In Syria, the overlap of flask and bowl designs was much greater. Designs 236, 238-240 and 274-277 occurred on both. In the Transjordan, only the concentric circles are found currently on bowls while the flask decoration is considerably more elaborate and continues for a longer time.

---

[1]Reference has been made above to the recent preliminary reports from Buseirah, see p. 59, footnote 2.

[2]Glueck, *BASOR*, CLXXXVIII, Part I, 8-15.

[3]It has been stated above that at Deir 'Allā painted decoration becomes extremely rare after phase E.

[4]Albright, *TBM*, I, pl. 30:2, 4, and 5.

TABLE 5. PALESTINIAN – SYRIAN IRON AGE DECORATIVE DESIGNS

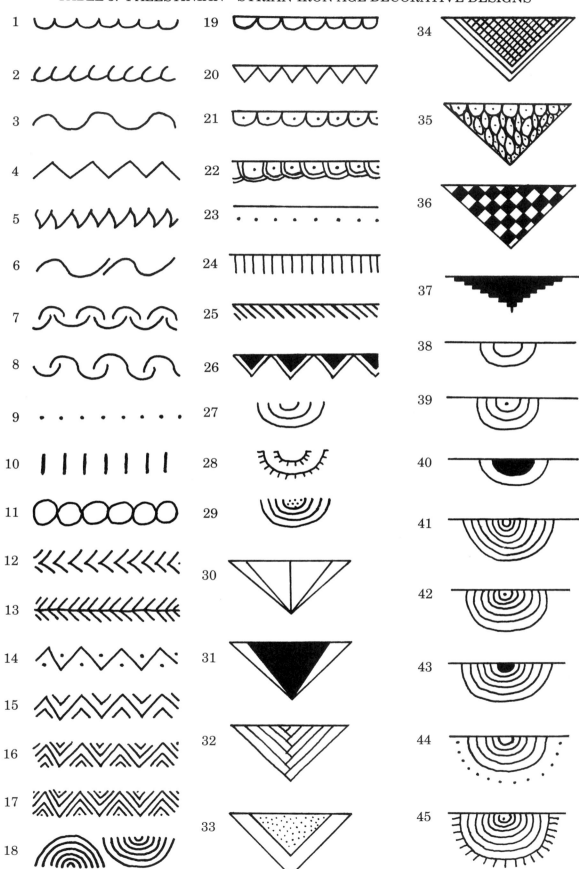

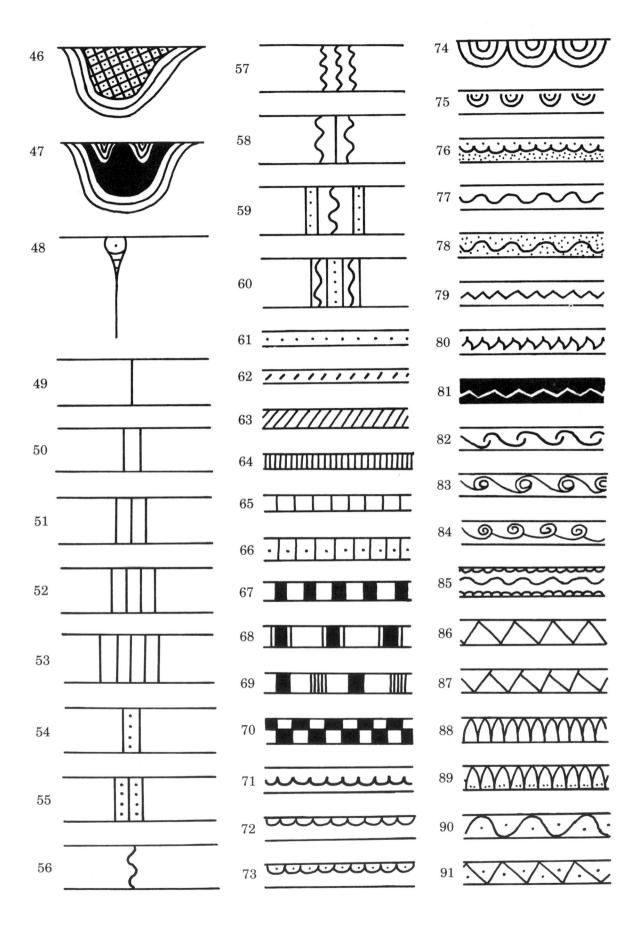

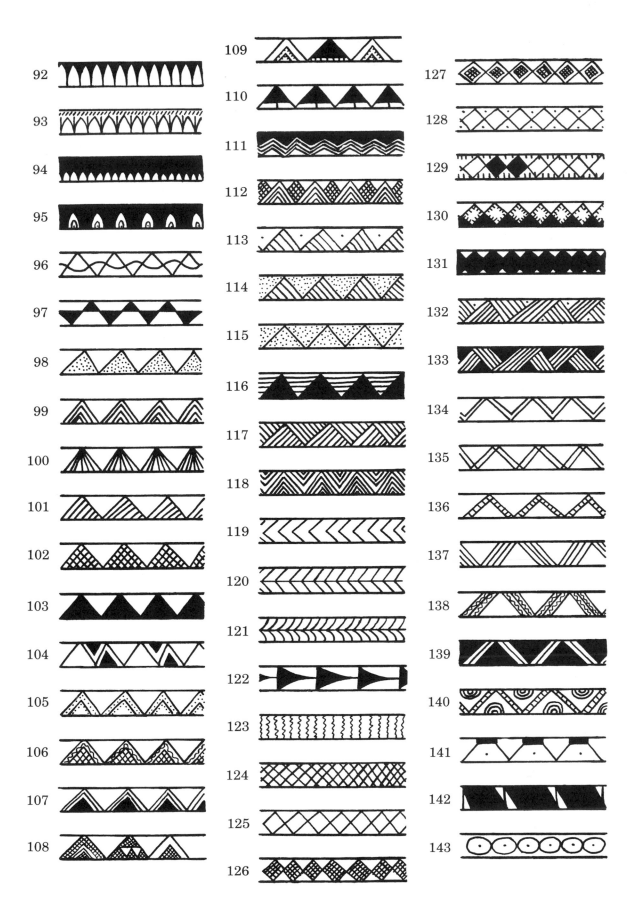

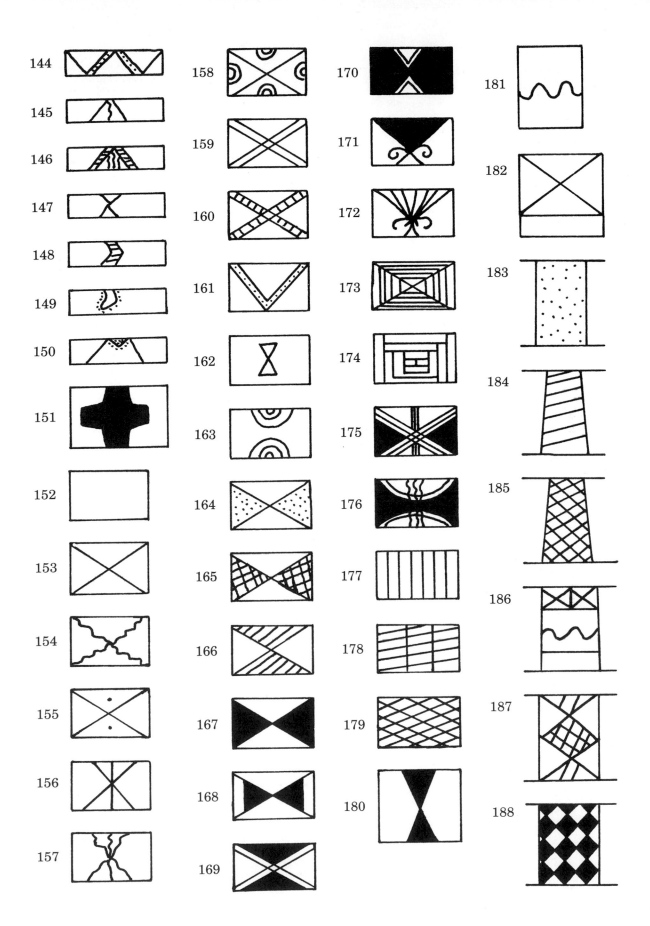

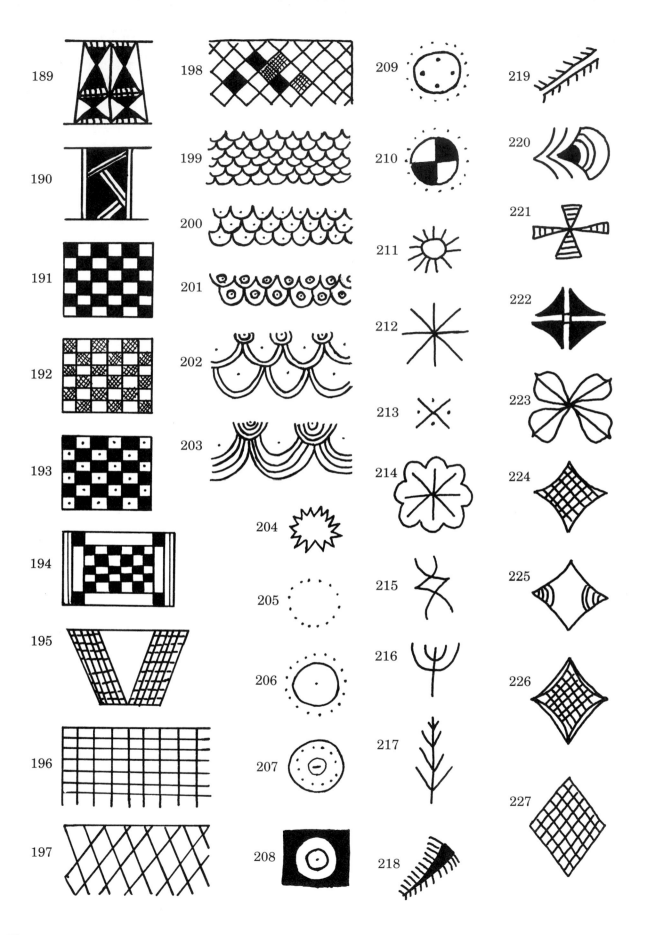

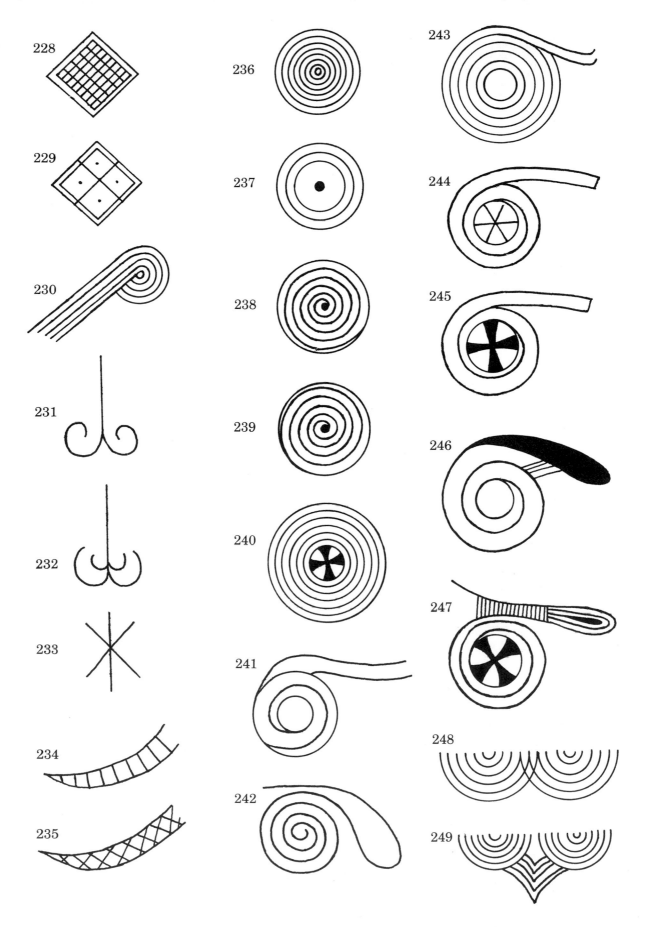

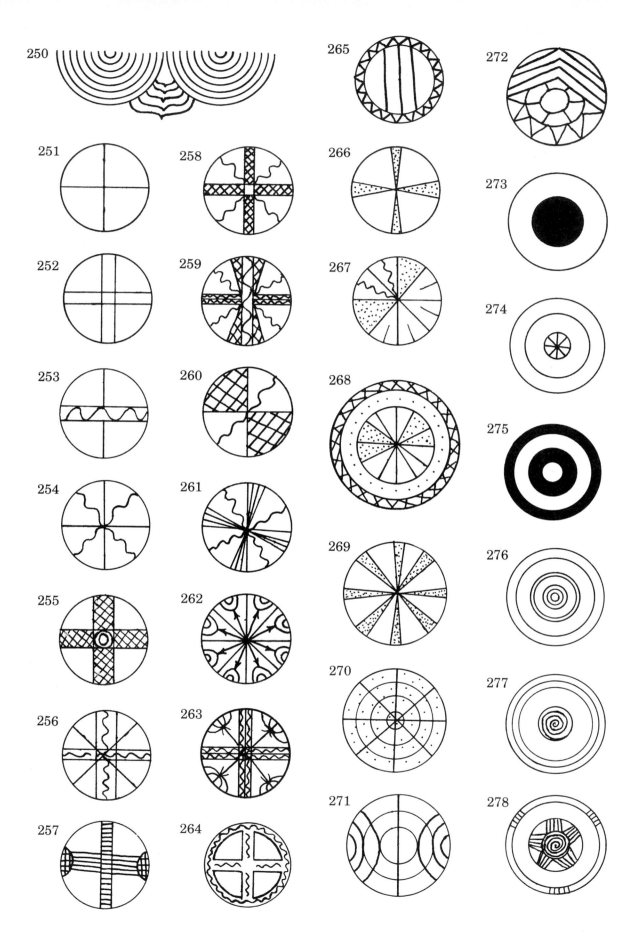

250

251

252

253

254

255

256

257

258

259

260

261

262

263

264

265

266

267

268

269

270

271

272

273

274

275

276

277

278

Design Number	A Philistine Pottery From	B Non-Philistine Pottery From	C Lebanese, Syrian Pottery From	D Cilician Pottery From	E Transjordanian Pottery From
1			Hama ⊗	Tarsus x	
2				Tarsus x	
3	Ashdod	Timna x	Tyre x / Hama ⊗		
4		Timna x			
5				Tarsus x	
6		Megiddo x			
7		Qurayyah x		Tarsus x	
8		Timna, Qurayyah x / Ashdod o			
9		Timna, Qurayyah x			
10		Ashdod o			
11			Hama x		
12	Ashdod				
13	Ashdod	Megiddo x / Ashdod o	Amuq ⊗ / Hama x		
14		Timna x			
15		Timna x / Qurayyah x			
16		Qurayyah x			
17		Qurayyah x			
18				Tarsus x	
19	Ashdod	Timna x / Ashdod o			
20		Timna x			
21	AS, Nasbe, Ashdod				
22			Amuq ⊗		
23		Timna x			AN o
24	Megiddo	Timna x	Amuq ⊗		DA B x
25			T.Khazel		
26	Ashdod				
27				Tarsus x	Sahab x
28		TBM x			
29	Ashdod				
30					DA B x
31	Ashdod				
32			Amuq		
33			Amuq ⊗	Tarsus x	
34				Tarsus x	
35	Ashdod				
36				Tarsus	
37					AA, AN o
38		Timna x			
39	Ashdod				
40		Ashdod o			
41	Far'ah(S)	BS, Qurayyah x	Amuq x	Tarsus x	DA B x
42	Ashdod	Timna x	Amuq x		
43	AS, TBM, Nasbe, Megiddo, Ashdod,	Megiddo x			
44				Tarsus x	
45		BS x	Amuq ⊗		
46	Ashdod				
47	Ashdod				
48		Timna x			
49	Ashdod	TBM, Megiddo x	Amuq, Hama ⊗	Tarsus ⊗	
50	AS, TBM, Gezer, Nasbe, Ashdod	TBM, Megiddo, Timna, Qurayyah x	Hama x / Amuq ⊗ / Tyre, T.Khazel o	Tarsus ⊗	
51	Ashdod	TBM, Megiddo, BS, Timna x	Amuq, Hama ⊗	Tarsus ⊗	Sahab x
52	TBM, Ashdod	TBM, Timna, Megiddo, x	Amuq, Hama ⊗	Tarsus ⊗	DA C x / TK o
53	Ashdod	Ashdod o			
54			Amuq, Hama x		
55			Hama x		
56	Ashdod	TBM, Megiddo x	Hama ⊗		DA A, B, C x
57	Ashdod				
58			Hama o		
59			Hama x		
60			Hama x		
61		Timna x	T.Soukas, Amuq x / Tyre o	Tarsus ⊗	K.Shedeiyed x / TK, Buseirah o
62			Hama ⊗	Tarsus x	
63		BS, Megiddo x	Amuq,		DA B x / TK, AA, Buseirah o
64		BS, Qurayyah x / Ashdod o	Amuq, Byblos, / Hama ⊗	Tarsus x	DA C x / TK, AA, Buseirah o
65	Ashdod	Timna x			Buseirah o
66		Timna, Qurayyah x	Amuq x		
67		Qurayyah x			TK, AA, Buseirah o
68					Buseirah o
69			Hama x		
70			Hama x		
71			T.Ashtara, Amuq x		DA B x
72	AS, TBM, Nasbe Ashdod		Amuq x	Tarsus x	
73	AS, Nasbe, Ashdod				
74					Sahab x
75			Amuq o		
76			Amuq ⊗		
77	Ashdod Megiddo	Ashdod, BS, Timna x	Amuq, Hama, / T.Asharah ⊗	Tarsus o	Sahab / DA B, D, E x
78			Amuq x		
79		Timna x			
80			Amuq x		
81		Timna x			
82		Timna, Qurayyah x			
83		Timna x			
84		Qurayyah x			
85				Tarsus x	
86	Ashdod	AS, Megiddo, Timna x / Ashdod o	Amuq, Hama ⊗ / Tyre o	Tarsus x	DA B, JN, K.Shedeiyid x
87	Far'ah(S)	BS, Timna x	Amuq ⊗	Tarsus x	
88		Timna x			
89		Timna x			
90			Amuq x		
91					Buseirah o
92		Timna x			
93		Timna x			
94	Ashdod	Timna x			
95		Qurayyah x			
96			Hama x		
97			Hama o		
98			Hama x / Amuq ⊗	Tarsus x	Dhiban x
99			Hama x / Amuq ⊗		TK o
100			Hama x		
101			Hama x		
102		BS, Megiddo x	Amuq x / Hama ⊗		
103	BS, DA Ashdod, Megiddo	BS, Megiddo x / Ashdod o	Hama x / Amuq o		DA B,C,D,E x / Buseirah, TK o
104		Timna x			
105			Amuq		
106			Hama x		
107	AS, Gerar	Megiddo x		Tarsus x	

Design Number	A Philistine Pottery From	B Non-Philistine Pottery From	C Lebanese, Syrian Pottery From	D Cilician Pottery From	E Transjordanian Pottery From
108			Hama x		
109			Hama x		
110					Nebo x
111			Tyre o		
112			Hama x		
113			Hama x		
114			Hama x		
115			Amuq o		
116	Ashdod				DA A x
117	BS	K.Tuleil x	Amuq ⊗	Tarsus x	
118			Amuq x	Tarsus x	
119	AS,Ashdod, Gezer	Timna, Qurayyah x Ashdod o	Tyre x Amuq ⊗	Tarsus x	
120	Ashdod,Nasbe		Amuq ⊗	Tarsus x	
121				Tarsus x	
122		Qurayyah x			
123	Ashdod				
124				Tarsus x	
125	Ashdod, Megiddo, Nasbe	BS, Megiddo, Timna x	T.Asharah x Amuq, Hama ⊗	Tarsus ⊗	DA B, Nebo, Madeba x AE, Dhiban, Taiwilan o
126			Hama x		Nebo x
127	Ashdod	BS,Megiddo x Ashdod o	Hama ⊗ Amuq o	Tarsus ⊗	
128			Amuq x		
129					Nebo x
130				Tarsus o	
131				Tarsus o	
132	Ashdod				
133	Adhdod				
134			Amuq, Hama ⊗		TK o
135		Megiddo x	Amuq ⊗		DA D x
136				Tarsus x	TK o
137		BS, Megiddo x	Hama ⊗	Tarsus x	
138			Hama x		
139		Megiddo x			
140		Megiddo x			
141				Tarsus o	
142		Timna x			
143		Timna x			
144			Hama ⊗		
145					DA B x
146					DA B x
147			Hama x		
148			Amuq x		
149			Amuq x		
150			Hama o		
151					Nebo x
152		Timna x			
153		TBM, Megiddo Timna x	Amuq, Hama ⊗	Tarsus ⊗	Buseirah, Dhiban, TK o
154			Amuq x		
155		Timna x			
156		TBM, Megiddo x	Amuq o		
157		BS x			
158			Amuq x		
159		Megiddo x	Amuq x		
160			Amuq x		TK o
161		BS x		Tarsus x	
162			Amuq o		
163		Megiddo x			
164				Tarsus x	
165			Amuq, Hama ⊗		
166			Amuq o		
167		AS, Megiddo x	Hama x Tyre o	Tarsus o	Dhiban ⊗
168			Amuq x		

Design Number	A Philistine Pottery From	B Non-Philistine Pottery From	C Lebanese, Syrian Pottery From	D Cilician Pottery From	E Transjordanian Pottery From
169		Timna x	Amuq x	Tarsus x	
170			Amuq x		
171		Megiddo x			
172		Megiddo x			
173			Amuq o		
174			Amuq o		
175	Ashdod				
176	Ashdod				
177		Ashdod o			
178	Megiddo x				
179		AS,Megiddo, TBM,Timna x			Dhiban x Buseirah,TK o
180		Qurayyah x	Hama x Amuq ⊗		
181			Hama o		
182			Hama x		
183	Ashdod				
184			Hama ⊗		
185		AS, BS x Ashdod o	Hama ⊗ Tyre o		
186			Hama x		
187			Hama o		
188		Megiddo x			
189			Hama o		
190	Ashdod	Ashdod o			
191	AS,Ashdod, Nasbe	BS, Megiddo x	Amuq, Hama ⊗		DA A,E x
192			Hama o		
193				Tarsus o	
194				Tarsus o	
195		Megiddo x			
196		BS, Megiddo x	Amuq ⊗		DA B, D, E; JN; K.Nahas x
197	Ashdod	BS,Megiddo x Ashdod o	Amuq, Hama o		DA A, D, J, L x Saliyeh, Dhiban o
198				Tarsus o	
199				Tarsus x	
200				Tarsus x	
201			T.Khazel		
202	AS, Gezer, Ashdod				
203			Amuq x		
204		Timna x			
205		Timna x			
206			T.Hammam	Tarsus x	
207		Timna x			
208		Timna x			
209				Tarsus x	
210				Tarsus x	
211					DA B x
212		Timna x			
213		Timna x	Amuq o		
214		Timna x			
215				Tarsus x	
216					DA C x
217					MB x
218			Hama ⊗		
219			Amuq o		
220				Tarsus x	
221			Amuq o		
222				Tarsus o	
223				Tarsus o	
224	Ashdod, Megiddo			Tarsus x	
225				Tarsus x	
226		Ashdod o			
227	Ashdod				
228	AS, TBM		Amuq o		
229	Far'ah(S)		Amuq o		
230				Tarsus ⊗	

Design Number	A Philistine Pottery From	B Non-Philistine Pottery From	C Lebanese, Syrian Pottery From	D Cilician Pottery From	E Transjordanian Pottery From
231			Hama ⊗		
232			Amuq x		
233				MA x	
234			Amuq,Hama x		
235	Nasbe		Amuq x		
236	Ashdod	BS, TBM, Megiddo x	Amuq, T.Hammam ⊗ T.Ashtara o	Tarsus x	DA A, JN, MA,Sahab x
237	Ashdod	Ashdod o			
238	AS, TBM, Ashdod, Nasbe,Megiddo	TBM, Megiddo x	Amuq ⊗	Tarsus x	DA E, MA, Sahab x
239	AS, TBM, Ashdod, Nasbe Megiddo	Megiddo x	Amuq ⊗ T.Khazel	Tarsus x	
240		Megiddo x	Amuq x Hama, Tyre, T.Soukas o	Tarsus x	
241	Ashdod				
242	Ashdod				
243	Ashdod				
244	Far'ah(S)				
245	AS, Ashdod Far'ah(S)				
246	Ashdod				
247	Ashdod				
248			Hama o		
249	Far'ah(S)				
250	AS				
251					Sahab x

Design Number	A Philistine Pottery From	B Non-Philistine Pottery From	C Lebanese, Syrian Pottery From	D Cilician Pottery From	E Transjordanian Pottery From
252		AS, BS x	Hama x		AA, AC o
253					Sahab x
254			Amuq x		
255		TBM, Megiddo x			
256			Amuq ⊗		
257			Hama x		
258			Hama o		
259			Hama o		
260			Hama ⊗		
261		Megiddo x			SC o
262					JN x
263		TBM x			
264					MA x
265					JN x
266					MA x
267					JN x
268					Sahab x
269					Sahab x
270					JN x
271					JN x
272					JN x
273					Sahab x
274			Amuq ⊗		
275			Amuq, Hama x		
276	Ashdod	Ashdod o	Amuq x		JN x
277	Ashdod		Amuq, Hama o		
278		Megiddo	Amuq		

KEY

x   = occurring in Iron I
o   = occurring in Iron II
⊠   = occurring in both Iron I & II

AS   = Ain Shems
BS   = Beth Shan
JN   = Jebel Nuzha
MA   = Madeba Tomb A
MB   = Madeba Tomb B
TBM = Tell Beit Mirsim
TK   = Tell el Kheleifeh

From the later half of our first sequence on, wide bands are not as common as earlier and usually occur only as the framing lines of a painted band[1] or as the center line of a three line group.[2] On plate 41 of *EEP*, IV, Glueck illustrates the wider early banding from Jordan Valley sites which is the same as on contemporary sherds from Bethel.[3] Only our sherd number 434 illustrates this type of decoration. It is possible that the Dhiban bowls (Reed and Winnett, *Dhiban*, I, pl. 77:14 and 15) should be dated this early also. At Tell Beit Mirsim (*TBM*, I, pls. 30A and 31B), Albright illustrates the beginning of the line painting which persists throughout the period. This is well illustrated on the line-painted jugs, juglets, and bottles of Sequence II, in some sherds of the Amman 1969 sounding to be discussed below, and in the Amman body sherds illustrated on nos. 70:434-436, 439, 454, and 71:459-473. Numbers 71:462 and 463 represent band-painted bottle sherds of type 17. Number 71:473 is a sherd of an imported Cypriote juglet with black paint on a red-burnished surface, while number 71:472 on the same plate illustrates how close in line and feeling this juglet is to our types 13 and 14 juglets, which are probably of local manufacture. Here we have black lines on a dark tan burnished surface. Number 71:471 has black paint on a tan unburnished surface and, like Albright, *TBM*, I, plate 30:3, represents a local product in which the lines are not quite as crisp and the paint not as uniform as the Cypriote vessels. Almost all the lines on the Amman sherds mentioned so far were black. The sherds nos. 71:435, 436 and 442, however, have lines of dark red to reddish-brown paint. The use of this color may have been stimulated at a time when red-burnished vessels became popular. Number 71:435 is unburnished while the others are burnished, and the paint on this sherd seems to be applied over a coarse and not very hard fired ware. Similar painting and ware are illustrated in Glueck, *EEP*, II, on plates 28A:2-4, 6-9, 12, 13, and 16-18 and 28B:22, 24, and 29.

Banded Decoration Effected by Incision

Contemporary with the parallel-line decoration in our Sequence II, there seems to be an attempt to create the same appearance by light and shadow effect rather than paint. The number of lines which are grouped and the zones of lines are identical to the painted technique and the effect is certainly similar, as is illustrated by the sherds nos. 69:420-428. It is obvious that these incised lines are not the traces of strings used to hold the vessels together until they were fired, but rather that they are intended as decoration. Several

sherds with such incised-line decoration were found in the 1969 Amman Citadel sounding, so we can trace this decoration back at least to the tenth century B.C. Since this decoration occurs primarily on larger vessels which are found only in small numbers in tombs, its virtual absence from our Sequence II does not rule out the continuation of such decoration to a late date.

Parallel-Line Decoration With Colored Bands Between the Lines

The Use of Black Lines on White-Painted Bands

The elaboration of the line decoration, discussed above, by applying it over a white band is one of the hallmarks of Transjordanian pottery. This method is most popular in the early and middle range of our second sequence and dies out in the late range. The examples from the 1969 Amman sounding will be discussed below. This type of decoration is well illustrated in the Sahab B and Amman A tombs. It is found primarily on jugs types 12-14, 22, 23; small jar and juglet types 12, 14-18 and jar types 1, 6 and 8; while the incised-line decoration on jug types 3 and 4 gives the same effect as the painting. It occurs only occasionally on bowls. The cross decoration on the two bowls of type I is interesting in that it does appear from time to time on low bowls but with other peculiarities specific to various periods.[4] The sherds nos. 70:448 and 449 is the best representation of this decoration we can illustrate. Except for Amman N and the Meqabelein tomb, this decoration usually occurs, as it does here, over a red wash. Number 70:451 seems somewhat faded, but the decoration is placed on a buff rather than red surface. It would be tempting to consider this in the late range, but similar examples from the Amman 1969 sounding indicate that such variation can be found among the earliest examples of this type of decoration.

In several cases, white wash seems to be applied before burnishing and the burnishing seems to have been done while the paint was still wet. The black bands do not show the smearing effect evident in the white, but often tend toward a grey color (nos. 433, 437, 438, 70:452, 453 and 455-58). Numbers 433, 437 and 438 illustrate the

[1]Figures 60:18; 61:12, 13, and 14; also Albright, *TBM*, I, pl. 30:3.

[2]Figure 60:1, 19, 20, 26, and 27; also Albright, *TBM*, I, pl. 31:35.

[3]Kelso, *Bethel*, pl. 39.

[4]We saw it first on MB II bowls and then on twelfth century bowls.

application of this decoration to rims where the wash is also very thinly applied.

Examples of the "typical" Transjordanian decoration can be found at many sites in Palestine, but are rare occurrences at each site: Tell Abu Hawam in level 3,[1] Megiddo from tomb 63G,[2] from level B$_3$ at Tell Beit Mirsim,[3] Tell en Naṣbe,[4] and El Jib (Gibeon).[5] Several examples of this painting technique are found in Syria, but all are from Tabbat al Hammam. One complete vessel, a large krater with a triple-loop base, illustrates it best[6] and numerous unpublished sherds from levels 3 and 4 bear the same decoration. This decoration is not found in the Amuq or at Tarsus, where numerous painted sherds were excavated, suggesting that its use did not extend this far north. No mention of it has yet been made from Tell Khazel, Tell Soukas, or the Phoenician coast, so the extent of its use on the east coast of the Mediterranean is uncertain. Similar decoration occurs later (fifth-fourth centuries B.C.) at Motya, a site originally founded as a Phoenician colony.[7] The "smear" type has good parallels at Tell Beit Mirsim, where all are early and come from level B$_3$,[8] and at Tell en Naṣbe.[9]

Transjordanian illustrations of this type of decoration are among the Moabite and Edomite sherds illustrated by Glueck and were first designated as such by Albright in 1924.[10] Albright did not illustrate his sherds, so the majority of such sherds are available only in Glueck's survey volumes (EEP, I: pls. 22:1-6, 8-10, 16, and 17, 27 and 37; 23:1, 4, 5, 9-12, 15, 17, and 18; EEP, II: pl. 27A:4 and 11; and EEP, IV: 42:2). We have mentioned the Madeba examples above and they are included in our chart. No painted sherds have yet been published from the 1965 and 1966 excavations at Umm el Biyara, or the 1968 and 1969 excavations at Taiwilan, but examples have recently been published from Buseirah.[11] A good percentage of Glueck's painted sherds were found at Taiwilan. Most of the middle and late sequence tombs of the Amman district contain some pottery bearing similar decoration. Amman A and B and Sahab B have the greatest number of vessels with such decoration.

Most of the sherds with very thin white bands, which basically belong to this type, seem to date toward the end of the use of this decoration type. Such sherds come primarily from Edom[12] where black dots were also placed on the white line (design 61).

The black line on white-painted band decoration is found occasionally on the rim of jars or bowls,[13] but the greatest number and variety are presently illustrated by our Amman sherds (nos. 433, 437, 438 and from the Amman 1969 sounding). Bichrome rim decoration with black strokes painted over a white band across the rim is found occasionally.[14] It is rarely found in Palestine.[15] Examples are described below from the Amman 1969 sounding and an additional example is illustrated as no. 443. From the tombs of the Amman district, this decoration is found on middle range type 3 and 4 cups. Our no. 444, which is similar to an example from Deir 'Allā in phase B.[16] Other similarities between decorated sherds from our 1969 Amman Citadel sounding and Deir 'Allā examples are most frequent in phases E-G.[17]

Occasionally, the decoration is a combination of the two types discussed and consists of lines in both directions, as illustrated by Glueck in EEP, II, plate 27:13, 19, 21, 22, and 24.

The Use of Red, Brown, and Black Lines or Bands for Decoration

The decorative use of red or brown bands, usually bordered by black or dark brown lines, is far

---

[1]Amiran, APHL, p. 290, fig. 251.

[2]Engberg and Shipton, MEG, I, pl. 158:16.

[3]Albright, TBM, I, pls. 31:44; 36:10.

[4]Wampler, Naṣbe, pl. 88:1, 2, 11, and 21.

[5]Awni K. Dajani, "An Iron Age Tomb at Al-Jib," ADAJ, II (1953), pl. IX:28.

[6]Robert J. Braidwood, "Report on Two Sondages on the Coast of Syria, South of Tartous," Syria, XXI (1940), 192, fig. 5:2.

[7]Several examples are illustrated in Donald Harden, The Phoenicians (London: Thames and Hudson, 1962), photograph no. 114. The vessel illustrated on the left stands closest to some of the Tabbat al Hammam sherds while the other two represent the lighter variety as in our no. 453.

[8]Albright, TBM, I, pls. 24:35, 36; 31:35.

[9]Wampler, Naṣbe, pl. 88:4, 15, and 21.

[10]William F. Albright, Excavations and Results at Tell el-Fûl (Gibeah of Saul) ("AASOR," IV; New Haven: ASOR, 1924).

[11]Bennett, Levant, VI, figs. 15 and 16; Levant, VII, figs. 5-8.

[12]Glueck, EEP, I, pls. 22:2, 13, 19, 34; 23:22, 23, 24, 28, and 29; and Glueck, BASOR, CLXXXVIII, fig. 4:7a and b and fig. 1:11.

[13]Glueck, EEP, I, pl. 22:4, 6; II, pl. 27:11, 18, 20, and 28.

[14]Glueck, EEP, II, pls. 27:13, 22, 23, 25, 27, and 30; 28:20, 28.

[15]Yadin, et al., Hazor, III-IV, Plates: pl. CCXIII:2 from Str. IX of Area B; and Hamilton, QDAP, IV, 22, no. 77 and p. 29, no. 153.

[16]Franken, DA, pl. 50:64.

[17]Ibid., pl. 59:55, 69, 74, 79, 85, 92, 102, and pls. 60:20; 61:79; and 64:68 and 76.

less frequent in the Transjordan than the black-on-white decoration. This is a reversal of the frequency in which these decorations are used in Palestine, though in general even there this decoration does not occur in great abundance. In Syria, it is weakly attested throughout Iron II and on the Phoenician coast it seems, on the basis of the evidence available to date, to be the normal decoration.[1] The Amuq examples are too numerous to mention here, but this situation is presently unique for Syria and no good examples can be found at Tarsus. There are many examples on display in the museum of the American University of Beirut and similar painted decoration on jars is a frequent feature found on Punic pottery.[2] In Palestine, a few clear examples can be cited from Tell en Naṣbe,[3] Hazor,[4] and Tell Abu Hawam.[5]

The majority of the Transjordanian examples come from el Medeiyineh and Sâliyeh in Moab.[6] It is impossible to say whether these sherds might date back as early as LB II, but they also would not be out of place in an Iron I context. This decorative color combination is rare in the Amman district and most of the examples belong in the late range of our second sequence. This is presently a peculiarity of this district and does not argue for a similar date for this decoration in Moab and elsewhere. On the contrary, the Syrian, Phoenician, and Palestinian examples argue that this decoration was common throughout Iron II.

Banded decoration with the same color scheme occurs about as frequently in Palestine on the inside of burnished bowls as it does on the body of jars and jugs discussed above. Here the decorative effect is created by applying the normal red slip, occurring so frequently on bowls, in bands and letting the body appear in reserve between them. In some cases, the greatest part of the particular vessel is covered with the red slip,[7] while in others the reverse is true.[8] This decoration occurs on very fine thin bowls of the type called "Samaria ware." The same type of decoration, however, occurs on bowls made of fine but softer ware, of considerably greater thickness. Examples of the "Samaria ware" can be found as far north as the Amuq,[9] and occur at Tabbat al Hammam, Khalde,[10] Hazor,[11] Megiddo,[12] and many other sites. The thicker ware is not available from as many sites, but is present in considerable quantity at Tell Ta'yinat in the Amuq (with isolated examples from Chatal Hüyük and Tell Judeideh), from Tarsus,[13] an isolated sherd from Tabbat al Hammam, from Hazor,[14] Tell Abu Hawam,[15] and Megiddo.[16] The Palestinian examples and some of the Amuq sherds come from Iron I contexts and seem to date to the time when red-burnished bowls were coming into use. At Tell

Ta'yinat, examples were found in early Iron II contexts but the majority of these sherds must be dated to the end of Iron II. It is often difficult to give an exact date to this type of decoration without some other peculiar feature, like rim profile, to give a firmer date. No examples of "Samaria ware" have yet been found in the Transjordan, but one example of the other type mentioned above has been found and comes from level IV at Tell el Kheleifeh.[17]

Other Painted Decoration

A number of other decorative motifs have been found on pottery in the Transjordan but their dating has been a problem. Most of these were published by Glueck from his survey finds or from his excavations at Tell el Kheleifeh and most were attributed to Iron I. Recently, Glueck has redated

---

[1] Illustrations of this decoration from the Phoenician coast can best be seen in photographs, Saidah, *BMB*, XIX, pl. VI:48, 49, 52, 56-58 and now also in Chapman, *Berytus*, XXI, 60-61.

[2] Cintas, *CP*, pls. LXVI:233, 92, 47, 325b; LXVII:230, 212; LXX:2; LXXVII:128; LXXXIV:199, 212, 225, etc.

[3] Wampler, *Naṣbe*, pl. 87:20 and 23.

[4] Yadin, *et al.*, *Hazor*, III-IV, pls. CCXIV:24; CCXV:26, CCXXI:4, 9; and CCXXVIII:3.

[5] Hamilton, *QDAP*, IV, pl. XIII, no. 62, 79, and pl. 24:97.

[6] Glueck, *EEP*, I, pl. 23:3, 5, 6, 10, 16, 18, 19, 20. Plate 22:15 is the same as our no. 17 on fig. 50 which, however, seems to be LB II.

[7] Crowfoot, Crowfoot, and Kenyon, *SS*, III, fig. 19:1 and 3.

[8] Yadin, *et al.*, *Hazor*, III-IV, pls. CCXIV:24 and CCXXIII:19. Both are from Area B and from Str. VII and VB respectively.

[9] To be published shortly from the Oriental Institute Syrian Expedition.

[10] Saidah, *BMB*, XIX, 61, no. 10.

[11] Yadin, *et al.*, *Hazor*, I, pl. LIV:6 as well as the other bowls cited above.

[12] Lamon and Shipton, *MEG*, I, pl. 25:57.

[13] Goldman, *Tarsus*, II, pls. 74:637 and 640; 124:637, and similar decoration on a jar, pl. 59:123.

[14] Yadin, *et al.*, *Hazor*, II, pls. LIII:22 and LI:3.

[15] Hamilton, *QDAP*, IV, pl. XIV and p. 29, nos. 153 and 155.

[16] Lamon and Shipton, *MEG*, I, pl. 23:12 and the chalices pl. 33:15 and 17.

[17] Glueck, *BASOR*, CLXXXVIII, Part II, fig. 5:6. The Buseirah material now provides additional examples, as mentioned below on p. 86, footnote 12.

much of this material to the end of Iron II.[1] We have discussed some of the level IV pottery from Tell el Kheleifeh above with only slight disagreement with his seventh to sixth-century B.C. date. On the whole, Glueck's reassessment of the pottery seems to be more correct than his earlier treatment, though the earlier date is probably still applicable to a few sherds. His reassessment was based on new evidence for the date of the settlement at Umm el Biyara and, recently, the late Iron II date of the material at Taiwilan and Buseirah supports his lowered dates. With the Deir 'Allā material now available for Iron I, some sherds published from Tell Ashtarah in southern Syria, and more pottery published from Beth Shan, the Iron I period is better known. The excavations at Ashdod[2] have provided more evidence on the repertory of Philistine pottery and the large quantity of Iron Age painted pottery from the Amuq will be available soon in publication to amplify a picture similar, in many respects, to what is available from Tarsus. When all of this material is examined, as well as that from the Amman district and other Transjordanian pottery in the sequences laid out above, the difficulty of making a judgment based on painted decoration alone becomes clear. It now seems that many motifs must continue throughout Iron I and II, though best represented at the beginning and end of this time range. In such cases, one must rely on other features or associated pottery to determine the date of these sherds.

A few general remarks are in order before we discuss individual motifs. Beth Shan and Deir 'Allā, in particular, illustrate that a painted pottery tradition, to some extent linked to the L.B. traditions but with many new features, existed in areas not influenced by Philistines but possibly affected by other groups of sea peoples. The decorative motifs on pottery of the twelfth and eleventh centuries B.C. at Tarsus and the Amuq reveal considerable overlap with those found on Philistine pottery. The background from which the potters were operating must have been the same. The question is: how many of the new features must be attributed to the invading sea peoples? The sea peoples undoubtedly had their effect, but when one considers the amount of imported Mycenaean pottery that has been found throughout Palestine, especially at places like Megiddo, Dothan, Gibeon, Lachish; in Syria at Tell Soukas and Minet el Beidah; in the Jordan Valley at Pella; and at the airport "temple" in Amman, one wonders what effect the cutting off of the supply of such pottery would have had. The greatest quantity of such pottery is found in special contexts, the airport "temple" in Amman, or most frequently in tombs. It almost seems that in LB II very little local effort was directed to producing fine and delicately decorated vessels. If the supply of such vessels had been cut off from the inhabitants of Syria, Palestine and the Transjordan before some of the fine Cypriote Iron Age vessels were available, one would expect that they would be forced to produce their own if the demand continued to be what it had been. It would be logical to expect that they would adapt some of the decorative motifs which had been popular on some of the best and most desirable fancy vessels in use previously. It would be impossible to discount the influence which the Sea Peoples must have had in the formation and development of the new pottery repertory, particularly in the spread of the "Granary" Type, but when one considers the number of peoples involved in relation to the influence they could possibly have had, it seems that other factors must have been working at the same time.

The unpublished Amuq material provides some interesting parallels to the situation in the twelfth century and seems to support the picture as it is indicated by Megiddo, Deir 'Allā, Timna and Beth Shan. We will pull together the various arguments on this problem in our conclusion, but need to indicate here as much as can be adduced from the painted decorations. Area II at Chatal Hüyük provides the best stratigraphy and the most abundant pottery evidence for our problem. This evidence is supplemented and substantiated by pottery from the other excavated areas at Chatal Hüyük. The Iron Age sequence begins in level 10 of Area II.

A specific style of painted decoration is evident here which has good parallels in level VII at Megiddo, level VI at Beth Shan, and the latest L.B. and phases A to D at Deir 'Allā. The most characteristic feature is the use of very dense or compact decoration in the painted areas. The painted lines are usually quite thick and seldom very steady. The vessels on which this decoration is found are usually thick and the surface is frequently burnished.[3] Many of the decorative designs found in our chart are already present. Two noteworthy features are the occasional use of dots or stippling as fill, which continue from L.B., and the occasional use of open-field filler decoration.

In the next level (9), designs like numbers 1-3, 5, 7, 18, 22, 24, 27, 41, 42, 44, 45, 72, 74, 75, 158, 199, 200, 203, 220, 238-40, 248, 277 and 278 are used very frequently and are for the most part attributable to Aegean influence. The pottery seems better made and the lines and painting are finer. The paint is more dense and usually shows a gloss. According to the excavators, bichrome painting is not used. Burnishing is infrequent and the thick ware of level 10, with its characteristic painting, is rare. The designs found in 10 continue to occur alongside those mentioned above, but even these are usually better executed.

In level 8, little imported ware is found in contrast to its occasional appearance in 9 and 10. The designs in use in 9 continue but the lines are noticably less fine and crisp than earlier. There is also a noticeable difference in the combination of designs. The amount of painted decoration does not seem to be less than before. In level 7, the painted tradition continues fairly strongly, but is usually more careless and is clearly being displaced by the red-burnished technique. At this point bichrome painted sherds, quite normal in Iron II, also begin to occur.

This is but the briefest outline, but it is enough to illustrate three important points. First of all, there is the fact of a strong painted tradition existing already in the twelfth century B.C. prior to the strong Greek influence. Secondly, the painted tradition remained strong and did not change greatly from the introduction of Greek influence until the red-burnished technique became popular. Thirdly, in the Iron I phase N, local pottery is purely monochrome decorated.

The parallel line decoration, primarily of the kind discussed above, found so frequently in Palestine, for example at Megiddo, Beth Shan, and Beth Shemesh, and also in the Transjordan at Jebel Nuzha and Deir 'Allā, is found at Hama, in the Amuq and also rarely at Tarsus. The use of this decoration on bowls currently has more elaborate examples in Palestine and Syria than in the Transjordan. The chart illustrates the overlap between the areas with designs 236-40 and 274-77 occurring at Ashdod, Ain Shems, Beth Shemesh, Deir 'Allā, Jebel Nuzha, Madeba, Megiddo, Tell en Naṣbe, Tell Beit Mirsim, Sahab, Chatal Hüyük, Hama, Tell Ashtara, Tabbat el Hammam, Tell Khazel, Tell Soukas, Tarsus and Tyre. Even the more elaborate bowl number 278 from the Amuq has a close parallel at Megiddo in Stratum VIB.[4]

Discussion of Designs

Table 5 provides a fairly comprehensive compilation of the most important decorative motifs to be found on pottery of the Iron Age in Palestine and Syria[5]. This of course, omits the banded and

at Beth Shan and are illustrated on figs. 22:26, 52:2, and 55:4 and 6 of James, *IABS*.

Interesting individual parallels link the three sites. The large bowl sherd on fig. 49:15 of James, *IABS*, has exact parallels at Chatal Hüyük. The bowl, fig. 50:17 of the same publication, is paralleled at Megiddo, though here it is from level VI and is decorated in bichrome. These are some of the best examples found in Palestine of the usual M.B.-L.B. Syrian decoration still in use in Iron I. Also, there is a very distinct use of parallel rows of impressed rope decoration which appears at this time at Beth Shan (James, *IABS*, fig. 55:5), Chatal Hüyük, Tarsus (Goldman, *Tarsus*, II, pl. 55:1), and other contemporary sites.

[4]Loud, *MEG*, II, Plates, pl. 74:11.

[5]Reference was made above to the pottery recently published from Timna and Qurayyah. We consider this material so important to our discussion here that we have made an exception to confining updating information to the footnotes. We have expanded our Table 5 to include decorative designs from six sites: Timna, Qurayyah and Sahab for Iron I, Ashdod for Iron I and II, and Dhiban and Buseirah for Iron II. New designs have been added to the chart and references to designs already included have been incorporated in the chart.

Rothenberg indicates that painted pottery was not present in the XIX*th* dynasty phase of the temple at Timna (Rothenberg, *Timna*, p. 155) which then puts the painted pottery purely in an Iron I context and prior to the period of Philistine domination in Palestine. Comparisons with other designs in our Table 5 show that roughly half have parallels while the remainder are primarily closely related variations. The repertoire from Timna and Qurayyah then seems richer and more innovative, with a frequent use of bichrome painting. The color range is not similar to that of the Philistine wares. Whether this is primarily due to methods of local manufacture and firing is not now clear but the colors and the use of light paint on a dark band as shown on Rothenberg, *Timna*, plate XXIII, are quite similar to the fourteenth to thirteenth century late derivatives of Mitannian decoration in North Syria.

The decoration is confined primarily to painted bands, with wider bands divided into metopes being uncommon (as noted below). The presence of narrow decorated bands of similar patterns on Egyptian vases and New Year's bottles indicate a possible stimulus for their adoption. The chart also indicates that by the eighth and seventh centuries B.C. very little new has been added in the way of designs at Buseirah and Tell el Kheleifeh, while the use of narrow bands of decoration still predominates. A good example of the inventiveness in the application of decoration is the use of an increased number of designs on the inside of bowls which in other locations is limited, extremely simple or purely liniar, if used at all.

"Midianite" wares seem to fit well into the overall picture we have abstracted in our conclusions for the twelfth century B.C. Such wares illustrate a very rich tradition which is clearly related to the general tendencies and repertoire of designs exhibited as far as Cilicia in southern Anatolia, but still with a great deal of local expression which limits the number of exact parallels.

[1]*Ibid.*, pp. 8-38.

[2]Moshe Dothan and David N. Freedman, *Ashdod*. Vol. I: *The First Season of Excavations, 1962* ("Atiqot," Vol. VII; Jerusalem: The Department of Antiquities and Museums, 1967) and Moshe Dothan, *Ashdod*. Vols. II-III: *The Second and Third Seasons of Excavations, 1963, 1965, Soundings in 1967* ("Atiqot" Vols. IX-X; Jerusalem: The Department of Antiquities and Museums, 1971).

[3]Jars like nos. 3 and 4 on pl. 64 and kraters like nos. 2 and 4 on pl. 56 or 13 and 16 on pl. 69 illustrate examples found at Megiddo from levels VII A and B (Loud, *MEG*, II, Plates). Similar kraters are found in level VI

parallel-line decoration discussed above and also the depictions of human and animal forms, which occur only in very rare instances. Only a small portion, just less than one-fourth, of the motifs in the chart can be illustrated on pottery from the Transjordan. An examination of the chart shows how much variation existed within quite fixed limits. What the chart does not show, however, is the great frequency with which most of the basic designs occur. No attempt was made to adhere to a consistent scale in the presentation of the motif.

Human and Animal Designs

Only on a "Philistine" spouted jug from Deir 'Allā are birds used as a part of the painted decoration. No other bird or animal figures are yet found on Iron Age pottery in the Transjordan. The human figure is only slightly better represented. One sherd of a stand from phase D at Deir 'Allā[1] shows the stick figure representations of several men. Similar schematic decoration is used in the depiction of two pairs of combatants on the flask (no. 94) from the Jebel Nuzha tomb. Human and animal figures are extremely rare on non-Philistine Iron Age pottery in Palestine. In Lebanon, birds are frequent on the few published sherds available. Birds also occur in the Amuq and at Tarsus but are not at all frequent. Hama provides the greatest number of examples of birds as well as a large number of other animals and fish.[2] In only a few of the examples of birds from these sites is there anything similar to the characteristic depiction of Philistine birds or even their Mycenaean prototypes. It is difficult to assess the birds on the Deir 'Allā jug because they are very crudely drawn, but the manner in which the wings are made and the zoning on the bodies demonstrates a similarity to the representation on Philistine pottery.

The stick men of Deir 'Allā and the Jebel Nuzha tomb have their counterparts at Hama and in the Amuq. They also are presently confined to the first two centuries of the Iron Age.[3]

Flask and Bowl Decoration

Figure 30:17-34 indicate that some of the most elaborate local painted decoration from the beginning of the Iron Age is to be found on flasks. The chart illustrates the most common tendency of dividing the circular areas of the sides of the flasks into pie-shaped wedges. The cross-line decoration, which was mentioned above, forms one of the most common organizational schemes for bowl decoration and most designs expand in elaboration from that point. Though the similar-

ities are clear, the flask decoration comes toward the beginning of Iron I while the bowls, exemplified by design numbers 254-56, 274-78 come from the end of Iron I. The Jebel Nuzha tomb illustrates best the bowl decoration from the beginning of Iron I with the varied arrangement of concentric circles. When the elaborate flask designs are no longer popular, the simpler spiral and concentric circle designs become the standard for the rest of the Iron Age. Designs 254, 256, 257, 259 and 275-77 illustrate the elaboration of the cross-line motif on bowls from Syria found primarily at the end of Iron I and the beginning of Iron II.

Turning to individual designs, numbers 257, 271 and 272 represent the greatest departure from those which are most common but they are executed within the frame of concentric circles. Design number 264 is the closest flask design to the cross motif so usual on the bowls. Design number 266 is the creation of a maltese cross by stippling alternate wedge-shaped areas. The maltese cross is very popular on flasks in Syria (design no. 240) and is most popular on Iron I flasks. In designs 244, 245, 248 we see it at the center of a spiral from the side of a bowl. The last important feature of note is the use of dots as a space-filling device. We saw this in the Late Bronze Age and it seems to continue frequently early in Iron I. Designs 29, 76, 78, 98, 115, 164, 183 and 266-70 represent best a similar occurrence in other contemporary designs.

Philistine Pottery and Decoration

We have indicated above our reasons for including the designs found on contemporary Philistine decoration in our chart. The amount of actual Philistine pottery found in the Transjordan is almost negligible. Only one relatively complete vessel has been found, a side-spouted one-handled jug from Deir 'Allā, which has already been mentioned above. Franken states that several Philistine sherds were also found. Unfortunately, he has presented line drawings of them without further description, and has left the discussion of the Philistine problem at Deir 'Allā for a future volume. As a result, we are somewhat limited in handling the problem but in the para-

---

[1]Franken, *DA*, fig. 57:51.

[2]Fugmann, *Hama Cem.*, p. 97, design nos. 100-12.

[3]Birds and humans are also found on decorated vessels from Timna, Rothenberg, *Timna*, fig. 47. None of the representations are complete. Humans are represented as stick figures, in one example apparently with a decorated robe, and the birds seem to be roosters rather than the birds represented on Philistine pottery.

graphs below we will discuss the difficulties of accepting this designation on the basis of the information now available.

Three points seem clear and must be mentioned here. The following characteristic features of Philistine pottery are not found on vessels bearing the similar designs illustrated in our chart from Syria and Cilicia: (1) the use of a white or creamy slip beneath the painted decoration, (2) the primary use of bichrome decoration, and (3) the use of the same range of colors. This is not the place to go into detail on these points, but the distinction must be made here because the painting tradition exemplified in Syria and Cilicia seems to be similar to that which is found in parts of Palestine. Unfortunately, only two outlying areas, the Amuq and Tarsus, provide ample material to date. The pottery which is available from sites like Hama, Qatna, Tell Soukas, Tell Khazel, Byblos, Tyre and Tell Ashtara, though scantily illustrated at present, illustrates that such painted pottery existed there also. The "Philistine" strainer jug from phase B at Deir 'Allā is considered an import by Franken. The scarcity of Philistine pottery at Deir 'Allā, if it is indeed Philistine pottery, is understandable when one considers how little of this type of pottery reached Beth Shan (24 miles away on the other side of the Jordan) at about the same time, despite the fact that the Philistines exerted control as far as Beth Shan for some time. The Deir 'Allā jug has the typical features of Philistine pottery with mat bichrome decoration in red and black over a white slip. The vessel shape is represented frequently among Philistine vessels. The lack of care in the execution of the vessel is interesting and it does not represent the best Philistine effort. We have mentioned above the representation of birds in one decorated band on the jug. The rest of the decoration consists of designs which can be found on our chart as common throughout Syria and Palestine. The parallel lines alternating in color between red and black are frequently found on the necks and shoulders of jars in phases A to E.

Dr. Franken's lack of discussion and description of the sherds which he lists as Philistine is unfortunate for us in that this comes to the heart of our argument. None of these sherds seem to be bichrome in the way they are drawn. Since there is no color description, it is impossible to tell whether a white slip is present or whether they are actually identical in paint and surface treatment to the other decorated sherds which are not classed as Philistine but considered local. It seems probable that they are similar to the other local painted sherds but are classed as Philistine on the basis of decoration. If this is the case, we would be inclined to eliminate the few Philistine

sherds which are said to be present at Deir 'Allā and, thus, weaken even further the evidence for Philistine interaction with the Transjordan.

Basically, two designs are illustrated as "Philistine decoration," and one design is said to be found on a "Philistine bowl." The first is the checkerboard pattern which our chart illustrates as quite common in Syria and Palestine in non-Philistine contexts. It occurs at Deir 'Allā in phase A, apparently on locally made pottery. The other design is the concentric arcs, number 41. Again, the chart illustrates the geographical distribution of this design and its variants. Number 43 is more common on Philistine vessels than any of the others, especially when the central half circle is painted a different color from the arcs.

A compass does not seem to be used in the creation of these arcs as it is later in the case of number 248 on Greek Cycladic cups, or when a full circle, rather than half circle, is represented on Cypriote and related wares toward the end of Iron I.[1] The scale pattern and variants (nos. 99-203) are a closely related multiplication of the concentric-arc designs and very common on Philistine pottery. Again, the design cannot be designated as Philistine since it has a wider popularity. The basic designs (nos. 199 and 203) were used on Mycenaean IIB and C pottery and, unlike the checkerboard motif, illustrate a Greek design which took root in Syria and Palestine.

The "Philistine bowl," with tripod-loop base, of phase B at Deir 'Allā is not a shape which is particularly associated with the Philistines (examples can be found with Philistine decoration) but rather seems to be a normal part of the ceramic repertory in Syria as well as the Transjordan in the Iron Age. The absence of bichrome painting, where a considerable area of the vessel is decorated and preserved, is the strongest argument for assuming that the other "Philistine" sherds come from vessels decorated in a similar style. The similar rim of a bowl, on the same plate (fig. 52:3) as the tripod-loop bowl and with decoration covering the same area, indicates that if one were to disregard the designs, the "Philistine" sherds would be indistinguishable from the other decorated sherds at Deir 'Allā.

In contrast, it will be interesting to know the color description on the jars and jugs with bichrome decoration to see if it corresponds to the range of Philistine colors or if it corresponds to the color range familiar in Syria, and probably to be seen as a continuation and, often, degenerate modification (as is evident in the sloppy work on

---

[1]This decoration with the use of a compass does, however, already occur in the twelfth century in Greece and a "belly-handled amphora" with such decoration has also been found at Chatal Hüyük in the Amuq.

most of the Deir ʿAllā vessels) of the L.B. painted tradition.

Remaining Designs with Iron I Contexts

It will be shown below that the great majority of the Iron Age decorations were geometric, with simple strokes or curves in considerable repetition, and most frequently arranged in single or multiple bands. Horizontal decorated bands are most frequent and, even where vertical bands are used, they are usually framed by horizontal elements. The bands vary in composition, as the chart shows, with either a continuous design like numbers 1-8, 11-17, 19-26 and 61-143, or broken up with a combination of designs. In the latter case, the designs may be spaced fairly wide apart or tightly together within the bands. Many of the designs fall into small metope-like areas as are illustrated by designs 152 to 179. The designs 49-60 may be used as dividers between metopes or independently in less compactly decorated bands (occasionally, horizontal patterns among those illustrated as designs 61-143, or simplifications or abbreviations of these designs, were used in a similar fashion).

Less frequent than the decoration schemes just mentioned is the application of decorative designs to broader areas. Designs 180-95 illustrate what could be considered expanded metopes while designs 196-98 illustrate decoration which covered large areas or even entire vessels.

Little use is made of mechanical devices, like a multiple brush or fast wheel, in creating the designs. Some of the horizontal bands may have been made on a slow wheel, but most of the designs had to be executed freehand. It is interesting that, despite this, the decoration is predominantly geometric and the instances of isolated decoration or the placing of designs in an open field are extremely rare. The few examples which exist from the Transjordan have already been mentioned. The combat scene on the Jebel Nuzha flask (no. 44, = fig. 30:20) is the only design truly in a free field. The birds on the Deir ʿAllā Philistine jug are closer to this than anything else, but even they are forced into a densely decorated band. The sherd upon which design 216 is found is too small to indicate the relationship it may have had to other decoration, if any at all. Designs 27-48, 204-30 and 248-50 represent geometric motifs which occur singly or in sparsely decorated bands and, on occasion, with less restrictions. Designs 231-233 are often free of restricting lines and extend down from the base of a vertical handle onto the wall of a jar, krater, or jug. In some cases, they are free of restriction; in others, they fill a vertical void between two areas of decoration and, in still other cases, they cut across horizontal deco-

ration which circumscribes a vessel. They are repetitive in most details and there are fill motifs and some multiple wavy lines (multiples in bichrome of no. 56) used as dividers. Only 233 has been found in the Transjordan, on a flask (no. 82, = fig. 30:34) from Madeba tomb A. The evidence for 231 and 232 is primarily Syrian but it does occur on kraters from Beth Shan and Megiddo.

Some designs, like numbers 19-26, 30-48, are found positioned above or pendant from a line. They may be bordered by a second line so that they stand within a band, but this is less common. Design 24 is most frequently used at the junction of the neck and shoulders of jars and is primarily Syrian, but one example is present from Deir ʿAllā (phase B, Franken, *DA*, fig. 51:62). Many of the wavy-line designs (nos. 1, 2, 5-7) are found primarily in Syria but apparently are influenced by a class of Greek vessels. An example was found in Palestine at Megiddo.[1]

A number of the designs in our chart have a long previous history in Syria and Palestine. In some cases, they are used in the same manner as the prototypes while in others they have been modified. We mentioned above the use of the checkerboard design (variations of this are found in nos. 36, 46, 70 and 191-94). We have seen this used as a panel decoration since MB II when it occurred at Amman. The Philistine adaptation of this motif is usually done with the squares in two colors. This motif is occasionally rendered in bichrome in Syria but its usual rendering is in monochrome. The two monochrome sherds from Deir ʿAllā have already been mentioned.

Also dating back to the Middle Bronze in Palestine and Transjordan, but even earlier in Syria, is the wavy line between parallel straight lines (designs 56 and 77). During Iron I, there is considerable variation in this design, as seen in numbers 56, 57, 59, 60, 71-73, 76-90, 92-94, 96, 176 and 186. Deir ʿAllā itself provides numerous examples with considerable variation.

There are many examples of gentle curves in the rendering of the wavy lines and there is a conscious spacing between it and the bounding parallel lines. One sherd from phase B at Deir ʿAllā shows the very kinky line (no. 80) which is a characteristic peculiarity of the wavy line decoration in this period. In one case, the curve is reduced to a zig-zag formed by straight line strokes which connect the parallel lines, numbers 86 and 87. This is most frequent in the Iron I decoration of Syria, though it does appear occasionally earlier. The most characteristic use of this design during Iron I is two-fold. The first is a dense covering of the surface in a sloppy manner, appar-

---

[1] Design no. 6 is found in Str. VII B at Megiddo (Loud, *MEG*, II, pl. 63:1).

ently having been done with a very thin paint. A good example of this is from phase G at Deir 'Allā (Franken, *DA*, fig. 65:54).[1] The second is the use of wide bands with the wavy line swinging sharply to touch both sides. Again, the paint seems to have been quite thin when applied. The best illustration of this is jug number 54 from the Jebel Nuzha tomb where the design that was produced is the same as that on a jar from Hama.[2] In the Hama jar, the entire exterior surface is covered with this decoration. The effect of the design is similar to that of a net covering the surface. This net effect, produced in this case by parallel intersecting lines, can be found on another jug from the Jebel Nuzha tomb (no. 55 = fig. 26:33). It covers almost the entire surface of this jug, except for an area around the neck where a curving line heightens the effect of a net draped over the jug. We will say more about the use of net-like designs below.

Similar to the zig-zag line decoration is its elaboration by the use of parallel lines as in numbers 99, 105, 118, 134-39 and 144. Unlike the plain zig-zag, this decoration is one of the most frequently used in Syria during the Middle and Late Bronze Ages. Number 135 illustrates its presence at Deir 'Allā in phase D (Franken, *DA*, fig. 57:49) and the Amuq provides good contemporary parallels.

Another long-standing design on pottery from Syria and Northern Mesopotamia is number 102. The very common use of hatching of geometrical areas is mentioned below, but its use in a row of triangles is very common, dating back into the neolithic period in Syria. As is quite evident from our chart, there is great variation in the way in which such rows of triangles were treated. The triangles may be painted solid in one color or filled with hatching, cross-hatching, parallel or radiating lines, zigzags, dots, stippling, checkerboard, or in several other ways. The bands may have the decorated triangles on a base line or pendant from a line. They usually occur in horizontal bands but can also be found in vertical bands. At Deir 'Allā, only numbers 103 and 116 are found and constitute some of the least elaborate groups. Number 116, however, is bichrome with alternating red and black triangles and is one of the decorations found on the Philistine jug.[3]

Pendant triangles with stippled fill are found on a jar from Dhiban. Most of the Amuq examples of this decoration come from late in Iron II, but the Iron I date of the Dhiban jar is unquestionable. The handles are typical for Iron I as is the profile of the rim, which is very close to the jar rims common in Megiddo VIB[4] and the contemporary krater rims from Megiddo[5] and Deir 'Allā.[6] A krater from tomb 73 at Megiddo[7] illustrates a contemporary Palestinian example. The best

parallel for the flat-topped rim is found at Tell en Naṣbe, where the identical profile also occurs.[8] The band above the triangles is decorated with metopes that are filled by cross-hatching. This decoration is also very common in Iron I.

The cross-hatching of restricted framed areas is a simple and extremely common decoration in Iron I. It is used at this time in a greater variety of ways than previously and it remains popular in Iron II. The areas decorated in this manner include bands (no. 124), metopes (no. 179), trapezoids (no. 185), and entire surfaces of vessels (no. 197), as well as other designs: 34, 102, 106, 108, 112-14, 126, 127, 165, 187, 224, 226-28, 235 and 268. Its use on the inside of bowls is illustrated at Hama (nos. 257-60) and the same idea is applied to bowls in Palestine (no. 255) at Tell Beit Mirsim,[9] and the metope decoration occurs at Tell el Kheleifeh.[10] At this site, however, the metope as well as the banded decoration seems to have been found in later contexts and will be discussed below. The chart illustrates that more than the presence of this decoration is needed to determine the date of the vessel on which it is found. We have mentioned above the appearance of this fill in metopes on an Iron I jar from Dhiban. A second sherd from Dhiban illustrates the decorated band. Two colors, orange and black, are used here but, as with the Tell el Kheleifeh sherds, this may be from Iron II since the sherd is

---

[1]Several good parallels from Palestine are to be found at Megiddo from tomb 48 (Guy and Engberg, *MEG T*, pl. 60:5) and from Ain Shems (Grant and Wright, *AS*, IV, pl. XXXCIII:3).

[2]Fugmann, *Hama Cem.*, p. 93, fig. 129. There are several other good examples from Hama of horizontal bands, with the zig-zags drawn in a similar manner. These are illustrated in the same volume on p. 57, fig. 55; p. 60, fig. 63; p. 91, fig. 127; and p. 93, fig. 128. Good examples were also found in the Amuq. (A registered example is no. B1116 from Chatal Hüyük area V, level 2.)

[3]It is interesting, from the point of view of overlap between designs, how designs like 99, 107, 112, and 118 can be treated very similarly to the concentric arc designs 18, 37-45, 74, and 248-50. Also, designs 74, 92-94, 97 and 125-31 are filled in a manner similar to the rows of triangles.

[4]Loud, *MEG*, II, Plates, pl. 73:6 and 8.

[5]Guy and Engberg, *MEG T*, pl. 73:3.

[6]Franken, *DA*, (phase C) fig. 55:1 and 2; (D) fig. 57:43, 44; (E) fig. 59:111, 112 (H) fig. 66:56, 67:37, 75.

[7]Guy and Engberg, *MEG T*, pl. 64:35.

[8]Wampler, *Naṣbe*, pl. 1:6.

[9]Albright, *TBM*, I, pl. 30:2, 4, and 5.

[10]Glueck, *BASOR*, CLXXXVIII, Part I, 19, fig. 5:1a and 2.

said to come from a wheel-made vessel. (The orange and black crossing lines, however, are common at the end of Iron I in the Amuq and at Tarsus.) Other decorated bands of this type were found at Tell el Ghayalā in the Jordan Valley,[1] phase B at Deir ʿAllā,[2] and at Taiwilan near Petra.[3]

Several examples of the use of cross-hatching on broader areas have been found, at Deir ʿAllā in phases B and D[4] and possibly at Taiwilan.[5] Another example from phase J at Deir ʿAllā is on a sherd which also contains a rim section and provides an excellent parallel for both decoration and rim with a sherd from Tell Beit Mirsim, level B.[6] Closely related to this cross-hatching is the use of a mesh with horizontal and vertical lines replacing the diagonal ones. Again, the examples come from Deir ʿAllā phases B, D, and E[7] and from Khirbet esh Shedeiyid in the area of ancient Edom.[8] The latter sherd best illustrates a broad, overall pattern.

Metope Decoration

We have mentioned, in general terms, the popularity of the use of the metope-like areas in decorated bands of Iron I and II and specific instances of their use in the Transjordan. Our chart reveals that this method of organization of banded decoration had a greater significance in Syria and Palestine than is currently illustrated by our evidence in the Transjordan. To some extent, decoration in earlier periods was organized in a similar manner, but it did not become popular in Palestine and Syria until the very end of LB II (thirteenth century B.C.). In the twelfth century B.C., the organization of bands into a series of metope-like areas is clearly established, but often somehow seems accidental. In subsequent centuries, the bands containing metopes are often narrower and the metopes more consistently rectangular. Such decoration becomes more popular on jars and bowls, while its earlier use was confined almost exclusively to kraters. The use of the metope-like areas then becomes an obvious means of organizing decorative units. Current evidence indicates that this had taken place at the end of Iron I. Almost all of design numbers 152-79 exist from the beginning of the period. Those which are first present at the end of Iron I and in Iron II in Palestine and Transjordan are relatively few, and represent some of the simplest designs. Many of these designs become a normal component of Cypriote and Greek geometric decoration. It would be fruitful to compare the overlap of designs found on Greek, Cypriote, and Syro-Palestinian vessels but this is beyond the scope of our study here.

Designs 153 and 156 are found on non-Philistine pottery of levels B_{3-2} at Tell Beit Mirsim.[9] The occurrence of design 179 at Dhiban represents the only clear and demonstrable early Transjordanian example for the use of the metope. Only a few sherds have currently been published from Timna. Design 169 is found on two of these. On another sherd a band is filled with a repetition of design number 213. The largest panel on this same sherd has a larger metope design with number 50 as a divider, but it is impossible to reconstruct the design from the photograph. There is enough here, however, to see that it is the same as that published by Glueck in *BASOR*, CLXXXVIII, Part I, figure 4:5. On plate 23, number 23, of *EEP*, I, Glueck illustrates a sherd decorated with what seems to be metopes filled with design 153 and separated by number 50. This sherd, however, may not belong to Iron I. All the other examples seem to be later.[10]

Similar to the use of the metope design is the fill of triangular areas with various decorations. The same idea present in the Deir ʿAllā phase B designs (nos. 145 and 146) also appears on a krater from level VI at Megiddo,[11] design 140.

Late Decoration

There are only a few examples at the end of the Transjordanian Iron Age sequences which illustrate more than band or line-painted decoration on red-burnished vessels.[12] There are enough examples to demonstrate, as we indicated above, that the repertory of designs which existed at the beginning of the Iron Age continued to its end. We have been able to list only a few sherds from the Transjordan that were decorated in the typical Iron II bichrome color scheme common farther north. Bands of decoration still occur. Design 124 is found at Dhiban,[13] Taiwilan,[14] and Amman (tomb E, No. 155). Design 125 was found on a jug from Meneʿiyeh.[15] Designs 68 and 99 also have isolated examples at Tell el Kheleifeh.[16] Several examples of the metope designs were also found with examples of numbers 52, 153, 160, and 179 from Tell el Kheleifeh.[17]

Very narrow bands of horizontal decoration, found occasionally in early contexts, are very frequent at this time. As the quality of the throwing of vessels improved the tendency to use minute painted decoration, probably with the help of the wheel, increased. Designs 61, 64, and 67 appear frequently at Amman, Tell el Kheleifeh, and Khirbet esh Shedeiyid.[18] Similar decoration outside the Transjordan finds its best parallels in northern Syria at Tell Halaf on vessels from the end of the Assyrian period.[19]

Some aid in dating these wares is given by the color of the paints and slips as well as by the thickness of the vessels. Most of the sherds are still heavy and occasionally carry the burnish and color range common on vessels for the greater portion of Iron II. Some peculiarities can be traced back to the end of Iron I but become common at the end of the Iron Age, like the use of narrow bands of painted decoration which was found on bowls like our type XXXVII. On the other hand, features which are common on vessels of later periods already occur as is the case with the small jar on figure 4:5 of Glueck, *BASOR*, CLXXXVIII, Part II. It illustrates a shape which is common in the Nabataean period, but its presence here is unquestionable. The decorated jar necks illustrated in the same monograph, in Part I on figure 4:3 and 4, seem to be contemporary as far as ware and painting are concerned.

Finally, two types of decoration must be mentioned in rounding out our survey. These are presently found only in the Amman district. The first is the use of a closely spaced series of dots, usually on a fine rib on the outside of a vessel. This is found on bowl 72 from Amman tomb N (fig. 32:35) and cup (type 3) number 11 from tomb A (fig. 33:46). It is closely related to design 61 but without the bordering lines, no. 9.

The second design is used in various ways and can be considered the most characteristic on painted pottery from the Amman district. This is the crow-step number 37. It occurs occasionally in the tombs, where it is confined to our late range, and four examples are present in our Amman sherd material. In three examples, it is found in black paint directly on the red slip of red-burnished bowls or in the case of number 70:450 on the side of a larger vessel. In bowl number 6 from tomb A (fig. 33:18), it is on the rim and confined to a circular band. On number 447 it is inverted and, rather than being framed by a solid line at the base, there is a row of dots at a rib on the vessel's carination which serves the same

metope.

[11]Loud, *MEG*, II, pl. 85:5.

[12]Pottery drawings have been included in the second and third preliminary reports from Buseirah. As is the case at Tell el Kheleifeh and Amman, a good deal of painted decoration occurs here. Only one vessel is illustrated with a wide decorated band and contains designs 153 and 179 in metope arrangement. Two vessels seem to indicate red or brown painted bands framed by black lines and there seem to be a number of examples of the white band between black lines, on a red surface. Frequent use is made of parallel line decoration on the outsides of deep bowls. The lines are spaced over the surface singly or in multiple groupings, as is found on vessels of similar shape at Ashdod: M. Dothan, *Ashdod*, I, figs. 37:20; 42:3-6 (on red slipped and burnished surfaces); *Ashdod*, II-III, figs. 40:3, 4; 53:16, 17; 88:20; 94:6 (all on red slipped and burnished surfaces) and 59:15. Most common is the use of narrow bands of decoration, as was the case at Tell el Kheleifeh, and seemingly a continuation of the tradition of painted pottery illustrated earlier at Timna. The specific designs are indicated on Table 5. Most of the common designs were already present at Timna. Also present here is the use of groups of short parallel lines across the rims of bowls or triangular section jar rims similar to those found at Amman (sherd nos. 343, 344, 365, 443 and 56:351) and elsewhere. Two black-burnished bowls have been remarked upon above. Six bowls are decorated on the interior with black, and black bands or black paint and reserved cream bands on red-burnished wares. These bowls are similar to the variety discussed above on p. 77-78 realted to, but of thicker ware than "Samaria ware" bowls. Finally, two very fine, thin bowls are illustrated with a line of mold-impressed animal designs set in horizontal bands. This decorative treatment is unique in Iron Age Transjordanian pottery. See Ephraim Stern, "New Types of Phoenician Style Decorated Pottery Vases from Palestine," *PEQ*, CX (1978), 1-21 for the mention of some parallels. We would consider the current evidence so scanty that Phoenician, as opposed to Edomite, origin of this style of decoration cannot be demonstrated conclusively.

[13]Reed and Winnett, *Dhiban*, I, pl. 78:5.

[14]Glueck, *EEP*, II, pl. 27:1, 6, and 10.

[15]Glueck, *BASOR*, CLXXXVIII, Part I, fig. 1:1.

[16]*Ibid.*, figs. 4:3 and 4:5 respectively. Several designs are also effected by incision rather than painting. Number 86 (Glueck, *BASOR*, CLXXXVIII, Part I, fig. 5:7) is found on a late Iron II (probably sixth century) bowl. Design no. 134 is found at the base of the neck of a ring-burnished jar of reddish-brown ware.

[17]*Ibid.*, figs. 1:2 and 5:1a, 2.

[18]*Ibid.*, figs. 1:2, 4:5; Part II, fig. 4:5 and 6. Amman tomb N (in silver), Harding, *AN*, pl. 7:31; Glueck, *BASOR*, CLXXXVIII, Part II, figs. 1:11 and 4:5. Amman tomb A:7 and A:17, and Glueck, *BASOR*, CLXXXVIII, Part II, fig. 4:3. A number of additional examples are now available from Buseirah, see Bennet, *Levant*, VI, figs. 15:11, 12, 14; 16:3; and *Levant*, VII, figs. 7:7, 12, 14; 8:6, 10.

[19]Barthel Hrouda, *Tell Halaf*, Vol. IV (Berlin: Walter de Gruyter, 1962), pls. 59:110 and 60:130.

---

[1]Glueck, *EEP*, IV, pl. 61:5.

[2]Franken, *DA*, fig. 52:3.

[3]Glueck, *EEP*, III, pl. 27:1, 6, and 10.

[4]Franken, *DA*, figs. 51:27; 57:46.

[5]Glueck, *EEP*, II, pl. 27:7.

[6]Albright, *TBM*, I, pl. 25:19.

[7]Franken, *DA*, figs. 51:55; 57:8, 50; and 60:33.

[8]Glueck, *EEP*, II, pl. 27:3.

[9]Albright, *TBM*, I, pls. 25:4 and 24:15 respectively.

[10]The additional designs which have been added to Table 5 were taken primarily from Rothenberg, Timna. The designs illustrated so far are organized primarily in horizontal bands, usually framed bands. There are a number of independent designs and a small percentage use the metope organization. When the metope is used, it is quite simple: one is empty, one cross-hatched and four designs, including the one mentioned above in the text, are variations of an x-filled

purpose. Number 450 is a fragmentary portion of this design. This same design occurs on a bowl of type X which we discussed as peculiar to our late sequence. In this case, number 72 from Amman N, we have red paint on a brown-burnished slip. On no. 446 we have the crow-step pendant from the rim. The paint is black, but the ware is covered with a pinkish-cream slip. On jug number 107 (=fig. 36:13) from Amman N, it appears in a painted band with reddish-brown lines on a buff surface.

The remainder of the vessels or sherds showing this design have the crow-step in bichrome decoration on a painted band. In one case, no. 70:445, the band is brown, the crow-step and confining lines are black, and the vessel's surface color is tan. The ware is similar to number 446 on the same figure. In both of these cases, the color of paint and ware is a departure from what is normal in Iron II. Number 70:445 is reminiscent of Hellenistic wares and paint while number 446 is equally similar to Persian period pottery. The final example comes from a two-handled jug where the design is found on the black-white-black banded decoration of the type we discussed above.[1]

The use of the crow-step in decoration raises some interesting questions of relationships which unfortunately cannot now be answered, but which must be mentioned because of their implications. The crow-step is primarily an architectural decoration and appears most frequently in Mesopotamia in Neo-Assyrian times and continues in use well into the Roman period.[2] It was a characteristic of Nabataean decoration which continued in use in the areas strongly influenced by the Nabataeans well into Roman times. It is found on most of the earlier facades at Petra and Madain Saleh,[3] and at places like Khirbet et Tannur, where it is used in the temple precinct. It is very interesting to see the use of this decoration at the edge of the roof line of temples at Palmyra and Ba'albek. This suggests a connection not only with the Nabataeans but with the culture of the caravaneers who traversed the Transjordan and the eastern deserts. The crow-step design can be seen in Assyrian reliefs in the crenelations at the tops of walls and towers as well as decoration in palaces, namely, the palace of Sargon II at Khorsabad and later, in the Persian period, at Persepolis. In some of these depictions, the crow-step is simplified to a row of triangles.

The instances of the use of such a motif on pottery or vessels of other materials, are extremely rare. An exhaustive search for parallels has yielded very little. At the palace in Khorsabad, the crow-step is used with medallions and other designs as painted decoration. There it constitutes a decorative motif but again has an archi-

tectural context. In the Amuq at Tell Ta'yinat, some currently unique impressed decoration has been found. These pieces are quite distinct from the style of impressed wares common in Sassanian and Parthian pottery in Mesopotamia, examples of which also occur in the Amuq. The examples, however, are clearly early and were usually found on very large basin-like vessels. The designs are identical with those common on the Khorsabad wall decorations. One of the designs is the crow-step. Such impressed designs provide the best parallels to the Amman painted crow-step designs.

Other evidence from Amman indicates that the crow-step was sometimes used for more than simple decoration. In several instances it is used as an insignia. The hats on several riders on horse-and-rider figurines have such crow-step insignias. The first one to be published was from Meqabelein. In the rider's hat, there is a design which is called a "splodge" by Harding.[4] The same decoration appears on the riders from tomb F. In these examples the design in the hat, however, is clearly a crow-step. A careful look at the photograph of the Meqabelein rider and the examination of the original in Amman leaves no doubt but that the "splodge" is in actuality a crow-step. The possibility that the crow-step is somehow associated with cavalry[5] is also indicated by its use on the saddle of the horse figurine from Amman tomb F (fig. 86:9).

---

[1]Only one other example of decoration within this black-white-black banded decoration is found, i.e., at Sâliyeh in ancient Moab. In this case, there is a net design over the white band. The lines of this net are formed with black lines in one direction and red lines in the other (Glueck, *EEP*, I, pl. 23:25).

[2]Edith Porada, "Battlements in the Military Architecture and in the Symbolism of the Ancient Near East," *Essays in Architecture in Honor of Rudolf Wittkowen* (London: Phaedon Press, 1967), pp. 1-12. Giovanni Garbini, "The Stepped Pinnacle," *East and West*, IX (1958), 85-91.

[3]RR. PP. Jaussen et Savignac, *Mission archéologique en Arabie*, Vol. II, *Atlas* (Paris: Librairie Paul Geuthner, 1914), pls. XXXVI:2, 3; XXXVIII:2; XXXIX; XL; XLII:2; XLVI-LIV.

[4]Harding, *QDAP*, XIV (1950), 46.

[5]The crow-step can also be found as a decorative design on garments: F. Thureau-Dangin et Maurice Dunand, *Til Barsib* ("Haut-commissariat de la République française en Syrie et au Liban. Service des antiquitiés Bibliothéque archéologique et historique," Tome XXIII; Paris: Librairie Orientaliste Paul Geuthner, 1936), pl. LI. Richard D. Barnett, *Assyrian Palace Reliefs* (London: Batchworth Press Ltd., 1960), pls. 12 and 51, where this design is used on the dress of infantry and archers. The use of the crow-step in Persian period and later crowns in Iron is discussed in Edith Porada, *The Art of Ancient Iran* (London: Methuen, 1965), pp. 158-60, pl. 45.

CHAPTER VII

AMMAN CITADEL (JEBEL EL QALA')
IRON AGE REMAINS

Introduction

We have refrained from bringing the sherd material into our discussion to any great extent so that all the Iron Age sherds from Amman could be presented in one unit. The sherds have been typed together with the whole vessels and grouped as logically as possible.[1] In some cases, the same type encompasses sherds of different dates, but fortunately this happens only rarely. Our discussion will be primarily by periods, discussing the material contemporary with each of the two sequences and the sherds and stratigraphic evidence from the Amman 1969 sounding. We will discuss the sounding material first because it stands between the two sequences and contains some sherds from each of them. Also, it is placed first because a description of the stratigraphy is necessary and this would disrupt the discussion if placed elsewhere. We have not included a complete catalogue and description of each sherd here as it would be far too cumbersome, but have included group or type discussion of wares, surface finishes, etc., in their stead.

Architecture and Stratigraphy

The plan on figure 5 illustrates the remains of the Iron and Bronze Age defense systems which have been cleared outside the northern "Hellenistic-Roman" defense wall of the Amman Citadel. The Bronze Age walls have been discussed above. No clearance has yet been made of any Iron Age defense walls near Area III. The plan, figure 5, illustrates clearly that the arc of the Iron Age wall, as determined in Areas I and II, could not have gone with walls D, E, or F in Area III without some abrupt changes of direction as well as upward shift in height. It is impossible to reconstruct the circuit of the Bronze Age walls, but they were founded on a ledge of bedrock a meter and a half or more higher than and inside the line of the Iron Age wall. According to the levels, the line of the Bronze Age wall may have intersected the "Hellenistic-Roman" wall just east of its northwest tower. North of the line of bedrock connecting Areas II and III there is a sharp drop. The Iron Age wall stood north of and below this ledge,

while the Bronze Age walls may well have followed its line and stood upon it.

It is impossible to say now whether we have to deal with a solid or casemated Iron Age wall. Wall C confronts us with the problem since it runs out at right angles to the main wall. If the wall is casemated, Area III may well indicate its thickness. There are about 6 m. between the inner face of stones in Area III, wall G, and the outer line of wall H. This would give 2 m. thickness to the actual parallel walls, with 2 m. width for the rooms between them. This agrees well with the dimensions illustrated for Area II where

---

[1] It has been possible to classify the complete bowl shapes and the bowl sherds from Sequence II in one series of numbers. Roman numerals are used for the types here. The same was not possible with the remainder of the sherds and vessels. It was possible to subdivide the whole vessels of Sequence II without great difficulty and arabic numerals are used for the types of each class of vessel. The Sequence I vessels have been divided into classes, but few of them have been typed. There is considerable variation within classes of vessels in this sequence but to label each variation as a type would necessitate the creation of far too many types. To create very general type groupings is also not satisfactory since it would then be difficult to make meaningful distinctions.

The remainder of the sherds have been typed consecutively. We have tried, as much as possible, to go from open to closed shapes and added special shapes at the end. These sherd types have also been designated by Roman numerals and, where it is possible to ascertain clearly the class of vessel to which they conform, we have included such designations in our discussion.

the wall thickness is normally 2 m.[1]

Area II

Very little remains in this area of the portion of the city that once stood outside the line of the "Hellenistic-Roman" fortification. Only a few places remain where bedrock is not exposed or only thinly covered by earth. We mentioned above that a limited amount of work can still be done around Area III. In Area II, even less still remains to be excavated. Most of the area had already been cleared by the Department of Antiquities early in the 1960's to give a better view of the "Hellenistic-Roman" wall. Several Iron Age layers were cleared. A small portion of this area had been left undisturbed and it was evident that good stratigraphy still existed here. An examination of the edges of the unexcavated area showed that a portion of a defense wall still stood here. The Bronze Age walls had been cleared in the fall of 1968 and the date of this undisturbed stretch of wall was unknown. There was a possibility that its excavation could, in a week's time, yield firm dating evidence. The sherd material from this sounding, as well as the arguments presented above, show that a complicated settlement history existed at this north end of the citadel and that the portions of walls we excavated were clearly tenth to ninth century B.C.

Since the amount of undisturbed deposit was quite limited, we had to work to save every scrap of pottery. Our main objective was to cut and draw a section against this wall which would show the stratification related to it. The nature of the area, however, provided considerable difficulty. Figures 11:1-4 and 17:1 and 2 show that the stratified deposit was in a long narrow area. The

lead to a natural supply of water. The tunnel does lead to a large underground chamber where the main hall is ca. 17 m. long and 6 m. wide with four bays leading off to form an H-shaped plan. The bays range in size from 3 x 4 m. to 4 x 6 m. but are cut close to the full height, 7 m., of the main chamber. (The arc of the ceiling is the same as found in L.B. tombs with corbeled roofs at Ugarit, or as found in the postern gate and tunnel at the same site. It is also found in the gallery of the Megiddo water system.) There is, unfortunately, no artifactual evidence for dating this huge chamber as nothing unusual was noted nor kept from its clearance. The only things that seem to have been found in relation to this clearance were from near the entrance of the chamber. These are a large collection of sculpture, including the statue of Yereah-'Azar. What existed above the level of the stairs, where the tunnel reaches the stairs, is problematic since this is built over by a modern entrance to the chamber. The stairs leading down to the floor of the chamber have been completely rebuilt. The tunnel and chamber are shown on fig. 10.

Since there is no evidence for habitation after the ninth century, in the portion of the Iron Age city which we are discussing here, the latest use of the tunnel must be put at this date. The construction of the chamber may well have been later and certainly it does not date as early as the tunnel. There is considerable difference in the workmanship of the two constructions. The tunnel (like that at Siloam or Megiddo) had been left with rough sides and there was no attempt at creating straight lines or smooth flowing curves. The chamber, on the other hand, shows the results of a greater interest in surface finish and line. The walls, though not perfectly straight, are carefully shaped and smoothed. There is a plaster covering on most of the chamber's surface and on the bays, but it would have to be analyzed to determine when it was applied. The use of the tunnel as a main entrance to the chamber is possible, but another entrance would be more suitable. If the date of the sculpture from this area does bear on the date of the chamber, it would indicate a use after that of the tunnel.

If the chamber is later, we have no evidence at present to show where the tunnel originally led. If the tunnel led to a smaller chamber, this chamber was removed when the larger one was built. It is also possible that the tunnel was merely a sally port or secret exit and nothing more. If the latter were the case, however, why was the chamber cut at this spot? We have remarked that the tunnel did not lead to a natural supply of water. The large chamber could very well have served as a cistern, but only the entrance could have served as an inlet for water, as no other inlets are to be found. There is no evidence on the walls of water having stood inside the chamber. Water would have to be transported mechanically to fill the chamber, and though possible, this would seem to be unlikely.

The other possibility, which I hesitate to suggest, is that the statuary did originally come from this chamber and that it had a special and perhaps religious function. Whether this would also have been the case for the tunnel and its original use is equally questionable. A minute re-examination of this system must be undertaken to see if any other evidence is still to be found to help solve the problems outlined here.

---

[1] In one place there is a slight widening, probably to deal with the irregular line of bedrock. We will deal with this problem in detail below.

We must mention one feature outside of the designated areas which must have been closely related to the defense system. This is a tunnel cut into bedrock in the center of our area. Unfortunately, the tunnel is fairly clean of dirt or deposit, and the entrance has long been visible and choked with fairly modern debris. It would be unexpected if excavation would yield enough information to date the cutting of the tunnel. One fact, however, is clear; the entrance to the descending stairway was inside both the Bronze and Iron Age cities. The tunnel, which ran from the base of this stairway, came out on the other side of both the Bronze and Iron Age fortification walls. The function of the tunnel is enigmatic. One is reminded of the water systems at Gibeon, Jerusalem, Megiddo, and recently at Hazor. Unfortunately, the tunnel (ca. 2.00 m. high) does not

area we excavated was 13.5 m. long[1] and 6 m. wide at the widest point, but only 4 m. wide or less for roughly the western two-thirds of the area. Erosion in the area caused sloping sides to the standing sections (fig. 11:2), so the highest portions of the western section were even narrower than the figure given. In the eastern higher part of our area, what looked like isolated stones turned out to be the line of a wall, wall J (fig. 11:3), with a second wall (K) arcing toward it from the south. Wall K was poorly preserved with a heavy scree of rubble and plaster south of it. Both of these walls belong, according to a preliminary analysis of the pottery, to the Abassid period. In this area, our section was kept as close to the north edge as possible and we then dug in from it as close to wall J as was possible (fig. 12:1).

In the western part of the area, we laid out our section line (fig. 11:4) as close to the edge as possible, but without going so far as to miss any of the layers. Since the area was eroded on a fairly steep slope to the north, it was difficult to gain very fine subdivisions of the material. The layers encountered here were designated one (surface), five, and eight. Layers 5 and 8 were then further subdivided after the section had been drawn and the divisions clearly seen (figs. 12:3, 4; 13:3, 4). Under layer eight we had come on a stone pavement in two levels which we did not want to destroy, so we drew the section first and removed it to get the plan of what went with this paving. We were surprised to find a second wall, wall C, at the south of the area and this explained why the whole area had not eroded away completely.[2] Fortunately, wall C did not extend far beyond our section line so the section was re-established (fig. 11:3) and we dug the remaining area to bedrock. At this depth, we could cut a clear face much farther to the north and could see the remaining layers clearly so that they could be removed one by one (fig. 11:4) up against our section (fig. 15:1, 2, and 4). A portion of the upper pavement was left standing, however, in case it went with something deeper and since the time allotted to excavation was running short. This accounts for the way in which we have drawn the center portion of our section.

The sequence of occupation in the area, then, from bedrock is as follows. The section of bedrock directly west of wall B was level. Whether this had been done intentionally was impossible to determine from the small area exposed. Farther west, bedrock was very irregular and dropped off steeply near the end of the preserved north face of wall C. A light colored, yellowish-brown clayey soil (layer 17) filled in most of the uneven areas. The remaining layers (through 5 d) ran up against wall B.[3]

Layer 16 was a very fine hard grey soil and may have been a leveling course for two successive rough layers, layers 14 and 13 above. These loci contained considerable gravel and may have been successive pavements. Layer 11 contained considerably more pottery than the lower loci and would seem to represent occupation debris. Layer 11 is the last locus to go with the original phase, Period I, of the fortification.

The fortification wall, wall B, was founded on bedrock and its base was stepped, depending on the contour of bedrock. Some fairly large stones were used in its construction (see plan for size). These stones had been roughly shaped and were laid in four courses with a total preserved height of over 1.75 meters. Only one special feature was preserved on the outer face of this wall. It was a shallow buttress (its west face is shown with a dot-dash line on the plan) which extended 40 cm. from the wall face and was most probably 2.00 m. wide.[4]

The top of layer 11 represents a fairly level sur-

---

[1] The section does not show this entire length because to do so we would have had to undermine wall J.

[2] Unfortunately, little can be expected north of the area in which we worked or directly west of it. At the west a road comes very close to the area which was standing before excavation. At the north everything has been removed for the foundations of a building, which is one of a number which stand between the area shown on our plan and the intersection of two of the roads which surround the citadel. These modern destructions of the ancient archaeological remains will probably make it impossible to answer a number of our outstanding questions. The only advantage to the neighboring apartment building was the use of its roof as a platform from which to photograph the progress of the excavations.

[3] The numbers of the layers against the wall itself are different from those to the west because this area had to be dug separately. This was done in an attempt to gain as much pottery as possible in this area without undermining the large stones above. Some levels had to be lumped in the digging but the section showed clearly how they corresponded to the divisions to the west.

[4] It is difficult to speculate about the placement of such a buttress since so little of the wall is preserved and its southern portion is destroyed. The wall thickens as it extends to the south because bedrock moves away from the line of its western face. We have reconstructed a curved wall though in all probability such a wall never existed. It is probable that the wall consisted of relatively straight segments between buttresses. It is, however, impossible for us to show this in our plan since there is no indication of the dimensions or spacing of the buttresses. The preserved face of wall B actually shows little curve and thus a slight change in the direction of the wall face to the next tower is to be expected. We have reconstructed an arc only to give a general idea of the position of the wall.

face upon which the one rebuilding of the fortification, Period II, took place. The most important feature was the founding of wall C. This wall was built at almost a right angle to wall B, against the buttress.[1] Its thickness was 2 m. and only one course of stones was well preserved. Unfortunately, the western end was broken when the modern road was constructed. A pavement of small and medium-sized stones in two levels stretches north of wall C and west of wall B. This pavement seems to end in a fairly straight line at the west. No large stones which may have continued the north face of wall C were found west of this point. Consequently, west of this point we seem to be past the face and into the center filling of another wall parallel to wall B. Unfortunately, there is not sufficient evidence to be able to state this unequivocally. The step in the pavement is 25 cm., with the higher portion to the east against wall B. A large stone forms the northern portion of this step while medium-sized stones continue it southward. The width of the upper pavement (i.e., east-west) varies from ca. 1.20 to 1.35 m. and the width of the lower pavement is at least 1.50 m. Layer 10 continues under and forms the bedding of wall C and the large stone in the step between the pavements. Layer 8 and its subdivisions form the occupation layers which built up between wall C and the level of the higher pavement. The narrow bands of soil which comprise layer 8 were only about 30 cm. thick and were extremely rich in sherds. The three layers above this, sublayers 5 b, c and d, represent the destruction of this second and final phase of the defense walls. Sublayer 5 d contained far more pottery than the other two layers. It seems that in the later periods the defense walls were swept clean down to the top of sublayer 5 b. This surface continued the level of the bedrock to the east and gradually sloped down from that level.

A layer of reddish-brown soil covered this destruction level. Sublayer 5 a, of wall B, was a continuation of layer 7. Unfortunately, no worthwhile stratigraphy was found east of wall B, as layer 21 represented an extremely small area with only a few associated sherds. Layers 4 and 6 run up against wall K but still contain considerable Iron Age material which must either have been churned up from below or scattered from later levels that have been removed entirely from the area.

Interpretation of Area II Walls

Since the area has been so badly destroyed, it is very difficult to make a valid reconstruction. The Period I fortification presents no difficulties with a solid wall face and shallow buttresses at inter-vals. Period II presents some difficulties with the addition of wall C. It would be unusual to have any non- military structure added to the outside of the defense wall. Since we do not know how this wall ends, whether with a right angle, a curve, or joining a cross wall, we must mention the implication of each possibility but cannot make a final judgement. It is possible in the first two instances to have a square (or rectangular) or rounded tower of which we have the portion of a side. The former seems most likely.

It is possible that rather than a tower we have to deal with a gateway. All sorts of possibilities present themselves. Since wall B shows no break in the excavated area, an indirect entrance gateway would seem to be the best proposal.[2] Examining the topography of the area, a location for a gateway at this point would be suitable. The citadel hill joins Jebel Hussein a short distance to the northwest with a narrow land bridge between the two hills. Moving further east or southwest along the fortification would make access to Jebel Hussein more difficult. The slopes of Jebel Qala' drop sharply here and leave only enough room for a narrow road at the base of the walls. The problem with this proposal is that if a gateway existed here in Period II, one would expect the same to have existed in Period I. There is no evidence for a gateway anywhere close by in Period I and, since there is no evidence for a complete revision of the defenses in Period II, one cannot expect a new gate to have been opened in a new location. This is especially true in that wall C is not founded on bedrock as would be expected for such a structure.

In view of this, a third possibility would be that the remains of Period II were part of a casemate wall. We mentioned this above in conjunction with Area III. Such an interpretation, unfortunately, has its difficulties also. The width of a total wall of between seven and eight meters seems excessive, especially with a minimum of three meters represented by two levels of pavement between the inner and outer walls. It is hoped that some clues remain in the area to solve these problems but the prospects for this are not good.

---

[1]The buttress is an integral part of wall B and, though we did not reach its base, we followed it through three of the wall's four courses. It clearly continued on down while wall C obviously stopped at the level of layer 10.

[2]Only a few gateways exist that would be valid in reconstructing a gateway here. The most suitable reconstruction would have to be something along the line of the gateway at Bethel (Kelso, *Bethel*, pl. 101). Unfortunately, the date causes a difficulty here since it is dated to the Middle Bronze Age.

Area I

When the remains of the wall in Area II were first recognized, an examination was undertaken to see if other sections of it were preserved. A portion of wall, and the promise of more in a jumble of stones, was found about 30 meters to the south, just around the northeast corner tower of the "Hellenistic-Roman" fortification (fig. 17:3 and 4). A modern wall, which is impossible to date presently, had been built up against the face of the "Hellenistic-Roman" fortification. The area has been disturbed by the building of a modern road, which can be seen in the photographs, as well as by the construction of a stairway leading to the top of the citadel. In the course of these projects, the modern wall against the face of the "Hellenistic-Roman" wall had been undermined and large sections of it had gradually fallen away. It was this erosion which made it possible to see traces of the Iron Age wall.

During the week Area II was excavated, some time was spent cleaning up Area I and making several small sections against the walls. The continuation of the line of the Iron Age wall of Area II was followed for almost 20 meters. The wall was preserved at both ends of this stretch but completely destroyed in between them. We could, however, trace its line clearly because it followed the edge of a ledge in the bedrock. At the south end, four courses of stone were preserved (fig. 18:1) while at the north (fig. 18:3 and 4) five and parts of a sixth were preserved. Nothing was preserved outside the wall at the south end, where it obviously continued to curve and go under the Hellenistic-Roman wall. The small cut at the northern section of this wall produced no stratified material remaining outside the wall. There was a very compact layer of yellow sand, on bedrock, which ran up against the lowest course of stones in the wall. The layer above this was mixed with modern debris.

Both at the north and south, there was a hard white clayey layer (similar to the material which had been used in the construction of the M.B. glacis) which came up against the inside of the Iron Age wall. Beneath this was a very compact layer of gravelly soil with medium to small-sized stones. We cut a section through this clayey material against the face of the "Hellenistic-Roman" wall (fig. 18:2). We were puzzled to find that the white clayey soil came directly against the later wall and that this wall did not rest on bedrock at this point, but on the gravelly layer described above. Unfortunately, all the soils we were working through were very nearly sterile. Consequently, we have no ceramic aids for dating any of the walls or layers in our Area I clearance.

When the modern wall fell away in this area, it revealed a difference in the size and shape of stones in the lowest courses of the "Hellenistic-Roman" wall and our clearance uncovered still another type of masonry beneath that. The chronological significance of these changes is impossible to document at this point. The thickness of stone courses, the use of bossed stones, and the manner in which headers and stretchers are arranged are quite variable in the construction of this wall (see fig. 17:3). Despite this, the five lowest courses are drastically different from the construction above. Starting from the bottom there is a row of two stretchers and a header, .55 x .40 x 1.00 m. The next row is a course of headers, .40 x .55 m. The faces on these stones are rough but there is a hint of a boss and margin on some stones. The next three courses seem to form an entity where bosses are clearly evident and margins usually shaped on the four edges of a face. The size of these stones is .35 x .55 x 1.65 m. Much larger stones were used higher up in the wall. The three courses of bossed stones look like good Hellenistic construction, but may date as early as the Persian period. The two lowest courses do not conform clearly to specific known masonry types in Palestine. They may date in the Iron Age or they may merely have been rougher stones used as foundation stones which were covered and, thus, did not require a finish like the others. Since the sizes do not correspond to those above, however, this does not seem to be the best interpretation. The only solution to the problem lies in digging inside the defense wall and examining the stratigraphy adjoining it. This would not be an easy task since close to 20 m. of archaeological deposit would have to be removed to reach the level of these stones.

Interpretation of Area I

Looking at this area in relation to Areas II and III, it seems that the following reconstruction is the most plausible. The white clayey soil in the area may be the remains of the Middle Bronze defenses which, as we saw from Area III, lie inside the line of the Iron Age wall and probably on the next step up in the bedrock. This wall must, here, lie inside the Hellenistic-Roman citadel. The Iron Age wall was founded upon bedrock and either cut into the earlier defense system or in places built directly against it. Both of these walls were curved, or at least had only small straight segments as opposed to the later long straight lines of wall. The "Hellenistic-Roman" wall may have been founded on the line of an earlier wall in this area which, in places, destroyed portions of the previous defense walls. The M.B. glacis material may or may not have been disturbed and redeposited in this process depending upon how the foundations were laid. The fact that the late wall does not reach bedrock in the small area we opened is probably explained by the contour of bedrock. The inside line, and probably most of the wall, can be expected to have rested on bedrock, but there probably was a dip in the bedrock here which had not been considered sufficiently great to require blocking.

The Extent of the Iron Age Citadel in Amman

More excavation is needed to determine where the defense wall stood from the end of the ninth century B.C. and later. It is possible that the wall exposed in Area II may have continued in use beyond our Period II, but that all remains of this have been obliterated by later building operations. The next problem to be solved in this connection is the date of the founding of the line of what we have been calling the "Hellenistic-Roman" wall. At present, we would shy away from a hypothesis on this matter in relation to what is known of the history of the city of Amman. Several possibilities would present themselves, but it would be better to leave them in abeyance until more information is available.

In examining the circuit of the Amman Citadel walls, there seems to be another place where the earlier cities extended outside the line of the Hellenistic-Roman citadel. This is at the southwest corner of the site where the slopes do not fall off as steeply as elsewhere. Unfortunately, no excavation has been undertaken here.

While the Department of Antiquities was clearing portions of the late walls at the southeast corner of the middle plateau of the citadel in the spring of 1969, earlier walls were also encountered. The sherds related to these walls were Iron Age so the extension of the city to this point, at least, seems assured.

Pottery from Area II

We have shown above that only two phases of the fortification wall have been preserved in this area. The limited remains indicate that only a relatively short time range is represented. Since contemporary material is rare in the Transjordan at present and published stratified material is nonexistent, it is a temptation to extract more information from it than is warranted. A statistical count of all rim, base, and decorated sherds was made in the field. This will not be presented here because the number (close to 750 tabulated sherds) is not sufficient for reliable statistical conclusions. Less than ten percent of the typed

sherds have a limited time range, namely, they are not present through the entire sequence of layers. These sherds do provide important information in that some of the types represented here occur only in the very lowest layers and others only in the highest layers.[1]

The sherds have been divided into five major groups: bowl rims, jar rims, bases, painted sherds, and miscellaneous decorated sherds. They are arranged in the illustrations according to the layers in which they were found.

Bowl Sherds

The variety of bowl shapes from this sounding is not great. The variation within types is limited and there is considerable similarity of sherds within particular types which makes it difficult to attribute them to one class or the other.

The simplest bowls are represented by bowls of type XII, nos. 52:141 and 156, with gently curved sides and rounded rims, and type XI, nos. 61:124, 142 and 154 with gently curved sides and pointed rims. Since the size of the rim sherds is rather small, it is often difficult to distinguish such sherds from those of shallower bowls with sharper curves or angles to the sides (type XXVIII) no. 53:193. The same difficulty occurs with flat-ended straight rims (type II) like nos. 168, 183-85, 195 and 61:169, and bowls with greater curve to the sides (type XVI) like nos. 129 and 61:127. A unique thickened version is illustrated by no. 132. The five rim types mentioned here constitute about forty-five percent of the bowl sherds.

The most popular rims fall basically into two groups and comprise the greater part of the remaining bowl rims, about thirty-seven percent. The first group consists mainly of type XXIV, nos. 158, 61:162, and 194. This is a thickened rim, usually with flat top, that shows a bulge both on the inside and the outside. The wall of the bowl is turned up, usually in a sharp curve or angle, to a position close to vertical. Type XXII illustrates a

---

[1] Limited statistics cannot be relied upon to show the comparative frequency of certain common types. The number of sherds from Period II is roughly 49 percent of the total, while Period I provides only about 22 percent. About 26 percent of the total came from post Period II layers, and this includes only the Iron Age sherds. These percentages would have to be taken into account in interpreting the other statistics. The relatively low number of sherds from Period I, just over 150, argues against any serious dependence upon statistics from this sounding. There are, however, a number of important instances where there is such a great disparity in the frequency of sherds, in early as opposed to late levels, that the significance is obvious.

variant where the thickening is somewhat rounded and primarily on the inside nos. 145, 52:150 and 62:186. The other group is formed primarily of type XXV rims. These are very similar to XLV (no. 151), except that the rim is usually slanting outward with most of the thickening of the rim on the outside (nos. 61:136, 52:137). There are several sherds which show the variants illustrated by type III, nos. 128 and 52:135.

The bowl shapes we have mentioned are all quite simple. This may be the result of the potters using earlier pottery techniques which were adapted to the production of quite thin-walled vessels.[1]

Despite many worn sherds, it is certain that better than ninety percent of the bowls were burnished. There is no evidence for wheel burnishing, but spiral burnishing does seem to occur. Hand burnishing is usual and some sherds seem almost polished on the whole surface. It is difficult to say if any pattern burnishing was used.

In some examples there are differences in color between the insides and outsides of vessels but these are not normal. In some cases, the use of a slip or wash is obvious. In others, only microscopic analysis would determine whether a slip was employed or whether the surface color was actually due to the firing of the clay without further treatment. Less than one quarter of the sherds had a plain tan, light brown, buff, or grey surface similar to the color of the ware of the vessel. The remainder had either red or orange surface color. The red was dominant, comprising half of the total sherds, while roughly another quarter of the sherds had an orange to orange-brown surface. Further statistical breakdown would not be valid. There does not seem to be a significant change in the colors found within the time range of Periods I and II. The preference for the use of a red surface contrasts sharply with the practice at Deir 'Allā through phase L, where sherds with surfaces in the red to orange color range were in the minority. The surface color and burnishing technique of the sounding sherds seem to agree well with what is present at Tell Beit Mirsim, in B_3 and A_1, and in contemporary levels on other sites in Palestine. In level IIa at Ain Shems, Wright notes a mottled appearance on vessel surfaces in the middle of the tenth century due to a thin application of paint. We have many examples of this from our sounding, also.

Only a few of the bowl sherds from the sounding were over 1 cm. in thickness with most of them ranging between .6 cm. and 1 cm. thick. This seems to put most of them in the type 4, thin-walled bowl category at Deir 'Allā. Parallels to all our shapes can be found at Deir 'Allā. This may be due primarily to their simplicity. The simple type XI, XII, XVII, and XXIX bowls can be found at Madeba and Jebel Nuzha, but as noted above, the red color would seldom be present and in these examples burnishing would usually be absent. The thickened rim types do not occur in these tombs. The low straight-sided bowl, types I and II, however, are rare at Deir 'Allā. They are both well represented in Sequence II (fig. 32), as we mentioned above. Bowl types XXIV and XXV and their variants occur with some frequency at Deir 'Allā, but seem to have their best parallels in the middle range of Sequence II (figs. 32 and 33), where the colors and burnish are also normal.

The typical sinuous-sided bowls or slightly carinated bowls with out-flaring rims so common in the first sequence, including Deir 'Allā, are virtually absent in our sounding. Sherd no. 151, type XLV, illustrates a buff ware burnished example of a slightly flaring version of type XXV. Number 61:166 represents the other example of a bowl rim that approaches this type. It seems to come from a taller vessel with a narrower neck than is common in Sequence I, however.

Only a few other rim types remain to be discussed. These represent the extremely rare examples of more elaborate rims. Two, numbers 181 and 62:191, are similar to the type XXVI bowls, with a ridge below the rim on the outside. The appearance of sherds of type V, like no. 192, is of great importance because they are distinctive and we have seen middle-late range Sequence II examples from Sahab B and Amman N above. There are no examples from Period I, so it seems that this type was introduced during Period II. A similar rim profile occurs on larger vessels of type LXIV which are also found only in Period II, paralleling the position of the type V bowl rims.

Finally, we must mention a feature occasionally found on bowls in this sounding, namely, a knob or knobs applied to the side of a bowl just below the rim. This feature appears in both periods. Examples are illustrated on nos. 128, 129, 161, 194, 53:193, 61:159, 160 and 63:233. The most frequent shape is pinched so that it has a longer vertical than horizontal axis. Two examples show a fairly uniform cone, nos. 194 and 61:160, while one has its major axis running horizontally and thus forms a miniature ledge handle. Such knobs are common at Tell Beit Mirsim

---

[1] No analysis has yet been undertaken, but this fact in itself makes a strong argument that the potting methods were still at a stage similar to those in use during phases A - L at Deir 'Allā. There, mold and coil-made vessels were used almost exclusively. When one compares these sherds with those to be discussed below, it is obvious that in the latter the fast wheel was skillfully employed, while here, in contrast, it obviously was not.

in level B₃,[1] at Ain Shems in II,[2] and Gibeah in level II.[3] These are only a few illustrations of such knobs on contemporary bowls. They are often considered to be the ends of bar handles. It is impossible to prove the contrary at Amman because of the small size and the position of the break on the sherds, but it seems unlikely, as is the case on the Gibeah sherds cited. There is considerable variation in the rim shapes on which such knobs appear. The parallels cited in our discussion of the bowl rims indicate that the pottery is still strongly Iron I, but features common to Iron II have begun to appear.

Deep Bowls, Jar, and Other Rim Sherds

Great difficulty was encountered in attributing small or coarse sherds to either jar or bowl types. This was the case above with some of the vessels encountered in Sequence I and there is an even greater problem in classifying sherds unless large quantities are available. Only if such quantities are available can one hope to make such fine distinctions as have been made in the Deir 'Allā publication. The use of the fast wheel for most of the second sequence pottery eases this difficulty somewhat, in that the profiles are much better defined and thus are easier to systematize. In this section, we have grouped the remainder of the rim sherds which do not have painted decoration. Their number is considerably less than the bowl types discussed above, by a ratio of roughly three to eight.

We have mentioned the type LXIV rims above as similar to the type V bowl rims but on larger vessels. The best examples of our type XLIV rims are illustrated as nos. 67:376 and 377. The surface color is a mat, medium red and no burnishing is detectable. Two grooves are spaced at the top and bottom of the exterior surface of these rims. The later variations of this type are illustrated as nos. 657-59. A related thicker, heavier rim, type LXX, is illustrated by nos. 63:247, 250 and 64:263. The ware is brown and has a heavy inclusion of grit similar to that used in cooking pot wares. This rim has good parallels at Deir 'Allā and is important in that it is a new feature appearing in phases K and L. The Deir 'Allā profiles are found on kraters.[4] Grooved krater rims were also found at Irbed in tomb B. Some of the Madeba kraters, illustrated with our Sequence I vessels, have rims which closely resemble the ones under discussion and can also be classed as type LXX. This information helps define a restricted date range of less than two centuries for these vessels and lends further support to our arguments above concerning their chronological position.

The deep bowl of type LXIII is illustrated by

nos. 237 and 62:206, the latter rounded variant of which is currently found only in the Transjordan. The example from layer 5 d is similar to the later bowls with rounded rim and body profile. The sherd from layer 11 has a higher and straighter rim with less angle at the bend between rim and body. In this, it is closer to similar deep bowl sherds type 3 d at Deir 'Allā, than the later sherd. There is some variation in profile within this Deir 'Allā type[5] and the best parallels come from the last published phase, phase L.

Almost half of the sherds which concern us in this section belong to rim type LXVI. It is difficult to classify these rims since no whole vessels with such rims have been found. Nothing is published from Deir 'Allā which is in any way similar to these rims. The interior ledge rim must be seen in the context of the hole-mouth jars, types LXXV to LXXX, to be discussed below. The use of red slip and burnishing, however, is infrequent in the latter, but occurs in almost all cases of the type LXVI rim. The angle of the rim, its width and its thickness vary somewhat but with no apparent significance. Such sherds are present in both Periods I and II and, though they are not more frequent in Period I, the number is very high in comparison with Period II (when the difference in the total number of sherds of each period is considered).

It is difficult to attribute this high vessel form with narrow neck to either a bowl or a jar form because no complete examples have been found. It is possible, though we have no evidence, that these represent earlier versions of our cup types 3 and 4. These cup types are the only examples we have for the use of an inverted rim on a small vessel of relatively fine ware. One sherd of the profile type LXXX, which is found on such cups, was found in the surface layer (no. 64:268). It must be considered post Period II since no similar rim profile is present elsewhere in the sounding.

---

[1] Albright, *TBM*, I, pl. 25:12 and 37.

[2] Grant and Wright, *AS*, IV, pl. XLIII:16 and 17.

[3] Sinclair, *Gibeah*, pl. 16:6.

[4] Franken, *DA*, fig. 73:2, 4, and 5-8; fig. 75:93.

[5] The Deir 'Allā parallels to the peculiar feature of a "straight collar-shaped rim," are said to fall exclusively in phase G and later, with the earlier examples probably attaining this shape accidentally (Franken, *DA*, p. 138). An examination of the published profiles shows only one good example, for our purposes, from phase G (*ibid.*, fig. 64:45), but even it, like many of this type of sherd, shows the profile which we have classed as our type LXXI. Only in phase L are there good and plentiful parallels to the sherds with which we are concerned here (*ibid.*, figs. 74:68, 69, 71; 77:32-34).

High-necked Jars or Jugs

A very small percentage of the sounding sherds illustrates jars or jugs with high necks. The few sherds which do occur are found both early and late. Numbers 62:197, 198; 64:259, 282 and 287 represent thin-walled examples which can be attributed to our type LVII. They all have a ridge about 3 cm. from the top and two have a second smaller ridge about halfway between the top and the major ridge. It is difficult, because of the size of most of the sherds, to determine if they come from jugs or jars and whether they represent the neckridge vessels so frequent at the end of our Sequence I and later. The general features of these rims can be found among the Deir 'Allā subtypes. The same problem exists in finding parallels at Deir 'Allā for jar sherds of normal thickness (nos. 62:199; 63:236 and 64:283). There are good Palestinian parallels for these rims from the end of Iron I.[1]

Grooved jar rims (repeating the rim treatment of type V bowls and type LXIV deep bowls) are illustrated by sherds nos. 67:374 and 375. The insides of both rims are concave. No. 67:374 is covered with a heavy red slip while no. 67:375 is of tan ware which is without slip. Painted black and white decoration adds to the rippled effect of the grooved surface.[2] Both of these sherds are later than Period II and come from a pit which contains only Iron II pottery.

"Collar-Type" Rims and Related Rim Types

Three recent publications (*Bethel, Beth Zur,* and *Gibeah*) have re-examined the "collar-type" rim in Palestine. We will not involve ourselves in this discussion other than to place the examples we have in the context of that discussion. With but one exception, our examples do not conform to the most frequent ones of this type, but seem rather to belong to its latest derivations. The isolated example, no. 395 from layer 6 (which is post Period II but a layer containing considerable earlier pottery) represents the "collar-type" jar well known from the excavations at Seilun (Shiloh)[3] and now well illustrated in the Transjordan at Sahab.[4] We can illustrate only one additional unstratified example from Amman, no. 629, so cannot make a significant contribution to the discussion of this vessel type other than to illustrate a series of later variants which occurred over a long period of time. It is interesting that this rim type is present in our sounding but is not found among the Sequence I shapes and that no exact parallels exist at Deir 'Allā.[5]

A "lower heavy rolled rim" appears at Bethel late in Iron I and is the closest parallel to the majority of our rims.[6] The form with a lower profile, exemplified by our number 64:256, is classed with these rims though it is substantially different.[7] The unstratified examples of type LX jars from Amman, which are illustrated below, are primarily of this variety. The examples from Beth Zur for this low type of rim are illustrated by Sellers, *et al., BZ,* on plate 21:7 and 8. These sherds are dated to 825 B.C. or later on the basis of parallels from 'Ain Shems,[8] though there they are much more rounded and the rib which indicates the collar is usually absent. The greatest number and the closest parallels to our sherds come from Tell en Naṣbe.[9]

Other examples of an "intermediate" type of this rim are our nos. 64:257 and 262. These have a v-shaped groove at the side of the rim. They occur at Beth Zur[10] where they are dated to the tenth century. The highest locus of Period II, layer 5b, contains another variant of this rim type, type LXXV, shown on no. 254. This small rim with pointed top is covered with a red slip and is burnished. The best parallel examples are from 'Ain

---

[1]Kelso, *Bethel,* pl. 56:20, 21, and Wampler, *Naṣbe,* pl. 18:311 (where it is given a very long date range).

[2]One other example of a ribbed jar rim must be mentioned here. It occurs on jug no. 53 (= fig. 36:19) from Amman tomb D. It is interesting that this rim should occur in the earliest tomb of our Sequence II, and is one of the few shapes that come from that tomb.

[3]See further comments on p. 102. The best examples from Seilun are now illustrated in: Marie-Louise Buhl and Svend Holm-Nielsen, *Shiloh* (Copenhagen: National Museum, 1969), Pls. 15:186-189 and 16:190-192. Similar jar rims are dated Iron I-II (nos. 31 and 243) and Iron II (no. 6) and illustrate the difficulty of interpreting the chronological significance of the Seilun pottery; see Rudolph H. Dornemann, review of Buhl and Holm-Nielsen, *Shiloh* in *JNES,* XXXI (1972), 384-385.

[4]Moawiyah M. Ibrahim, "The Collared-rim Jar of the Early Iron Age," in *Archaeology in the Levant,* edited by Roger Moorey and Peter Parr (London: Aris and Phillips, 1978), 116-126.

[5]A collar occurs on two storage jars from Deir 'Allā but they are very early, phase A, and seem to be isolated occurrences. The rim profiles above the collar are not unusual at Deir 'Allā, however, and are not like the normal rims of the "collar-type" rim in Palestine.

[6]It "came into use and continued through Iron I_2 and Iron I_3." Kelso, *Bethel,* pl. 63.

[7]*Ibid.,* pl. 57:2.

[8]Sellers, *et al., BZ,* pl. 46.

[9]Wampler, *Naṣbe,* pls. 3:44; 4:59; 5:63 and 66.

[10]Sellers, *et al., BZ,* pl. 21:19 (= fig. 7:19).

Shems in level IIc[1] and from Tell en Nasbe.[2]

In summary, the parallel material suggests that our rims are to be dated to the end of Iron I, more precisely, in the last half of the tenth century B.C., and at the very beginning of Iron II, probably the first quarter or possibly the first half of the ninth century B.C.

"Cylindrical-Jar" Rims and Related Rim Types

The Palestinian evidence for cylindrical jars indicates that they are later than the "collar-type" rims and are clearly Iron II. Both "collar-type" and "cylindrical-jar" rims occur in Period II. Some related types seem to indicate a transition between the two. A few of the late variety of "cylindrical-jar" (or hole-mouth) rim types (LXXVIII and LXXIX) were found in Period II. We will say more about these below and note here, primarily, that this seems to be their earliest occurrence. These rims (nos. 63:243, 64:264-66 and 65:288) are characterized by a broad inturned ledge with a minimal ledge or rib at the outside of the rim at the point where the vessel closes sharply inward.

We must discuss first among the variants those rims which are similar to Palestinian sherds and have been cited as later derivations of the "collar-type" rim. Our type LXXVII, which is illustrated on nos. 63:216, 227, 228 and 65:290, has numerous good parallels; the clearest of these are from Bethel[3] and are attributed to Iron II. Our examples were found in Period II or later.

A majority of the remaining rims are variations of this type. The prime difference is in the treatment of the exterior of the rim at the point where it turns inward. These rims seem to have been formed either by folding the clay over to the outside of the vessel and pressing it against the wall, or by adding a band of clay to the top of a slightly inturned jar wall. In one case, the rim has a fairly high step on the outside which is finished with a straight, nearly vertical side, type LXXVI (nos. 207, 208; 62:201, 209; 63:218, 226; 64:251 and 279). In one example, the step was nearly eliminated when the end was pressed smooth against the jar wall (no. 63:241). In several other examples, the exterior fold of clay was not secured to the vessel wall and a space was left between the fold and the jar wall (nos. 62:202, 203; 63:242 and 65:289). This last variety resembles another tenth century (and later) version of the "collar-type" rim; the best examples of this type are found at 'Ain Shems in level IIb.[4] Numbers 62:210 and 211 have less pointed, blunted exterior ledges, as is also the case in number 6 of the parallels listed from 'Ain Shems.

All the variants of the "cylindrical-jar" rim,

discussed in the last paragraph, are found in Periods I, II and later; in all but one case, there are very few examples from Period I. The exceptions are the type LXXVI rims which occur in roughly equal numbers in Periods I and II. Four of these rims, numbers 62:203; 63:226, 247 and 64:251, illustrate the incised-line decoration at the edges of the upper surface of the rim which was also characteristic of the deep bowls, type LXIV. The fact that this decoration occurs primarily on these rims (which also seems to be the earliest) is significant in that it may shed some light on the derivation of the grooved cylindrical rims in Palestine. In most cases, the grooves on the Palestinian vessels are not done as carefully as the Transjordanian examples and are often minimally represented. Good Palestinian parallels are published for most of the "cylindrical-jar" rims illustrated here.[5]

A number of small jars with "cylindrical-type" rims have also been found. Some of these come close to the profile of the deep bowl rim, type LXVI. Red wash is extremely rare on these sherds. The basic difference is that the tops of the rims are more horizontal than the type LXVI examples and there are no thickenings on the inside where the rims turn to the inside. Most frequently, there is a little groove at the outside of the rim, just below the angle of body and rim, type LXVII (nos. 63:217, 220, 229, 232; 64:252, 253 and 270). Occasionally, there is a small ledge projecting at this point (no. 276). A rounded rim of similar profile also has the v-shaped incised line at the junction of rim and body. This rim, type LXVII (no. 64:269), may belong to a deep bowl.

The ware color of all of the "cylindrical-jars" sherds is brown to red-brown. The bodies of all sherds show a heavy inclusion of sandy grit. In many cases, the upper surface of the rim is burnished but only rarely is burnish found elsewhere on the sherds. There are several examples of conical knobs at the top of the body wall as was the case on the small bowls discussed above.

The date of the rims discussed in this section coincides, for the most part, with that of the rims in the previous section. The overlap of features within the subtypes of the "collar-type" rims and the "cylindrical-jar type" rims, makes this overlap in time understandable. The presence of the

---

[1]Grant and Wright, *AS*, IV, pl. LXV:5 and 11.

[2]Wampler, *Nasbe*, pl. 5:72.

[3]Kelso, *Bethel*, pl. 41:18, 27, 31, 34, and 38.

[4]Grant and Wright, *AS*, IV, pl. XLVII:1, 2, 6, 8, and 9.

[5]Wampler, *Nasbe*, pl. 24:388, 389, 390; pl. 25; and pl. 26:421, 428, 432, 434, 437; Grant and Wright, *AS*, IV, pl. LXV:18-34, Sellers, *et al.*, *BZ*, fig. 15:1-4, etc.

late variety of "cylindrical-jar" rims, of the type LXXVIII, only in Period II indicates once more that our area must have continued in use for some time during the ninth century B.C.

Miscellaneous Jar Rims and Cooking Pots

Only two other jar rim types, LXII and LXXIII, remain to be mentioned. Type LXXIII (no. 63:249) will be discussed with other examples below and type LXII represents a very simple rim, possibly a simplified rendering of the "collar" type. Its distinguishing feature is a deep groove about one centimeter below the top of the vessel (nos. 63:248, 64:261 and 64:281).

Only three sherds that could be classed as cooking pot rims were found in the sounding (nos. 62:213, 214; and 64:260). All of the examples are very small. A double groove on the outside is common to all of them. Unfortunately, we can say nothing about the height or shape of the pots to which these rims belong. Their profiles, however, show that they were probably in keeping with the ribbed-rim profiles of similar Palestinian pots. The sides of these vessels slanted inward and the tops of the rims are rounded, similar to the tenth to eighth century cooking pot rims in Palestine. They are not as vertical as the eighth century and later ribbed rims. Numbers 62:214 and 64:260 are basically the type of triangular rims which are common earlier in Iron I and which constitute the bulk of the three types of cooking pot rims at Deir 'Allā. Since the sherds have not been subjected to microscopic analysis, it is impossible to say specifically which Deir 'Allā type is represented in either sherd. Grooving on the Deir 'Allā rims is not deep enough to be noticeable on many of the profiles and this feature must have become common after phase L. Wright's comments on the cooking pots from 'Ain Shems indicate that the same is true at this site.[1] The earlier profile of the rim is said to continue in IIa. Several good parallels to our sherds, illustrated on pl. LXIII:33 and 34 (Grant and Wright, *AS*, IV), are attributed to IIa and early in IIb. There, "in the late tenth century or early ninth century this form is gradually displaced by one which has a grooved rim.[2] Similar rims are well illustrated at other Palestinian sites. Sherd no. 62:213 is a variation in which the curve at the inside of the rim follows the curve of the exterior of the rim. A sherd from Tell en Naṣbe illustrated on plate 47:1007 (Wampler, *Naṣbe*) provides a good parallel for this variation.

Finally, there are a number of rims which conform to a similar type and which may be early variants of cup types 3 - 5 illustrated above in figures 33 and 34. The examples shown here (nos. 63:235 and 64:275) are red-washed and burnished

sherds, but several of the painted rims (nos. 343, 344, 365 and 66:351) seem to come from vessels of a similar shape. The diameters of these vessels range from 10 to 20 cm. It is possible that they represent jar rims but the quality of the ware and the size of the rims, in relation to their diameter, make this seem unlikely. A larger portion of the profile is preserved on the decorated rim illustrated below (no. 443).

Bases

Very little modification seems to be evident in the base sherds between Periods I and II. If, in that case, one disregards the stratigraphy, it is interesting to see the distribution (see Table 6). It is important to note the very low number of ring bases as this was also the case in our Sequence I material. The percentage of flat bases is high, but not surprising. The surprising fact is the high percentage of disk bases or variants thereof — fifty-seven percent. In our Sequence II pottery, the disk base was most common and the ring base was rare. It is impossible to say that this is a peculiarity of the time range covered by our sounding, because the exposure is so limited. As we discussed above, the situation is different here from what exists at Deir 'Allā. Certainly, parallels for our disk bases exist in Palestine but the percentages are unknown.

TABLE 6.   Tabulation of Amman Citadel 1969 Sounding Base Sherds

Type	Kind of Base	Number of Sherds	Percentage of Total
1	Round base	6	3%
3	Flat base	46	30%
4	Disk base	62	36%
7	Grooved-disk base	7	3%
8	Stepped-disk base	30	18%
10	Ring base	15	9%
	Miscellaneous	3	1%
	TOTAL	169	100%

Type 4 is a very low disk base with only a slight rounding at the side (nos. 300, 305 and 315). Only a few examples were found with more pronounced rounding (nos. 65:298 and 320). In most cases, the

---

[1]Grant and Wright, *AS*, V, 138.

[2]*Ibid.*

bases have quite level bottoms but occasionally the cross-section shows a very slight concave arc (nos. 304, 307 and 321).

The only noticeable development occurs in the stepped-disk bases. Most of these bases are very shallow with a slight step, but in the later layers a number of examples show greater relief and a more pronounced step. Stepped-disk bases continue to occur through Sequence II.

The miscellaneous bases represent individual specific base types. One is a high ring base from layer 11, Period I, and is similar to the bases found earlier in the Jebel Nuzha tomb and in Madeba tomb A (JN 12, 41, 36, 42, 38; and MA 58 = figs. 21:10-14 and 23:14 respectively). Another is a flat base of a straight-sided, rectangular or square vessel, possibly like the one from which the painted corner sherd no. 65:314 came. The other base is a high ring or low pedestal foot. It is from layer 5, Period II, or later. It may have come from a bowl since it is covered with a red wash.[1]

Sherds with Painted Decoration

Since we have discussed all the other painted pottery from the Transjordan above, we will not go into detail on many of the sherds here and can limit our reference to parallels. The number of and variety of sherds with painted decoration from such a small sounding are impressive. Most of the decoration is, however, simply that of painted bands or lines.

Period I

Twice as many painted sherds were found in Period II as in Period I, but even this small number from Period I is significant. Unlike the few decorated vessels of Sequence I, the sounding sherds were primarily bichrome. Three sherds are distinguished by having their surface covered with a white slip. Two were of rather heavy ware (nos. 66:334 and 340) and had cross-hatched designs in red and black. On no. 66:334, lines of the mesh are not straight but curved. Some of the areas between the lines may have been filled with additional designs, but this has worn off to such an extent that it is impossible to interpret. The color combination corresponds to what we considered typical of Philistine pottery above, but neither sherd comes from a vessel which could be considered a common Philistine shape. Number 66:334 must come from a box-shaped or similar type of vessel. The sherd is flat and has part of a rounded corner (at the left in the illustration). The smaller sherd, no. 66:340, is an odd-shaped corner fragment. The closest parallel to this

sherd is from Tell Beit Mirsim in level B_3. It is a similar curious corner sherd with a cream slip, but only black paint was used in the cross-hatching. The larger sherd has good parallels from Chatal Hüyük in the Amuq, from area IV, where the sherds were found in an early Iron II context. One of these sherds is from a vessel with flat sides. Its painted decoration is black and red but little of the underlying slip (which is tan) shows through. A second sherd has a rounded corner and the same colors of paint are applied to a light cream surface.[2] Thus, the few parallels that can be found do not indicate that these sherds must be dated in the eleventh century when Philistine decoration was most common in Palestine.

Sherd no. 66:346 is of tan ware with white slip and black decoration. The decoration here is similar to that found on Cypriote jugs with two wide black bands framing an area of thin black lines. There are a series of black dashes, one above the other, between this decorated band and the handle of the jug. The decoration was applied in a very distinctive fashion and it is equally noticeable on the vessels which are cited as parallels. In most cases, it seems as if a wide black band was painted on the vessel and then the center was wiped out with a rough surface or comb, to leave thin black lines in reserve. The lines are not as fine and uniform as they are on Cypriote or later locally manufactured wares that are closely related to Cypriote vessels. Here the line is uneven, as if the paint had been applied unevenly with a thin, runny paint. The same effect is to be found at Megiddo,[3] Beth Shemesh,[4] Hama,[5] Tabbat al Hammam (unpublished) and Tell

---

[1] Such high-footed bowls are not represented elsewhere in the sounding and are not found in Sequence II. The rims are usually simple like that on no. 544, type XXVIII of our unstratified sherds. The popularity in the use of this bowl comes from a period when our Amman material is weak, namely, late ninth and eighth century. This bowl type seems to be popular in the ninth century at Samaria in Period III (Fawzi Zayadine, "Tomb du Fer II à Samarie — Sebaste," *RB*, LXXV [1968], figs. 5:5-7 and 6:1-3), and in the eighth century, primarily in Periods V-VI (Crowfoot, Crowfoot, and Kenyon, *SS*, III, 147). It seems to be most common in the north of Palestine.

[2] Many examples of a mesh pattern composed of red and black lines were found at Chatal Hüyük and other Amuq sites. These examples are contemporary with the sherds cited here.

[3] Guy and Engberg, *MEG T*, pl. 72:1 (from tomb 221B).

[4] Grant, *Beth Shemesh*, I, pl. XIX, tomb 11.

[5] Fugmann, *Hama Cem.*, fig. 242. The vessel illustrated comes from level E on the tell at Hama.

Ta'yinat.[1] The Beth Shemesh example may be earlier than Iron I, but it seems best to date it with the others.[2] An early tenth century date would best accommodate most of the examples.

Sherd number 66:335 is a fragment of a bowl rim with a tan surface color. There is a series of concentric bands of black, white and red paint below the rim on the inside of the vessel. The decorative pattern of a white band with black framing lines, which we above considered so typical for the Transjordan, is present already in layers 14 and 13. The surface color of these sherds is pink (14) and tan (13).[3] This decoration appears on three sherds which come from a single vessel (nos. 66:347-49). The surface of the vessel has a brown slip and is burnished. Three thin black lines were painted on the white band and a black band was painted lower down on the vessel. The appearance of this decoration on a brown-burnished surface cautions against trying to date Period I too early.

Two sherds, nos. 66:336 and 341, illustrate the color scheme popular in Palestine and Syria as a carry-over from the Late Bronze Age. The surface color is tan and the decoration consists of a band painted in a deep red color, framed by thin black lines.

Several additional decorated rim sherds were also found. Number 66:345 is a type LXXIV jar sherd which is burnished and has a red-orange surface color. Grey-black bands run around the diameter of the vessel on the top of the rim. The other two sherds, numbers 343 and 344, have short lines painted across the rim at right angles to the diameter. On number 344, only black lines are preserved because of the sherd's small size, but both red and black lines appear on number 344.

Period II

Some of the decoration on Period II sherds is similar to that on some of the Period I sherds we have mentioned above and there are some unique pieces. There is another burnished example of a jar rim, type LXXIV, no. 67:370. The paint is a deep red color. There are two bands at the base of the exterior step of the rim and painted slashes across the top of the rim. The smaller rims with painted slashes across the top, nos. 365 and 67:351, are essentially the same as the earlier ones. There are eleven examples of the white band with black lines painted on it. The largest sherds have a tan surface and the colors are subdued so that the white is faint and the black tends to grey, nos. 66:355, 67:372, 373 and 374. The last mentioned sherd is apparently a unique jar rim where the band is painted near the tip of the rim and the central white band is broken, not by

black lines, but by shadows caused by a ribbing of the surface. The top of a second decorated band is preserved at the bottom portion of this sherd.[4] The remaining body sherds with this type of decoration are darker in surface color, from brown to red-brown, the black lines are preserved as grey, and the white has almost disappeared, nos. 66:352, 358, 359; 67:366 and 373.

There are two small, horizontal-ledge rim bowl sherds with pink surface colors, which have this type of decoration preserved in brighter colors. Two sherds decorated with black and red bands were found, nos. 66:354 and 356. The latter example is curious in that the bands on this jar rim are extremely narrow and the red shades to an orange-red color. Since this decoration is so fine, it is difficult to be certain of parallels when sherds are only illustrated in photographs.

The remaining types of painted decoration did not occur in Period I. Number 67:371 illustrates a burnished sherd with a dark red slip on which a black line has been painted along the top edge of the rim. Traces of this decorative practice were found on other sherds, but this is difficult to illustrate in photographs. Such decoration is most often executed on the simple type XI or type XII bowl rims.

---

[1]This is an unpublished sherd from the second floor level of room g in Hilani I which dates to the ninth century B.C.

[2]Two earlier vessels with similar painted bands are found at Gezer (Amiran, *APHL*, p. 219, fig. 199) and Abu Hawam (Hamilton, *QDAP*, IV, 37, no. 230). The shape of these vessels, however, indicates that they are very late L.B. or very early Iron I. The paint seems thinner, less shiny, not as dark as the good L.B. imports, and they seem to indicate transitional forms which could possibly be put in the twelfth century.

[3]We have discussed above the occurrence of such decoration, with the earliest examples coming from Tell Beit Mirsim B₃ and contemporary levels elsewhere. The excavations at Tell Qasile further substantiate this early occurrence, where it appears on a jar in level X. This level is considered post-Philistine and pre-Israelite (late eleventh and early tenth century). In Iron I, this decoration seems to be popular both in Palestine and the Transjordan. There seem to be a number of examples from many Palestinian sites but it is impossible to say if, at this time, it was more common in the Transjordan. We have more examples from our sounding than have been published from any single contemporary Palestinian site. It is clear that this decoration continues to be popular in the Transjordan during Iron II, while in Palestine it is only rarely found at that time.

[4]Number 67:375 illustrates a similar ribbed rim, but from a vessel of smaller diameter. The closest parallel for such a rim in Palestine is on a jug from Tell en Naṣbe (Wampler, *Naṣbe*, pl. 38:677), but the rim diameter here is still smaller.

Several sherds have brick-red ware and surface color, and are decorated with black lines (nos. 67:361, 368 and 369). Number 67:361 is a sherd from the neck of a jug. Such a profile has not yet been found on a complete vessel. The same shape and decoration appear at Bethel.[1] The other two sherds are bowl sherds with concentric bands on the inside. Similar decoration has been discussed above as quite frequent early in Iron I. The difference is that, unlike the early bowls, where dark bands are painted on a light-colored ware, the surface color of the late Iron I examples is dark. In our case, it is brick red and has a smooth surface which, however, is not burnished. The red is a deeper, more even color than is found on the red bowls discussed above. A similar bowl is again found at Bethel (fig. 65:34), but better examples are found at Tell Beit Mirsim,[2] where the ware is medium to dark brown with dark red paint (apparently like our no. 67:370). One of the Tell Beit Mirsim sherds is said to be lightly burnished, while the other two are said to be wet-smoothed. The latter would be similar to the technique applied to our sherds. The Tell Beit Mirsim sherds are dated to level B$_3$, while the Bethel sherds are merely considered Iron I without further discussion.

One sherd, no. 66:353, represents a change from the predominantly banded decoration we have discussed. It is impossible to say what was represented and whether it was more than a geometric design. The paint is the same as we have seen on some of the sherds above. It is deep red on a tan surface and there are two patches of white paint. Another unique sherd is no. 66:350, which seems to be a jar sherd. The ware is tan, but the paint, which covers the top of the rim, is purple and the area covered by this paint is burnished.

Finally, the remaining sherds are once more band painted but they seem to represent, though weakly, a still different tradition from any discussed above (nos. 66:360 and 67:363, and one unillustrated sherd). These sherds have a cream to white slip upon which are painted red bands (bright medium red) bordered by grey-black lines. The color combination is similar to sherds nos. 66:334 and 340 discussed above. This all brings to mind the painted pottery on a white slip which was noted by Olávarri at Aro'er, but unfortunately not illustrated in his preliminary report.[3] If that is the case, we have to deal here with a little known variety of pottery in the Transjordan and the similarity of the color combination, if our sherds are indicative, to Philistine pottery may prove significant either for cultural influences or chronological purposes. The dating for the *floruit* of Philistine pottery is usually considered late twelfth through eleventh century, with few examples of the characteristic wares occur-

ring later. The band painting and cross-hatched painting on thick vessels are, however, not characteristic of Philistine pottery. We may have to deal with a tradition influenced from the coast, but well established as a component of the local Transjordanian repertory.

Miscellaneous Shapes and Types of Decoration

Number 67:376 is a portion of a trough spout. The spout is open at its attachment to the body of the vessel and there is no strainer produced by perforating the vessel wall where the spout is attached. Unlike the strainer spouts discussed above, such spouts are quite rare.[4] Numbers 67:378 and 380 are the legs of tripod bowls. Number 67:379 represents a pinched knob handle placed just below the rim of a bowl which is shown in section.

Numbers 67:377, 381-398 illustrate sherds with incised or impressed decoration. Number 67:381 is a small buff-ware sherd with an incised grid pattern. Number 67:393 is a red-burnished sherd with an applied clay ring. This is not a base, but apparently decoration applied to the wall of a fairly large vessel. Number 67:394 has three rows of impressed decoration in a unique pattern. Number 67:395 is the portion of a "collar-type" jar rim bearing three incised circles and possibly the edge of a fourth. It is curious that this decoration, which one would expect to be unique, actually has a number of Palestinian parallels. It occurs on similar rims from Gibeah[5] and Seilun (Shiloh).[6] A similar sherd was also found on the surface of Tell Safut not far from Amman and also at Sahab.[7]

It is, of course, impossible to say at present whether these were decorations or purposefully executed signs. A considerable number of such signs are illustrated among our sherds and were

---

[1]Kelso, *Bethel*, pl. 39:33.

[2]Albright, *TBM*, I, pl. 30:25 and 26.

[3]A published example of such decoration seems to be illustrated in Glueck, *EEP*, I, pl. 23:20.

[4]They appear in the Amuq and elsewhere, but often with a dark red-burnished slip on vessels which are Anatolian or strongly influenced from that area. Our example is buff colored with no special surface finish.

[5]Sinclair, *Gibeah*, pl. 20:2.

[6]Hans Kjaer, "The Excavation of Shiloh 1929," *JPOS*, X (1930), 101, fig. 8, and 108, fig. 11.

[7]See reference on p. 97, footnote 4.

found on handles, bases and rims. There is no need to describe these further as they are clear on the photographs.

The letter *'aleph* is clear on no. 67:392 and a *taw* (if that is what was actually intended rather than a simple x) on no. 67:387. What looks like the letter *shin* on several rim sherds (nos. 67:385, 388, 390 and 396) is actually quite doubtful. It may instead be part of a numerical system with V providing one numeral and a simple line another. In several cases, especially number 67:390, the two V's seem intended as separate signs. Number 67:386 is a simple line, and on one of the sherds from the sounding we clearly have VI. The small conical holes (and similarly the incised circles on the "collar-type" jar rim mentioned above) may have been designed for similar numerical usage.[1]

Additional signs which were found on sherds from Area III are illustrated as no. 68:401.[2] Two sherds with the remains of inscriptions were found. Number 68:399 is a jar handle, which originally had an inscription indicating ownership: "---ח‎ל‎," belonging to Ḥ---," where only the first letter of the name is preserved. This sherd was found in layer 5c and belongs to Period II. Numer 68:400 was found in layer 4, a post-Period II context. The inscription is incised on the inside of a bowl with a step-disk base (type 8). Again, we seem to be dealing with names and only the center two letters can be read with relative certainty: "...(?)‎ן‎צ‎(צ‎)...," name x (ending in *ṣadê*), son of name..." It is interesting that the Phoenician-Hebrew form *ben* is used here and not the Aramaic *bar*.

Three handles illustrate the placements of thumb impressions at the point where they join the vessels. A number of such marks and signs are present in almost every excavated late Iron I site in Palestine. The sherd, no. 67:389 is the pierced disk base of a bowl.

Two other types of sherds which were also found in the sounding must be mentioned here. The first is a sherd of black-burnished ware. None of this pottery was found in either Period I or II but the sherd was found in a post-Period II locus. We have no evidence, then, for extending this decorative practice earlier than the middle of the ninth century B.C. The other type is illustrated by body sherds decorated with parallel incised lines. Such sherds are found only in Period II.

Area III Iron Age Sherds

The sherds found in the Iron Age levels of Area III seem, on preliminary examination, to correspond exactly with those which we discussed from Area II. Many of the jar rims LX, LXIII, LXIV, LXVI, LXXI, LXXIII, LXXIV, and LXXV are present as well as characteristic bowl rims II, XI, XII, and XXIV. The same range of base types was found, as well as the small legs for tripod-based cups. The variety of painted decoration was more restricted but no new type was found. One unique piece was the leg of a red-burnished, probably three-legged, bowl.

---

[1]It is curious that among our signs we can illustrate I, V, X, and M, and one wonders if this may not be more than a coincidental similarity to the Roman system of numbers.

[2]These are illustrated here with the permission of Mr. Mohammad Odeh of the Department of Antiquities of Jordan.

CHAPTER VIII

UNSTRATIFIED SHERDS FROM THE
AMMAN CITADEL
(JEBEL EL QALA')

Find Spots

We have alluded above to the sherd material presented in this chapter. Many of the types presented here were illustrated as complete vessels in our corpus. A number of types, however, were not represented there or were represented by isolated examples. In this chapter, we will document a considerable portion of the unstratified sherds collected from the Amman Citadel. The amount of variation within each type is well illustrated. A few types found in the corpus were not present but it is clear from the material presented here that many of the types found in tombs do not represent specialized tomb pottery, but are found as occupation debris on the citadel. Since most of the sherds to be discussed here are unstratified, we will not attach a list of find spots or loci, where they are available, but deal with them entirely on a typological basis. The writer spent a good deal of time on the site from September, 1968, to May, 1969, in excavation and exploration, and this material was gathered both during formal excavation and informally during that time. In our discussion, we will bring in the published sherds from elsewhere in the Transjordan and arrange our discussions, as much as possible, according to parallels with our two sequences and our 1969 citadel sounding.

During the fall of 1968, a modest joint excavation was undertaken on Jebel el Qala' by the American Schools of Oriental Research, the University of Jordan, and the Department of Antiquities of Jordan. The co-directors of the expedition were myself, Dr. Ida Suliman, and Dr. Fawzi el Fakharani. Mr. Safwan et Tel was the representative of the Department of Antiquities. The squares excavated by the joint expedition are shown on the site plan, figure 4, as Areas IV to VII. Only one good pre-Hellenistic locus was encountered, despite the fact that bedrock was reached in every area (not every square) of excavation. In the Roman Temple Area, bedrock was reached in both Temple Trenches I and III (equal Areas V and IV respectively). Considerable Iron Age and earlier pottery was found, but all of it came from mixed fills.

In the series of squares excavated on the second plateau (Area VII), we went down to bedrock against the foundation wall of an early Byzantine building. Unfortunately, the foundations of this building also went down to bedrock and little of the earlier levels had been left undisturbed in the area we were able to excavate. In our other area of excavation, we cleared most of square S.E. 8-15 and 16 down to bedrock (Area VI). Several channels were found cut into the bedrock. These led to a bag-shaped cistern that was hollowed out of bedrock. Most of the capstones were still in place over the cistern and sealed with a thick red-orange clay. This locus, the original sealing of the cistern, contained only Iron II pottery. The cistern was a disappointment in one respect, namely, all the original water channels had been blocked, a new opening had been created, and most of the debris that had collected in the original use of the cistern, or immediately following that use, had been removed when the cistern was cleaned out and replastered. The vessels found in the cistern dated to the third and second century B.C. Only sherds of earlier periods were found, some of which were embedded in the final plaster coating. A number of Iron Age walls were encountered at one of the corners of this square but all the floors and associated layers had been disturbed by pits and later burials.

A considerable amount of the pottery we are illustrating here was found while a pay-loader was widening a section of the road (the area is marked "road cut" on fig. 4) which cuts across the citadel. My excavation foreman, Mustafa Tawfiq; two volunteers, William Dornemann and John Parssinen; and myself aided the Department of Antiquities inspector, Mohammad Abu Saleh, in watching the progress of the work, collecting pottery, and steering the work clear of stratified deposits. Huge Hellenistic and Roman tipped fills were encountered in most of the area and, fortunately, stratified occupational debris was encountered in only a few places. Most of these areas contained house walls of the Iron Age.

The majority of the unstratified sherds is contemporary with Sequence II. A few of the types are contemporary with our 1969 sounding pottery, and nothing can be placed earlier. The wares of all normal-thickness vessels are fairly consistent. They are fired to a uniform color across the cross sections of the sherds. The colors range from an occasional orange-brown to an occasional dark brown, with the greatest percentage of the wares being light brown to tan. Exceptions to this are the black and light cream wares which are discussed separately below. Normally, a fairly high percentage of white, apparently limestone, grit is used. In the sherds of heavier wares, and on the unburnished or hand-burnished sherds, the surface is usually pock-marked, apparently by the eruption of the surface as these grits expanded during firing. This could be observed occasionally on wheel-burnished vessels, but usually between the burnish lines or where the burnish was applied before the vessel was sufficiently dry (causing a smeared burnish). In the very thin wares, grit is still often used but it is finer and less noticeable. This may be a result of the change to a cleaner clay more suitable for use on the fast wheel. Several examples of late Iron Age wares are included and the composition of the clay contrasts sharply with that which was used earlier. The colors are lighter (light pink, light orange, or yellow) and the clay is very finely levigated.

Bowl Types

Types Contemporary with Sequence I and the Amman Citadel 1969 Sounding

The number of sherds which fall into this time range is quite limited (nos. 502-509, 511; 72:510). Most frequent among them are sherds with the simple rim profile of type XI. All but one of these sherds (no. 507) are burnished and only this sherd and no. 508 have a red to red-orange slip. The red slip argues against a dating much earlier than the materials from the 1969 sounding. Type XI bowls are present through the middle range of Sequence II, but the hand burnishing indicates a date well before the end of this range. The sherds of type XII (like no. 512) are also hand-burnished and red-washed, so the argument for their dating is identical with that of type XI.

The type XIV sherd, no. 511, is very distinctive but presently has no Transjordanian counterpart. The same profile with heavy ribbing was found at Bethel[1] and is attributed to Iron I. A similar dating for our sherd is most likely.

We have mentioned bowl types I and II in our discussion of the 1969 sounding and particularly the Sequence II material (p. 50). There is variety in the burnishing, nos. 476 and 481 being hand burnished, number 475 hand polished, and numbers 474, 477, 478, 479, 480, 483 and 71:482 wheel burnished. The wash and burnish are applied only on the inside and just over the edge of the rim on the wheel-burnished examples, as is illustrated in numbers 480 and 71:482. Since wheel burnishing was extremely rare in Periods I and II of the 1969 sounding, most of these rims must be placed in Sequence II, probably in the middle and late ranges (as indicated by the Amman C, E, Sahab B, and Meqabelein occur-

rences). The down curve in the type I rims, nos. 474, 475 and 477, supports the late date, as the best parallels are from Meqabelein (nos. 45 and 46) and Amman E (no. 154). We can illustrate several examples of such type I, low, straight-sided bowls or plates, numbers 474, 475 and 477 and an example found in our 1969 Amman sounding, no. 61:134.

In the discussion of the sounding sherds, we considered a number of rim types that were basically variants of types XXIV and XXV. None of the same variant types are represented among the unstratified sherds, but several other variants as well as examples of the main types XXIV and XXV are present. Numbers 532, 533, 536, 538; 73:535 and 537 illustrate type XXIV. The knob below the rim, the ware, and profile indicate that no. 73:537 is probably contemporary with the sounding but it is blackened by fire so the burnish is obscured. Type XVIII rims., nos. 528 and 529, have profiles which are basically similar to that of type XXIV but each has a groove below the exterior ledge at the top of the rim. The color and ware are similar to that of the 1969 sounding sherds but they are thicker than the type XXIV and XXV sherds and are not burnished. The type XIX rim, no. 530, is also a thicker sherd which was not fired to a uniform color throughout its cross section. It has a grey core, and a tan surface, and has been wheel burnished.[2] There is no conclusive evidence in the way of parallels to secure the date of these rims precisely but, on analogy with the sherds discussed immediately above, an early-middle Sequence II date seems most plausible.

Number 539 is a wheel-burnished, red-washed example of type XXVI. The burnishing indicates that it is later than the sherd of this type from the 1969 sounding (number 62:182). The profile is much more clearly defined here than in the sounding sherd and is clearly parallel to the bowl rim from Amman tomb C, no. 39 (= fig. 41:10).[3] The dating of our sherd and that from Amman C seem to coincide. The examples of rim type XXVII exhibit a similar inturned rim (nos. 540-542 and 73:543), but with a different profile which did not appear in the 1969 sounding.[4] This

---

[1] Kelso, *Bethel*, pl. 40:13 and 18.

[2] This thick-ware sherd has good parallels at Umm el Biyara (Bennett, *UB*, figs. 3:2, 4, 15; and 4).

[3] Sahab B:20 (= fig. 41:8) is slightly different in profile (the rib being separated more from the rim) but is close enough to be classed as type XXVI also.

[4] A somewhat similar rim, however, was found in Period II of the 1969 sounding but it seems to have belonged to a jar. No rib is illustrated on this sherd and the groove below the rim is small and sharp.

profile currently is found only infrequently in the Transjordan, but is very common in Palestine. In Palestine,[1] the rim does not turn in as far as our examples, the bowl usually seems to be deeper, and the rib beneath the rim is almost always absent. The date range in Palestine is not very precise, as such bowls are found throughout Iron II. Both rim types XXVI and XXVII, illustrated here, seem to show Transjordanian (or possibly just Ammonite) peculiarities. The exaggerated incurve and the exterior rib beneath the rim are features which are common on the type 3 cups and on the types LXVII and LXVIII jar rims (which are found only infrequently elsewhere).

Two other rim types of quite simple profile, types XVII (nos. 525-527 and 73:524) and XLV (no. 549), seem to fall in the time range of the sherds which we are discussing in this section. Palestinian parallels within this time range could be cited, but the simplicity of the rims makes reliance on such parallels doubtful. None of the rims are burnished.

Finally, there is a single example of rim type XXVIII (no. 544). No examples of this simple pointed bowl rim with upturned, near vertical, sides were found in the 1969 sounding. Bowls with a less sharp angle appeared in Irbed (IA, 10; IB, 3-5, = figs. 21:24, 23, 22, and 20:25 respectively) and represent earlier versions of this type.[2] This rim seems to be most popular in Palestine during the ninth and eighth centuries B.C., but it usually had a much longer vertical side and less pointed rim. Our sherd here, then, seems to fall beween the earlier and later types, which would place it contemporary with the 1969 sounding or slightly later (i.e., mid-ninth century).[3]

Bowl Types Which Appear in Red-, Black-, and Cream-Burnished Wares

The majority of our unstratified bowl sherds fall into this category. We have cited above, in the discussion of Sequence II tombs from the Amman district, four of the five types to be considered here. The few examples of types XV and XLVI-XLVIII are enough to establish their position in the middle and late ranges. Very few examples of these rims are, at present, found outside of the Amman district. For most of these types, we have illustrated a considerable number of profiles and photographs since they are currently so poorly documented. This evidence clearly demonstrates the complete overlap between the red and black-burnished sherds of these types. In fact, almost all of the black-burnished rims have exact parallels in red-burnish. The burnish in all cases is wheel burnish, but in some cases the burnish

lines have become broad and/or have unburnished areas between them. There are only a few examples of the cream-colored ware and it does not seem to be present in the published material. We have only four sherds of such ware; three are of type XLVII and one of type XLVI. The intentional color variation on these bowls indicates considerable sophistication in the firing techniques, matching the sophistication evident in the mastery of the potter's wheel which is evident in other forms. The black bowls (and the other shapes to be discussed below) are of a very dark grey or black ware. In most cases, the white grits normal in the red-burnished bowls occur here also. In a few cases, the clay is better levigated and has little grit inclusion. The surface color is usually dark grey where the surface was not burnished. It seems that the black and red bowls were identical in ware and burnishing technique, and that the difference between them was the result of firing in a reducing or oxidizing atmosphere respectively. All four light cream-colored sherds are wheel burnished and identical in color of surface as well as core. Two sherds are of very fine, clean ware while the other two are of normal ware. Again, the color difference here was a result of the firing process. Apparently, an oxidizing atmosphere was created in the kiln but higher firing temperatures were also used than were normal for the red and black bowls. The type XV and XLVII bowls were found in the middle range of Sequence II and types XLVIII and XLVI only in the late range.

---

[1]Albright, *TBM*, I, pls. 61-63; III, pls. 22 and 23. Kelso, *Bethel*, pls. 62:2-16; 63:22; and 64:1 and 2. Lamon and Shipton, *MEG*, I, pls. 25:64, 65; 27:84, and numerous other examples. Examples closer to some of the Palestinian bowls were found at Dhiban, Reed and Winnett, *Dhiban*, I, pl. 74:7 and 8.

[2]A similar bowl was found in Str. III at 'Ain Shems, Grant and Wright, *AS*, IV, pl. LXXI:20, and is dated Iron Ia-b by Wright.

[3]The absence in the 1969 sounding of high-ring or low pedestal bases of sizes that are usually found on these bowls, also argues against the presence of this type of bowl. It is not out of the question that these bowls are contemporary at least with Period II of our sounding, since the earliest Samaria examples come from tombs. The sherds of this type found in excavations on the tell come from Str. VI-IV which agree in date with similar sherds from Tell Far'ah (north) in period II (dated by de Vaux as 800-722 B.C.), de Vaux, *RB*, LIX (1952), 569, fig. 8:6 and 13.

Rim Type XV

The only example of the type XV rim found in Sequence II is no. 6 from Sahab B (= fig. 32:42). The ware and color are interesting in that the ware seems to be that of our black-burnished sherds, but the black surface color appeared only on the interior of the bowl while the exterior was pink. We shall see a similar color combination on sherds discussed below, and this peculiarity is also illustrated on a number of other vessels from the middle and late ranges of Sequence II. Many of the black-burnished bowl rims of this type are from small bowls (nos. 516, 518 and 73:521-23), as is the case for the Sahab example. Only one larger sherd is black burnished (no. 513) and has a bar which is much wider than on the other examples. Two black-burnished sherds are from deeper bowls, nos. 513 and 517. One heavy ware sherd with a red wash has very low sides and a broad, wide bar (no. 514), bowls are of thicker ware and enough was preserved of the section of two of them to show that the sides of these bowls are quite low. Both examples (nos. 516 and 73:522) are of the usual tan ware, have a brick-red color slip, and are not burnished. The first has a flattened bar and the second has patches of black.[1] Rims of this type are occasionally found on bowls with bar handles. If such handles are not considered, the parallels are few. The best example of a rim parallel to ours comes from Tell en Naṣbe.[2]

A question concerning the significance of the black-burnished bowls is raised by the finding of the fragment of a grey marble bowl, probably of local stone, in 1969 in the road cut. The rim on this bowl, no. 805, is identical with the type under discussion. The shape of this bowl, with its short sides, corresponds to the shape of sherds nos. 515 and 518. The surface of the bowl has been polished to a lustrous sheen. The existence of basalt bowls imitating the typical profile of red-burnished Iron Age II bowls is attested in Palestine. A particularly close example to our fragment was found at Tell el Qiṭaf near Beth Shan and was also dated late in the Neo-Assyrian period.[3] The question which comes to mind in relation to this bowl is: is the black-burnished ware actually an imitation of vessels in dark stone? We have already discussed this question to some extent above in the treatment of the black-burnished bowl of type IX from tomb Amman C. The evidence presented in this section indicates that the possibility for an affirmative answer is very good.[4]

Rim Type XLVII

Two examples of this rim type were also found in Sahab B, numbers 14 and 15 (= fig. 33:24 and 25). Interestingly enough, number 14 is of buff ware with traces of burnishing, while number 15 is black and has circular burnishing. The variations of the rounded, out-curved rims of this type are illustrated as nos. 584-95; 75:596. The other features which occur frequently are a flattened, near vertical end to the rim and impressed grooves either on this flat end or just below the curve of the rim on the outside. The latter feature is a degeneration of the burnishing technique. Only one example of the black-burnished technique is found here, no. 591, but there are cream-colored sherds, nos. 589, 594 and 74:596. The remaining sherds have the usual tan ware with red slips ranging in color from orange-red to brick-red. The profiles of sherds nos. 590, 591 and 593 are close to those of sherds illustrated from Tell el Kheleifeh, level IV, even though these sherds belong to jars.[5] The angle of our rims is different, but otherwise the profiles are close and the ribbing is also present.[6]

---

[1] The latter peculiarity is evident on a number of sherds of type XLVI, but it is difficult to say what caused the paint to be so flaky and varying in color and, also, whether this was created intentionally.

[2] Wampler, *Naṣbe*, pl. 63:1443. Also, see the article by Amiran cited in the next footnote for similar profiles on basalt and pottery bowls.

[3] Ruth Amiran, "A Late Assyrian Stone Bowl from Tell el Qiṭaf in the Bet-She'an Valley," *Atiqot*, I-II (1955-1959), 129-32. A second example was much more elaborate than the one cited above. It had tripod feet formed as bull's feet, which merged into duck heads that ran up the side of the bowl. Both bowls are considered as: "not only Assyrian in style, but were imported into Palestine from Assyria or from an Assyrian province."

[4] It should also be noted that the base on this stone bowl is a double-stepped disk, which we saw in the 1969 sounding and will see as quite common in the Amman district in our discussion of bases below. Sherd no. 514 also had a similar base. The inner disk is not shown in the profile but its start is evident at the edge of the sherd.

[5] Glueck, *BASOR*, CLXXXVIII, Part I, 19, fig. 5:5 and 11.

[6] The profiles of the sherds illustrated as nos. 586 and 587, in particular, have a wider popularity. As is the case with the type XLVIII rims below, several good parallels can be found which must date around 600 B.C. (see p. 109). Crowfoot, Crowfoot, and Kenyon, *SS*, III, 126, fig. 11:16 (period VII) and Joseph Naveh, "The Excavations at Meṣad Ḥashavyahu—Preliminary Report," *IEJ*, XII (1962), 101, fig. 4:3. Transjordanian parallels are illustrated in Glueck, *EEP*, II, pl. 23:2, 17-19.

Rim Type VI

No parallels exist for this rim type so we cannot give it a more precise date range than that covered by the black-burnished bowls. The black-burnished example (no. 498) has an almost exact counterpart in red-burnish (no. 499).

Rim Type XLVIII

Most of the bowls of this type are low and, like a number of the XLVII bowls, have short sides. The rims are much more of a ledge than is the case for type XLVII bowls, and the tops of the rims are rounded. The ends of the rims always extend considerably beyond the sides of the bowls, while in type XLVII the diameter at the end of the rim is about equal to that of the greatest diameter on the side of the bowl. The sherd, no. 601 is the only black-burnished example in the group. Numbers 597-600 have red-burnished surfaces while the others are tan, with 598 having brown beneath the spaced burnish lines and no. 599 being burnished only on the inside. A low-sided bowl of this type, close to nos. 599 and 600, was found at Meqabelein (no. 64, = fig. 33:27). The type XLIX bowl, AN:68 (= fig. 33:26), is a distinctive profile but also very similar to the bowls we have just cited.

A number of parallels can be found at the few Palestinian sites on which the late seventh and sixth centuries B.C. are well represented. The best parallels are from Meṣad Ḥashavyahu,[1] level V at Engedi,[2] and Stratum III at Beth Zur.[3] A similar small bowl was found at Chatal Hüyük[4] and is the best example of the black-burnished ware found at any of the Amuq sites (see below for the examples from Tell Ta'yinat). The upper surface of the rim is decorated around the circumference by a continuous row of incised concentric circles. This is currently the only Syrian parallel for such a bowl, but similar bowls also appear in Cyprus at Salamis and are dated primarily around 600 B.C.[5]

Rim Type XLVI

Many more examples of this type of bowl were found in the Amman district tombs than any other type discussed in this section. All the examples, as the corpus shows, come from Amman N and the Meqabelein tomb. The number of our illustrated sherd examples (nos. 447, 550-56, 558-68, 573-76, 579-83; 56:570; 74:557, 569-72, 577 and 578) indicates a similar popularity for this bowl type on the Amman Citadel. Many of the sherd profiles bear some resemblance to sherds of other types, chiefly type XLV, but all of them are characterized best by the label, "step-rim." Most of the red-burnished rims need no special mention as they conform to the same range of color, ware, and burnish that we have stated above as normal for the sherds in this section. Two sherds, nos. 562 and 576, show the peculiarity which we noted above for no. 73:521, namely, the slip is flaking off in an abnormal manner and the color of the slip is uneven, with streaks of black and red. The black-burnished sherds are shown as nos. 555, 557-60, 563, 577 and 580, and number 578 is the one cream-burnished sherd.

We have been able, in this section, to cite only a few Palestinian parallels. The same is true for type XLVI rims and our only good Palestinian parallel is from Gerar. It is published with a plate full of Assyrian period bowls dated around 700 B.C. Several other bowls on this plate come close in profile to our "step-rim" but are actually closer to type XLVII rims. No black-burnished ware is mentioned, but "creamy-white" is.[6] A rim of similar profile was also found at Deir 'Allā in the Jordan Valley.[7] Syrian parallels are more numerous. Similar rims appear among the sherds from Tabbat al Hammam,[8] where their ware and surface color are orange-tan and they are wheel burnished inside and out. Similar sherds are found in the Amuq at Tell Ta'yinat in the latest Iron Age levels. Almost all of the examples were of red to

---

[1]Naveh, *IEJ*, XII, 101, fig. 4, no. 6. The examples with a similar shape, but with the ledge of the rim bent down against the side of the bowl, nos. 9, 11-13 on the same figure, are more common in Palestine.

[2]Mazar, Dothan, and Dunayevsky, *Atiqot*, V, 63, fig. 15:2.

[3]Sellers, *et al.*, *BZ*, fig. 18:1-4.

[4]Registered sherd b518 from the surface of Area IV.

[5]Vassos Karageorghis, *Excavations in the Necropolis of Salamis*, I ("Republic of Cyprus, Ministry of Communications and Works, Department of Antiquities, Salamis," Vol. III; Nikosia: Published for the Republic of Cyprus by the Department of Antiquities, 1967), pl. CXXV:31, 83, 118 (other similar bowls, but with less rounded rims, are also found in Tomb 3, which is dated around 600 B.C.), pl. CXXXIII:42 (the only example from tomb 31, and also the earliest, placed in the first half of the seventh century B.C.), and pl. CXLIX:145, 148-50, and 155 (from tomb 50 and dated early in the sixth century B.C.). The one example from tomb 31 should possibly be placed as late as possible since the great concentration of such bowls seems to fall in tombs that date several decades on either side of 600 B.C.

[6]Petrie, *Gerar*, pl. LXV:17 and pp. 23-24.

[7]Glueck, *EEP*, IV, pl. 132:7.

[8]Area X, level 4.

orange-burnished ware, but one, from floor 1 in Area XIII, is identical to our no. 578 and is of equally fine cream-burnished ware. Furthermore, Ta'yinat is important for the sherds under discussion in this section since, in the same late levels just mentioned, the equivalents of our Amman black-burnished sherds also occur. Again, the overlap within certain types of black and red-burnished bowls is clear, but the black sherds are not numerous.[1] The presence of the cream-colored sherd with an exact correspondence in profile indicates that the sophistication and experimentation evident at Amman is not confined to that area, but is an indication of the general level of ceramic technology in the seventh and sixth centuries B.C.

The existence of the black and cream-burnished bowls in the Transjordan, of the types mentioned here, is poorly attested outside of the Amman district.[2] There are two possible reasons for this: first, such bowls are confined to the Amman district and, second, the Amman district habitation layers and tomb deposits from which they came are later than the material published so far from other sites. The lack of such sherds so far at Umm el Biyara and Tell el Kheleifeh argues that regional variation must play some role. The presence of such sherds in the Amuq suggests a possible connection with the north. The absence of such sherds at any site which was occupied to the end of the eighth century, but not later, indicates that these special types were first produced around 700 B.C. No such sherds were found at Tell er Rumeith which is said to have been abandoned around 733 B.C.[3] Both possibilities mentioned above may, then, prove to be partially correct.[4] Tell Deir 'Allā was inhabited down to the fifth century, but we must await more information on the pottery from that site to know whether the sherd types in question here appear that far west.[5]

Thin-Walled Bowl Sherds

Most of the bowl types in this section have been discussed in detail in the Sequence II and Amman sounding chapters. Therefore, little more than a brief description of additional examples is necessary here. Bowl types IV and V are illustrated on nos. 487-89, 492-97; 72:490 and 491; all sherds are of tan ware, have a red slip, and show fine wheel burnishing. The range of both types was seen to be the middle and late ranges of Sequence II, with type V probably beginning earlier. No parallels can presently be shown to exist elsewhere, but several bowls at Tell el Kheleifeh may belong to type IV. It is a distinct possibility that these bowls, particularly

type IV, are the forerunners of the later, thin-ware Nabataean bowls.

The sherd, no. 501, is an isolated example of rim type X. Only one example of such a bowl (MA 25 = fig. 32:34) has been found outside of the Amman district, where the examples clearly fall within the late range of Sequence II. The surface treatment of such bowls varied. In some cases, they were red or brown burnished, one had more elaborate decoration, and the rest had no particular surface finish. Our sherd is of tan-colored ware with few grits and has a grey and brown surface color which is mat and without burnish.

The sherd, no. 545, type XXIX, is thicker than the sherds mentioned so far in this section. Its ware and surface are cream-colored, but not as light as the special sherds mentioned in the previous section. The fineness of the ware suggests that this bowl falls very late in the Iron Age, probably Persian period, but no good parallels can be cited.

The sherd, no. 548, type XXXVIII, is presently

---

[1]Only a few examples are present in the sherd collection at the Oriental Institute of the University of Chicago, but the expedition records indicate a noticeable quantity of such sherds in the latest Iron Age levels. Most of the Ta'yinat examples do not have the dark colors that are present in Amman and tend more to a grey color. The similarity with the technique of the Amman sherds is quite clear, however.

[2]See p. 120, footnote 1, for discussion of recently published pottery from Heshbon.

[3]Lapp, *RB*, LXXV, 98. The late Dr. Paul W. Lapp examined a number of the black-burnished sherds from Amman illustrated here and stated that he had not found similar sherds at Tell er Rumeith.

[4]Two black ware bowls are illustrated among the sherds from Buseirah, Bennett, *Levant*, VII, 8, fig. 5:6 and 10. The profiles are similar to our type XXIV, particularly no. 158 but this profile did not occur in black-burnished ware in Amman or Heshbon (as published to date, see below). If the Buseirah black ware bowls correspond to our black-burnished ware, it is important to see such bowls occurring so far south and apparently in pre-seventh century B.C. context. We await further information on the range of forms occurring in this ware, their frequency of occurrence and their chronological range, so that we can compare them to the Amman and Heshbon materials.

[5]Franken, *VT*, XVII, 480. A recent preliminary report on the renewed excavations at Deir 'Allā illustrates a black-burnished bowl with a profile similar to our type XLIX, as well as a similar bowl in orange-burnished ware. Several other late Iron Age vessels are illustrated from level III (apparently fifth century B.C.), including a decanter, a bowl of our type X and a handleless jar; Henk J. Franken and Moawiyah M. Ibrahim, "Two Seasons of Excavations at Tell Deir 'Allā, 1976-1978," *ADAJ*, XXII (1977-1978), 57-80.

the sole example of the "Assyrian period" bowl best illustrated at Tell Far'ah (north) and at Tell el Kheleifeh. This sherd is a typical example of such bowls in that it has grey-brown ware and surface color, and has wheel burnishing both inside and outside. The burnishing lines are spaced, with unburnished areas in between. Parallels for this bowl type are indicated on p. 175.

The bowl type XXXVII (no. 547) is more closed than any of the other bowls considered among the unstratified sherds. Amman A:18, figure 33:9, is the only Transjordanian parallel. No good parallels can be cited from Palestine, but good parallels can be found as far away as Tarsus and the Amuq. The Chatal Hüyük examples are of Iron II date and the Tarsus examples are dated to the sixth century B.C.[1]

Miscellaneous and Late Types

The bowl type XXXI (no. 546) has an elaborate profile that must be classed by itself. No parallels exist for such a bowl. The ware and flaking slip, however, are identical to those described above for the sherds illustrated on nos. 516, 521, 562 and 576; thus, we may date it to Sequence II.

We have discussed above, pages 86-87, the decoration on the bowl which is classed as type XXXIV, no. 70:446. The surface color, ware color, and fine levigation of the ware are similar to that of the Persian period. The decoration indicates that it should not be placed very late in that period, at least until the Persian period is better documented.

One of the latest Iron Age II bowl types that has been found so far in Amman is type VII, no. 500. This is the bowl which is usually considered to be characteristic of the Persian period. Recently the date of such bowls has been pushed back slightly and they must be considered to have come into use in the Neo-Babylonian period.[2] It seems doubtful that they can be brought far back into the Neo-Assyrian period. We can conservatively date these rims to the sixth century B.C. Number 500 is made of the creamy-white ware and is burnished.

Jars, Deep Bowls, and Other Rim Sherds

Unlike the bowl rims, curiously, most of the jar rims seem to fall within Sequence I and primarily in the range of our 1969 sounding. The remaining shapes do not cluster at any particular time and are only represented. We have discussed above (pages 89 and 95) the difficulties of ascertaining, in many cases, the complete shape to which these rims belong and that this makes classification of sherds and whole vessels in one typology impossible. Many of the profiles illustrated here have been dealt with in detail above, so our discussion in most cases will be kept to a minimum. We will first discuss rim types which appeared in the 1969 sounding. In this discussion, we will follow the order in which types were presented above (pp. 94-103) to facilitate cross-reference. This will be followed by a discussion of other rims which are related to this group but not found in the 1969 sounding. Finally, we will discuss later rim types.

Rim Types Present in the 1969 Sounding

Some, but not all, of the sherds to be discussed in this section are actually contemporary with the 1969 sounding material. The remainder are later examples which illustrate the longevity of some of the sounding types.

Types LXIV and LXX

The double-grooved rim, type LXIV, is illustrated as nos. 657-59. The ware and burnish are finer than the 1969 sounding examples. All of the examples are nicely wheel-burnished, have orange-brown slips on normal tan wares and have the typical double groove on the exterior surface of the rim. The stances of the rims vary from an inward tilt, no. 658 to an outward tilt, no. 657. No examples of such rims have been found among the Sequence II vessels, so this type may have gone out of use during the eighth century B.C.

The type LXX rims are represented by number 682. It has a rib at both, top and bottom, on the outside of the rim, with a slight groove inside each rib.

Type LXIII

A majority of our examples are of tan ware and surface color, nos. 650, 651, 654-56; 77:649, 652

---

[1]Goldman, *Tarsus*, III, Plates, pl. 87:1214 (which is band painted) and pl. 88:1243 (which is wheel burnished).

[2]A date not far removed from 600 B.C. has been argued for such bowls from Engedi (Mazar, Dothan, and Dunayevsky, *Atiqot* V, 65, fig. 16:1 and 2), Meṣad Ḥashavyahu (Naveh, *IEJ*, XII, 101, fig. 4:16 and 17), and Salamis (Karageorghis, *Salamis*, I, pl. CXXV:4, 6, 144, from tomb 3).

and 653. Three of these have an accentuated depression between rim and body, numbers 651; 77:652 and 653. Number 77:649 is black burnished but the ware is a light greyish-tan, rather than the deep grey of the sherds discussed above. Of the remaining three examples, nos. 654-56, the first two are wheel burnished with brick-red and orange slips respectively. Number 654 is very similar to the rim from sub-layer 5d of the 1969 sounding, except for the wheel burnish. Number 656 has a different surface treatment. The core of the sherd is dark grey with medium amounts of various sizes of sand grits. The burnish lines are spaced as we have seen frequently on late Iron II sherds. The unburnished portions of the surface are red-orange in color while the wider burnished areas shade from orange to grey-brown.

This rim type was not found in either Sequence I or II but has parallels on other Transjordanian sites. A number of such rims were found by Glueck during his survey. Some were found at Khirbet el Far'ah, Khirbet Daḥaḥah, and Taiwilan[1] in ancient Edom[2] and at Deir 'Allā and Tell el Mazar in the Jordan Valley.[3] The Edomite sherds were also often decorated with parallel-painted lines (esp. Glueck, *EEP*, II, pl. 24:1 and 3). This decoration occurs here also on other bowls.[4] The two Jordan Valley sherds are decorated with a white band bordered by black lines, a type of decoration which we discussed above.

Type LXVI

Numbers 662-65, 667-73; 78:666, 674 and 675 illustrate this type. Numbers 673; 78:674 and 675 have incised lines just under the in-turn of the rim, on the outside. This was also true on several of the 1969 sounding rims.[5]

Type LV

Rims of this type are represented as nos. 661 and 58:660 and are paralleled in the 1969 sounding (see p. 97 above). The ware and surface colors are brown, tan, and grey. This rim type has a characteristic ridge at the bottom of the rim and then one or more minor ridges or deep incised lines between the bottom ridge and the top of the rim.

"Collar-Type" Rims and Related Rim Types (Types LX, LXXIV, LXXV, and LXII)

All of the unstratified type LX rims have paral-

lels in the 1969 sounding (nos. 633-35, 638-45; 77:636 and 637) and, in all but one case, they represent a very low thick rolled rim.[6] The exception is number 633 which is smaller than the others and has a red-burnished slip. Such a slip is extremely unusual on this type. Four rims, numbers 641-44, are of the v-grooved type (p. 97 above) and no actual collar is preserved. Deep grooves beneath the heavy roll of the rim indicate the collar on most of the remaining sherds.

One example each of types LXXIV and LXXV were found in the sounding, but one is post-Period II (sublayer 5a) and the other, from layer 5 before its subdivision, was most probably also post-Period II. None of these rims appeared in the Sequence II tombs so we must suppose, temporarily, a mid-ninth to mid-eighth-century B.C. date for them. Both small rims do resemble the "collar-type" rims, as does the larger one of type LXXIV. The larger type LXXV rims seem typologically to stand between the "collar-type" and "cylindrical-jar" type rims. The rims of both types are triangular in cross section and the basic difference between them is that on type LXXIV the top of the rim is formed by the base of an inverted triangle, while in type LXXV it is formed by the outward protruding apex of the triangle. Most of these rims bear painted decoration and are illustrated with the painted sherds (nos. 437-40, 442; 70:436 and 53:441). Number 693 is a red-burnished (on the outside) example of rim type LXXV. Numbers 437 and 440 are the other sherds of this type. They have a pinkish-brown surface color and the outsides of the rims are burnished. The slanting portions of the rims, on the inside were apparently covered with a whitish slip (some of which has subsequently been worn off) with three brownish-black bands painted on it. The upper rim surface of the type LXXIV rims, nos. 438, 442 and 70:441 have the same blackish

---

[1]Glueck, *EEP*, II, pl. 24:1, 3, 7, and 8.

[2]Similar sherd profiles are now illustrated from Dhiban in Tushingham, *Dhiban*, II, figs. 1:67, 69, 70 and 24:24; and from Buseirah in Bennett, *Levant*, VI, fig. 15:4; *Levant*, VII, fig. 5:11 and 13.

[3]Glueck, *EEP*, IV, Part II, 132:5 and 6.

[4]*Ibid.*, pls. 23:8 and 24:5, 6, and 11.

[5]We remarked above that similar rims were rare elsewhere but examples from Tell Safut (unpublished) and Balu'a (Crowfoot, *PEFQS*, LXVI, pl. II, fig. 2:13) illustrate that they do exist outside Amman. Safut must be considered on the very border of the Amman district but Balu'a certainly is not. Palestinian parallels for such rims, however, do not exist.

[6]A complete vessel with a rim of this type is published from Balu'a. *Ibid.*, pl. III, figs. 1 and 2.

bands on a white slip. There are traces of burnishing, but primarily on the outside over a medium to light brown slip. Number 693 has no painted decoration. It is of pinkish-brown ware with considerable white grit and is burnished lightly on top of the rim. On the exterior, light grooving replaces the burnishing.[1]

Rims similar to our larger examples, with the definite triangular shape and painted decoration, currently have no good parallels. They seem to represent a vessel type which is currently not represented by a complete vessel shape in the Amman district.[2]

Two additional examples of the type LXII grooved rim, which was also present in the 1969 sounding, are illustrated as nos. 77:647 and 648.

"Cylindrical-Jar" Rims and Related Rim Types (Types LXXVII, LXXVI, LXXVIII, LXXIX, and LXXX)

There is little more to add to the discussion of types LXXVII and LXXVI above and the parallels cited there. The rims, nos. 696 and 697 represent the type LXXVI grooved rims. Numbers 698-706 represent the most common type LXXVII rims, while nos. 707-12 represent the plain rims with straight sides or sides which flare slightly because they were not pressed down fully.[3] Only a few of the type LXXVII rims show signs of burnishing, and where it occurs, it is confined to the top of the rim.

The wider rims of types LXXVIII and LXXIX usually occur late in Iron II in Palestine and "cylindrical-jar" rims occur primarily from the eighth century B.C. and later. In general, our evidence is similar to that from Palestine, though the wide rims can occur at an earlier date, as they did in the 1969 sounding. There are few well-dated Palestinian parallels to our wide rims but the angularity in the bend of the rim, as found especially in our examples nos. 714 and 715, provides a criterion for a seventh-century early sixth-century B.C. date.[4] The one complete Transjordanian example of a hole-mouth jar was found in Amman tomb N (fig. 41:5), where both the broad rim and sharp inturn are illustrated.[5] This, then, is in keeping with the Palestinian evidence. At Lachish, the wide rims under discussion are attributed to hole-mouth jars, class S.8, and are assigned to the beginning of the sixth century B.C.[6] The type LXXIX profile is distinguished by the groove on the rim and the up-turn of the end of the rim. All but two of the sherds of both of these types are of the same ware that we have seen as normal for Iron Age sherds. Their color range is from brown, to tan, to grey, and the white grits appear in good quantity, as is normal.

The sherds, numbers 713 and 714, seem to be of a later ware. Their clay is better levigated, though still sandy textured, and the white grits are sparse (almost absent in no. 713). Number 714 has a tan slip, which has partially flaked off, and number 713 has an orange-brown surface color.

The other inturned ledge rim belongs to type LXXX. The one rim of this type found in the 1969 sounding was post-Period II. It was from a medium-sized vessel and had sharp corners like three unstratified red washed and burnished sherd fragments which are too badly preserved to illustrate. The rims illustrated here, nos. 718-22 and 80:723 are, for the most part, from larger vessels. In some cases, the rib at the incurve of the rim was purely that, while in other cases it seemed to have been created more by the formation of a step in the side of the rim (no. 720). Numbers 718, 719 and 721 are burnished both inside and out while the other rims have merely a few burnished strokes. The only good example of this rim type to be found in Palestine is a deep bowl from Stratum VIII at Hazor.[7] This is the only rim type belonging to a large vessel for which we presently have black-burnished examples (nos. 718 and 80:723). The best Sequence II example of this rim form was found in the Sahab tomb B, number 20 (fig. 41:8), and it was also black-burnished. The other Sequence II example of this rim type, belonging to the middle range, is the deep bowl number 39 from AC (fig. 41:10). The color variation on this sherd is interesting in that the outside is brown, the inside light pinkish-brown,

---

[1]We have noted this above on several occasions and considered it as usually representing a late degeneration of the spaced-burnish technique.

[2]Complete vessels (or nearly complete) with type LXXIV or LXXV rims are represented in the Madeba district: Piccirillo, *LA*, XXV, figs. I:8, II:3 and Tav. II:9, 10; and at Buseirah: Bennett, *Levant*, VII, 12, fig. 7:7.

[3]Similar rims from Tell Jellul (unpublished) and Balu'a (Crowfoot, *PEFQS*, LXVI, pl. II, figs. 1:1, 2, and 2:1, 2) should be mentioned.

[4]Sellers, *et al.*, *BZ*, p. 57, where other references are also cited.

[5]Several large hole-mouth jars are now published from Buseirah: Bennett, *Levant*, VII, 22, fig. 14:9 and 10. The profiles of these rims are closest to our earlier type LXXVII sherds, specifically no. 711.

[6]Olga Tufnell, *Lachish*, Vol. III: *The Iron Age* (2 parts; "The Welcome-Marston Archaeological Research Expedition to the Near East," III; London: Oxford University Press, 1953), Text, p. 316; Plates, pl. 97:537, 540, 541, and 543. This rim is considered characteristic of level II at Lachish.

[7]Yadin, *et al.*, *Hazor*, II, pl. LIV:25.

and the core dark grey. A number of other sherds in this section, as well as some of the sherds of type LXVI, illustrate this same feature. On many such vessels, incomplete oxidizing of the clay resulted in light to dark grey cores. This is the same color range found on the interior of the black-burnished vessels mentioned above. In some cases, especially where there are strokes of burnishing, the same black color is attained as was common on the black-burnished bowls, while in others, the grey is much lighter than has yet been found on such bowls.

Rim number 722 has a smaller diameter than the others and seems to be an example of our type 3 and 4 cups, especially like AE 47, 56, 129 (= fig. 34:8, 11, 9) and AB 53 (= fig. 33:48) which all have a prominent rounded rib. The other larger rims, however, belong to vessels of larger diameter, 28 to 32 cm. as opposed to 19 cm. Our rim type is best illustrated in Sequence II by such cups, but our sherd material supports the few examples which indicated its use on other shapes. Both kinds of rims are found in the middle range of Sequence II, but seem to disappear at the beginning of the late range of Sequence II and are replaced by cup type 5.

Other Iron I Rims and Rims Similar to the 1969 Sounding Types

There are a number of other rim types which must be considered as contemporary with our Sequence I or the 1969 sounding, but which are not illustrated there. While some closely resemble types already discussed, others do not. We will discuss first those which are similar to rim types discussed above.

Rim Types LVIII, LXXII, and LXXIII

All of these rims represent additional variants of the "collar-type" rim. Type LVIII rims, nos. 629-631, represent a high "collar type" in contrast to the low-collar rims illustrated thus far (with only one exception). We mentioned above that the low "collar-type" rim is a transitional form and our type LVIII is similar to a variety of the earlier form of such rims in Palestine.[1] Only the incised rim from layer 6 of the 1969 sounding, no. 395, represents a rim of type LVIII.[2]

The simple profiles of the type LXXII rims, nos. 688 and 689, resemble Early Bronze hole-mouth rims more than the Iron Age rims of similar name. The ware, grits, and surface color (tan ware with many white grits and a red wash) are clearly Iron Age. The profile, with thick rounded

top and grooving near the top, seems like a simplification of the low thick rolled-over "collar-type" rims illustrated above. The only parallel which helps to establish a date for this type is from Dhiban[3] and is dated to the end of Iron II.[4]

The type LXXIII rim, no. 690, represents a very small portion of a basically triangular rim of heavy ware. Several similar rims were found at Umm el Biyara[5] and one example is published from Dhiban.[6] The date range, then, seems to be about late ninth century to mid-seventh century B.C. for this specific rim type, which appears to be primarily Tranjordanian. A similar rim profile occurs most frequently at Deir 'Allā as a cooking pot rim (type la with a range from phase A to G),[7] but also on deep bowls.[8] Our sherd is not as coarse as the cooking pot examples, but is more like the deep bowls.

Rim Types LXVIII, LIX, LVI, and LI

The single type LXVIII rim resembles some of the type LXXX rims. The inturn on the top, however, is more pronounced and angular, forming a second rib. The lower rib is not accentuated. Similar rims were found in the 1969 sounding but on smaller bowl shapes, nos. 182 and 62:191.

Type LIX is a very simple jar rim, no. 632, on

---

[1]Loud, *MEG*, II, pl. 83:4 (from Str. VI); Kelso, *Bethel*, pl. 56:1-3 and 6 (from Iron I$_{1-3}$ levels), and the rims from Seilun (Shiloh) mentioned above on pp. 97 and 102.

[2]A number and variety of "collar-type" rims were found at Tell Safut in the spring of 1969. (Tell Safut is situated about 10 km. west of Amman on the slope of the hills overlooking the fertile Belqa Valley.) The rims found here were of the high "collar type" (type LVIII, one of which was mentioned above as having incised circles on the rim similar to the sherd from our 1969 sounding), low "collar-type" rims (type LX, similar to those discussed in this chapter and the 1969 sounding), and a very narrow, late version of a "collar-type" rim as is illustrated from Str. II at 'Ain Shems (Grant and Wright, *AS*, IV, pl. XLVI:1 and 2) and also in Glueck, *EEP*, IV, pl. 139:3.

[3]Reed and Winnett, *Dhiban*, I, pl. 76:3.

[4]*Ibid.*, p. 76.

[5]Bennett, *RB*, LXXIII, 391, fig. 4:2-4.

[6]Reed and Winnett, *Dhiban*, I, pl. 73:12. Additional examples from Dhiban are illustrated in Tushingham, *Dhiban*, II, fig. 1:24-26 and 34.

[7]Franken, *DA*, figs. 56:37, 38 (phase D); 59:2, 8 (phase E); 61:36 (phase F).

[8]There is no consistency in the type on which it occurs, but it appears on various sub-types of the type 1 and 2 deep bowls. Franken, *DA*, figs. 49:17 and 18 (phase B); 59:35 (phase E); 64:21 (phase G).

which the neck is terminated without a particular profile being given to form a rim. We have mentioned a number of complete vessels above from Mt. Nebo which had similar rims and were dated to Iron I.[1] The ware of our sherds is that used for most of the "collar-type" rims.

A similar ware is found in the type LVI rims which seem to belong to handled, deep bowls which, in profile, resemble kraters. A handle seems to have been broken off at the right of sherd no. 628. A similar profile, again, can be found at sites in the Wadi Arabah and dates to Iron I.[2] Number 76:627 is similar to 628 but is neither as thick at the top nor grooved (and is from a narrow necked jar). Again, parallels from the Wadi Arabah seem good.[3]

The type LI sherds, nos. 604, 56:602 and 75:603 are from vessels of differing proportions but all have simple, usually flaring rims with rounded tops.[4] Few parallels can be cited for number 604,[5] but the shape should be illustrated.[6] Number 75:603 represents a thicker rim with a red-brown, burnished slip.

Rim Types LII, LIV, LXIX, and LXXI

Deir 'Allā parallels can be cited for most of the rims in this section but similar profiles also occur much later. In types LII and LIV, similar profiles can be found in early Hellenistic contexts, while types LXIX and LXXI are not that late, they date in the second half of Iron II. We can state here what seem to us to be the closest parallels, but must defer any final attribution to a time when these types occur in clearly stratified deposits.

All of the type LII rims seem definitely to be made of the typical Iron Age ware with the usual concentration of white grits. Deir 'Allā parallels can be found in phases B, C, and J,[7] while similar late rims can be found at Beth Zur.[8]

The type LIV rims, nos. 614, 615, 618; 57:619; 76:616, 617 and 622, are more numerous and difficult to attribute. There are better early and late parallels. The majority of the rims still seem clearly to be of Iron Age ware but some, numbers 615 and 76:617, are better levigated and have fewer grits. These rims can be subdivided as follows: (a) those which are undercut beneath the out-flaring ledge (nos. 615; 57:622 and 76:616),[9] (b) those which have the ledge pressed tight to the neck (nos. 618 and 619),[10] (c) those which have the ledge pressed tight to the neck and are finished off straight, nearly vertical on the outside (no. 614),[11] and (d) those which are pressed tight at the rim and are somewhat squared with a rounding on the outside.[12] The early parallels for sub-

---

[1]The ware seems to be similar to many of the Iron I sherds from the Wadi Arabah. For the rim profile see

Rothenberg, *PEQ*, XCIV (1962), pl. XI:11.

[2]Rothenberg, *PEQ*, XCIV (1962), pl. XI:17.

[3]*Ibid.*, pl. XI:15, 16, and 18.

[4]Similar simple but smaller rims can be illustrated, for example, at Tell en Naṣbe on one-handled pots (Wampler, *Naṣbe*, pl. 46:969-71), cooking pots (*ibid.*, pl. 49:1031), cups (*ibid.*, pl. 44:927-31), conical jars (*ibid.*, pl. 26:438, 439), pitchers (*ibid.*, pl. 31:541-49; pl. 32:554-56; pl. 33:571), and jugs (*ibid.*, pl. 34:601; pl. 35:612). Many of these do belong to Iron I.

[5]Franken, *DA*, pl. 62:17 (from phase F) and Sellers, *et al.*, *BZ*, fig. 8:24; both belong to Iron I.

[6]See the discussion below for jar types LII and LIV which may be Iron I, but such rims also appear in the Hellenistic period. Number 604 could possibly be dated this late, though the ware does not seem to be significantly different from normal Iron I.

[7]Franken, *DA*, figs. 51:31-32, 40, 42; 57:36; 67:53, 55, 56; and 70:38.

[8]The Hellenistic rims vary with rounded-topped rims earlier (third century) than the squared-off rims (end of third and second centuries B.C.). See Sellers, *et al.*, *BZ*, pp. 71, 72, and fig. 22:1 and 3, though such rounded rims also begin earlier, but with shorter necks, fig. 21:7 and 8. Similar rims will, upon further excavation, probably prove to be common late in Iron II. A large number of such rims were found in debris which was cleaned out of a cistern at Khirbet Mudhmar (3 km. southwest of Tell Safut). There were a number of other rim profiles of exactly the same ware, but the most characteristic (and clearly late Iron II) were some hole-mouth rims of type LXXVIII.

[9]Franken, *DA*, figs. 47:5 (phase A), 50:103 (phase B), 57:38 (phase D); Yadin, *et al.*, *Hazor*, III-IV, pl. CCIX:13 (Str. IX), for early examples; and Wampler, *Naṣbe*, pls. 27:450 and 28:476, for late examples.

[10]Franken, *DA*, figs. 46:70, 72, 74-76, 83, 84 (phase A); 50:101, 104; 51:29, 30 (phase B); 54:99 (phase C); 55:35, 36 (phase D); Yadin, *et al.*, *Hazor*, III-IV, pls. CLXVII:4-6; CLXVIII:7, 18, 19, 22 (Str. XII); and Lamon and Shipton, *MEG*, I, pl. 21:123 (Str. V) for early examples, and Kelso, *Bethel*, pls. 68:18-25; 69:5, 6, 9, 10, and 11, for late examples. Franken, *DA*, fig. 50:102 is a good parallel for our 66:15, but Kelso, *Bethel*, pl. 68:21 and 22 are also good parallels.

[11]See Franken, *DA*, figs. 50:100 and 51:29 (phase B), and Yadin, *et al.*, *Hazor*, III-IV, pl. CLXVII:2 (Str. XII) for early examples and Kelso, *Bethel*, pl. 68:1-5, 9-13, and 16 for late examples. A similar rim on a conical jar at Tell en Naṣbe (Wampler, *Naṣbe*, pl. 27:444) is given a date range from 600 B.C. to Hellenistic.

[12]There are no good parallels from Deir 'Allā, but the rim is found early at Hazor in Str. XII (Yadin, *et al.*, *Hazor*, III-IV, pl. CLXVII:7). This rim is also found in the Persian period at Hazor, Str. II (*ibid.*, pl. CXC:12) and, like the rims discussed immediately above, also has Neo-Babylonian - Hellenistic parallels on cylindrical jars at Tell en Naṣbe (Wampler, *Naṣbe*, pl. 27:446, 447, and 451). Hellenistic rims of this type are well illustrated at Bethel (Kelso, *Bethel*, pls. 68:6, 15; 69:1 and 12).

types a and b fall at the beginning of Iron I but we would prefer a date consistent with the latest examples at the end of Iron II until their appearance in stratified contexts permits precision in the matter.

Rim types LXIX (nos. 677, 678, 680, 681; and 58:679) and LXXI (nos. 683-86) are related and come from jugs, narrow-necked jars or larger deep bowl or krater forms, though the latter are less common. In both cases the ware is rather coarse, reddish-brown to dark brown in color, and includes considerable black and white sandy grits. It strongly resembles cooking pot ware, but is not quite that coarse. The type LXIX rim slants inward while type LXXI is tilted in on a slight curve. Both rims have rounded tops and type LXXI is somewhat thicker, with a fairly straight outer face. There is usually one slight groove near the top of this outer surface (on type LXXI) and occasionally an even less pronounced groove near the bottom. Type LXIX is much simpler, with a depression between the rounded top of the rim and a rounded rib.

It is difficult to find good parallels to the type LXXI rims. The best available are of a larger diameter (ca. 20-34 cm. as opposed to 13-18 cm.) and are found on deep bowls type 3a at Deir 'Alla.[1] (Some of the jugs to be discussed below as the best parallels for type LXIX rims have a few variants closer to type LXXI, but this comparison is not very convincing.) Better parallels, on medium sized vessels, are found on the late Iron II and Iron III cooking pots. Many of these rims are ribbed more than our examples, but some good parallels can be cited at Tell el Far'ah (north),[2] 'Ain Shems,[3] and Tell Beit Mirsim.[4] It is difficult, on present evidence, to determine where these rims belong but the later date now seems preferable. On figure 28, we illustrated some two-handled jars from Madeba which we placed at the very end of our Sequence I. Jar numbers 4 to 7 on figure 28 have rim profiles similar to type LXIX. Unfortunately, we were unable to find good parallels for them.

The rim, no. 681, is clearly a jug with the top of the handle attached at the neck ridge. The rim, number 78:679, is unquestionably from a similar vessel. The low and pronounced rib differs from our other examples. Jugs of similar profile, but with the handle extending to the top of the rim rather than to the neck ridge, are very common late in Iron II.[5] The handle joining at the neck ridge, an earlier feature, is usually found on smaller jugs and on decanters. An exact parallel for rim no. 681 is found at Megiddo in Stratum V[6] and corresponds well with the examples illustrated above for the end of our Sequence I. Our remaining examples attributed to type LXIX cannot comfortably be attributed to jugs because of

their thickness and inward incline. Similar rims are found at Engedi in Stratum V (630-582/1 B.C.) and are attributed to vats.[7] The diameters and inward incline of the rims are similar. The date, then, overlaps with that of the jugs mentioned above and we have seen the application of similar rims to different vessel shapes. The vessel designated "vat" by Mazar at Engedi is similar to the Umm el Biyara vessels with the type LXXIII rim mentioned above. Interestingly enough, our type LXIX does occur on such a vessel ("vat") at Umm el Biyara also.[8] The Engedi examples would, then, date just after the one from Umm el Biyara.

In summary, it seems plausible that the date of the type LXIX rims, nos. 677, 678 and 58:680 can be confined to Iron II and they belong to the end of that period. Such rims must be contemporary with the late range of our Sequence II, despite the fact that they were not illustrated in that body of material. The two jug rims, nos. 681 and 78:679, on the other hand, are probably best attributed to the end of Iron I.

Jug Rims

Only four other jug rims were found: two, type LXXXI, with narrow necks and two, type LXXXV, with considerably wider necks. The rims within each type are almost identical in profile. The high, rounded rims (nos. 724 and 80:725 type LXXXI) are typical Iron Age ware and they are burnished. The only parallels for such rims are also from the Transjordan.[9] The

---

[1]Franken, *DA*, figs. 46:12-16 (phase A); 49:41-44 (phase B); 54:8-12 (phase C); 56:50-53 (phase D); 59:44-49 (phase E); and 61:53-56 (phase F). Type 3a deep bowl rims continue in phase G and then their numbers taper off considerably. From G on, however, their profiles are no longer similar to our rims. Now see Tushingham, *Dhiban*, II, figs. 1:29-32 and 18:15 (a complete form which resembles the Palestinian cooking pots just cited) for parallels to our type LXXI rims.

[2]de Vaux, *RB*, LIX (1952), 571, fig. 9:4.

[3]Grant and Wright, *AS*, IV, pl. LXIV:28.

[4]Albright, *TBM*, I, pl. 55:11 and 12.

[5]We will cite only a few examples here: Albright, *TBM*, I, pl. 58:4, 5, 7-9; Grant and Wright, *AS*, IV, pls. LXV:38, LXVII:10; and Wampler, *Naṣbe*, pl. 33:584-88.

[6]Lamon and Shipton, *MEG*, I, pl. 22:129.

[7]Mazar, Dothan, and Dunayevsky, *Atiqot*, V, 75, fig. 21:9-14.

[8]Bennett, *RB*, LXXIII (1966), 389, fig. 3:12.

[9]Glueck, *EEP*, II, pl. 24:14, and *EEP*, III, pl. 19:5.

type LXXXV rims, nos. 731 and 80:732, however, have good Iron I Palestinian parallels.[1] These jugs are similar to some of the globular one-handled jugs in the Madeba Museum which we have illustrated on figure 26:21, 22, and 24. We have placed them late in our Sequence I and commented that they probably continued in use early in Iron II.

Cooking Pot Rims

We have illustrated only four Iron Age cooking pot rims, nos. 727-29 and 80:726. It would be an overrefinement at this point to divide these rims into many types, but one rim clearly must be separated from the rest and, thus, no. 729 has been designated type LXXXIII, while the remainder are labeled type LXXXII.

The type LXXXIII rim was found on a middle range, Sequence II cooking pot from Sahab B, no. 67 (= no. 41:4) and parallels indicated a date after 700 B.C. Though the grooved rims of type LXXXII cannot be paralleled with any accuracy, one expects that they are contemporary with our 1969 sounding and continue for about a century later. At the upper end of this time range, some of the rims of the latest phases at Deir 'Allā[2] seem similar (though no real parallels are present), and our rims can be considered, basically, like the triangular type which comprises most of the Deir 'Allā examples. On the other hand, grooving is popular on the two-handled deep cooking pots of the late Iron II in Palestine (which, however, are more vertical than our rims) as well as on those similar to our type LXXXIII, but with a taller and wider rim.[3] The short, near vertical stance above the carination of no. 727 is a feature most frequently found in Iron I, while the considerable incline and lower carination on no. 728 is more common in Iron II. It is possible that since we have seen considerable popularity in the use of grooved rims in late Iron I and early Iron II contexts in the Transjordan, we may find that we have here a cooking pot rim which is peculiar to this area and exhibits the grooving popular on other forms.[4]

Krater

Only one krater sherd is included in our unstratified material, no. 730, type LXXXIV. The rim is plain with a flat top, vertical side, and a line indicating a slight collar at the base where it joins the body of the vessel. This profile is identical to that of some of the kraters from the Madeba Museum, figures 23:29 and 24:1 (from Madeba B) and 24:2. Another krater, figure 23:30, has a pro-nounced rib at the base of the rim and the Irbed B kraters, figure 24:3 and 4, are essentially the same with the addition of grooving to the rim. The kraters from Madeba tomb A are also similar, figure 23:23, 24, 26 and 28, though many of the rim tops are rounded and the base of the rim is not accentuated. A middle to late Iron I date, probably tenth century B.C., seems best for our no. 730.

Cups

Two sherds of type 1 cups are illustrated, nos. 734 and 80:733 (= sherd rim type LXXXVI). We have discussed such cups at length above (pp. 52 and 99) and need add little more here. Our no. 734 corresponds exactly in form to the cups illustrated on figure 33:38-41 from the Amman district, especially number 40 (SB:71). The ware and surface color are also identical. The Umm el Biyara[5] and the Tell el Kheleifeh cups[6] are more like our no. 80:733. These cups have outtilted lips with the greatest diameter at the top of the rim rather than that at the carination of the body (the next widest point). The Tell el Kheleifeh and Umm el Biyara cups, on the whole, have shorter bodies and handles which project further than the type 1 cups exemplified by no. 734. Both subtypes of these cups seem to be contemporary, in the first half of the seventh century B.C., and sherd no. 80:733 argues against making a geographical distinction between subtypes (as one may have supposed on the basis of the other Amman district vessels).[7]

---

[1]Kelso, *Bethel*, pl. 40:5; Sellers, *et al., BZ*, pl. 22:1.

[2]Franken, *DA*, figs. 61:43 (phase F); 66:40 (phase H); 69:46, 47, 49, and 50 (phase J); and 74:52 (phase L).

[3]Albright, *TBM*, I, pl. 55:2 and 5.

[4]Only a few grooved cooking pot rims with profiles similar to our Amman examples have come to our attention. They were found at Tell Jellul near Madeba (unpublished). A number of other cooking pot rims found at this site represent the Iron I triangular rims common at Deir 'Allā, though they have not been examined to see to which Deir 'Allā type they may conform. Other contemporary cooking pot rims are illustrated in Glueck, *EEP*, IV, pl. 139:2, 6, 7, and 8.

[5]Bennett, *RB*, LXXIII, 387, fig. 2:1, 3 and 389, fig. 3:7, 8.

[6]Glueck, *BASOR*, CLXXXVIII, Part II, fig. 3:1-4.

[7]The cup with out-tilted rim and projecting handle may prove to be a type with an earlier history and is also present at Dhiban, Tushingham, *Dhiban*, II, fig. 1:13.

Juglets

The juglet rims and bases, illustrated as nos. 463, 735-40 and 71:462 correspond to vessels discussed above: no. 735 with Sequence I juglets (= sherd type LXXXVIII, fig. 38:7-10); no. 736 with type 9 juglets (= sherd type LXXXIX, fig. 39:36-38); no. 737 with type 2 juglets (= sherd type XC, fig. 38:7-10); nos. 739 and 740 with type 1 juglets (= base type 15, fig. 38:2-6 and 23); and nos. 463, 738 and 71:462 with the type 17 and 18 juglets (= base type 14, figs. 39:1-41). The juglet bases bear the unusual feature of very thick bottoms which may prove to be a chronological indicator, but which is very poorly attested at present. Number 735 illustrates the Sequence I, late Iron I, juglet with the top of the handle attached at the middle of the cylindrical rim, figure 26:3-16. We have illustrated only one such jug from the Amman Museum, figure 26:9, and the rest are from outside the Amman district. Similar juglets, however, did appear in Amman G and Sahab C, but are unpublished.

Miscellaneous Rims, Handles and Bases

Type LXXXVII Rims

This rim, illustrated with the painted sherds, no. 443, represents an unusual profile. Sherds with similar profile and painted decoration were found in both Periods I and II of the 1969 sounding but suggest little of the vessel's complete shape, nos. 343, 344, 365; and 66:351. The diameter of the rim, the incurve at the top, and the perforated hole indicate that this may be an earlier strainer type for which we presently have no evidence in the Amman district, but this profile seems to be present on strainers from the Mt. Nebo tombs, nos. 20 and 84, and indicates a date at the end of the ninth or beginning of the eighth century B.C.[1]

Handles

Numbers 742, 745, 753; 81:741, 743, 744 and 746-52 illustrate the unstratified handles. Numbers 742, 745, 81:741, 743 and 744 have a rounded section, number 746 is formed of two round bands of clay, and numbers 753 and 81:747-52 have oval sections. Numbers 742, 745, 81:741, 743 and 744 come from jugs and juglets, and numbers 753 and 81:747-52 from jars.

Bases

The unstratified bases substantiate our com-ments above concerning the 1969 sounding sherds (pp. 99-100). The ratio of disk bases to other bases is even greater here. The 1969 sounding evidence shows clearly that this preponderance of disk bases is not entirely fortuitous or the result of chance involved in the collection of these sherds. The dating of the unstratified sherds is rather difficult in most cases and currently the profiles rarely aid us. The wheel-burnished examples are securely placed in Iron II and the sharp angles and corners on some profiles, evidence for turning on the fast wheel,[2] indicate a similar date. The only rounded base is illustrated as no. 754. Since the surface color is tan and it has been hand burnished, a late Iron I date seems most suitable. Only a few ring bases were found. On smaller vessels, the ring has a triangular cross-section, type 9 (nos. 791 and 83:792-94) while most of the larger bases have basically a rectangular cross-section, type 10 (83:796 and 797). Only one larger ring base has a triangular cross-section, no. 795, and this is somewhat rounded.

The greatest number of bases have simple disks. These have been subdivided into those which are extremely shallow, type 2, those with straight sides and squared corners, type 3, and those with rounded sides and corners, type 4. There is a wide range of dates for each of these types so that ware, color and burnishing procedure are more significant than shape for use as a dating criteria.

Type 2 bases, nos. 755-57, 759-61, and 81:758, 762 are extremely low disk bases. The four Iron I examples are hand burnished, nos. 755, 756, 759 and 760. Wheel-burnished, late Iron II bases are illustrated as nos. 757, 761 and 81:758, 762. All are from fine wheel-made bowls; nos. 757 and 81:758 are cream wares and nos. 761 and 81:762 are black wares.

Type 3 bases, nos. 763, 765 and 81:764, 766, 767 all seem to be wheel-burnished and date to Iron II. They are all normal disk bases with straight sides and slight concavity to the base. One sherd, no. 81:766 is of a fine cream ware and one, no. 81:767 which has a spaced wheel burnish, is of

---

[1]Saller, *LA*, XVI, 207, fig. 16:21, 22; 268, fig. 31:3, 269, fig. 32:4, 5.

[2]We presently know nothing about the technical means by which the bases were produced, whether the bottoms of the vessels were closed by a slab of clay, whether an actual ring or disk of clay was added to an already closed base, or whether the base was worked by pinching or scraping from the wall of an already closed vessel. Such differences in manufacture may be the reason behind some of the type distinctions, but no technical analysis has been undertaken.

pinkish-orange ware. The remaining sherds are tan to light brown in color. Two sherds, nos. 765 and 81:764 are of somewhat coarser ware and come from larger vessels than the other three bowl sherds.

Type 4 bases, nos. 768-70; 60:772 and 82:771, 773-76, are either flat disks or have a slight concavity at the base, nos. 769, 770 and 772. On two examples the disk is set off from the body of the vessel by a distinct groove. The two larger bases again seem to be late Iron I. They are of plain light brown wares and have traces of hand burnish. Two of the smaller bases, nos. 770 and 82:771, are of light brown wares and have traces of hand burnishing. A third hand-burnished sherd is heavily burnished, virtually hand polished, no. 82:773, and has a dark red-brown surface color. These three bases also date to the end of Iron I. The three remaining type 4 bases date to the end of Iron II and show the characteristic spaced wheel-burnish which was common at that time. The colors are also typical for this time range: no. 82:774 is pink, no. 82:775 is black and no. 82:776 is cream.

The type 5 bases, nos. 82:777-79, are basically flat, but there is a gentle rounded curve forming the transition from bowl wall to base. Number 82:777 apparently comes from a jug which has vertical burnish strokes on its sides. Numbers 82:778 and 779 come from shallow bowls where red-orange slips were applied inside and out, but not over the entire base. On number 82:778 the slip stops at a deep groove and there is a similar groove on the jug sherd, number 82:777. On both bowl sherds, however, the bases are also burnished and the wares are clearly late Iron II. The type 6 bases, nos. 780 and 781, are similar to type 5 with a groove on the base of both examples, but in this case the groove is near the edge of a definite disk base. The ware is similar to that of the sherds we have placed late in Iron II.

Base type 7, nos. 782-86, 788 and 82:787, is the "step-disk" that we have seen in tombs of the late range of Sequence II, but which also appeared earlier in the 1969 sounding (see pp. 99-100 above).[1] The profiles of all these bases have very sharply defined steps in contrast to the slight steps with very low profiles, common in the 1969 sounding. The burnishing and ware, present on all examples, are of the type seen frequently in late Iron II. Number 783 exemplifies the creamy-white burnished ware and number 784 has a similar texture, but a light pink color.

The type 8 base is closely related to type 7 except that here the steps rise up the side of the vessel, as if in superimposed layers, and the corners are not brought down to the same plane as the bottom of the base. All examples again seem to be late Iron II. Numbers 83:789 and 790

illustrate two such sherds and no. 514 illustrates such a base on a sherd where an almost complete section is preserved. The grey marble bowl, no. 805 also has a base of this type.

Miscellaneous Bases

Type 11, no. 798, seems to be the portion of a high pedestal base or a stand. Type 12 represents the leg of a tripod bowl, no. 83:799,[2] and type 13 represents the leg of a tripod cup, no. 83:800, and could belong to any of the types we have discussed above.

Miscellaneous Sherds

Four lamp fragments, illustrated as nos. 83:801-804, are from the portion of the lamp where the walls were pinched in to form the nozzle; thus, it is impossible to attribute them to either a specific type or date.

Summary

The sherd material presented in this chapter, in conjunction with the 1969 sounding sherds, expands considerably the number of significant shapes which can be illustrated from the Amman district. We are occasionally able to indicate examples of complete forms to which our rims or base profiles belonged, but most of our sherds illustrate types not documented in the sequences above. Types represented by rare examples in the corpus are given better documentation here by numerous examples. To some degree this seems to be attributable to vessels occurring on the tell which were not commonly placed in tombs, and the reverse, that the tomb material in many shapes may represent special, rare, or more

---

[1]Tell Safut and Tell Jellul provided good examples of several types of disk bases of the types under discussion here. Our type 7 "step base" was found at both sites and an example of the grooved rim, type LVI, was also found at Jellul. A number of plain rounded-side disk bases, type 4, were found at Safut.

[2]See figs. 22:46-51; 33:42-49; 34:1-10, 13-19, and p. 102 above for more discussion of such bowls.

costly vessels.[1]

We noted above, without finding a good explanation, that a very high percentage of our bowl profiles from unstratified contexts are Iron II, primarily late in that period, while Iron I is very poorly represented, except for types that are illustrated in the 1969 sounding. The non-bowl shapes are more evenly distributed but many of the clearly definable types, in contrast to the bowls, can be attributed to Iron I. The 1969 sounding material is of great importance to us in providing a firm position from which to build our discussion. Very few early Iron I shapes, as illustrated by the Jebel Nuzha tomb in Amman, can be distinguished and only a few shapes clearly preceded our 1969 sounding material. The sounding, then, forms an effective upper limit for us, as the middle and late range of Sequence II present a well documented lower limit. We have a number of forms which were found in the 1969 sounding and, fortunately enough, have later variants, as determined by clay or surface treatment. As a result, we are able to show a continuation of forms. In some cases, such types continue to the end of Iron II while others extend only into the presently ill-defined and ill-represented late ninth and eighth centuries B.C.

In the bowl shapes, specifically, we have several of the simple rims common in the 1969 sounding, types XI, XII, XXIV, and XXV. Only a few types, like type XIV, can be cited as contemporary but not illustrated in the 1969 sounding.

The most significant group of bowl rims are those bearing a feature which is currently best illustrated at Amman, namely, the firing of typical red-burnished bowls to a black or creamy-

---

[1]A significant body of comparative material has recently been published from the excavations at Heshbon, Edward N. Lugenbeal and James A. Sauer, "Seventh-Sixth Century B.C. Pottery from Area B at Heshbon," *Andrews University Seminary Studies*, X (1972), 21-69 and pls. A-C, I-XI. We are including reference here to the pottery types represented at Heshbon rather than adding individual footnotes above. The Heshbon pottery tradition is extremely close to that from Amman. Only a few forms present at Heshbon were not present in Amman and a number of forms illustrated by limited examples at Heshbon could be included because of the stratigraphic context. In our unstratified Amman materials some poorly illustrated parallel forms were not included in our discussion and illustration, because there was insufficient basis to include them in this time range. The Heshbon evidence allows us to expand our Amman repertoire slightly.

The predominant rim profiles are bowl types I, IV, XII, XV, XVIII, XLVI, XLVIII (using Amman type numbers) with the greatest number attributable to types XLVI and XLVIII at both sites. Jar and other profiles are represented by types LII, LV, LVIII, LX, LXII, LXIII, LXXVII with type LXXVIII occurring in greatest number. Most of the bases illustrated fall within our types 3, 7 and 9. In the case of those types which are illustrated with numerous examples, a comparison shows nearly the same range of variations at the two sites. There are few forms at Heshbon that we would place solely in our late range of Sequence II, particularly absent are a number of characteristic forms that we would place latest in this range. The greatest concentration would rather fall contemporary with our middle range of Sequence II, the most common forms

being those which continue into the late range.

Black-burnished wares occur but only in two of the bowl forms in which they occurred in Amman, types XV and XLVI. A lighter shade of vessel color, dark grey, occurs most frequently. This is rare in bowl forms in Amman and where this color occurs (most commonly on the interior of large jar forms, as indicated above) it seems unintentional or the result of less precision being exercised in the firing process. Again we are inclined to place the Heshbon black- and grey-burnished wares as early as possible in the period when such wares were common, in a developmental stage. White ware sherds (apparently corresponding to what we have discussed above as cream-burnished wares) are not found among the type XV and XLVI sherds. White and very pale brown sherds occur in twelve other forms, only one of which, type XLVII, occurs in black- and cream-burnished wares at Amman. More examples are necessary to document the overlap and peculiarities of the white- and black-burnished wares and to shed more light on the question of the earliest appearance of these wares.

The sherd profiles on plate V:291-304 represent a cooking pot type which currently has no parallels in Amman and few good Palestinian or Transjordanian parallels. It is striking to see such cooking pots at Heshbon since their major occurrence is in northern Syria. This type is very similar to the normal Iron II cooking pot in the Amuq.

Our inclination is to see the Heshbon material as running parallel to our middle range and continuing early in our late range of Sequence II. A date range of mid-eighth century through late seventh century would then seem most appropriate to us on present evidence.

white color.[1] Unfortunately, such important characteristic wares are currently not well illustrated elsewhere in the Transjordan, nor for the most part are the shapes on which they occur. There are a large number of the special black-burnished type in the Amman district, but only a few of the creamy-white. As far as occurrences elsewhere are concerned, however, there are more and better examples of the creamy-white ware at Gerar and as far north as the Amuq, while only the Amuq provides examples of the black variety. The presence of such rims in our Sequence II, middle to late range, provides a longer time range for such vessels in Amman than currently seems present elsewhere. The creamy-white ware parallels are very late in the Neo-Assyrian period, while several other specific bowl profiles, like types XLVII, XLVIII, and a variety of XLVI, have parallels in Palestine and as far away as Cyprus, with a date probably ranging around 600 B.C. (a few decades on either side).

A series of thin-walled bowls must be considered the second most significant group. Type XXXVIII represents the profile of an Assyrian period bowl found on many sites: Tell Far'ah (both north and south), Tell Gemmeh, Engedi, Tell el Kheleifeh, Samaria, Tell Ta'yinat, and elsewhere. The very thin bowls, types IV, V, and X, are presently of strictly local importance and, together with the black or creamy-white ware bowls, indicate that the potter's art reached a very high level of proficiency in the seventh and sixth centuries B.C. in the Amman district.

We have illustrated jar shapes which also range in date from our 1969 sounding material to early in the Persian period. The most significant among these are the rims which clustered around the "collar-type" rim and those which are related to the "cylindrical-type" or hole-mouth rims. We are able to provide only a few examples of forms which predate our 1969 sounding material, especially the high "collar-type" rim, type LVIII. The end of Iron II is well represented with an ample selection of type LXXVII to LXXIX rims. The grooved rims, types LXIV, LXX, and LXXI are well represented in the 1969 sounding, but we are able to define the time range and variety of such rims more clearly here.

Grooved rims are present on the few cooking pot rims which otherwise add little information beyond what was present in our corpus. Similarly, the shapes LXXXV, LXXXVI, and LXXXVIII to XC merely illustrate types that are documented in the corpus and discussed earlier.

We illustrated the decided preference in the Amman district for the disk base or modification thereof. This preference was already noted in the 1969 sounding materials and continued through Iron II. We added examples of a number of base types not present in the sounding and were able to illustrate a number of examples of several types which were popular at the end of Iron II.

---

[1]We have speculated above that the incentive for producing the black bowl variants may have been an attempt to imitate dark stone vessels (basalt, marble, or some other grey-black stone). Another possibility suggests itself, namely, that this is an attempted imitation of Greek black-glazed vessels. If this is so, one would expect this phenomenon to have developed in another area, preferably along the Mediterranean coast. Also, imitation presumes a familiarity with seventh-sixth century imported Greek pottery. Unfortunately, this cannot be documented at present and it is extremely doubtful that significant amounts of such pottery will be found in the Transjordan (if none have to date, despite the amount of pottery available from this date range) contemporary with the introduction of black-burnished wares around 700 B.C. We must presently, on the basis of arguments presented above, consider it most probable that we have here the imitation of dark stone bowls in pottery.

CHAPTER IX

We have devoted a considerable amount of space above to the sherds and pottery vessels available to us from the Transjordan. This evidence far exceeds that which is available from other classes of objects and from architectural remains. Our discussion in this chapter will be brief and constitute a summary of the information available on the topic. The limited material consists of portions of the following: defense walls; several fortresses; large, official buildings; domestic buildings; a number of "megalithic" towers and settlements; and the ground plans of tombs.

Remains of Fortification Walls and Fortified Settlements

A number of Iron Age buildings, portions of buildings and smaller areas containing structural remains have been excavated in the Transjordan. At Dhiban,[1] Amman,[2] Khirbet al Hajjar,[3] Aro'er, Tell er Rumeith and Tell el Kheleifeh,[4] portions of walls and their foundations, constructed of roughly shaped and often crudely squared stones, were uncovered. The remains of numerous settlements of similar stone construction have been encountered throughout the Transjordan in the course of surveys by Conder, Mackenzie, Albright, de Vaux, Glueck, Mittmann, and others. Many of these structures, often called megalithic, have been considered Iron Age on the basis of ceramic finds. The theory has been proposed,[5] and is repeated in recent dicussions,[6] that in the early Iron Age a series of such structures ringed the ancient capital Rabbat Ammon and thus formed an outlying defense perimeter. Unfortunately, the facts used to substantiate such a theory are extremely scanty and as more evidence comes to light considerable doubt is cast on it. In most cases, the settlements are badly eroded and yield very little pottery.[7] In too many cases, Roman or Byzantine pottery is far more common than any identifiable Iron Age pottery (though on many sites there is unmistakable Iron Age pottery). The major problem, then, is whether we really have a unified defense system of one

period or merely a scattering of sites of various periods, ranging in date from the Chalcolithic to Turkish. If a site was reused and rebuilt, to what date can we attribute the full extent of the building remains which we see at any given location? It seems equally probable today that in the Iron Age we had a scattering of minor settlements on the hillsides around Rabbat Ammon (as there probably were in most periods) which had very little military or strategic value, which were perfectly viable entities in relatively stable periods and were subjected to military pressure only for

---

[1] Reed and Winnett, *Dhiban*, I, 14-16.

[2] This has been presented in Chapter VII above.

[3] Thompson, *BASOR*, CCVII, 27-34.

[4] The last three sites are discussed in the next section.

[5] Glueck, *EEP*, III, 163. "Furthermore, the large number of these strongly built EI sites in the 'Ammân region indicates the intricate development of the defense organization which was perfected then, and points to the intensive cultivation, as do many terraces from the EI period, of the fertile slopes they guarded. Only thriving communities could have afforded to build such numerous and strongly built settlements and fortresses, and only a dynamic people and kingdom could have had the ability to erect them."

[6] Landes, *BA*, XXIV, 76. "Ammonite architecture is not characterized by any notable artistic features or striking decorative motifs. The Ammonites built primarily for shelter and protection. But the number and strength of their fortresss dwellings, together with the conscious plan manifest in their arrangement and system, point to a dynamic civilization with a well-organized center of political authority. And the effectiveness of their defensive setup is attested by the fact that, as we know, only once in some six centuries of Ammonite history was the ring of defenses around their capital at Rabbath-Ammon ever breached and the capital itself besieged and taken."

[7] Usually the pottery which is found is so badly weathered that it is virtually useless for dating purposes.

very brief and limited periods of time.[1] Only further excavation designed to ascertain the period or periods of use and the size, nature and duration of the settlements within each specific period, will eventually settle the matter. Some outlying fortresses can well be expected to have existed around Amman in periods when the population density of the district was heavy. The answer to the question of whether or not the number of strongly fortified settlements that existed at any particular date was large enough to support the hypothesis of an elaborate defense network surrounding Amman, does not now exist and considerable concentrated effort will be required before it can be found. Excavations at Balu'a, Dhiban, Tell es Sa'idiyeh, Deir 'Allā, Umm el Biyara, Taiwilan, Sahab and Buseirah have exposed architectural remains, probably within fortified settlements. Fairly simple domestic remains were encountered in almost all cases, the major exception being Buseirah where portions of fortification walls were excavated. At Buseirah, a series of buildings, building levels and rebuildings have been encountered which date in their primary use to the seventh century B.C. but continue in use into the Persian period.[2] Several large, official or sacred buildings were found on the acropolis of the site. The last major building, Building A, measures 48 by 36 meters and the larger structure beneath it measures 77 by 38 meters. The foundation thicknesses vary from 1 to 2 meters and extend above floor level to different heights. Good white plaster was found on

outside the tower; see Boraas, *ADAJ*, XVI. A few sherds dated to Iron II (seventh-sixth centuries B.C.) were found in stratified contexts in soundings at Rujm el Malfuf south: Thompson, *ADAJ*, XVIII. Iron Age I sherds were also found on this site as well as later fifth century B.C., Byzantine and Ayyubid-Mamluk sherds. Thompson also excavated at Khirbet el Hajjar and dated a tower on that site to the seventh-sixth centuries B.C. An Iron I settlement (twelfth-tenth centuries B.C.) had been established on a natural hill and a second period of occupation dated to the seventh-sixth centuries B.C., prior to the construction of the tower. Sherds of the beginning of Iron II were found on the site, as were later Byzantine sherds; Thompson, *BASOR*, CCXXVII.

Explorations on a number of sites south of Amman yielded Byzantine sherds in one instance and primarily Early Bronze in another (which also yielded some Iron Age and Byzantine sherds). Even farther south, some hours were spent at Meqabelein but we could not examine the most important parts of the site. Here, there actually seemed to be a whole series of low mounds which seemed to belong to different periods. The area which looked like the acropolis was, unfortunately, inaccessible. Mamluk, early Islamic, Byzantine, Roman, and some Hellenistic sherds were found in various places as well as a great number of both Iron I and II. A number of clear thirteenth century sherds were also found in one area.

Finally, as we mentioned above, some time was spent collecting sherds at Khirbet Mudhmar. Here the majority of the sherds were definitely Iron Age but of both Iron I and II. Late Roman pottery was also present on this site. This site, like Meqabelein, must be considered in the Amman district but could not strictly be considered a border fortress of Amman itself, since it is far closer to the sites of Sweileh and Safut (which is about 2 km. distant but on the slope of the hills overlooking the valley in which Khirbet Mudhmar is situated). (Meqabelein, Sahab, Safut, and other tells must be considered in the Amman district but probably as dependent settlements around the capital at Amman.) It would be extremely enlightening to find out the function of Khirbet Mudhmar and its relationship to Tell Safut and Rabbat Ammon, especially since its position is such that it blocks access into the valley from Safut and Sweileh (or, conversely, it blocks the approach to these sites) and does not serve a defensive function for the northern or western portions of the valley (particularly for access up the Wadi Zerka). If the site did have a prime military function, it could have served to defend the Amman district or it could equally have served as an opposing outpost.

Any datings by style of architecture must now clearly be avoided since it seems that we cannot distinguish clearly between Early Bronze, Middle Bronze, Iron Age, Roman, or Byzantine "megalithic" structures. There are clear resemblances in the construction of the Area I and II Iron Age walls at the north end of Jebel Qala' (Amman) and Aro'er or Khirbet Mudhmar. On the other hand, one is hard pressed to distinguish walls such as these from the Jebel Qala' Middle Bronze walls or the Rujm Malfuf Roman construction.

[1]Between 1965 and 1969, the writer made trips to many of the different towers and settlements around Amman. On most of them, an hour of searching by several individuals yielded only a handful of sherds and only a small number of these were in good enough condition to be identified. The sherds that could be identified were usually Roman, Byzantine, or Islamic. Many hours were spent collecting pottery at one of the sites, halfway between Amman and Khirbet Sar, which was being destroyed to make room for new houses and roads. The search here yielded mostly late Roman and Byzantine pottery. A few Iron Age sherds were found here, but most of them were turned up where the bulldozer was cutting into the lowest accumulations and into virgin soil. Closer to Amman, at a point about 2 km. northeast of Rujm Malfuf and only about one-half kilometer north of the same highway, heavy occupation debris of the Mamluk and early Islamic periods was found on the slopes and near the crest of a low hill. A handful of Iron Age sherds was also found.

During the summer of 1969, a sounding was made at one of the so-called Iron Age settlements that had long been considered the most typical and best preserved example. The preliminary report on the excavation of Rujm el Malfuf north indicates two periods of Roman occupation extending to bedrock in areas inside and

[2]Bennett, *Levant*, IX (1977), 3.

some of the room and courtyard floors and walls. Fill created by the collapse of walls into rooms and courtyards indicates that part of the superstructure was of mud brick. The plans are not yet fully articulated as far as walls and doorways are concerned, but a major feature seems to be a large courtyard around which rooms are arranged on four sides.

Building B foundations were sunk into a fill which apparently forms the base of the acropolis. The acropolis is set off from the lower plateaus of the city by a defense wall, and a heavy stone wall surrounds the site. Domestic architecture was encountered outside the acropolis area, but at least one building of substantial size was also excavated.[1] In general, its plan resembles that of the buildings on the acropolis.

Though a fortification wall was not excavated at Tell es Saʿidiyeh, a long and initially covered stairway connected the top of the acropolis with the foot of the tell at the Jordan Valley on the west side. The stairway must have been planned in conjunction with the city's defenses. Its side walls and floor were built with stones and a mud brick wall down its center helped support its roof. The stairway is dated to the twelfth through ninth centuries B.C.[2]

Remains of Three Fortresses

Two fortress sites have been excavated near the northern and southern extremities of our area, and a third, Aroʿer, near its center. In the north at Tell er Rumeith, a portion of a fortress has been excavated. The excavator, P. W. Lapp, estimated that one-fifth of the area of the superimposed fortresses has been excavated so far. The four phases of fortress occupation at the site are dated between the end of the tenth century B.C. and 733 B.C. The first fortress, level VIII, is said to be Solomonic with a Palestinian orientation in its ceramics, but this changes in VII, and seems to continue until V, to a Syrian orientation and, one must suppose, Aramean domination. The size of the level VIII fort was estimated at 32 x 37 m. and this was expanded to a larger fort with casemated walls covering an area of 42 x 43 m. in level VII. Several of the entrances into the fort from the north have been excavated.[3] It is not clear at present what type of occupation was enclosed within the fortress and whether contemporary settlement is also to be found outside the fort walls, forming, for example, an outer city.

In the south, four main fortress levels were excavated at the much discussed site of Tell el Kheleifeh.[4] Here, in the first level, a tall central building was surrounded by an open court which in turn was enclosed by a casemate wall (with the rooms of the casemate opening into the court and with recesses on the outer face). The gateway into the fortress was at the northeast. The central building had in the past been interpreted as a "smelter,"[5] but is now considered a "storehouse-granary."[6] In the second period, a larger area was enclosed within a new defense wall. The "storehouse-granary" was preserved but now situated against the northern corner of the new defenses; thus, a portion of the old defenses lay outside the new line and was no longer used. The new wall was solid and had a sloping glacis against its outer face. This glacis ended against a second, narrower wall and a second glacis extended outside of this wall.[7] The new gateway, now off-center in the southwest side, consisted of two sets of guard rooms which stood inside the line of the heavy wall. No plan has yet been published for the later fortresses, but we have dealt at length above with the published pottery from level IV.

The level I fortress is still considered Solomonic, and that of level II a rebuilding under Jehosaphat (who reigned in Judah between 873 and 849 B.C.). The constuction methods employed in these fortresses seem to substantiate this date.[8] We have seen above (pp. 45-46) that the mines at Timna, which were also considered Solomonic and contemporary with the earliest occupation of Tell el Kheleifeh, have now been shown clearly to date two centuries earlier. We must now await further publication of Rothenberg's finds and the re-evaluation of Glueck's material as a result. If the Solomonic date is substantiated, a new search must be initiated to find the mines used at the time of Solomon.

The fortress at Aroʿer was small but well built, measuring roughly fifty by fifty meters square. The outer wall is an impressive structure constructed of courses of very large, squared stones. The major occupation of this "fortress of Mesha"

---

[1]*Ibid.*, p. 8.

[2]James B. Pritchard, "Two Tombs and a Tunnel in the Jordan Valley: Discoveries at Biblical Zarethan," *Expedition*, VI (1964), 3-5.

[3]Lapp, *RB*, LXXV, 98-105.

[4]For a bibliography on the articles concerning this site, see the excavator's latest appraisal in: Nelson Glueck, "Ezion-geber," *BA*, XXVIII (1965), 70-87.

[5]*Ibid.*, p. 73.

[6]*Ibid.*, p. 81.

[7]Glueck cites similar defense systems on sites in Moab, *BA*, XXVIII, 84.

[8]*Ibid.*

is dated between the middle of the ninth and the beginning of the sixth centuries B.C., though there is no conclusive archaeological evidence for the destruction of the fortress. An Iron I occupation underlies this phase and continues after a Late Bronze Age phase.[1]

Remains of Private Houses

House remains were excavated at several sites: Aro'er, Balu'a, Dhiban, Tell es Sa'idiyeh, Deir 'Allā, Umm el Biyara, Taiwilan, Sahab and Buseirah (in Areas C and D). At Aro'er,[2] Balu'a,[3] Dhiban,[4] Sahab,[5] and Buseirah there are walls and foundations of roughly shaped stone. Stone walls and foundations were also found at Taiwilan[6] and Umm el Biyara,[7] but differed considerably in construction because of the kind of stones used and the means employed for shaping the stones. At these two sites, sandstone was broken, along natural cleavage lines, into thin flat slabs of varying thickness (from 1 to 15 cm).[8] Portions of several architectural units were excavated at Umm el Biyara and the following characteristic features were illustrated: the predominant use of long rectangular rooms, the use of common walls in adjacent units, and the joining of most building units to each other. The little that has been published from Taiwilan indicates a similar building practice which, since it is largely determined by the building material, can be expected to be common at least in the western portions of ancient Edom.[9]

Remains of domestic and industrial buildings, pits, pavements and storage caves were excavated at Sahab. Extensive settlement of the twelfth century B.C. was encountered on five scattered areas of the site. After a major destruction, occupation was reduced to a few scattered buildings in the eleventh century B.C. Late in Iron II, primarily in the seventh century B.C., a well planned settlement existed on the site but over a much more restricted area than the Iron I settlement.[10]

Tell es Sa'idiyeh and Tell Deir 'Allā, as Jordan Valley sites, present a different picture with the predominant use of mud brick and only occasional use of stone as foundation courses for important walls. An area of private houses was exposed at Tell es Sa'idiyeh, and four occupation levels of the ninth and eighth centuries B.C. were encountered. In each level, the houses were built along streets and in the third and fourth levels the six houses cleared all conformed to the same ground plan.[11] We discussed briefly above (pp. 39-40), the architectural remains which have been published from the Iron I phases at Deir 'Allā. We can only add here that structures continuing the occupation sequence to the fifth cen-

tury B.C. have been excavated in the last seasons. One of these buildings was apparently a shrine whose walls were covered with whitewash and then written upon in Aramaic script in red and black paint.[12]

Tomb Plans

Most of the pottery discussed above in our corpus came from tomb groups. Unfortunately, only a few of these had plans which were in any way informative. Many of the chambers were roughly cut and with oval ground plan, or they merely seemed to be natural caves. In two cases, two

---

[1]Olávarri, *RB*, LXXII, 77-94 and *RB*, LXXVI, 230, 231 and pl. I.

[2]Olávarri, *RB*, LXXII, 80-84.

[3]Crowfoot, *PEFQS*, LXVI, 76-84.

[4]Reed and Winnett, *Dhiban*, I, 14-16.

[5]See footnote 1 on p. 10 for references.

[6]Bennett, *RB*, LXXVI, 386-90.

[7]Bennett, *RB*, LXXIII, 378-84 and pls. XIV, XV, XIX, and XX.

[8]*Ibid.*, p. 378.

[9]Glueck, *EEP*, II, 30, fig. 13.

[10]Ibrahim, *ADAJ*, XIX, 55-61 and *ADAJ*, XX, 69-79 and 82.

[11]Pritchard, *RB*, LXXIII, 574-76. In James B. Pritchard, "A Cosmopolitan Culture of the Late Bronze Age," *Expedition*, VII (1965), 26-33 a block of twelve row houses is mentioned. They are said to be identical in size (17 by 24 feet) and plan with six on each side with a common wall serving the backs of the units. In each unit one enters a courtyard from the street. A row of wooden or brick pillars supports a roof over part of the courtyard and a small room is situated at the rear of the unit. Mud and reed impressions were found in the heavily burned remains of the roofs. This complex is dated to the eighth century B.C. Five large circular "bread ovens" were found to the west of one of the parallel streets and a large collection of loom weights in one house indicated a specialized use of that unit.

In the highest level of the tell, a large, official building had been constructed in the fourth century B.C., James B. Pritchard, "The Palace of Tell es Sa'idiyeh," *Expedition*, X (1968), 20-22. The palace, possibly the residence of a certain Jakinu if the inscription on an incense altar is indicative, is a square structure measuring roughly 71 feet on a side. Massive walls divide the building into a central courtyard and seven surrounding rooms. The rooms and courtyard were all paved with small stones.

[12]Henk J. Franken, "Texts from the Persian Period from Tell Deir 'Allā," *VT*, XVII (1967), 480-81 and Jacob Hoftijzer and G. van der Krooij, *Aramaic Texts from Deir 'Allā* (Documenta et monumenta orientis antiqui," 19; Leiden: E. J. Brill, 1976).

rooms were attached: Irbed tombs A and B and Nebo tomb number 20. Amman E and N were elongated oval chambers with no special features, but N had a better shaped doorway and an open area cut into the rock in front of the entrance.

The five tombs which can be differentiated from the above all had a bench or benches in the main chamber. Irbed C was the simplest of these and had a bench opposite the entrance, though the shape of the chamber was a simple oval not very different from the tomb chambers mentioned so far. However, this tomb is important in that, unlike most other tombs, part of it had not been disturbed. A skeleton was found on the bench with a number of vessels next to the skull.[1]

Tomb AA has a unique plan.[2] The chamber is nearly a rectangle, but it is somewhat wider at the back of the tomb. There is a separate rock-cut entrance area and two "cupboard-like" recesses were cut into the side walls of the tomb at the back (giving the plan a T-shaped appearance). The bench is long, narrow, and very low. It stretches along the south wall from the entrance to the cupboard, is 20 cm. wide, and reaches a maximum height of only 7 cm. The cutting of the tomb was very rough.

The two Dhiban tombs[3] were almost identical in plan. The corners of the tombs were rounded so that the plan was closer to an irregular oval than a rectangle. There was a drop in level from the shaft to the level of the chamber and stairs spanned this vertical distance in J3. A rectangular depression extended into the chamber from the doorway and was of the same width. There was a second, deeper, half-oval depression at the back of the chamber. The higher portions of the chamber floor, then, formed three connected benches. A major difference between the two tombs was that in J3 the benches were built of stone while in J1 they were cut into bedrock. At Meqabelein, the shaft had been destroyed but there was a similar depression (or "shallow gangway"[4]) extending into the tomb from the entrance. The depression at the rear, however, is lacking and as a result the plan takes on a square shape. Iron Age bench tombs have also been found in Palestine, but since the number of our Transjordanian examples is so few it would be dangerous to say much concerning similarities or cross-connections.[5] Also, the number of Palestinian rock-cut tombs, which would serve as comparisons, is quite small and thus makes our problem of interpreting the significance of any connections either extremely difficult or uncertain.[6]

No detailed plan illustrating the location of every object has yet been published for an Iron Age Transjordanian tomb. In most cases, the tombs were badly disturbed and unfortunately, as a consequence, it is difficult to say whether any consistency existed in the placement of specific classes of objects or of the bodies. It does seem that all of the tombs were used for multiple burials and in some cases a large number of interments must have been made.[7]

Concluding Remarks

This summary indicates that we know very little so far about Iron Age architectural practices in the Transjordan. Some regional variation is already obvious and is based upon the most readily available building material in a specific area. Considerably more excavation and publication are needed before a significant contribution can be made to the understanding of the architecture in the Transjordan and its relation to practices in the surrounding areas.

---

[1]R. Dajani, *ADAJ*, XI, 88-89.

[2]Harding, *QDAP*, XI, 67-68.

[3]Reed and Winnett, *Dhiban*, I, 57-60 and pls. 94-96. A third tomb, J2, is mentioned here but it apparently was never finished nor used.

[4]Harding, *QDAP*, XIV, 44.

[5]*Ibid.*, pp. 58-59. Two additional tombs with Iron Age materials, published in 1970 and 1972, must be added to our earlier discussion. Both provide additional illustrations of the use of benches as a specific feature of Transjordanian Iron Age tombs. The chambers are different in plan, as are the placement of the benches along the base of the walls of the irregular chamber of tomb F and the different size benches along the side walls of tomb C. The use of a "gangway" in the Dhiban and Meqabelein tombs may be related to the two pathways which cross at the center of tomb C, one stretching from the entrance to the rear wall (and the base of a "chimney") and the other connecting the side benches. Similar to Sahab tomb B, but previously unique there, are "chimney"-like structures in tombs C and F which link the tomb chambers, apparently to what would have been the contemporary ground level above. R. Dajani notes a higher accumulation of debris under the "chimney" in tomb C, including a preponderance of the latest materials found in the tomb. A substantial drop from the entrance to the floor of tomb C is a feature also noted in the Dhiban tombs. For the details and dimensions published so far concerning Sahab tombs C and F see: R. Dajani, *ADAJ*, XV (1970), 29-30 and Ibrahim, *ADAJ*, XVII (1972), 31-34.

[6]Stanislao Loffreda, "Iron Age Rock-cut Tombs in Palestine," *LA*, XVIII (1968), 244-87.

[7]The only attempt at estimating the number of burials in a tomb was made for tomb J3 at Dhiban (Reed and Winnett, *Dhiban*, I, 59). The teeth found in this tomb were examined and at least 45 adults are said to have been represented.

CHAPTER X

IRON AGE SMALL OBJECTS
AND SCULPTURE

The discussion in this chapter will center primarily on two classes of objects, terra-cotta figurines (and molds for the production of such figurines) and sculpture. These represent a majority of the pieces of Iron Age plastic arts preserved from the Transjordan. Though the sculpture has been published, it has not been discussed extensively. Only a few pieces of sculpture were found outside of the Amman district, so we have illustrated all the Amman pieces here (all but figs. 91:1 and 92:3 are reproduced from our own photographs) to facilitate the discussion. We have also illustrated, in our plates, the figurines and molds from Amman tomb F as well as figurines found in Amman in 1968-69. Some unique items are presented here, but serve to illustrate the major figurine types that are available to date from the Transjordan. The material from the other sites will also be brought into the discussion. Since, once again, most of these objects come from unstratified contexts, a typological discussion is imperative.

Figurines

Most of the figurines to be considered here fall into three groups: (1) female figurines; (2) male figurines, and (3) animal figurines. Careful examination reveals changes in the style of representation but the subject matter in each group is very limited; namely, virtually all the female figures are women carrying tambourines, virtually all the male figures are horsemen, and virtually all the animal figures are horses. On human figurines, the use of molds is usually restricted to the face while the body is usually shaped by hand. The only exception are a number of the earliest type of female figurines where the entire front side was impressed in a mold.

Female Figurines

It is only with the publication of figurines from Mt. Nebo, Deir 'Allā, and Irbed that enough figurines are available so that a comparison of similar features is valuable. Such an examination shows that virtually all female figurines conform to a specific type, namely, a woman playing a tambourine. The figurines published earlier by Glueck and others were fragmentary and did not allow the reconstruction of the type of figurine to

which they belonged. An analysis of the decorative details, facial features, etc., leads to a threefold subdivision which seems to have chronological significance.

Group I

No figurines have been published so far for the first half of Iron I. Neither the Jebel Nuzha tomb nor the Madeba tombs provided an example, nor did phases A through L at Deir 'Allā. The earliest examples which provide sufficient information are found in tomb A at Irbed. Similar figurines have been found at Deir 'Allā, but the scanty information available indicates only that they are Iron Age and must be later than phase L.[1] A surface find from Jebel Qala[2] illustrates the following features which are also common on the other examples of this group.

A mold is usually used and the features on it are accentuated primarily by the use of line rather than by plastic shaping or modeling of planes. The preserved portion of this figurine is from the shoulders to just below the waist. The tambourine is held over, and covers, the left breast.[3] The left hand supports it from underneath and the right hand, positioned against its lower left quadrant, is shown as if steadying or beating it. The palms of both hands are against the tambourine. The edge of the instrument is formed by three concentric raised circles with a row of dots between the inner two. (The Beth Shan figurine[4] and the larger Irbed figurine, IA:16, which conform to this type, have dotted decoration on the center portion of the tambourine also.) Two rows of the decorated skirt are illustrated. Each row is indicated by two parallel lines; the upper one is filled with a

---

[1]No information is available on their stratigraphic position other than that they are Iron Age and apparently did not belong to the earliest levels. Franken, *VT*, X, pl. 13 and XI, pl. 19.

[2]Register no. A. C. '68:17. See fig. 89:3.

[3]Musicians are presented in procession on several carved ivory pyxides at Nimrud. Richard D. Barnett, *The Nimrud Ivories* (London: British Museum, 1957), pls. XVI, XVII. Here, fully clothed musicians play tambourines which are depicted both as plain disks and as disks with decorated borders, similar to those illustrated on our figurines.

[4]James, *IABS*, fig. 112:5.

line of dots while the other is filled with a row of triangles. (The Beth Shan figurine has two more rows with a repetition of the dots, row three, and triangles, row four. This extends so far below the waist that the representation of a decorated skirt, and not merely a waistband, is obvious.) Three lines at the right wrist represent two bracelets and four lines on the upper right arm indicate three armlets. The right breast is shown but was not well impressed by the mold. The Beth Shan and other figurines show, by analogy, that it was probably bare, as was the entire torso above the waist. Two narrow plaits of hair, which fall at either side of the head on the Beth Shan figurine and reach to the breasts, are barely visible at the top of the Amman figurine.

The same details are found on the Irbed figurine IA:16, but it seems to be badly worn and the drawings and photograph are not very clear. The smaller Irbed figurine, IA:29, seems to be of a similar type, but is less well preserved and the tambourine seems to have been broken off. Another similar figurine was found near Mt. Nebo. Only the tambourine, hands, armlet, and ends of the plaits of hair are preserved.[1]

The head of the Beth Shan figurine is also preserved and helps us to attribute several figurine heads from Deir 'Allā to this group.[2] On the Beth Shan figurine, the elongated almond-shaped eyes are surrounded by a ridge, the nose is destroyed, the mouth is fairly wide, and the ears cannot be seen in the photograph. The most important feature is the high hat. There is a band, again decorated with dots, above the forehead and a higher portion of the hat extending above it. Two figurine heads[3] and a mold[4] from Deir 'Allā also illustrate hats, but each has a slightly different decoration. The figurines are of the crude style also present at Amman, Mt. Nebo, Irbed, and Beth Shan, but the mold is much more delicately executed.[5] It is difficult to determine whether the illustration of different types of hats was intentional or whether they are all merely a depiction of the *polos* so frequently found on Canaanite and Phoenician ivories.[6] The eyebrows and ears are clearly depicted on these heads and the plaits of hair (which like the Beth Shan figurine are decorated with hatching) are also preserved on the mold. The ends of the hair are turned around into small circular curls which seem to be diminutive "Hathor curls."[7] These figurines are presently isolated examples in the Transjordan. The Deir 'Allā mold is broken below the shoulders, but a necklace with a circular pendant is worn between the breasts by the woman who is represented.

A similar necklace is present on another Deir 'Allā figurine of this type,[8] but several other variations are illustrated here. This figurine is not mold-made but the decoration is incised. Bracelets and armlets, indicated on both arms, are depicted by parallel incised lines with dots between them. A collar-like necklace and the cord of the necklace with the pendant are also shown in this manner. The hands hold a small tambourine in the usual manner and both breasts are indicated. The lower portion of the body is also unclothed while the dotted and the triangle bands, found on the skirts of the other figurines, have been combined in a waistband formed by triangles with dots at their centers. One would not expect any significance in the use of such simple patterns of decoration, but the repetition is noteworthy.

In contrast to some of the figurines to be discussed below, all of these figurines must be considered as plaques and apparently were not intended to stand by themselves. It is unfortunate that few of the figurines to be discussed below are preserved below the waist. Presently, it seems that the one Deir 'Allā figurine represents the only Transjordanian example in which a woman is depicted as completely unclothed. Another nude female figurine from Deir 'Allā

---

[1]Oswald Henke, "Zur Lage von Beth Peor," *ZDPV*, LXXV (1959), pl. 46.

[2]Henk J. Franken and C. A. Franken-Battershill, *A Primer of Old Testament Archaeology* (Leiden: E. J. Brill, 1963), pl. XV.

[3]*Ibid.*, pl. XV:A.

[4]*Ibid.*, pl. XV:B.

[5]Though this mold has much in common with the figurines under dicussion here, its finer execution indicates that it is later than the others. Unfortunately, no good stylistic criteria are present to indicate how much later it should be dated.

[6]The earliest ivories upon which it occurs are at Meggido: Gordon Loud, *Megiddo Ivories* ("OIP," LII; Chicago: University of Chicago Press, 1939), no. 291 on pp. 43, 186; no. 295 on pp. 38, 173; no. 342 on pp. 2, 4. There are several examples at Tell Halaf: Felix Langenegger, Karl Müller, and Rudolf Naumann, *Tell Halaf II, Die Bauwerke* (Berlin: W. de Gruyter, 1950), pl. 59:2, 3. The most numerous examples are from Nimrud, of which only a few examples are cited here: Max E. L. Mallowan, *Nimrud and Its Remains* (London: Collins, 1966), pl. 3, figs. 146, 147, and 150, and particularly Barnett, *The Nimrud Ivories*, pl. 105 and pls. LXX:S183; LXXII:S179, 190-96, 198, 200, and 201; LXXIII:S197, 202-205, 206, 208, 209, 212, etc. In most of the Nimrud examples, the *polos* is worn by a naked female employed as a caryatid figure either single or in pairs. It is interesting that in none of the cases cited here is the naked woman with *polos* shown holding a tambourine, so the examples from the Transjordan and Beth Shan would show a unique combination.

[7]Barnett, *The Nimrud Ivories*, p. 37.

[8]Franken, *VT*, X, pl. 13a.

may represent a further variation of this type.[1] This figure seems to be kneeling on one knee and holding a baby (covering the left breast with the child rather than the tambourine). The child reaches up with both arms to hold the woman's breasts and its face is also presented full front. The reason for considering this figurine with the other nude figurines at Deir 'Allā (in the group under discussion) is obvious when compared with another figurine from Beth Shan.[2] This figure shows both the tambourine and an infant held over the left breast. The two necklaces of the Deir 'Allā figurine are present as well as the waistband and undraped lower portion of the body. The emphasis on the use of the line is also obvious. The Irbed and Beth Shan examples indicate a date between the late eleventh and early ninth centuries B.C. for this group of figurines.

It is not possible to explain this combination of features, any more than it is to identify the person or deity represented. It is now possible only to note the particular features in order to gain information on the stylistic and chronological development of the figurines. Hopefully, information will become available to shed some light on their interpretation. On the basis of analogies with the well known Phoenician ivories, the tambourine players can be considered to depict entertainers, and possibly priestesses who entertain for a god, but they most probably do not represent divinities. The figurines with child are another matter, however.[3]

Group II

The second group of figurines are or seem to be characterized by a simplification and slight modification of the group just discussed. They represent the next chronological stage which would date provisionally from the late tenth century to the eighth century B.C. Two examples, one from Mt. Nebo[4] and one from near Kerak,[5] illustrate mold-made figurines (probably to be used as plaques as were all the examples above). The details indicated by incised lines are rare and little in the way of clothing or jewelry is shown. Waistbands are indicated but little is preserved below them, so it is impossible to say whether this part of the body was clothed. The upper body also is not clear, but we suppose that it was unclothed. The hands hold a small object in the same manner as the tambourines were held. The hair falls to the breasts and is hatched on the Kerak figurine. No hat is illustrated here. The ears, rounded eyes and eyebrows, mouth and chin resemble the manner of depiction used in the group I figurines, except that there is complete reliance on modeling of the surface instead of outlining the features with definite lines.

The remaining figurines in this group were not intended as plaques, but were designed to stand erect on the hollow clay cones which formed the bodies. A similar type of figurine in Palestine has been called "pillar figurine."[6] Two other figurines from Mt. Nebo may represent a variation of this type which is normally dated to the eighth and seventh centuries B.C.[7] As in the Palestinian examples, each head is molded separately, with a pin or tenon formed from the clay at the bottom in place of a neck. The pin is inserted into the body of the figurine and a band of clay, pressed into the joint, forms the neck and holds the pieces together.[8] In Palestine, either the body is a solid cylinder of clay with a depression at the top to take the head and a slight hollowing out and flaring at the base to form a stand or, less frequently, the body is hollow.[9] The bodies of the Mt. Nebo figurines are hollow cones. The arms, breasts,

[1]Franken, *VT*, X, pl. 13b, and Franken and Franken-Battershill, *A Primer of Old Testament Archaeology*. Unfortunately, the captions are not consistent and illustrate the difficulty in identifying the figures involved because they are not well or clearly molded. It seems likely, though, that rather than having a "monkey seated on the lap of a seated female figure" (Franken, *VT*, X) or the "figurine of a monkey with child" (Franken and Franken-Battershill, *A Primer of Old Testament Archaeology*), we have simply a clumsily depicted naked woman holding a naked child.

[2]James, *IABS*, pl. 111:6.

[3]An attempt at classifying female figurines and examining them to see if they can be identified with any deities mentioned in written texts is undertaken in James B. Pritchard, *Palestinian Figurines in Relation to Certain Goddesses Known through Literature* (New Haven: American Oriental Society, 1943).

[4]Glueck, *Other Side*, p. 152, fig. 82.

[5]*Ibid.*, p. 153, fig. 83.

[6]Pritchard, *Palestinian Figurines*, pp. 56-58.

[7]Saller, *LA*, XVI, 260-63. The figurines cited here are illustrated on fig. 28:1 and 2. Number 1 is taller and holds a tambourine, but in no. 2 the tambourine has been broken off.

[8]Albright, *TBM*, III, 138-41.

[9]Thomas A. Holland, "A Study of Palestinian Iron Age Baked Clay Figurines, with Special Reference to Jerusalem: Cave 1," *Levant*, X (1978), 121-54 provides a valuable statistical compilation of the Palestinian material according to quite specific typological categories. The Transjordanian evidence is included, except for the Amman evidence presented here for the first time. At the present time, it does not seem profitable to subdivide the basic groups we have indicated until more evidence is available from the Transjordan.

and tambourine (broken off on no. M2001) are hand modeled on the body and the skirt is represented by a ledge that flares above the base. The facial features and representation of the hair are the same as on the Kerak figurine, including the hatching on two plaits of hair at the sides of the face and the narrow rounded ledge of hair above the forehead (which was probably rounded off at the top when the edges of the figurine were smoothed to obliterate the traces of the edge of the mold).[1] The reason for the lack of detail in the molded face or on the body is now clear. These figurines, as was the case in Palestine, were painted. The body was covered with a white slip representing a garment and the face was painted red-brown. In Palestine, yellow paint was preserved in a few instances and was apparently used to indicate jewelry.[2] The Amman figurines, which will be discussed below, were all decorated with paint, but with a single exception they were decorated in a different color scheme.

Two almost identical figurine heads found at el Medeiyineh and Balu'a probably belonged to this class of figurine, as one of them has the pin for attachment to the body preserved.[3] The face and hair of these figurines are similar to those discussed above, and particularly to the plaque figurine from Mt. Nebo. The only unusual feature here is the depiction of the large, awkward ears.

The remaining figurine of this type is a surface find from Jebel Qala', illustrated on figure 89:2. It is badly broken in places, but enough characteristic features are present to classify it. The right arm is missing and it is difficult to determine whether the projection on the figure's left side represents a breast or a tambourine. Since it projects farther from the body than is normal for tambourines on the plaque figurines and is more like the pronounced breasts on the Mt. Nebo "pillar figurines," we must assume that a breast was intended. This assumption is further substantiated by the fact that, like the Nebo "pillar figurines," only the face was pressed in a mold while the body was hand formed. The color scheme was the same as that found on the "pillar figurines." This figurine must, however, be a late example of this class because the hair style now seems to be fuller around the neck, it does not come down so far on the shoulder, and also the incision on the mold is far more delicately executed. These features are characteristic of the latest group of figurines. The eyes are not formed as they are on the later examples, however, since they are still represented in an almond shape and bulging. No separate lines indicate the eyebrows, but the eyelids are now intentionally indicated though the pupil is not. A tentative date for this figurine (together with fig. 89:1 to be discussed below) can be given as around 700 B.C.

Group III

Finally, the latest group of figurines is illustrated by fragments and molds from tomb F in Amman. Two head fragments are illustrated in three views each on figure 87:4 and 5, and two tambourines, with attached hands, are illustrated in front and back views, figure 87:6 and 7. Two complete molds and one fragmentary one are illustrated on figure 88:1-3. The backs of the molds are shown at the top, the decorated sides are in the middle, and clay impressions are at the bottom of the page. A careful examination of the figurine heads from the tomb shows that they illustrate the same features present on the molds (indicating a homogeneous group), but none of the figurines were produced from these specific molds.

Turning first to the figurines, it seems most likely that they also belonged to "pillar figurines."

The break at the neck of figure 87:4 shows the pin for attachment to the body. Some of the clay which held the two portions of the figurine together is preserved on the figure's left side. The tambourine and hands are modeled clearly but were not impressed in a mold. The color scheme is different from what we have seen thus far. The dark red wash now seems to cover the entire figurine, with special features accentuated by black and white paint. The painting on the faces follows the impressed detail but the amount of detail present on the mold seems to be far more than is required on such figurines. Some of it is clearly used. The pupil of the eye is painted black and the paint fills a small mold-made hole. The almond-shaped eyes are painted white and surrounded by black paint which covers the eyelids. The line impressed in the cast, as a fine ridge

---

[1]Illustrations of a similar hair style can be found in Assyrian art but even more striking are their use in the strongly Assyrian-influenced Urartian art. A number of the bronze "siren" heads attached to bronze cauldrons are very much like the heads on the Kerak and Mt. Nebo (tomb) figurines. See especially Maurits N. van Loon, *Urartian Art, Its Distinctive Traits in the Light of New Excavations* ("Uitgaven van het Nederlands Historisch-Archaeologisch Instituut te Istanbul," XX; Istanbul: Nederlands Historisch-Archaeologisch Instituut, 1966), pp. 107-109. It is interesting in connection with our figurines that parallels need not be drawn as far away as Urartu. Van Loon argues that the "siren" attachments on cauldrons, with facial features similar to the figurines under discussion here, were produced in "workshops in the Taurus area west of the Euphrates" (p. 108).

[2]Albright, *TBM*, III, 14c.

[3]Glueck, *EEP*, I, 25, fig. 7a and b.

around each eye to indicate the eyelid, is not picked up in paint. The hair, delicately indicated on the molds, can barely be seen on the figurines as it is entirely obscured by paint. A headband seems to be indicated above the forehead with the usual white paint bordered by black. The hair at the sides of the face is painted black and indicates that, as is true with the sculptured heads to be discussed below, the headband did not extend down at the sides of the face.

That jewelry was also indicated by the characteristic white band framed in black, is illustrated by the bracelets on the wrists of the hands against the tambourines. One can only suspect that armlets and some kind of necklace would also have been shown in this manner. The decorated band found on the earliest figurines was also present here as paint, but on the edge rather than the side of the instrument.

Figurine Molds

The mold which resembles these figurines most closely is figure 88:1, but it could not have been used to produce them because it is slightly larger. The faces on figure 88:2 and 3 are smaller and have different features. The mold, figure 88:2, resembles most closely the group II figurines. The great difference between these molds and the figurines discussed above is that the peculiar features present here are not normally found in figurines but are characteristic of carved ivories. Despite this great similarity, there are no exact duplicates for any of our figurines or molds in ivory. In other words, no specific ivory has the same combination of features as those illustrated here. All of the individual features can be paralleled, however.

Hair Styles

The molds, figures 88:1 and 2, had relatively simple hair styles. In both cases, they seem to have been parted in the middle with three locks of hair (shown on top of the head) which curve down behind the ears and alongside the face. On number 2, the hair is longer at the sides than on the other molds and extends to the shoulders in fairly narrow tresses. In this respect, mold number 2 most closely resembles the figurine heads from this tomb as well as the four double-faced stone heads discussed below. On molds 1 and 3, the hair falls to just below the level of the chin but is puffed up and each lock ends in a curl. Mold number 3 also has a more elaborate arrangement on top of the head. At first glance one is reminded of the frontlet found on some of the ivories depicting the "woman in the window" motif or the "naked goddess,"[1] especially since the necklace and earrings shown on this mold can be found on such ivories,

also.[2] An earring with three balls pendant from a crescent is found only on a horse frontlet decorated with a "naked goddess" found at Nimrud (earrings with two balls pendant from a crescent are more common) and at Arslan Tash.[3] In place of the frontlet, our mold shows four vertical locks of hair, each ending in a curl. Another unusual feature is the narrow, vertically hatched band of hair which forms a narrow bang across the forehead.

Facial Features

The depiction of the eyes is uniform on the three molds. The eyes are not large, as is often the case on ivories, but in normal proportion to the rest of the face. They are almond shape and the lids are depicted as a narrow ridge around the eye. This ridge does not actually merge in a point at the sides of the face but rather as two parallel lines,

---

[1] Barnett, *The Nimrud Ivories*, pl. XCIII:S334o and pl. LXIII:S146. Mallowan, *Nimrud and Its Remains*, p. 212, figs. 148, 149, 152; p. 213, fig. 156; p. 539, fig. 458; p. 583, fig. 549.

[2] Choker necklaces of this type, with three bands, are frequently shown on ivories but usually the center strand is a row of dots. See our discussion below concerning the female stone heads where such necklaces are shown. Ivory no. S226, illustrated in Barnett's *The Nimrud Ivories*, pl. LVII, from the Southeast Palace (Burnt Palace), is an isolated example of the plain necklace. It is often difficult to tell, in cases where only head and neck are shown, if we are really dealing with the depiction of necklaces or the decorated fringe on the top of a garment. Similar decoration is shown as the upper border of garments in many instances (pls. III:C4, C8; XII:F2; XVI:S3; XXIII:S26; XXVI:S20; XXVII:S12a; LXXXVIII:S293; etc.). The only earrings with three balls pendant from a crescent are found on horse frontlets: Barnett, *The Nimrud Ivories*, LXIII:S146, and possibly Mallowan, *Nimrud and Its Remains*, p. 583, fig. 549. It seems to us that these should be distinguished from the earrings worn by Assyrian kings, illustrated on pl. 8 of Barthel Hrouda, *Die Kulturgeschichte des assyrischen Flachbildes* ("Saarbrücker Beiträge zur Altertumskunde," II; Bonn: Rudolf Habelt Verlag, 1965), no. 24, but closer to the later no. 33 (see pp. 55-57) attributed to the time of Sargon II. The earrings on the double female heads, discussed below, are similar to those on the mold shown on fig. 88:3, but are elongated and pendant from the bottom of the crescent (and not partially from the sides). This seems to be in keeping with the tendency found at the end of the Assyrian empire, illustrated by Hrouda's pl. 8:43.

[3] François Thureau-Dangin, A. Barrois, G. Dossin, et M. Dunand, *Arslan-Tash* ("Haut-commmissariat de la République française en Syrie et au Liban. Service des antiquités Bibliothèque archéologique et historique," XVI; Paris: Librairie Orientaliste Paul Geuthner, 1931), pl. XXXVI:56-58.

with one on top of the other. The pupils are depicted as dots in 1 and 3, while the presence of the same in number 2 is difficult to determine. The eyebrows, which appear as ridges in the casts, follow the contour of the upper eyelid and have squared off ends. The noses do not always come out well in the cast but on the figurines from this tomb (where they came out better than on our casts) their short, slightly rounded, quite graceful forms are indicated. The cheek bones are high and the cheeks are nicely modeled, as is the short, slightly pointed chin. There is a slight smile on the lips, which are tight, not very wide, and, like the chin and nose, slightly pointed.

Ears

The ears, as on most of the figurines from the Transjordan, seem to have presented the greatest problem to the artist. In some cases, this difficulty seems less pronounced when the object is viewed in three dimensions rather than in a drawing or photograph. Mold number 2 seems to be most successful in that the ears are normal, in proportion to the face, and are shown as would be expected when the face is seen from the front. In number 1, the ear is much larger than normal and turned so that it is seen from an angle that is normal if one were viewing the face from the side.[1] The ears on number 3 are also larger than normal and turned as in number 1. This point must be stressed, since the same difficulty is present on the sculptured female heads below and was noted above on the figurines from Balu'a and el Medeiyineh. The problem exists primarily because the artist seems to be handling his subject as if he were forced to work in two dimensions rather than three. If his mold could be made so that the side of the face could be properly presented, his problem would have been eased, but since he apparently felt this was not possible, and it was essential that the ear be depicted clearly, he tried to solve his difficulty as best he could. As can be seen here, some solutions seem more successful than others.[2]

A number of features present on the molds and figurines from tomb F are unique when compared with the other figurines discussed above. Similar features are also found on figurines from Meqabelein. It would seem that such features, as well as the change in color scheme, are characteristic of the latest Iron Age figurines available from the Transjordan. The above analysis and interpretation of the figurines seem valid, but an assessment of their date in comparison to the date of the carved ivories showing similar stylistic features raises some difficulties. An examination of ivories produced in Syria, Phoenicia, and Palestine does not help our chronological situation considerably. There is still room for increased precision in dating ivories, as far as stylistic fea-

tures are concerned. Generally, no greater precision than a 150-200 year range for specific features is possible, though even such a time range is not always secure. Features like the earrings and necklace[3] on the mold, figure 88:3, or the curls[4] on figure 88:1 and 3 can be found in ivories at Nimrud. It seems, however, that little evidence for their date is available other than that they were collected with the other ivories of the Southeast (Burnt) Palace between the years 722 and 612 B.C.,[5] when that palace flourished, or that they were found in Fort Shalmaneser, which flourished in the seventh century B.C. before its major destruction in 612 B.C.[6] How much earlier the ivories were actually carved before they were deposited in these palaces, or how long similar modes of representing specific details or patterns were in use (whether for 50, 100, or 150 years) is still a question open to considerable debate. Certain features, like the almond-shaped eyes, the way the eyelids and eyebrows are depicted, the hair style of figure 88:2, and the depiction of the pupil of the eye, are discouragingly common features on ivories and can be found as early as the twelfth century in ivories from Megiddo.[7] Features like the rounded eyes without the representation of pupils, as was common on many of our earlier figurines, can also be found on ivories.[8] In some instances, there may be a chronological coincidence in the occurrence of this feature on figurines and ivories but the matter is presently far from clear.

In light of these facts, it is obvious that extreme caution must be exercised in generalizing from the distinctions outlined above for figurines, and in applying these generalizations to other art objects. The evidence is limited and more information may change the picture completely. It does not seem, however, that this analysis will prove to be far wrong since its application to Palestinian material seems valid also. Presently, it must suffice to say that the new features present on the figurines from Amman tomb F were heavily influenced by artistic conventions previously established for carving on ivory and softer materials. Many of the new features that were introduced in this way were not actually necessary and could not be used to good advantage on figurines whose function had not changed drastically. This is best illustrated by the seeming uselessness of much of the detail present in the molds. The new painting tradition seemed intent on accentuating some details, but for the most part it served to obscure much of the mold-impressed detail. The use of the white and black band-painted decoration on red-washed pottery vessels was discussed above and it was shown to be an established Transjordanian decorative scheme for around five hundred years. There are no instances of the application of this scheme to figurines for this length of time but, rather, only for such an occurrence at the very end of Iron II. It is interesting that a cult stand with caryatid female figurines dating to the seventh century B.C. was found at Salamis[9] in Cyprus and was decorated with the same color scheme. The bodies of the women are painted red, as is most of the stand. Several white bands bordered by black bands ring the stand at the top and bottom, but, most importantly, the whites of the eyes are indicated in white, and the lids, eyebrows, and pupils are painted in black. The hair is also painted black. (The photographs and drawings are too indistinct to permit a more detailed discussion.) Similar painted decoration is found on figurines at Tabbat al Hammam in Syria, but these figurines are dated somewhat earlier.[10]

Miscellaneous Female Figurines

Two other figurine heads and a figurine mold which represent women have been found, but there is no indication that these also belonged to women holding tambourines. They are included here to round out the discussion of female figurines. One of these figurines is from Amman and indicates a number of features not represented above.[11]

The hair style is unique. There is a row of dots over the forehead which reminds one of the tufts of hair on the Palestinian figurines mentioned below (p. 137), but here they are smaller and more numerous. The rest of the hair arrangement is not similar to the normal Palestinian depiction of hair on such figurines, which is usually interpreted as representing a wig. The hair seems to reach the shoulders and seems to be hatched like on the longer locks of the Kerak and Madeba figurines (the published photograph is so dark that it is difficult to see much of the detail). The row of dots over the forehead is otherwise unique on figurines and very rare elsewhere. It is, however, found on the stone female heads from Amman and will be discussed below. Mr. Ma'ayeh mentions that above this band is a veil which covers the top of the head.[12] The face and especially the chin are shorter than usual, making the face much more rounded and puffy. The lips are wider than usual but show a slight

---

[1]The fact that we have only a fraction of the mold may exaggerate this effect in the photographs, since the nose and ear would not normally be in a plane perpendicular to a frontal line of sight but in a receding plane.

[2]The depiction of ears in side view, next to (and in roughly the same plane as) the face in front view, is a common feature of Egyptian art. Successful and unsuccessful attempts to deal with this problem can be illustrated on Egyptian works of art. See William Stevenson Smith, *The Art and Architecture of Ancient Egypt* (Baltimore: Penguin Books, 1965), p. 47 and pls. 67-69a, 114a, 138, and 139 for some of the less successful solutions to this problem.

[3]See p. 133, footnote 2.

[4]Similar curls are quite rare. Two ivories from Arslan Tash show them on "women in the window" ivories, Thureau-Dangin, *et al., Arslan-Tash,* pl. XXXVI:56-58. Two other examples can be found at Nimrud, but there two rows of curls are shown, one above the other, as if at the bottom of two different lengths of hair, Mallowan, *Nimrud and Its Remains,* pl. V and p. 587, fig. 555.

[5]Mallowan, *Nimrud and Its Remains,* pp. 203-210. Many of these ivories seem to date to the eighth century B.C. on the basis of parallels elsewhere; see Robert H. Dyson, "Review of *Nimrud and Its Remains,*" *AJA,* LXXIII (1969), 79-80.

[6]Mallowan, *Nimrud and Its Remains,* p. 373.

[7]Loud, *Megiddo Ivories,* no. 342, pls. 2, 4; no. 295, pls. 38, 173a and b. The narrow eyes with large pupils (especially noticeable when the pupil inlay is preserved) are different from what is found on the later ivories. Barnett, *The Nimrud Ivories,* pls. IV:C12-15; V:C16; LIX:S100h; LXIII:S146; LXX-LXXV; XCIII, etc. It is sometimes difficult to make a distinction between the earlier and later ivories in the representations of the eye and this may be further complicated by the manner in which it is shown on full front poses, as opposed to the representation of faces in profile. *Ibid.,* I:C62, A1, 14; III:C1, 4, 8, 10; XIX:S13, etc.

[8]*Ibid.,* pls. XVII:S3; XVIII:S1; XXXI:S18; XXII:S2, 4; XXIII:S26, 28, etc. (also on pls. X:F1; XI:F3; XII:F2; etc., where the ivories are, however, done in the Assyrian style).

[9]Karageorghis, *Excavations in the Necropolis of Salamis,* I, 57, pls. LXXIX and CXXXVII.

[10]Braidwood, *Syria,* XXI, 197, fig. 9.

[11]The figurine is published in a note by Farah S. Ma'ayeh, "Recent Archaeological Discoveries in Jordan," *ADAJ,* IV-V (1960), 114 and pl. III:2, where its find spot is described as exactly the same as that for tomb AE, but this figurine is not mentioned in the latter publication.

[12]The existence of veils on such figurines is often difficult to establish since they are usually indicated on surfaces which have been smoothed or obscured by the artisan, but may well represent imperfect impressions. In this case, the interpretation of a veil seems valid, but like on the figurine from Nebo tomb 84, no. 1072, the interpretation of a veil is somewhat more difficult to make. Another problem that must be mentioned in connection with our figurines and the use of a veil is whether these figurines were truly intended to be naked or whether they were intended to be covered with a very thin see-through garment. The fact that the Nebo figurines have their bodies covered with a white slip indicates that this is a distinct possibility.

smile. The nose seems to be larger than illustrated on other Amman figurines. The eyes have the pupil, lids, and eyebrows that we saw on the tomb F molds and figurines, but they seem to be rendered slightly different and are formed with thicker lines. The ears are well represented, being in proper proportion to the rest of the face and not turned toward the front.

The eyes, short hair, and rounded face make it tempting to date this figurine as late as the sixth century, on analogy to the female limestone heads to be discussed below.

The other figurine and mold to be discussed here are from Deir 'Allā and are unlike anything discussed so far.[1]

The mold shows more detail than the figurine fragment and the lines are much finer. The eyes are small and are taken up almost entirely by the thickness of the incised line, leaving little for the eye proper. On the figurines, small dots are placed between paired arced lines to indicate the pupils. On the mold, wide hatched bands seem to indicate heavy bushy eyebrows while on the figurines they are indicated as heavy crescent-shaped ridges. The hair is illustrated in bunches, apparently curls, at the top. In both cases, little space is left for a forehead but on the mold three strands of hair parted in the center are shown between the curls and the eyes. It is impossible to describe from the photograph how the hair was arranged at the side of the face. There seems to be a choker necklace on both pieces (neither is absolutely certain and the one on the figurine seems to be applied in paint) and a second pendant necklace is indicated on the mold.

These are the salient features of the two pieces, but it is impossible to date them without more information because of the unique style. The contacts which do exist with the other figurines are not strong enough to support a convincing argument for their date.

Finally, a number of very crude, handmade figurines found near Buseirah must be mentioned.[2] It is not necessary to go into great detail here other than to say that three of the four figurines served as stands for lamps, so that the lamps formed hats on the figures. The lamps are good Iron Age types. On the best preserved figurine, the breasts are modeled as well as hands holding a tambourine. The one figurine without the lamp was made in two parts, joined by a tenon, and only modeled breasts remain on the body. Glueck assigns a ninth to eighth century B.C. date to such "lamp goddesses."[3]

Male Figurines

The number of male figurines is less than half that of the female figurines and figurine molds, ten as opposed to twenty-one (not counting the crude "lamp goddess" figurines), but seven of them are late. Despite this, a development similar to that outlined for the female figurines is indicated. The earliest were again found at Deir 'Allā and represent merely the torsos from which heads and legs have been broken off.[4]

Like the female figurine torsos mentioned above, these are also hand modeled and the details that were indicated were incised into the wet clay before it was fired. Both figurines are naked. One has no decoration whatsoever, while the other has a waistband and possibly a necklace. On the latter, the arms are broken off, but on the former they seem to have been indicated only as stubs.[5]

The other figurine which does not date late in Iron II was found at Khirbet el Medeiyineh.[6]

The eyes, ears, and nose are shown as larger than normal, the hair style is unique, and a beard seems to be indicated by a piece of clay added at the chin. The eyes are bulging and the eyelids are indicated. The depiction of the eyes and eyebrows is closer to our figurines 89:1 and 2 than to any others, and the mouth is also similar. Glueck mentions two intentional incisions on the right cheek and there are marks on the cheeks of number 89:1, but it is impossible to say if they were intentional. The headgear is presently unique. It seems to be a cloth, like the modern kafiyeh, which covers the hair, except at the sides and "is held on by an 'uqal, tied in front with a bow knot."[7] It is further indicated by lines of brown paint. The hair, which hangs down to the level of the chin, is like that on the sculptured head number 92:3 (see below) and together they

---

[1]Franken, *VT*, X, pl. 14a (terra-cotta head) and b (mold and cast).

[2]Glueck, *Other Side*, p. 151, fig. 80, and p. 152, fig. 81.

[3]*Ibid.*, p. 151.

[4]Franken and Franken-Battershill, *A Primer of Old Testament Archaeology*, pl. XIV:B.

[5]Male figurines with arms reduced to little stubs can be traced back at least to the end of the Syrian Early Bronze Age at Selenkahiye, Maurits van Loon, "First Results of the 1967 Excavations at Selenkahiye," *AAS*, XVIII (1968), 28, and Hama, Fugmann, *Hama*, II, fig. 85:3A586, 3A399, 3A685 (Niveau J5); fig. 98:3A199, and fig. 106:5A468 (Niveau J1). Since male terra-cotta figurines are relatively rare in comparison with female figurines, it is not possible to trace a continuation of specific types for male figurines, as one can to a large extent with the female figurines.

[6]Glueck, *EEP*, I, 23, fig. 6a and b.

[7]*Ibid.*, p. 23.

comprise the only illustration so far of such a hair style in the Transjordan.

A unique figurine was excavated in the eighth century B.C. level III at Tell es Saʿidiyeh. It is six inches high, has a hollow body and a head modeled with the addition of clay pellets for the eyes and ears. A strand of clay circles the top of the head to indicate a headdress. Two arms are modeled at the front with hands at the neck clutching what seems to be part of a bag which is slung over the shoulder and attached to the back of the figurine. The body and head are decorated with white, black and red-brown paint. Pritchard's interpretation of this unique figurine as the representation of a traveler seems very appropriate.[1]

Unlike the long plaits of hair common in the Transjordan, the most common hair style in Palestine is the tufted Egyptianizing wig.[2] Whether the Transjordan pieces were actually intended to represent wigs is not certain. They are both clearly longer than the Palestinian wigs and the tufts of hair come up against and somewhat beneath the ears (indicating that it is not a wig), while in Palestine the ears are almost always covered by the wig. In this respect, the Transjordan may be following or paralleling a Syrian practice[3] where the ears may be covered or uncovered, but the latter is the normal. On most Palestinian figurines, there are four rows of tufts below the hairline on the forehead, while on the head under discussion there are six. There is no evidence presently that would help to reconstruct the type of body to which this head was attached. A date in the middle of the eighth century B.C. seems to be most probable for this figurine. The tufted hair style is best documented for the eighth and seventh centuries B.C.,[4] but how frequently it was used before the eighth century B.C. is uncertain at present.[5]

The figurine, figure 89:1, already shows the shorter, shoulder-top length hair style that seems to gradually replace longer plaits or bunches still common during the eighth century B.C. This hair style is only occasionally found on ivory carvings. It usually appears with those faces on which the pupils of the eyes are not indicated.[6]

Figure 89:1 is clearly related to the horse rider figurines to be discussed below and represents the earliest Transjordanian example of this type known to date. The bulging, slanted eyes, surrounded by the ridge representing the eyelids, are similar to those on the figurine just discussed. The hair style here is in keeping with the Assyrian tradition with drop-shaped bunches of hair curving down from behind the ears.[7] It is impossible to tell if the beard was indicated on the mold as a narrow hatched band. Beards are very frequently depicted this way on the later Persian period rider figurines.[8] Like the female figurines, tentatively dated to ca. 700 B.C., and later, the red, black, and white color scheme is applied here also. The beard is represented by a black line which is swung in an arc over the chin from one cheek to the other. A single stroke then connects the center of the lower lip with the line at the chin. The mustache illustrated on the figurine, figure 87:3, does not seem to be represented here, as is also the case on figure 87:1 and 2. The painted decoration in all respects resembles that on the figurine, figure 87:2 below. Though the pupil of the eye was not impressed by the mold, it was indicated by a painted black dot.

The conical cap with rounded top has a long history in Syria and Palestine on clay and metal figurines.[9] The Amman district horse and rider figurines are the largest such group of figurines in Palestine or Syria that can be assigned a date prior to the Persian period. In the Persian period, and lasting into the Hellenistic period, such figurines are extremely common at many Syro-Palestinian sites and also in Mesopotamia. The clay, modeling, and style of the Amman figurines are clearly still within the Iron II tradition and are very different from the Persian period

---

[1]James B. Pritchard, "An Eighth Century Traveler," *Expedition*, X (1968), 26-29.

[2]Tufnell, *Lachish*, III, Plates, pl. 31:1-5, 9-13; Albright, *TBM*, III, pls. 54:B1-8, 56:1-5; 57:C:1-3, and many examples from other sites.

[3]This is illustrated only on ivories at this point: Barnett, *The Nimrud Ivories*, pls. III:C1; XVI and XVII:S3; XXIII:S28a; XXVII:S12a; XXVIII:t and y; LIX:S100g, 101, etc.

[4]Saller, *LA*, XVI, 262-63.

[5]Pritchard, *Palestinian Figurines*, pp. 23-27, 56-57.

[6]See ivories C1 and S3 cited in footnote 3 above.

[7]Henri Frankfort, *The Art and Architecture of the Ancient Orient* (Baltimore: Penguin Books, 1955), pl. 82.

[8]Pézard, *Qadesh*, pl. XXI:1 and 2. Hrouda, *Tell Halaf*, IV, pl. 17:137, 140.

[9]Loud, *MEG*, II, Plates, pls. 235:23; 237:30; 238:30 in bronze. Loud, *Megiddo Ivories*, pls. 22 and 32 (a small low, but still pointed cap) on incised ivories. Frankfort, *Art and Architecture of the Ancient Orient*, pl. 142 in bronze. Fugmann, *Hama*, II, fig. 85:3A685, 3A659 (Niveau J₄), fig. 98:3A199 (Niveau J₂) in pottery and fig. 124:S768 in bronze. Braidwood and Braidwood, *Amuq*, I, pls. 57-59 in bronze.

figurines.[1] Only on Cyprus, primarily at Ayia Irini, is there a large number of figurines which can be dated earlier than the Persian period[2] and contemporary with ours. A great variety is present in the figurines represented there. Some exhibit features similar to ours, but they are totally within a different tradition.[3] Restricting the discussion to a single feature, there are some caps or helmets depicted on male figurines which are quite close to ours, though they do not form a dominant type.

Similar helmets also occur on Assyrian,[4] Babylonian,[5] Neo-Hittite,[6] and Persian[7] reliefs. In most cases, however, they are unusual, infrequent, or non-native features.[8] The usual Assyrian helmets, for instance, have their own peculiarities and development. Their tops are more pointed; in the ninth century they are not very pronounced and have sides that taper gracefully to a point.[9] In the eighth-to-seventh-centuries B.C. type, the point becomes elongated to form a short spike.[10] Two Urartian bronze helmets found at Karmir Blur illustrate the latter type and are inscribed with the names of eighth century B.C. rulers.[11]

The Urartian bronze helmets and some of those illustrated on the Assyrian reliefs[12] illustrate zones of decoration in bands at the base of the helmet. This may be what the painted decoration on figure 87:2 and 3 is intended to show. On these figurines, there is a band over the forehead, similar to that on the female figurines figure 87:4 and 5, but enlarged by the addition of a vertical band reaching to the top of the helmet. The helmet is shown differently on figure 87:1, where a triangular area covering most of the front is painted in the usual manner with white outlined in black. A similar division is also indicated on the Sakjegözü and Ayia Irini helmets which we mentioned

tions the cavalry contingents in the Aramean forces opposing Shalmaneser and the Assyrian reliefs illustrate cavalry extensively), and it would be difficult, in this light, to see in our figurines anything other than the representation of local people as cavalrymen.

[2]Gjerstad, et al., The Swedish Cyprus Expedition, Vol. II, Part II, pp. 642-850.

[3]Ibid., pls. CLXXXIX; CXCI; CXCII:1, 2; CXCIII:1, 2; CXCIV:3, 6; CXCVI; CXCVII; and CCXV:1.

[4]Richard D. Barnett and M. Falkner, The Sculptures of Aššur-Naṣir-Apli II, Tiglath-Pileser III and Esarhaddon (London: British Museum, 1962), pls. CXXIV, CXXV. Wallis Budge, Assyrian Sculptures in the British Museum, Rein of Ashur-Nasir-Pal, 885-860 (London: British Museum, 1914), pls. XVII, XXIII, XXV, XXVI. W. L. King, Bronze Reliefs from the Gates of Shalmaneser King of Assyria B.C. 860-825 (London: British Museum, 1915), pls. III, V, VII-X, XIV, etc. (with numerous examples).

[5]Frankfort, Art and Architecture of the Ancient Orient, pl. 120.

[6]J. Perrot and C. Chipiez, History of Art in Sardinia, Judea, Syria and Asia Minor (London: Chapman and Hall, Ltd., 1890), II, 65, fig. 279 (illustrating a relief from Sakjegözü). Anton Moortgat, Tell Halaf, III (Berlin: Walter de Gruyter, 1955), pls. 16B, 25, and 26.

[7]Erich F. Schmidt, Persepolis I ("OIP," LXVIII; Chicago: University of Chicago Press, 1953), pl. 31, on tribute bearers from Babylon, but there is a tassel here hanging down from the point of the helmet. On pl. 32, Syrian tribute bearers are depicted with a similar shaped cap but it is illustrated as if made of a band of cloth wrapped around like a turban. The shape and lack of tassel bring such helmets closer geographically to the Transjordan. As was the case in the Babylonian helmets, the Syrian helmets are not new but only rarely depicted earlier. In the bronze reliefs of Shalmaneser from Balawat, which we mentioned above in footnote 1 (in pl. XIV cited there), men from Tyre and Sidon are shown wearing the same type of helmets. Once again, in this case also, we have a close parallel in shape but a long time range of about 500 years for the use of this type of wearing apparel. It seems that we have to deal with conservative features of dress that must be treated carefully for chronological purposes.

[8]A number of distinctive helmets which seem to be localized in specific areas can be identified. As examples, we cite two types here: first, a helmet which is usually squat and has a sphere at the top, D. G. Hogarth, Carchemish, Part I: Introductory (London: British Museum, 1914), pls. B9, B11, and B14, and second, the crested helmet, Hrouda, Die Kulturgeschichte des assyrischen Flachbildes, pp. 132-33 and pl. 23:1-3, 15-20.

[9]Hrouda, Die Kulturgeschichte des assyrischen Flachbildes, pp. 132-33 and pl. 23:1-3.

[10]Ibid., pp. 132-3 and pl. 23:5-13.

[11]Massino Pollottino, "Urartu, Greece and Etruria," East and West, IX-X (1958-59), 30-34.

[12]Hrouda, Die Kulturgeschichte des assyrischen Flachbildes, pl. 23:1-3, 5, 11, 12, 14.

---

[1]The Amman figurines are of the normal Iron Age ware discussed above in connection with the pottery vessels. The Persian period figurines usually have a very yellow pink ware with a cream to yellow slip or surface color. This ware is well levigated and seldom has grit inclusion. The body of the rider and of the horse are handmade, as in our examples, but it was shown above that this tradition of horse and rider figurines, as well as female figurines, can be traced back to the end of Iron I and can no longer be considered unique for the Persian period. The face, beard, and helmets are depicted entirely different, as illustrated on the plates cited above in footnote 8, p. 137. The Persian period figurines seem, then, to perpetuate a long established type. Any speculation as to the identification of these riders with specific peoples in the Persian period, like the Scythians, cannot be pushed back into earlier periods. Historically, cavalry played an important part in warfare, at least by the time of Shalmaneser III (Pritchard, ANET, pp. 278-79, men-

above[1] as similar in shape to those of the Amman figurines. The crow-step designs in black against the white painted portions of the helmets are clear on figure 87:1 and 2. This design was discussed on page 87 above, where it was used frequently with the same color combination we have here. Parallels for the use of this design were also cited, but these appeared primarily on architecture. There are two instances where the crow-step is used on clothing and these bring us closer to its use here. One is on an ivory from the Southeast Palace at Nimrud[2] and the other appears as decoration on a garment shown in a mural from Til Barsib.[3] It is interesting to note the use of the crow-step on the crowns of Persian and later kings.[4] It is quite probable that the crow-step motif here, or even more generally when it is used on wearing apparel, is a sign of royalty. Whether a king is represented here as in Persia would, of course, only be speculation. It may be true that most of the male figurines from Palestine and Syria represent gods or kings, but the representation of the king in an equestrian role in a frequently occurring figurine type does not seem probable. The cavalry, however, as the earlier charioteers or *mariyanu*, may have represented an elite class[5] that in the Amman district may have been associated with a crow-step emblem.

Finally, there are a few more details on figurines, figure 87:1-3, which we have not mentioned so far.

> The ears are represented as over-sized, and are only rotated slightly into the frontal plane. The hair at the sides of the face hangs down straight in three locks and just touches the shoulders. The painting over the eyes makes them larger than the mold impression and, thus, they seem larger than natural. The black-white-black band, which rings the body just below the shoulders, is also found at Meqabelein and seems to be added more for decorative purposes than to represent something like a band on a garment.

The facial features need not be cited in detail nor need more be said about the hair style, since they are identical to those on the two female figurines, figure 87:4 and 5, described above. All of these figurines (male and female) may have been made in a single mold and the little variation which can be noted seems to be no more than what should normally be expected in separate impressions of a single mold. It is important to note that one mold could be used to produce both male and female figurines. An examination of the figurines published at Lachish,[6] indicates that the same thing was done here, though it was not suspected earlier. Figures 6 to 8 on the Lachish plate cited also have pointed tops which probably

represent helmets. The face and hair, which are mold impressed, are identical to that on the common female figurines.[7] The tufted rows of hair above the forehead were a little more awkward to adapt for use with a helmet than the locks of hair on the Amman figurines. The implication of these comparisons is that the Transjordanian figurines are not isolated examples (though for the time being the clearest examples) of such helmeted male figurines in the Syro-Palestinian area before the Persian period.

Two complete horse and rider figurines were found in the Meqabelein tomb (and one other unpublished example is on display with them in the Amman Museum). All of these figurines represent the details of modeling we have discussed for the tomb F figurines. The two painted heads, just mentioned, have the same helmet design as our 87:1. The Meqabelein example is said to lack beard or mustache (if this has not been worn off), but the unpublished example is like 87:3 with mustache and beard. In all other respects, the heads seem to be identical. The horses and human bodies are handmade.[8] The horses will be discussed below. The riders' bodies were depicted as sitting directly against the horses' necks and no saddles are indicated. The left hands, which apparently held the reins, are placed just below and behind the horses' ears while the right hands are at the sides and apparently hold whips. The thighs and knees are shown extending straight out from the body, as in a sitting position, and the lower part of the legs and the feet hang straight down against the horses' flanks.

Summary of Human Figurines

In the discussion above, a sequence of features was observed which provided a chronological progression in both male and female figurines. Almost all the female figurines belong to the "tambourine-player" type. They are always unclad above the waist, but sometimes are clad on the lower part of the body. A majority of the male

---

[1]See footnotes 3 and 6, p. 138.

[2]Barnett, *The Nimrud Ivories*, pl. XCIV:S336d, e (where it is shown as decoration on a dress or skirt).

[3]Thureau-Dangin and Dunand, *Til-Barsib*, pl. LI.

[4]Porada, *Ancient Iran*, pp. 152-56.

[5]Donald J. Wiseman, *The Alalakh Tablets* (London: British Institute of Archaeology at Ankara, 1953), p. 11.

[6]Tufnell, *Lachish*, III, Plates, pl. 31.

[7]*Ibid.*, pl. 31:1-5, 9-14.

[8]Harding, *Meqabelein*, p. 46.

figurines belong to the horse and rider figurine type. At present, the following sequence is indicated. No figurines are presently available for the twelfth and eleventh centuries from the Transjordan. In the tenth and early part of the ninth centuries B.C., figurine plaques were produced both by hand modeling and by pressing in a mold. In both cases, the features were indicated by the use of strong incised or impressed lines. A second group of figurines overlaps somewhat with the first, but continues in use into the eighth century B.C. In this group, there is a dependence on modeling the surfaces rather than an emphasis on lines. The details previously brought out by lines were probably still indicated, but with paint. Some plaque figurines are still found but most of our examples now seem to be made to stand on a base and have only their faces impressed in a mold (in the case of female figurines these are the "pillar figurines"). The color scheme is white for the handmade bodies and red for the faces. The use of yellow for hair or jewelry, as in some cases in Palestine, or black for the hair, as is used later, is not yet documented. The only unusual painted decoration is the brown bands on the headpiece of the male figurine from el Medeiyineh.

The final group would seem to have little overlap with the preceding groups. We would tentatively date the earliest examples to around 700 B.C. and consider that they continued through the sixth century B.C. In this group, the modeling of the surfaces of the mold-made portions is still excellent (even the handmade features are very well executed) but details, once again, are represented with a heavy dependence on lines rather than modeling. Many of the hair and facial features illustrate stylized patterns which seem to have been adopted, in the preparation of these molds, from the long established traditions of the ivory carver. Some of the increased detail from these molds was adopted and accentuated on the figurines by paint (like the pupils and lids of the eyes and the outline of the hair at the sides), while other details were obscured or ignored (as was true of the strands and curls in the hair and of the eyebrows. Thus, it is clear that greater detail was produced by the mold than was necessary for the purposes for which the figurines were intended. A new scheme of painted decoration is presently illustrated in the Transjordan only in the Amman district, but is similar to the black-white-black band decoration discussed above as characteristic on pottery vessels of the Transjordan in the Iron Age. A wider geographical use of this color scheme is indicated by examples from Syria, at Tabbat al Hammam, and from Cyprus, at Salamis.

Finally, it must be pointed out that figurines of the horse and rider type, as well as of the woman with tambourine type, were found in tombs. In Palestine there was no consistency in this practice, which differed from site to site. At Gibeon and Samaria, figurines are not present in tombs but they are at Megiddo, Gezer, and Beth Shemesh.[1] This indicates that such figurines can play a part (but not necessarily always) in mortuary cults. There is slight evidence, which we tend to favor, that in each type of figurine (with the possible exception of a few unusual examples) human and not divine beings are represented. Consequently, no attempt has been made to identify the figurines with specific divine personalities, which would presently be impossible in the Transjordan, but rather we would see these figurine types as illustrations of individuals who belong to socially honored or elite groups.

Animal and Miscellaneous Figurines

Only a few animal figurines from the Transjordan do not represent horses. A catalogue and discussion of such animal figurines yield very little important information, so they will be omitted from the discussion. Only those figurines found in Amman tomb F have been included so that a complete discussion of that tomb is available here.

Horse Figurines

Examples of horse figurines, both with and without riders, have been preserved. The horses are entirely handmade with the most care given to the formation of the mane and head. On most examples, trappings and some facial features are indicated by painted decoration. Only a few examples were either not decorated with paint or their paint is worn off. Most of the figurine fragments illustrate the same details that are found on the complete figurines from the Meqabelein tomb, as well as our figure 86:9.

Figure 86:5 illustrates a portion of the hindquarters and tail of a horse figurine and figure 86:7 illustrates the conical legs with rounded bottoms of a similar figurine (both from tomb F). The legs were not made to be uniform. On most figurines, the horse's chest is depicted as thick and heavy. The two horse heads, figure 86:6 (from tomb F) and figure 89:6 (from the road cut[2]), show prominent manes which stand out on the necks and drop steeply onto the foreheads. The pointed ears are suggested on figure 86:6, as are the eyes, which seem normally to be applied as pellets and

---

[1]Saller, *LA*, XVI, 262-63.

[2]Registration number A.C. '69:29.

occasionally, as here, are smoothed into the head. The muzzle is slightly elongated. (Only on one of the Meqabelein horses (no. 38) are the mouth and nostrils indicated by incision.) The surface find, figure 88:6,[1] is badly weathered but the tail and leg stumps are still clear, as is the attached clay at the back which represents the seated rider and possibly his left arm hanging down at the side. Two figurine fragments in a similar state of preservation are published by Glueck as coming from el Medeiyineh.[2] One riderless horse, figure 86:9, was found in tomb F and the head of a larger, hollow horse figurine, figure 89:5, was found in mixed fill, but near bedrock, in the 1968 excavations.[3] These figurines conformed to the same style of modeling that was described above. Only one other riderless horse is published from the Transjordan, so far, and this is from Mt. Nebo tomb 84.[4] On the whole, its features are similar to those described here but some details, particularly the facial features, are different. The eyes are incised holes, the muzzle is short and squared, and the less pronounced mane does not arch very high above the ears.[5]

Two basic schemes of color decoration were used on these figurines. The one is the black-white-black decoration against a pink or red background, as can be seen on the riders in tomb F and the Meqabelein figurines. The other is black paint on a white slip that covers the entire figurine. The harness on the head received a fairly uniform treatment. Paint is preserved on the eyes, but it is always worn off to such a degree that the original manner of application is not clear. The shock of hair from the mane, which rests on the forehead, is always painted but, again, always too indistinct to interpret. Paint usually encircled the eyes and a line is drawn from under the eye over to, and across the mouth. From the corners of the mouth, two intersecting lines are drawn across the head to the top of the opposite eye. The two triangles formed in this manner at the top of the head are filled in with paint. The reins are not further indicated in paint on the figurines with riders, but on figures 86:9 and 89:5 some additional decorative trappings are indicated by two lines, with dots between them, which encircle the neck.[6] The last mentioned figurines are white-slipped and have the decoration applied in black paint. This was true also on the Mt. Nebo figurine.[7] The head, figure 89:6, also has a white slip[8] but the decoration is bichrome in grey and red-brown. Here, unlike the other figurines, there seems to have been less of an attempt at indicating the actual harness than at decorating the head. The paint has been badly weathered and is very light, but the bands cross in different places and the triangles at the sides, rather than the top of the head, are filled in with paint. An eight petaled rosette is painted directly on the nose. On the presently available horse and rider figurines, painted decoration is confined to the head. On the riderless figurine, figure 86:9, painted decoration on the back indicates a blanket.[9] The

edges of the blanket are shown by black lines and diagonal lines (crossing in the center) connect opposite corners. The four triangles formed in this manner are divided in half by lines perpendicular to the blanket border. A crow-step design was placed at each of the four intersections of these lines and the blanket border. The two fragments, figure 86:5 and 7, have painted lines on the bodies which may also belong to such blankets. Number 5 has a white slip, but the surface of number 7 is pink. It is possible that it was originally covered with a white slip which has subsequently worn off.

The depiction of a blanket on the back of figure 86:9, and the possibility of the same on two other fragments, indicate that the mode of riding was the same in Amman as it was in Assyria. It would seem that these horses were also intended for riding (spare horses for the riders?) and are not draught horses. Early Iron Age examples of horse and rider figurines are rare, but they do occur elsewhere. The best early example is a head from Hama[10] which corresponds in details of mane, head shape, and painted trappings. This head

[1] Registration number A.C. '68:23, surface find.

[2] Glueck, *Other Side*, pp. 156-57, figs. 87-88.

[3] Registration number A.C. '68:87, from square S.E. 9-30.

[4] Saller, *LA*, XVI, 261 and 263, fig. 28:3.

[5] Another head fragment was found at Sâliyeh, Glueck, *Other Side*, p. 155, fig. 85a. It also has an incised eye and possibly a mouth indicated, but the mane is more clearly indicated than on the Nebo horse.

[6] On the right side of fig. 89:5, there is another pellet of clay applied between the eye and ear, at the intersection of two painted lines. This must represent a knob, possibly decorated, which was intended to hold the harness together.

[7] Saller, *LA*, XVI, 263.

[8] It is too early to say if there is any significance in the two color schemes. The number of examples is far too small to say that the riderless figurines always had a white slip upon which the other painted decoration was applied, and that the horse and rider figurines had the black-white-black band decoration against a reddish background. It is possible that the latter color scheme is relatively new on figurines at the time of the deposit of objects in the tomb, while the former scheme had a longer history.

[9] Hrouda, *Die Kulturgeschichte des assyrischen Flachbildes,* p. 152 and pl. 30:6, 8 mentions the use of blankets on horses used for riding, as they are shown on Assyrian reliefs. It is interesting to note Hrouda's remark that in contrast to Scythian riding practice, where a primitive saddle was used, this was not the Assyrian practice.

[10] Fugmann, *Hama*, II, 193, fig. 245:5B125 O 15 (from "Période E").

must be dated before 720 B.C., which is the date ascribed to the destruction of the building level in which it was found. The number and sophistication of the horse and rider figurines in the Transjordan are significant and, though there is no literary evidence to bear it out, they seem to indicate that cavalry played an important role in this area.

Other Animal Figurines

Two other figurines found in Amman should be mentioned. Figure 86:10, from tomb F, indicates a monstrous creature which is extremely difficult to identify.

> The color scheme is the black-white-black bands on light red background. It has a long neck, pointed head, and short muzzle. The ears are broken off but the eyes and the head band are indicated by painted pieces of applied clay. The mouth and nostrils are indicated by incision and there is a black band encircling the neck. At the back of the figurine is a high piece of clay with a white band framed by two black bands. A horse is certainly not represented here and the only possibility seems to be a camel with rider. This interpretation, which does not look plausible at first glance, seems likely on the basis of unpublished camel and rider figurines from the Amuq. On the horse and rider figurines, the seated figures are placed tightly against the horse's neck while it would seem that here, the rider's body merges with the hump behind which he or she sits. One would have to consider that the rider's body (not indicated by any special details) is preserved to just below the shoulders and above this we would have a mold impressed face. The awkward placement of the rider at the back of the figurine is attested by the Amuq figurines.

It would not be surprising to find camel and rider figurines in Amman earlier than the Persian period (at which time they frequently occur alongside horse and rider figurines). It does not seem justifiable, however, to follow up this argument on the basis of one questionable example and additional evidence must be awaited.

The second fragment is also difficult to interpret.[1] It is the hollow base for a figurine, but only the front part of the leg and the foot are preserved. The figurine seems to have been a *couchant* animal. The ware is light grey and the slip is grey-black. Such a dark-colored slip on a figurine is unparalleled at present.

Miscellaneous Figurine and Mold Fragments

There are a number of additional figurine and mold fragments from tomb F. Two pieces, figure 86:3 and 4, represent plaque fragments which were pierced for suspension. Number 4 is plain except for a line incised after firing, but number 3 has been cast in a mold and brown-black paint is applied over the ridged molding on the left side. Unfortunately, the fragments are too small to identify the objects to which they belong. Figure 86:8 may simply represent a pendant, but such a simple shape in terra-cotta would be unusual and it is possible that it is a figurine arm that was attached to the body by a fastening through the hole. At Megiddo, clay pieces in the shape of legs were found with similar holes pierced through at the top.[2] The three photographs each for figure 88:4 and 5 indicate the back, front, and clay impression of two molds. Number 4 may represent a portion of a fish and number 5 a Bes figure. This deity is too common to comment on extensively here, but it is far more frequent as a small amulet than as a molded figure. The interpretation of the other fragment is more difficult. At first one is tempted to see in it the portion of a wing of a sphinx, griffin, or winged-genie form. Closer examination indicates that such most probably was not the case. The indication of what one would consider the feathers oriented in two different directions is not usual and the size of the area covered by the scale pattern is too great. The scale pattern is quite normally indicated at the tops of the wings and close to the point where the wings touch or attach to the body. The arced sides of the scales usually point down, except when used in plant or other motifs like the depiction of a mountain. The proportionate area covered by the scales suggests the representation of a fish and the lines at the edge are not feathers but fins. Such an indication of a fish is again not extremely unusual, but is unique if represented in plaque form.[3]

Other Terra-Cotta Objects with Applied Plastic Decoration

Two classes of objects are mentioned here: first a number of apparent model shrines which presently are more numerous in the Transjordan than elsewhere and, second, a number of sarcophagi on which human features have been molded.

---

[1] Registration number A.C. '69:30.

[2] Loud, *MEG*, II, Plates, pl. 206:49 and 61. Here, these pieces are considered to be amulets.

[3] See the discussion of fish indicated on ivories in Barnett, *The Nimrud Ivories*, pp. 57, 95, 199, and the examples no. S110a-f on pl. LXI.

Terra-Cotta Shrines

A number of terra-cotta "shrines" have been found, or are said to have been found, in the Transjordan. Only one of these was found in one of the tombs we discussed above in our Sequences I and II, tomb AE.[1] Two examples are clearly from the Transjordan but their provenience is unknown. An unpublished example is on display in the Amman Museum and the other was published in 1944 by J. H. Iliffe and is dated to the tenth to ninth centuries B.C.[2] Four such model shrines have also been found at Deir 'Allā, but in the destruction of the L.B. temple complex.[3] Some of them seem to date early in the twelfth century but others are probably earlier. These shrines are mentioned only to indicate the present evidence for the range of time such shrines were in production as well as to stress their clear association with a sacred area. The designation of such pieces as model shrines is in keeping with Iliffe's and Franken's discussions and is supported by the analysis of their ornamentation.

The shrine published by Iliffe is like the Deir 'Allā shrines in that it has rounded sides and a knob handle at the top. It was made as if it were a jar built up by a potter. The opening at the top, however, was closed and instead an opening was created in the side. The façade on Iliffe's shrine, attached against the opening at the side, is far more elaborate than any of the Deir 'Allā examples, though one of the latter was fitted with a door and lugs that would hold a rod to secure the door. The other two shrines were roughly box-shaped with one side open.

The shrine from Amman tomb E was decorated with lines of brown-black on the back and sides, but had nothing in the way of a façade indicated at the front. The primary interest and importance of the shrine published by Iliffe and the one on display in the Amman Museum are their façades. On Iliffe's shrine are two columns *in antis* (but connected to the door jamb by a piece of clay halfway up the column) which support elaborate capitals and a rectangular beam that stretches across the front. Above the door and between the capitals, a dove figurine has been attached.[4] Iliffe cites the proto-Ionic volute capitals from Samaria and Megiddo as architectural parallels for the lower portion of this capital. To this, one can now add the finds of such capitals at Ramat Raḥel[5] and Hazor,[6] but even more important for our concerns was the discovery of such a proto-Ionic capital by Glueck at Meḍeibî' in the Transjordan.[7] Quadruple volutes are frequently found on other art objects in Palestine and Syria and are indicated in the same way, with the out-turned volutes at the bottom and the in-turned volutes at the top. A seal in the Amman Museum, number J2825,

shows a worshipper kneeling on one knee before a similar quadruple-voluted column. A similar placement of volutes (occasionally in greater multiples but conforming to the same pattern) can be found at Megiddo,[8] Lachish,[9] Arslan Tash,[10] and Nimrud,[11] to list only a few examples. It is probable that this model was produced when such capitals were still more decorative than structural in use.[12] One can easily suspect that on such a model the artisan would be inclined to indicate a common decorative motif, frequently employed on other small objects but not yet employed structurally. The fact, as Iliffe points out, that the stone capitals

---

[1]R. Dajani, *ADAJ*, XI, pl. I, fig. 1 and IV:130.

[2]J. H. Iliffe, "A Model Shrine of Phoenician Style," *QDAP*, XI (1944), 91-92 and pl. XXI.

[3]Franken, *VT*, XI, 365 and 368; Franken, *VT*, XIV, 422.

[4]Iliffe points out (Illife, *QDAP*, XI, 91-92) the association of Astarte with the dove and the occurrence of doves or dovecotes on incense and offering stands. This is further supported by the presence of naked female figurines on the façade of the other model shrine discussed here.

[5]Yohanan Aharoni, *Excavations at Ramat Raḥel* (Rome: Centro di studi semitici, 1962), pl. 11:1.

[6]Yadin, *et al.*, *Hazor*, III-IV, pls. CCCLXII and CCCLXIII.

[7]Glueck, *EEP*, I, 68, fig. 26.

[8]Loud, *Megiddo Ivories*, pls. 6:13-15; 34:165, 166; 35:167.

[9]Tufnell, Inge, and Harding, *Lachish*, II, pl. XIX:17.

[10]Thureau-Dangin, *et al.*, *Arslan-Tash*, pls. XXVII:22; XLV:97 and 98.

[11]Barnett, *The Nimrud Ivories*, p. 32, fig. 1:D8, G6a, S19, and S309.

[12]Iliffe, *QDAP*, XI, 92. "It would seem as if we had here that stage of evolution before the palm-tree motif had crystallized inevitably into the form which it eventually took as the Ionic capital; when the idea of using it at the top of a column had suggested itself, but the final stylized form was still the subject of experiment. That is if we take this model shrine as reflecting to any extent the contemporary trends in architecture, which seems justifiable. A further indication that the volutes are decorative and not yet structural members is perhaps to be seen in the fact that they are *appliques* and not yet double-sided or free-standing, a feature which they share with those on the Megiddo shrines and the above mentioned stone capitals from Megiddo and Samaria. We can see the architect still at the stage of trying out various patterns based upon his observation of the palm-tree. It will be noticed also that the columns forming the façade of the shrine, and standing so it were *in antis*, are connected half-way up with the walls by a thick supporting bar."

are only carved on one side is a very strong argument that all of the Iron Age examples were not yet employed as capitals of free-standing architectural elements; they still had a basically decorative function as engaged columns or pilasters. That the columns, here, are not indicated as free-standing is thus informative. Also, proto-Aeolic capitals from Golgoi[1] lend additional support to our restatement and updating of Iliffe's argument, in that they illustrate in stone the decorative double volutes like those on some of the Megiddo, Arslan Tash, and Nimrud ivories. Here also the volutes are carved on only one face so that the pieces are not free-standing architectural elements.

A shrine very similar to the one in the Amman Museum is on display at the American University of Beirut Museum.[2] The shapes of both shrines are similar and the room that they enclose is fairly shallow. No special features are indicated on the Amman Museum shrine, while a molded door frame is indicated on the American University of Beirut Museum shrine. In both cases, the female figurines flank the door openings and are attached to the door jambs. They are not depicted as serving an architectural purpose as caryatid figures. The fertility aspect, depicted by the dove on the previously discussed shrine, is thus stressed much more heavily here.

A figurine fragment from Amman tomb C[3] combines features of all the shrines, indicating that all the symbolism points to fertility and that the shrines are all indicative of a similar cult. This figurine is broken at the hips, but the white painted body shows a distended abdomen, supported by both hands. The breasts, one of which has broken off, were applied as clay pellets. Above the head

> is a head-dress, consisting of four up-turning spirals set at right angles to each other; another identical group of spirals, somewhat smaller, was also found, but does not fit on the first one, though the breaks on the top of this show clearly that another similar group surmounted it.[4]

Two tiers of volutes are thus a distinct possibility, as is the pair of figurines. The combination of the votutes, and the naked, pregnant figure ties together the symbolism on the previously discussed shrines. The column with volute capital may represent a symbol of fertility, i.e. the common "tree of life" motif. The volutes over the head of the tomb A figurine do indicate that we are dealing with a caryatid figure. An analysis of the features of the figurine's face provides some interesting conclusions. The face is painted red, and the eyes are indicated in white paint with the pupils in black paint. The surprising features are the black beard and mustache which indicate an hermaphrodite deity.[5] Harding's suggestion that the:

> Mesha stele mentions Ashtor-Khemosh, a deity apparently combining the female aspects of Ashtor with the male ones of Khemosh[6]

may be a solution to this difficulty, if one accepts that:

> our figurine might well represent some such combination.[7]

There is very little information available to help with the interpretation of these shrines and to give an indication of their intended use. Little can be said of the temple or shrine which they represent since only a small single room is indicated and the emphasis seems to be placed on the façade. Temples with two columns *in antis* have a long history in Palestine and Syria[8] and the best Iron Age example was found at Tell Ta'yinat.[9] The architectural, as opposed to the decorative, aspect of this façade and that of the proto-Ionic capitals have been discussed above. None of the proto-Ionic capitals found to date can be clearly associated with temple architecture. Thus, the symbolic value of the palm-tree or "tree of life" motif seems to have a more general use (as is also indicated by the great variety of ways it is used as

[1]Sabatino Moscati, *The World of the Phoenicians* (London: Weidenfeld and Nicolson, 1968), translated by Alastair Hamilton, p. 107, fig. 30 and pl. 3.

[2]Dimitri Baramki, *The Archaeological Museum of the American University of Beirut* (Beirut: American University, 1967), *Corrigendum*, p. 3. The shrine is object no. 46 in case 27A.

[3]Harding, *ADAJ*, I, 37 and pl. XIV.

[4]Harding, *ADAJ*, I, 37.

[5]The color scheme which seems to indicate a transition between our group II and III figurines was also noted on the figurine, fig. 89:2, which was dated around 700 B.C. The fact that the pupils are indicated but the eyelids are not, and the eyebrows are shown as ridges, further illustrates the features in common with the Amman figurines. The chronological placement of this tomb above (from the point of view of ceramic style), substantiates this dating.

[6]Harding, *ADAJ*, I, 37.

[7]*Ibid.*

[8]Rudolph H. Dornemann, "The Architecture of the Temples of Bronze Age Palestine and Syria" (unpublished M.A. dissertation, Department of Oriental Languages and Civilizations, University of Chicago, 1965), pp. 13-50 and 65-86; also, Th. A. Busink, *Der Temple von Jerusalem*, Band I: *Der Temple Salomos* (Leiden: E. J. Brill, 1970), pp. 367-511.

[9]Richard C. Haines, *Excavations in the Plain of Antioch* ("OIP," XCV; Chicago: University of Chicago, 1971), II, pl. 103, 106 and 107.

decoration on other objects), though when used as decoration on a temple or shrine the interpretation should probably be considered more strictly connected with aspects of fertility. It must be noted here that these figurines did not support anything, as in the case of the hermaphrodite figurine, and cannot be considered as caryatid figures but merely as attached at the front. This must be kept in mind in relation to our discussion of possible caryatid figures below.

The question which must be considered here is: what purpose did these shrines serve and do any similar objects exist whose function is known? Any answer concerning the purpose must remain very speculative, but it is tempting to associate these shrines with the stone *aedicule* and the related *naos cippi* in Phoenicia and the Phoenician colonies. Here temple or shrine façades are the main feature. Two columns supporting an entablature are normal[1]; women occasionally replace the columns as caryatids[2] and a female figure is sometimes found in the doorway.[3] It is possible for both sexes to be represented here and they are found in a variety of poses.[4] The Phoenician *aediculae* were frequently found as the main shrine (occasionally shrines) of large enclosed sacred precincts.[5] The *naos cippi* found at Carthage, Motya, and other Phoenician colonies were usually found in association with urns bearing the remains of human sacrifices placed in the sacred precinct or *topheth*. The sacrifices at Carthage were originally made to Baal Hammon, but eventually the goddess Tanit was also worshipped by that practice.[6] Though evidence for human sacrifice is not indicated in the Phoenician sacred areas, the practice of erecting votive monuments is.[7] In fact, this practice dates back at least to the Middle Bronze Age Obelisk Temple at Byblos, where the same idea of a small raised shrine at the center of a sacred court containing commemorative monuments is also present. The practice of placing a *naos cippus* in such a sacred area is also illustrated at this early date in this temple area.[8]

The fact that child sacrifice was practiced in the Transjordan[9] and is associated with Khemosh, an aspect of whom seems to be represented by the figurine from Amman tomb C, indicates that the Transjordan shared the underlying religious practices of the Phoenician and Punic world. The preservation of features of these religious practices in the Transjordan in the Hellenistic and Roman periods indicates that they were an integral part of the culture.[10] These interesting connections help shed some light on what otherwise is a very dark or blank cultural picture, but they do not help in explaining the use of our terra-cotta shrines. They are, perhaps, best interpreted as a poor man's substitute for the stone monuments found elsewhere and their inclusion in tombs, unconnected with a sacred precinct, divests them of a use for votive display, though they could retain a commemorative function. The similarities to the *aedicule* and *naos* are too close not to be noted and to give some background for a more complete understanding in the future.

Anthropoid Sarcophagi

The final group of objects upon which plastic decoration was applied is a number of anthropoid sarcophagi. Portions of five sarcophagi were

---

[1]Moscati, *The World of the Phoenicians*, pp. 45-47, 152, and pls. 2, 24, 25, 30, 41, 52, and 56.

[2]Anna Maria Bisi, *Le stele puniche* (Roma: Istituto di studi del Vicino Oriente, 1967), pls. II and XXIV:2 (from Susa).

[3]Moscati, *The World of the Phoenicians*, pl. 41. The woman is holding a disk in front of her which raises the question of an association with our tambourine players.

[4]How much of this variation appears on later stelae, and how closely the earlier ones may confine their representation to the worship of Tanit or a related goddess is an unknown at present.

[5]The Phoenician sites are briefly discussed in Moscati, *The World of the Phoenicians*, pp. 45-47. At Ayia Irini in Cyprus, the same arrangement was also present; Gjerstad, *The Swedish Cyprus Expedition*, Vol. II, Part II, pp. 642-850.

[6]Moscati, *The World of the Phoenicians*, p. 142.

[7]*Ibid.*, p. 46.

[8]Maurice Dunand, *Fouilles de Byblos* (Republique libanaise. Ministère de l'instruction publique et des beaux-arts, Direction des antiquités, Étudés et documents d'archéologie," III; Paris: Librairie d'Amérique et d'Orient Adrien Maisonneuve, 1950), Tome II, Atlas, pls. XXXII:1, XXXIII:1, 3.

[9]Judges 11:30-40; II Kings 3:27; Lev. 18:21; II Kings 16:3, 23:10; II Chron. 28:3 and 33:6.

[10]Similar perpetuation of religious practices is clearly illustrated in the Punic area in the Hellenistic and Roman periods. Also, in this connection, it can be noted that Classical temple complexes in Syria-Palestine often exhibit peculiar local features and the idea of surrounding the temple with a large enclosed precinct is illustrated most clearly in the Baal Temple at Palmyra, the Artemis Temple at Jerash, etc. Even closer to the older sacred areas are the Nabataean shrines like Khirbet et Tannur, where a small raised shrine stands in a large open-air court enclosed by a temenos. Furthermore, some of the frequent motifs found on the *naos cippi* and the later stelae, like the groups of obelisks, appear frequently in Nabataean iconography at Petra and Medain Salih. In fact, one could see in the elaborate funeral façades at these cities a perpetuation in colossal form of the earlier, smaller *naos*.

found in the Amman district and seem to date to the tenth century B.C.[1] A later eighth-century B.C. example was found in tomb J3 at Dhiban.[2] There had been a considerable change between the two types of sarcophagi, but the continuation of the tradition is obvious. Fragments of either sarcophagi or coffins, like those found in Amman tomb N (which seem to indicate the observance of Assyrian burial custom in the use of deep basin-like coffins),[3] were found in tomb 84 at Mt. Nebo.[4] The coffins have not been reconstructed, but since the tomb contents were eighth to seventh centuries B.C., Saller supposed that the later Amman N coffin type was probably present here. Fragments of anthropoid coffins were also found in the Late Bronze-Iron I tombs at Pella excavated by the Department of Antiquities.[5] Pritchard notes an unusual burial practice in two of his tombs at Tell es Sa'idiyeh in which a body "had been wrapped in cloth and then encased in a block of bitumen—apparently in an attempt at mummification of the body."[6]

The earlier Amman district sarcophagi are about two meters in length and are cylinder-shaped. The head-end of each is rounded off and wider than the foot-end, which is squared. The opening, at the head, was covered by a fitted lid. It was this lid which bore most of the decoration. In tomb A at Sahab, about the only thing which has been preserved is a lid, figure 89:4, upon which a face had been modeled.[7] Two of the sarcophagi from Amman tomb G[8] also bore similar faces, but three were plain. The two which did have faces, also had arms modeled at the sides of the body portion of the sarcophagus; these extended out straight at the sides, with the fingers of the hand crudely rendered against the body. Paired lugs, one on the lid and one on the body, were placed so that the lid could be fastened to the body. Four handles were spaced along each side of each sarcophagus to facilitate carrying. One of the coffins with a plain lid had sixteen additional handles spaced in two rows on its bottom. These handles apparently served as legs to raise the coffin above the floor of the tomb.

The Dhiban sarcophagus is considerably different. Instead of a cylindrical shape, there is an elongated box with rounded ends. The lid is not confined to the head portion, but covers the full length of the box. The loop handles are absent but there are four ledges, two near the bottom and two near the top, by which the lid can be removed. The face is indicated very schematically at one end of the lid.

The styles in which the faces are rendered on the Sahab and Amman lids are basically very similar, but there are differences. It is impossible at this point, however, to attach any meaning to these differences.

The noses in both cases are prominent, pointed, and have the nostrils pressed into the clay. The mouth is straight and the lips have a puckered appearance. The eyes bulge and the eyebrows are thick and broadly arced. The ears, integrated into two of the attachment loops on the Sahab lid, are indicated by wide ledges at Amman. The beard is indicated by a slight change in the level of the surface at the bottom and an incised line at the top at Sahab. The incised line is missing in the Amman example, so it is hard to tell if a mustache was also intended here. In both cases, the point of the beard is formed by one of the attachment loops. The Sahab lid had a pointed top with a fourth attachment lug placed there. The top of the Amman example is rounded and only a narrow forehead is indicated. Six pairs of small attachment lugs were used to secure this lid. The Amman lid gives the impression of a sleeping person, while the Sahab lid indicates a person who is awake.

The Dhiban face is framed by a horseshoe-shaped ridge. A prominent triangular nose, on which the nostrils are also impressed, is centered near the top of the horseshoe and two small pellets of clay form the eyes. The mouth is indicated by two narrow bands of clay beneath the nose and an arc between the ends of the horseshoe forms the beard. Thus, the features noted above seem to be indicated here in a very abstract manner.

When Albright published the Sahab lid, he made the obvious association with similar decorated lids found in Palestine and as far away as the Sudan, dating between the thirteenth and tenth centuries B.C. These coffins and associated

[1]Khair N. Yassine, "Anthropoid Coffins from Raghadan Royal Palace Tomb in Amman," *ADAJ*, XX (1975), 57-68.

[2]Reed and Winnett, *Dhiban*, I, 59-60, pls. 96 and 97.

[3]Harding, *AN*, pp. 59-60 and 67.

[4]Saller, *LA*, XVI, 289-90.

[5]This was brought to my attention by Dr. Mohammad Khair Yassine, a former member of the Department of Antiquities of Jordan, and currently chairman of the Department of History and Archaeology at the University of Jordan.

[6]James B. Pritchard, "New Evidence on the Role of the Sea Peoples," *The Role of the Phoenicians in the Interaction of the Mediterranean Civilizations*, ed. by William A. Ward (Beirut: American University of Beirut, 1968), p. 108.

[7]William F. Albright, "An Anthropoid Clay Coffin from Sahab in the Transjordan," *AJA*, XXXVI (1932), 295-306.

[8]Four of these sarcophagi are on display in the Amman Museum.

material have been reappraised in considerable detail by Trude Dothan,[1] as well as in articles by Wright.[2] Albright was quite cautious about the association of these lids with the Philistines, in his initial comments on the Sahab lid.[3] Similar caution was expressed by Petrie and Naville in their statements on the Palestinian coffins at the same time. Albright later accepted the arguments of Dothan and Wright that Philistines are to be seen as connected with these anthropoid coffins and that initially these probably belonged to mercenary troops in Egyptian employ.[4] It is difficult to take sides in the matter because there are good arguments on both sides. It is impossible to deny, as Albright points out, that clay coffins were the poor man's substitute for more elaborately decorated wooden coffins in Egypt, and that by the Egyptian New Kingdom, the middle and poorer classes were imitating the burial practices previously confined to the upper classes. He cites other examples of clay anthropoid coffins which have not been illustrated, but which may have been distinct from those found associated with Palestinian or Philistine pottery. He points out that the use of anthropoid coffins is not attested in the Aegean world. Francis James finds considerable Egyptian influence in the pottery, small objects, and inscriptions from the Beth Shan tombs with anthropoid coffins and the earliest tombs containing anthropoid coffins at Far'ah (south) and Lachish.[5] She finds nothing in the way of artifacts or pottery to support an attribution of these burials to Philistines and can find only one sherd painted with Philistine decoration in Level VI on the tell, that is, the level contemporary with most of these tombs.[6] The new type of tomb which appears at this time has also been associated with the Philistines, but Albright noted the absence of parallels for it in the Aegean world.[7] Stanislao Loffreda, in his examination of the developments in the construction of burial chambers, comes to the same conclusion.[8] He sees the new tomb types as local developments, in the coastal area, of tomb types that had been common since the Hyksos period.

Certainly these burials must be seen in a context of Egyptian cultural influence. The coastal area of southern Palestine was strongly influenced by Egyptian cultural and political domination during the New Kingdom. The provincial capital at Gaza must have served as a transfer point through which the Nile Delta area and southern Palestine maintained close cultural contact and through which the mutual exchange of cultural influences occurred. The Philistine settlers in this area most probably became an integral part of this Egyptian presence and can only with difficulty, and by means of very specific objects, be clearly identified during the period in which Egypt maintained strong control.

In the specific case of the anthropoid coffins, it is very difficult not to accept the identification of the "highly stylized almost grotesque" decoration on some of the lids with representations of Sea Peoples.[9] The other coffins present a greater difficulty. The ones from Lachish and Far'ah (south) are also stylized, but are quite different.[10] They bear features which are usually found on Egyptian coffins.[11]

---

[1]Trude Dothan, *The Philistines and Their Material Culture* (Jerusalem: The Bialik Institute and the Israel Exploration Society, 1967), in Hebrew with English summary; "Philistine Civilization in the Light of Archaeological Finds in Palestine and Egypt," *Eretz Israel*, V (1958), 55-56; "Archaeological Reflections on the Philistine Problem," *Antiquity and Survival*, II, no. 2/3 (1957), 151-64.

[2]G. Ernest Wright, "Philistine Coffins and Mercenaries," *BA*, XXII (1959), 54-66; "Fresh Evidence for the Philistine Story," *BA*, XXIX (1966), 70-86.

[3]In a more recent discussion of the problem Albright seems to accept Dothan's and Wright's arguments; William F. Albright, "Syria, the Philistines and Phoenicia," *CAH*, Vol. II, Chapter xxxiii (revised edition; Cambridge: Cambridge University Press, 1966), pp. 24-33.

[4]Wright, *BA*, XXII, 65-66.

[5]James, *IABS*, pp. 136-38.

[6]The tombs are now published in Oren, *The Northern Cemetery of Beth Shan*.

[7]Albright, *AJA*, XXXVI, 301.

[8]Loffreda, *LA*, XVIII, 282-87. The same conclusion was arrived at independently by William H. Stiebing, Jr., "Another Look at the Origins of the Philistine Tombs at Tell el Far'ah (S)," *AJA*, LXXIV (1970), 139-44.

[9]In T. Dothan, *Antiquity and Survival*, II, 153 the coffins are said to be associated with the Philistines, but the arguments of James and more recently Oren, *The Northern Cemetery of Beth Shan*, 135-39 and 148-49, are quite strong. They deny that Philistines were at Beth Shan at this time because there is a lack of supporting archaeological evidence (cf. the total absence of real Philistine ware in the Northern Cemetery and on the tell at Beth Shan, and the fact that the headgear indicated on the "grotesque" coffin lids are not specific to the Philistines but are also used for other Sea Peoples, specifically the Denyen).

[10]Petrie, *Beth Pelet*, I, pl. XXIV, and Tufnell, *Lachish*, IV, pls. 45 and 46.

[11]Édwouard H. Naville and F. Griffith, *The Mound of the Jew and the City of Onias: Antiquities of Tell el Yahudiyeh* (London: British School of Archaeology in Egypt, 1887, 1890), pl. XIV:2. Flinders Petrie, *Tannis*, II (London: British School of Archaeology in Egypt, 1888), pl. I:17.

The short Osirid beard normally represented on male sarcophagi in Egypt is shown, as well as a wig (as at Lachish and the lid from tomb 562 at Tell Far'ah [south]). These coffins seem to be the earliest and, if one considers them to be Philistine coffins, then, the earliest examples seem to be closest to what one would expect the Egyptian prototype to have looked like. On the other hand it would seem more logical to consider those coffins with the depictions of the beards and wigs to have been used for the burial of Egyptians and that the Philistine coffins were based on such models.[1]

The remaining lids are rendered much more realistically and, usually, are so individualistic that they seem to approach portraiture. Trude Dothan suggests that these lids represent women and this is quite possible, but whether they were Philistine, local, or Egyptian women cannot be clearly demonstrated. A word of caution should be inserted by stressing the point that, except in ritual scenes, the Egyptian male is always clean-shaven and most of the sea peoples are depicted this way also, as is the case on the "grotesque" lids.[2] The possibility that Egyptian males are depicted there can possibly be eliminated, since, as indicated above, one would expect that on a sarcophagus they would be shown with the Osirid beard. The style of modeling on these lids has been compared with that illustrated on the gold masks from Mycenae.[3] The same realistic plastic molding of the facial features can, however, also be found in contemporary Egyptian art and is best illustrated by Hathor mask fragments and

Dothan, "Anthropoid Clay Coffins from a Late Bronze Age Cemetery near Deir el-Balah (Preliminary Report II)," *IEJ*, XXIII (1973), 129-46 and pls. 33-44; and I. Perlman, F. Asaro and Trude Dothan, "Provenance of the Deir el-Balah Coffins," *IEJ*, XXIII (1973), 147-51.

The reports deal with fifty anthropoid coffins and an assemblage of fourteen through early twelfth century B.C. artifacts including Cypriote, Mycenaean III A and B, and Egyptian imports alongside the local wares which are primarily storage jars, bowls, dipper-juglets and flasks. A rich and varied group of alabaster vessels, jewelry and royal scarabs of Thutmoses III, Amenhotep II, Thutmoses IV, Amenhotep III (and his queen Tiye), Seti I, Ramses II (the most numerous) and Ramses IV were found.

The coffins provide the earliest examples found in Palestine and are divided into two groups. The first group has a mummy shape on which the head and shoulders are delineated. This is a type of coffin which was not known before from excavations in Palestine and is the predominant type here. The second group, the coffin type previously known from Palestinian sites, is found in only five examples.

The majority of the lids are done in a naturalistic style and a few in a "grotesque" style. The molded decoration is confined to the lid, except in the few cases where feet are also indicated. The more elaborate lids closely follow the Egyptian prototypes in wood, cartonnage and stone. All the coffins are made locally and a number of Egyptian features are found on all lids, namely, lotus-flowers, the usual hand and arm positions (in some examples the hands are holding religious symbols), wigs and Osirid beards. Paint is preserved in many cases.

Dothan concludes her discussion of anthropoid coffins with the following statements: "The earliest known appearance of anthropoid burials in Canaan (fourteenth to the end of the thirteenth century B.C.) occurred at Deir el-Balah. Its last phase overlaps the early group of anthropoid burials at Beth Shean, and leads up to the transitional Late Bronze Age-early Iron Age burials of this type from Tell Sharuhen and Lachish tomb 570. . . . All these are most probably attributable to Egyptian officials or garrisons stationed in Canaan. . . . The later group (twelfth-eleventh centuries B.C.), consists of the 'grotesque' coffins from Beth Shean and the Philistine burials at Tell Sharuhen. These show that the burial custom was adopted by the Sea People, the Philistines, who were probably first settled as mercenaries in Egyptian strongholds in Palestine by Ramesses III after the defeat of the Sea People, *ca.* 1190 B.C., in the battles depicted on the walls of his temple at Medinet Habu (T. Dothan, *IEJ*, XXIII [1973], 146)." Our most serious reservation with the above is in the role of the Philistines, in keeping with the arguments we have stated above.

---

[1]The bitumen burials at Tell es Sa'idiyeh can be used in this same line of argument. The practice of mummification in Palestine should be expected to have been carried out either under strong Egyptian influence or by Egyptians who felt they had no chance of having their bodies returned to their native land for interment. Such a practice in the Jordan Valley, where bitumen can be procured at the south end of the Dead Sea, can be seen as an attempt at using local materials as a substitute method. Since the practice is influenced by Egyptian custom, it is impossible to say at this point whether Egyptians, Sea Peoples, or local people were buried in such a manner. The possibility of seeing Sea People or Philistine burials here, seems most unlikely to us. Why should they try to imitate a burial practice that was foreign to them in still another foreign country? Tentatively, it would seem most plausible to see this as an adaptation by the local population.

The exciting finds at Deir el Balah. have expanded our knowledge of anthropoid coffins in a critical geographical area 14 km. southwest of Gaza. Trude Dothan, "Anthropoid Clay Coffins from a Late Bronze Age Cemetery near Deir el-Balah (Preliminary Report)," *IEJ*, XXII (1972), 67-72 and pls. 9-13; Trude

[2]Like the three Beth Shan lids illustrated in Wright, *BA*, XXII, fig. 2:1-3 and Oren, *The Northern Cemetery of Beth Shan*, figs. 52:1-4, 53:4, 78:1-3, 79 and 80.

[3]Henry Schliemann, *Mycenae* (New York: Benjamin Blom, Reissued 1967), pp. 289, no. 474 and p. 312. Georg Karo, *Die Schachtgräber von Mykenai* (München: Verlag F. Brackmann, A.-G., 1930, 1933), pls. XLVII-LII.

Hathor capitals at Timna,[1] and similar capitals at Sherabit el Khedaim in Sinai.[2] Here the features are, however, indicated more precisely. For instance, fine lines are used to outline the eyes, to indicate the eyelids, and in the handling of the nose which is not as pronounced or angular as it often appears on the lids. The rounded features and primary reliance on modeling are clearly evident on the lids, masks, and capitals.

With this background, the discussion of the Transjordanian coffin lids is clearer. The Amman district lids resemble most closely the last-mentioned "realistic" type. The Amman lid would seem to be more stylized than that at Sahab, but a similar variety in the manner of depiction is evident at Beth Shan also. The unusual feature, here, is the depiction of the full beard. The use of this style for showing a male would then be unique, if we accept Trude Dothan's view. The addition of the beard makes this lid look very much like the so-called gold "mask of Agamemnon" from Mycenae; but, in view of the way men are depicted on the other lids that are extant, a chronological gap of more than 200 years, and the absence of any similar piece in Palestine, we must consider, with Albright, that this is a Semitic feature. The lack of a mustache on the Amman lid fits well with the local representation as we have seen it on figurines and as we shall see below in sculpture; namely, that both styles of wearing the beard (with or without mustache) are accepted as normal in the area. In speculating on the influences indicated by these lids, there seem to be several alternatives. These lids could have been inspired by the Philistines or used by Philistines in the Transjordan, or they could have been inspired by Egyptians or used by Egyptians. The appearance here of local peculiarities, which cannot be found in Palestine, probably indicates early examples of a local variant tradition which could go back to the time of Egyptian dominance and continuing to the time in which sculptured heads were depicted in a similar manner in stone (see below, p. 161).

This local tradition is further emphasized by the difference in the placement of the arms. In Palestine, Egypt, and the Sudan, the arms are only found on the lids and usually in an awkward and stylized manner. In Amman, two sarcophagi show that the hands were not placed on the lids but at the sides of the body portion of the sarcophagus. Unlike the usual Egyptian practice of crossing the arms on the chest, as is done on some of the other lids, or of bringing the arms across the chest toward each other but not usually touching, the arms are here represented as straight out along the sides. The fact that the Amman district sarcophagi actually date later than the Palestinian examples is significant, particularly as they do not represent stylized, degraded, or abstracted types. It is difficult, then, for us to see strong Philistine influence here as we were not able to see it in the ceramic material.

The Dhiban lid does not add very much to our discussion, since it is later than the Palestinian or Amman district examples and illustrates an even greater abstraction of the essential features of the head than is in evidence elsewhere. The change in the lid shape is noteworthy because it is obvious that a different type of coffin was now preferred, but the tradition of anthropoid coffins was still so strong that a head was indicated to keep within that tradition also.

Other Small Objects

It is impossible and unnecessary to go into great detail here concerning the numerous other objects found to date in the Transjordan. The compilation of a summary catalogue will not be attempted here, since its value would be quite doubtful. We will mention here only those items which are unusual and of special interest, or those which have special chronological significance.

Iron I Objects

Small objects are numerous, but quite repetitious in the tombs of this period. The best collections are presently from Madeba tomb A[3] and Sahab tomb C[4]. Most of the metal objects are of bronze: knives, straight toggle pins, arrowheads, spearheads, bracelets, anklets, earrings, finger-rings, razors, and armor scales. Precious metals are very rare and iron is somewhat more frequent, but a very poor second place. One curved piece of iron was found in the Jebel Nuzha tomb[5] and two bracelets and two finger-rings were found in Madeba tomb A. These pieces are important because of their twelfth century B.C. date and in that they seem to be used as an infrequent substitute for common bronze forms. It is very doubtful that in these instances iron could be considered as a precious metal.

The most interesting objects are pieces of bronze that were used as armor scales and several complete bronze vessels found in the Jordan

---

[1]Rothenberg, *ILN*, Nov. 15, 1969, pp. 32-33, figs. 6-8.

[2]Flinders Petrie, *Research in Sinai* (New York: E. P. Dutton, 1906), figs. 95, 100, 103, and 104.

[3]Harding, *MA*, pp. 31-33, 40-41.

[4]see R. Dajani, *ADAJ*, XV.

[5]R. Dajani, *JN*, p. 52.

Valley. Several pieces of bronze with holes and central ribs were found in Madeba tomb A[1] where they are called "attachments for the chains to dagger sheaths,"[2] but numerous similar pieces were found at Deir ʻAllā in the latest L.B. levels and are considered armor scale.[3] The similarity to the portions of armor found in Cyprus[4] allows one to reconstruct the method of attachment of the individual scales into an armor vestment, and indicates that all the pieces mentioned here from the Transjordan served the same function.

James B. Pritchard has published a tomb, number 101, from Tell es Saʻidiyeh in which a large number of bronze objects were found. These include a cauldron of hammered metal with handles, a bronze tripod to which a bowl was riveted, a large bowl or laver with handles, a smaller bowl, a strainer with loop handle, a juglet with pinched lip and twisted handle, and a bronze lamp.[5] Pritchard stresses that: "Traditional pottery forms, such as bowl, tray, strainer, juglet and lamp, were reproduced in metal."[6] There were actually very few pottery objects in the tomb and most of the metal vessels seemed to form a very distinctive group, namely, a wine service. One of the pottery store vessels and two juglets may also have had an associated use. Similar wine services, or portions thereof, are cited from contemporary levels at Beth Shan and Megiddo, and more importantly from Tell Mazar, situated between Tell es Saʻidiyeh and Deir ʻAllā.[7] Gold, silver and electrum were also found in this tomb but, interestingly enough, iron was not present.

Several carved ivory objects were found. Two are called flasks and one is a small dish which was fitted with a sliding cover, and a spoon. These were considered as "probably used to contain and dispense cosmetics."[8] Numerous beads (571) were found in this tomb also. Beads, amulets, and scarabs were found in the Madeba tomb. The identifiable scarabs are said to be Hyksos, XIXth Dynasty and Ramesside types.[9] The amulets are of the Egyptian types which continue to occur in later tombs also, most notably, the *uzat* eye amulet.

Iron II Objects

Some of the small objects remain constant throughout the Iron Age and are equally well represented in the latest tombs. There are, of course, some changes in style and some new forms appear. The changes are obvious, since the majority of the preserved objects come from the end of Iron II. The lack of objects from late Iron I and early Iron II leaves little that would show a transition or development within forms. Most of the tombs, like Amman A-F, Sahab A-C, and

Irbed A-C, contain only a few metal objects.

The bracelets, earrings, and finger-rings of the early tombs continue to occur as do a bronze strainer and two bronze bowls at Meqabelein, which seem to represent part of a "wine service." Iron objects, though not numerous, show a variety of forms but knife blades are most common. Precious metals are extremely rare, except for the richest tombs AN and M. The most significant new metal forms are bronze mirrors (AE and M), fibulae, new types of arrow points, long bronze kohl sticks, and some new types of finger-rings and earrings. Many of the new types are found in the two tombs richest in objects and date late in the seventh and early in the sixth centuries B.C. Most of these objects, like the glass bottles and the horse and rider figurines, are better documented (and normally are considered to belong) toward the end of this time range, primarily in the Persian period. More will be said about this below.

Fibulae are present in most tombs and are clearly a class of object which did not occur earlier. The main type represented is the knee fibula with molded, encircling rings. The dating of the tombs to which these fibulae belong agrees well with the dates of their most common occurrence elsewhere; that is, it overlaps the eighth and seventh centuries B.C.[10] Several of the fragments of the earlier arc-topped fibulae occur in Mt. Nebo tomb 20. This tomb is said to begin in the ninth century and such arc-topped fibulae continue to be common in the eighth and seventh centuries.[11] A fibula of this type is also found in the Meqabelein tomb.[12] A stamp seal in a bronze setting is suspended from the narrow pin portion, and illustrates the practice of wearing a stamp seal as an

---

[1]Harding, *MA*, pl. V:189-94.

[2]*Ibid.*, p. 32.

[3]Franken, *VT*, XI, 367; *VT*, XIV, 420.

[4]It was found at Idalion. Gjerstad, *et al.*, *The Swedish Cyprus Expedition*, Vol. II, Part II, pp. 538-39, pl. CLXXII.

[5]Pritchard, "New Evidence on the Role of the Sea Peoples in Canaan at the Beginning of the Iron Age," pp. 102-103.

[6]*Ibid.*, p. 108.

[7]Franken, *VT*, X, 387.

[8]*Ibid.*, p. 102.

[9]Harding, *MA*, p. 33.

[10]David Stronach, "The Development of the Fibula in the Near East," *Iraq*, XXI (1959), 180-206.

[11]Saller, *LA*, XVI, 198-99.

[12]Harding, *M*, pl. XIII:2.

ornament attached to a garment. A modification of the latter type, namely, a high loop-top fibula, is found as a fragmentary piece in AN. An eighth to seventh-century date is again given for parallel finds elsewhere.[1]

With the exception of a few items, the metal objects and the other small objects which we have quickly reviewed here pose a dating problem similar to that illustrated by the pottery vessels. It was noted that there are some pottery forms which have a range of popularity between the end of the Neo-Assyrian period and the Persian period. Only a few good arguments could be found which would allow us to place these vessels late in that time range, while the best parallels seemed to indicate dates closer to the beginning of that range. The analysis of a number of the gems in tomb AN leads to a similar conclusion by indicating a date just prior to 600 B.C. The partial overlap of AN and M is indicated by numerous items which are similar, but in addition, by a series of objects which indicate a continued use of the Meqabelein tomb. Again, the ceramic repertory, the similarity of the ceramic assemblage, and the lack of concrete Persian period pieces argue that the time range of the Meqabelein tomb must be placed within the Neo-Babylonian period.

Dealing first with the earliest objects, we have a number of gems which fit best in a Neo-Assyrian context. One of these, a small seal fitted on a silver ring, is read "belonging to 'Adoni-nur servent of 'Ammi-nadab." An Ammi-nadab is mentioned in an inscription of Ashurbanipal dated to ca. 667 B.C.[2] but the inscribed bottle found at Tell Siran indicates that there were at least two Ammonite rulers with this name.[3] On the basis of parallels to the ceramic materials from tomb AN, we would identify the Ammi-nadab of the seal impression with the second Ammi-nadab and date the seal around 635 B.C. Other seals from this tomb, numbers 3, 5, and 6, are also quite clearly Neo-Assyrian in date and two of these are also inscribed with personal names. Number 2 mentions a Shub-El and number 3 mentions Menahem son of Yamin.[4] Only one, number 4, an octagonal stamp seal decorated with the conventionalized depiction of a ritual scene, is incised with straight lines and drill holes which are so common in the Neo-Babylonian period. A more delicately cut seal, which is almost identical in the way the worshipper and the symbols are indicated, was found in the Meqabelein tomb.[5] The other AN objects paralleled in the Neo-Babylonian and Persian periods are a trilobate "Scythian" arrowhead, a silver bowl, and a fragment of a small glass vase.[6] Sixth to fifth centuries B.C. and post-exilic parallels are cited for similar arrowheads at Deve Hüyük, Athlit, and Tell ed Duweir.[7] The silver bowl, number 33, seems to be identical in profile to one found at Kamid el Loz.[8]

The glass vase fragment is similar to a complete vase from Meqabelein. A second glass vase at Meqabelein is an imitation of the alabastron, a form which is also reproduced in pottery in this tomb. Though the techniques involved in the production of alabaster vessels were quite old,[9] the

[1]Stronach, *Iraq*, XXI, 190-95. The AN example is closest to Stronach's Type III (fig. 7:3), and is a variety of the triangular fibula.

[2]Landes, *BA*, XXIV, 80.

[3]See the discussion on p. 58.

[4]Harding, *AN*, pp. 52 and 53.

[5]Harding, *M*, p. 46 (number 33). Numerous seals, either bearing inscribed names (written in the local script) and other designs or merely designs, have been attributed to Transjordanian findspots. These, for the most part, are similar to the gems from tombs AN and M. Many of these objects come from Amman, in particular see the Neo-Babylonian seal with two cuneiform signs published by Rafiq W. Dajani, "A Neo-Babylonian Seal from Amman," *ADAJ*, VI-VII (1962), 124, 125, and fig. 8; and Phillip C. Hammond, "An Ammonite Stamp Seal from Amman," *BASOR*, CLX (1960), 38-41. Other objects are stated to have been found at sites like Petra (Godfrey R. Driver, "Seals from Amman and Petra," *QDAP*, XI [1945], 81-82, pl. XVIII:Petra Seal) and Adolf Reifenberg, *Hebrew Seals* (London: The East and West Library, 1950), no. 36 from Irbed (nos. 27 and 35 are said to be Ammonite and nos. 3 and 28 are merely called Transjordanian). Additional seals are identified as Ammonite or Moabite in Nahman Avigad, "Ammonite and Moabite Seals," *Near Eastern Archaeology in the Twentieth Century*, edited by James A. Sanders (Garden City: Doubleday and Company, Inc., 1970), pp. 284-95.

We mentioned above the seal impressions of Qos-gabr at Umm el Biyara (Bennett, *RB*, LXXIII, 399-401) and Qôs-'anal at Tell el Kheleifeh (Nelson Glueck, "The First Campaign at Tell el-Kheleifeh (Ezion-geber)," *BASOR*, LXXI (1938), 15, 16, and fig. 6; "The Topography and History of Ezion-geber and Elath," *BASOR*, LXXII (1938), 11-13 and fig. 3; "The Second Campaign at Tell el-Kheleifeh (Ezion-geber: Elath)," *BASOR*, LXXV (1939), 30). A stamp seal with the typical stylized altars, stands, and symbols was found at Taiwilan with eighth-seventh century pottery, Bennett, *RB*, LXXVI, pl. VI.

[6]Harding, *AN*, pp. 55 and 56, nos. 30, 33, and 42 respectively.

[7]*Ibid.*, pp. 70 and 71.

[8]Rolf Hachmann and Arnulf Kuschke, *Bericht über die Ergebnise der Ausgrabungen in Kamid el-Loz (Libanon) in den Jahren 1963 und 1964* (Bonn: Rudolf Habelt Verlag, 1966), fig. 26:7.

[9]Corning Museum of Glass, *Glass from the Ancient World* (Corning: The Corning Museum of Glass, 1957), pp. 13-29.

specific shape found here enjoyed a period of popularity which coincides with the date range of the objects under discussion here. The examples from AN and M are some of the earliest examples within this time range.[1] The two silver earrings (no. 4) have very good parallels at Kamid el Loz[2] and two silver finger-rings (nos. 5 and 6) are done in a similar heavy style with the application of small pellets for decoration. Bronze kohl sticks were found both in the Meqabelein tomb and in a tomb at Kamid el Loz.[3] The seal number 10 has a good parallel, again at Kamid el Loz.[4] The bronze suspension loop attached through the center hole of the seal is the same and both seals illustrate similar scenes. At Kamid el Loz, a central hero fighting two steers is depicted. At Meqabelein, the central hero is holding an antelope by a hind leg in each of his raised hands. The costumes and hair styles are not identical. On the Meqabelein seal, a series of lines and dots, indicating either a sacred tree or cult symbols, separate the antelopes on both sides of the composition.[5]

The Athlit, Kamid el Loz, and Deve Hüyük material was also found in tombs which have a date range that overlaps both Neo-Babylonian and Persian periods. Specific examination of some of these tombs yields objects which can be dated quite closely but, for the most part, it is very difficult to distinguish between the two periods. The date range here is usually supported on the lower side by the pottery, which is closer to Persian period than to the preceding Iron II. As was stated above, the ceramic evidence in the Amman district works in the opposite direction and indicates that some of the earliest objects of these specific types are being dealt with here. The detailed discussion of horse and rider figurines illustrated exactly the same point.

In conclusion, mention must be made of sixteen enigmatic objects which were found primarily in Amman tomb F. The most likely use of these objects was as instruments to shape or burnish pottery vessels during manufacture. The size of these objects ranges from 3.4 by 4.3 to 6.0 by 10.2 cm. and the thickness is between 0.4 and 1.0 cm. A roughly centered, circular hole (between 1.1 and 1.7 cm. in diameter) had been pierced through them before firing. These pieces were slightly rounded on one side, both at the central hole and on the edges, while the other side was either flat or curled up slightly with a sharp ridge either around the hole or around the edge. There were three distinct shapes: (1) an elongated oval (figs. 85:3, 4 [6?]; 86:1 and 2), (2) a rectangle (fig. 85:8 and 10), and (3) a "combination form" with rounded top and straight bottom. Four of these pieces (figs. 85:1, 3, 10, and 86:2) had signs or letters incised on them before firing, and one (fig. 86:1) had a feather (?) and a branch (?) incised on it after

firing. In all cases, the signs were placed on the flat side. Many of the pieces showed wear from use. Two similar objects (fig. 84:8 and 9) made of polished bone were also found and had elongated rectangular shapes. A portion of a pottery weight, possibly a loom weight, was also found in this tomb (fig. 85:9).

The only parallels to be found for these sixteen terra-cotta and two bone objects are from Megiddo and Meṣad Ḥashavyahu. At Megiddo, these objects are called "felucca" and their dating is a problem.[6] The similar objects from Meṣad Ḥashavyahu are called "polishing implements."[7] The rarity of such objects adds to the difficulty of giving an explanation for their use but, on the other hand, their presence at Meṣad Ḥashavyahu provides a good link for chronological purposes and supports our contention of a date around 600 B.C.

[1]Don Barag, "The Glass Aryballos," *Atiqot*, V (1965), 58-59.

[2]Hachmann and Kuschke, *Kamid el-Loz*, fig. 20:6 and 7.

[3]*Ibid.*, fig. 29:11 and 12. Similar objects are rare in Syria and Palestine, so the parallel is significant despite the differences, namely, the notched ends and incised bands at Kamid el Loz as opposed to the plain rods with flattened spoon-shaped ends at Meqabelein.

[4]*Ibid.*, figs. 22:11, 29:6.

[5]We should mention here the two other published cylinder seals from the Transjordan. Both are given eighth-seventh century dates and are executed in a rather severe incised-line style, and both show ritual scenes and symbols. One is from Tell es Sa'idiyeh: James B. Pritchard, "A Cosmopolitan Culture of the Late Bronze Age," *Expedition*, VII, No. 4 (1964), 32. The other is from tomb 20 at Mt. Nebo: Saller, *LA*, XVI, 187-92 and fig. 7. The symbol and carving on this seal are very similar to that on the stamp seal from Taiwilan mentioned above.

[6]The Megiddo felucca have been dated to LB II, where some may belong. Most of these objects, however, come from tomb 63 which has a mixture of pottery and is said to have been used as a workshop in the Iron Age. Nos. 5526 and 3925 are dated LB II (?) and I would suspect they should really be placed with the M.I. material. It is interesting that in 63F, which is mostly a LB II deposit, a red-burnished jug sherd was found with the black-white-black decoration that, as we have seen above, is so characteristic of the Transjordan. Guy and Engberg, *MEG T*, pl. 158:1, 16, 18, and 20.

[7]Joseph Naveh, "The Excavations at Meṣad Ḥashavyahu," *IEJ*, XII (1962), 97.

Stone Sculpture

With the exception of the Balu'a stele and the sculptured head from the area of ancient Moab which is in the American University of Beirut Museum,[1] all the Iron Age sculpture available from the Transjordan comes from the Amman district. Twenty-eight out of more than thirty of these sculptures have been found since 1950.[2] This makes Amman the most important site on either side of the Jordan River for such Iron Age artistic production. On sites like Carchemish, Tell Halaf, Zincerli, Hama, Ta'yinat, Sakjegözü, etc., most of the sculpture was used as architectural decoration or in the decoration of stele, but few pieces were designed to be free-standing. At Amman, the opposite is true; most of the pieces are intended to be free-standing and only the four double-faced female heads seem to have been intended for architectural purposes. The function of the Amman sculptures would, then, seem to be quite different from that of most of the Neo-Hittite pieces.

The Amman sculptures exhibit a very cosmopolitan flavor. Stylistic features are present which can be attributed to Egyptian and Mesopotamian influences but, on the whole, these are to be expected, as they are also characteristic of Syro-Palestinian art.

Balu'a Stele

The second earliest example of stone sculpture in the Transjordan was found at Balu'a.[3] This monument has been re-examined and exhaustively restudied by William A. Ward and M. F. Martin.[4] The main tenets of their arguments are summarized in the following four points. (1) The inscription panel and the relief were produced at the same time and the relief panel was not placed on an older inscribed stele as a number of other scholars have suggested. (2) The speculation concerning the nature of the inscription must, for the most part, be dismissed because it was done on the basis of extremely poor photographs. Since the inscription is difficult enough to work with first hand, the use of photographs only compounds the problems. Ward and Martin conclude that the inscription may well represent a local attempt at writing Egyptian. They think a number of the signs can clearly be identified and that there is a possibility of reading the name Thutmose.[5] (3) The garments and other stylistic features indicate a date range of 1309 to 1151 B.C. (Seti I to Ramses III) and only one feature, the headdress worn by the king, indicates a more precise date, the reign of Ramses III.[6] (4) Finally, they argue that:

[1]See illustration in Siegfried H. Horn, "The Crown of the King of the Ammonites," *Andrews University Seminary Studies*, XI (1973), pl. XX:8.

[2]Fourteen of these pieces are illustrated on our figures 90-94. Figure 92:2 is piece D published in Richard D. Barnett, "Four Sculptures from Amman," *ADAJ*, I, 36, pl. XIII.

Figure 92:3 is piece B, *ibid.*, pp. 34-35, pl. XI and inscription on pl. XIII.

Figure 92:4 was found about ten years later near the spot where the four pieces published by Barnett were found; Farah S. Ma'ayeh, "Recent Archaeological Discoveries in Jordan," *ADAJ*, IV-V (1960), 114-5 and pl. IV:1.

Figure 90:1 has recently been published in Nabil Khairi, " 'Aragan Statue," (in Arabic), *ADAJ*, XV (1970), 15-18, pls. 1 and 2. The site of 'Aragan is directly south of Amman.

Figure 90:2 is unpublished.

Figure 90:3 is piece C, Barnett, *ADAJ*, I, 36, pl. XII.

Figure 91:1 is piece A, *ibid.*, p. 34, pl. X.

Figure 91:2 and 3 are unpublished.

Figure 91:4 Barnett, *ADAJ*, I, 34, footnote 1, by editor, stated to be in the Amman Museum.

Figures 93 and 94 are four heads, labeled A-D for convenience in discussion and in keeping with their published sequence. They are briefly published in Safwan Kh. Tell, "New Ammonite Discoveries" (in Arabic), *ADAJ*, XII-XIII (1967-68), 9-16 and pls. 1-4.

Now see also Fawzi Zayadine, "Recent Excavations on the Citadel of Amman," *ADAJ*, XVIII (1973), 27-28, 33-35 and pls. XXI-XXIII and Pierre Bordreuil, "Inscriptions des Têtes à double Face," *ADAJ*, XVIII (1973), 37-39.

Two additional sculptured heads which have not been illustrated previously, are now illustrated in Horn, *Andrews University Seminary Studies*, XI (1973), pls. XVII:2 and XIX:5. The first is a basalt head which is in the British Museum and the second a limestone head in the Amman Museum.

Two statuettes have recently been found at Khirbet el Hajjar, seven kilometers southwest of Amman, Moawiyah M. Ibrahim, "Two Ammonite Statuettes from Khirbet El-Hajjar," *ADAJ*, XVI (1971), 91-97 and pls. 1-3. In addition Ibrahim mentions fragments of 12-13 broken statuettes from Abu 'Alanda, seven kilometers south of Amman, *Ibid.*, p. 95. One head from this group has been illustrated in Horn, *Andrews University Seminary Studies*, XI (1973), pl. XX:7.

[3]G. Horsfield and L. H. Vincent, "Une stele Égypto-Moabite au Balou'a," *RB*, XLI (1932), 416-44.

[4]Ward and Martin, *Balu'a*, pp. 5-29 and pls. I-VI.

[5]If an Egyptian pharaoh were intended here, the latest, Thutmose IV (1413-1405), would create some difficulty in placing the stele better than a century earlier than Ward and Martin would like to put it.

[6]Ward and Martin cite Driton's identification of this headdress with the Shasu who are shown as the enemies of Ramses II and III on temple reliefs in Egypt. They tend to favor this interpretation over the one which associates it with the Sea Peoples, especially the Shekeles and Teresh, as Wainwright suggests.

It seems to us that the Balu'a stele could only have been carved at a time when Egypt was a power to be reckoned with, when Moab was thoroughly aware of the presence of considerable Egyptian strength in Palestine and when there was the possibility of Egyptian intervention in east Jordan itself.[1]

They then present arguments supporting their conclusions that:

East Jordan had a sedentary population throughout the Egyptian empire period and, except for a few scattered decades, Egyptian power in Palestine was firmly entrenched throughout this age. Egyptian objects in east Jordan spread from the Hyksos age to the late Empire and beyond, and references in Egyptian inscriptions are too vague to allow us to say anything beyond the mere fact that there is slim evidence of Egyptian influence in Moab and possible references to military raids into east Jordan. We can, however, indicate the earliest and latest possible date for the Balu'a stele.[2] [See item 3 above.]

It is important to make only a few more observations which call attention to features and influences which can also be noted on some of the sculpture we will discuss below. Ward and Martin point out in their discussion that a thorough understanding of Egyptian representation is indicated in the representation of the garments, the use of specific symbols, and the attitude and placement of all three figures.[3] The canon of proportions and the manner in which the relief is executed, however, show clear local workmanship. This is further illustrated by the fact that the Egyptian elements seem to be fully integrated into the composition and easily presented side by side with features and symbols of obvious local significance. One could go so far as to say that a local art style of a very highly Egyptianized character is illustrated here.

Male Statues or Statue Fragments from the Amman District

Four complete statues, a single headless body, a single body fragment, and at least eight heads come under this heading, and can be divided into three groups: (1) an Egyptianizing group, (2) a Transjordanian group, and (3) a Syrian group. There are many overlapping features within these groups, but they all, like the Balu'a stele, represent the production of a local school which has incorporated Egyptian elements to varying degrees. It is interesting that unlike Phoenician artistic production, which welded features borrowed from other areas into a distinct style of its own, we have here a less integrated style in which

the local craftsmen were not strong enough to impose themselves sufficiently on their subject matter to obscure the foreign elements and reshape them as their own.

Individual features on these sculptures may help in the dating of a specific piece, but it is difficult to indicate much that would be useful in making chronological distinctions. For now, these pieces must be considered to date within Iron II and confined primarily to the eighth and seventh centuries B.C.

The find spots of most of these pieces are problematical or unknown. Less than half of the Amman Citadel pieces, however, were found at the north end of the citadel, near the modern entrance into the large underground chamber that we discussed above on page 90.

Group 1

In this group of one complete statue and two heads, illustrated on figure 90, Egyptian influence can be seen most clearly, but it is somewhat deceptive because the details are not rendered with great precision.[4]

The Egyptian influence is most striking in the complete statue. The pose, with clenched hands held at the sides, left foot forward, and the back attached to a pillar, is clearly similar to Egyptian practice which existed from the Old Kingdom period on[5] and is not common elsewhere. The body proportions conform to those found on Egyptian sculpture, but the head is disproportionately large. The feet are bare as is the upper body above the waist, except for the indication of a wide Egyptian necklace. A skirt is frequently found on such Egyptian statues (as indicated by the parallels cited in the footnotes), but the style depicted here is un-Egyptian. It resembles instead

---

[1]Ward and Martin, *Balu'a*, p. 19.

[2]*Ibid.*

[3]*Ibid.*, p. 22.

[4]At least one of the statuettes and a majority of the thirteen fragments mentioned in footnote 2, p. 153 above, must now be included here also. A detailed analysis of the recently discovered pieces from Abu 'Alanda is necessary before they can be incorporated into our discussion. The pieces are very broken and the surfaces badly worn or abraided.

[5]Jean Capart, *L'art égyptien*. Tome II: *La statuaire* (Bruxelles: des Etabl. Vromant, S.A., 1948), pls. 236, 237, 240, 241, 304, 366, 379, 383, and 394, and J. Vandier, *Manuel d'archéologie égyptienne*. Tome III: *Les grandes epoques: La statuaire* (Paris: Editions A. et J. Picard et Cie, 1958), pls. IV, V, VII, XVII, XVIII, XXV, C, CI, CXXXII, etc.

the garments illustrated on Syrian reliefs and on the Assyrian monuments. The major difference is that these garments, which show the right leg uncovered to the thigh and the left leg almost completely covered, usually cover the entire body or represent a draped shawl,[1] and are not shown as a skirt or kilt. There seems to be a combination of elements here.[2] The same is true of the head. The facial features are un-Egyptian and resemble those of Yereah-'Azar (see fig. 92:3 and the discussion below) but no beard is shown. The hair is depicted in the fashion of an Egyptian wig but, as we remarked above concerning the figurine from el Medeiyineh, pages 136-37, the ear is shown in conformity with local practice. Some hair seems to show below the ears and, if this is the case, the same hair style as on figure 90:3 seems indicated. The depiction of the tufts of hair as individual curls is also un-Egyptian, but occurs quite frequently on North Syrian reliefs and sculpture.[3] The mouth is straight and the lips and nose are fairly heavy. The eyes and eyebrows (represented by a ridge) are similar to those on the other heads where provisions were made for inlaid eyes.

This statue, then, shows a combination of features which is presently quite unique.

Similar composites based on Egyptian styles and motifs are, of course, characteristic of Phoenician art, but there are no features here which could be considered Phoenician. This piece must, then, be seen as an example of another Egyptianizing, syncretistic style which has incorporated specific Assyrian elements that were also being adopted at this time in North Syrian art. It is impossible to tell if paint was applied to the figure. There is a dark stain in places on the soft yellow-white stone, but this seems to be due to weathering.

The facial features of figure 90:2 are much the same as those discussed above.

Sockets were cut for inlaid eyes but the inlays intended for them have not been preserved. It seems that a short hair style is intended, but it is possible that this is not fully represented and, like on figure 90:1, the head and body may have been attached to a post that came up against the lower part of the head at the back. The hair is shown in rows across the head but individual tufts of hair, as on figure 90:1 and 3, are not indicated.[4] A row of very small tufts, however, seems to be depicted on the forehead beneath the lowest hair row. (See the discussion below for figure 92:3 on the style of hair in strands that seems to be the same as here.) The color of the stone and results of the weathering are the same here as on figure 90:1.

The remaining head in this group, figure 90:3, has been discussed to a large degree above. The eyes were also originally inlaid and were not as large, in proportion to the face, as on the other pieces. The lips and cheeks are modeled so as to indicate a smile. The chin does not jut out as on some of the other heads, but is pulled back so that the beard would seem to have formed a smooth transition from the face to chest. The beard is indicated by smaller rows of narrow tufts than the hair. A similar beard is shown on an ivory plaque found at Nimrud.[5] There, the men also have tufted hair and the ears are not covered. The hair is not shown, however, in rows of tufts which line up both horizontally and vertically as in this Amman example, but the vertical rows are staggered so that alternating rows line up vertically. Unlike the figurines, the hair style on this head can be seen all around and the concentric rows of tufts observed from the top converge at the center in an eight petaled rosette. The only other evidence, in addition to that given above, upon which a date for this head can be based is the manner in which three heads are rendered in profile on a Carchemish relief.[6] Here the hair tufts are arranged in rows but each tuft is shown as a curl, like those discussed above as parallels for figure 90:1. Otherwise, the profile and slant of the forehead and chin are similar to what is shown here. Akurgal indicates a date range of 850-700 B.C. for this relief and other sculpture which is of a similar style. A date of ±900 B.C., however, is suggested by H.G. Güterbock in the dating of the Carchemish long wall reliefs to

---

[1]Hrouda, *Die Kulturgeschichte des assyrischen Flachbildes*, p. 31.

[2]Rare examples of similar skirts on men are found on several ivories at Nimrud, which Mallowan considers Phoenician. These men also wear the wide necklace and the atef crown. Mallowan, *Nimrud and Its Remains*, pp. 541-42, 509; figs. 469, 470, and 481.

[3]Ekrim Akurgal, *Die Kunst der Hethiter* (München: Hirmer Verlag, 1961), pls. 118, 119, 121, 122, 124 (from Carchemish); 126, 127, 129, 130 (from Sam'al); 133 (from Sakçegözü); 138, and 139 (from Maraş). Their date range here is ninth to seventh centuries B.C., but such curls are considered to be characteristic of his "Assyrisierende Stil, Erste Phase" (850-745 B.C.). There are a number of ivories from Nimrud on which individual curls are illustrated. Some show a long spring-like curl while others show a tight curl which is little more than a spiral (as is the case in Amman). Barnett, *The Nimrud Ivories*, pl. LIX:S95, and Mallowan, *Nimrud and Its Remains*, figs. 383, 384, 385, 402, and 409.

[4]It is possible that the hair was originally rendered in a manner similar to the beard of 90:2 but that the vertical divisions have been lost as a result of weathering.

[5]Mallowan, *Nimrud and Its Remains*, p. 579, fig. 539.

[6]Akurgal, *Die Kunst der Hethiter*, pl. 117.

which the cited Carchemish relief belongs.[1]

Group 2

Again, there are one complete statue and a number of heads, in this case four. The fourth head is not illustrated here but is in the British Museum and was recently published.[2] Figure 91:1 is of basalt, while the others are limestone. The most characteristic feature which marks these pieces as a separate group is the Egyptian *atef* crown which they wear. This and the stance of figure 91:1 are the only Egyptian features present here. The statue, figure 91:1, is very much lacking in detail. A sparseness of detail can be found on some of the basalt sculptures at Carchemish,[3] but it is not as extreme as here. Rather, it is similar to the treatment of the heads on figure 91:2 and 3 and suggests that figure 91:1 was never finished.[4] The missing details may be reconstructed from the statues of Yereaḥ-ʿAzar, since it corresponds exactly in both stance and dress.

The feet are again shown bare; the garment and shawl will be discussed below in connection with Yereaḥ-ʿAzar since more details are present there. The right hand is straight down at the side with clenched fist, while the left hand is held at the front, also with a clenched fist, as if holding something but nothing is indicated. The beard alone is indicated here, as in figure 91:4, without mustache (which is indicated on figure 91:2 and 3). The mouth is small, straight, and puckered in appearance; the nose is broken, the eyelids are merely ledges over the eye sockets, and the eyes, almond-shaped and slightly rounded, are raised above the sockets. The ears are placed directly beneath the feathers of the crown. This crown is very squat, as is also the case for figure 91:2 and 3, and thus different from the similar crown worn by the female deity on the Baluʿa stele.[5]

The *atef* crown is not commonly found on men in sculpture in Palestine and Syria.[6] It can be found on Iron Age ivories of Phoenician style on both men and human-headed sphinxes.[7] The crown is unique in its use in the Transjordan.[8] There is only scanty evidence for the identification of the person wearing the crown. The bare feet indicate that a mortal, rather than divine being, is depicted. Only later, in the Persian period, are figurines of seated men (wrapped in cloaks) found wearing similar *atef* crowns of an elongated shape like our figure 91:4 (but on these figurines the point of the crown extends beyond the top of the feathers[9]). Finally, the short, heavy representation of the figure itself must be mentioned. As in the statue discussed above, the sculptor did not trust the strength of the stone at the feet and ankles, and left a block of stone behind the heels for support. Another indication that the statue is unfinished may be seen by the fact that the hem was not carried around to the back of the statue.

The other heads show a variation on the same theme. As we mentioned, figure 91:2 and 3 have mustaches. The beards on figure 91:3 and 4 have the peculiarity, occasionally illustrated on figurines also (fig. 87:1 and 3), that the upper line of the beard is drawn up in a point, on the center of the chin, to touch the lip. As on figure 87:3, the mustache does not touch the beard, which seems to be confined to the angle of the jaw. The eyelids are indicated by incised lines in figure 91:2, where they are larger than on any of the other heads, and the eyebrows are indicated by incised arcs. Figure 91:3 would seem to be somewhat

---

[1]Hans G. Güterbock, "Carchemish," *JNES*, XIII (1954), 102-14.

[2]See footnote 2 on p. 153 above for a reference to the recent pulbication by Horn.

[3]Akurgal, *Die Kunst der Hethiter*, pls. 110-14.

[4]R.D. Barnett suggested, when he published the statue, that the reason it looks the way it does is that unlike the statue of Yereaḥ-ʿAzar, which was carved on soft limestone, this statue was carved out of hard basalt. The fact that much more detail is indicated on the other basalt heads shows that this should probably be expected here also if the statue had been finished. Barnett, *ADAJ*, I, 34.

[5]Ward and Martin, *Baluʿa*, p. 16. "The crown worn by the Baluʿa goddess is that normally worn by Osiris in Egyptian reliefs and paintings. However, it is quite significant to note that Canaanite goddesses are frequently found in Egyptian reliefs wearing this crown, so that the Baluʿa goddess fits into a well-known category of divine female figures."

[6]Rare early examples of seated, though unidentifiable, gods were found at Minet el Beidah and Ras Shamra in a Late Bronze Age context: Claude F.A. Schaeffer, "Les fouilles de Ras Shamra-Ugarit, septième campagne (printemp 1935)," *Syria*, XVII (1936), pl. XV:3 and "Résumé des resultats de la xxiiie campagne de fouilles à Ras Shamra-Ugarit (automne 1960)," *AAS*, XII-XIII (1961-1962), 191 and fig. 6.

[7]Mallowan, *Nimrud and Its Remains*, figs. 469, 470, 504, 525, and pl. IX.

[8]Siegfried Horn suggests that it was the crown of the Ammonite king; for his arguments see: Horn, *Andrews University Seminary Studies*, XI (1973), 170-80 and pls. XVII-XX.

[9]Ora Negbi, "A Deposit of Terracottas and Statuettes from Tell Sipor," *Atiqot*, VI (1967), 17 and pl. XI:67. Nahaman Avigad, "Excavations at Makmish, 1958," *IEJ*, X (1960), 93 and pls. 9:B, 10A. Maurice Chehab, "Les terres cuites de Kharayeb," *BMB*, X (1951-52), Text; XI (1953-54), Plates, pp. 17, 20, Kh. 39-45, pl. VII:2. The men represented on these figurines may well be identified with the god Osiris, but such an identification is unlikely for the Amman sculptures where another interpretation of the crown is necessary.

later in that the eyes and eyebrows are indicated by low, raised flat planes, as if to imitate inlays. The ears are treated differently on each head. In all cases, except figure 91:3, they are oversized and made to protrude as far as the feathers. Finally, like on the head figure 90:2, figure 91:2 has a narrow band of small curls indicated over the forehead. A head with similar *atef* crown is illustrated in the collection of the American University of Beirut Museum and is said to come from ancient Moab.[1] It is closest in modeling to figure 91:3, but the crown is higher and narrower at the top (not as exaggerated as fig. 91:4) and the eyes, though smaller and well proportioned, are executed like on figure 91:2. The proportions of the crown are similar to 91:2 and 3, though somewhat narrower and higher. The feathers on all three crowns are similar, with an incised line following the edge of the feathers.[2]

Group 3

In this group, we have one complete statue, one almost complete body portion of a second, and the upper torso of a third. Once again several Egyptian features are present but, on the whole, these pieces reflect strong influence from the north. The complete statue of this group is identified by its inscription as that of Yereah-ʿAzar, an official of the king Ammi-nadab.[3]

The positions of the hands and feet on figure 92:3 and 4 are identical and the same as on figure 91:1 above. The only difference here (also different from fig. 90:1) is the cylindrical piece grasped in the right hand. In this respect, the artist seems again to be following Egyptian conventions.[4] The undergarment on figure 92:3 is a short-sleeved, ankle length "tunic of crinkly material, probably the fine linen of Egypt, girt with a girdle, and wrapped round with a shawl."[5] The ends of the girdle and the tassel are decorated, as is the shawl (with three wavy lines running the length of the shawl and a fringe which is decorated along one long edge). The "tunic of crinkly material" is represented by narrow fluting on the statue over its lower part and on the arms. These same features, again, were present on figure 91:1 but without incised decoration. On both of these statues and on figure 92:2, the shawl is wound in the same manner. It is wrapped around the waist, behind the back and over the right shoulder. A tassel at the corner of the shawl lies against the upper part of the chest, at the right side.

The torso fragment figure 92:2 was enhanced with the addition of paint; red-orange is preserved on the undergarment (and possibly other

²Three additional heads have recently been illustrated by Horn and one of the two statues from Khirbet el Hajjar should be grouped here also, see footnote 2 on p. 153 above. Horn's head no. 5 from Amman should be classed with our figs. 91:2 and 3 as far as the details of the eyes, eyebrows, beard with point on chin, mustache, proportions of crown and outlining of the feathers on the crown. The fine modeling of the features is closer to 91:3 but the elongation of the face and the over-sized almond-shaped eyes are distinctive features. The Abu ʿAlanda head once had inlaid eyes, is without mustache and has a fairly long beard. The proportions of the crown and the flattened, plain feathers most resemble our 91:1. The British Museum head (Horn's no. 2) is the only other piece in basalt beside our 91:1. The features are badly worn but once had inlaid eyes and a medium sized beard, the proportions of the crown and outlining of its feathers resembles those on our 91:2 and 3, the head from the A.U.B. Museum and the Ammonite head numbered 5 by Horn. The Crowned figure from Khirbet el Hajjar bears strong resemblance to the Amman statue fig. 91:1. The crown is similar, with only minor variations. The costume is similar but badly abraided so details are difficult to ascertain. A curve is cut in the hem of the garment so that it touches the ground at the back but reveals the bare feet at the front. The hand positions are similar but the right arm is curiously elongated. Few details are shown at the rear of the statue. The second statue from Khirbet el Hajjar has been considered female by Moawiyah Ibrahim. This is certainly possible but far from certain. The statue is bare-headed and shorter than the crowned statue. The face is badly destroyed but does not seem to have been bearded. The position of the right arm is different from the other statues by being placed at the chest in the same fashion as the left arm, rather than being held at the side. None of the above mentioned features provide conclusive proof that the individual represented was female. Rather, beardless males are commonly depicted in Syrian and Assyrian reliefs. The ear rings on this statue are similar to those of the Amman female heads (see below) but are also found on fig. 90:1. The individual strands of hair are depicted much like on fig. 92:3 though the strands are decorated with vertical incised lines, rather than with hatching, and the strands end in curls. The curls are rendered in a fashion similar to that on our figurine fig. 88:1. It is difficult to differentiate the features of the costume from that represented in figs. 91:1 and 92:3. It is thus quite possible that a male of different rank or station is presented here rather than a female, but it is difficult to be certain in the matter.

³An important new reading of the Yereah-ʿAzar inscription has appeared in Fawzi Zayadine, "Note sur l'inscription de la statue d'Amman J. 1656," *Syria*, LI (1974), 129-36. Here Zayadine reads: [. . .] SW YRḤʿZR/ [BR Z] KR BR SNB, ". . . of Yarah-ʿAzar son of Zakir (?), son of Shanib." He argues that the statue represents the Ammonite king and the inscription identifies this individual and lists his father and grandfather as well.

⁴See the statues, pls. 236, 237, 240, 241, 304, and 394 cited in footnote 5, p. 154 above.

⁵Barnett, *ADAJ*, I, 35.

¹Baramki, *The Archaeological Museum of the American University of Beirut*, p. 39.

TABLE 7. DIMENSIONS OF DETAILS ON THE AMMAN DOUBLE-FACED, FEMALE HEADS

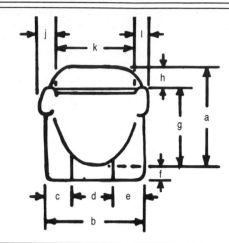

	Head A	Head A(rev)	Head B	Head B(rev)	Head C	Head C(rev)	Head D	Head D(rev)	Average Dimension	Variation
a	25.5	26	26.5	25.5	27.9	27.4	26	25.9	26.3	2.4
b	18.5	18	23	20.5	21.4	21.3	22*	22*	20.8	5
c	6	6	6	6	6.8	6.9	6	5.4*	6.1	1.5
d	7	7	8	8.5	7.7	7.7	7.8	7	7.8	1.5
e	5.5	5	6	6	6.9	6.7	6*	5.4	6	1.9
f	6	6	6	6	5	5.3	6	6.5	5.8	1.5
g	14	14.5	15	14.5	14.8	15.2	15	14.7	14.2	1.2
h	5.5	5.5	5.5	5	6.1	6.9	5	4.7	5.8	3.4
j	2.5	3	4	3.5	2.4	3.5	3.5	4*	3.3	1.5
k	14	14.5	15.5	15.5	16	15	15*	14*	14.4	2
l	2.5	3	3.5	3.3	2.7	2.8	3.5*	4	3.2	1
									Average Variation	2.1

All dimensions are given in centimeters.
*Indicates reconstructed dimension.

areas), and the scales indicated on the fringe are alternately red and black (or dark blue). The only other interesting feature on this torso is a wide armlet (apparently originally in open work), indicated on the right arm.

The statue, figure 92:3, holds a lotus flower in the left hand, while figure 92:4 holds something more difficult to interpret (but it may be a stalk which branches out into blossoms and buds at the top). The garment of figure 92:4 is completely different and a narrow shawl is indicated. Very delicate lines indicate the pattern of this garment, which is skin-tight, short-sleeved and ankle length, with a fringe at the bottom. The narrow shawl is composed of a band decorated with a series of squares and a fringe which is pendant from it.[1]

Only on figure 92:3 is the head preserved. "His jutting chin is covered with beard, and his eyes, which were once inlaid, must have looked very lively. His hair is carefully formed into long corkscrew curls, bound at the forehead with a cord, below which they fall on to his shoulders. Two small curls fall before his ears, in the Syrian manner."[2] The rows of the hair at the front are indicated like on figure 90:2, but there the corkscrew curls were not indicated, nor was the headband. The head is proportionately far too large for the body and the large, full head of hair is also disproportionately large for the face. The eyes are larger than normal, the nose is broken and a slight smile is represented on the somewhat puffy lips. Despite the busy incised details of the hair and beard, the face is rendered by subtle modeling which gives a realistic quality to the slightly sunken cheeks, high cheek bones and broad forehead. A strong, intense personality is portrayed through a balance of awkwardness and dignity which seems to reflect an attempt at a realistic representation of this individual.

The few Egyptianizing features that could be identified were mentioned above. It is interesting that most of these features, when they occur in North Syria, are considered determinants of an "Aramaic" style of art.[3] Shawls, of course, are common on sculptures in Syria, Babylonia, and Assyria, but their appearance in Syria is apparently one of the clothing features which becomes popular in the eighth and seventh centuries B.C., under Assyrian influence. The shawl on figure 92:2 seems to be of the type most frequently illustrated in the north. It seems to be narrower and swung in wider arcs, so that one would expect it covered most of the body.[4] The scale fringe on top is unusual; it is usually found at the bottom of such shawls. Figure 92:3, also, has a similar fringe at the top of the shawl. This shawl and the similar one on figure 91:1 are unusual in that they are confined to the upper portion of the body and only come slightly below the waist.[5] This

[1]A similar shawl is illustrated on the bronze figure of a courtier from Toprak-Kale (van Loon, *Urartian Art*, pl. XVI). Here the stance, hand positions, general proportions, and fine linear details are also similar to our fig. 92:4.

[2]Barnett, *ADAJ*, I, 34.

[3]Akurgal, *Die Kunst der Hethiter*, pp. 100-105. The pleated garment, the lock of hair in front of the ears, the headband holding back long curls, and the holding of lotus flowers, "offenbar das Zeichen königlicher Würde," (p. 101) are all good indicators.

[4]Akurgal, *Die Kunst der Hethiter*, pls. 106, 107, 109, 121, and 129.

[5]*Ibid*., pls. 125, and possibly 130 and 131, though 130 seems to be held with a fibula rather than merely being draped.

may well prove to be a local habit of dress. The presence of a wide shawl on this statue most probably indicates a person of higher rank than the individual represented on figure 92:4.[1] Barnett points out the "block-like, four-square conception of the human figure"[2] with its oversized head and feet, and notes that, in these respects, it resembles some North Syrian sculptures. Finally, the hair style with long corkscrew curls is again considered by Akurgal as a characteristic feature of his "Assyrisierende Stil, Zweite Phase"[3] (745-700 B.C.), which agrees with Barnett's assessment on the date of this statue. Such curls, without the spiral terminations usually found in North Syria,[4] continue to be used on the latest "Aramaic style" sculptures at Karatepe, dated around 700 B.C. The garment on figure 92:4 can have a similar eighth century B.C. date range, but can also be found in contexts a century earlier or later. Similar garments and belts can be found on Assyrian palace reliefs[5] and in North Syria.[6]

Female Heads

These four heads were found near the middle of the south edge of the second plateau on the Amman Citadel and were reused as building material for a Hellenistic drain in Area VIII.[7] The heads were carved on yellowish-white limestone. They are preserved to the bases of their necks, and faces were carved on both sides. At the top of each head, was a cylindrical hole averaging around 4.0 cm. in diameter (see the group photograph with mirror on top of fig. 93) which must have been intended for fastening the head to something. The faces had inlaid eyes, and probably eyebrows, and the necklace was also decorated with inlays.[8] The eye inlays were in three pieces. The lids and pupils were black and in one piece. The eyes were formed by two white inlays on either side of the pupil. The faces must have been intended to be identical but despite this are very individualistic. Some differences in style and manner of carving can be detected though, on the whole, the basic details are carried out in a similar manner.

All four heads show the following details on both sides. The fairly long necks are adorned with choker necklaces, consisting of two lines at top and bottom framing three circular inlays. The inlays were probably in two pieces, a black one which probably had a smaller white inlay in a central hole (this piece, however, was not found). Three or four straight strands of hair extended below the ears, framing the necks. The oversized ears, which varied considerably in size from head to head, are either question mark (B and D) or number 9 (A and C) shaped. An earring, consisting of a crescent and three pendants, was worn on each ear. The hair is shown on top as parallel

strands crossing from one side of the head to the other, on heads B, C, and D, but radiating from the center hole on head A. Bands hold the locks of hair in place and are separated from the foreheads by narrow rows of pellets which seem to represent small curls. The almond-shaped inlays for the eyes have been discussed above. The nose has been destroyed in each case. The lips are quite delicately shaped and drawn up at the sides to form slight smiles. High cheek bones are suggested with delicate modeling and the chins are slightly pointed.

Despite this repetition of features, it must be noted that the artist either did not try, or was not able, to produce very exact duplicates. For the most part, the faces are the most uniform pieces. On heads B and D, the tops, in front view, are fairly level with rounding close to the sides. Head A is somewhat more rounded but uneven, while head C shows a smooth arc without noticeable flattening. The hair at the side comes down straight on B, but slants out slightly on the other heads. The greatest difference is found in the depiction of the ears, which, as we noted above, was also a major problem on the figurines. In all cases, they are positioned higher on the head than is normal or natural. Quite possibly this is a carry-over from the positioning of ears on the Hathor heads. On heads A and D, the ears were rotated completely into the frontal plane and were most pronounced. Head C is closest to normal and head B is in between. Head C has a strikingly different appearance from the other three,

---

[1]Maurits van Loon, "Dress—Ancient Mesopotamia," *Encyclopaedia Britannica* (Chicago: Encyclopaedia Britannica, Inc., 1969), VII, 678-79.

[2]Barnett, *ADAJ*, I, 35.

[3]Akurgal, *Die Kunst der Hethiter*, p. 97.

[4]*Ibid.*, pls. 129 and 134.

[5]Barnett, *Assyrian Palace Reliefs*, pls. 90, 91, 94, 97, 107 (for long, fringed garments) and 53, 59, 130 (for shoulder-strap and belt).

[6]Akurgal, *Die Kunst der Hethiter*, pls. 118, 126, and 127.

[7]The Department of Antiquities had excavated a square up against the city wall in this area and, as they were beginning to encounter Iron Age levels, suspended work. While guiding a group of students in this area, I accidentally discovered a piece of head D as a building stone of the drain. Further examination and excavation of the drain by Safwan Tell and Mohammed Odeh of the Department of Antiquities, produced the remaining heads. The heads have been published in a brief note, accompanied by photographs for A-C, in Tell, *ADAJ*, XII-XIII, pls. ٤-١.

[8]The inlays were marked, but all of them were not removed for examination so no pattern to their placement was clear. Two of the letters seemed to be mirror images of other signs. The signs represented are: 𐤆, 𐤉, 𐤀, 𐤌, 𐤔, 𐤉, 𐤏, 𐤑 and 𐤑. *Ibid.*, p. ١١.

and the ears are the major reason for this. Unlike the ears on the other heads, the ears on C do not protrude from the side, but are kept within the outline of the hair. In the side view, one, two, and three strands of hair separate the ears of front and back on A, B, and C respectively. On the one side of D on which the ears are preserved, the ears from the opposite faces are connected in one unit without division by hair strands, and the hair is depicted in narrower strands than usual beneath them. The lines and curves of the hair on head C seem much more graceful and better executed than on the other heads, but this is somewhat deceptive because the obtrusive ears do not break up the composition. The ears are smallest on head C, but are placed in the same position just beneath the headband. This gives the effect of raising the ears.

Table 7 indicates measurements of general and specific features on these heads and clearly illustrates the degree of variation. The average difference in the size of particular features is just over 2 cm. We must mention in this respect that all the heads, except C, are very close to 26 cm. in height, and head C is about 2 cm. larger. There is greater variation in the head widths. Also, the sizes of features on opposite sides of a head can vary as much as they can from head to head.

It is difficult to find good parallels for these heads in stone sculptures, ivories, or any other artistic medium on other sites. Individual details can be found, but they appear only rarely. The stylistic peculiarities of these heads can be paralleled better on figurines or other sculptures from Amman than they can be from any other site. This provides one of a number of arguments indicating that these pieces, and the others discussed above, represent a local school of art. It is difficult to find good parallels in the ivory carvings which show faces carved in a full frontal view. We have discussed such pieces above in connection with figurines and molds from Amman tomb F, and on page 161 below. The choker necklace is shown on mold figure 88:3, but the beads are not indicated. Such a choker necklace is rare on the Syro-Palestinian ivories. In most of the "women in the window" heads, the necks are too short for a necklace to be shown, though on occasion they are shown on the necks of women portrayed in the ivories from Nimrud and elsewhere.[1] Necklaces are often shown on other female figurines, but they are usually more elaborate, or hang lower on the neck or below it.[2] The hair style at the side of the head resembles that on figurine 88:2, where the parting of the hair strands also resembles head A. The earrings are like those depicted on the mold of figure 88:3 (see parallels cited above), and the row of pellets above the forehead is found on the figurine head published in Ma'ayeh, *ADAJ*, IV-V, 114 and plate III:2. This feature is rare

elsewhere, but parallels can be found.[3] The headband is also indicated on the figurines 87:4 and 5. The practice of holding strands of hair in place is also found on the statue of Yereah-'Azar (though there the locks are hatched). The indication of strands of hair across the top of the head is also shown on figure 90:2. Similar headbands can be found on ivories, but with various hair styles.[4] The hair style with the headband is best illustrated on Phoenician champleve ivory plaques, like the one illustrated in figure 478 of Mallowan's *Nimrud and Its Remains*.

The proportions of face and ears on the Syro-Palestinian ivories are like head C, where the ears stay within the outline formed by the hair. The only good parallels for similar difficulties in handling the ears are commonly found on North Syrian sculptures, best exemplified at Carchemish[5] and Tell Halaf.[6] Heads A, B, and D also have the same rough or awkward character that characterizes much of the North Syrian sculpture in the ninth and eighth centuries B.C. Head C, on the other hand, seems to draw its inspiration more from Phoenicia. This point is made most emphatically by the great similarity that exists between head C and terra-cotta female *protomae* found at the Phoenician colonies of Carthage and Moyta.[7] The *protomae* show much stronger Egyptian influence, but the modeling of the face is very close. The hair at the sides, the headband, and the row of small curls illustrated schematically over the forehead, provide striking resemblances to head C.

Function of the Heads

Two unusual features of these heads suggest their use; namely, the fact that they are double-faced and that they have circular dowel holes at their tops. A number of sculptured, carved, or modeled objects can be cited which illustrate

---

[1]C. Decamps de Merzenfeld, *Inventaire commenté des ivoires phéniciens et apparentés découverts dans le Proche-Orient* (Paris: E. de Boccard, 1954), pl. CIX, no. 984; Barnett, *The Nimrud Ivories*, pl. LXX:S185.

[2]*Ibid.*, pls. LVII:S226; LVIII:S96; LXIII:S146; LXX:S172, 173, 183; LXXI:S176, 182, etc.

[3]*Ibid.*, pls. XVIII:S1; XIX:S13; XXI:S18; LXXIII:S204 a and b.

[4]*Ibid.*, pls. XVIII:S1; XXVI:S20; XXVII:S12; etc. On Assyrian style ivories, see pls. X:F1; XI:F3; XII:F2; CXV:I1; CXIX:V8.

[5]Akurgal, *Die Kunst der Hethiter*, pl. 109.

[6]Moortgat, *Tell Halaf*, III, pls. 110, 130, 133, 146.

[7]Moscati, *The World of the Phoenicians*, pls. 60 and 62.

multiple heads or bodies back to back. A stand from Salamis, with two naked women attached, was discussed above.[1] A large number of ivory pieces (probably for attachment to furniture) found at Nimrud (and fragments available from other sites) represent naked women or clothed men standing back to back.[2] Occasionally only the heads are preserved, and on these pieces the whole body may not have been depicted. One can group all of these as caryatid figures, since they form a unit, stand on some type of base or floral element, and have a capital placed over the head (either directly on the head or on a hat, normally a *polos*).[3] The imitation of architectural elements is clear, but there is little evidence that such features were ever employed in the decoration of buildings. A second group of well documented, architecturally used sculptural heads illustrate an Egyptian practice of long duration. The head of the goddess Hathor is frequently used to ornament capitals in her temples. One, two, or four faces may be displayed on a capital. The multiple-headed capitals are not used on façades, but as supports for total or partial roofs, inside rooms or courtyards. The closest examples (geographically) to our area were found at the temple at Sherabit el Khedaim in Sinai,[4] and fragments of similar capitals have been found at the temple excavated by Rothenberg at Timna.[5] On the pillar capitals, Hathor is normally depicted with cow's ears, and often with hair shown in strands as on the heads being discussed (this is normal when the "Hathor curls" are not used).

The above parallels suggest quite clearly that the Amman heads also had an architectural purpose. The fact that they are finished off to a flat surface at the bottom, with the hair and neck terminating in the same plane, indicates that, like the Hathor capitals, most probably only the heads were depicted here and not busts or complete bodies. On the other hand, we are reminded of the shrines, discussed above, on which naked women were shown against the door jambs. We commented above that these female figures were not shown as if they were intended for structural purposes or as parts of columns supporting a façade. Consequently, we cannot use these shrines as an argument for a reconstruction that would make these heads part of a temple façade. The fact that the heads have two faces also argues against this possibility since, as we have seen, there is no evidence in Palestine for the use of free-standing, as opposed to attached, decorative elements on a façade during the Iron II period. The application of double-faced heads on a façade also does not seem reasonable, since such a location could hardly allow easy viewing of the rear face. The best alternative for the use of these heads, then, seems to be a use similar to that of the Egyptian Hathor head capitals.[6]

Date of the Female Heads

The similarities we noted to the other Amman sculpture and figurines, and to the Syro-Palestinian ivories, indicate that these heads must be dated in the Iron II period. One can only surmise that the four heads came from the same building and suppose that, since they were collected (probably not very far from the spot where they were originally used) for use in the same portion of an underground channel, their original use involved the whole group. Even if these assumptions are accepted, there is no reason to assume that the heads were all made at the same time.[7] It is also possible that more heads, yet to be found, existed in the building. It has been noted that there are many features which group heads A, B and D together, while head C is somewhat different. The slightly larger size of C indicates that it could have been used in a different room, though the slight 2 cm. variation should have made little difference.

The main question is whether the heads should be considered as contemporary and the differences due to different stylistic features, or whether the differences represent changes which have chronological significance. Heads A, B, and D are somewhat rougher and more archaic looking than C and resemble, in some details, the figurine heads attributed to Group II and figurine mold 88:2.

---

[1]Karageorghis, *Excavations in the Necropolis of Salamis*, p. 57, pls. LXXXIX and CXXXVII.

[2]Barnett, *The Nimrud Ivories*, pls. LXXII:S206; LXXIV:S207; LXXVI:S221; LXXXVIII:S293; LXXXIX:S294; and XCI.

[3]*Ibid.*, pls. LXXVII-LXXIX and XCII.

[4]Petrie, *Researches in Sinai*, figs. 95, 100, 103, and 104.

[5]Rothenberg, *ILN*, Nov. 29, 1969, pp. 28-29 and *Timna*, pl. 78.

[6]The reconstruction of a series of heads in metopes is possible, so that one would see the architectural equivalent of the "woman-in-the-window" motif so common on Syro-Palestinian ivories. Since no depictions of such a motif on an architectural façade exist, one could postulate their placement at the sides of the building. In this case, the chance of an illustration being preserved in a work of art is not great. Unfortunately, there is also no architectural evidence for such a reconstruction, so it is still best to rely on the Hathor head parallels.

[7]If the building to which they belonged had several phases of rebuilding, one could easily assume that in any particular phase some older capitals could be reused, but placed with newer ones.

Though head C diverges in the direction of later facial depictions, the other heads need not actually be much earlier. They could well be contemporary but preserving older stylistic features. Head C can be dated closer than the other heads, primarily by the *protomae* that we cited from Motya and Carthage. The punic *protomae* are dated to the sixth century B.C. Such a date would be in keeping with the figurine and mold, fig. 88:1 and 3, from tomb F, which exhibit similar features and, together with the Meqabelein tomb, should be dated early in the sixth century B.C. Whether the other three heads can be dated this late is difficult to say, though certainly there is no evidence to date them later. If one disregards the ears, the appearance of these heads comes much closer to C than one would expect and suggests that their dates should be kept fairly close together. The presence of peculiarities common to North Syria alongside Egyptian or Phoenician elements was also evident in the other pieces of sculpture and did not seem to indicate different chronological phases. There is no reason to see any chronological differences here either, except that one would expect all the heads to have been as similar as possible, if they were intended to be displayed together. Consequently, we are inclined to date head C early in the sixth century B.C. and the other three heads to the seventh century B.C.

Concluding Statement Regarding the Amman Sculpture

The discussion above has centered on particular features which would help in dating the pieces under consideration. A date range of ninth to sixth centuries B.C. seems appropriate for most of the sculptures and in some cases we were able to be more precise. A cosmopolitan flavor is evident, if the pieces are considered as a whole, but they all bear the definite stamp of local workmanship. The greatest similarities to these sculptures were from inland Syria and it is curious that, both for the figurines and the sculpture from Amman, the best parallels for specific details come from a limited number of ivories found at Nimrud. This, coupled with the fact that it was possible to isolate Egyptianizing features coming more directly from Egypt than by way of the Phoenician coast, indicates that eventually the art of this area should be distinguishable both from that of northern Syria and the Phoenician coast.

In light of the additional pieces of sculpture which have been published recently, it seems worthwhile to point out a number of features which may provide more precise dating criteria. Comparisons with Syrian sculpture is greatly facilitated by the recent publication of Orthmann's book on late-Hittite Art.[1] Variations can be noted in the details of the crowns and their proportions, the proportions of the figures themselves, the use or non use of inlaid eyes and the rendering of beards and moustache. If a development can be traced, it would seem that the block-like, squat, awkward rendering of fig. 91:1 would be at the beginning, followed by the Khirbet el Hajjar pieces. Figures 90:1 and 92:1 (belonging to groups 1 and 3 respectively) are more normally proportioned (except for the head of the latter) and proportionately thinner, though still stiff and formal. The use of inlaid eyes seems to be a later feature. Figure 91:3 is transitional in this respect, using relief to render the eyes but giving them the same appearance as the inlaid heads. The rendering of the eyes on the figurines noted above represents a similar and possibly related change. The proportions and incised detail of the crowns common to the second group also seem to show a development. The broad, squat crowns (on fig. 91:1 and the Khirbet el Hajjar figure) seem to be early and the narrower, elongated crowns (on fig. 91:4 and the British Museum head) seem to be late. Incised lines outlining the feathers seem to occur primarily on the figures of intermediate date.

The Amman sculptures do not get as massive or awkward in proportions or as rough and crude as many examples of North Syrian sculpture, though tendencies in that direction can be noted (figs. 92:3 and 91:1). On the other hand, there are no sculptures here which show the polished late eighth to sixth century Assyrianizing style that becomes popular in North Syria, but again tendencies in that direction can be noted also (figs. 90:3 and 92:2-4).

The manner in which influences from the surrounding areas are combined on the Amman sculptures is often unique but it is not carried through consistently and integrated into a definite style, as was done in Phoenicia. It is impossible at present to indicate the extent of the area over which such art objects were produced. One would doubt that the Transjordan, as we are considering it here, would have formed a definable cultural unit in itself rather than one which was included with the inland area of southern Syria, but not enough evidence is available to make such speculation worthwhile.

[1] Winfried Orthmann, *Untersuchungen zur späthethitischen Kunst* ("Saarbrückner Beiträge zur Altertumskunde," Band 8; Bonn: Rudolf Habelt Verlag, 1971). Also, for an expanded discussion of Iron Age sculpture of Syria-Palestine see the University of Saarbrucken dissertation of Ali Abu Assaf of Damascus.

The information that might help to determine the function of these pieces has been discussed. It seemed most plausible to assume an architectural purpose for the four female heads and that they were used as capitals, in the fashion of the Egyptian Hathor capitals. The fragments of male sculptures probably belonged, like the complete examples, to statues. Some of these were fashioned as a single piece and others were made in two parts, with separate heads fitted into sockets on the body portion. The attitude of most of the figures, the fact that the feet, where preserved, are bare, and the portion of an inscription on one statue, indicate that they were used as votive offerings in temples or shrines. Thus, unlike much of the North Syrian sculpture, the Amman pieces would seem to have had greater religious significance and were employed more directly with religious structures or areas.[1]

It is surprising that despite the small amount of excavation that has been carried out in the Transjordan in comparison with Palestine, considerably more sculpture has been found. If we are correct in assuming a religious function for the Amman pieces, then it is difficult not to associate this difference, between Palestine and Transjordan, with the Biblical injunction against the portrayal of the human form.[2]

[1]Their function would seem to be within a long tradition that stretches back into the third millennium B.C. and has its best parallels in the Sumerian sculptures of Mesopotamia.

[2]Ex. 21:5, Lev. 26:1, Deut. 4:16-19.

CHAPTER XI

CONCLUSIONS

In the preceding chapters, the archaeological evidence for the Bronze and Iron Ages has been surveyed comprehensively within the limits imposed by the state of publication of the various sites concerned. In the introductory sections we pointed out the limitations imposed by the often scanty or geographically scattered nature of the information and the effect this consequently must have in the statement of any conclusions. The discussions of general questions, implications, and interpretations have been limited to those issues which helped clarify the analysis of the evidence and the understanding of specific artifacts. As noted in the introductory sections, the discussion of history (to the limited extent that historical facts are available) has been used chiefly to provide a framework within which the archaeological evidence can be understood.

The Bronze Age

The evidence at hand is not yet sufficient to allow a delineation of all the characteristics and peculiarities of the Bronze and Iron Age cultures of the Transjordan. It is possible that the character of the two ages was strikingly different and that there was minimal continuity from one to the next. It is not yet possible to prove or disprove such a possibility. The remarks on the Bronze Age had to be limited because the evidence is limited. All phases of the Early Bronze Age are present in the Transjordan, but too little material is available to proceed very far in judging the relative density of populations in specific periods or in specific areas. The population seems to have clustered in urban centers, but it remains to be seen, after more excavation has been undertaken, whether or not it will be possible to distinguish between urban and non-urban populations, a possibility suggested by Paul W. Lapp.[1]

The presence and importance of non-urban populations are critical problems for consideration of the Middle and Late Bronze Ages. The views of Nelson Glueck, William F. Albright, and others, were considered above, namely that there was a considerable decline of population in the Transjordan between 2000 and 1300 B.C., primarily in the area south of the Amman district, and a less lengthy decline between 1800 and 1300 B.C. in most of the remaining areas of the Transjordan. Glueck indicated that some settlement did continue in a few major centers but considered that the Transjordan was inhabited primarily by non-urban populations during those periods in which the population density was very low. The review of the evidence that has come to light since Nelson Glueck's survey has led to the favoring of the view, currently expressed by W. A. Ward and M. F. Martin, that a settled, urban civilization continued to exist and play a role in the Transjordan through the Middle and Late Bronze Ages, even though the number of sites may have decreased after the Early Bronze Age in most portions of the Transjordan.

The ceramic evidence and scarabs scattered over the entire area of the Transjordan and the evidence for fortified cities make it increasingly difficult to deny the presence of settled, urban populations during the Middle Bronze II and Late Bronze I periods. As discussed above, there are rich Transjordanian deposits which contained imported Mycenaean and Cypriote vessels of types common in Palestine. The imported vessels occur here in equally high concentrations as in contemporary deposits from major sites in Palestine. Though the material which documents LB II (as presently known) is not as widely distributed as that for the Middle Bronze II period, it clearly documents the continuity in urban settlement.

The Biblical account of the invasion of Israelite tribes into portions of the Transjordan indicates that a settled urban population existed in the area at the time. If the theory of Nelson Glueck, *et al.*, were to be followed, it would be necessary to see a sudden upsurge of urban settlements during the thirteenth century to accommodate the Biblical record (if this is indeed the time at which an invasion took place). No evidence is found for such an upsurge in the number of settlements. The clear Late Bronze assemblage which is present (rather than the transitional but primarily Iron I assemblage originating in the thirteenth century which Glueck's hypothesis would lead one to expect) may well be considered to have belonged to the populations which the Israelite tribes encountered. The changes from L.B. to Iron I will be discussed below and the character of the twelfth century assemblage will be reviewed. The observations on the nature of the Egyptian influence during the XIXth and XXth Dynasties in relation to the Deir 'Allā, Beth Shan, and Timna finds will be reiterated below, but we must acknowledge its existence in the Late Bronze Age

---

[1]Paul W. Lapp, *The Dhahr Mirzbâneh Tombs*, pp. 96-97 and 114-16.

also. A different setting for the incursion of the Israelites is posited here, in order to consider that it occurred during the end of the Late Bronze Age while most of Palestine was firmly under Egyptian control and the Transjordan was exposed to Egyptian influence. The extent to which the Israelite invasion led to the decline of the Late Bronze civilization or was responsible for its replacement by the Iron I civilization cannot be stated until more detailed documentation is available from sites which were occupied during this time.

Iron Age

In the discussion of the archaeological material, we have seen that the published artifacts do not document the entire Iron Age uniformly. The discussion of the pottery demonstrated that the evidence is concentrated in specific date ranges. In order to gain as much information as possible from the ceramic evidence, the discussion was based on typological considerations. In this way, the pattern into which the evidence was grouped could be observed. In the case of the whole vessels, the material clustered into what was called Sequence I and Sequence II. These sequences were not identified with the Iron I and II designations because that could mislead the reader into assuming that the periods were represented uniformly. The information clustered in Iron I and the end of Iron II. The pottery of the tenth century, the end of Iron I, is considerably different from that which preceded it in Iron I; it shows more of a continuity with the pottery of the first centuries of Iron II. The clustering of vessels and sherds in the seventh and sixth centuries B.C. formed another clear unit. Whether or not a gradual evolution of forms preceded the establishment of this assemblage is uncertain because of a scarcity of material.

The ceramic evidence and other objects indicate that in the following discussion it is most convenient to consider the Iron Age in three divisions: (1) twelfth and eleventh centuries, (2) tenth to eighth centuries, and (3) seventh and sixth centuries.[1] The artifactual evidence will be discussed first and then it will be related to the historical framework. Following this discussion, some of the general problems which the historical and archaeological materials raise will be considered briefly.

Twelfth and Eleventh Centuries B.C.

We will begin our remarks with the metal which serves as the hallmark of the period under discussion. Unfortunately, no firm conclusions can be drawn on the manner in which iron was made or used on the basis of the few published pieces. All that can safely be said is that, though the use of iron was rare, it did not seem to have been developed specifically for the manufacture of new luxury items. It was, however, used as a substitute metal for the manufacture of items normally produced in bronze in the same size and shape.

In the discussion of the ceramic materials, it was shown that distinct Late Bronze and Iron I pottery assemblages existed in the Transjordan as they did west of the Jordan. For the Bronze Age, the presence of such an assemblage can only be indicated and nothing can be said concerning its geographical distribution. A number of L.B. pottery forms continue into Iron I and, as is to be expected, the closest relationship is found in the earliest Iron I material: the Jebel Nuzha tomb and Deir 'Allā levels A-D. The transition from L.B. is not yet clear in all details. The full publication of the evidence from Deir 'Allā, Tell es Sa'idiyeh, Pella, and Timna should solve many of the outstanding problems. On the basis of the information presently available from these sites, together with the published material from Megiddo and Beth Shan, it seems that it may soon be possible to identify clearly a distinct assemblage confined to the twelfth century B.C. The Deir 'Allā evidence raises the question of placing the transition from L.B. to Iron I precisely at 1200 B.C. It has been noted above that Franken considers that his L.B. occupation lasted down to about 1170 B.C. at Deir 'Allā. This is indicated most clearly by the appearance of an inscription mentioning Queen Taousert of the XIXth Dynasty in the final L.B. destruction. In the final decades of this settlement, vain attempts had been made to rebuild the temple area which had been violently destroyed (probably by an earthquake). The ceramic evidence of this final phase seems to show a significant difference from what preceded it. If full publication substantiates

---

[1]We do not intend here to create a Transjordanian Iron I, II, and III or Early, Middle, and Late Iron. First, it would be premature to make such a division and second, it would be contrary to our desire to avoid a proliferation of period divisions as defined by individual scholars. As we discussed in our introduction above, we would rather see the stress fall on peculiarities of each century for the purposes of dating and identifying artifacts, and leave the divisions to be named and defined by characteristic historical situations: (1) period of an incipient Iron Age assemblage, (2) period of local individualism, and (3) period of Mesopotamian control within provincial organization, or some similar divisions.

this, Deir 'Allā will be a key site for understanding this period.

Irrespective of these problems, the characteristics of the twelfth century B.C. Iron I assemblage are clearly present by about 1150 B.C. (future work will have to indicate how close to 1200 B.C. they can be dated and we expect their appearance will probably be quite close to the date). The major characteristics which distinguish Iron Age I from Late Bronze are: the use of iron, the absence of imported Cypriote pottery, the absence of imported Mycenaean pottery, the presence in the twelfth century B.C. of a distinctive style of painted pottery, and the incorporation of Egyptian art elements into local artistic production (illustrated in the manufacture by local artists of an Egyptianizing stele at Balu'a, and Hathor capitals and masks at Timna). The most characteristic shapes in L.B. which continued in use were painted flasks, dipper juglets, kraters, lamps with rounded, up-curved sides, a modification of the L.B. carinated bowl (which became the characteristic Iron I "wavy profile rim" bowl) and local imitations of L.B. Mycenaean pyxides and stirrup vases. The most significant innovation is the use of simple vessel forms, like simple round-sided bowls with simple rims. These simple bowls and other forms are made in the poorest and crudest technique that can be found for better than a thousand years earlier and later. The amount of decorated pottery seems to diminish to the point of relative infrequency by the end of the twelfth century B.C. but a repertoire of designs seems to be perpetuated through Iron I and II.

One of the most significant changes is the sudden absence of imported Mycenaean and Cypriote pottery vessels. Unfortunately, there is no evidence from the Transjordan which helps us understand this occurrence, so it must be seen in the context of historical events that are taking place in Palestine. A final answer is not yet possible, but several different views of the situation which have been proposed by different scholars were outlined. The greatest portion of our discussions concentrated on those aspects of the problem which affected the interpretation of the archaeological material. These discussions need not be repeated, but the various arguments must be brought together.

In the discussion of the Balu'a stele above, pages 153-54, the argument of Ward and Martin was cited to the effect that such a monument could only have been erected when Egyptian control of Palestine was firm and the cities of the Transjordan were well aware of this domination. The presence of the stele shows that Egypt must have exerted at least some cultural and artistic influence on the Transjordan,[1] and this agrees with the continuing presence of Egyptian influence in the later sculpture from the Transjordan. In these later sculptures, it is not clear where the inspiration for the Egyptian features originated, since it does not seem to come by way of Phoenicia. Either it must be accounted for by more direct contacts or by the continuation of an older tradition that was well acquainted with Egyptian artistic production. Unfortunately, no further information is available with which to follow up any such speculation.

The other artifactual evidence suggests that Egyptian influence in the Transjordan was minimal and was concentrated primarily in the Jordan Valley. These objects are closely associated with a body of material from the other side of the valley and from the Wadi Arabah, and their interpretation should be similar also. These problems have been discussed above on pages 145-49, in the discussion of anthropoid coffin lids and the two Tell es Sa'idiyeh burials in which mummification was attempted by wrapping the bodies in linen and covering them with bitumen. The whole question of Egyptian domination is connected with the question of Philistine penetration into this area, and this must also be seen in the light of the discussion on pages 81-83 above, concerning the painted pottery in the Transjordan.

If these arguments are consolidated, it is possible to reconstruct the following. The international commerce, which apparently was still at a high point in the thirteenth century B.C., as evidenced in the Transjordan by tomb material from Pella and Irbed and by the deposits at the "temple" at the Amman Airport, came to a very abrupt end. As noted above, there were only a few survivals in the way of Mycenaean vessel types, which most probably were produced locally. Up to this point, the imported pottery seemed to have had a limited effect on the local pottery shapes and decoration. In the twelfth century, when imported vessels are virtually absent in both Palestine and Transjordan, Aegean motifs become common in the local painted pottery traditions of Palestine and Syria. Discussed above (pages 78-80) were several alternative possibilities which could explain this. Pottery decorated with the typical decoration of red and black paint on a white-slipped background did not become popular immediately when the Philistines settled in Palestine, but was associated primarily with the period of their dominance under a confederation of city-states. Consequently, it is quite possible that many Aegean motifs on Palestinian Iron I pottery (particularly the earliest examples) were not Philistine-inspired, but that the inspiration

_____

[1]See footnotes on pp. 61-63 above for recent additions on this subject.

came from some other source (or sources).

During the period of Egyptian dominance in Palestine, in the first half of the twelfth century, the cultural influence of the Philistines, even on ceramic styles, may have been extremely small (whether or not they served as mercenaries in the Egyptian army).[1] This can be verified at many sites in Palestine, most notably at Tell Beit Mirsim where the pre-Philistine Phase B_1 contrasts with the Philistine domination period, B_2. There were some noticeable additions in the repertoire of painted designs and a greater precision in the painting (probably as a result of Greek influence), but seemingly these represented outside influences incorporated into a local tradition. An interesting fact, also, is that the decoration was consistently carried out in monochrome and in a range of colors quite different from those found on Philistine pottery. Illustrated in chart form was the overlap of designs found on Philistine and non-Philistine pottery of the Iron Age, and a continuity was seen in the designs present in Syria in Iron I and II. The painted tradition that was noted at Megiddo in Strata VIIA-VI, Beth Shan VI, Deir 'Allā, and Timna (together with the Transjordanian sites, which have consistently been considered contemporary with the Timna occupation and which cannot be shown to be Iron II) seemed to be within the painted tradition as defined in Syria, and true Philistine pottery was exceptionally rare at these sites.[2] The situation in Syria seems to clarify the picture of what is happening in the Transjordan and the Jordan rift (as well as that indicated at Megiddo). The most complete evidence from Syria is from the Amuq, where, as we pointed out above on pages 79-80, a strong native painted tradition existed already in the twelfth century, prior to the arrival of strong Greek influence.

At Timna and Deir 'Allā, the painted pottery was found side by side with the simple, usually undecorated, roughly made pottery that is best exemplified by the material found in the Madeba tombs and at Tell Beit Mirsim in Stratum B_1. The sequence is longer at Deir 'Allā and here the painted pottery virtually ceases early in the eleventh century B.C. On almost all Transjordanian sites, there is a gap in the evidence for painted pottery in the eleventh century B.C. The continuity of designs on the painted pottery, between the twelfth, tenth, and seventh centuries, indicates that this tradition must have been fairly constant and maintained somewhere without drastic change for a considerable length of time, despite the scantiness of the evidence.

The poorly made, undecorated, common pottery represents a clear break with L.B. traditions and indicates considerable isolation and parochialism in Palestine and Transjordan. On the other hand, the painted pottery seems to illustrate a continued, though diminished and probably otherwise considerably changed, contact between the Transjordan and Syria. In Palestine, the situation seems somewhat different. The situation in the Esdraelon, as exemplified by Megiddo, is similar to that in the Jordan rift but in the hill country the parochial, isolated nature of cultural remains occurs earlier. It forms a sharp contrast to the former L.B. assemblage and is without noticeable transition to, or particular derivation from, the culture of the surrounding valleys. When outside influence becomes noticeable in the hill country, it is the result of expanding Philistine influence.

In the Jordan rift, the situation in the twelfth century is much more complex and seems to be bound up with the mining and working of metals in the area. The Timna mines, long thought to have been worked in the tenth and ninth centuries (on the assumption that they were originally used under the instigation of King Solomon), have proved, instead, to have been worked principally in the closing centuries of the Egyptian Empire, between the reigns of the Egyptian Pharaohs Seti I (1309-1291) and Ramses V (1145-1141). The portions of furnaces and slag which were found in phases A-D at Deir 'Allā show that the refining and smelting of copper was not confined to the south, though this activity is here attributed to itinerant smiths (see p. 39). The richness of the finds of copper or bronze objects at Tell es Sa'idiyeh and Tell Mazar indicates clearly that the copper or bronze production was not solely geared for foreign consumption, but that a significant number of the vessels and utensils which were produced became a part of the local assem-

---

[1]The recent evidence mentioned above indicates an elaborate "Midianite" painted pottery tradition at Timna, closely related to that farther east as represented at Qurayyah. If the evidence from the Timna temple is supported by evidence from other sites, then we will have come some way in clarifying our problems. The Timna evidence now suggests that the painted pottery belongs to the beginning of the twelfth century, exists under Egyptian domination, and is clearly to be differentiated from the later Philistine pottery.

[2]In Palestine, non-Philistine Iron Age painted pottery is not plentiful and is most common only at the end of Iron I. It seems to be more plentiful in the Transjordan and the Jordan Valley.

blage.[1] It is difficult to separate this metal-working activity from Egyptian inspiration, and this must be seen in the context of the heavy concentration of Egyptian objects and customs in the area, including objects inscribed with Egyptian hieroglyphics, Egyptian scarabs and amulets, Egyptian-influenced art styles, Egyptian-influenced burial practices (mummification and the use of anthropoid coffins), Egyptian pottery, and other lesser items. How much additional influence was exerted by Egyptian mercenaries (specifically the Philistines) or how much of the Egyptian influence was mediated by these people is difficult to say. Again, we will not repeat the arguments advanced above, but it should be stated that certain characteristics were undeniably due to Philistine influence, while many features could equally well or even more plausibly be attributed to Egyptian or local practice.[2]

Much of the preceding discussion has centered on the Jordan rift. It is essential to understand the situation on the west bank of the Jordan in order to understand and interpret the material available from the east bank. Glueck interpreted the evidence from his survey as documentation of a flourishing period of early Iron Age settlement in all portions of the Transjordan and dated it between the thirteenth and the eighth centuries B.C.[3] We have just summarized the information which indicates that the Late Bronze and Iron Age assemblages must now be considered quite distinct. The twelfth century B.C. material cannot be accepted as essentially transitional in nature but is already clearly Iron I. There does seem to be a heavy concentration of Iron I settlements, but it is not possible to say how many were contemporary in any particular decade and it is not known if the majority had their beginning in the twelfth century as opposed to the tenth. Is the

such vessels were not commonly available, it would be difficult to accept such a possibility; but if such vessels can be shown to be quite common, then such an interpretation becomes extremely plausible.

[2]The new evidence noted above in footnotes, supports the previous conclusions stated here. Clearly the Egyptian occupying forces had a greater impact on the material culture of the Palestinian coast, the rift valleys and the southern Transjordan than has previously been acknowledged. The twelfth century B.C. painted pottery traditions, as indicated at Timna and Qurayyah, as well as the anthropoid coffins from Deir el Balah, show that a review of previous interpretations of materials from Tell Far'ah (S), Lachish, Beth Shan and related sites is in order. A preoccupation with Philistine influence must be put aside to give due consideration to Egyptian and local features. Established Egyptian influence continuing into the Iron Age in the areas just mentioned, provides us with a reasonable background for the Egyptian influence in art objects later in the Iron Age. This occurrence is difficult to explain satisfactorily by any other means.

The connection of iron working with the Philistines is another major problem. Biblical references seem to indicate a monopoly by the Philistines of the technology involved in the use of this metal (I Sam. 13:19-22) and this, and its implications, have been stressed in the historical discussions of many scholars (for example, see Albright, "Syria, the Philistines, and Phoenicia," p. 33). As in much of the discussion above concerning the Philistines, the unknown factors are considerable and widen the range of possible interpretations. The Egyptian presence at the Timna mines has been stressed above, and it seemed reasonable to attribute most of the actual labor and technological abilities to the local, probably Edomite, populace. But, could the Philistines have had a particular interest in this area also and had a hand in the activities here? Here we have the introduction of an unknown factor and it would seem best not to see any such activity unless there is some clear archaeological evidence for it. Nelson Glueck's survey of the eastern portion of the Arabah, and the wadi beds leading into it, yielded settlements and evidence of mining activity contemporary with that at Timna (we assume that this activity continued through Iron II, but no evidence is available to support this). The slag from these sites is very interesting in contrast to that from Timna because, according to Glueck, iron could be extracted as easily as copper and some of the slag obviously resulted from the extraction of iron (Nelson Glueck, "The Recently Discovered Ore Deposits in Eastern Palestine," BASOR, LXIII [1936], 4-8). Was this a prime source upon which the Philistine "monopoly" of iron depended or were the Philistines not at all the only ones who could work this metal? Is there really some fact to the iron bedstead of Og, King of Bashan, which stood in Amman, and does this indicate that some artisans in the Transjordan (not only Edom) knew the techniques required for the production and handling of this metal? Unfortunately, the question can only be raised and considerable directly focused research will be necessary to find an answer to it.

[1]In this light, one can view in a different way the problem, mentioned above, of filling the void which occurred when Mycenaean pottery was no longer imported. It is true that the bronze vessels probably did not replace earlier vessels item by item but, rather introduced a luxury item of a different kind. The "wine services" of Tell es Sa'idiyeh and Tell Mazar (possibly still to be found as late as Amman tomb N) are illustrated in use by nobility or royalty in paintings and ivories of the Late Bronze Age in Palestine and the New Kingdom in Egypt. Thus, the incorporation of such a service in a tomb inventory may well indicate a newly acquired prestige item in this area. If finer vessels were produced in copper, and in good supply, it is easier to understand why there was no great impetus to produce finer pottery vessels. Also, this could possibly provide a key for understanding the origin of the red-burnished technique. It has been suggested that red-burnished wares were finished in this manner as an imitation of polished bronze or copper vessels. If

[3]Glueck, EEP, III, 269.

upsurge of settlements to be seen as a continuation beyond the end of L.B. or the introduction of Iron II? The socio-economic conditions and relative parochialism of the Palestinian hill country seem to exist in the Transjordan to some extent, but they are modified by a closer contact with Syria as illustrated by the painted pottery tradition. Distinctions between Palestine and Transjordan are best documented at Deir 'Allā and are more difficult to make elsewhere. Only detailed pottery studies on other sites, similar to those undertaken on the Deir 'Allā material, will provide the information that is needed to understand any differences that may exist between Palestine and Transjordan. This information would also indicate whether the Jordan rift must be considered as a separate unit or as connected with one or the other side.[1]

The eleventh century is not well represented, and thus the introduction of the red-burnished technique on pottery vessels, which comes into use at some point during this century, cannot yet be documented. Deir 'Allā spans most of this interval, but the lack of description of individual sherds makes it impossible to trace this development. There are parallels, however, between the pottery of the latest published phases (from J on) and that of Irbed tombs A-C, and these are best characterized by the juglets with elongated cylindrical necks with the handles attached at the middle of the neck. Some of the shapes of the Irbed tomb pottery resemble those frequently found in Philistine pottery and indicate a date in the second half of the eleventh century B.C. The simple forms of the vessels from the Madeba tombs continue, but here the red-burnished technique is already well established. The Amman sherd material provides several shapes, as does that from Balu'a, Aro'er, Dhiban, Nebo and Sahab, but without published stratified materials it is impossible to form significant conclusions. Nothing can be said as yet about individual kingdoms confined to specific geographical areas, nor is it possible to lend any further understanding to the interpretation of the Biblical accounts dealing with the activities of the Israelite judges in the Transjordan.

Tenth to Eighth Centuries B.C.

Once again, surface surveys indicate extensive occupation in the Transjordan, but published tomb material is relatively scarce and most of the artifacts from excavated sites that have occupations which span this period have not yet been published. Consequently, as shall be shown more fully below, it is difficult to draw many general conclusions at the present time. The pottery sequence, however, is fairly clear and the 1969 Amman Citadel sounding, though only a small operation, yielded a substantial body of evidence and provided a good basis for illustrating the evolution of ceramic forms. It has been possible to amplify this information by using it as a starting point for the typological arrangement of similar forms that came from unstratified contexts on the citadel. Together, this information should provide a larger and more relevant body of material than has previously been available for study in the Transjordan.

The stratigraphy of the 1969 sounding (Area II on fig. 5) was clearly subdivided into two periods. The first was composed of layers which came up against the outer face of the defense wall, wall B (see fig. 6), and the second was composed of layers associated with the use of this wall after the rebuilding of the defense system, as characterized by the addition of wall C. The length of time covered by both periods was fairly short and, consequently, no radical shift can be noted in the pottery. There were, however, a number of shapes which did not continue in use through both periods and thus provided criteria for discriminating a sequence of forms. On the whole, the character and even the peculiarities illustrated here were very close to that of the material from the hill country in Palestine (as illustrated by Tell Beit Mirsim B_3-A_1 and contemporary deposits on other sites like Tell en Naṣbe, Gibeah, Bethel, Ain Shems, and Gibeon). The stage in the sequence of the red-burnished pottery was identical, with hand burnishing and occasionally polishing being used almost exclusively. The pottery was still handmade and no imported pottery was found, though it did appear at other sites in the Transjordan at this time. The characteristic high "collar-type" rim of the eleventh century is not found here (though there were some unstratified examples or examples found in mixed debris), but a large number of the transitional low "collar-type" rims common in the tenth and early ninth centuries in Palestine were common. The "cylindrical-jar type" rims that were to be popular from the ninth century on in Palestine were found in both periods, but the related wide

---

[1]It does not seem that the Jordan Valley was ever consistently associated only with the region to the west or that to the east. This status probably changed from period to period and future research must be oriented not to generalizations, but to understanding separately the situations existing at different times. It is understandable that at most times the Jordan Valley formed a distinct unit in the way in which influences from east and west were combined here. Future research must take this into consideration.

interior-ledge hole-mouth jar rim that is common late in Iron II had already appeared in Period II. There were other examples of very close correspondences in peculiar rim types, such as bowl rim type XIV. The most popular red-burnished bowl rims (types XXIV and XXV) can be paralleled in Palestine. Similar forms are indeed very popular in Palestine, but exact parallels are rare, though this may be deceptive because of a partial void in the Palestinian repertoire. A similar problem exists with the low, open bowls (or plates) types I and II, which are more clearly shown to be currently much better represented in this period in Syria than in Palestine and continue, though modified, into our Sequence II.

Some features, like the simplicity of most of the rims and the clear preference for disk or flat bases, are in keeping with tendencies noted at Madeba and Irbed. The parallels between the 1969 sounding sherds and those of the published Deir 'Allā phases were not as close as one might have expected. This is due partially to the fact that the two sequences do not overlap; rather the sounding begins with Period I, dating just after the end of the published Deir 'Allā phases. A number of definite parallels do occur but many more shapes are from similar types, rather than types which correspond exactly in all the nuances of profile. The lack of color description and the multiplicity of types in the Deir 'Allā publication provide an additional obstacle in judging correspondence between the sites.

There are a number of distinct rim profiles which are extremely rare outside the Transjordan and must be considered as characteristically local. These are particularly the rim types LXVI and LXIII, and the grooved rims LXIV and LXX. Most of these profiles are well illustrated in the unstratified sherd material from Amman and seem to continue in use later than the date of the material from the 1969 sounding, but they are not found in Sequence II. A significant, but limited number of profiles which were found only in Period II of the 1969 sounding, continued in use into Sequence II. The most important of these is a very thin-ware bowl sherd of type V rim profile, which shows that a gradual and not a sudden improvement in techniques was responsible for some of the very thin and fine wares of the late range of Sequence II.

The fragments of painted pottery from the 1969 sounding were extremely enlightening. Some of these sherds were quite small, but their number was unexpectedly large, and they displayed an interesting variety. The decoration, with few exceptions, was simple and for the most part was done in bichrome. Most of these sherds were separated into four groups. (1) The simplest were sherds decorated with black or grey lines, usually on a dark red, unburnished surface, for which good parallels could be found in Palestine. (2) There were sherds with a white slip, and red and black decoration. These recalled the typical Philistine color scheme, but our examples were either too simple for more specific attribution or non-Philistine in design. The date of these sherds is later than the period in which Philistine pottery was most popular in Palestine, so any connection is doubtful. The painted sherds with a white slip found at Aro'er are not yet published in detail, so it is not possible to say whether they are similar to the ones found at Amman. If a similarity could be shown to exist, this would demonstrate a little known type of decorated pottery which may be unique to portions of the Transjordan. (3) There were red-washed sherds on which bands of white paint, framed by black lines, had been applied. This decoration is commonly associated with the red-burnished pottery and seems to come into use with it. It is well represented at this time in Palestine also, but only with a limited number of examples from any particular site. In the ninth century B.C., this decoration, and in fact most painted decoration, becomes very rare in Palestine, but in the Transjordan painted decoration on pottery vessels remains popular. This particular color scheme is by far the most popular in the Transjordan and can be cited as one of the hallmarks of this area. How wide a popularity this type of painted decoration originally had is difficult to say, though isolated pieces, mostly later than those from the 1969 sounding, can be found in Phoenicia and the Phoenician colonies. Only at one Syrian site, Tabbat al Hammam, has similar decorated pottery been found in any quantity. Finally, (4), a number of sherds with a light brown or tan slip were decorated with red-brown bands bordered by black or dark brown lines. This color scheme is reminiscent of the Late Bronze decorating tradition, but it continued to be popular to the end of Iron II in Syria and Phoenicia.

The study of the painted pottery and sherd profiles indicates that there were many features linking the Amman material with that of Syria and Palestine. The contact with Palestine was close, while that with the north was far less pronounced. Balancing this closeness with Palestine was a significant number of features which indicate an expression of individuality in Amman. As in the preceding centuries, there still seemed to be a parochial character to the assemblage, as opposed to the involvement in a broader international sphere that is evident at the end of Sequence II (which will be stressed below). The scanty contemporary material available for the tenth and ninth centuries B.C. from elsewhere in the Transjordan seems to substantiate a similar generalization for the entire area. In the south, the pertinent levels of the fortified settlement at Tell el Kheleifeh are not yet fully published, but a Palestinian orientation seems indicated. In the north at the fortress of Tell er Rumeith, though again full publication is not yet available, the excavator, Paul W. Lapp, stated that level VIII, the original Solomonic building of the fortress, had a Palestinian orientation in its ceramics while the next levels indicated a Syrian orientation.

The excavations at these two fortified sites indicate that it should be possible to make a good beginning at placing the archaeological evidence within the framework of the historical references found in the Biblical sources. No attempt will be made to evaluate the correctness of Glueck's identification of his site with Ezion-Geber - Elat, but certainly the remains at Tell el Kheleifeh must be seen in the context of the Biblical references to King Solomon's trading and mining expeditions, which concentrated in that general area, and the references to the activities of later Judean kings. Similarly, Tell er Rumeith must be seen in light of the border struggles between the Aramean state centered in Damascus and the kingdom of Israel. Deir 'Allā, Tell es Sa'idiyeh, Dhiban, and Aro'er are less helpful at present in accomplishing this purpose, but the 1969 sounding in Amman must be considered in the context of the Biblical references to the time of David and Solomon. It has been seen that there was no significant break between Periods I and II in our 1969 sounding and that it spans much of the tenth century B.C. and continues on into the ninth century. The one historical event in this period which would be expected to leave a decisive mark on the archaeological remains is the capture of the city by the Israelites under David around 980 B.C. It would be difficult to see this event as the reason for the rebuilding of the defense wall before Period II, primarily because that would shift the date of Period I too early and cause an unexplainable length for Period II (if compelled to extend it into the ninth century). A destruction of the Period II city by David is also extremely unlikely as it would force most of Periods I and II into the eleventh century, which the ceramic evidence will not allow. A very plausible solution, however, would be to see the "original" building of Period I as the rebuilding of the city after the capture by David. A date around 980 B.C. for the building of wall B would suit the archaeological evidence and the rebuilding in Period II would be a minor undertaking that took place just before or around 900 B.C.

David apparently assumed the kingship in Amman himself and it remained a separate kingdom rather than part of the administrative organization of the state of Israel. How long this situation lasted under later Israelite rulers is not certain. Only two other items may be noted here: (1) the close and friendly ties that first existed between David and the Ammonite state under the ruler Nahash, and (2) the strong treaty relations that existed between Amman and the Aramean states to the north which prompted the exertion of considerable energy and the expenditure of considerable resources on their part to protect their Ammonite ally from the Israelite menace.

A basic Palestinian orientation of the ceramic material in the tenth century would then be in keeping with the historical references. At the present state of knowledge, it is impossible to make distinctions within the Transjordan between different sections and it certainly would not be valid to make such an attempt until a sufficient and well published body of evidence was available from each area. The past designations of Edomite, Moabite, and Ammonite painted wares can no longer be substantiated and, though new distinctions may arise as the result of increased information, it is necessary for the time being to be content with the documentation of features which demonstrate a common tradition in the Transjordan. The 1969 sounding sherds and the unstratified sherds from Amman have yielded examples of decorated pottery which duplicate most of the decoration types published presently from the other two areas. Most of the so-called Moabite painted sherds seem to resemble the types found in the 1969 sounding, while most of the so-called Edomite sherds either belong to the twelfth century painted pottery tradition discussed above (and best illustrated at Timna and Deir 'Allā) or are similar to the painted sherds common at the end of Iron II. A chronological difference may actually provide the basis for these distinctions rather than a regional difference, and the fact that most of the published painted sherds from the Transjordan can be paralleled from the 1969 sounding sherds, the unstratified Amman sherds, or the Amman district tomb pottery underscores this contention.

Few small objects are available for the tenth and ninth centuries, though they are more abundant in the eighth century. In the tenth and ninth centuries, what is available in the way of objects and pottery does not indicate an assemblage as polished or sophisticated as that available for the seventh to sixth centuries B.C. A number of ninth century inscriptions on stone are now available, from Dhiban, Kerak, and Amman, which help somewhat in understanding this period. The two inscriptions which are long enough to provide sufficient material for analysis indicate that the language is a local dialect of Canaanite.[1] While the Mesha stone inscription is written in a "Hebrew script," the Amman Citadel inscription is considered to be written "in a characteristic Aramaic hand of the ninth century B.C."[2] The Kerak inscription closely resembles the Mesha stone.[3] The text of the Mesha stone indicates an intense local nationalism and the language of the above-cited inscriptions indicates, similarly, the use of a native and not a foreign mode of expression. On the other hand, the distribution of the various scripts indicates the extent of the cultural spheres of influence which connected specific localities with surrounding nations. To this extent the literary and archaeological information can be paralleled, but with the limited nature of this information it is presently not possible to extend our speculation much further.[4]

The archaeological information available for the ninth century B.C. is quite limited and difficult to assess, but in the eight century B.C. it begins to increase. At this time there are indications that it will be possible to distinguish peculiarities within different parts of the Transjordan, when presently excavated materials are published and have been supplemented by further excavations. In the Amman district, the middle range of our typological Sequence II begins in the last third or quarter of the century. Tomb materials from Mt. Nebo and Dhiban are closely related to this and can be used to illustrate a typologically earlier stage, which we would consider to cover primarily the first half of the eighth century B.C. There are many forms here which did not appear earlier and which are poorly represented or absent from our 1969 sounding. Some of these forms seem to be Transjordanian and are rare in Palestine. In most cases, there is no clear evidence for the date when these forms were introduced. In the ninth and eighth centuries B.C., the shapes gradually became more sophisticated in Amman, and hand-burnishing gave way to wheel-burnishing, though indications of wheel-thrown vessels seem to be present only toward the end of the eighth century. There is a greater continuity in the heavier, larger vessels and profiles like types LXII, LXVI, LXX, and LXXIV-LXXVIII which continue on, though occasionally with modifications in the profile, from the time of the 1969 sounding and now normally occur with a wheel-burnished surface. The bowl rims, on the whole, are still not very distinctive or elaborately profiled and thus are more difficult to trace. In fact, it is difficult to document the emergence of the types which become popular

---

[1]Concerning the Mesha stone, A. H. van Zyl states, "In certain respects Moabite has an affinity with Ugaritic, in others with Phoenician, and in still others with Hebrew, while all these languages are closely related in numerous other aspects. Therefore Moabitic is rather to be considered as a dialect of the Canaanite language, which is related to all other languages that belong to this group." A. H. van Zyl, *The Moabites* ("Pretoria Oriental Series," III; Leiden: E. J. Brill, 1960), p. 188. The same general affinities seem to be illustrated in the Amman Citadel inscription as is evident by the designation of its language as Ammonite (Frank Moore Cross, Jr., "Epigraphic Notes on the Amman Citadel Inscription," *BASOR*, CXCIII [1969], 17). How closely related the two languages were must await further study and, probably, more inscriptional material.

[2]Cross, *BASOR*, CXCIII, 17. Further discussions of the Amman Citadel inscription have appeared: William F. Albright, "Some Comments on the 'Ammān Citadel Inscription," *BASOR*, CXCVIII (1970), 38-40; Giovanni Garbini, "La lingua degli Ammoniti," *Annali del Instituto Orientale di Napoli*, XXX (n.s. XX) (1970), 249-58; J. Teixidor, "Bulletin d'épigraphie, no. 60," *Syria*, XLVII (1970); L. Palmaitis, "The First Ancient Ammonite Inscription of the I Millennium B.C.," *Vestnik drevnei istorri*, CXVIII (1971), 119-26 (in Russian); R. Kutscher, "A New Inscription from 'Amman,"

Qadmoniôt, V (1972), 27-28 (in Hebrew); Émile Puech and Alexander Rofe, "L'inscription de la citadelle d'Amman," *Revue Biblique*, LXXX (1973), 531-46; and Adriaan van Selms, "Some Remarks on the Amman Citadel Inscription," *Bibliotheca Orientalis*, XXXII (1975), 5-8.

An inscription on a bronze bottle found at Tell Siran, on the outskirts of Amman to the northwest, contains the names of several previously unknown rulers of Ammon which have now been added to our Table 3. The excavations at Tell Siran are described in Thompson, *ADAJ*, XVIII, 5-14 and pls. I-X. The inscription on the bronze bottle is published in Fawzi Zayadine and Henry O. Thompson, "The Ammonite Inscription from Tell Siran," *Berytus*, XXII (1973), 115-40 and Henry O. Thompson and Fawzi Zayadine, "The Tell Siran Inscription," *BASOR*, CCXII (1973), 5-11. Additional comments on the inscription are presented in Frank Moore Cross, "Notes on the Ammonite Inscription from Tell Sīrān," *BASOR*, CCXII (1973), 12-15.

[3]William L. Reed and Fred V. Winnett, "A Fragment of an Early Moabite Inscription from Kerak," *BASOR*, CLXXII (1963), 1-9.

[4]A recent attempt at shedding more light on the Mesha stone, its purpose and historical context is found in Max Miller, "The Moabite Stone as a Memorial Stela," *PEQ*, CLX (1974), 9-18.

in the middle and late range of Sequence II.[1]

The tomb deposits at Mt. Nebo and Dhiban, together with some of the level IV pottery from Tell el Kheleifeh, provided a number of forms that were not common earlier or later. The most important of these was a large number of censers, one-handled cups, and juglets (jugs occurred rather infrequently). The cups and censers sometimes overlapped in profile, with the major difference being the perforations on the latter. The cups were the forerunners of the type LXXXVII forms which were found in the middle range of Sequence II. A few censers were already found at the end of Sequence I, but seem to have their greatest popularity in the ninth and eighth centuries B.C. Some of the latest censers have profiles resembling the tripod cup types 3 and 4, which are common in the middle range of our Sequence II. The difference in the intended use of the perforated and nonperforated cups is not clear, but only the latter seemed to continue in use long after the end of the eighth century. The types 3 to 5 cups were always red-burnished, but the earlier cups and censers were often covered with a white slip. The use of a white slip may prove to be a very significant peculiarity of specific areas at this time. The red-burnished technique is not noted at all at Aro'er and is less popular as a surface finish than white slip on many shapes found in the Mt. Nebo tombs. Similar white or cream slips are present in the Amman district, but here red-burnishing is most common on the material presently available (which is scanty for the ninth and eighth centuries B.C.). How much this white slip is restricted to certain shapes and certain chronological periods is presently unknown since it is not well documented, but it is something which must be watched carefully in the future.[2]

The decanters, jugs, and juglets provide the best shapes that can be paralleled in Syria, Phoenicia, and Cyprus. The number of jugs that are documented between the tenth and eighth centuries is rather small compared to earlier and later periods, and it is very difficult to fill this range with existing sherd profiles. The early Sequence I jugs were primarily an extension of the L.B. tradition. The Irbed tombs provided some examples for the end of that sequence which were very diagnostic and had good parallels in Palestine. The decanters and jugs are best illustrated in material from the Nebo tombs, and in examples in the Madeba Museum. For the most part, the decanters parallel those found in Palestine and are more numerous than the jugs. Most of the jugs have a neck ridge and the top of the handle is attached at this point. These jugs could be considered to be imports from Cyprus or Phoenicia, but the ware and rough execution of most of them suggest local imitations. Only two one-handled black-on-red Cypriote juglets occur and these constitute the only indisputable Cypriote imports. The two-handled Cypriote-like[3] juglets, which are so numerous in the middle and late ranges of Sequence II, and also in the Dhiban tombs, are clearly later than the one-handled variety (as is also the case in Palestine and Cyprus). The Nebo and Dhiban tomb materials show an evolution from the shape of these juglets to the shape with the tall neck common in the middle range of Sequence II. Ceramically, these jugs and juglets are the best illustrations of foreign contacts. The limited number of early examples is again indicative of a somewhat isolated, parochial assemblage. The ridge-handled jugs and two-handled juglets, however, indicate a greater contact with neighboring areas. The question of local as opposed to foreign manufacture of these vessels raises more problems than can be solved at this point. A plausible explanation which might be advanced is that these vessels contained a commodity which was becoming a major component of trade through this area and

---

[1]It is tempting to distinguish between some types of vessels found only in tombs and others found only in occupation debris. The number of heavy vessels found in occupation debris is considerably greater than that of smaller vessels. "Collar-type" rim vessels are not illustrated from tomb deposits and hole-mouthed or "cylindrical-jar type" rims are rare. Certain forms, like rim types LXII, LXIV, LXVI, LXX and LXXII, have not yet been found in tombs. On the other hand, the numbers of jug, juglet, and censer sherds found in occupation debris are presently quite small. The analysis, however, indicates that a good part of this may be due to the accident of discovery—whether, for instance, kitchen areas are being excavated on a tell as opposed to public gathering areas. Another factor to be considered is whether or not we can prove an exact temporal overlap between the tomb and tell material in a restricted geographical area. That this is obviously not the case in many instances can be seen from the scattered nature of the evidence in most periods. Consequently, it is possible only to point out the alternatives but further evidence must be awaited. In this case, a considerable overlapping of stratified occupation deposits and tomb deposits, that could be analyzed statistically, would be needed in order to obtain trustworthy results.

[2]If it can be documented clearly that this type of surface finish is the continuation of a practice popular in the Transjordan since the Middle Bronze period, the implications of the continuity of cultural features will be highlighted.

[3]We say Cypriote-like because the similarity is clear but it is not at all certain that they actually come from Cyprus. The later jugs seem to be distinct in ware and paint from Cypriote juglets, and their large number indicates a local product used as a container for some popular commodity in this area.

that a rapid growth of this trade can be seen in the eighth century.

Only one other pottery form need be pointed out here and that is the type XXXVIII bowl. Examples of similar profiles have been found at Engedi, Tell Gemmeh, Tell Far'ah (north), and Samaria in Palestine, and are capable of being dated very closely between 725 and 700 B.C.[1] These bowls have been associated with Assyrian palace ware, but they are clearly a local imitation.[2] This form is very common at Tell el Kheleifeh, so much so in fact that there seems to be some experimentation with the form and, in some cases, assimilation to the profile of other local vessels. A sherd of this type from Amman illustrates the wider distribution of the shape. Table 8 provides a review and summary of pottery forms from the Transjordan and an indication of their chronological occurrences.

The historical texts show that in the eighth century, Assyria brought the lands neighboring on the Transjordan into almost total subjugation, with Damascus being made a province in 732 B.C.[3] and Samaria in 721 B.C.[4] The Transjordanian states were not touched by the might of the Assyrian armies but appeased the conquerors with timely tribute. Aramean power in the north was crushed and what remained of the Judean state could no longer pose a lasting threat. In this manner, it seems that the shackles were gradually removed and the Transjordan was gradually able to move away from the parochialism that had been evident for centuries.

The Transjordanian states had not, according to the historical references, succumbed continually or ever entirely to outside domination. There was a constant shift in relative strengths and the local kingdoms reasserted themselves when conditions allowed. When these kingdoms were dominated either by one of the Syrian or Palestinian states, the local monarchies were usually maintained and only rarely were rulers deposed in favor of provincial governors sent by the conquering state. The payment of tribute to Assyrian overlords, who maintained the previous local royal administrations in these kingdoms, seemingly was a small price to pay for the relative security which paved the way for growing prosperity. The bowl type mentioned above is a clear indicator of things to come in the way of influence from Assyria as a result of the new political situation.

Some specific items have been pointed out above that illustrate the distinctness of the Transjordan, despite many close ties with Palestine. The most significant and clearest examples that illustrate this difference have been held until the end of the discussion in this section, namely, the objects of art. The most important of these objects are the sculptures found in Amman. Only a few pieces can be attributed to the seventh or sixth centuries B.C, while most of the others are dated earlier. These pieces were discussed above, pages 154-59, and we will summarize that discussion briefly here. The majority of the pieces represented human male figures and were separated into three groups. All three groups exhibited noticeable Egyptian influence, but it was surprising to note that this influence was not mediated to this area by way of the Phoenician coast. The features characteristic of Phoenician art were absent, for the most part, and it was felt that the manner in which the Egyptianizing features were displayed illustrated a distinct style which was part of an inland, rather than coastal, tradition. The independent contact with Egypt either was very direct or was based on a longstanding Egyptianizing artistic tradition, like that illustrated considerably earlier by the Balu'a stele. Though additional evidence is needed, there seemed to be enough evidence to suggest that these pieces should be seen in connection with a South Syrian school of art.

The first group of sculptures was classed as Egyptianized. It was surprising to see that, despite an obvious dependence on Egyptian canons, the execution of many details was totally un-Egyptian. Some of these details were helpful in giving a closer date to these pieces (all were found without suitable archaeological context), since comparable features occur on fairly precisely dated North Syrian or Assyrian sculpture, or on Phoenician or Syrian style ivory carvings. This was the earliest of the three groups, with dates that seemed to range between the late ninth and the eighth century B.C.

The second group is best described as typically Transjordanian. The most characteristic feature linking these pieces was the Egyptian atef crown that they are each shown wearing. A date range of ninth to sixth century had to be assigned to them and a number of specific features where indicated that seem to be more precise chronological indicators. A fragmentary head (on display in the American University of Beirut Museum),

---

[1]Crowfoot, Crowfoot, and Kenyon, *SS*, III, 97-98.

[2]These bowls seem to stand even closer to the metallic prototype that is suggested for the palace ware vessels. The color and burnish could be an attempt at reproducing the color of such vessels.

[3]H. Tadmor, "The Southern Border of Aram," *IEJ*, XII (1962), 115-21.

[4]"Texts from Hammurabi to the Downfall of the Assyrian Empire," trans. A. Leo Oppenheim; *Ancient Near Eastern Texts*, ed. James B. Pritchard (2nd ed.; Princeton: Princeton University Press, 1955), pp. 284-85.

TABLE 8. SUMMARY OF POTTERY

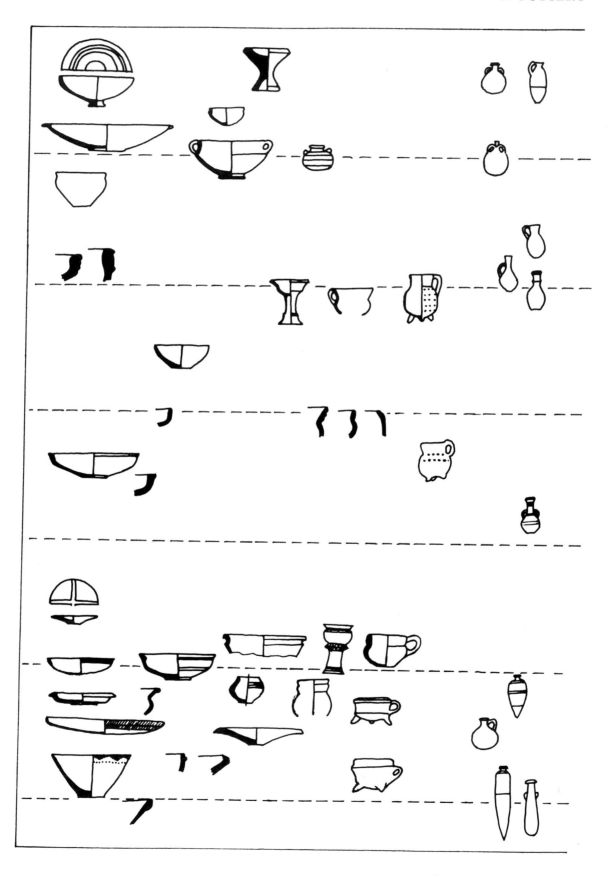

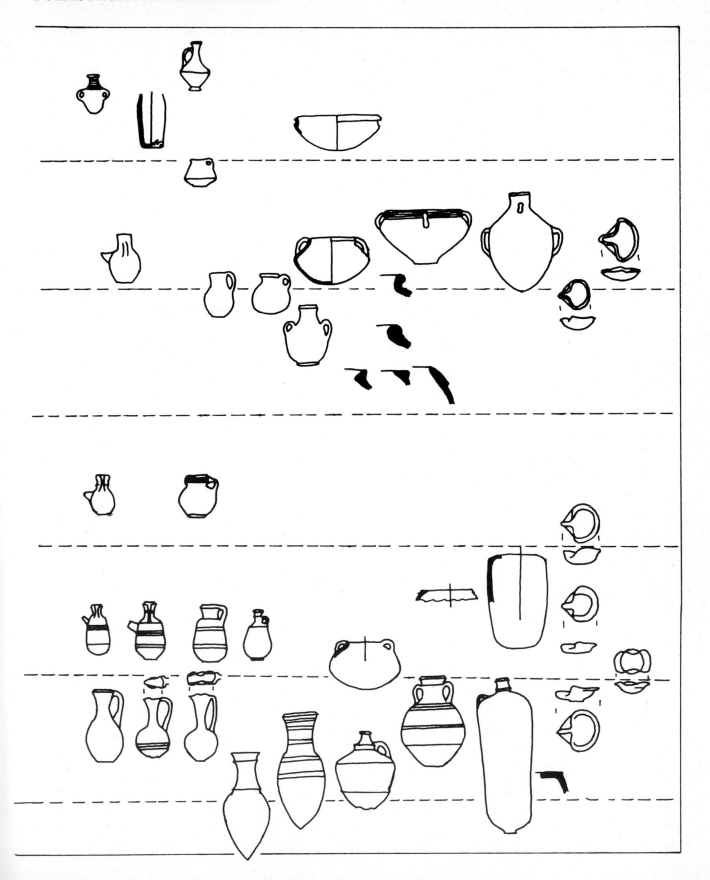

which could be attributed to this group, is said to have been found in ancient Moab and thus provides our only possible example of sculpture from another portion of the Transjordan.

The third group is not easily given a descriptive label but is most closely linked with the sculptures of North Syria. As a unit this group can be dated later than the others, with a date in the second half of the eighth century for the earliest piece, a roughly 700 B.C. date for the statue of Yareaḥ-'Azar,[1] and a probably seventh-century date for the other piece. The Assyrian influence, increasingly noticeable on the North Syrian sculptures after ca. 750 B.C., is also obvious in these pieces.

In all three groups, it is clear that the sculptures were made by men who were well acquainted with the art styles of the neighboring areas. It is undeniable that the pieces were local products. The combinations of features cannot be explained in any other way. The cosmopolitan character of the Amman sculpture is noteworthy. It is also clear, however, that despite this acquaintance with foreign art styles, the local sculptors were not skilled enough to weld these features into an integrated, polished and clearly articulated style as was done in Phoenicia.

In conclusion, these sculptures indicate that a local art style did exist in the Transjordan in the Iron Age. Most of the pieces seem to date to a period of increased freedom and prosperity in the area, namely, the eighth century B.C. The apparent use of these sculptures as votive objects, places them within the context of a long-standing Near Eastern practice. The lack of similar objects from Palestine, despite the great amount of excavation which has been undertaken there, is in need of explanation. It has been suggested above, that the explanation for this may lie in the Biblical injunctions against the depiction of the human form. This would have curtailed the production of such sculpture in Palestine, while the kingdoms of the Transjordan, which did not share the same religious scruples, would have been free to continue in the exercise of age-old customs.

Seventh and Sixth Centuries B.C.

A larger body of material is available for the seventh and sixth centuries B.C. in the Transjordan. The variety is greater and it can be handled with greater precision than the earlier materials. It has been shown above that the level of the material culture of the area seems clearly to be on the rise in the eighth century B.C., but this merely seems to be a beginning. There is an abundance of indicators to this effect in the archaeological remains, namely, the presence of new metal

objects, gems and seals, small glass vessels, stone alabastra, male and female figurine types, some stone sculpture, a great variety of ceramic forms (in many of which a development can be traced), and an increase in the use of painted decoration on terra-cotta objects and vessels. Only a few of these items will be mentioned here in review to illustrate the nature of this assemblage. The ceramic evidence will be mentioned briefly and then some of the other items. The ceramics will be discussed in three groups: (1) those indicating very close contact with Mesopotamian pottery, (2) those illustrating wide foreign contacts (often the imitation of foreign shapes but in local wares and with a decidedly local character), and (3) those illustrating profiles of purely local character which, however, also show the rich variety of forms in the local assemblage. Most important among the first group are the fragments of Assyrian palace ware in tomb AN. The pointed vases (fig. 40:1-6) from tombs AN and M have a distinct Mesopotamian character and parallels were cited in Assyria and Babylonia. Many of the other jar forms (fig. 40:7-11, 15-17) are equally well documented in Mesopotamia. The imitation alabastra in pottery (fig. 39:42-51) are distinctive Egyptian forms, but are common throughout the Near East from Egypt to Babylonia.

Many other pottery forms are common in the Assyrian period but show a less pronounced Mesopotamian character. These forms, the second group, must be regarded as indicators of the cosmopolitan character of local assemblages, like that of the Amman district. Those areas which chose to play an active role in the new political framework that emerged in the last century of the Assyrian empire, seemed to share many features not directly attributable to Assyrian influence but illustrated as common features between local assemblages.

The eighth-century two-handled, Cypriote-like juglets which are common throughout our middle range have been mentioned above, but they are gradually displaced by handleless, small, pointed bottles, figure 39:1-38, which appeared already in a few examples in the Dhiban tombs. On present evidence, these juglets must be considered primarily Transjordanian since they are plentiful here, but extremely rare in Palestine. How they relate to Syrian ceramics is still unclear but the connections are firmer than with Palestine. It was mentioned above that numerous examples were fund in the Amuq, where they were deco-

---

[1] A date in the first third of the seventh century B.C. would be required if we accept Zayadine's new reading in *Syria*, LI and would substantiate the date previously assigned to the statue.

rated in a variety of ways, and the form overlapped with a specific form of glazed vessel that is best paralleled in seventh-century contexts. The elongated shape of similar pointed flasks illustrates a tendency which is noted in Neo-Babylonian and Persian contexts in Mesopotamia.

The major jug type and a two-handled, ridge-necked amphora type are related to Phoenician shapes. It must be noted, however, that we had more examples of these vessels in a few Amman district tombs than could be illustrated elsewhere, and that the ware and painted decorations were in keeping with local practice and production. Consequently, we must conclude that, until further information warrants a change, these illustrate local forms. The two-handled, ridge-necked amphora was present in the middle range of Sequence II and in tomb AN of the late range. It appeared already in Palestine at Tell el Far'ah (north), together with the bowl type XXXVIII, in the last quarter of the eighth century B.C. Its continuation in the seventh century is clearly indicated at Amman. The one-handled jugs of the types illustrated on figures 34:20-36:11 are usually considered to be Phoenician, but only a few published examples are available from that area and few have been found in Palestine. The number illustrated above is considerable but represents only a small portion of such jugs found in the Amman district, when the unpublished vessels are taken into account. There is a noticeable evolution in the form and an indication that most of the Phoenician jugs have a different, quite distinctive profile. The comparative material is too scanty to pursue such details, but it is obvious that these jugs form an important part of the local Transjordanian repertoire of forms. A large number of decanters was found in the Transjordan, but their profiles and quantity are consistent with those found in Palestine and Syria.

There are a number of vessel types which could be discussed in connection with the second or third group. The unifying characteristics of these vessels are features which resulted from firing practices employed in their manufacture. The surface treatment of these vessels is related to the normal Iron II red-burnishing technique and provides an important variation. Some of the shapes involved seem to have a restricted, local popularity, but very exact parallels have been found to others at Tell Gemmeh on the Mediterranean coast and in northwest Syria, in the Amuq. Apparently, very simple techniques were used to create a striking range of colors on these vessels. The ware, surface burnish, and possibly even slip seem to have been identical when these vessels were formed, but in one case the vessels were fired in a reducing atmosphere so that a black color was produced. The normal red surface color was the result of firing under oxidizing conditions and the third color, creamy-white, was apparently the result of more complete oxidation of the ware, possibly firing at a higher kiln temperature. Parallels for the creamy-white wares were numerous and the black wares are well represented only in the north. The Amman sherd material illustrated a complete overlap in forms, wares, etc., between the bowls of different colors. As far as the black sherds are concerned, the Amman examples are more successfully produced than those in the Amuq, which usually tend more to a grey color and sometimes to an unevenly reduced, mottled color. The identity of techniques is indisputable. In addition, the Transjordanian black-burnished ware is not confined to a single or limited range of shapes, as it is in other areas to bowl and/or juglet forms but rather is used on a wide range of vessel shapes (large jars of various profiles [especially the sample illustrated on fig. 84:1], rims of types LIII and LXXX, lamps and juglets, as well as bowls). It is suggested that the incentive for the conscious production of the black bowls may have been the imitation in pottery of basalt or dark stone vessels.

The most important point to be stressed in this context is the degree of sophistication in the potter's art which these products demonstrate. Considerable skill and knowledge are required to produce the color variations intentionally as crisp, uniform colors, and not to produce a great variety of two-tone or intermediate tone vessels at the same time. The great technical competence of the potters in the Transjordan should be stressed with an additional illustration by mentioning a second class of vessels (confined to the third group). In this case (illustrated in bowl types IV, V, VIII-X), the potter's ability to throw very fine and sophisticated vessels is evident. Only bowl type V has a long history, but it and type IV are especially important in that they clearly seem to be the forerunners of similar, though somewhat thinner, bowls which are one of the most obvious indicators of the Nabataean ceramic assemblage. The dipper juglets, other bowls, lamps, cooking pots, and other miscellaneous forms have been considered in detail above. They need not detain us here other than to note that they round out this assemblage and, on the whole, provide a continuity with what is available in Palestine. The only other form that must be mentioned separately, in conclusion, is the tripod cup. This form, like its apparent forerunners, is typically Transjordanian and cannot be paralleled elsewhere. The purpose of these cups is unknown but it was noted that types 3 and 4 were confined to the middle range of Sequence II, while type 5 was another clear indicator of the late range.

The review of the ceramic forms, their variety

and some of their international parallels, clearly illustrates what can also be seen in the small objects (pp. 149-52 above), in the latest of the sculptures, and in the figurines, namely, that we are dealing here with a very rich assemblage. The list of tribute paid to Ashurbanipal[1] indicates that Ammon had to pay twice the amount required of any of her neighbors and that all the Transjordanian kingdoms paid a higher tribute than the Palestinian kingdoms. It is tempting to see the amounts of the tribute payments as illustrations of the relative wealth of these areas, if they were based on an ability to pay. If, however, the amount of tribute required of a nation was adjusted to take into account the relative loyalty of that nation, it would be difficult to assess the meaning of the amounts of tribute stated in the annals. Any attempt at comparing the Amman district material with the rest of the Transjordan leads to equally inconclusive results.

Quite simply, sufficient evidence is not yet available. Many of the local peculiarities present in the Amman district are also to be found in tomb material illustrated in the Irbed Museum. The Dhiban tombs, though none dating to the seventh century has been found, indicate a high level of prosperity in the preceding century and a similar assemblage to that present in Amman.[2] At Umm el Biyara, some of the peculiarities of the Amman district assemblage were not evident,[3] though the occupation dated to the first half of the seventh century B.C., and the pottery seemed to be closer to the earlier vessels from Dhiban. Here, as at Dhiban and Mt. Nebo, it is difficult to tell if the assemblage differed substantially from that at Amman. Tell el Kheleifeh is extremely valuable in this respect in that a number of the peculiarities otherwise illustrated only in the Amman district can be found here also.[4] This, together with the fact that pointed vases like those illustrated on figure 40:1-6 were also found at Tell Arad and are considered Transjordanian, is another indication that much of the material presently illustrated only in the Amman district will prove to be fairly standard throughout the area.[5]

It was difficult to assign precise dates to the late range of our Sequence II, particularly to its end. The problem stems from the difficulty in distinguishing between the end of the Neo-Assyrian period, the Neo-Babylonian period, and the Persian period. The Neo-Babylonian and Persian periods are poorly represented in Palestine and, even where shapes are present that illustrate clear Mesopotamian influence, there is little basis for precision in making distinctions. Many of the artifacts published in the Meqabelein tomb, in particular, have their best parallels in tomb finds in Syria which date to the Neo-Babylonian

or Persian period. On these sites, it is difficult to separate the two periods as the pottery wares, surface finish, etc., characteristic of the Persian period clearly begin earlier. In Syria, the overlap of the main Iron II assemblage with that of the Neo-Babylonian is vague. In the Transjordan, the opposite is true. It is difficult to extend tomb AN much beyond the end of the Neo-Assyrian period, or extend its chronological range very far in either direction beyond the second half of the seventh century B.C. There are too many pottery forms and small objects which require a date in the second half of the seventh century B.C., a date which would fit Ammi-nadab II if that is indeed the ruler mentioned on the inscribed seal of Adoni-nur.[6] That the Meqabelein tomb is part of the same assemblage as tomb AN, though slightly later, is unquestionable. Some pieces in tomb AN also seem to belong in a Neo-Babylonian context. As a result, some overlap between these tombs is evident and AN seems to extend down in date to around 600 B.C., while the earliest features present in M cannot have originated much before that date. The ties to the Iron II tradition in these tombs are obvious, but no firm idea exists of the character of the Persian period in this area.

Some of the arguments above will be reviewed by mentioning again only some of the details concerning the terra-cotta figurines.[7] The same

---

[1] Pritchard, *ANET*, p. 301.

[2] In some vessels closer Palestinian ties were indicated at Dhiban, but in general there was no great difference.

[3] More parallels are cited in the text of the preliminary report, however, than are illustrated in profile drawings.

[4] The selection of pottery published from the recent work at Buseirah expands the basis of our knowledge beyond what was previously available from Tell el Kheleifeh.

[5] The greatest indication of distinctively local wares is present at Tell el Kheleifeh where a crude handmade pottery with point-incised decoration is found, as well as the use of a "dentiled ornamentation" attached to the carination of certain vessels. The former pottery is also found in the Arabah and the Negev. Tell el Kheleifeh, of course, lies in the Arabah and contacts with the neighboring Negev are to be expected. The second of these wares, however, seems to illustrate an Edomite peculiarity which has not been found elsewhere. This would then be one of the few good indicators which can presently be isolated as characteristic of specific kingdoms in the Transjordan.

[6] See the discussion on p. 58.

[7] For the similar arguments that can be propounded, on the basis of particular small objects, see our discussion above, pp. 151-52.

sophistication in manufacture that was evident in the repertoire of ceramic forms can also be illustrated on figurines, when the figurines of the seventh and sixth centuries B.C. are compared with earlier figurines. In keeping with the practice of earlier centuries, the bodies of the figurines were molded by hand while the faces were impressed in a mold. Changes were noted in the way details were shown. Earlier incised-line detail had given way to a surface where features were formed by modeling and the details rendered by paint. This tradition was modified by a change of color scheme around 700 B.C. and the painted details, though summarily represented, were well done in the seventh century B.C. The modeled features impressed by the mold became very elaborate in the seventh century B.C. Some of the details, like the pupils of the eyes and the eyelids, were highlighted by the painted decoration. The fine line detail seemed more elaborate than was necessary for such figurines since features like eyebrows, strands and curls of hair, etc., were obscured or ignored when the paint was applied. The examination of the figurines and molds found in Amman tomb F advanced our study considerably. It is evident that the representations on the molds had been done in conformity with artistic patterns worked out by ivory carvers. Though no exact parallels can be found for these molds, it is possible to illustrate parallels to specific details on ivories from Arslan Tash, Samaria, Nimrud, and Khorsabad. It is clear that the same mold could be used for both male and female figurines. Sex was normally indicated by details which were added by hand modeling or by painted decoration.

We will ignore the female figurines here for review purposes. Almost all of the male figurines were equestrian. The importance of the horses was further illustrated by the fact that the majority of the animal figurines were horses (some with riding blankets on their backs). Horse and rider figurines are very common in the Persian period but not earlier. The presence of such figurines in Amman tombs A, F, an unpublished tomb, and the Meqabelein tomb, documents a significant pre-Persian period occurrence of their use. The ware, paint,[1] and molded details are all in keeping with similar features in the preceding centuries and are clearly different from what is normal in the Persian period. Thus, it seems perfectly justifiable to date these figurines, and the tomb deposits in which they occurred, to the Neo-Babylonian period. By the seventh century B.C., cavalry played an important role in ancient warfare and cavalry contingents are enumerated in the Assyrian records.[2] There is little evidence that Amman was in any way especially associated with cavalry, but these figurines certainly seem

to indicate that such was the case.[3]

It is clear that the rich seventh-century assemblage continued on into the sixth century without drastic change. No clear Persian period forms are found in any of the tombs and only a few sherds, with shapes or wares that were identifiable as Persian, were found in our unstratified sherd collection. A few other profiles, like the hole-mouth jar rims types LXXVII and LXXIX, clearly come down into the sixth century and may extend into the Persian period. There were a number of black-glazed sherds which dated to the Persian period

---

[1]The painted decoration is the white-painted band with black bordering lines that proves to be so characteristic of the Transjordan. These figurines illustrated, in the emblem in some of the riders' hats and the blanket of one of the horse figurines, another decorative design found on Transjordanian pottery but not elsewhere, namely, the crow-step. We discussed parallels to this design in other than painted decoration and cited some references to fuller discussions of this motif. The exciting feature for the Transjordan is that this "crow-step" design is closely associated with the later Nabataeans. This indication of continuity is yet another example of a long-standing tradition in the Transjordan which formed part of the background for the Nabataean civilization.

[2]The horse and rider figurines common in the Persian period may in some way be connected with the representation of Scythian mercenaries. Since there is evidence that the Scythians already appeared as mercenaries in the Neo-Babylonian army (van Loon, *Urartian Art*, pp. 22-25) it could be argued that these Amman horse and rider figurines also represent Scythians. This does not seem likely since these figurines do not seem to be a foreign element or represent foreigners. We have seen how the depiction of the facial features is closely related to the artistic styles best illustrated on Phoenician-Syrian ivories. The use of cavalry is mentioned in Assyrian annals as a significant part of any army in the ninth century and this was probably true earlier also. The riding style that we mentioned in connection with the horse blankets argues for a continuation of the Assyrian-type cavalry in these figurines. There seems to be no reason, then, to find any connection between the rider figurines of the Amman district and the Scythian cavalry, though some stimulation in regard to the manufacture of such figurines may have come from foreign sources.

[3]In this context, Albright's reading of the title on the statue of Yereah-ʿazar (Barnett's transcription in the original publication of this statue has been followed here, but O'Callaghan and Albright read it slightly altered as *Yarahʿazar) as RB RKSN*, "Chief of the Horse," should be noted. William F. Albright, "Notes on Ammonite History," *Miscellanea Biblica B. Ubach* (Barcelona: Montisserrati, 1953), p. 135. If the reading proposed by Zayadine, *syria*, LI is accpeted, Albright's interpretation would no longer be valid, see p. 157, footnote 3.

also, but so far the evidence is not abundant. Persian period material is present on the Citadel in Amman and is distinct from that with which we are familiar through the Neo-Babylonian period. Persian period pottery and Greek imported wares of that period were also found at Tell el Kheleifeh but have not been published. A sizeable official building at Tell es Sa'idiyeh has been attributed to the Persian period. Aside from this material, little more can presently be said about the presence of Persian period artifacts in the Transjordan.

The four double-faced female heads found on the Amman Citadel in 1968 must be mentioned again. They indicate that the production of stone sculpture in Amman continued into the Neo-Babylonian period and continued to exhibit features common on the earlier sculptures from Amman. The faces and other features on both sides of the heads were obviously intended to be identical, but each had a distinct individual character because of the lack of precision in rendering the details. One of the heads was clearly different from the others in its appearance, primarily because of a change in the positioning of the ears. This once more illustrated what was pointed out above, namely, that the work of the local sculptors never crystallized into a uniform, consistent style. The manner in which these faces were depicted was similar to that found on local figurines and the Amman tomb F figurine molds. Similarly, they also are ultimately not to be traced back to a style of depiction that had been worked out for sculpture, but to the full front rendering of faces on ivory carvings. Multiple heads or multiple caryatid figures in ivory are well illustrated as ornamental features for furniture but, though the stone heads seemed to have had an architectural function, they do not seem to have been used as parts of caryatid figures. Examples were cited of naked caryatid figures used on model temple façades but, again, these heads did not seem to have been used in this manner. Each head seems to form an independent unit, as is the case with Egyptian Hathor capitals, rather than part of a complete human figure. The presence of such capitals at Sherabit el Khedaim in Sinai, at Timna, and in the Phoenician colonies illustrates that such capitals need not have been unknown to the people of Amman. Also, the fact that the heads are to be seen in the round with faces on front and back sides, argues against their use in a façade but rather for their use as roof supports in a room or colonnaded courtyard (or portico), like the Egyptian Hathor capitals.

General Concluding Remarks

The preceding discussion stressed the archaeological information that was available from various areas in the Transjordan. In the introduction, it was pointed out how the geography of the Transjordan lent itself to the division of the area into separate kingdoms, and how the historical references constantly refer to these divisions and the struggles between the kingdoms and their neighbors. In general, it was possible to make some distinctions which indicated the association of specific artifacts or building methods with specific areas, but these were limited. It seems impossible to interpret any area differences properly without a continuous artifactual sequence and enough documentation from each area to determine the specific diagnostic features of its assemblage. Only when this is available can an attempt be made to define an Edomite or Moabite, as opposed to Ammonite, assemblage or to understand the nature of the settlements in the Jordan Valley, the Irbed district, or the hill country of Gilead. Once the characteristics of these six major areas are clear, it will be possible to determine the nature and strength of outside influence within each area. When the documentation reaches this level, sufficient information will be available to make some basic correlations between the archaeological information and the historical records. As long as this is not the case, it would be well to exercise extreme caution in discussing area differences and to avoid stressing distinctions for the time being.

In our discussion we emphasized those features which were common to many of the areas, features which could safely be designated as Transjordanian. Some features stood out as characteristic of the Transjordan when comparisons were made with the materials from the surrounding areas, specifically Palestine, Syria and the Phoenician coast. Specific points of similarilty and their chronological importance were also noted in this comparison. It was felt that this, at present, is all that can be accomplished with the information available, and that we have been successful in this respect. For the future and for any attempt at additional subdivisions and more precise distinctions, it is necessary to wait until the sequence of assemblages has been worked out in each geographical area of the Transjordan.

The question always arises in the Transjordan as to whether both settled and nomadic social elements existed in the same area at a particular date, and what their relative strengths and the nature of their contacts were. It is known that almost all of the Iron Age sites discussed were walled settlements and there is no information to suppose that they were other than settlements of sedentary peoples who supported themselves primarily on the agricultural yields of their lands.[1] No information is available in the archaeological evidence that would form a basis for distinguishing between settled and nomadic elements in the population.[2]

In this concluding chapter, some general observations on the nature of foreign contacts were repeated and the evidence for such contacts was reviewed briefly. An involvement in Late Bronze Age international trade gave way very quickly to a very parochial outlook throughout the area, and in the tenth century to a clear Palestinian orientation. Both this orientation and the parochialism gradually broke down by the eighth century B.C., when the area began to flourish. Foreign features, most clearly evident in the art styles, increased significantly but were definitely kept in control either by local artisans or by local tastes. The art styles and early history of the Iron Age indicated the absorption of many Egyptian features. These features were perpetuated locally at least into the seventh and sixth centuries B.C. when the area was drawn once more into the sphere of international trade in a significant way. The cultural orientation, however, was new, as it shifted gradually toward the land of the conqueror as is indicated by pottery styles, jewelry, architecture, etc., and even burial practices.[3] It is difficult to separate the cause of this upsurge from the political situation in which the Transjordanian states happily worked within the framework of the conqueror's organization and benefited by the contacts that were brought with it. This was in sharp contrast to Palestine where a great part of the efforts and resources of the area were consumed in resisting the Assyrian and Neo-Babylonian states. Thus, the rulers in Palestine placed obstacles in the way of an increased contact between geographical areas which was fostered by the dominant super-state.

The archaeological finds do not yet illustrate clearly the role played by the trade routes in the Transjordan, nor do they unambiguously document the commodities which passed over these roads. The historical information suggests that the Transjordan was more stable than Palestine in the eighth through the sixth centuries B.C. If this was so, then trade routes through the Transjordan would have been preferred over a route through the center of Palestine or even the Jordan Valley. The trade route along the Mediterranean coast also continued to provide an important route. The spice trade of Arabia must have crossed Edom in its land route and from there it could have branched to the north or continued west. When Palestine did not dominate this trade, and that from other areas to the south and southeast, the Transjordan could make a greater profit in the handling of these commodities. Perhaps the items which are described as the trade commodities handled by King Solomon would be the same

items that were later transferred via the Transjordan. Gold, in particular, is stressed but almug wood, precious stones,[4] silver, ivory, apes, peacocks,[5] myrrh, and spices[6] illustrate the possible variety of the goods which could have been handled. It is difficult to connect any of these commodities specifically with any of the vessels we have discussed above, with one exception.[7] It is difficult to avoid connecting the great quantity of juglets in some way with this trade. The most likely solution would be the use of these juglets for the transport of scented oils, quite possibly myrrh-scented oils.[8]

It is interesting to note that it was possible to

---

[1]Even Amman, which is supposed to be a city-state based primarily on trade, is said in II Chronicles 27:5 to have paid a tribute of "ten thousand cors of wheat and ten thousand of barley" besides one hundred talents of silver. This tribute was repeated for a total of three successive years. On the assumption we are inclined to make, that this grain represents local produce and not stores gathered through trade, it follows that in normal years Amman should not have needed to import basic food stuffs, but was easily able to sustain itself.

[2]Some evidence on this subject should be published soon and a careful search may provide more. In the spring of 1966, Dr. George E. Mendenhall excavated a cistern at Umm Rujum on the outskirts of Amman. This cistern contained an Arabic inscription on its walls and is dated to the seventh century B.C. ("Archaeological News: Amman—Iron Age Arabic Inscription Discovered," *ADAJ*, XI [1966], 104). This may be seen as evidence for nomadic Arabs moving into the Amman area, and seen in connection with the eventual occupation of Amman by people from the east with camels, around 600 B.C., as is mentioned by Ezekiel (Ezekiel 25:3-5).

[3]The coffin found in AN is of a type common in Assyria and apparently fragments of similar coffins were found in Mt. Nebo tomb 84, Saller, *LA*, XVI, 289-90.

[4]I Kings 10:11.

[5]I Kings 10:22.

[6]I Kings 10:25. Whether the garments, horses, and mules mentioned here were also exchange commodities would be more speculative. The horses are a good possibility, however, in view of their possible importance in Amman.

[7]A second possibility is seeing some connection between the censers and tripod cups and the burning of aromatic spices obtained from Arabia. This is a possibility but, in that case, we have the consumption of a luxury item as a common cultural feature in this area, rather than evidence for its use as a trade commodity. Since the Transjordan is closer to the source of supply, it is of course possible that it enjoyed the use of the commodities which we expect should have been one of its major transport items.

[8]Gus W. Van Beek, "Frankincense and Myrrh," *BA*, XXIII (1960), 85.

illustrate only minimal contact with the Phoenician coast or Cyprus, and no evidence for Greek pottery is available as late as the sixth century B.C. This indicates that the Transjordan was part of an inland trade route which did not have its primary northern contact with the coast in Phoenicia but farther north in Syria. Its southern connection was with the southernmost Palestinian seacoast cities. Significant Mesopotamian parallels indicate that, like the later Nabataeans and Palmyreneans, the route was primarily inland and oriented toward Mesopotamia. It was possible to cite some parallels with Phoenicia and the Phoenician colonies, but the inclination was to stress the probable South Syrian connections of the local art styles. The contacts with Phoenicia and the west concerned features that were shared by South Syria and Phoenicia, and probably were not more direct than that.

The appearance of Greek pottery in the Transjordan in the Persian period would seem to indicate a wider sphere of international contacts than had existed earlier and probably also illustrates the increased cosmopolitan nature of an empire which was larger than any that had existed previously. The scanty evidence from Amman and the unpublished material from Tell el Kheleifeh do not allow more of a statement than that Greek imports exist, though more should be expected to become available with increased archaeological activity, since the historical references lead us to expect this (at least in certain parts of the Transjordan). We have mentioned a number of times that specific features which later were characteristic of the Nabataean civilization were already present at the end of the Iron Age in the Transjordan. It does not seem plausible to see the Nabataeans solely as invaders from the desert who filled a virtual vacuum. They do not really appear very foreign or unrelated to the area they eventually controlled, but seem to have maintained many of the customs and practices of their forerunners, just as they also took over their inland trade route.

BIBLIOGRAPHY

Books

Aharoni, Yohanan. *Excavations at Ramat Raḥel.* Rome: Centro di studi semitici, 1962.

_____. *The Land of the Bible.* Translated by A. F. Rainey. Philadelphia: The Westminster Press, 1967.

Akurgal, Ekrim. *Die Kunst der Hethiter.* München: Hirmer Verlag, 1961.

Alami, Yusuf; Dassel, Peter; Zayadine, Fawzi; and Balqar, Siham. *The Ancient History of Amman.* Department of Antiquities, 1975.

Albright, William Foxwell. *Archaeology and the Religion of Israel.* 5th ed. New York: Anchor Books, 1969.

_____. *Excavations and Results at Tell el-Fûl (Gibeah of Saul).* (Annual of the American Schools of Oriental Research, Vol. IV.) New Haven: American Schools of Oriental Research, 1924.

_____. *From the Stone Age to Christianity.* 2nd ed. New York: Anchor Books, 1969.

_____. *The Archaeology of Palestine.* 5th ed. Harmondsworth: Penguin Books, 1969.

_____. *The Excavations of Tell Beit Mirsim in Palestine.* Vol. I: *The Pottery of the First Three Campaigns.* (Annual of the American Schools of Oriental Research, Vol. XII.) New Haven: American Schools of Oriental Research, 1932.

_____. *The Excavations at Tell Beit Mirsim.* Vol. IA: *The Bronze Age Pottery of the Fourth Campaign* (Annual of the American Schools of Oriental Research, Vol. XIII.) New Haven: American Schools of Oriental Research, 1933.

_____. *The Excavations of Tell Beit Mirsim.* Vol. II: *The Bronze Age.* (Annual of the American Schools of Oriental Research, Vol. XVII.) New Haven: American Schools of Oriental Research, 1938.

_____. *The Excavations at Tell Beit Mirsim.* Vol. III: *The Iron Age.* (Annual of the American Schools of Oriental Research, Vols. XXI-XXII.) New Haven: American Schools of Oriental Research, 1943.

_____. *The Jordan Valley in the Bronze Age.* (Annual of the American Schools of Oriental Research, Vol. VI.) New Haven: American Schools of Oriental Research, 1926.

Amiran, Ruth. *Pottery of the Holy Land.* New Brunswick: Rutgers University Press, 1970.

Baramki, Dimitri. *The Archaeological Museum of the American University of Beirut.* Beirut: American University, 1967.

Barnett, Richard D. *Assyrian Palace Reliefs.* London: Batchworth Press, Ltd., 1960.

_____. *The Nimrud Ivories.* London: British Museum, 1957.

Barnett, Richard D., and Faulkner, M. *The Sculptures of Aššur-Naṣir-Apli II, Tiglath-Pileser III and Esarhaddon.* London: British Museum, 1962.

Bisi, Anna Maria. *Le stele puniche* (Studi Semitici, No. 27.) Roma: Istituto di studi del Vicino Oriente, Università di Roma, 1967.

Braidwood, Robert J., and Linda S. *Excavations in the Plain of Antioch.* (Oriental Institute Publications, Vol. LXI.) Chicago: University of Chicago Press, 1960.

Brunton, Guy, and Engleback, Reginald. *Gurob.* London: British School of Archaeology in Egypt, 1927.

Budge, Wallis. *Assyrian Sculptures in the British Museum, Reign of Ashur-Nasir-Pal, 885-860.* London: British Museum, 1914.

Buhl, Marie-Louise, and Holm-Nielsen, Svend. *Shiloh.* Copenhagen: National Museum, 1969.

du Mesnil, du Buisson. *Baghouz.* Leiden: E. J. Brill, 1948.

Burckhardt, John Lewis. *Travels in Syria and the Holy Land.* London: John Murray, 1822.

Busink, Th. A. *Der Temple von Jerusalem.* Band I: *Der Temple Salomos.* Leiden: E. J. Brill, 1970.

Capart, Jean. *L'art égyptien.* Tome II: *La statuaire.* Bruxelles: des Établ. Vromant, S.A., 1948.

Cintas, Pierre. *Ceramique punique.* (Publications de L'Institut des Hautes Études de Tunis, Vol. III.) Paris: Librarie C. Klincksieck, 1950.

Cleveland, Ray L. *The Excavation of the Conway High Place (Petra) and Soundings at Khirbet Ader.* (Annual of the American Schools of Oriental Research, Vols. XXXIV-XXV, Part II.) New Haven: American Schools of Oriental Research, 1960.

Conder, Major C. R. *The Survey of Eastern Palestine.* Vol. I: *The 'Adwân Country.* London: The Committee of the Palestine Exploration Fund, 1889.

Corning Museum of Glass. *Glass from the Ancient World.* Corning: The Corning Museum of Glass, 1957.

Cowley, Arthur E. *Aramaic Papyri of the Fifth Century B.C.* Oxford: Oxford University Press, 1923.

Crowfoot, J.W.; Crowfoot, G. M.; and Kenyon, Kathleen M. *Samaria-Sabaste.* Vol. III: *The Objects from Samaria.* London: Palestine Exploration Fund, 1957.

Davice, A., *et al. Missone archeologica italiana in Siria, Rapport preliminare della campagna 1966 (Tell Mardikh).* (Universitat degli studi di Roma, Serie archeologica, No. 13.) Roma: Istituto di studi del Vicino Oriente, 1967.

Decamps de Mertzenfeld, C. *Inventaire commenté des ivoires phéniciens et apparentés découverts dans le Proche-Orient.* Paris: E. de Boccard, 1954.

Dothan, Moshe. *Ashdod.* Vols. II-III: *The Second and Third Seasons of Excavations, 1963, 1965, Soundings in 1967.* (Atiqot, Vols. IX-X.) Jerusalem: The Department of Antiquities and Museums, 1971.

Dothan, Moshe, and Freedman, David N. *Ashdod.* Vol. I: *The First Season of Excavations, 1962.* (Atiqot, Vol. VII.) Jerusalem: The Department of Antiquities and Museums, 1967.

Dothan, Trude. *The Philistines and Their Material Culture.* Jerusalem: The Bialik Institute and the Israel Exploration Society, 1967. In Hebrew with English summary.

Dunand, Maurice. *Fouilles de Byblos.* Tome II: *Atlas.* (République libanaise. Ministère de l'instruction publique et des beaux-arts. Direction des antiquités. Études et documents d'archéologie, Tome III.) Paris: Librairie d'Amérique et d'Orient Adrien Maisonneuve, 1950.

Duncan, J. Garrow. *Corpus of Dated Palestinian Pottery*. London: British School of Archaeology in Egypt, 1930.

Franken, Henk J. *Excavations at Tell Deir 'Allā*. Vol. I. (Documenta et monumenta orientis antiqui, Vol. 16.) Leiden: E. J. Brill, 1969.

Franken, Henk J., and Franken-Battershill, C. A. *A Primer of Old Testament Archaeology*. Leiden: E. J. Brill, 1963.

Frankfort, Henri. *The Art and Architecture of the Ancient Orient*. Baltimore: Penguin Books, 1955.

Fugmann, Einar. *Hama, fouilles et recherches de la Fondation Carlsberg 1931-1938*. Vol. II, Part I. (Nationalmuseets skrifter, Vol. IV.) København: Nationalmuseet, 1958.

Giveon, Raphael. *Les bédouins Shosou des documents égyptiens*. Leiden: E. J. Brill, 1971.

Gjerstad, Einar, *et al. The Swedish Cyprus Expedition*. Vol. II, Part 2. 4 vols. Stockholm: The Swedish Cyprus Expedition, 1948.

Glueck, Nelson. *Explorations in Eastern Palestine*. Vol. I. (Annual of the American Schools of Oriental Research, Vol. XIV.) New Haven: American Schools of Oriental Research, 1933.

_____. *Explorations in Eastern Palestine*. Vol. II. (Annual of the American Schools of Oriental Research, Vol. XV.) New Haven: American Schools of Oriental Research, 1934.

_____. *Explorations in Eastern Palestine*. Vol. III. (Annual of the American Schools of Oriental Research, Vols. XVIII-XIX.) New Haven: American Schools of Oriental Research, 1939.

_____. *Explorations in Eastern Palestine*. Vol. IV. 2 parts. (Annual of the American Schools of Oriental Research, Vols. XXV-XXVIII.) New Haven: American Schools of Oriental Research, 1951.

_____. *The Other Side of the Jordan*. New Haven: American Schools of Oriental Research, 1940.

_____. *The River Jordan*. Philadelphia: The Westminster Press, 1946.

Goldman, Hetty. *Excavations at Gözlü Kule, Tarsus*. Vol. II: *From the Neolithic through the Bronze Age*. Princeton: Princeton University Press, 1956.

_____. *Excavations at Gözlü Kule, Tarsus*. Vol. III: *Iron Age*. Princeton: Princeton University Press, 1963.

Grant, Elihu. *Beth Shemesh (Palestine): Progress of the Haverford Archaeological Expedition*. Haverford: Privately Published, 1929.

Grant, Elihu, and Wright, G. Ernest. *Ain Shems Excavations (Palestine)*. 5 vols. Haverford: Privately Published, 1931-39.

Guy, P. L. O., and Engberg, Robert M. *Megiddo Tombs*. (Oriental Institute Publications, Vol. XXXIII.) Chicago: University of Chicago Press, 1938.

Hachmann, Rolf, and Kuschke, Arnulf. *Bericht über die Ergebnisse der Ausgrabungen in Kamid el-Loz (Libanon) in den Jahren 1963 and 1964*. Bonn: Rudolf Habelt Verlag, 1966.

Haines, Richard C. *Excavations in the Plain of Antioch*. Vol. II (Oriental Institute Publications, Vol. XCV.) Chicago: University of Chicago, 1971.

Haller, Arndt. *Gräber und Grüfte aus Assur*. (Wissenschaftliche Veröffentlichung der Deutschen Orient-Gesellschaft, Band 65.) Berlin: Verlag Gebr. Mann, 1954.

Harden, Donald. *The Phoenicians*. London: Thames and Hudson, 1962.

Harding, G. Lankester. *Archaeology in the Aden Protectorates*. London: Her Majesty's Stationery Office, 1964.

Helck, Wolfgang. *Die Beziehungen Ägyptens zu Vorderasien im 3. und 2. Jahrtausend v. Chr.* (Ägyptologische Abhandlungen, Band 5.) Wiesbaden: Otto Harrassowitz, 1962.

Hennessy, J. Basil. *The Foreign Relations of Palestine during the Early Bronze Age*. London: Bernard Quaritch, Ltd., 1967.

Hestrin, Ruth. *The Philistines and the Other Sea Peoples*. Jerusalem: The Israel Museum, 1970. Hebrew and English.

Hoftijzer, Jacob and van der Kooij, G. *Aramaic Texts from Deir 'Allā*. (Documenta et monumenta orientis antiqui, Vol. XIX.) Leiden: E. J. Brill, 1976.

Hogarth, D. G. *Carchemish*. Part I: *Introductory*. London: British Museum, 1914.

Hrouda, Barthel. *Die bemalte Keramik des zweiten Jahrtausends in Nordmesopotamien und Nordsyrien*. (Istanbuler Forschungen, Band 19.) Berlin: Verlag Gebr. Mann, 1957.

_____. *Die Kulturgeschichte des assyrischen Flachbildes*. (Saarbrückner Beiträge zur Altertumskunde, Band 2.) Bonn: Rudolf Habelt Verlag, 1965.

_____. *Tell Halaf*. Vol. IV. Berlin: Walter de Gruyter, 1962.

James, Frances. *The Iron Age at Beth Shan: A Study of Levels VI-IV*. Philadelphia: The University Museum, University of Pennsylvania, 1966.

Jaussen, et Savignac, RR. PP. *Mission archéologique en Arabie. Vol. II: Atlas*. Paris: Librairie Paul Geuthner, 1914.

Karageorghis, Vassos. *Excavations in the Necropolis of Salamis I*. (Republic of Cyprus, Ministry of Communications and Works, Department of Antiquities, Salamis, Vol. III.) Nicosia: Published for the Republic of Cyprus by the Department of Antiquities, 1967.

Karo, George. *Die Schachtgräber von Mykenai*. München: Verlag F. Brackmann A.-G., 1930, 1933.

Kelso, James L. *The Excavations of Bethel (1934-1960)*. (Annual of the American Schools of Oriental Research, Vol. XXXIX.) Cambridge: American Schools of Oriental Research, 1968.

Kenyon, Kathleen M. *Excavations at Jericho*. 2 vols. Jerusalem: British School of Archaeology in Jerusalem, 1960 and 1965.

King, W. L. *Bronze Reliefs from the Gates of Shalmaneser King of Assyria, B.C. 860-825*. London: British Museum, 1915.

Lamon, Robert S., and Shipton, Geoffrey M. *Megiddo I, Seasons of 1925-34, Strata I-V*. (Oriental Institute Publications, Vol. XLII.) Chicago: University of Chicago Press, 1939.

Langenegger, Felix; Müller, Karl; and Naumann, Rudolf. *Tell Halaf*. Vol. II: *Die Bauwerke*. Berlin: Walter de Gruyter, 1950.

Lapp, Paul W. *The Dhahr Mirzbâneh Tombs*. (American Schools of Oriental Research Publications of the Jerusalem School, Archaeology, Vol. IV.) New Haven: American Schools of Oriental Research, 1966.

Loat, William L. A. *Gurob*. London: Bernard Quaritch,

1905.

van Loon, Maurits. *Urartian Art, Its Distinctive Traits in the Light of New Excavations.* (Uitgaven van het Nederlands Historisch-Archaeologisch Instituut te Istanbul, Vol. XX.) Istanbul: Nederlands Historisch-Archaeologisch Instituut, 1966.

Loud, Gordon. *Megiddo Ivories.* (Oriental Institute Publications, Vol. LII.) Chicago: University of Chicago Press, 1939.

_____. *Megiddo II Seasons of 1935-39.* (Oriental Institute Publications, Vol. LXII.) Chicago: University of Chicago Press, 1948.

McCown, Donald E., and Haines, Richard C. *Nippur I.* (Oriental Institute Publications, Vol. LXXVIII.) Chicago: University of Chicago Press, 1967.

Mallowan, Max E. L. *Nimrud and Its Remains.* 3 vols. London: Collins, 1966.

Matthiae, Paolo. *Ebla, un impero ritrovato.* Turin: Guilio Einaudi, 1977.

May, Herbert G. *Oxford Bible Atlas.* London: Oxford University Press, 1962.

Mittmann, Siegfried. *Beiträge zur Siedlungs- und Territorialgeschichte des nördlichen Ostjordanlandes.* (Abhandlungen des Deutschen Palästinavereins.) Wiesbaden: Otto Harrassowitz, 1970.

Moortgat, Anton. *Tell Halaf III.* Berlin: Walter de Gruyter, 1955.

Moscati, Sabatino. *The World of the Phoenicians.* London: Weidenfeld and Nicolson, 1968.

Naville, Édwouard H., and Griffith, F. *The Mound of the Jews and the City of Onias: Antiquities of Tell el Yahudiyeh.* London: British School of Archaeology in Egypt, 1887, 1890.

Noth, Martin. *The History of Israel.* 2nd ed. New York: Harper and Brothers, 1960.

Oren, Eliezer D. *The Northern Cemetery of Beth Shan.* Leiden: E. J. Brill, 1973.

Orthmann, Winfried. *Untersuchungen zur späthethitischen Kunst.* (Saarbrückner Beiträge zur Altertumskunde, Band 8.) Bonn: Rudolf Habelt Verlag, 1971.

Ottosson, Magnus. *Gilead: Tradition and History.* (Coniectanae Biblica: Old Testament Series, No. 3.) Lund: C. W. K. Gleerup, 1969.

Perrot, J., and Chipiez, C. *History of Art in Sardinia, Judea, Syria and Asia Minor.* Vol. II. London: Chapman and Hall, Ltd., 1890.

Petrie, Flinders. *Kahun, Gurob and Hawara.* London: K. Paul, Trench, Trübner and Company, 1890.

_____. *Ancient Gaza IV.* London: British School of Archaeology in Egypt, 1934.

_____. *Beth-Pelet I (Tell Fara).* London: British School of Archaeology in Egypt, 1930.

_____. *Gerar.* London: British School of Archaeology in Egypt, 1928.

_____. *Researches in Sinai.* New York: E. P. Dutton, 1906.

_____. *Tannis.* Vol. II. London: British School of Archaeology in Egypt. 1888.

Pézard, Maurice. *Qadesh.* (Haut-commissariat de la République française en Syrie et au Liban, Service des antiquités et des beaux-arts, Bibliothèque archéologique et historique, Tome XV.) Paris: Librairie Orientaliste Paul Geuthner, 1931.

Porada, Edith. *The Art of Ancient Iran.* (Art of the World, Vol. XVI.) London: Methuen, 1965.

Porter, Bertha, and Moss, Rosalind L. B. *Topographical Bibliography of Ancient Egyptian Hieroglyphic Texts, Reliefs, and Paintings.* Vol. VII: *Nubia, the Deserts, and Outside Egypt.* Oxford: Griffith Institute, Ashmolean Museum, 1962.

Pritchard, James B. *Palestinian Figurines in Relation to Certain Goddesses Known through Literature.* New Haven: American Oriental Society, 1943.

_____. *The Bronze Age Cemetery at Gibeon.* Philadelphia: University of Pennsylvania Museum, 1963.

Reed, William L., and Winnett, Fred V. *The Excavations at Dhibon (Dhībân) in Moab.* (Annual of the American Schools of Oriental Research, Vols. XXXVI-XXXVII.) New Haven: American Schools of Oriental Research, 1964.

Reifenberg, Adolf. *Hebrew Seals.* London: The East and West Library, 1950.

Reuther, Oscar. *Die Innenstadt von Babylon (Merkes).* (Wissenschaftliche Veröffentlichung der Deutschen Orient-Gesellschaft, Band 47.) Leipzig: J. C. Hinrichs'sche Buchhandlung, 1926.

Riis, Poul J. *Les Cimetières à Crémation: Hama, fouilles et recherches de la Fondation Carlsberg 1931-1938.* (Nationalmuseets skrifter, Vol. I.) København: Nordick Forlag, 1948.

Rothenberg, Beno. *Timna: Valley of the Biblical Copper Mines.* London: Thames and Hudson, 1972.

Saller, Sylvester J., and Bagatti, Ballarimino. *The Town of Nebo (Khirbet el-Mekhayyat).* (Publications of the Studium Biblicum Franciscanum, No. 7.) Jerusalem: Franciscan Press, 1949.

Schaeffer, Claude F.-A. *Ugaritica.* Vol. II. (Institut français d'archéologie de Beyrouth, Bibliothèque archéologique et historique, Tome LXVII.) Paris: Librairie Orientaliste Paul Geuthner, 1949.

Schliemann, Henry. *Mycenae.* New York: Benjamin Blom, Reissued 1967.

Schmidt, Erich F. *Persepolis.* Vol. I. (Oriental Institute Publications, Vol. XLVIII.) Chicago: University of Chicago Press, 1953.

Shipton, Geoffrey M. *Notes on the Megiddo Pottery of Strata VI-XX.* (Studies in Ancient Oriental Civilization, No. 17.) Chicago: University of Chicago Press, 1939.

Sellers, Ovid R., et al. *The 1957 Excavation at Beth-Zur.* (Annual of the American Schools of Oriental Research, Vol. XXXVIII.) Cambridge: American Schools of Oriental Research, 1968.

Sellin, Ernst. *Tell Ta'annek.* (Denkschriften der Kaiserlichen Akademie der Wissenschaften in Wien, Philosophisch-historische klasse, Band 50.) Wien: Carl Gerold's Sohn, 1904.

Sinclair, Lawrence A. *An Archaeological Study of Gibeah (Tell el Fûl).* Part I. (Annual of the American Schools of Oriental Research, Vols. XXXIV-XXXV.) New Haven: American Schools of Oriental Research, 1960.

Smith, George Adam. *Atlas of the Historical Geography of the Holy Land.* London: Hodder and Stoughton, 1915.

_____. *The Historical Geography of the Holy Land.* 7th ed. New York: A. C. Armstrong and Son, 1901.

Smith, Robert H. *Pella of the Decapolis.* Vol. I. Wooster:

College of Wooster, 1973.

Smith, W. Stevenson. *The Art and Architecture of Ancient Egypt*. Baltimore: Penguin Books, 1965.

Strommenger, Eva. *Gefässe aus Uruk von der neubabylonischen Zeit bis zu den Sasaniden*. (Ausgrabungen der Deutschen Forschungsgemeinschaft in Uruk-Warka, Band 7.) Berlin: Verlag Gebr. Mann, 1967.

Thompson, Thomas L. *The Historicity of the Patriarchal Narratives*. Berlin: Walter de Gruyter, 1974.

Thureau-Dangin, François, *et al. Arslan-Tash*. (Haut-commissariat de la République française en Syrie et au Liban. Service des antiquités. Bibliothèque archéologique et historique, Tome XVI.) Paris: Librairie Orientaliste Paul Geuthner, 1931.

Thureau-Dangin, François, and Dunand, Maurice. *Til-Barsib*. (Haut-commissariat de la République française en Syrie et au Liban. Service des antiquités. Bibliothèque archéologique et historique, Tome XXIII.) Paris: Librairie Orientaliste Paul Geuthner, 1936.

Tufnell, Olga. *Lachish*. Vol. III: *The Iron Age*. 2 parts. (The Wellcome-Marston Archaeological Research Expedition to the Near East, Vol. III.) London: Oxford University Press, 1953.

Tushingham, A. Douglas. *The Excavations at Dibon (Dhiban) in Moab: The Third Campaign 1952-53*. (Annual of the American Schools of Oriental Research, Vol. XL.) Cambridge: American Schools of Oriental Research, 1972.

Vandier, J. *Manuel d'archéologie égyptienne*. Tome III: *Les grandes époques: la statuaire*. Paris: Editions A. et J. Picard et Cie, 1958.

van Zyl, A. H. *The Moabites*. (Pretoria Oriental Series, Vol. III.) Leiden: E. J. Brill, 1960.

Ventris, M., and Chadwick, J. *Documents in Mycenaean Greek*. Cambridge: Cambridge University Press, 1956.

von Bissing, W. *Fayencegefässe*. Vienne: Adolph Holzhausen, 1902.

_____. *Steingefässe*. Vienne: Adolph Holzhausen, 1907.

_____. *Zeit und Herkunft der in Cerveteri gefunden Gefässe aus ägyptischer Fayence und glosiertem Ton*. München: Bayerischen Akademie der Wissenschaften, 1941.

Wampler, Joseph C. *Tell en-Naṣbeh*. Vol. II: *The Pottery*. Berkeley and New Haven: The Palestine Institute of Pacific School of Religion and the American Schools of Oriental Research, 1947.

Wiseman, Donald J. *The Alalakh Tablets*. London: British Institute of Archaeology at Ankara, 1953.

Yadin, Yigael, *et al. Hazor*. 4 vols. Jerusalem: Magnes Press, 1958-61.

Articles

Abou Assaf, Ali. "Der Friedhof von Yabroud," *Annales archéologiques Arabes Syriennes*, XVII (1967), 55-68.

_____. "Tell Aschtara in Süd Syrien. Erst Kampagne 1966," *Annales archéologiques Arabes Syriennes*, XVIII (1968), 103-22.

Aharoni, Yohanan, and Amiran, Ruth. "A New Scheme for the Subdivision of the Iron Age in Palestine," *Israel Exploration Journal*, VIII (1958), 171-84.

_____. "Excavations at Tell Arad," *Israel Exploration Journal*, XIV (1964), 131-47.

Aharoni, Yohanan; Fritz, Volkmar; and Kempinski, Aharon. "Vorbericht über die Ausgrabungen auf der Ḫirbet el-Mšāš (Tel Māśôś), 2. Kampagne 1974," *Zeitschrift des Deutschen Palästina-Vereins*, XCI (1975), 109-34.

Albright, William F. "The Archaeological Results of an Expedition to Moab and the Dead Sea," *Bulletin of the American Schools of Oriental Research*, XIV (1924), 2-12.

_____. "An Anthropoid Clay Coffin from Sahab in the Transjordan," *American Journal of Archaeology*, XXXVI (1932), 295-306.

_____. "Soundings at Ader, a Bronze Age City of Moab," *Bulletin of the American Schools of Oriental Research*. LIII (1934), 14.

_____. "Ostracon No. 6043 from Ezion-geber," *Bulletin of the American Schools of Oriental Research*, LXXXII (1941), 11-15.

_____. "Correspondence with Professor Einar Gjerstad on the Chronology of 'Cypriote' Pottery from Early Iron Levels in Palestine," *Bulletin of the American Schools of Oriental Research*, CXXX (1953), 22-26.

_____. "The Chronology of Middle Bronze I (Early Bronze-Middle Bronze)," *Bulletin of the American Schools of Oriental Research*, CLXVIII (1962), 36-42.

_____. "Syria, the Philistines and Phoenicia," *Cambridge Ancient History* Vol. II, Chapter xxxiii. Revised edition. Cambridge: Cambridge University Press, 1966, 24-33.

_____. "Some Comments on the 'Amman Citadel Inscription," *Bulletin of the American Schools of Oriental Research*, CXCVIII (1970), 38-40.

Albright, William F.; Kelso, James L.; and Thorley, J. Palin. "Early Bronze Pottery from Bâb ed-Drâ' in Moab," *Bulletin of the American Schools of Oriental Research*, XCV (1944), 3-13.

Amiran, Ruth. "A Late Assyrian Stone Bowl from Tell El Qiṭaf in the Bet-She'an Valley," *Atiqot*, I-II (1955-1959), 129-32.

'Amr, A. Jalil. "Excavations at Meqablein," *Annual of the Department of Antiquities of Jordan*, XVIII (1973), XLIII-XLVI.

Avigad, Nahaman. "Excavations at Makmish, 1958," *Israel Exploration Journal*, X (1960), 90-96.

_____. "Ammonite and Moabite Seals," *Near Eastern Archaeology in the Twentieth Century*, edited by James A. Sanders. Garden City: Doubleday and Company, Inc., 1970, pp. 284-95.

Barag, Don. "The Glass Aryballos," *Atiqot*, V (1965), 58-59.

Barnett, Richard D. "Four Sculptures from Amman," *Annual of the Department of Antiquities of Jordan*, I (1951), 34-36.

Bartoccini, Renato. "Ricerche e scoperte della missione italiana in Amman," *Bollettino dell'Associazione internazionale degli studi mediterranei*, I (1930), fasc. 3, 15-17.

_____. "Scavi ad Amman della missione archeologica italiana," *Bollettino dell'Associazione inter-*

nazionale degli studi mediterranei, III (1932), fasc. 2, 16-23.

Bartoccini, Renato. "Scavi ad Ammàn della missione archeologica italiana," *Bollettino dell'Associazione internazionale degli studi mediterranei*, IV (1933-34), fasc. 4-5, 10-15.

Ben-Dor, I. "Palestinian Alabaster Vases," *Quarterly of the Department of Antiquities of Palestine*, XI (1941), 93-112.

Bennett, Crystal -M. "Fouilles d'Umm el-Biyara," *Revue Biblique*, LXXIII (1966), 372-403.

_____. "Tawilan," *Revue Biblique*, LXXVI (1969), 386-90.

_____. "Buseira," *Revue Biblique*, LXXIX (1972), 426-30 and pl. XLIV.

_____. "A Brief Note on Excavations at Tawilan, Jordan, 1968-70," *Levant*, IV (1972), v-vii and pl. II.

_____. "Excavations at Buseirah, Southern Jordan, 1971: A Preliminary Report," *Levant*, V (1973), 1-11 and pls. I-VIII.

_____. "Excavations at Buseirah, Southern Jordan, 1972: Preliminary Report," *Levant*, VI (1974), 1-24.

_____. "Excavations at Buseirah, Southern Jordan, 1973: Third Preliminary Report," *Levant*, VII (1975), 1-19.

_____. "Excavations at Buseirah, Southern Jordan, 1974: Fourth Preliminary Report," *Levant*, IX (1977), 1-10.

_____. "Excavations at the Citadel (El Qal'ah), Amman, Jordan," *Levant*, X (1978), 1-9.

Boraas, Roger S. "A Preliminary Sounding at Rujm El-Malfuf, 1969," *Annual of the Department of Antiquities of Jordan*, XVI (1971), 31-45 and figs. 1-41.

Boraas, Roger S., and Horn, Siegfried H. "Heshbon 1968: The First Campaign at Tell Ḥesbân," *Andrews University Seminary Studies*, VII (1969), 97-222.

_____. "The Fourth Campaign at Tell Ḥesbân," *Andrews University Seminary Studies*, XIV (1976), 1-216.

_____. "The Fifth Campaign at Tell Ḥesbân," *Andrews University Seminary Studies*, XVI (1978), 1-200.

Bordreuil, Pierre. "Inscriptions des têtes à double face," *Annual of the Department of Antiquities of Jordan*, XVIII (1973), 37-39.

Braidwood, Robert J. "Report on Two Sondages on the Coast of Syria, South of Tartous," *Syria*, XXI (1940), 183-221.

Chapman, Susannah Vibert. "A Catalogue of Iron Age Pottery from the Cemeteries of Khirbet Silm, Joya, Qrayé and Qasmieh of South Lebanon," *Berytus*, XXI (1972), 55-194.

Chehab, Maurice. "Les terres cuites de Kharayeb," *Bulletin de Musée de Beyrouth*, X (1951-52), text, XI (1953-54), plates.

Coughenour, Robert A. "Preliminary Report on the Exploration and Excavation of Mugharat el Wardeh and Abu Thawab," *Annual of the Department of Antiquities of Jordan*, XXI (1976), 71-78.

Cross, Frank Moore. "An Ostracon from Heshbon," *Andrews University Seminary Studies*, VII (1969), 223-29.

_____. "Epigraphic Notes on the Amman Citadel Inscription," *Bulletin of the American Schools of Oriental Research*, CXCIII (1969), 13-19.

_____. "Notes on the Ammonite Inscription from Tell Sīrān," *Bulletin of the American Schools of Oriental Research*, CCXII (1973), 12-15.

Crowfoot, John W. "Soundings at Balu'ah," *Palestine Exploration Fund Quarterly Statement*, LXVI (1934), 56-63.

Culican, William. "The Graves at Tell Er-Reqeish," *The Australian Journal of Biblical Archaeology*, II (1973), no. 2, 66-105.

Dajani, Awni K. "An Iron Age Tomb at Al-Jib," *Annual of the Department of Antiquities of Jordan*, II (1953), 66-74.

Dajani, Rafik W. "A Neo-Babylonian Seal from Amman," *Annual of the Department of Antiquities of Jordan*, VI-VII (1962), 124-25.

_____. "An (EB-MB) Burial from Amman," *Annual of the Department of Antiquities of Jordan*, XII-XIII (1967-68), 68-69.

_____. "An Iron Age Tomb from Amman," *Annual of the Department of Antiquities of Jordan*, XI (1966), 41-47.

_____. "Iron Age Tombs from Irbed," *Annual of the Department of Antiquities of Jordan*, VIII-IX (1964), 99-101.

_____. "Jebel Nuzha Tomb at Amman," *Annual of the Department of Antiquities of Jordan*, XI (1966), 48-52.

_____. "A Late Bronze-Iron Age Tomb Excavated at Sahab, 1968," *Annual of the Department of Antiquities of Jordan*, XV (1970), 29-34.

Dayton, John E. "Midianite and Edomite Pottery," *Proceedings of the Fifth Seminar for Arabian Studies* (London: Seminary for Arabian Studies), pp. 25-38.

de Contenson, Henri. "Three Soundings in the Jordan Valley," *Annual of the Department of Antiquities of Jordan*, IV-V (1960), 12-31 and figs. 1-18.

_____. "The 1953 Survey in the Yarmuk and Jordan Valleys," *Annual of the Department of Antiquities of Jordan*, VIII-IX (1964), 30-46.

Dever, William G. "The EBIV-MBI Horizon in Transjordan and Southern Palestine," *Bulletin of the American Schools of Oriental Research*, CCX (1973), 37-62.

de Vaux, Roland. "La troisième campagne de fouilles a Tell el-Far'ah, près Naplouse," *Revue Biblique*, LVIII (1951), 393-430.

_____. "Les fouilles de Tell el-Far'ah, près Naplouse," *Revue Biblique*, LVIII (1951), 566-90.

_____. "Palestine during the Neolithic and Chalcolithic Periods," *Cambridge Ancient History*, Vol. I, Chapters ixb and v-viii. Revised edition. Cambridge: Cambridge University Press, 1966, 35-59.

Dothan, Trude. "Archaeological Reflections on the Philistine Problem," *Antiquity and Survival*, II, No. 2/3 (1957), 151-64.

_____. "Philistine Civilization in the Light of Archaeological Finds in Palestine and Egypt," *Eretz Israel*, V (1958), 55-56.

_____. "Anthropoid Clay Coffins from a Late Bronze Age Cemetery near Deir el-Balah (Preliminary Report)," *Israel Exploration Journal*, XXII (1972), 65-72 and plates 9-13.

_____. "Anthropoid Clay Coffins from a Late Bronze Age Cemetery near Deir el-Balaḥ (Preliminary Report II)," *Israel Exploration Journal*, XXIII

(1973), 129-146 and plates 33-44.

Driver, Godfrey R. "Seals from 'Amman and Petra," *Quarterly of the Department of Antiquities of Palestine*, XI (1945), 81-82.

Dyson, Robert H. "Review of *Nimrud and its Remains*," *American Journal of Archaeology*, LXXIII (1969), 79-80.

Edelstein, Gershon, and Levy, Shalom. "Cinq années de fouilles a Tel 'Amal (Nir David)," *Revue Biblique*, LXXIX (1972), 325-67 and pls. XVIII-XXVIII.

Franken, Henk J. "Excavations at Deir 'Allā in Jordan," *Vetus Testamentum*, X (1960), 386-93.

————. "The Excavations at Deir 'Allā in Jordan: Second Season," *Vetus Testamentum*, XI (1961), 361-72.

————. "The Excavations at Deir 'Allā in Jordan: 3rd Season," *Vetus Testamentum*, XII (1962), 378-82.

————. "The Excavations at Deir 'Allā, Season 1964," *Vetus Testamentum*, XIV (1964), 417-22.

Franken, Henk J. "Texts from the Persian Period from Tell Deir 'Allā," *Vetus Testamentum*, XVII (1967), 480-81.

Franken, Henk J., and Ibrahim, Moawiyah M. "Two Seasons of Excavations at Tell Deir 'Allā, 1976-1978," *Annual of the Department of Antiquities of Jordan*, XXII (1977-78), 57-80.

Fritz, Volkmar. "Erwägung zu dem spätbronzezeitlichen Quadratbau bei Amman," *Zeitschrift des Deutschen Palästina-Vereins*, LXXXI (1971), 140-52.

Garbini, Giovanni. "The Stepped Pinnacle," *East and West*, IX (1958), 85-91.

Garstang, John. "Jericho: City and Necropolis," *Liverpool Annals of Archaeology and Anthropology*, XX (1933), 3-42.

Glueck, Nelson. "Ezion-geber," *The Biblical Archaeologist*, XXVIII (1965), 70-87.

————. "Ostraca from Elath," *Bulletin of the American Schools of Oriental Research*, LXXX (1940), 3-10.

————. "Ostraca from Elath," *Bulletin of the American Schools of Oriental Research*, LXXXII (1941), 3-11.

————. "Some Edomite Pottery from Tell el-Kheleifeh, Parts I and II," *Bulletin of the American Schools of Oriental Research*, CLXXXVIII (1967), 8-38.

————. "Some Ezion-geber: Elath Iron II Pottery," *Eretz Israel*, IX (1969), 51-59.

————. "The Civilization of the Edomites," *The Biblical Archaeologist*, X (1947), 77-84.

————. "The First Campaign at Tell el-Kheleifeh (Ezion-geber)," *Bulletin of the American Schools of Oriental Research*, LXXI (1937), 3-17.

————. "The Recently Discovered Ore Deposits in Eastern Palestine," *Bulletin of the American Schools of Oriental Research*, LXIII (1936), 4-8.

————. "The Second Campaign at Tell el-Kheleifeh (Ezion-geber: Elath)," *Bulletin of the American Schools of Oriental Research*, LXXV (1939), 8-22.

————. "The Topography and History of Ezion-geber and Elath," *Bulletin of the American Schools of Oriental Research*, LXXII (1938), 2-13.

————. "Three Israelite Towns in the Jordan Valley: Zarethan, Succoth, Zaphon," *Bulletin of the American Schools of Oriental Research*, XCIII (1943), 2-23.

Güterbock, Hans G. "Carchemish," *Journal of Near Eastern Studies*, XIII (1954), 102-14.

Hadidi, Adnan. "The Pottery from the Roman Forum at Amman," *Annual of the Department of Antiquities of Jordan*, XV (1970), 11-15 and pls. I-VI.

Hamilton, R. W. "Excavations at Tell Abu Hawam," *Quarterly of the Department of Antiquities of Palestine*, IV (1935), 1-69.

Hammond, Phillip C. "An Ammonite Stamp Seal from Amman," *Bulletin of the American Schools of Oriental Research*, CLX (1960), 38-41.

Hankey, Vronwy. "A Late Bronze Age Temple at Amman: I. The Aegean Pottery," *Levant*, VI (1974), 131-59.

————. "A Late Bronze Age Temple at Amman: II. Vases and Objects Made of Stone," *Levant*, VI (1974), 160-78.

Harding, G. Lankester. "An Early Bronze Age Cave at El Husn," *Palestine Exploration Fund Annual*, VI (1953), 1-13.

————. "An Iron Age Tomb at Meqabelein," *Quarterly of the Department of Antiquities of Palestine*, XIV (1950), 44-48.

————. "An Iron Age Tomb at Sahab," *Quarterly of the Department of Antiquities of Palestine*, XIII (1948), 92-103.

————. "Excavations on the Citadel, Amman," *Annual of the Department of Antiquities of Jordan*, I (1951), 7-16.

————. "Recent Discoveries in Jordan," *Palestine Exploration Quarterly*, XC (1958), 10-12.

————. "The Tomb of Adoni Nur in Amman," *Palestine Exploration Fund Annual*, VI (1953), 48-75.

————. "Two Iron Age Tombs, Amman," *Quarterly of the Department of Antiquities of Palestine*, XI (1945), 64-74.

————. "Two Iron-Age Tombs in Amman," *Annual of the Department of Antiquities of Jordan*, I (1951), 37-40.

Harding, G. Lankester, *et al.* "Four Tomb Groups from Jordan," *Palestine Exploration Fund Annual*, VI (1953), 1-72.

Helms, Svend W. "Excavations at Jawa (A Preliminary Report)," *Annual of the Department of Antiquities of Jordan*, XVIII (1973), 41-44.

————. "Jawa Excavations 1974: A Preliminary Report," *Levant*, IX (1977), 22-35.

Henke, Oswald. "Zur Lage von Beth Peor," *Zeitschrift des Deutschen Palästina-Vereins*, LXXV (1959), 155-63.

Hennessy, J. Basil. "British Archaeology Abroad," *Antiquity*, XL (1967), 130.

————. "Excavations of a Late Bronze Age Temple at Amman," *Palestine Exploration Quarterly*, XCVIII (1966), 155-62.

Hentschke, Richard. "Ammonitische Grenzfestungen südwestlich von 'Ammān," *Zeitschrift des Deutschen Palästina-Vereins*, LXXVI (1960), 103-23.

————. "Ammonitische Grenzfestungen zwischen Wādi eṣ Ṣīr und Nā'ūr," *Zeitschrift des Deutschen Palästina-Vereins*, LXXIV (1958), 55-64.

Holland, Thomas A. "A Study of Palestinian Iron Age Baked Clay Figurines, with Special Reference to Jerusalem: Cave 1," *Levant*, X (1978), 121-54.

Horn, Siegfried H. "Excavations at Heshbon," *The Biblical Archaeologist*, XXXII (1969), 35-45.

————. "Three Seals from Sahab Tomb 'C'," *Annual of the Department of Antiquities of Jordan*, XVI

(1971), 103-106.

————. "The Crown of the King of the Ammonites," *Andrews University Seminary Studies*, XI (1973), 170-80 and pls. XVII-XX.

Horsfield, G., and Vincent, L. H. "Une stele Égypto-Moabite au Balou'a," *Revue Biblique*, XLI (1932), 416-44.

Huesman, John E. "Tell es-Sa'idiyeh," *Revue Biblique*, LXXV (1968), 236-38.

Iback, Robert, Jr. "Archaeological Survey of the Hesbân Region," *Andrews University Seminary Studies*, XIV (1976), 119-26.

————. "Expanded Archaeological Survey of the Hesbân Region," *Andrews University Seminary Studies*, XVI (1978), 201-14.

Ibrahim, Moawiyah M. "Two Ammonite Statuettes from Khirbet El-Hajjar," *Annual of the Department of Antiquities of Jordan*, XVI (1971), 91-97 and pls. 1-3.

————. "Archaeological Excavations in Jordan, 1971," *Annual of the Department of Antiquities of Jordan*, XVI (1971), 113-15.

————. "Archaeological Excavations at Sahab, 1972," *Annual of the Department of Antiquities of Jordan*, XVII (1972), 23-36.

————. "Second Season of Excavation at Sahab, 1973," *Annual of the Department of Antiquities of Jordan*, XIX (1974), 55-61 and 187-98.

————. "Third Season of Excavations at Sahab, 1975," *Annual of the Department of Antiquities of Jordan*, XX (1975), 69-82 and 169-78.

————. "The Collared-rim Jar of the Early Iron Age," *Archaeology in the Levant*, edited by Roger Moorey and Peter Parr. London: Aris and Phillips, 1978, pp. 116-26.

Ibrahim, Moawiyah M.; Sauer, James A.; and Yassine, Khair N. "The East Jordan Valley Survey, 1975," *Bulletin of the American Schools of Oriental Research*, CCXXII (1976), 41-66.

Iliffe, J. H. "A Model Shrine of Phoenician Style," *Quarterly of the Department of Antiquities of Palestine*, XI (1944), 91-92.

Kalsbeek, Jan, and London, Gloria. "A Late Second Millennium B.C. Potting Puzzle," *Bulletin of the American Schools of Oriental Research*, CCXXXII (1978), 47-56.

Kenna, V. E. G. "A L.B. Stamp Seal from Jordan," *Annual of the Department of Antiquities of Jordan*, XVIII (1973), 79 and pl. L:1.

Kerestes, Terry M.; Lundquist, John M.; Wood, Brian G.; and Yassine, Khair N. "An Archaeological Survey of the Three Reservoir Areas in Northern Jordan, 1978," *Annual of the Department of Antiquities of Jordan*, XXII (1977-78), 108-35.

Kitchen, Kenneth A. "Some New Light on the Asiatic Wars of Ramesses II." *Journal of Egyptian Archaeology*, L (1964), 47-70.

Kjaer, Hans. "The Excavations of Shiloh 1929," *Journal of the Palestine Oriental Society*, X (1930), 87-174.

Landes, George M. "The Material Civilization of the Ammonites," *The Biblical Archaeologist*, XXIV (1961), 65-86.

Lapp, Paul W. "The 1961 Excavations at 'Araq El-Emir," *Annual of the Department of Antiquities of Jordan*, VI-VII (1962), 80-89.

————. "Bâb edh-Dhrâ'," *Newsletter of the Ameri-can Schools of Oriental Research*, 1965, no. 8, p. 3.

————. "Bâb edh-Dhrâ' Tomb A76 and Early Bronze I in Palestine," *Bulletin of the American Schools of Oriental Research*, CLXXXIX (1968), 34-38.

————. "Tell er-Rumeith," *Revue Biblique*, LXXV (1968), 98-105.

————. "The Cemetery at Bab edh Dhra', Jordan," *Archaeology*, XIX (1966), 106-10.

————. "Palestine in the Early Bronze Age," *Near Eastern Archaeology in the Twentieth Century*, edited by James A. Sanders. Garden City: Double-day and Company, Inc., 1970, pp. 101-24.

Loffreda, Stanislao, "Iron Age Rock-cut tombs in Palestine," *Liber Annuus*, XVIII (1968), 244-87.

Lugenbeal, Edward N., and Sauer, James A. "Seventh-Sixth Century B.C. Pottery from Area B at Heshbon," *Andrews University Seminary Studies*, X (1972), 21-69 and pls. A-C, I-XI.

Ma'ayeh, Farah S. "Recent Archaeological Discoveries in Jordan," *Annual of the Department of Antiquities of Jordan*, IV-V (1960), 114.

Macalister, Robert A. S. "Some Interesting Pottery Re-mains," *Palestine Exploration Quarterly Statement*, XLVII (1915), 35-37.

Mackenzie, Duncan. "Megalithic Monuments of Rab-bath Ammon at Ammān," *Palestine Exploration Fund Annual*, I (1911), 1-40.

Mazar, Benjamin. "The Tobiads," *Israel Exploration Journal*, VII (1957), 137-45, and 229-38.

Mazar, Benjamin, *et al.* "En-Gedi," *Atiqot*, V (1966), 1-100.

McCreery, David W. "Preliminary Report of the A. P. C. Township Archaeological Survey," *Annual of the Department of Antiquities of Jordan*, XXII (1977-78), 150-62.

McEwan, C. W. "The Syrian Expedition of the Oriental Institute of the University of Chicago," *American Journal of Archaeology*, XLI (1937), 8-13.

Mellaart, James. "Preliminary Report on the Archae-ological Survey in the Yarmuk and Jordan Valley for the Point Four Irrigation Scheme," *Annual of the Department of Antiquities of Jordan*, VI-VII (1962), 126-57.

Miller, Max. "The Moabite Stone as a Memorial Stela," *Palestine Exploration Quarterly*, CLX (1974), 9-18.

Naveh, Joseph. "The Excavations at Meṣad Ḥashavyahu," *Israel Exploration Journal*, XII (1962), 89-113.

Negbi, Ora. "A Deposit of Terracottas and Statuettes from Tell Ṣippor," *Atiqot*, VI (1967), 1-27.

Noth, Martin. "Beiträge zur Geschichte des Ost-Jordanlandes," *Beiträge zur Biblischen Landes und Altertumskunde*, III (1949).

Oates, Joan. "Late Assyrian Pottery from Fort Shal-maneser," *Iraq*, XXI (1959), 130-46.

Olávarri, Emilio. "Sondages a 'Arô'er sur l'Arnon," *Revue Biblique*, LXXII (1965), 77-94.

————. "Fouilles a 'Arô'er sur l'Arnon," *Revue Bib-lique*, LXXVI (1969), 230-59.

Parr, Peter J. "A Cave at Arqub El Dhahr," *Annual of the Department of Antiquities of Jordan*, III (1956), 61-73.

Parr, Peter J.; Harding, G. L.; and Dayton, J. E. "Pre-liminary Survey in N.W. Arabia, 1968," *Bulletin of the Institute of Archaeology*, X (1972), 23-61 and pls.

1-31.

Peltenburg, E. J. "Al Mina Glazed Pottery and Its Relations," *Levant*, I (1969), 73-96.

Perlman, I.; Asaro, F.; and Dothan, Trude. "Provenance of the Deir el-Balah Coffins," *Israel Exploration Journal*, XXIII (1973), 147-51.

Piccirillo, Michelle. "Una tomba del Ferro I a Mafraq (Giordania)," *Liber Annuus*, XXVI (1976), 27-30.

———. "Una tomba del Ferro I a Madeba," *Liber Annuus*, XXV (1975), 199-224.

———. "Una tomba del Bronzo Medio a Amman," *Liber Annuus*, XXVIII (1978), 73-86.

Pollottino, Massino. "Urartu, Greece and Etruria," *East and West*, IX-X (1958-59), 30-34.

Porada, Edith. "Battlements in the Military Architecture and in the Symbolism of the Ancient Near East," *Essays in Architecture in Honor of Rudolf Wittkown* (London: Phaedon Press, 1967), pp. 1-12.

Prag, Kay. "The Intermediate Early Bronze-Middle Bronze Age: An Interpretation of the Evidence from Transjordan, Syria and Lebanon," *Levant*, VI (1974), 69-116.

Pritchard, James B. "Two Tombs and a Tunnel in the Jordan Valley: Discoveries at Biblical Zarethon," *Expedition*. VII (1965), 26-33.

———. "A Cosmopolitan Culture of the Late Bronze Age," *Expedition*, VII (1965), 26-33.

———. "Tell es-Sa'idiyeh," *Revue Biblique*, LXXIII (1966), 574-76.

———. "New Evidence on the Role of the Sea Peoples," *The Role of the Phoenicians in the Interaction of the Mediterranean Civilizations*, edited by William A. Ward. Beirut: American University of Beirut, 1968, pp. 99-112.

———. "The Palace of Tell es-Sa'idiyeh," *Expedition*, X (1968), 20-22.

———. "An Eighth Century Traveler," *Expedition*, X (1968), 26-29.

———. "On Use of the Tripod Cup," *Ugaritica*. Vol. VI. edited by Claude F. -A. Schaeffer (Institut Français d'archéologie de 'Beyrouth, Bibliothèque archéologique et historique, Tome LXXXI.) Paris: Librairie Orientaliste Paul Geuthner, 1969, pp. 427-34.

Puech, Emile, and Rofé, Alexander. "L'inscription de la citadella d'Amman," *Revue Biblique*, LXXX (1973), 531-46.

Rast, Walter E., and Schaub, R. Thomas. "Survey of the Southeastern Plain of the Dead Sea, 1973," *Annual of the Department of Antiquities of Jordan*, XIX (1974), 5-53.

Reed, William L., and Winnett, Fred V. "A Fragment of an Early Moabite Inscription from Kerak," *Bulletin of the American Schools of Oriental Research*, CLXXII (1963), 1-9.

Rothenberg, Beno. "Ancient Copper Industries in the Western Arabah," *Palestine Exploration Quarterly*, XCIV (1962), 6-71.

———. "King Solomon's Mines No More," *Illustrated London News*, November 15, 1969.

———. "The Egyptian Temple of Timna," *Illustrated London News*, November 29, 1969.

———. "Timna," in "Chronique archéologique" of *Revue Biblique*, LXXIV (1967), 80-85.

Rothenberg, Beno, and Cohen, Ezra. "An Archaeological Survey of the Eloth District and the Southernmost

Negev," *Museum Haaretz Bulletin*, X (1968), 25-35.

Saggs, H. W. F. "The Nimrud Letters 1952, Part II," *Iraq*, XVII (1955), 126-160.

Saidah, Roger. "Fouilles de Khaldé, rapport préliminaire sur la première et deuxième campagnes (1961-1962)," *Bulletin du Musée de Beyrouth*, XIX (1966), 51-90.

Saller, Sylvester. "Bab edh Dhra'," *Liber Annuus*, XV (1964-65), 137-219.

———. "Iron Age Tombs at Nebo, Jordan," *Liber Annuus*, XVI (1966), 260-63.

Sauer, James A. "ACOR, Amman: Director's Report 1976-77," *Newsletter of the American Schools of Oriental Research*, 1977, no. 7, p. 1-11.

Schaeffer, Claude F.-A. "Les fouilles de Minet el Beidah et de Ras-Shamra, quatrième campagne (printemps 1932)," *Syria*, XIV (1933), 93-127.

———. "Les fouilles de Ras Shamra-Ugarit, septième campagne (printemps 1935)," *Syria*, XVII (1936), 126-48.

———. "Résumé des résultats de la XXIIIe campagne de fouilles à Ras Shamra-Ugarit (automne 1960)," *Les Annales archéologiques de Syrie*, XI-XII (1961-1962), 187-96.

Schaub, Thomas R. "An Early Bronze IV Tomb from Bâb edh-Dhrâ'," *Bulletin of the American Schools of Oriental Research*, CCX (1973), 2-19.

van Selms, Adriaan. "Some Remarks on the Amman Citadel Inscription," *Bibliotheca Orientalis*, XXIII (1975), 5-8.

van Seters, John. "The Conquest of Sihon's Kingdom: A Literary Examination," *Journal of Biblical Literature*," CXI (1972), 182-97.

Smith, Robert H. "Pella (Tabaqat Faḥl)," *Revue Biblique*, LXXV (1968), 105-112.

Stern, Ephraim. "New Types of Phoenician Style Decorated Pottery Vases from Palestine," *Palestine Exploration Quarterly*, CX (1978), 1-21.

Stiebing, William H., Jr. "Another Look at the Origins of the Philistine Tombs at Tell el Far'ah (S)," *American Journal of Archaeology*, LXXIV (1970), 139-44.

Stronach, David. "The Development of the Fibula in the Near East," *Iraq*, XXI (1959), 180-206.

Tell, Safwan Kh. "Recent Ammonite Discoveries," *Annual of the Department of Antiquities of Jordan*, XII-XIII (1967-68), ١٢ - ٩ and pls. ٤ - ١ (in Arabic).

Thompson, Henry O. "Ammonites on Campus," *The Australian Journal of Biblical Archaeology*, II (1973), no. 2, 23-30.

Thompson, Henry O. "The Biblical Ammonites," *The Australian Journal of Biblical Archaeology*, II (1973), no. 2, 31-38.

———. "The Excavations at Tell Siran (1972)," *Annual of the Department of Antiquities of Jordan*, XVIII (1973), 5-14 and pls. I-X.

———. "Rujm Al-Malfuf South," *Annual of the Department of Antiquities of Jordan*, XVIII (1973), 47-50 and pls. XXVIII-XXX.

———. "The Ammonite Remains at Khirbet al-Hajjar," *Bulletin of the American Schools of Oriental Research*, CCXXVII (1977), 27-34.

Thompson, Henry O., and Zayadine, Fawzi. "The Tell Siran Inscription," *Bulletin of the American Schools of Oriental Research*, CCXII (1973), 5-11.

Thompson, R. Campbell. "The British Museum Excavations at Nineveh," *Liverpool Annals of Archaeology and Anthropology*, XX (1933), 71-186.

Thomsen, Peter. "Ausgrabungen in Ammân," *Archiv für Orientforschung*, XIV (1941-44), 102.

Toombs, Lawrence E., and Wright, G. Ernest. "The Fourth Campaign at Balâtah (Schechem)," *Bulletin of the American Schools of Oriental Research*, CLXIX (1963), 1-60.

Tufnell, Olga. "The Shihan Warrior," *Iraq*, XV (1953), 161-66.

Tushingham, A. Douglas. "Excavations at Dhibon in Moab, 1952-53," *Bulletin of the American Schools of Oriental Research*, CXXXIII (1954), 6-26.

van Loon, Maurits. "Dress—Ancient Mesopotamia," *Encyclopaedia Britannica* (Chicago: Encyclopaedia Britannica, Inc., 1967), VII, 678-79.

_____. "First Results of the 1967 Excavations at Selenkahiye," *Annales archéologiques Arabes Syriennes*, XVIII (1968), 5-32.

Ward, William A. "Cylinders and Scarabs from a Late Bronze Temple at 'Amman," *Annual of the Department of Antiquities of Jordan*, VIII-IX (1964), 47-55.

_____. "Scarabs, Seals and Cylinders from Two Tombs at Amman," *Annual of the Department of Antiquities of Jordan*, XI (1966), 5-18.

_____. "The Shasu 'Bedouin,' " *Journal of Economic and Social History of the Orient*, XV (1972), 35-60.

_____. "A Possible New Link between Egypt and Jordan during the Reign of Amenhotep III," *Annual of the Department of Antiquities of Jordan*, XVIII (1973), 45-46 and pl. XXVII.

Ward, William A., and Martin, M. F. "The Balu'a Stele: A new transcription with paleographic and historic notes," *Annual of the Department of Antiquities of Jordan*, VIII-IX (1964), 5-29.

Wilson, John A., trans. "The Story of Si-nuhe," *Ancient Near Eastern Texts*, edited by James B. Pritchard (2nd ed.; Princeton: Princeton University Press, 1955), pp. 18-22.

Wright, G. Ernest. "Archaeology of Palestine," *The Bible and the Ancient Near East*, edited by G. E. Wright (Garden City: Doubleday and Company, Inc., 1961), pp. 94-101.

_____. "Fresh Evidence for the Philistine Story," *The Biblical Archaeologist*, XXIX (1966), 70-86.

Wright, G. Ernest. "Philistine Coffins and Mercenaries," *The Biblical Archaeologist*, XXII (1959), 54-66.

Yassine, Khair N. "Anthropoid Coffins from Ragadan Royal Palace Tomb in Amman," *Annual of the Department of Antiquities of Jordan*, XX (1975), 57-68.

Zayadine, Fawzi. "Tomb du Fer II à Samaria-Sebaste," *Revue Biblique*, LXXV (1968), 562-85.

_____. "Recent Excavations on the Citadel of Amman," *Annual of the Department of Antiquities of Jordan*, XVIII (1973), 17-35 and pls. XI-XXVI.

_____. "Note sur l'inscription de la statue d'Amman J. 1656," *Syria*, LI (1974), 129-36.

Zayadine, Fawzi, and Thompson, Henry O. "The Ammonite Inscription from Tell Siran," *Berytus*, XXII (1973), 115-40.

Unpublished Material

Landes, George M. "A History of the Ammonites." Unpublished Ph.D. dissertation, Department of Near Eastern Studies, Johns Hopkins University, 1956.

FIGURE 1. GEOGRAPHICAL UNITS IN THE TRANSJORDAN

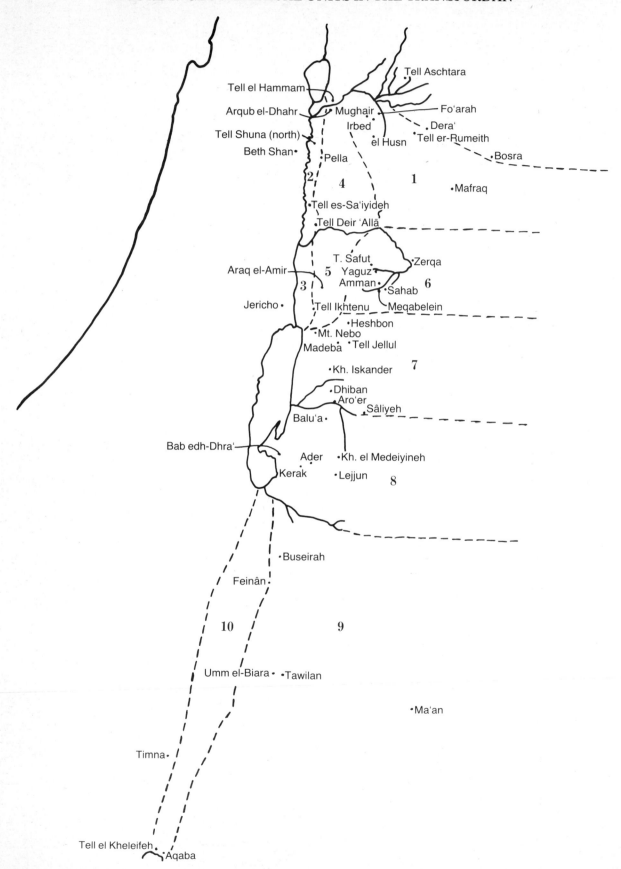

FIGURE 2. AMMAN DISTRICT, REGIONAL MAP

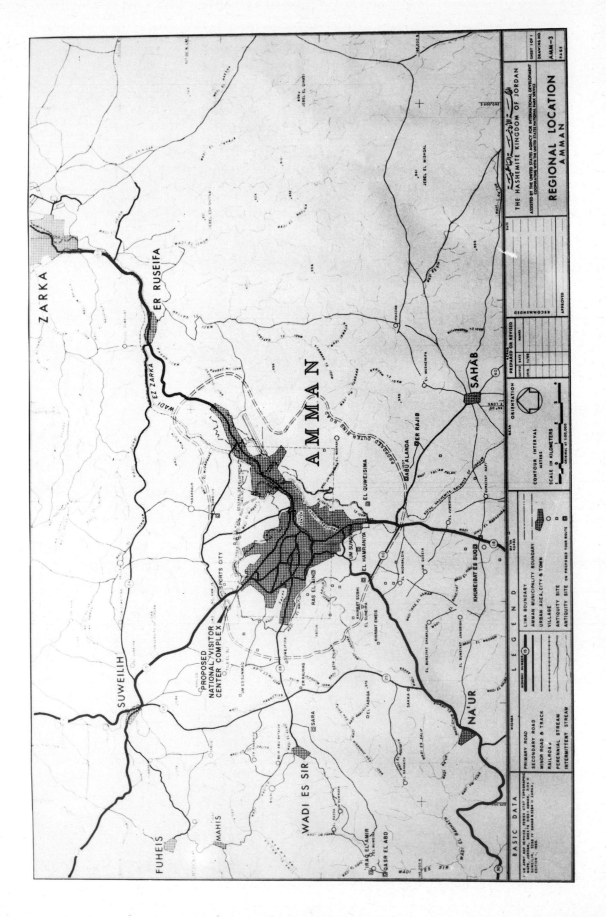

FIGURE 3. AMMAN JEBELS MAP

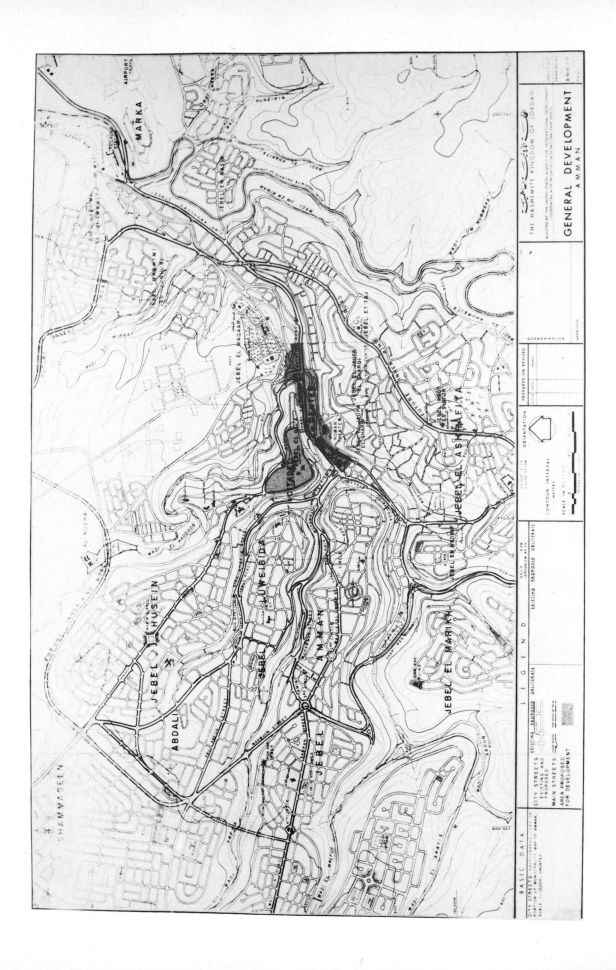

FIGURE 4. SITE PLAN ILLUSTRATING INVESTIGATED AREAS

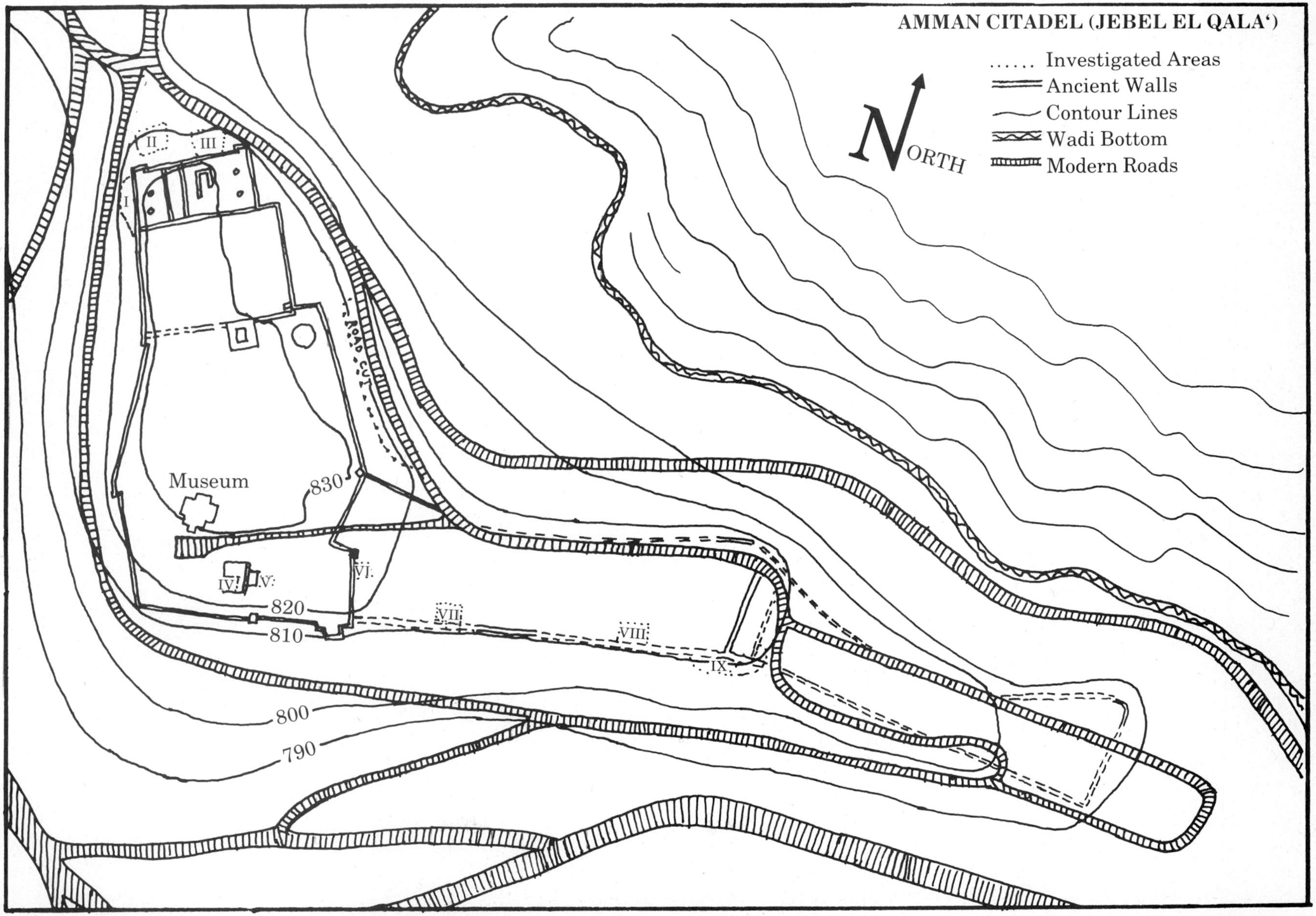

AMMAN CITADEL (JEBEL EL QALA')

..... Investigated Areas
═══ Ancient Walls
⌒ Contour Lines
▨▨ Wadi Bottom
▤▤ Modern Roads

197

FIGURE 5.

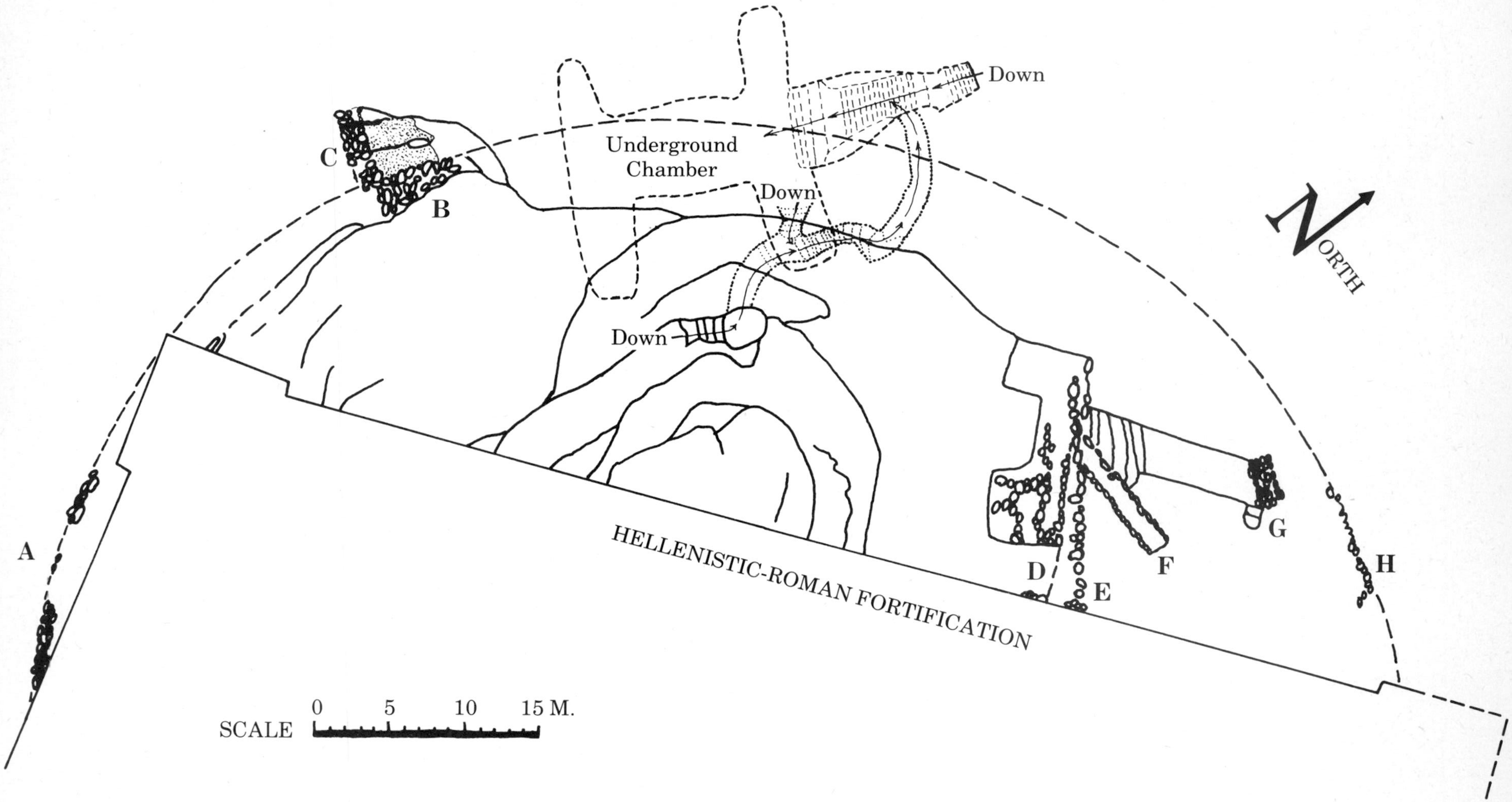

Down
Underground
Chamber
Down
Down
NORTH
A
B
C
D
E
F
G
H
HELLENISTIC-ROMAN FORTIFICATION
SCALE
0
5
10
15 M.

AMMAN CITADEL (NORTH END)
(EARLY WALLS ARE LABELED IN CAPITAL LETTERS)

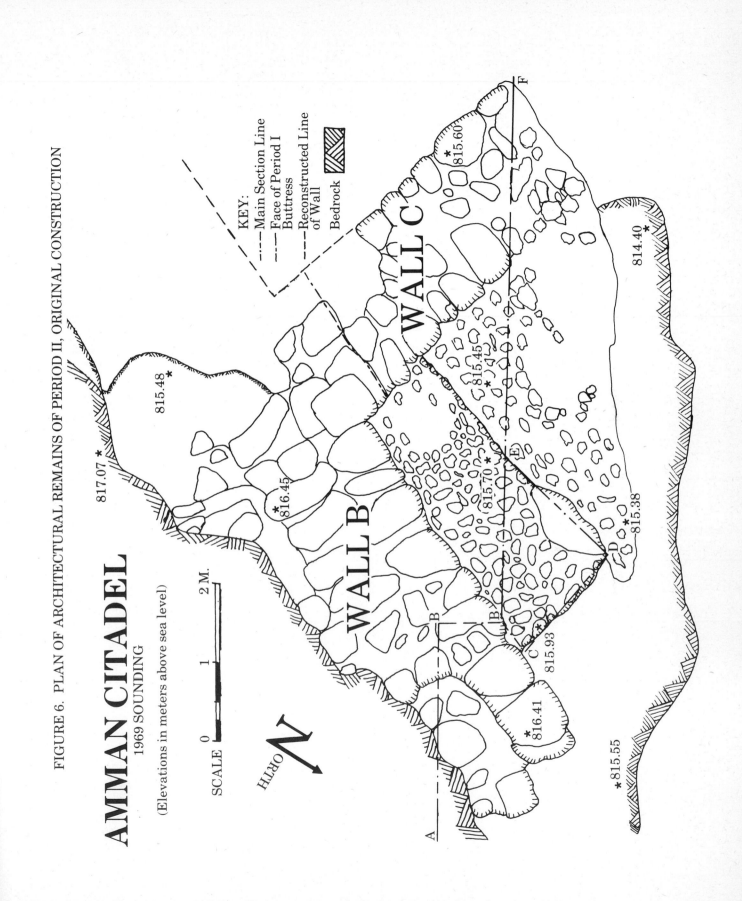

FIGURE 6. PLAN OF ARCHITECTURAL REMAINS OF PERIOD II, ORIGINAL CONSTRUCTION

AMMAN CITADEL

1969 SOUNDING

(Elevations in meters above sea level)

SCALE

0   1   2 M.

NORTH

KEY:
— · — · —   Main Section Line
— — — —   Face of Period I
            Buttress
— — — —   Reconstructed Line
            of Wall
⬚⬚⬚   Bedrock

WALL B

WALL C

817.07 *

815.48 *

* 816.45

* 816.41

815.60 *

814.40 *

815.45 *

815.70 *

815.38 *

815.93 *

815.55 *

199

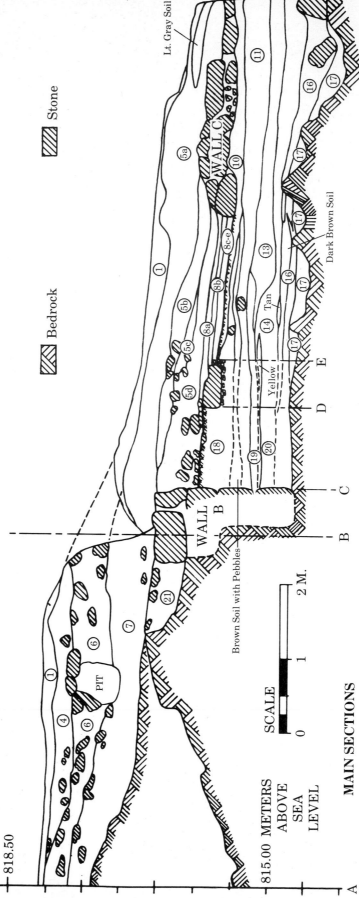

FIGURE 7.

LOCUS DESCRIPTIONS:

① Soft Brown Surface Soil
④ Soft Dark Brown Soil
⑤a Orange-Brown Soil with Medium Sized Stones
⑤b Brown Soil with Many Pebbles
⑤c Tan Brickey Soil
⑤d Red-Brown Soil with Many Small Pebbles
⑥ Soft Medium Brown Soil with Pebbles

⑦ Red Clayey Soil
⑧a Hard Light Brown Soil
⑧b Light Brown Soil with Many Small Pebbles
⑧c-e Orange-Brown, Brown and Light Brown Layers
⑩ Light Brown Soil and Gravel
⑪ Light Grey-Brown Soil
⑬ Dark Grey Soil and Many Pebbles

⑭ Light Grey Soil
⑯ Hard Dark Grey Soil
⑰ Very Hard Yellow-Brown Soil
⑱ Orange-Brown Soil
⑲ Light Brown Soil
⑳ Grey Soil
㉑ Red-Brown Soil

⬚ Stone

⬚ Bedrock

AMMAN CITADEL
1969 SOUNDING

MAIN SECTIONS

SCALE

0   1   2 M.

METERS ABOVE SEA LEVEL

818.50

815.00

200

2

1

4

3

FIGURE 8. Amman Citadel Area III: M.B.-L.B. Walls and Glacis

201

FIGURE 9. Amman Citadel Area III: M.B.-L.B. Walls and Upper Entrance to Underground Chamber

2

4

1

3

FIGURE 10. Amman Citadel Area III: Underground Passageways and Underground Chamber

2

4

1

3

FIGURE 11. Amman Citadel Area II: General Views from West and Start of Work on Main Section

2

4

1

3

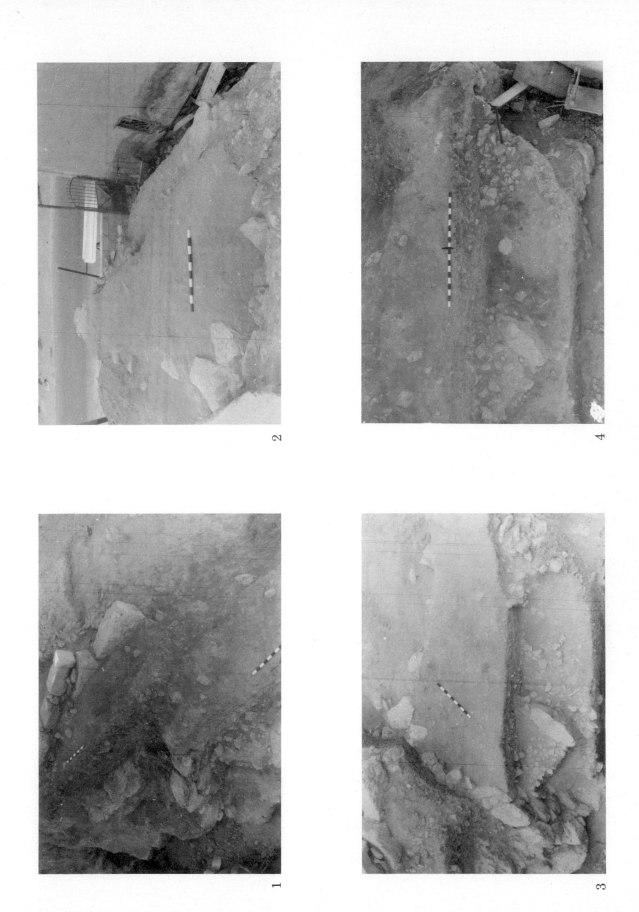

FIGURE 12. Amman Citadel Area II: Excavation of Section Through Period II

FIGURE 13. Amman Citadel Area II: Eastern Part of Main Section
Excavated to Bedrock, from North and Roman and Islamic Remains

2

4

1

3

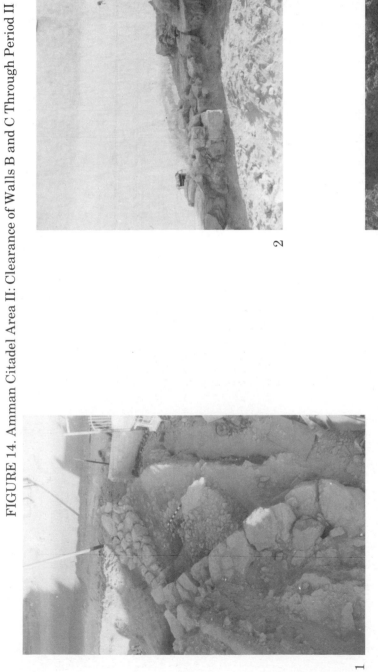

FIGURE 14. Amman Citadel Area II: Clearance of Walls B and C Through Period II

2

4

1

3

207

FIGURE 15. Amman Citadel Area II at End of Excavation: Re-established Section and General View

2

1

3

FIGURE 16. Amman Citadel Area II at End of Excavations

2

4

1

3

2

4

FIGURE 17. Amman Citadel Area II: General View at End
of Excavation and Area I: General View after Cleaning

1

3

FIGURE 18. Amman Citadel Area I: Trial Sections and Wall Exposures

1

2

4

3

2

1

FIGURE 19. Amman Citadel Area I: View of Section of Iron Age Wall

FIGURE 20. Sequence I: Small Bowls

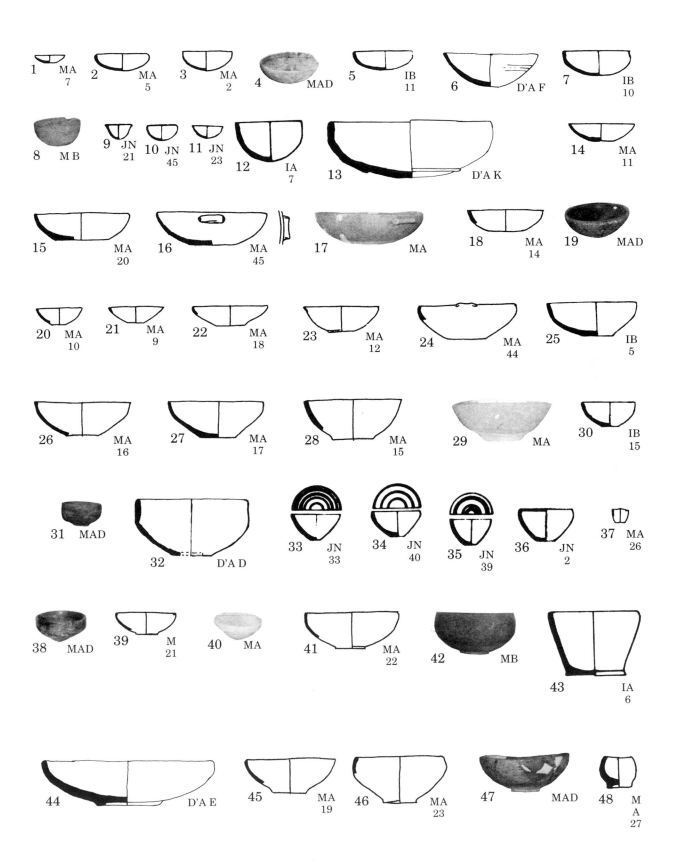

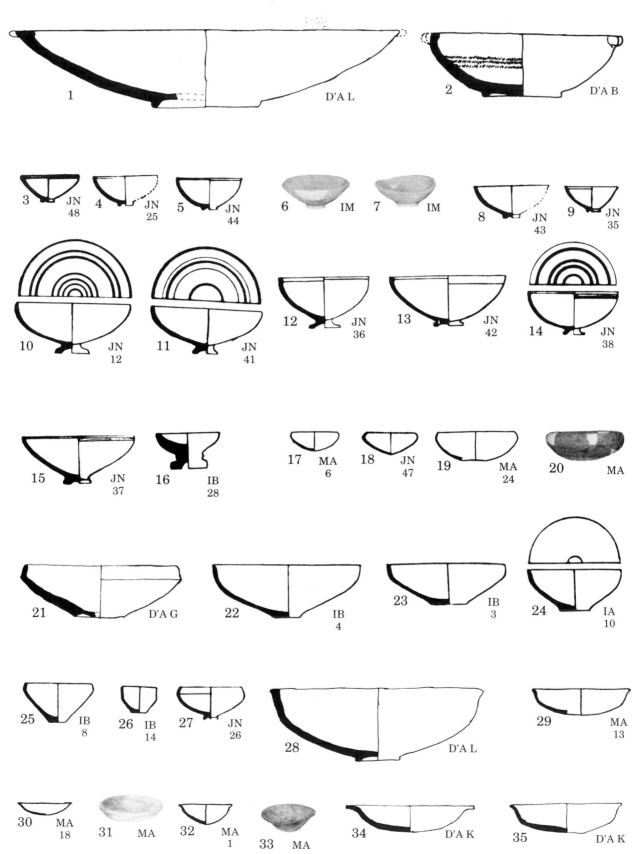

FIGURE 21. Sequence I: Small Bowls (Continued)

214

FIGURE 22. Sequence I: Small Bowls (Continued), Cups, and Strainers

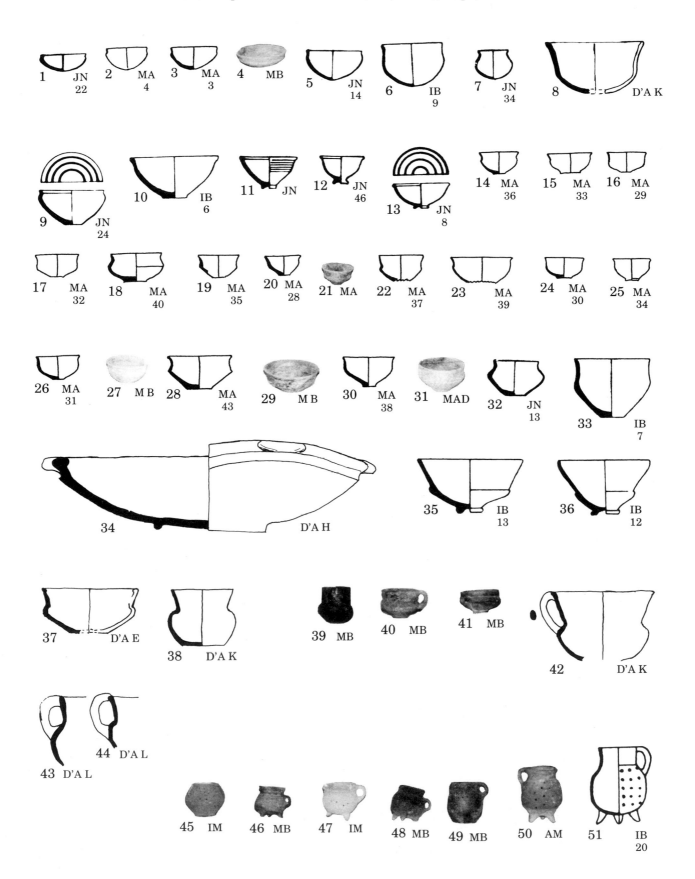

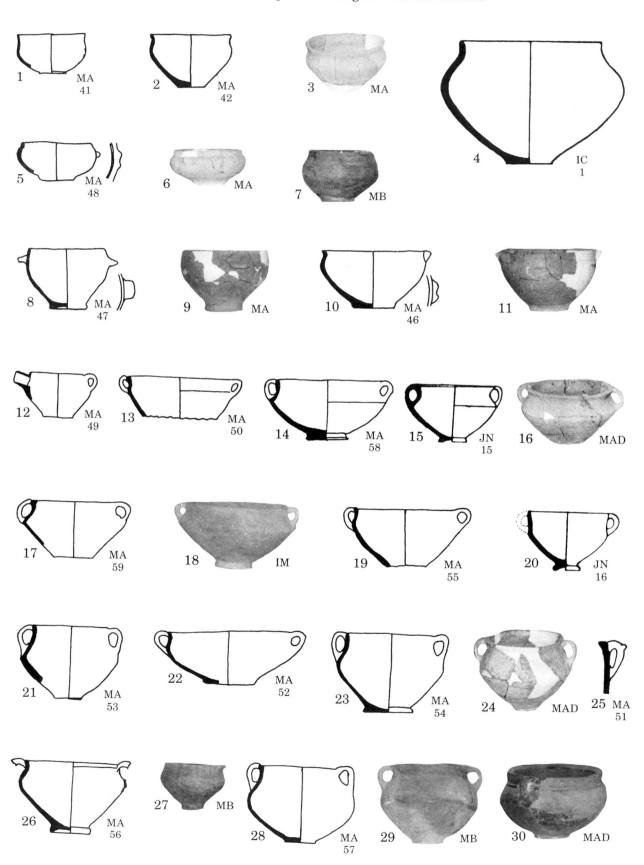

FIGURE 23. Sequence I: Large Bowls and Kraters

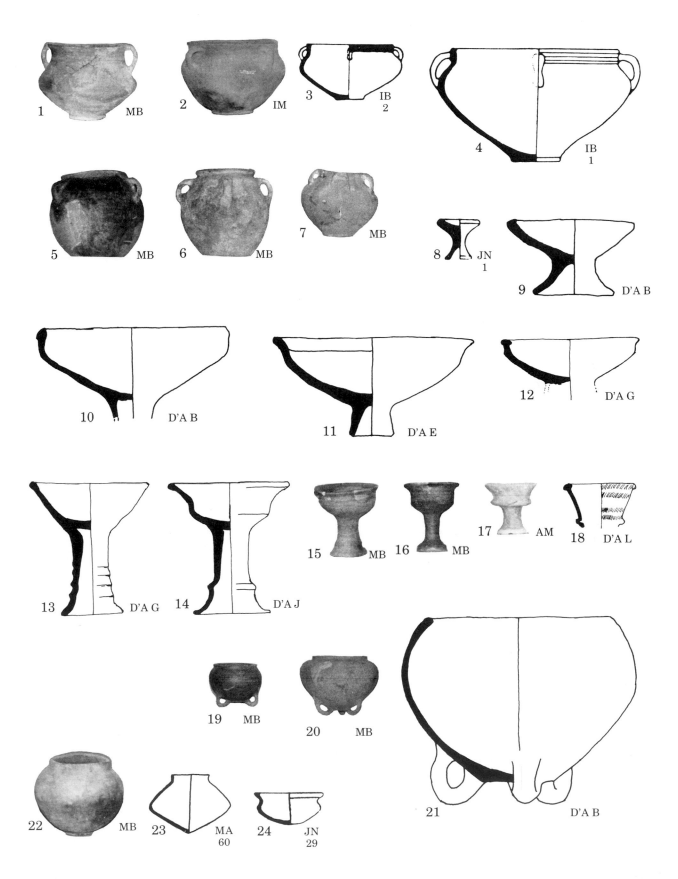

FIGURE 24. Sequence I: Kraters (Continued), Chalices, Loop-footed Bowls, and Cooking Pots

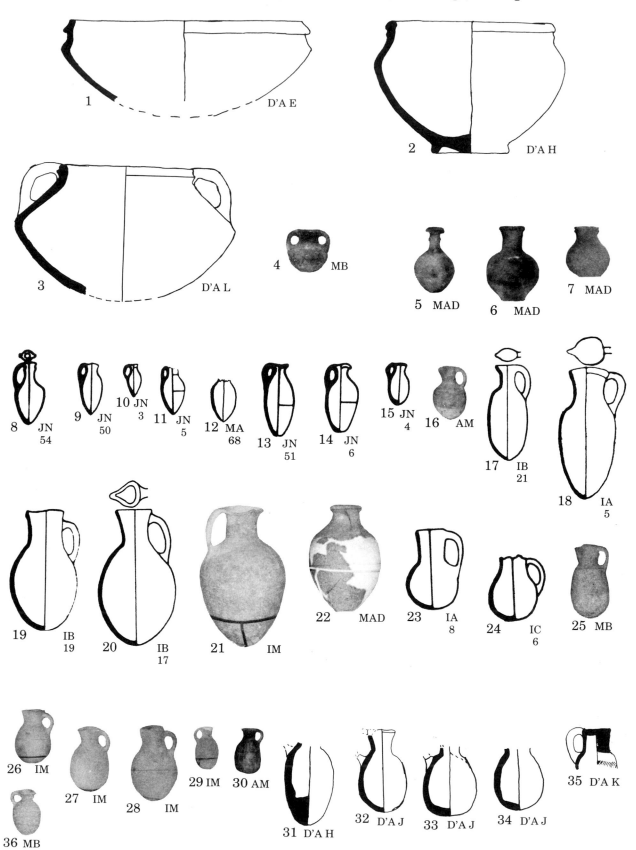

FIGURE 25. Sequence I: Cooking Pots (Continued), Small Jugs, and Juglets

FIGURE 26. Sequence I: Juglets (Continued), Large Jugs, and Jars

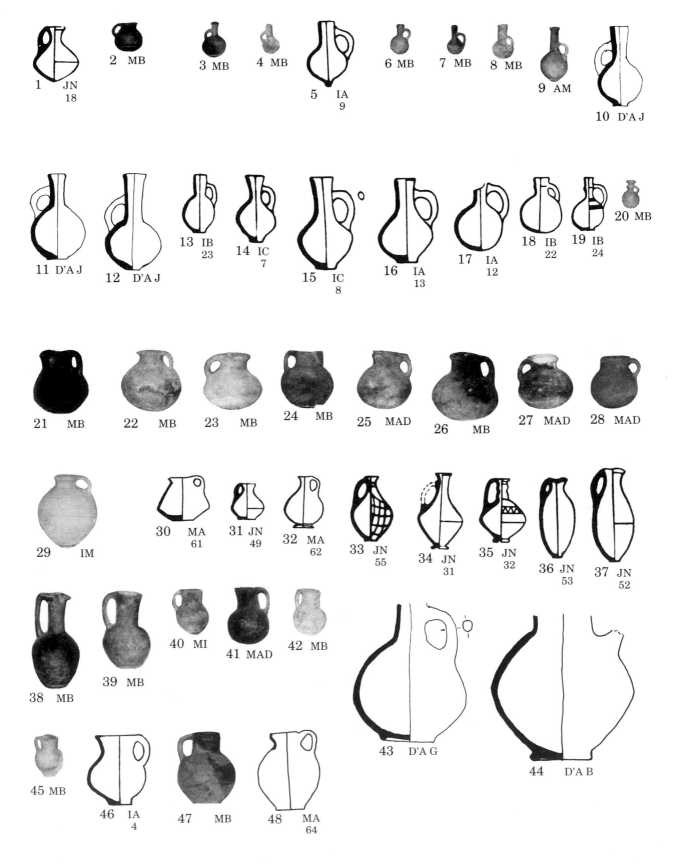

1 JN 18
2 MB
3 MB
4 MB
5 IA 9
6 MB
7 MB
8 MB
9 AM
10 D'A J

11 D'A J
12 D'A J
13 IB 23
14 IC 7
15 IC 8
16 IA 13
17 IA 12
18 IB 22
19 IB 24
20 MB

21 MB
22 MB
23 MB
24 MB
25 MAD
26 MB
27 MAD
28 MAD

29 IM
30 MA 61
31 JN 49
32 MA 62
33 JN 55
34 JN 31
35 JN 32
36 JN 53
37 JN 52

38 MB
39 MB
40 MI
41 MAD
42 MB
43 D'A G
44 D'A B

45 MB
46 IA 4
47 MB
48 MA 64

FIGURE 27. Sequence I: Jars (Continued), Decanters, Strainer Jugs, and Two-handled Jars

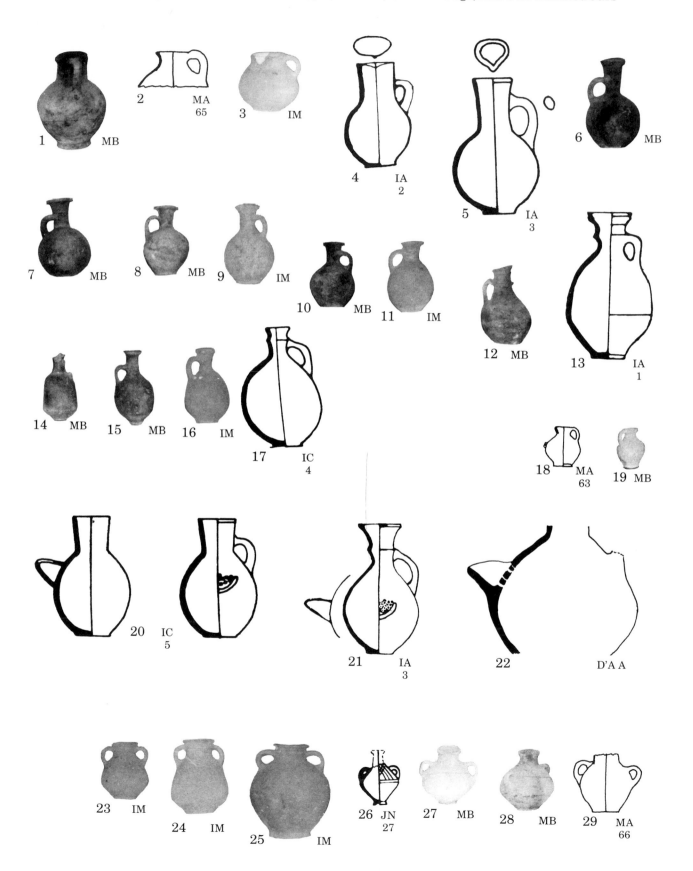

1 MB

2 MA 65

3 IM

4 IA 2

5 IA 3

6 MB

7 MB

8 MB

9 IM

10 MB

11 IM

12 MB

13 IA 1

14 MB

15 MB

16 IM

17 IC 4

18 MA 63

19 MB

20 IC 5

21 IA 3

22 D'A A

23 IM

24 IM

25 IM

26 JN 27

27 MB

28 MB

29 MA 66

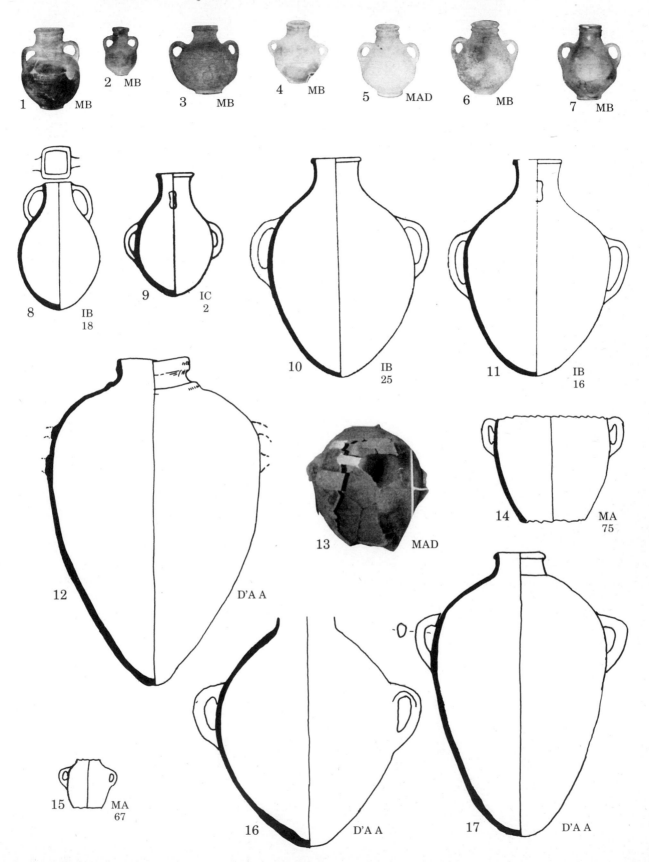

FIGURE 28. Sequence I: Two-handled Jars (Continued) and Storage Jars

1   MB

2   MB

3   MB

4   MB

5   MAD

6   MB

7   MB

8   IB 18

9   IC 2

10   IB 25

11   IB 16

12   D'A A

13   MAD

14   MA 75

15   MA 67

16   D'A A

17   D'A A

221

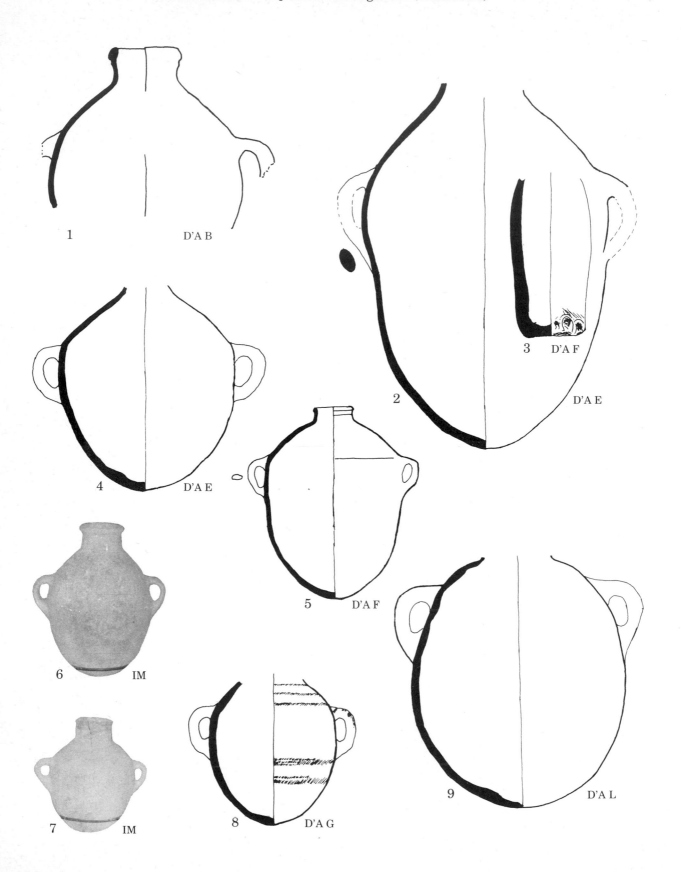

FIGURE 29. Sequence I: Storage Jars (Continued)

1   D'A B

2

3   D'A F

D'A E

4   D'A E

5   D'A F

6   IM

7   IM

8   D'A G

9   D'A L

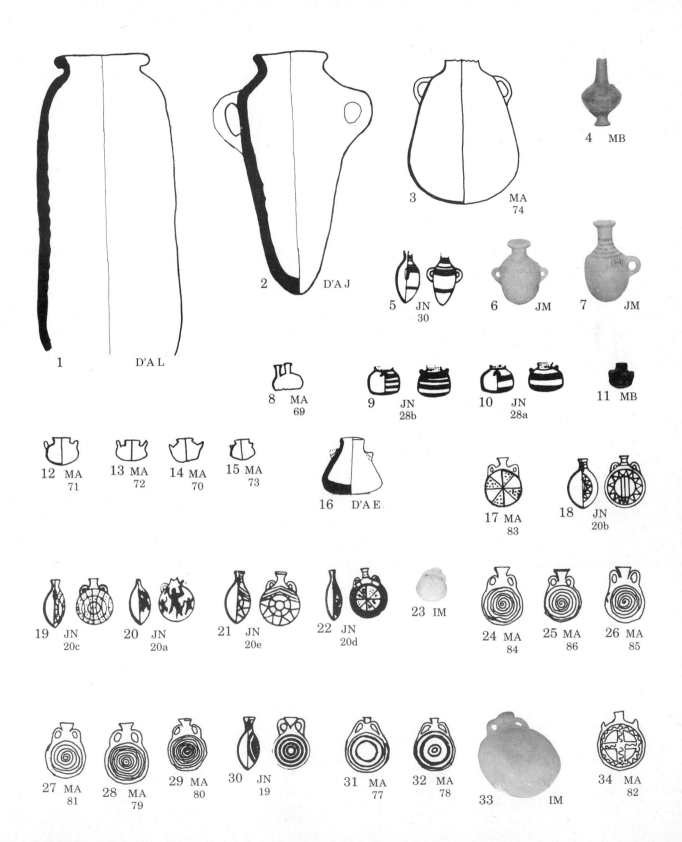

FIGURE 30. Sequence I: Storage Jars (Continued), Bilbil Stirrup Jar, Pyxis, Small Two-handled Jar, and Flasks

1   D'A L

2   D'A J

3   MA
     74

4   MB

5   JN
     30

6   JM

7   JM

8   MA
     69

9   JN
     28b

10   JN
     28a

11   MB

12 MA
   71

13 MA
   72

14 MA
   70

15 MA
   73

16   D'A E

17 MA
   83

18   JN
     20b

19   JN
     20c

20   JN
     20a

21   JN
     20e

22   JN
     20d

23 IM

24 MA
   84

25 MA
   86

26 MA
   85

27 MA
   81

28 MA
   79

29 MA
   80

30   JN
     19

31 MA
   77

32 MA
   78

33   IM

34 MA
   82

FIGURE 31. Sequence I: Lamps and Figurines

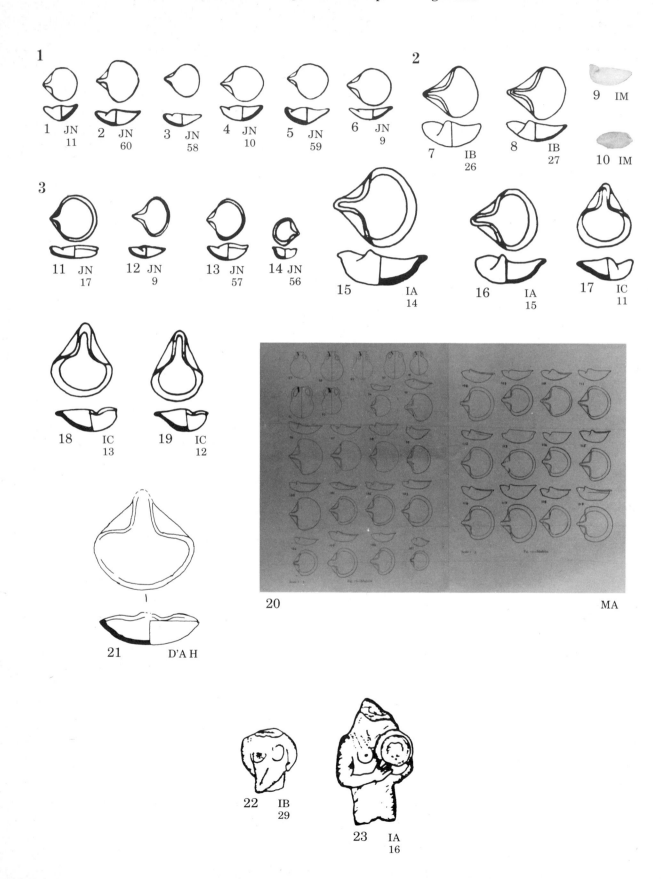

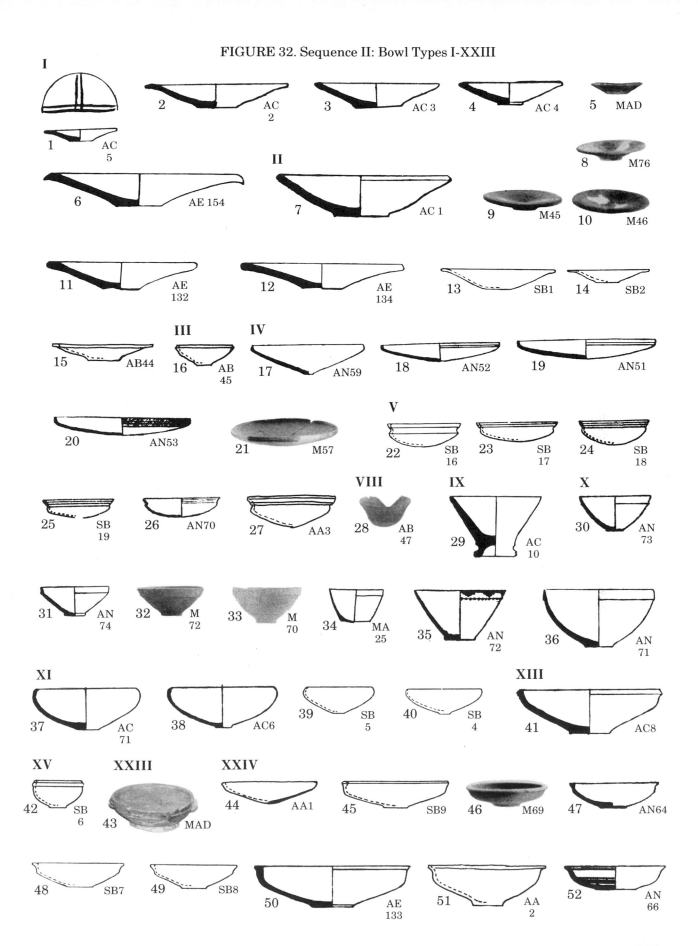

FIGURE 32. Sequence II: Bowl Types I-XXIII

FIGURE 33. Sequence II: Bowl Types XXIII-LXII, Chalices and Cup Types 1-3

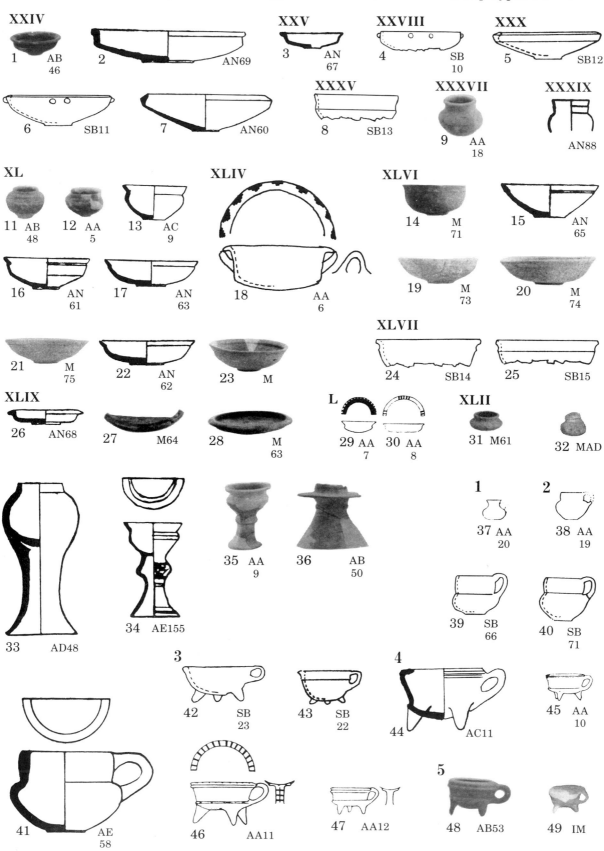

FIGURE 34. Sequence II: Cup Types 3 (Continued)-5 and Jug Type 1

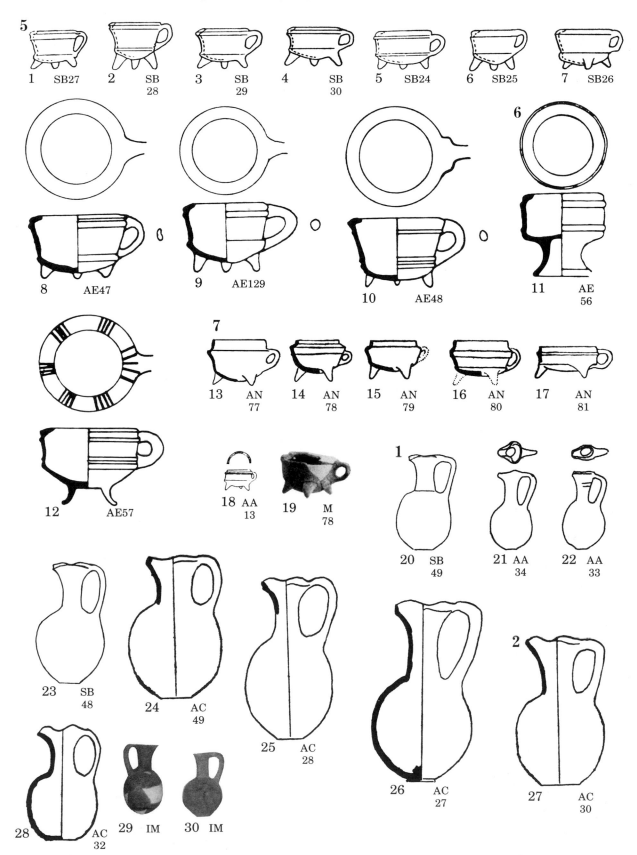

5

1 SB27 2 SB 28 3 SB 29 4 SB 30 5 SB24 6 SB25 7 SB26

6

8 AE47 9 AE129 10 AE48 11 AE 56

7

13 AN 77 14 AN 78 15 AN 79 16 AN 80 17 AN 81

12 AE57 18 AA 13 19 M 78

1

20 SB 49 21 AA 34 22 AA 33

23 SB 48 24 AC 49 25 AC 28 26 AC 27

2

27 AC 30

28 AC 32 29 IM 30 IM

FIGURE 35. Sequence II: Jug Types 1 (Continued)-4

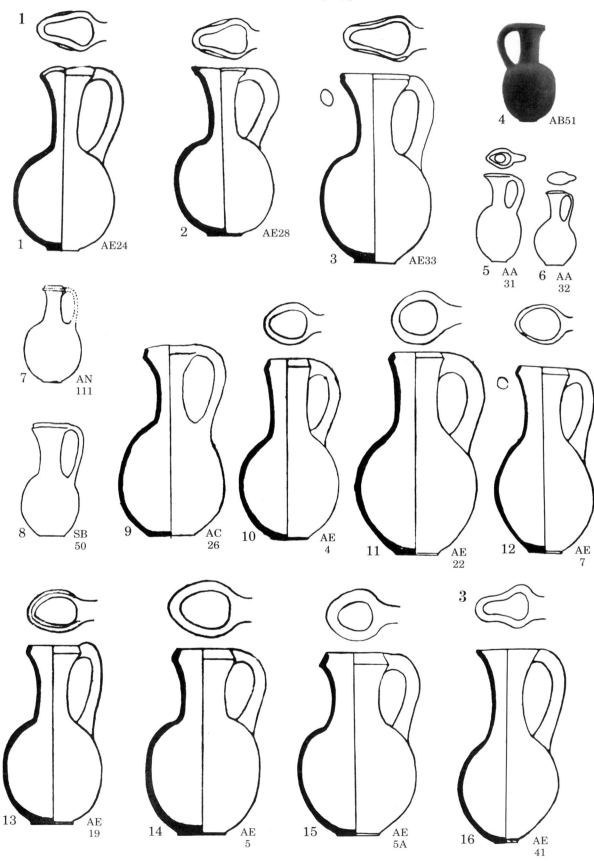

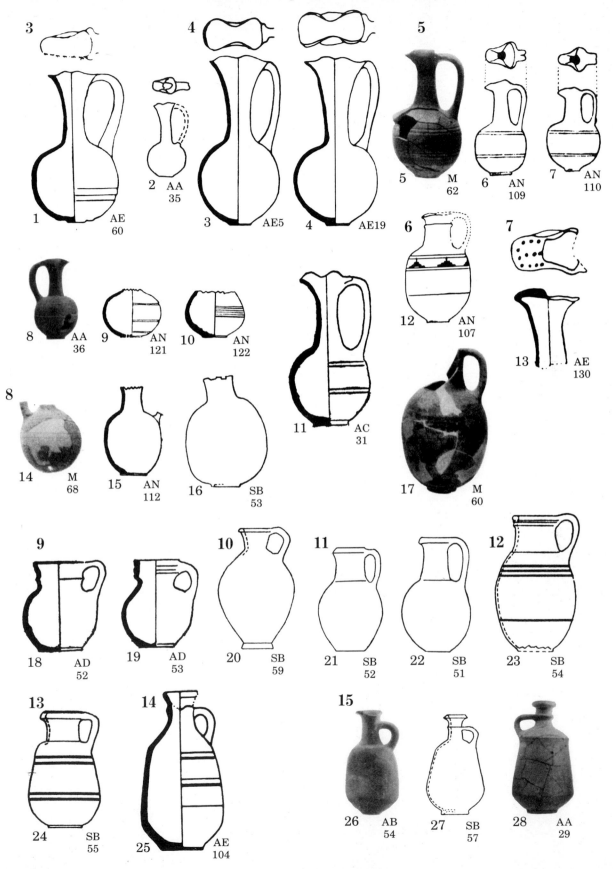

FIGURE 36. Sequence II: Jug Types 5-16

3

2   AA 35

1   AE 60

4

3   AE5   4   AE19

5

5   M 62   6   AN 109   7   AN 110

8   AA 36   9   AN 121   10   AN 122

6

12   AN 107

7

13   AE 130

8

11   AC 31

14   M 68   15   AN 112   16   SB 53

17   M 60

9

18   AD 52   19   AD 53

10

20   SB 59

11

21   SB 52   22   SB 51

12

23   SB 54

13

24   SB 55

14

25   AE 104

15

26   AB 54   27   SB 57   28   AA 29

FIGURE 37. Sequence II: Jug Types 16 (Continued)-27

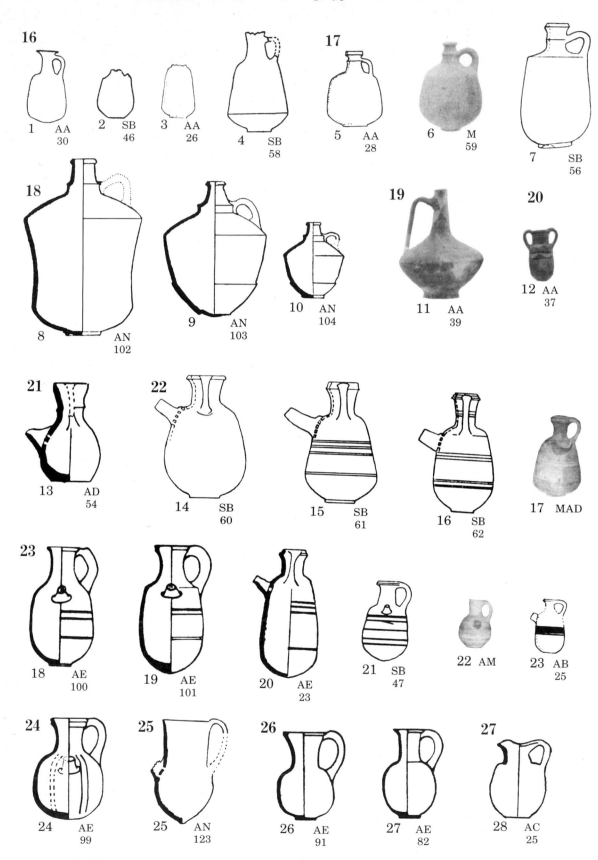

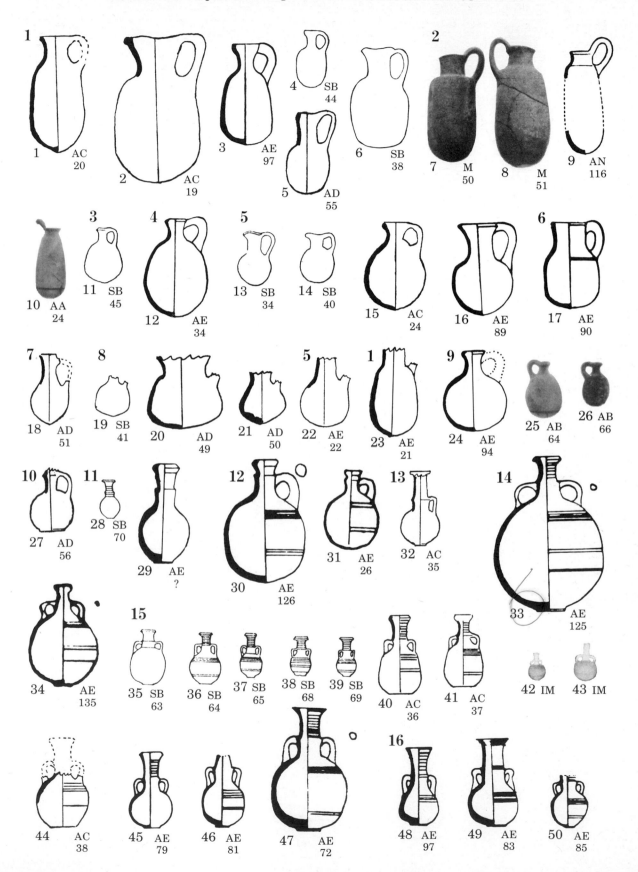

FIGURE 38. Sequence II: Juglet, Small Jar, and Bottles, Types 1-16

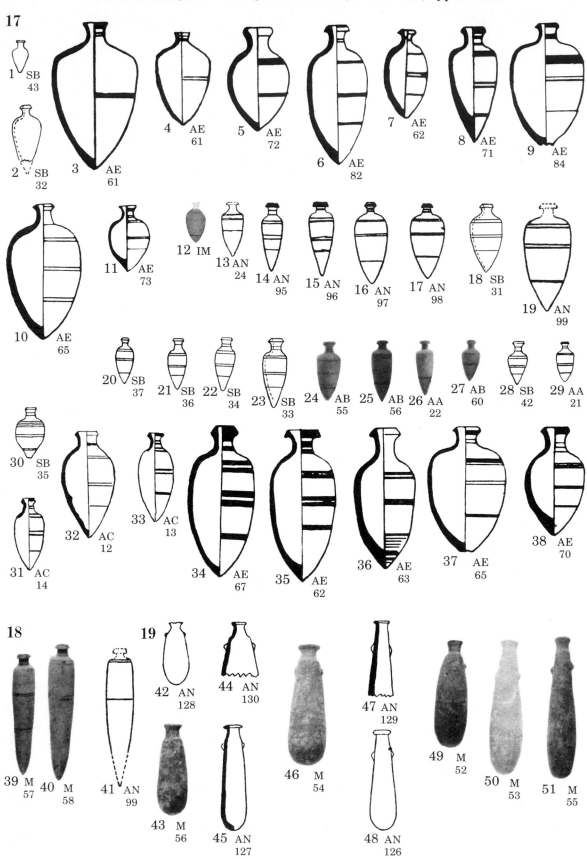

FIGURE 39. Sequence II: Juglet, Small Jar, and Bottles, Types 17-19

232

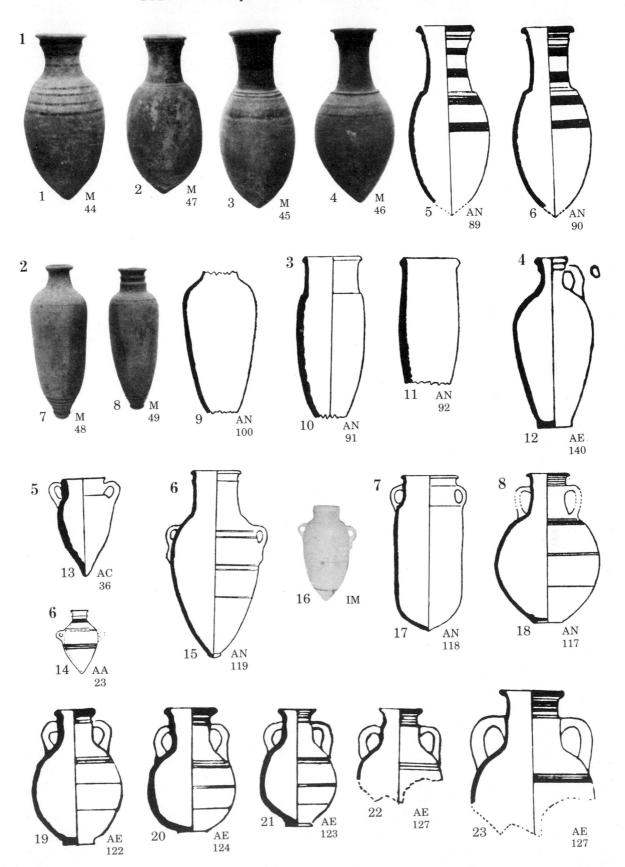

FIGURE 40. Sequence II: Jar and Amphora Types 1-8

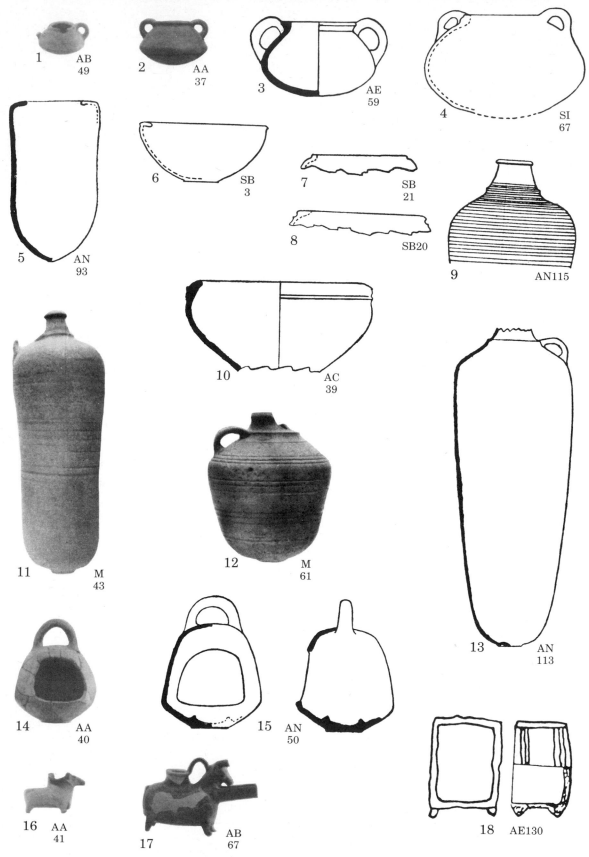

FIGURE 41. Sequence II: Cooking Pots, Storage Jars, Deep Bowls, and Miscellaneous

1 AB 49

2 AA 37

3 AE 59

4 SI 67

5 AN 93

6 SB 3

7 SB 21

8 SB20

9 AN115

10 AC 39

11 M 43

12 M 61

13 AN 113

14 AA 40

15 AN 50

16 AA 41

17 AB 67

18 AE130

FIGURE 42. Sequence II: Lamp Types 4-8

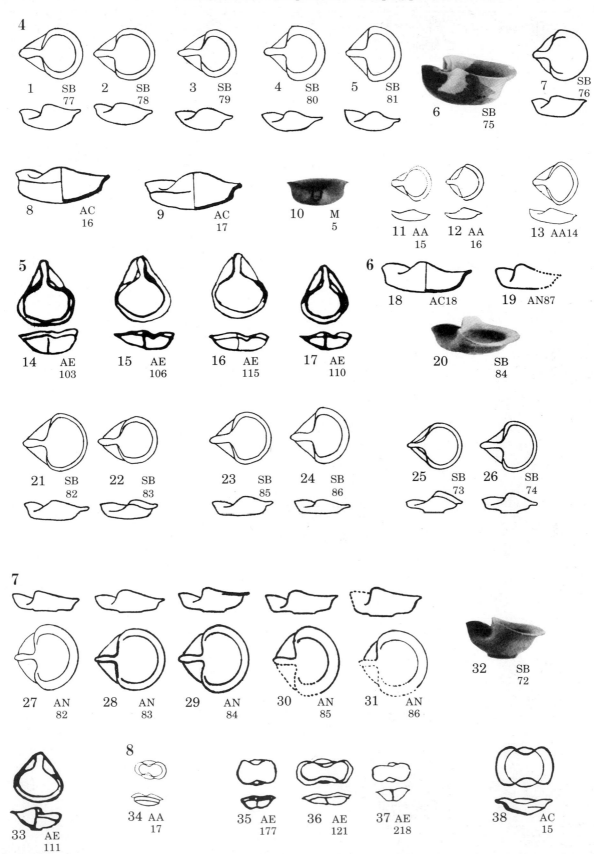

4

1　SB 77

2　SB 78

3　SB 79

4　SB 80

5　SB 81

6　SB 75

7　SB 76

8　AC 16

9　AC 17

10　M 5

11　AA 15

12　AA 16

13　AA14

5

14　AE 103

15　AE 106

16　AE 115

17　AE 110

6

18　AC18

19　AN87

20　SB 84

21　SB 82

22　SB 83

23　SB 85

24　SB 86

25　SB 73

26　SB 74

7

27　AN 82

28　AN 83

29　AN 84

30　AN 85

31　AN 86

32　SB 72

8

33　AE 111

34　AA 17

35　AE 177

36　AE 121

37　AE 218

38　AC 15

FIGURE 43. Sherd Profile Types I-XLVI

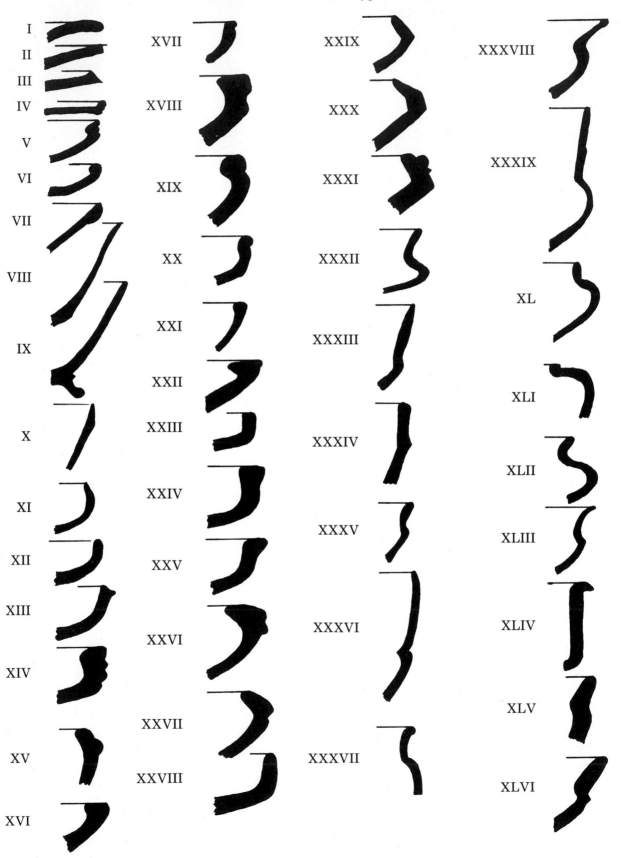

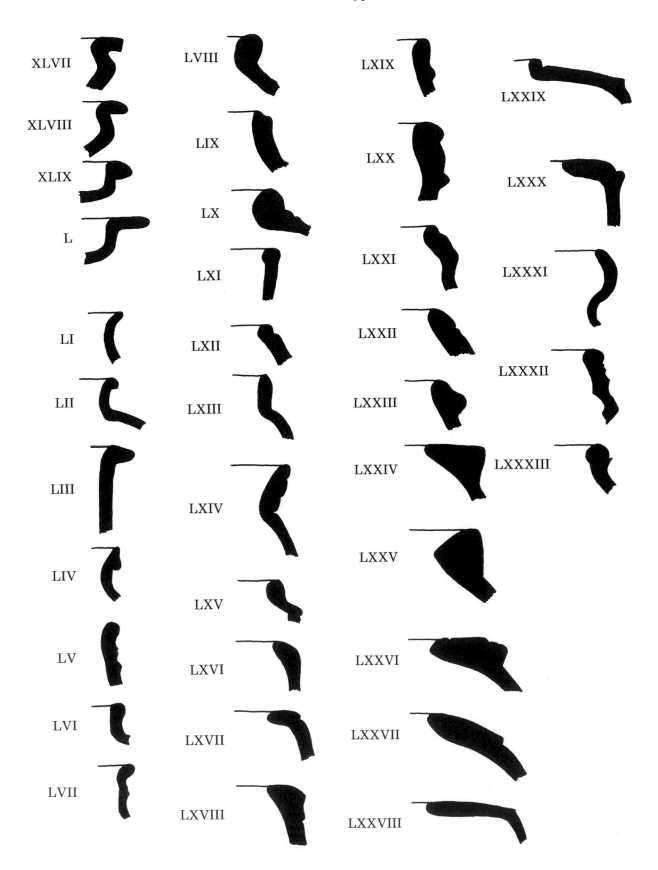

FIGURE 44. Sherd Profile Types XLVII-LXXXIII

XLVII

XLVIII

XLIX

L

LI

LII

LIII

LIV

LV

LVI

LVII

LVIII

LIX

LX

LXI

LXII

LXIII

LXIV

LXV

LXVI

LXVII

LXVIII

LXIX

LXX

LXXI

LXXII

LXXIII

LXXIV

LXXV

LXXVI

LXXVII

LXXVIII

LXXIX

LXXX

LXXXI

LXXXII

LXXXIII

FIGURE 45. Sherd Profile Types LXXXIV-XC and Base Sherd Profile Types 1-15

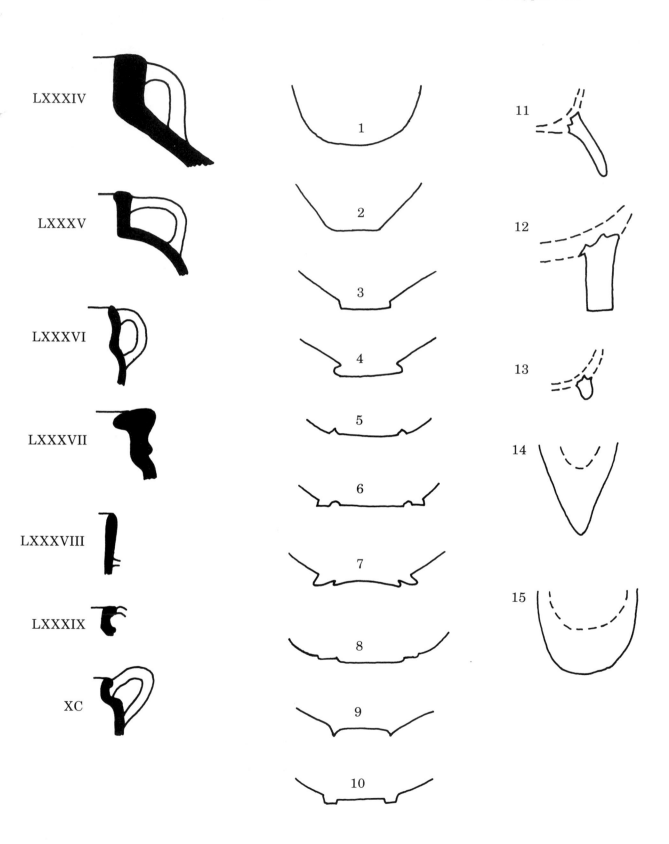

FIGURE 46. Amman Citadel: Early Bronze and Middle Bronze I Sherds

FIGURE 47. Amman Citadel: Middle Bronze I and II Sherds

240

FIGURE 48. Amman Citadel: Middle Bronze II Sherds

FIGURE 49. Amman Citadel: Middle Bronze II and Late Bronze Sherds

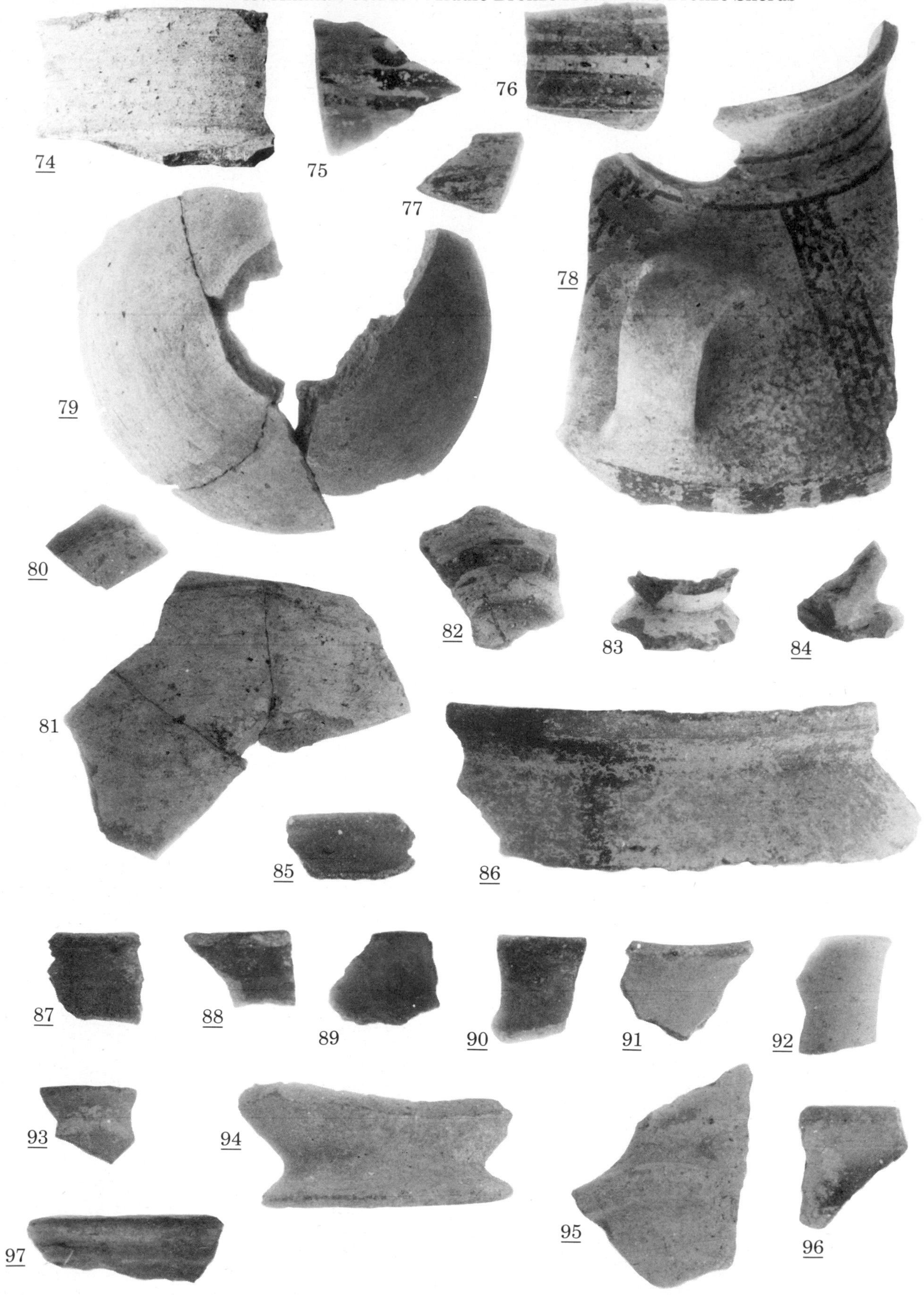

FIGURE 50. Amman Citadel and Jerash Museum Late Bronze Sherds

243

FIGURE 51. Amman Citadel: Bronze Age Sherd Profiles

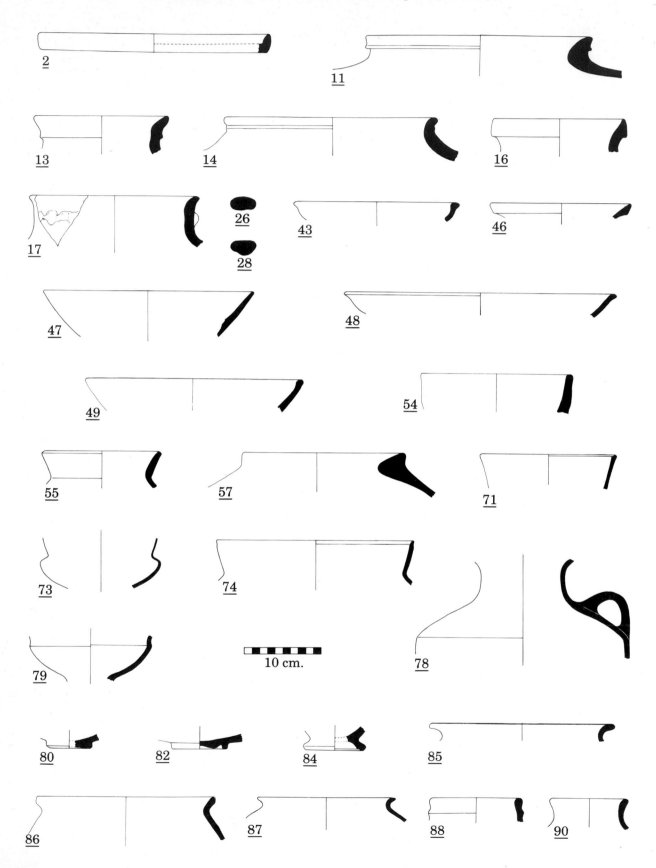

10 cm.

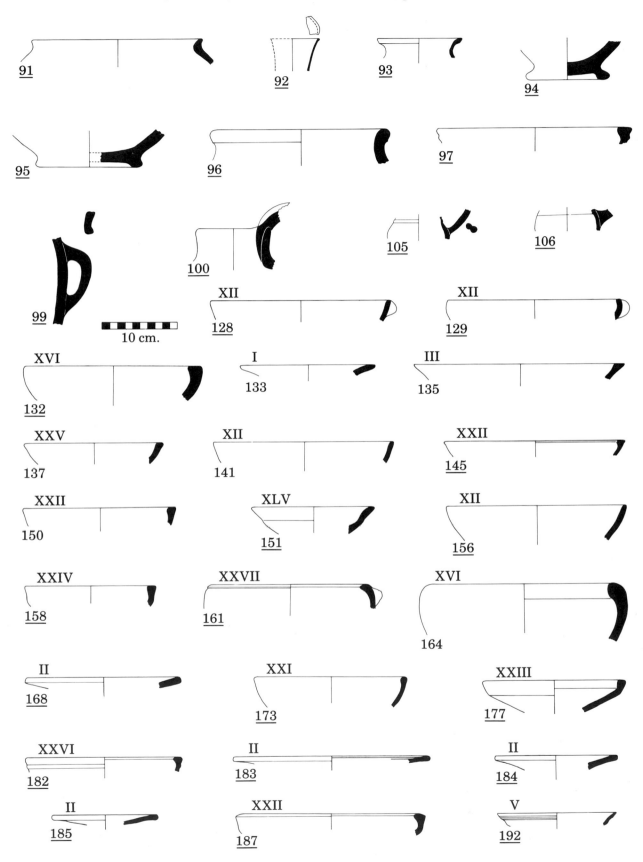

245

FIGURE 53. Amman Citadel 1969 Sounding Sherd Profiles, continued, and Type I Rim Sherd Profiles

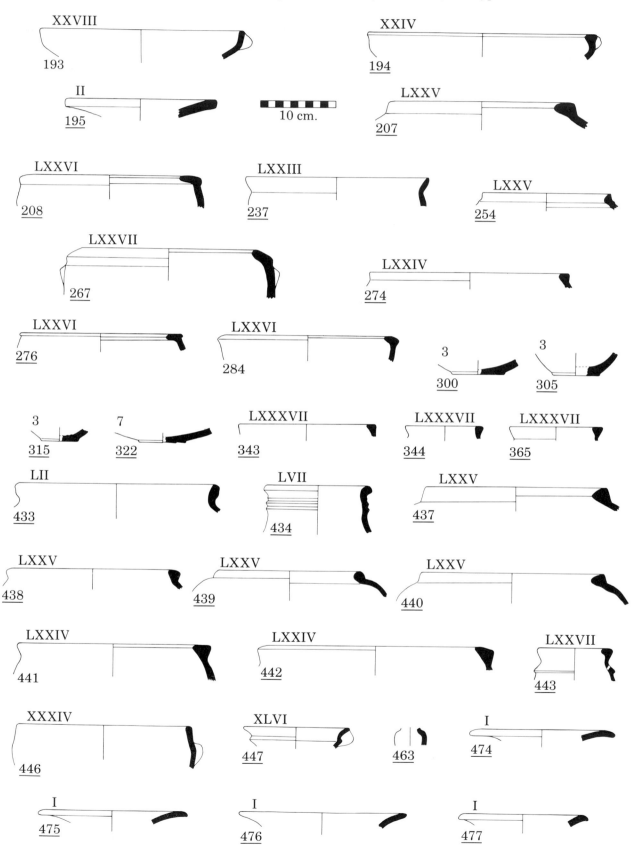

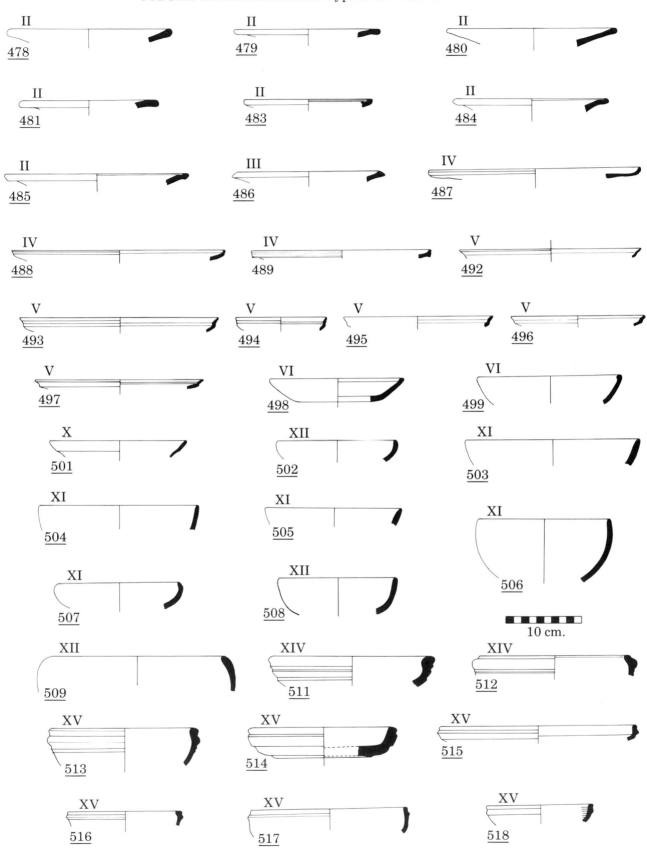

FIGURE 54. Amman Citadel: Type II-XIV Rim Sherd Profiles

10 cm.

247

FIGURE 55. Amman Citadel: Type XIV-XLVI Rim Sherd Profiles

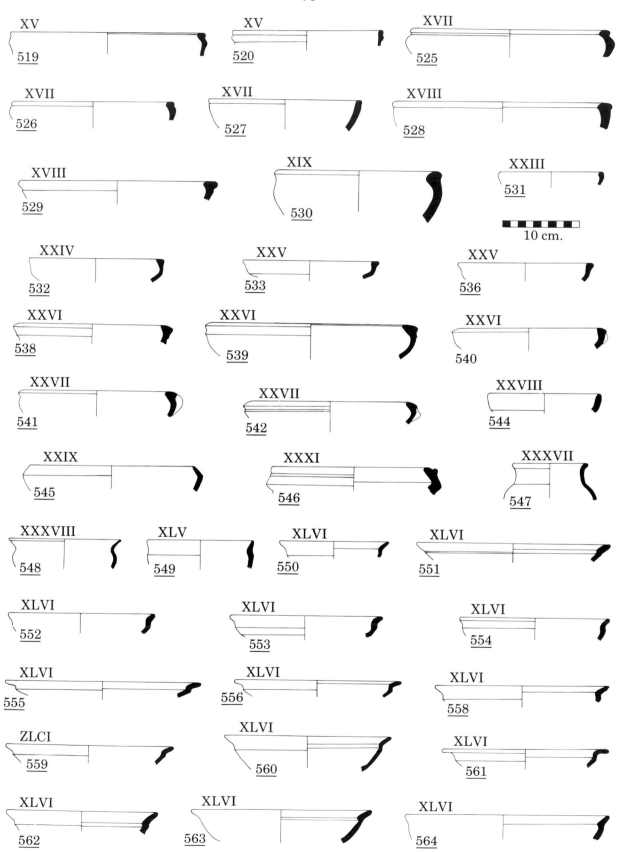

FIGURE 56. Amman Citadel: Type XLVI-LII Rim Sherd Profiles

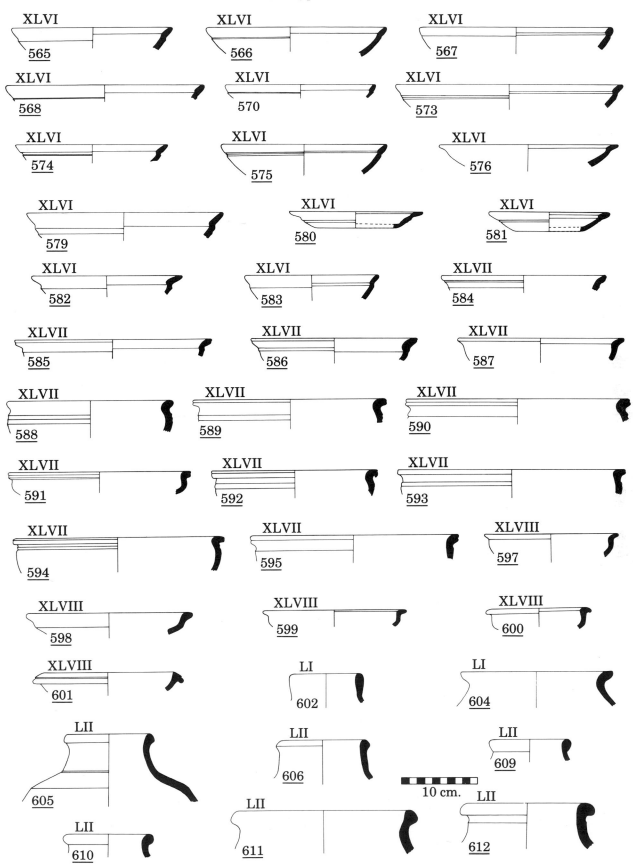

FIGURE 57. Amman Citadel: Type LIII-LXIV Rim Sherd Profiles

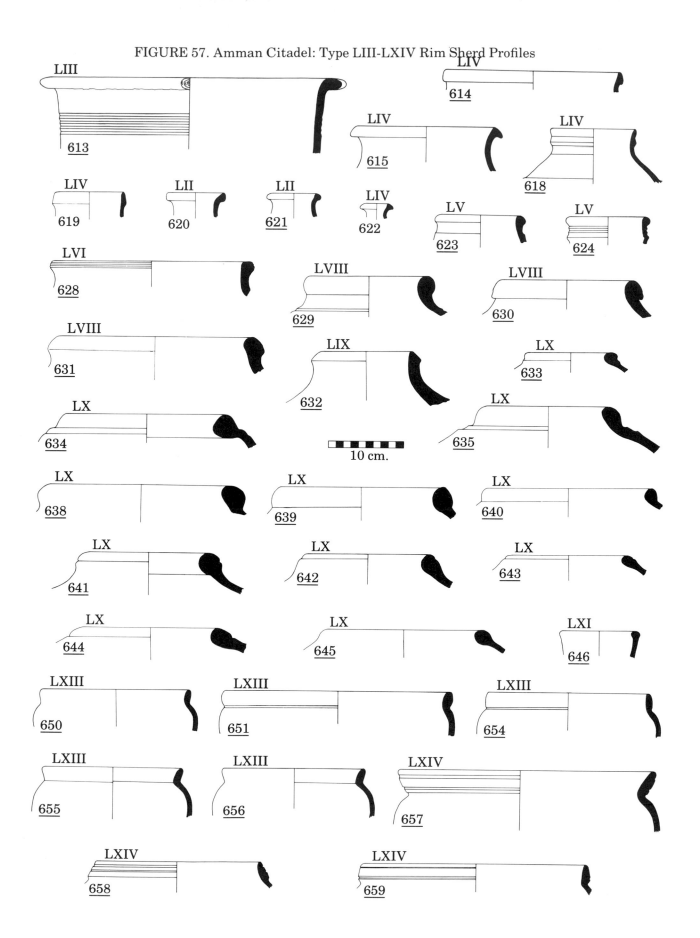

FIGURE 58. Amman Citadel: Type LXV-LXXVII Rim Sherd Profiles

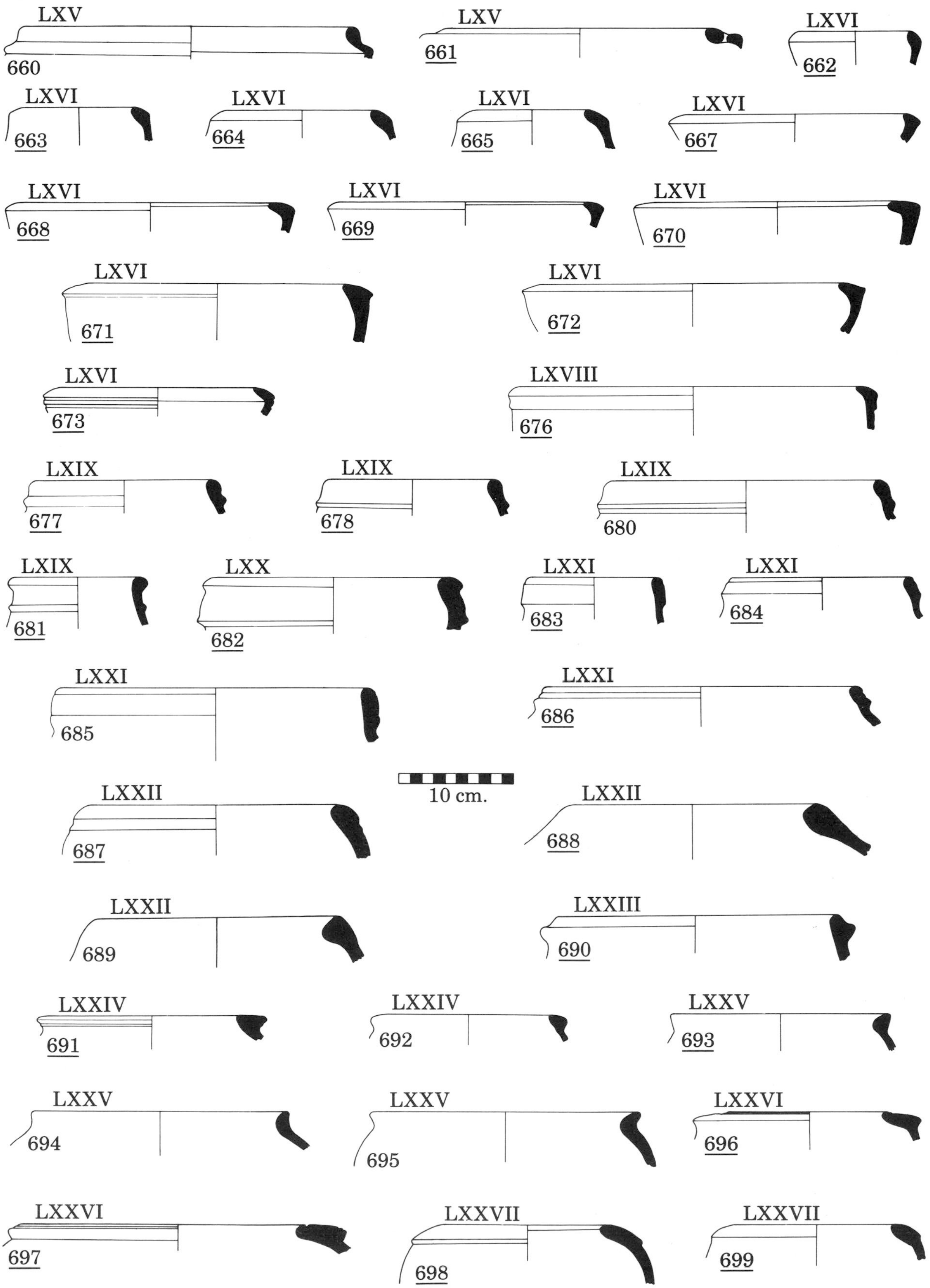

LXV
660

LXV
661

LXVI
662

LXVI
663

LXVI
664

LXVI
665

LXVI
667

LXVI
668

LXVI
669

LXVI
670

LXVI
671

LXVI
672

LXVI
673

LXVIII
676

LXIX
677

LXIX
678

LXIX
680

LXIX
681

LXX
682

LXXI
683

LXXI
684

LXXI
685

LXXI
686

LXXII
687

10 cm.

LXXII
688

LXXII
689

LXXIII
690

LXXIV
691

LXXIV
692

LXXV
693

LXXV
694

LXXV
695

LXXVI
696

LXXVI
697

LXXVII
698

LXXVII
699

FIGURE 59. Amman Citadel: Type LXXVII-LXXXIII Rim Sherd Profiles

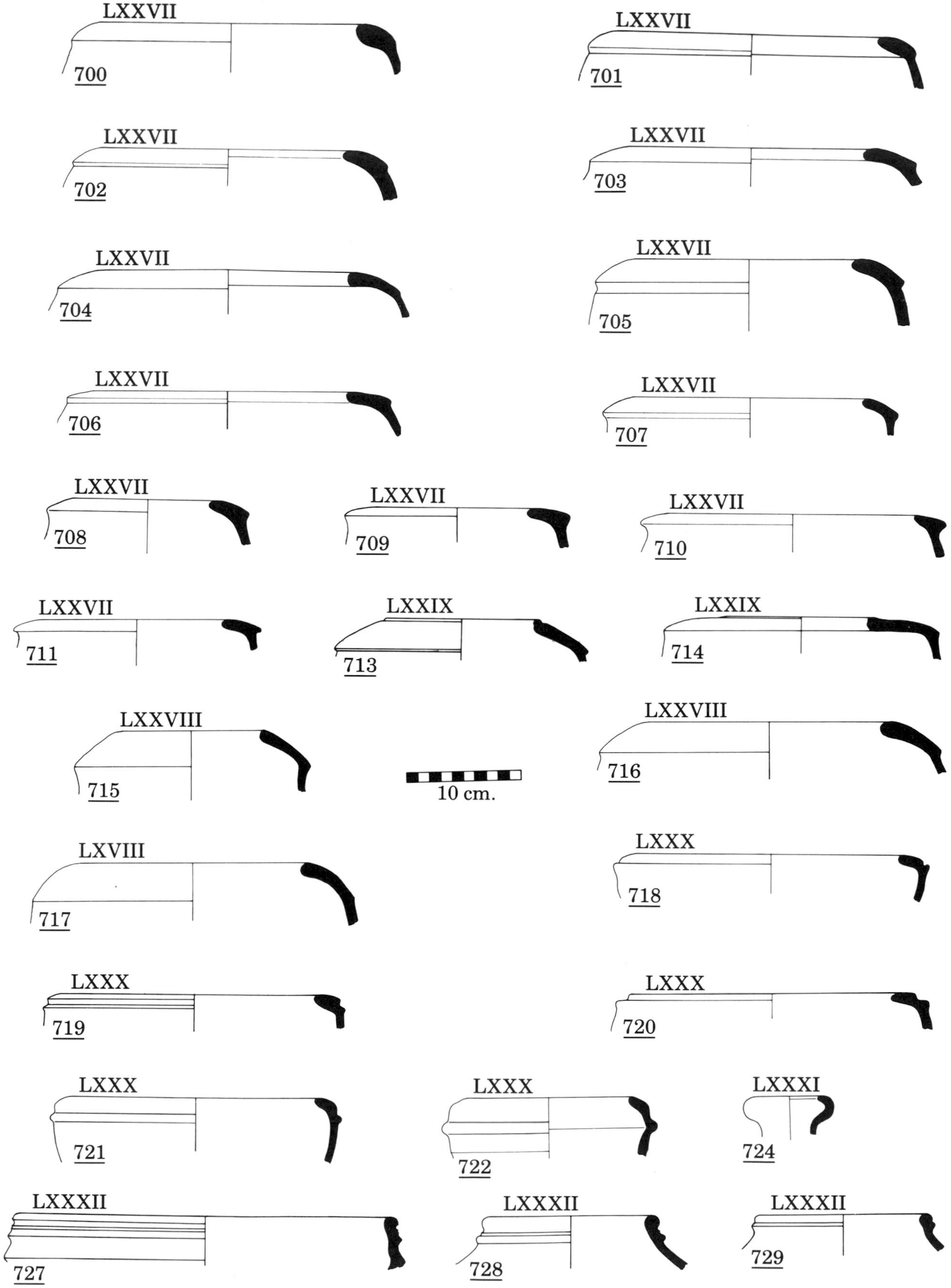

252

FIGURE 60. Amman Citadel: Type LXXXIV-XC Rim, Handle and Base Sherd Profiles

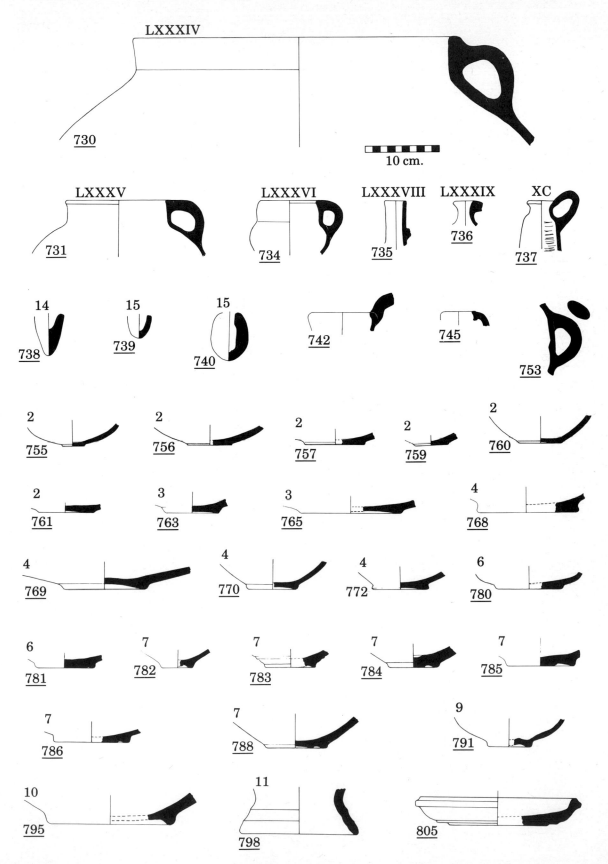

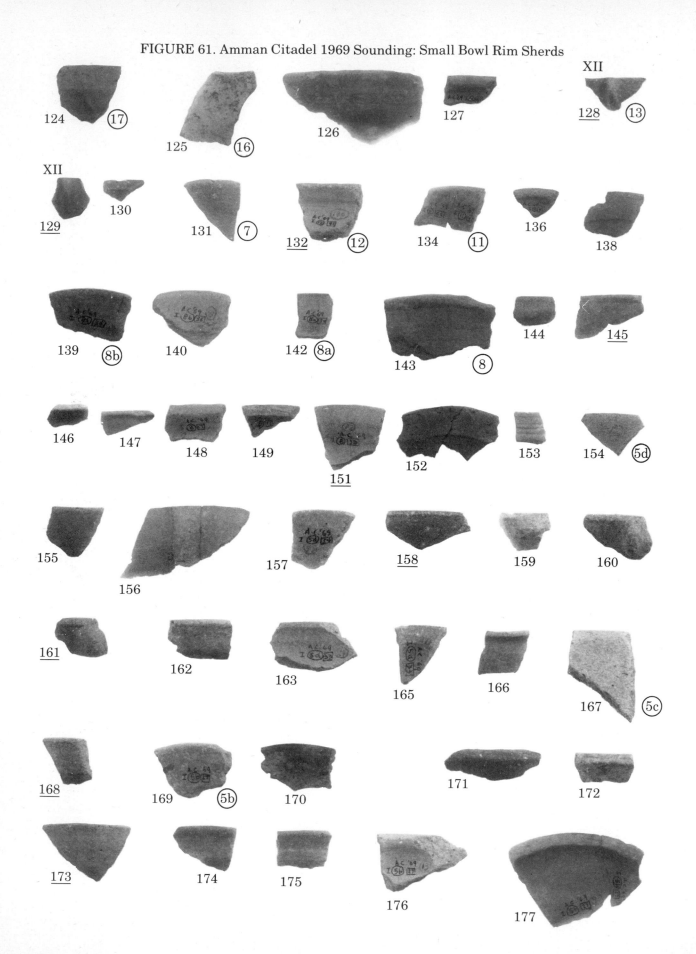

FIGURE 61. Amman Citadel 1969 Sounding: Small Bowl Rim Sherds

254

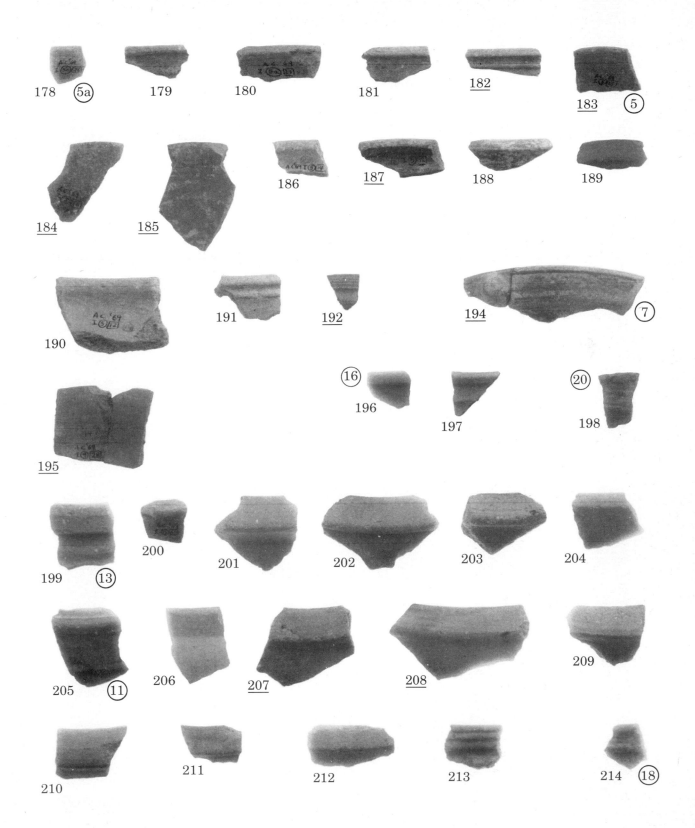

FIGURE 63. Amman Citadel 1969 Sounding: Large Bowl and Jar Rim Sherds

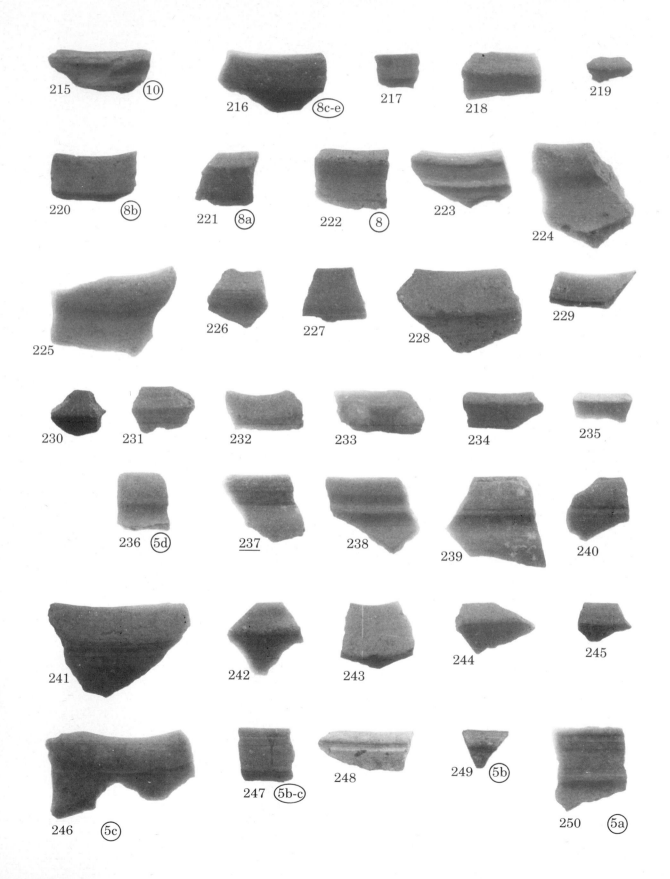

215 ⑩   216 ⑧c-e   217   218   219

220 ⑧b   221 ⑧a   222 ⑧   223   224

225   226   227   228   229

230   231   232   233   234   235

236 ⑤d   <u>237</u>   238   239   240

241   242   243   244   245

246 ⑤c   247 ⑤b-c   248   249 ⑤b   250 ⑤a

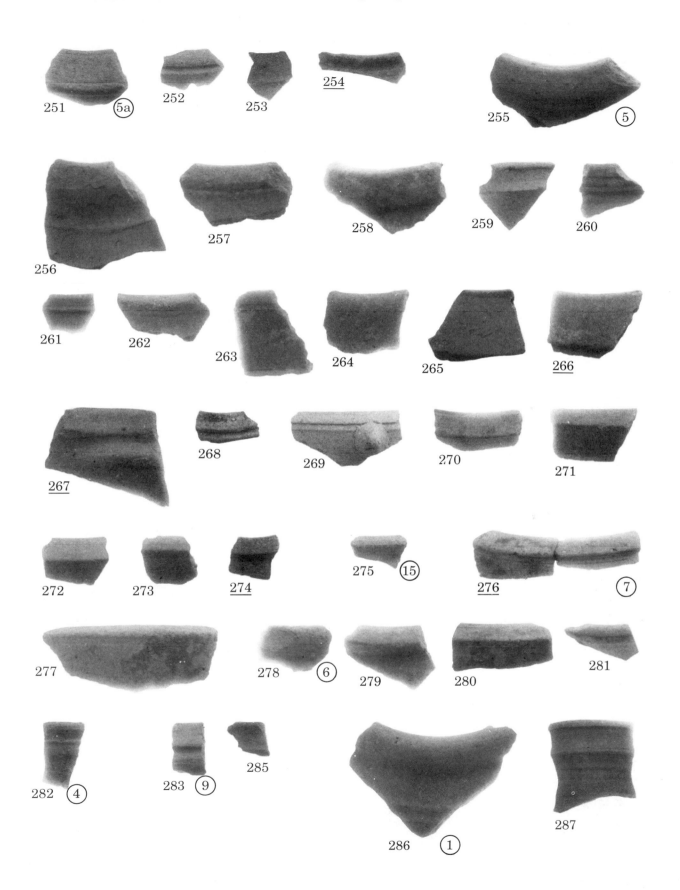

FIGURE 65. Amman Citadel 1969 Sounding: Jar Rims and Base Sherds

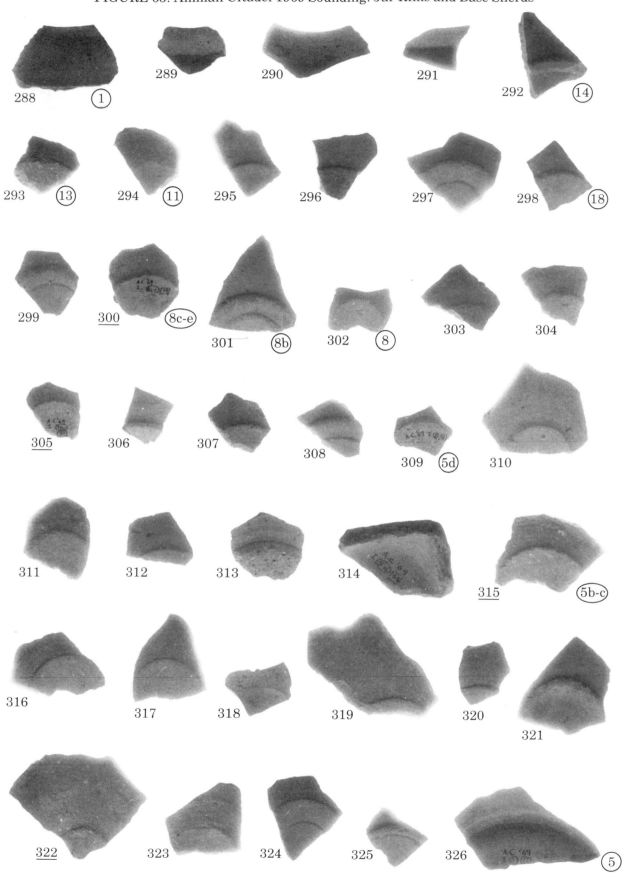

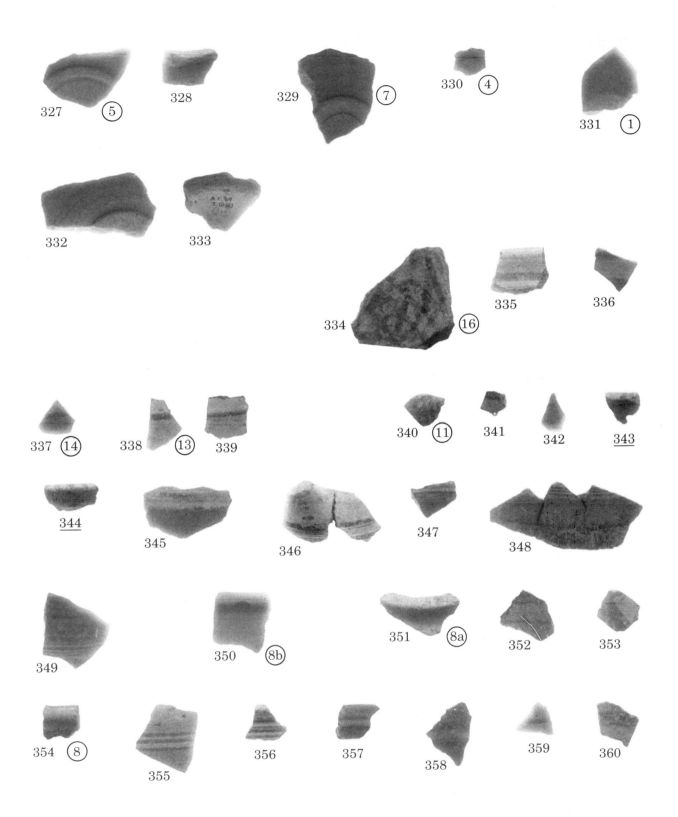

FIGURE 66. Amman Citadel 1969 Sounding: Base Sherds and Decorated Pottery

FIGURE 67. Amman Citadel 1969 Sounding: Decorated Pottery and Miscellaneous Sherds

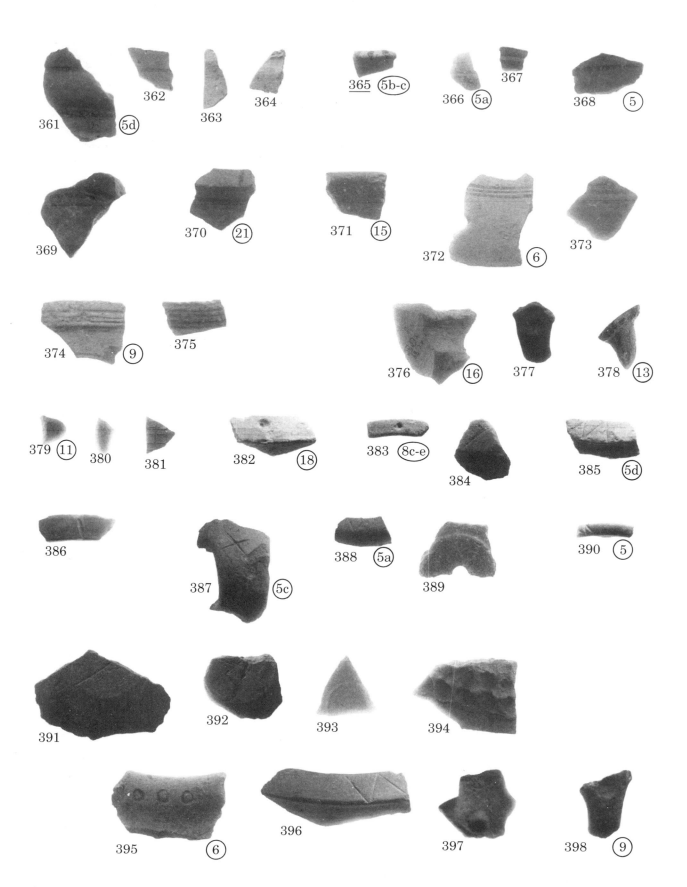

FIGURE 68. Amman Citadel: 1. and 2. Ostraca from 1969 Sounding. 3. Incised Marks on Area III
Iron Age Pottery. 4. to 7. Marked Bones and Stone Bowl Fragments from 1969 Sounding. 8. to 16.
Line-Painted Pottery, Various Locations

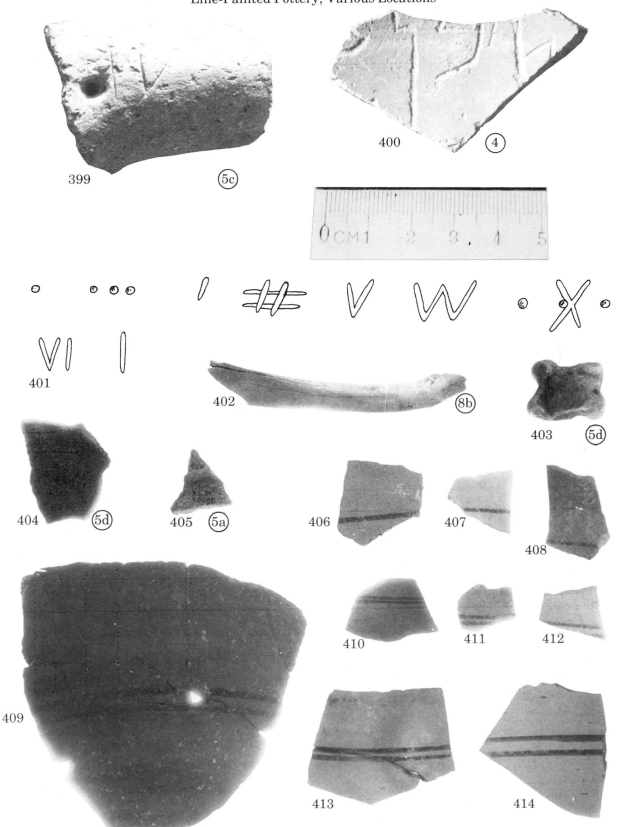

FIGURE 69. Amman Citadel: Line-Decorated Sherds

FIGURE 70. Amman Citadel: Sherds with Painted Decoration

FIGURE 71. Amman Citadel: Sherds with Painted Decoration and Type I-IV Rim Sherds

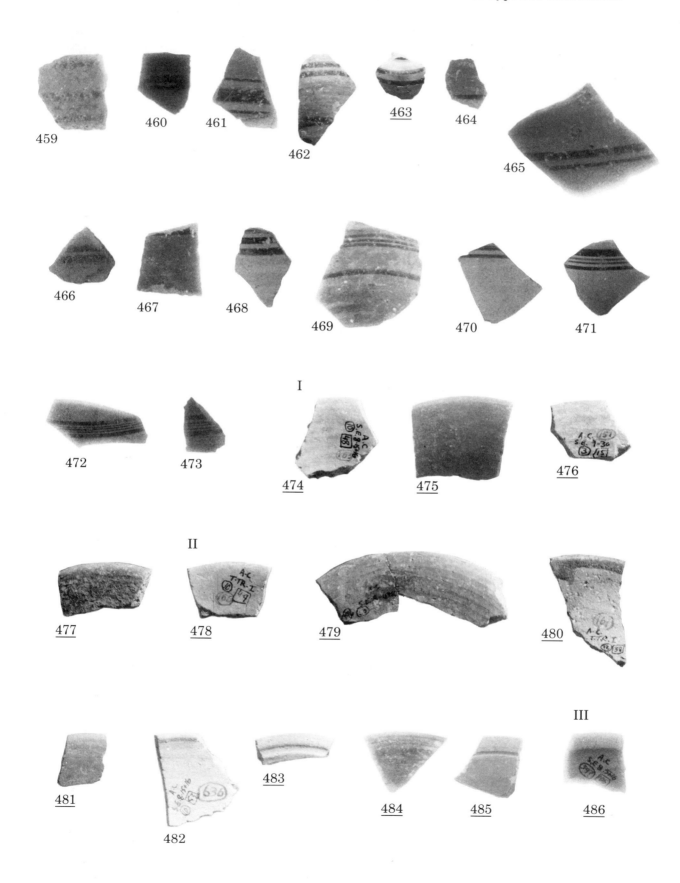

459 460 461 462 463 464 465

466 467 468 469 470 471

I

472 473 474 475 476

II

477 478 479 480

III

481 482 483 484 485 486

FIGURE 72. Amman Citadel: Type IV-XV Rim Sherds

IV

487

488

490

491

V

492

493

494

495

496

497

VI

498

499

VII

500

X

501

XII

502

XI

503

504

XII

505

506

507

508

509

XXVIII

510

XIV

511

XV

512

513

514

515

516

517

518

FIGURE 73. Amman Citadel: Type XV-XLVI Rim Sherds

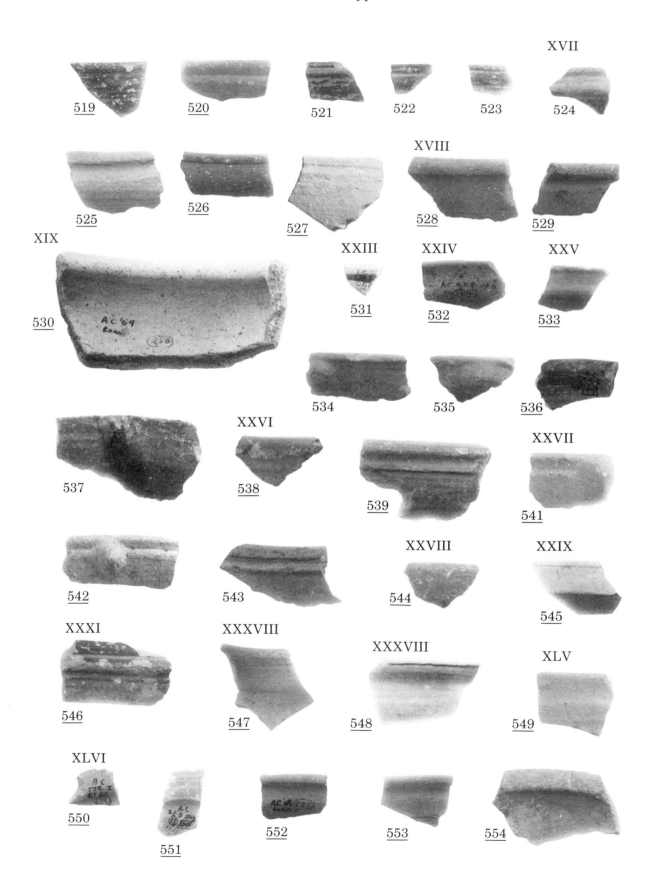

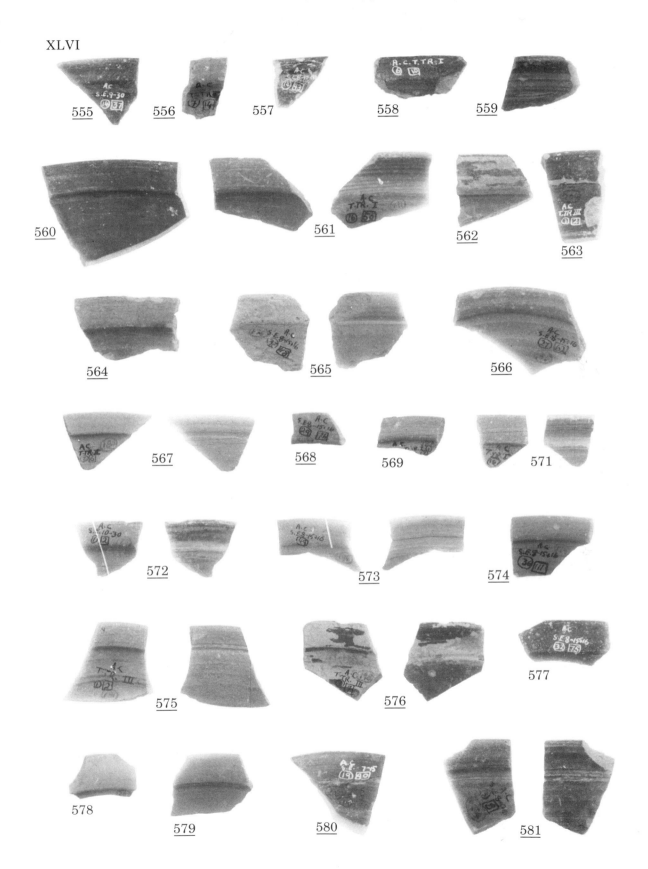

FIGURE 74. Amman Citadel: Type XLVI Rim Sherds

XLVI

555   556   557   558   559

560   561   562   563

564   565   566

567   568   569   571

572   573   574

575   576   577

578   579   580   581

FIGURE 75. Amman Citadel: Type XLVII-LI Rim Sherds

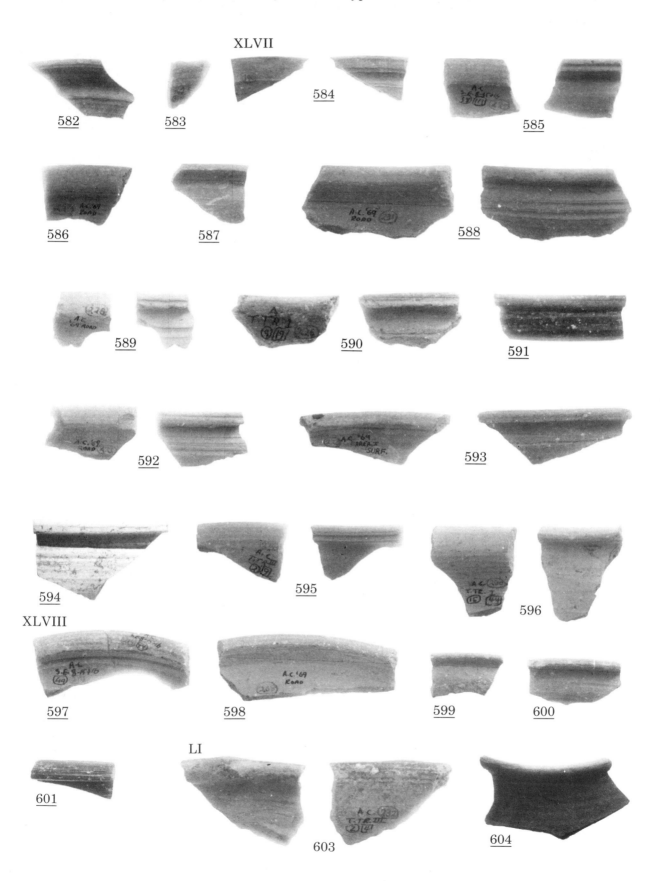

FIGURE 76. Amman Citadel: Type LII-LVI Rim Sherds

LII

<u>605</u>

<u>606</u>

607

608

<u>609</u>

<u>610</u>

<u>611</u>

<u>612</u>

LIII

<u>613</u>

LIV

<u>614</u>

<u>615</u>

616

LII

<u>621</u>

LV

<u>623</u>

<u>624</u>

625

617

<u>618</u>

LVI

626

627

<u>628</u>

LVIII

<u>629</u>

<u>630</u>

<u>631</u>

LIX

<u>632</u>

LX

<u>633</u>

<u>634</u>

FIGURE 77. Amman Citadel: Type LVIII-LXIII Rim Sherds

LX

635

636

637

638

639

640

641

642

LXI   LXII

643   644   646   647   648

LXIII

649

650   651   652   653

654

655

656

LXIV

657

658   659

LXV

661

270

FIGURE 78. Amman Citadel: Type LXIV-LXXV Rim Sherds

LXVI

662

663

664

665

666

667

668

669

670

671

672

673

LXVIII

LXIX

674

675

676

677

678

LXX

LXXI

679

681

682

683

LXXII

684

686

687

688

LXXIII

LXXIV

690

691

693

FIGURE 79. Amman Citadel: Type LXXVI-LXXXII Rim Sherds

LXXVI

LXXVII

<u>696</u>

<u>697</u>

<u>698</u>

<u>699</u>

<u>700</u>

<u>701</u>

<u>703</u>

<u>704</u>

<u>705</u>

<u>706</u>

<u>707</u>

<u>708</u>

<u>709</u>

<u>710</u>

<u>711</u>

LXXIX

712

<u>713</u>

<u>714</u>

LXXVIII

<u>715</u>

<u>716</u>

<u>717</u>

FIGURE 80. Amman Citadel: Type LXXXII-XC Rim Sherds and Handle Fragments

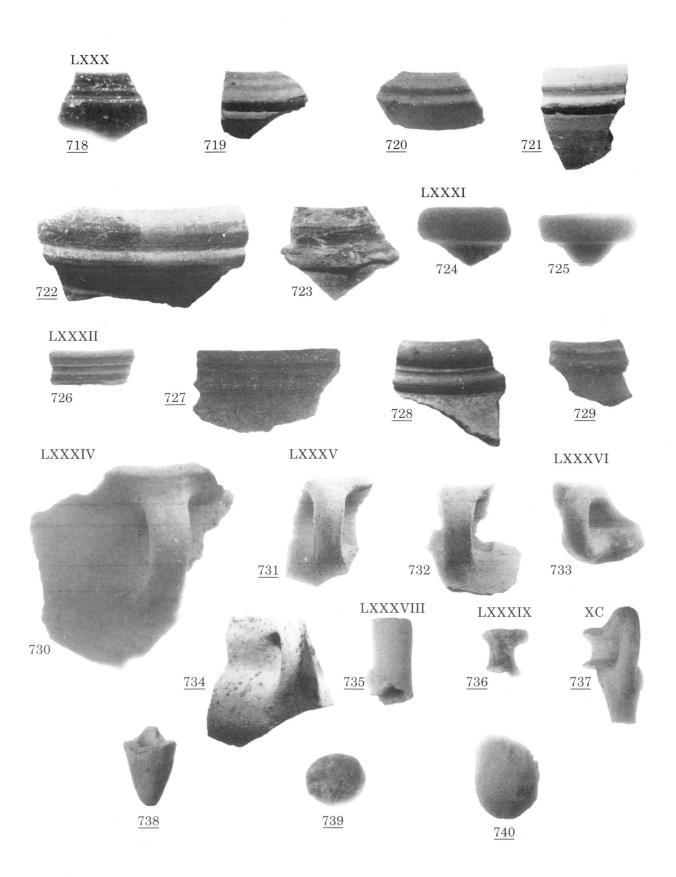

LXXX

718

719

720

721

LXXXI

722

723

724

725

LXXXII

726

727

728

729

LXXXIV

LXXXV

LXXXVI

730

731

732

733

LXXXVIII

LXXXIX

XC

734

735

736

737

738

739

740

FIGURE 81. Amman Citadel: Type 1-5 Base Sherds

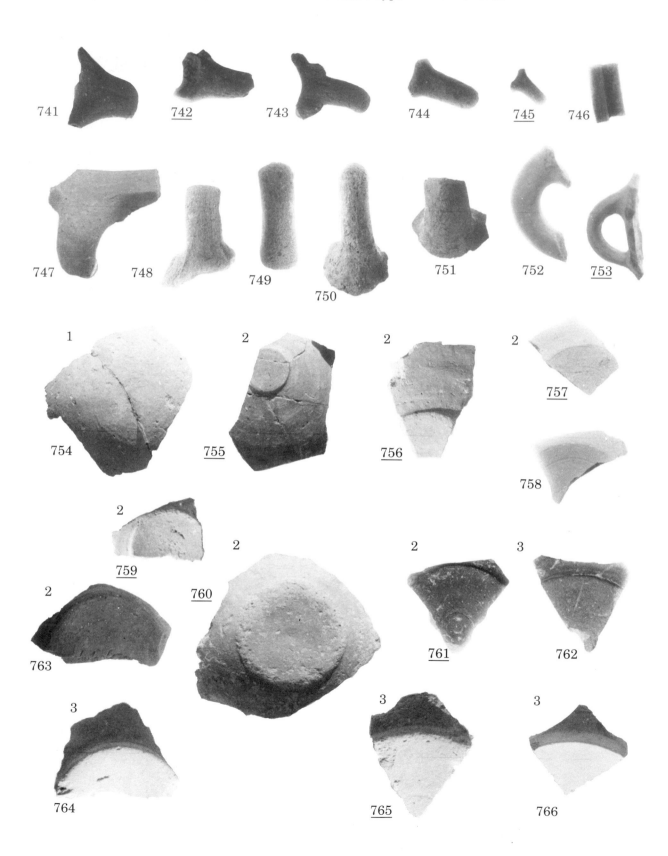

741   742   743   744   745   746

747   748   749   750   751   752   753

1   2   2   2

754   755   756   757

758

2

759

2   2   2   3

763   760   761   762

3   3   3

764   765   766

FIGURE 82. Amman Citadel: Type 5-9 Base Sherds

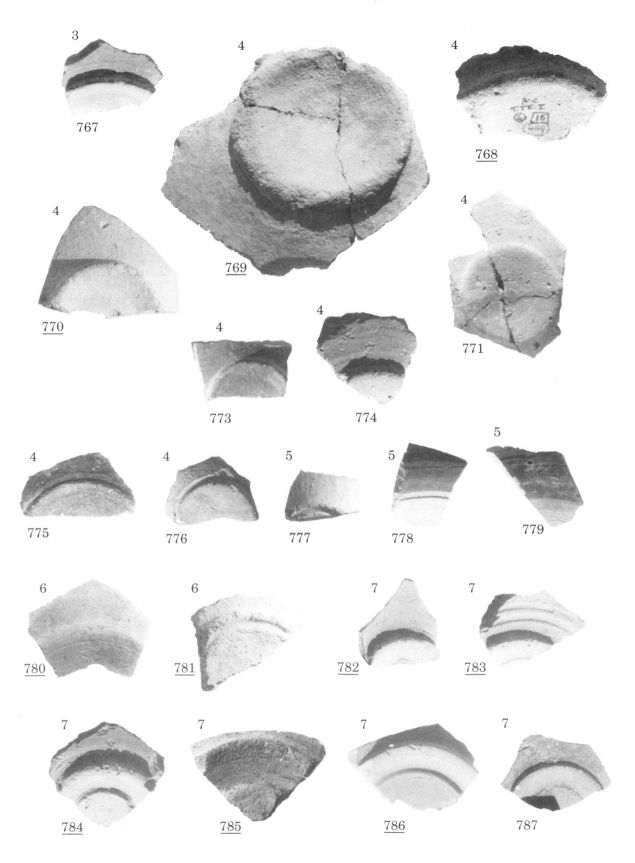

3
767

4
769

4
768

4
770

4
771

4
773

4
774

4
775

4
776

5
777

5
778

5
779

6
780

6
781

7
782

7
783

7
784

7
785

7
786

7
787

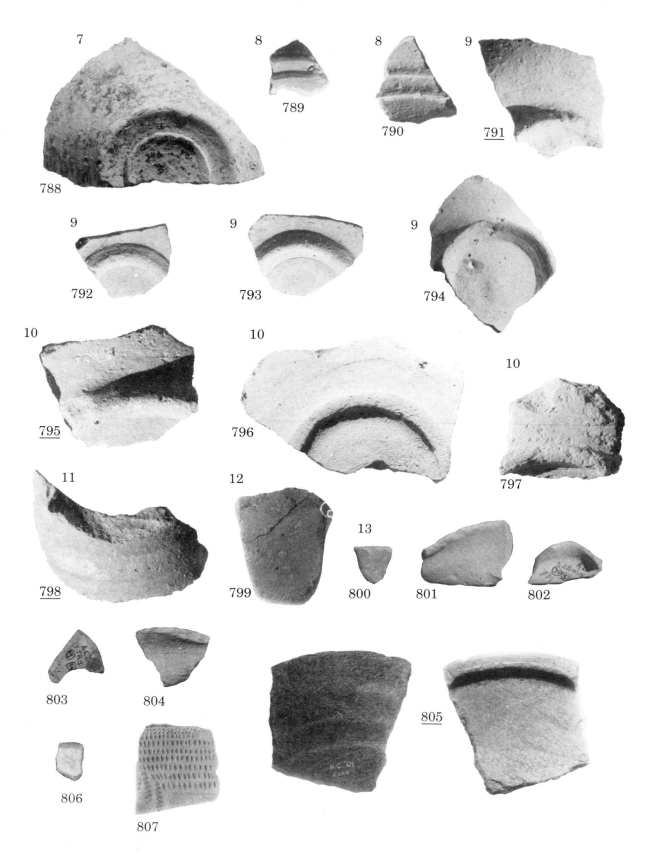

FIGURE 83. Amman Citadel: Type 10-13 Base Sherds, Lamp
Fragments, Stone Bowl Fragment, and Two Miscellaneous Sherds

7

788

8

789

8

790

9

791

9

792

9

793

9

794

10

795

10

796

10

797

11

798

12

799

13

800

801

802

803

804

805

806

807

FIGURE 84. Amman Citadel, Tomb F: Registered Pottery and Bone Objects

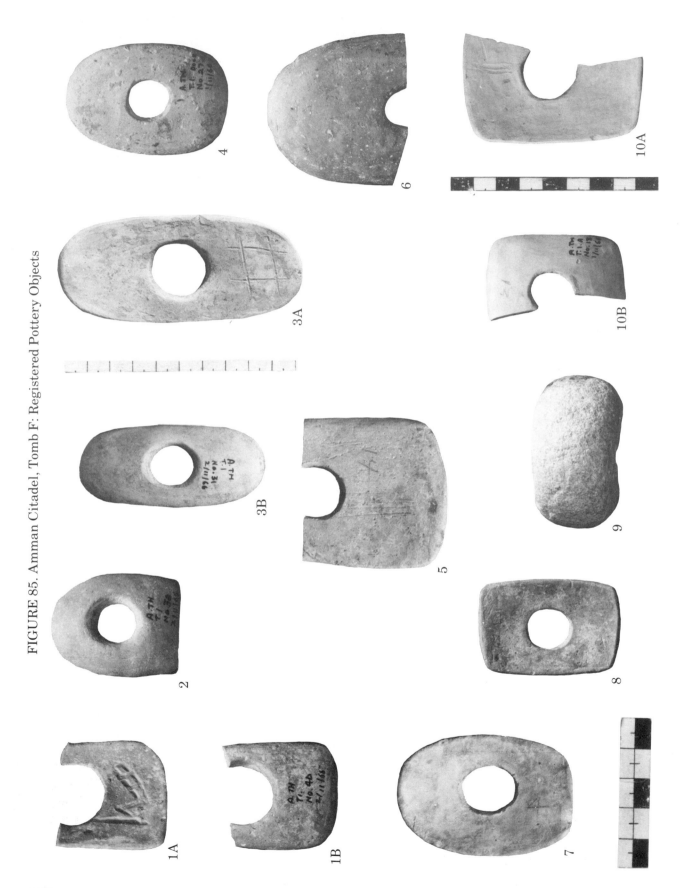

FIGURE 85. Amman Citadel, Tomb F: Registered Pottery Objects

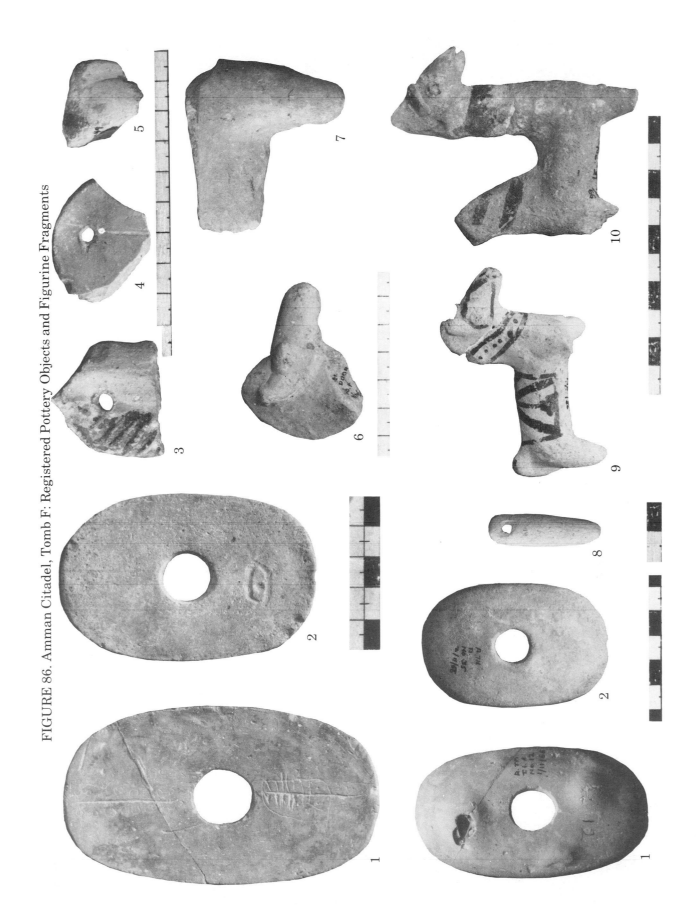

FIGURE 86. Amman Citadel, Tomb F: Registered Pottery Objects and Figurine Fragments

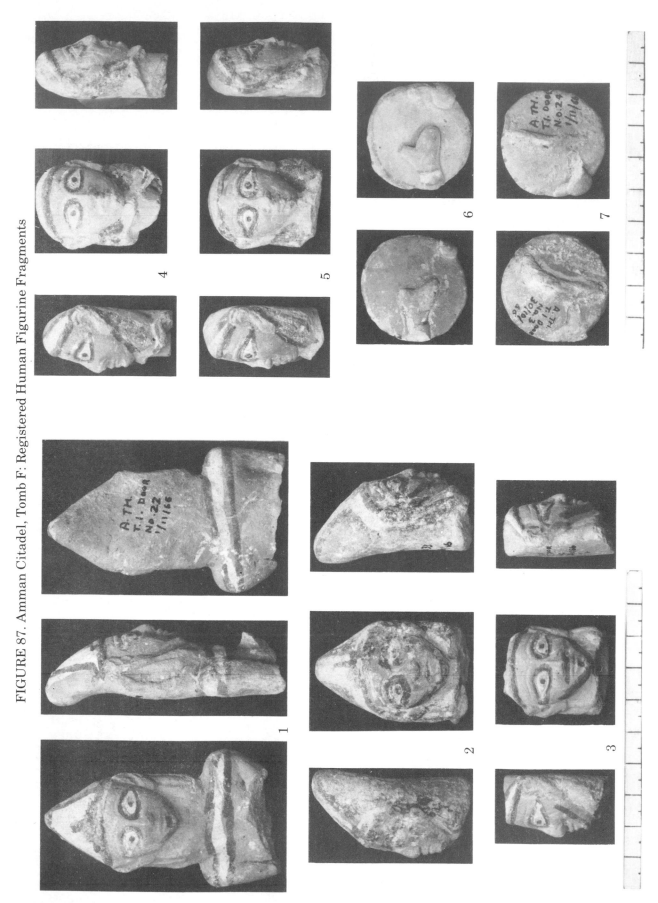

FIGURE 87. Amman Citadel, Tomb F: Registered Human Figurine Fragments

FIGURE 88. Amman Citadel, Tomb F: Terra-Cotta Molds, Mold Impressions, and Figurine Fragment

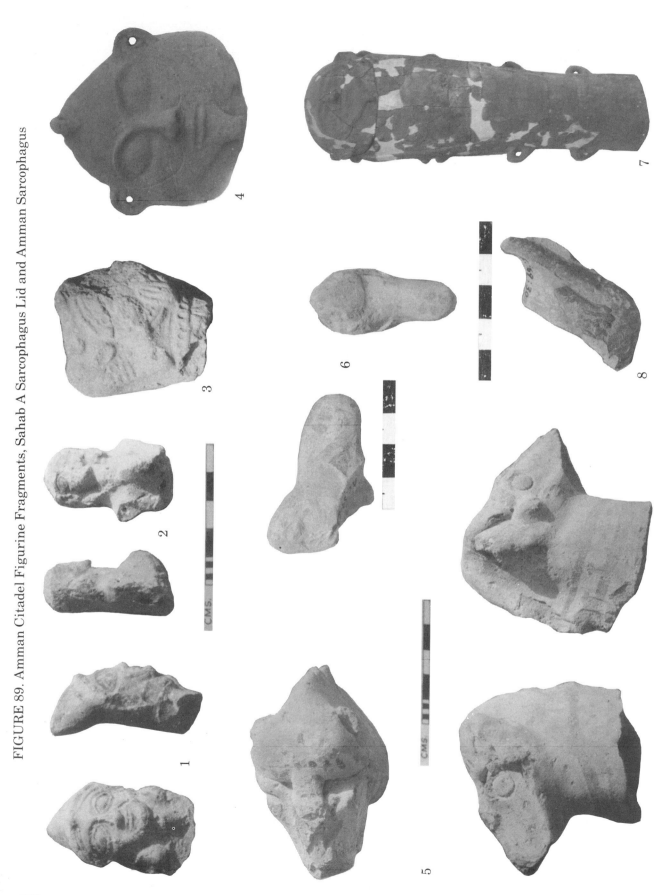

FIGURE 89. Amman Citadel Figurine Fragments, Sahab A Sarcophagus Lid and Amman Sarcophagus

282

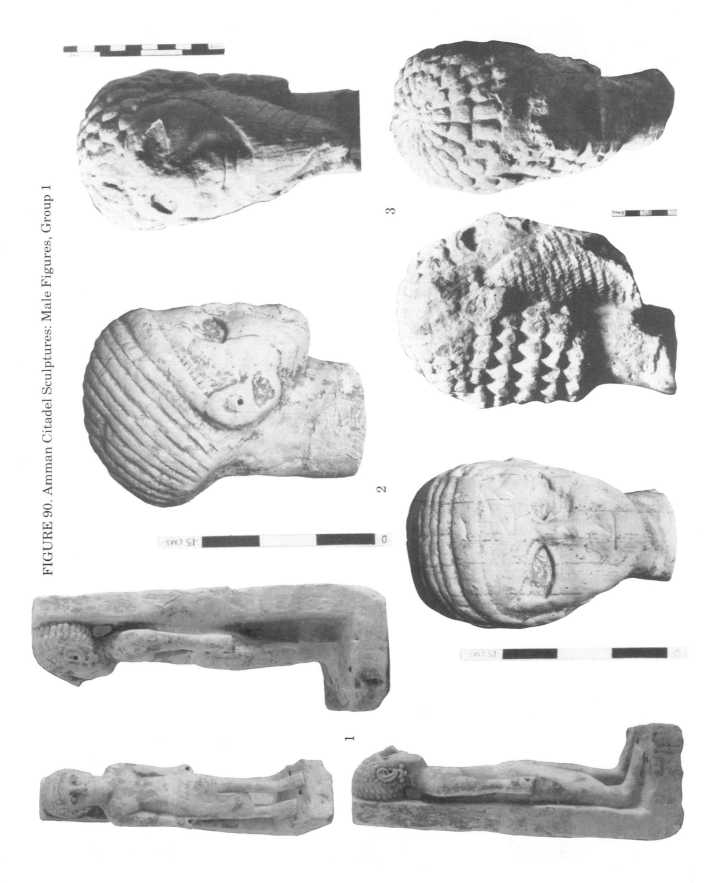

FIGURE 90. Amman Citadel Sculptures: Male Figures, Group 1

283

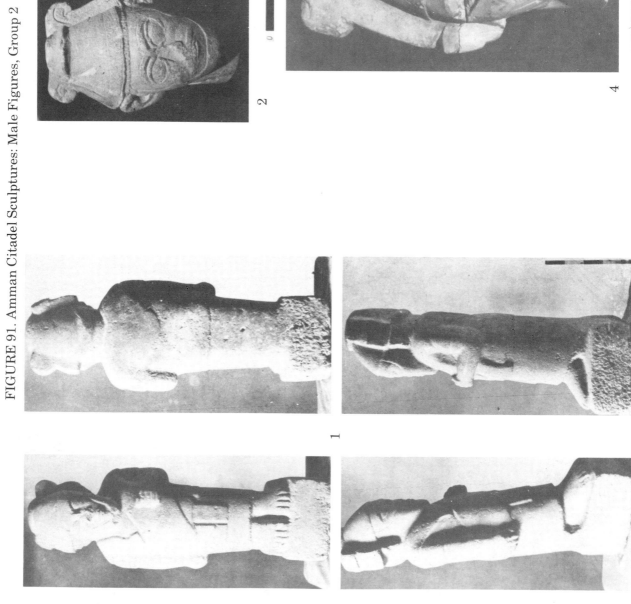

FIGURE 91. Amman Citadel Sculptures: Male Figures, Group 2

FIGURE 92. Dhiban Anthropoid Sarcophagus and Amman Citadel Sculptures: Males Figuress, Group 3

FIGURE 93. Amman Citadel Sculpture: Double-faced Female Heads

D   C   A   B

A
FRONT

B
FRONT

A
BACK

B
BACK

FIGURE 94. Amman Citadel Sculpture: Double-faced Female Heads

C
FRONT

D
BACK

C
BACK

B
FRONT   BACK

C
FRONT   BACK

A
FRONT   BACK

D
BACK   FRONT